The "Final Solution" in Riga

Studies on War and Genocide
General Editors: Omer Bartov, Brown University; A. Dirk Moses, University of Sydney

Volume 1
The Massacre in History
　Edited by Mark Levene and Penny Roberts

Volume 2
National Socialist Extermination Policies: Contemporary German Perspectives and Controversies
　Edited by Ulrich Herbert

Volume 3
War of Extermination: The German Military in World War II, 1941/44
　Edited by Hannes Heer and Klaus Naumann

Volume 4
In God's Name: Genocide and Religion in the Twentieth Century
　Edited by Omer Bartov and Phyllis Mack

Volume 5
Hitler's War in the East, 1941–1945
　Rolf-Dieter Müller and Gerd R. Ueberschär

Volume 6
Genocide and Settler Society: Frontier Violence and Stolen Indigenous Children in Australian History
　Edited by A. Dirk Moses

Volume 7
Networks of Nazi Persecution: Bureaucracy, Business, and the Organization of the Holocaust
　Edited by Gerald D. Feldman and Wolfgang Seibel

Volume 8
Gray Zones: Ambiguity and Compromise in the Holocaust and Its Aftermath
　Edited by Jonathan Petropoulos and John K. Roth

Volume 9
Robbery and Restitution: The Conflict over Jewish Property in Europe
　Edited by M. Dean, C. Goschler, and P. Ther

Volume 10
Exploitation, Resettlement, Mass Murder: Political and Economic Planning for German Occupation Policy in the Soviet Union, 1940–1941
　Alex J. Kay

Volume 12
Empire, Colony, Genocide: Conquest, Occupation, and Subaltern Resistance in World History
　Edited by A. Dirk Moses

Volume 13
The Train Journey: Transit, Captivity, and Witnessing in the Holocaust
　Simone Gigliotti

Volume 14
The Train Journey: The "Final Solution" in Riga: Exploration and Annihilation, 1941–1944
　Simone Gigliotti

The "Final Solution" in Riga
Exploitation and Annihilation, 1941–1944

Andrej Angrick and Peter Klein

Translated from the German by Ray Brandon

Berghahn Books
NEW YORK · OXFORD

First published in 2009 by
Berghahn Books
www.berghahnbooks.com

© 2009, 2012 The Society of Survivors of the Riga Ghetto, Inc.
© 2009, 2012 of the English-language edition Berghahn Books
First paperback edition published in 2012
Originally published as Andrej Angrick and Peter Klein,
Die "Endlösung" in Riga, Ausbeutung und Vernichtung 1941–1944
(Wissenschaftliche Buchgesellschaft, Darmstadt 2006)

All rights reserved. Except for the quotation of short passages for the purposes of criticism and review, no part of this book may be reproduced in any form or by any means, electronic or mechanical, including photocopying, recording, or any information storage and retrieval system now known or to be invented, without written permission of the publisher.

Library of Congress Cataloging-in-Publication Data

Angrick, Andrej, 1962–
 ["Endlösung" in Riga. English]
 The "final solution" in Riga : exploitation and annihilation, 1941–1944 / Andrej Angrick and Peter Klein ; translated from the German by Ray Brandon.
  p. cm. — (Studies on war and genocide ; 14)
 Includes bibliographical references and index.
 ISBN 978-1-84545-608-5 (hbk.)—ISBN 978-0-85745-601-4 (pbk.)
 1. Holocaust, Jewish (1939–1945)—Latvia—Riga. 2. Jews—Persecutions—Latvia—Riga—History—20th century. 3. Jewish ghettos—Latvia—Riga—History—20th century. 4. World War, 1939–1945—Deportations from Latvia. 5. World War, 1939–1945—Jews—Latvia—Riga. 6. Riga (Latvia)—Ethnic relations—History—20th century. I. Klein, Peter, 1962– II. Title.
 DS135.L32R5313 2009
 940.53'18094796--dc22

2009025148

British Library Cataloguing in Publication Data

A catalogue record for this book is available from the British Library.

Printed in the United States on acid-free paper

ISBN: 978-0-85745-601-4 (paperback)

Contents

List of Figures and Maps	viii
Foreword	ix
Abbreviations	xi
Introduction	2

Chapter 1
Latvia Caught between Two Dictatorships — 11

Chapter 2
Operation Barbarossa: Preparations for the German Attack on the Soviet Union — 35

Chapter 3
From the Pogroms to the Establishment of the Ghetto — 58

Chapter 4
Securing German Rule in Occupied Riga: The Period of the Large Ghetto for Latvian Jews — 93

Chapter 5
Murder on a Massive Scale: The Murder of the Ghetto's Latvian Jews — 130

Chapter 6
In Search of Territories for the "Final Solution": The Road to Riga as a Final Destination for Deportations — 175

Chapter 7
Plans for the Salaspils Camp — 197

Chapter 8
The Deportation of German Jews to Riga — 202

Chapter 9
The Salaspils Camp: A Place of Internment with Many Functions — 235

Chapter 10
German Jews Build Salaspils: December 1941–August 1942 — 248

Excursus I
SS Major Rudolf Lange and the Wannsee Conference — 260

Chapter 11
The Latvian Labor Market and the Compulsory Deployment of Jews in Riga — 265

Chapter 12
The Utilization of Jewish Assets and the Issue of Ghetto Administration — 287

Chapter 13
Ghetto Life and Forced Labor in Riga in Spring 1942 — 312

Chapter 14
The Turning Point: Operation Dünamünde at Jungfernhof and in the "Ghetto for Reich Jews" — 328

Chapter 15
Forced Labor and Annihilation in County Commissariat Riga City — 336

Chapter 16
Failed Resistance: The Tin Square Operation, October 1942 — 351

Chapter 17
Annihilation Instead of Forced Labor: Himmler's Struggle against Production Constraints and Armaments Interests in General Commissariat Latvia — 366

Chapter 18
Concentration Camp Kaiserwald and the Barrackings — 379

Excursus II
SS Second Lieutenant Fritz Scherwitz, The Commander at Lenta: A Biographical Sketch — 395

Chapter 19
The Decommissioning of Concentration Camp Kaiserwald, Evacuation, and Liberation — 405

Chapter 20
  A New Start and the Search for Justice   435

Chapter 21
  Conclusion   467

Glossary   471

Organizational Chart   473

Table of Ranks   474

Biographical Appendix   475

Archival Sources   481

Bibliography   486

Index   504

Figures and Maps

Map 1. Overview of the Baltic region in 1942.	1
Figure 4.1. At the ghetto fence.	112
Figure 4.2. On Ludzas St. inside the ghetto.	116
Figure 5.1. Friedrich Jeckeln in field uniform.	159
Figure 8.1. Page from an album showing the search of Jewish men in Würzburg on 27 November 1941, two days before their deportation to Riga.	207
Map 2. Map of the Riga Ghetto.	217
Figure 10.1. SS Technical Sergeant Otto Teckemeier in Salaspils.	252
Figure 10.2. Siegfried Kaufmann as camp policeman.	253
Figure 13.1. Part of the evacuated and devastated half of the ghetto.	315
Figure 13.2. Fetching water near the gallows on Tin Square.	319
Figure 15.1. Detail of Jewish forced laborers on the way to the workplace.	343
Figure 18.1. A flogging at Concentration Camp Kaiserwald.	381
Figure 18.2. Roll call in Concentration Camp Kaiserwald.	383
Figure 18.3. At the fence surrounding the site of the Concentration Camp Kaiserwald.	386
Figure 19.1. Children operation at a barracking in Riga.	409
Figure 20.1. Viktor Arajs.	454

Foreword to the English-Language Edition

The publication of this book was initiated by the New York-based Society of Survivors of the Riga Ghetto, which was founded in 1970 by Mrs. Lore Oppenheimer, a survivor from Hanover, Germany. This organization was one of the first of its kind, established long before "Holocaust" became a household word.

The Society at that time was made up of 400–500 members who had survived the Riga ghetto and various concentration camps in Latvia and beyond. We represented those who remained out of more than 20,000 deportees from "Greater Germany." But if not for a roll of the dice by the Gestapo in Berlin and a blockage of special trains for civilians in November 1941, the transports could have ended up in Minsk, and if not for a labor shortage in Riga, the number of survivors would have been zero. It also has to be emphasized here that the labor shortage (and the availability of an empty ghetto for our accommodation) was the result of the massacre of 27,800 Latvian Jews just before the arrival of the transports from the Reich.

In the beginning, the Society was mostly involved in tracking down ex-Nazi war criminals, many of whom were then living in the greater New York area. Society members also began publishing a quarterly newsletter, holding annual meetings, and collecting money for the assistance of the disabled in Israel – all of which continues to this day.

The idea to publish a book about the horrendous suffering that took place during more than three years of incarceration, slave labor, torture, and killing had been on the mind of the Society's president, Lore Oppenheimer, and vice-president, Herman Ziering, for many years. After three failed attempts, Mr. Ziering found a benefactor in Jan Philipp Reemtsma, who funded the authors, Andrej Angrick and Peter Klein, for their research and writing through the Hamburg-based Foundation for the Advancement of Research and Culture.

The result is a 520-page book that depicts in astonishing detail the fate of more than 20,000 German, Austrian, and Czech Jews, as well as that of tens of thousands of Latvian and Lithuanian Jews. The work at hand contains a thorough examination of the planning and implementation of the mass killings carried out by the SS, the deputized German police, and Latvian auxiliaries. It investigates the various roles of the military and civil administration in the exploitation of the Jews in Riga. Particular attention is given to the infighting over who had the "honor" of overseeing the "final solution of the Jewish question in Europe" on site in occupied Latvia and who was in charge of the assets left behind.

Because the book was written in German, it needed to be translated into English. The Society was able to acquire the services of Ray Brandon, an American living in Berlin. Mr. Brandon brilliantly completed the task in close collaboration with Mr. Angrick and Mr. Klein. The Society wishes to thank all three for a job that could not have been done better.

Now there is a comprehensive book of remembrance for future generations and a "bible" for researchers.

Bernd W. Haase
March 2009

ABBREVIATIONS

ABA	Army Clothing Office
BdS	territorial commander of the Security Police and Security Service
Berück	commander of rear area army group
CdS	chief of the Security Police and Security Service
EG	Einsatzgruppe
Ek	Einsatzkommando
HSSPF	higher SS and police leader
KdS	regional commander of the Security Police and Security Service
Korück	commandant of army rear area
OD	Order Service
OKH	High Command of the Army
OKW	High Command of the Wehrmacht
Orpo	Order Police
RFSS	Reichsführer-SS
RKO	Reich Commissariat Ostland
RM	reichsmark
RMbO	Reich Ministry for the Occupied Eastern Territories
RSHA	Reich Security Main Office
SA	Storm Troops
SD	Security Service
Sk	Sonderkommando
SSPF	SS and police leader
WBO	Wehrmacht Territorial Commander Ostland
WiG	Military District Territorial Commander in the General Government
WVHA	Economics and Administration Main Office

Map 1. Overview of the Baltic region in 1942. Cartographer, Peter Palm, Berlin.

Introduction

Even sixty years after the Second World War, hardly a day passes that we are not reminded in one form or another of the heinous acts of cruelty people were forced to suffer in German-occupied Europe. How could it be any other way? This chapter of history involves the lives of millions who were tortured and murdered, and who, if they survived, were frequently psychologically and physically broken, barely able to return to normality, imprisoned instead by the past they had experienced. But while the torrent of movies, documentary reports, and specialist books – in some cases with overstated audacious theses, such as the "discovery" of Hitler's homosexuality or Himmler's alleged murder at the hands of the British intelligence service – is owed to modern media society's demand for sensation, a growing number studies are once again addressing the protagonists of the "Third Reich," the machinery of murder and terror, and wartime events.

Despite this trend, it is still the case that, unlike research into the history of the concentration camps within the Reich, regional studies on the mass murder of the Jews of Eastern and Southeastern Europe are rare, and that such studies are unfortunately not in fashion in academia. This may be due to the fact that until most recently the history of the victims has been written primarily by survivors, because historians, for whatever reason, seldom took on the topic, or it happened, as in the case of H. G. Adler, that the historian, the contemporary, and the chronicler were the same person. However, many of the survivors who put pen to paper were initially motivated by their personal experience or felt compelled to submit to the public comprehensive accounts and narratives of their experiences. So long as enough authors from the survivors' generation were able to bear forceful witness to the crimes committed against them and at the same time to analyze these crimes and to put them in context, it would seem understandable that such authorities dominated this field of research for so long.

With the passing of time, however, much of what was still a part of memory in everything recounted in private conversation and public discourse becomes what is called history. This is accompanied by a loss of information about social milieus, political constellations, and the cultural

---

Notes for this chapter begin on page 10.

interaction of different ethnic groups. As is known, the past is unfamiliar territory; knowledge and social processes that were once considered self-evident, because they shaped everyday life and most of the population's perception of life, soon seem alien or unclear to us and in need of explanation. On the other hand, distance in time makes it possible to formulate and answer questions both more broadly and more pointedly. This is primarily owed to the release of new documents, that is to say, the historian's tools of the trade. Archival material considered explosive twenty years ago becomes freely available for analysis, because it clearly no longer gives cause for scandal. As a result, many things that were incomprehensible to contemporaries or were concealed from view are explained and move beyond the realm of speculation. This is in turn accompanied by a new evaluation of the protagonists. All of the above applies in general to the current direction of research into the crimes committed under National Socialism and in particular to the dreadful events that took place in Latvia and its capital in the years 1941 to 1944.

The New York-based Society of Survivors of the Riga Ghetto, founded in 1970, recognized very early on that it is necessary to take a comprehensive approach when examining these issues. The society believed that an exhaustive academic monograph on the Riga ghetto was the best way to oppose the process of forgetting in the long term and at the same time to press upon subsequent generations the barbaric character of Nazi Germany's occupation of Riga. The society initiated the work at hand, supported it, and at the same time watched over it with goodwill and critical commentary during the research phase. Against this backdrop, it was our desire to submit the first comprehensive history of the Riga ghetto, the people who lived there – and for the most part died there – the evolution of the crimes committed, and the perpetrators.

Although we could have begun our account with the capture of Riga and the murderous activity of the mobile task force Einsatzgruppe A and its Latvian auxiliary units, it seemed more suitable to expand our scope. To this day, questions concerning Latvian collaboration, the role it played in planning and implementing massacres and the extent of its intent to commit murder continue to stir controversy in Latvia as well as in the United States and Germany. In order to demonstrate the break with civilization that occurred in summer 1941, it was unavoidable that, as a matter of introduction, chapter 1 had to handle certain aspects of the history of independent Latvia, which tried to chart a course for itself between Nazi Germany and Soviet Russia during the 1930s. Only in this way could we illustrate that prewar relations between the Latvians and their minorities – which included both Germans and Jews – did not have to lead to mass murder: the shared interests and parliamentary alliances of the 1920s and 1930s could very well have made possible other courses of action. At the same time, however, it was also evident that the invading German troops did not import anti-Semitism and violent nationalism to Latvia; broad sections of Latvian society had developed their own animosity toward the Jews rather early on. In this respect, the Soviet occupation of Latvia in the wake of the Hitler-Stalin pact represented only a reinforcing factor. Without the incorporation of Latvia into the Soviet Union and the accompanying persecution of real or suspected opponents of the regime and their deportation to the Gulag, the unbridled outbreak of violence and destruction, the "campaign of revenge" carried out by Latvian nationalists in July 1941, would be inexplicable. It was therefore necessary to write about the Soviet occupation as well.

The same goes for German preparations for the invasion of the Soviet Union. The guidelines for this campaign of conquest and annihilation also had to be taken into consideration – even if this topic has been exhaustively discussed in the historiography – primarily so as not to relativize the role of Berlin and key ministries by omitting them. And the same can be said for the role of the Wehrmacht, the German armed forces. By now, it should not only be a matter of consensus in academia but common knowledge among the general public that the Wehrmacht's "shield of honor" did not go untarnished. But does that mean it is unnecessary for us to discuss the contribution and responsibility of individual Wehrmacht and Army units? Hardly. Therefore, we undertook to examine and assess the key role of individual combat formations as well as that of the military administration and economics offices in the persecution of Riga's Jews. After all, it was the latter that initiated the establishment of the Riga ghetto.

The main emphasis of our study, however, lies of course in the history of the ghetto itself, the deportation of German Jews to the east, and the camps near Riga where Jewish prisoners were abused and exploited for a very broad array of forced labor assignments. This is accompanied by tracing and assessing the roles and responsibilities of various occupational authorities, such as the Regional Commander of the Security Police and Security Service (*Kommandeur der Sicherheitspolizei und des Sicherheitsdienstes*, KdS), the Higher SS and Police Leader (*Höherer SS- und Polizeiführer*, HSSPF), and the territorial, regional, county, and local offices of the civil administration. The long-standing antagonisms and rivalries between various agencies and shifting alliances in the implementation of the "final solution" make up one of the themes that run throughout our account. While one group promoted a ruthless policy of annihilation, the other preferred the principle of selection. Complying with the needs of the Latvian labor market, the latter sought to leave a part of the Jews alive as forced laborers – at least initially – while those Jews considered "superfluous" were singled out and murdered.

Therefore, the narrative and analysis of the pogrom phase in Riga, the establishment of the large ghetto, and the massacres at Bikernieki and Rumbula take up a good deal of space, with the focus being on the fate of the Latvian Jews. At the end of chapter 5, a change of perspective takes place. With the arrival of German Jews in Riga, we try to outline the greater context and the Latvian capital's special place within the framework of the "final solution" and to trace the ordeal of those deported from their homes in the west. In this context, the camps Jungfernhof and Salaspils are at the center of attention, because the history of the ghetto cannot be told without reference to these places of internment. In general, the exploitation of human labor, the registration and confiscation of Jewish economic goods, and the perpetrators' strategies, as well as the encounter between German and Latvian Jews as a community of adversity, are granted considerable space in this account. With Operation Dünamünde, it becomes clear that German Jews were in no way to be spared from shooting operations, and that purely utilitarian considerations at first determined the course of "Jewish policy" in 1942, although the change of paradigm to a policy of annihilation was already becoming apparent. In this context, we go into the further development of the ghetto right up to its dissolution and the transfer of its inhabitants to Concentration Camp Kaiserwald, which was established in the summer of 1943. Inserted between these issues is a chapter on resistance in the ghetto and the subsequent Tin Square Operation.

It might have been possible to conclude with the subsequent chapters addressing Concentration Camp Kaiserwald and the barracking of its inmates at their worksites in and around the Riga vicinity, the attempt to destroy the evidence of the mass murder operations, and the evacuation of the Latvian capital. However, it would have been unhistorical to stop at this point. Although this book concerns the Riga ghetto, the history of its inhabitants' suffering was not limited solely to the Latvian capital; their ordeal continued in an unusually brutal fashion during and after evacuation. It was therefore impossible for us to omit the apocalyptic conditions at Concentration Camp Stutthof, near Danzig (Gdańsk), the destination of most of the Jews from the Riga ghetto, and the final throes of the "Third Reich."

The term "epoch" belongs to the terminology of the historian and serves to show the limits of a work, that is to say, to set off the period the historian seeks to explore and to bring order, his or her order, to the issues within these limits. However, anybody who has experienced history, shaped it, or above all suffered in the course of it is bound to show little understanding for such categorizations. The experiences of the Riga ghetto's Jews did not automatically disappear into the past with the collapse of the Third Reich. In fact, the memory of those experiences frequently became a defining constant in life later on and not a part of what is commonly called history. We are only all too aware of this fact and try to do it justice in our last chapter, where we briefly go into the lives of the victims as well as the perpetrators after the Second World War.

In writing this book, we could have fallen back on the different accounts and memoirs that have already shed light on diverse aspects of this topic in an impressive manner. Worthy of mention here are Hans-Heinrich Wilhelm's *Einsatzgruppe A der Sicherheitspolizei und des SD 1941/42* (unavailable in English) and Andrew Ezergailis's *The Holocaust in Latvia 1941–1944,* both of which can rightly be called standard works.[1] One recognizes the value of these books all the more when one reads in the more recent literature something from an acknowledged specialist well-versed in the sources, such as Klaus Jochen Arnold: "Here [in Riga] the establishment of a ghetto was strived for at the initiative of the Jews, who were trying to save themselves from looming annihilation."[2] As is clear in this example, there is no getting around the older literature when examining the German occupation of Riga. This literature is still relevant and will remain so in the future. Nonetheless, for the region around Riga and the Latvian capital itself, survivor narratives, for the most part, continue to shape the historiography.

In addition to the regrettably neglected later work by Alfred Winter[3] and the 1947 study by Jeanette Wolff,[4] the oft reprinted *Journey into Terror* by New York historian Gertrude Schneider stands out among the published memoirs by Jews who were deported to Riga from the west and survived. Due to her profession as a historian and her personal history as a former ghetto inhabitant, Schneider was not only able to explain the internal processes within the "ghetto for Reich Jews" in Riga's Moscow Suburb. She was also able to portray the fear and confidence, the despondency and hope that existed in the face of constant danger and exploitation. We may have succeeded in discovering a crucial contemporary document in the form of the ghetto journal kept by the Dortmund Group of deportees, but its entries, as a rule very brief, can be understood only with the background knowledge gained from Schneider's book and other written records handed down by survivors.

Fortunately, several counterparts to the work by Gertrude Schneider have come from surviving Latvian Jews as well. First and foremost is *Churbn Lettland* (unavailable in English) by Max Kaufmann. Kaufmann is at the same time chronicler and witness and, like no other, provides deep insights into the conflicts of conscience of the Jewish decision-makers in the ghetto. The memoirs of Bernhard Press hold similar value; his book, *The Murder of the Jews in Latvia: 1941–1945,* answers questions left open by Kaufmann. Both works ably combine into a cohesive whole the family biographies of their narrators and the history of the persecution of the Jews in Latvia. Third, there is Margers Vestermanis, another survivor, whose multifaceted essays are full of insight and moral authority and show great knowledge when handling juxtapositions such as mass murder and resistance or collaboration and solidarity in occupied Riga.

In addition to the aforementioned individuals, the Berlin historians Diana Schulle and Wolfgang Scheffler (d.) have also made a crucial contribution to research on the Riga ghetto. With their two-volume bilingual *Buch der Erinnerung*, they managed not only to clarify the arrival dates of deportation trains that had been incorrectly ascribed in the past; they also provided compelling empirical findings about the age structure and the number of survivors from each and every one of the twenty-five transports to Riga. The way this information is presented makes this book a unique source. It provides a scaffolding of data for many of our statements and makes it possible to verify contemporary documents. With this work, the historiography now has at its disposal a voluminous study that advances research both as a narrative and as an edition of source material.

Even if such impressive accounts of the Riga ghetto were available to us for consultation, it is self-evident that for a contemporary topic of such importance our own archival research was essential. For official documents, we were able to access the long-available files of the SS and police, the Wehrmacht, and the civil administration that are to be found in the Federal Archives (*Bundesarchiv*) and other German repositories. In addition, there were the records of the same said agencies scattered throughout the archive administrations in Russia, Latvia, and other former Socialist states. As "trophy files," these were for a long time largely inaccessible to historians; only since the collapse of Communism have they become available to academics. Records of the same provenance held at the YIVO Institute for Jewish Research in New York are also not to be underestimated in their importance. Although almost all of the institutions holding contemporary documents from the National Socialist era have opened their holdings to scholars, it must be noted that a large part of the files from those institutions and agencies responsible for the implementation of the "final solution" cannot be found. The existing sources for Einsatzkommando 2, KdS Latvia, HSSPF Ostland, or the formations of Latvian collaborators should not obscure the fact that the majority of these records are not available. Particularly painful is the loss of the Jewish Council's documents, because there is no replacement for these holdings that would allow us to fill in the gaps. For this reason, our account of the council's activities and functions as well as its members' strategies must inevitably remain unsatisfactory. Only the future will show whether all of the missing records from these agencies have been lost to researchers forever, or whether the studies that follow will be able to fill in the gaps based on new discoveries of files.

If the grand lines of policy could be reconstructed on the basis of the available state sources – and if the complex processes behind the forced labor measures in particular could be written only on the basis of such contemporary administrative files – it would in turn hardly be possible to depict the history of the genocide as a series of countless individual crimes without the use of postwar German court records. In extensive questioning, survivors, witnesses, and perpetrators were queried in detail. Only on the basis of their testimonies could the process of the Nazi policies of persecution and annihilation in Riga be reconstructed in all of its nuances. Even if the questioning sessions served primarily the investigation and prosecution of criminal offenses, the statements made also reveal astonishing things for historians. These forceful accounts by survivors – which no contemporary document can convey with the same intensity – are often the most important source of information available for determining the perpetrators' motives and assigning individual responsibility. In turn, it is also necessary for investigators to have contemporary documents on-hand during questionings – whether as a memory aid or as a means of reproach. The historian who undertakes the difficult matter of reconstructing and interpreting events is therefore just as unable to do without any of these sources as the jurist entrusted with investigating the criminal offense.

Unlike other historical accounts using West German investigations and court records concerning National Socialist crimes, there are not a lot of individual cases that involve the Riga ghetto. Instead, the first investigations of the Prosecutor's Office of the Free and Hanseatic City Hamburg were conducted in the first years of the postwar era and then merged into the large Riga case with the file number 141 Js 534/60. This mammoth case is relatively confusing even for a well-versed user, because under the aforementioned file number are numerous related cases and criminal offenses that were investigated independently of one another. For example, the investigation of Latvian collaborator Viktor Arajs actually forms a separate case. In addition, the Hamburg Prosecutor's Office investigated former members of HSSPF Ostland, the Territorial Commander of the Security Police and Security Service Ostland (*Befehlshaber der Sicherheitspolizei und des Sicherheitsdienstes Ostland*), Einsatzkommando 2, and KdS Latvia as well as additional police units. In addition to this large, complex case, it also proved necessary to analyze the criminal investigations of other prosecutor's offices, in particular those concerning members of the civil administration, Latvian self-defense formations, and Concentration Camp Kaiserwald, and to incorporate their findings into our narrative.

We thank Senior Prosecutor Helge Grabitz (d.) and Senior Prosecutor Jochen Kuhlmann from the Prosecutor's Office of the Free and Hanseatic City Hamburg for giving us the opportunity to look at and analyze their office's files. From the German justice system, we would like to express our gratitude to Prosecutor Franz-Josef Tönnies and the other employees of the Central Office of the State Justice Administration for the Investigation of National Socialist Crimes in Ludwigsburg, and to the staff of the Federal Archives branch now located there: Heinz-Ludger Borgert, Elke Bartholomä, and Rainer Juchheim. From the other branches of the Federal Archives, we would like to thank Carina Notzke and Helga Waibel (Freiburg), Marion Namsler and Sabine Kaulitz (Dahlwitz-Hoppegarten), and Regina Grüner, Lutz Möser, and Peter Klein (Berlin-Lichterfelde). We received valuable support from Gaby Müller-Oelrichs (House of the Wannsee Conference), Peter Grupp (Political Archive of the German Foreign Office), and Günther Friedrich (Bavarian State Archive, Nuremberg). In Latvia, Ira Zaneriba, Margers Vestermanis, Alexanders Bergmanis, and Rabbi Mordechai Glazman placed their considerable knowledge at our disposal. The Latvian Historical Commission gave us the chance to put parts of our book up for public discussion; we would therefore like to thank the organizers of the resulting conferences. In Moscow, Vladimir Kuzelenkov and Vladimir Korotaev (Central Archive of the Russian Armed Forces) let us view their holdings, while Olga Lapavok, as always, untiringly provided her services as interpreter.

From U.S. archives and institutions, Marek Web (YIVO Institute for Jewish Research); Martin Dean, Aaron Kornblum, Jürgen Matthäus, and Alexander Rossino (United States Memorial Museum, Washington); Bob Waite (U.S. Department of Justice); and the staff of the Captured German Documents section of the National Archives and Records Administration (College Park) provided much advice and assistance. For obtaining two important files, we thank Susanne Willems, Reinhard Müller, and Stephen Tyas, as well as Florian Dierl, who drew our attention to photos of Salaspils located in the Federal Archives Koblenz. During our stay in the United States in autumn 1998, we were granted the opportunity to join the Society of Survivors of the Riga Ghetto for their annual meeting. For their friendly reception and care, we would like to thank Lore Oppenheimer and her husband Leo Oppenheimer (d.) and in particular Herman Ziering (d.) and his wife Lee.

Katrin Reichelt, from whom a comprehensive study on Latvian collaboration is to be expected soon, researched, translated, and interpreted for us in the Riga archives with unyielding enthusiasm and was at the same time a critical discussion partner. She and her spouse Bob Waite were perfect hosts. At our side during the writing of this book were Gerlinde Angrick, Matthias Kamm, and Dorothea Walther. We received methodological advice, suggestions, and criticism from all of the "usual suspects": Martin Cüppers, Florian Dierl, Christian Gerlach, Alfred Gottwaldt, Marcus Gryglewski, Martin Hölzl, Michael Mallmann, Dieter Pohl, Stephen Tyas, Martina Voigt, and Michael Wildt. The Hamburg Foundation for the Promotion of Science and Culture enabled us to carry out all of the research in domestic and foreign archives free of all financial and temporal limitations. Without its support, this study would not have been possible in its present form. In addition, we are most grateful to Michael Mallmann for immediately making this book a part of his project and enabling its publication in the series "Publications of the Research Office Ludwigsburg of the University of Stuttgart." We thank Heidrun Baur of the Research Office Ludwigsburg of the University of Stuttgart for making the index as well as the publishing house Wissenschaftliche Buchgesellschaft in Darmstadt and its editor Daniel Zimmermann for accepting this book into its program.

Over the years, Wolfgang Scheffler, our teacher, accompanied and supported this study with considerable goodwill. Although we were all working on various projects related to the same topic, it never came to competition. The investigation of the crimes against the Jews in Riga between 1941 and 1944 always stood front and center for all of us.

Notes

1. Hans-Heinrich Wilhelm, *Die Einsatzgruppe A der Sicherheitspolizei und des SD 1941/42*, and Andrew Ezergailis, *The Holocaust in Latvia 1941–1944*. The precise bibliographical data for the works cited are to be found in the bibliography at the end of the book.
2. Klaus Jochen Arnold, *Die Wehrmacht und die Besatzungspolitik in den besetzten Gebieten der Sowjetunion*, 497, fn. 63.
3. Alfred Winter, *The Ghetto of Riga and Continuance*.
4. Jeanette Wolff, *Sadismus oder Wahnsinn*.

– Chapter 1 –

LATVIA CAUGHT BETWEEN TWO DICTATORSHIPS

In their turbulent past, the Baltic states, Latvia included, have always stood between Russia and Germany, an object coveted by each side in its drive for greater territory. In the process, Latvia's population and its elites – caught in the interplay of forces largely beyond their control – always endeavored to pursue a policy of their own between the power blocs, something that became a reality only after the First World War. On 1 August 1920, the Treaty of Riga was signed, which for Latvia meant a diplomatic success of the first order, and for the Soviet Union a painful loss of territory. For Moscow, however, Latvian independence seemed less of an evil than a western flank threatened by the Entente (meaning primarily Great Britain and France) and Germany or a Greater Poland expanded to include Latvia.[1] That same August, Germany and Latvia also signed a peace treaty. For Latvia, whose population consisted of 75 percent Latvians and Latgalians, it was at this point that the period of independence truly got underway. The country was recognized by the Allies on 26 January 1921 and by the United States on 22 July. Accession into the League of Nations finally followed on 22 September.[2]

As a young state, Latvia had first of all to constitute itself and to create loyal ministries that transcended thinking in terms of ethnicity, but were committed to the country, and to organize those ministries accordingly. A Latvian constitution was indispensable to this end. The constituents met for the first time on 1 May 1920. On 15 February 1922, the constitution, which drew on those of Switzerland, France, and Weimar Germany, was adopted. The parliament, or Saeima, was accorded decisive importance. The Saeima elected the head of state, and it controlled the judiciary as well, for it had to confirm the appointment of judges. The judges themselves were independent and beholden only to the law. The president in turn was also the commander in chief of the army and had the power to issue emergency decrees in exceptional cases, which – if they were to last – had to be confirmed by the Saeima later. The president's term of office was set at

---

Notes for this chapter begin on page 28.

five years, that of the Saeima at three years. A national flag – a horizontal white stripe between two fields of dark red – was designed based on a description found in a thirteenth-century chronicle. The state seal – featuring the Courland lion and the Livonia dragon – also adopted medieval motifs, which were to emphasize the long history of the new state, something more important than a modern constitution.

Numerous parties and groups of all hues took part in Latvian politics. The political left was represented in the Saeima primarily by the Social Democrats, who were split into two wings, a more moderate one and a more radical one, while the Communists played a certain role only within the union movement. The middle-class camp had a number of parties at its disposal, among which the Peasants' Union, founded in 1917 and led by the charismatic Kārlis Ulmanis, occupied a paramount position. The liberal electoral system also enabled marginal political groups – which included the country's Germans and Jews – to send representatives to the Saeima. Similar to the situation in Weimar Germany, no political orientation or – what was often the same thing here – national group could be excluded from political life. Some Germans and Jews were even appointed ministers. The Jewish group tried to offset possible disadvantages by forming alliances of necessity. Thus representatives of Agudat Israel made its influence felt in more conservative cabinets – frequently in concert with representatives of the German minority – while Zionists and Russian parliamentarians reached agreement in more left-leaning cabinets. Overall, however, the law of proportional representation impaired the government and the introduction of laws and led – as in Weimar Germany – to constantly shifting majorities and unstable alliances. For the minorities, this meant that something achieved by one cabinet was often repealed by the next cabinet. No real security existed.

Jānis Čakste, a former member of the Russian Duma and a Latvian diplomat, was elected Latvia's first president in 1922. The seat of government was established in Riga in the former castle of the Livonian Order, where Swedish and, later, Russian governors had also resided. This phase of Latvian independence – known as "the parliamentary epoch" – lasted sixteen years, during which priority was given to the reconstruction of the country, the development of its sovereignty, and the formation of a national identity. On 1 August 1933, a national penal code was passed. The university and technical school system was reformed with the nation in mind, and a national cultural fund was created. From this, the national-educational concerns of hundreds of public and school libraries were financed. Similar importance was given to forming an intellectual elite. Between 1919 and 1939, 6,841 students successfully completed their studies. Because university faculties lacked Latvian academics, these students, who were to form the national leadership of the future, often studied under Russian, Jewish, or German university instructors.

Economic life was governed almost completely by the market; state monopolies existed only for schnapps and flax (of which Latvia was Europe's leading producer). From these, the young state derived a considerable part of its income. Agriculture in this primarily agrarian country prospered – although a general agrarian reform, which affected primarily landholders, resulted in the appropriation of 1,300 estates without recompense. Latvian ports acted as transfer centers for goods throughout the year. Liepāja (Libau) and Ventspils (Windau) were free of ice during the winter, and if necessary, Riga's harbors could be made passable by icebreakers. By contrast, industry was still stuck in its infancy and frequently provided solely for Latvia's own needs. This may have been one reason why an industrial proletariat failed to take shape in Latvia. To the contrary, working conditions and social benefits (an eight-hour workday for blue-collar workers, six-hour workday for white-collar employees, job protection measures, modern health insurance, compulsory schooling, child support, maternity protection, etc.) – were so good that the Latvians enjoyed a high standard of living even when compared with their European neighbors.[3]

In the wake of the strengthening of the political right in Germany, the inclusion of the National Socialists in the government in 1933, and the consolidation of Stalin's position in the Soviet Union through the expulsion of all inner-party opposition, the year 1934 brought about radical changes to Latvia's form of government as well. The liberal electoral system's advantages of giving the minorities in the Saeima the chance to speak and to be heard were outweighed by the disadvantage of having too many parties. After the 1931 elections, twenty-seven groups were represented in the Saeima, several of which had just one member. This frustrated both government continuity and the implementation of election programs. Economic decline was accompanied by the Saeima's increasing inability to act. As a consequence of the world economic depression, demand from west European markets had fallen off, which led in turn to higher unemployment and a devaluation of the currency in Latvia.

This was accompanied by the organization of the extreme right in the form of the Thunder Cross (Pērkoṇkrusts), which was founded by Gustavs Celmiņš in 1933.[4] Like other ethno-nationalist, right-wing extremist movements, the Thunder Cross was organized along paramilitary lines, uniformed, and distinguished by anti-Semitic but also anti-German slogans. More important than closing ranks with the Fascist-oriented movements in other European countries, which were of course against Bolshevism and served only to a limited extent as role models, the only task of the Thunder Cross was the strengthening of Latvia, an undertaking seen in socially utopian, crudely romantic terms. Their rituals and form of greeting – the cry "Hail battle!" with an outstretched right arm – came across as imitative of the Hitler movement. The followers of the Thunder Cross movement never sought to become a broad-based people's movement, but among students and within cities, they enjoyed considerable popularity. Wherever political life was articulated in the cities, one heard their agitation against Jews and Germans, against corruption and the political establishment.

Such was the political atmosphere on 16 March 1934, when Ulmanis, who the year before had intervened on behalf of a change in the constitution with regard to the electoral system so as to create stable parliamentary majorities, was entrusted with forming a government. In addition to becoming head of government, he was to hold at the same time the office of foreign minister. An ostensible Communist uprising allowed him to declare a state of emergency on 15 May 1934. This, however, affected above all the followers of the Thunder Cross movement, which was subsequently banned. In this putsch, Ulmanis was able to rely on Minister of War General Jānis Balodis and the paramilitary Aizsargi. The sitting president, Alberts Kviesis, who also belonged to the Peasants' Alliance, followed Ulmanis's call for a government commission to shape legislation, whereupon the Saeima lost most of its significance. After Kviesis's term expired in April 1936, there was no new election for president. Ulmanis simply "took over" the office, seeing himself, similar to his role model Oliver Cromwell, more as a protector and a part of the parliament than as a dictator. He therefore disputed comparisons of his regime to that of Hitler's. Scholars differ over the possibility that Mussolini served as Ulmanis's role model.[5]

During this period of domestic political upheaval, Latvia's role between the power blocs changed. Once able to ascribe its founding and maintenance as a state to the stalemate between Germany, the Entente, and Soviet Russia after the First World War, Latvia found that this constellation no longer applied by the early 1930s. The rapprochement of Germany and the Soviet Union – manifested in the Treaty of Berlin of 24 April 1926 and the trade agreements of October 1925 – meant, at least at first glance, the loss of Latvia's special standing in alliance and military politics.[6] For the members of the Saeima and Ulmanis, it became clear that Latvia could no longer move back and forth between the power blocs, a situation that led to the conclusion of a treaty of non-aggression with the Soviet Union. In the following years, Latvia pursued a strict policy of neutrality in its foreign policy; the Baltic Entente, an alliance born of mutual interest with just Estonia and Lithuania, was expanded. Latvia and Estonia concluded pacts of non-aggression with the Reich only on 7 June 1939. Such a step would not have been considered necessary beforehand, because Germany's interests in the Baltic region were initially aimed at Lithuania and the Memel territory until its "return" and occupation by German troops in March 1939.[7]

As Germany reemerged as a military power and the Nazi regime revealed its aggressive character – as demonstrated in the annexation of Austria, the Sudetenland, and then the remaining Czech lands – a non-aggression treaty seemed sensible to the Latvian government. And even the German Foreign Office saw benefits in ratifying the treaties. Ever since a Communist putsch attempt in 1924 in Estonia, Berlin had maintained the best relations, also in military matters, with Tallinn, which tended to be skeptical of its large neighbor to the east; however the Foreign Office took the view that vis-à-vis Germany, Latvia followed "the line of a genuine policy of neutrality." Hitler therefore sought to tie the Baltic republic more closely to the Reich and used the occasion of a state visit by Latvian Foreign Minister Vilhelms Munters on 7 June 1939 to insist on intensifying economic contacts, pointing out "the usefulness of very long-term trade treaties." At the same time, conversation also turned to Russia, with Hitler disclosing that he "was extraordinarily poorly informed about Russia," and that the goals of the Russian leadership were enshrouded in secrecy. Munters must have been skeptical of the German dictator's remarks; Hitler also claimed that he did not want a war, but "Germany was not afraid of Russia." It was within this context that Hitler pointed out to Munters that Latvia would need weapons from Germany. In the summer of 1939, it seemed that the foreign policy interests of Latvia's powerful neighbors would force the country to lean more forcefully to one or the other side, for the room for diplomatic maneuver was becoming more limited.[8]

Latvia's domestic climate had changed as well. In his speeches, Ulmanis always spoke of a renewal of the parliamentary system and constitutional reform, but nothing ever happened in that respect. To the contrary, civil liberties, above all those of the minorities, were increasingly curtailed. Even the Peasants' Alliance, to which Ulmanis owed his political career, was disbanded. This applied all the more to the extreme political right. The followers of the Thunder Cross, inasmuch as they were not in prison, went underground. Astute observers could not help but notice that Ulmanis had appropriated many of their national demands – "Latvia for Latvians" – during his six years in power and even ruled according to the *Führerprinzip*. This meant restrictions on the freedom of the press as well as the dissolution of organizations considered hostile to the government and the confiscation of their assets by the state. The courts also ceased to function autonomously and were subjected to control from on high.

The economy was also increasingly centralized, which brought Ulmanis into conflict with the economic influence of businessmen. By founding cooperatives according to individual professions as a substitute for economic freedom (Chamber of Commerce and Industry, Chamber of Agriculture, Chamber of Artisans, Chamber of Labor, Chamber of Professions, Chamber of Writing and Art) and forming state-controlled corporations, the regime introduced a form of state capitalism between 1934 and 1938. Perhaps Ulmanis also thought that, with these chambers, he could create a kind of substitute parliament for that critical part of the population that mourned the loss of the parliamentary era – a democratic field of activity, something that would simultaneously distract such critics from major policy issues. What is relevant here is that Latvia, starting in the mid 1930s, started to overcome the global economic crisis – due in part to these newly created chambers – and to move its economy forward, a turnaround reflected in a noticeable increase in industrial jobs and a general shortage of workers. The latter increasingly led the agricultural sector to fall back on migrant workers from Poland. Not only did Latvia's domestic market profit from this; foreign trade in particular also grew, which, however, also underscored the Latvian economy's dependency on exports.[9]

With the rapprochement between Nazi Germany and the Soviet Union, at the end of which stood the conclusion of the Hitler-Stalin pact, the overall situation changed. In its expansion to the east, Germany had up to this point sought to close ranks with Poland strategically, something that was no longer practicable due to Poland's close ties to Great Britain.[10] Now, destroying Poland and temporarily securing the western flank stood in the foreground. This change on the political front required that Germany move quickly in approaching the Soviet Union, as preparations for the attack on Poland had been underway since April 1939 and were supposed to be completed by the end of August. On 26 July, Legation Counselor Julius Schnurre, the head of the East European Desk at the German Foreign Office, met Embassy Counselor Georgii Astakhov and Evgenii Babarin, the deputy chief of the Soviet trade representation, for dinner at the Berlin restaurant Ewest, where they discussed relations between their two countries. Schnurre spoke relatively freely about the big political picture – as he had been told to do – and let slip a few remarks that the relationship between the two dictators could clearly be better, for ultimately the ideological antagonisms had long ago become obsolete, something his Soviet interlocutors appreciated. Astakhov paid particular attention to the question of whether Germany's interests in the Baltic states and Romania went beyond purely economic issues, something Schnurre more or less denied. At the same time, Schnurre emphasized that the Reich sought nothing "that would endanger Soviet interests." Astakhov considered the conversation so valuable that he wanted to inform Moscow about it. In addition, it was important for him to know whether Germany's position would remain the same in talks at a higher level.

Schnurre confirmed this, but noted in his report to the Foreign Office that he considered Astakhov's course of action Soviet diplomatic tactics.[11]

Yet this interest was more far-reaching in nature. On 2 August, Astakhov was summoned to German Foreign Minister Joachim von Ribbentrop – which for a diplomat of comparably low rank was rather unusual. Ribbentrop explained to Astakhov that Germany would not yield with regard to Poland and the conflict over Danzig, and he assured him that Schnurre represented the Foreign Office's views regarding a rapprochement with the Soviet Union. Astakhov, said Ribbentrop, should report this to his superiors. On 3 August, Schnurre again approached Astakhov. In non-committal fashion, he suggested that the two countries put their political thoughts in a secret final protocol for the occasion of the ratification of an economic treaty, which had also been planned. At a hastily arranged meeting between the two on 10 August, conversation, which was supposed to be about economic issues, quickly came to revolve around German-Soviet political relations and the possibility of a German-Polish conflict. Astakhov signaled to Schnurre that the Soviet Union would be interested in intensifying its relationship with the Reich, while Schnurre emphasized that Germany was prepared "to grant the Soviet Union any desired security" and, where the inviolability of the Soviet Union's western border was concerned, could certainly do this better than Great Britain.

After that, things moved very quickly. Astakhov reported to Moscow on 12 August that the conflict between Germany and Poland was coming to a head, and that crucial events could materialize in a very short time. On 15 August, the German ambassador in Moscow, Friedrich Werner Graf von der Schulenburg, received a top secret telegram from the German foreign minister that instructed him to call on Soviet Foreign Minister Viacheslav Molotov. Schulenburg was then to read the telegram to Molotov. The contents of the telegram stated, in short, that Germany and the Soviet Union "stand opposite one another in separate and hostile camps" due only to ideological differences. Germany now wanted to change this, for "real antagonisms in interests" between the two states and "cause for an aggressive tendency on the part of one country against the other" did not exist. All questions of foreign policy such as "the Baltic Sea, the Baltic states, Poland, issues regarding the southeast, etc." could be regulated by means of mutual agreement, and genuine cooperation between the two states could be sought. Ribbentrop's telegram stressed that the Soviet government also desired "clarification of the German-Russian relationship," but the usual diplomatic channels worked too slowly in this case. For this reason, Ribbentrop recommended that he travel to Moscow as quickly as possible, in order "to lay the foundation for a final clearing up of German-Russian relations" in talks with Stalin.[12]

In Moscow, the offer was understood all too well; the indications of a German attack on Poland were not to be overlooked. At the same time, the idea that Great Britain and France's guarantee for Poland would be honored was not highly appreciated in diplomatic circles. Would the Soviet Union seize the opportunity and pull off a change of direction in foreign policy – for considerations of pure realpolitik at the exclusion of ideology – to the detriment of Poland? At first, Molotov informed the German ambassador on 16 August that he would gladly welcome an improvement in Germany's relations with the Soviet Union, and that he believed in the sincerity of the German offer. Any concrete agreements, however, must be discussed with his government, that is to say, with Stalin, and he cautioned that Ribbentrop's trip would therefore require certain preparations. This applied mainly, he added, should the conclusion of a treaty of non-aggression or similarly significant, concrete decisions be at issue. The next day, Schulenburg again visited Molotov and confirmed that the conclusion of a treaty of non-aggression was at issue, and if so desired, such a treaty could be limited to twenty-five years. Ribbentrop, for his part, had let it be known that he would board a plane at any time after 18 August and fly to Moscow – an unmistakable indication that war with Poland was looming. Still, Stalin hesitated, for he did not like to be rushed.

On the German side, time was of the essence. Ribbentrop once again sent Schulenburg to Molotov. In addition to a treaty of non-aggression, a "special protocol" was to be signed as well. The latter would regulate by mutual agreement various issues concerning both states' spheres of interests – the Baltic Sea area and the Baltic states being mentioned specifically. Anything more concrete, however, was only possible in a verbal exchange. After two visits on 20 August, Schulenburg reported that the Soviet government had agreed to a visit by Ribbentrop on 26 or 27 August. At the same time, he conveyed a Soviet draft of the treaty of non-aggression. Originally, Molotov did not want to commit to what was, from the point of view of the Soviets, an early appointment, one that, for the Third Reich, came too late. Therefore, on 20 August, Hitler sent a telegram directly to Stalin, explaining that "a crisis could break out any day" and asking in no uncertain terms that Ribbentrop be received on 23 August at the latest. Stalin underlined the decisive passages of Hitler's telegram and agreed to his request on 21 August.[13]

One hour after Ribbentrop arrived in Moscow, negotiations were already underway, and in the early hours of 24 August, the Treaty of Non-Aggression between Germany and the Union of Soviet Socialist Republics was signed. This pact was presented to the outside world as equivalent to the treaties Germany had concluded with Latvia or Estonia. More significant, however, was the highly secret protocol, which was but a few paragraphs long. In it, the geopolitical spheres of interest of both dictators were staked out. With regard to the Baltic states, Germany conceded that, in the event "of a territorial-political re-organization" of the Baltic states and Finland, Berlin had no interests in these areas; Lithuania's northern border represented "the border of the sphere of interests of Germany and the USSR." Ribbentrop telegraphed during a break in the negotiations that access to the ports of Liepāja and Ventspils was important to the Russians, something Hitler accepted. With regard to Poland, the two powers agreed to partition the country, with the rivers Narew, Vistula, and San acting as the border. With this in mind, the protocol was signed.[14] The first victim of this pact was to be Poland. Having nothing to fear, at least from the Soviet Union, Hitler was finally able to launch the invasion of Poland. On 1 September 1939, the Second World War began.

As is known, the campaign against Poland was a complete success of German arms and laid the foundation for the Wehrmacht's long-lasting aura of invincibility. While operations were still underway, however, the conquered territories quickly degenerated into a field of experimentation for National Socialist policies of annihilation. Once military administration had been replaced by civil administration, the Germans set about dismantling the Polish state. A part of the Polish territories (all or large parts of the western voivodeships) were annexed to the Reich, while the rest was used to form the General Government. In the weeks and months that followed, the systematic persecution of those groups declared enemies by the Reich Security Main Office (*Reichssicherheitshauptamt*, RSHA) and other Nazi organizations also increased. In addition to Jews and members of the Polish intelligentsia, which was to be annihilated completely in "extraordinary pacification operations," German euthanasia policy was expanded to include Poles. Special commandos "emptied" the nursing homes and killed those who were ill. In other respects, the technocrats of mass murder – meaning primarily officials from the RSHA, where the Security Police (the collective designation for the Gestapo and the Criminal Police) and the Security Service (the Nazi party's own intelligence service) had been merged into a single administration under Reinhard Heydrich since 27 September 1939 – began making the first plans to determine which tactics could best be applied in the envisioned large-scale annihilation, reassimilation, and resettlement measures. They gained much of the corresponding "experience" needed during the massive forced resettlement of Poles from the annexed territories.[15] The criminal organizations responsible for mass murder and "displacements of peoples" were to find application just under two years later in the Baltic as well, and the "knowledge" gained in Poland was to be used accordingly.[16] While Hitler and the Third Reich basked in the success of the Blitzkrieg, the Soviet occupation of eastern Poland had set in.[17] Stalin then made his move, step by step, to implement the pact with

Germany with regard to the Baltic states and to carry out his expansion to the northwest.

The Latvian foreign minister, Vilhelms Munters, may have assured the German ambassador in Riga, Hans Ulrich von Kotze, that Latvia felt "in no way affected" by the German-Soviet treaty of non-aggression, but he ultimately desired a statement to the press that this accord "does not infringe on the independence, integrity and security of the Baltic states." When the German ambassador responded that everything had been settled by the German-Latvian treaty of non-aggression of 4 June 1939, and that statements going any farther would be inopportune, the Latvian government must have felt its fears completely confirmed. Kotze could not avoid reporting the Latvians' irritation and anger toward Germany and their concerns about a Russian invasion. But for the German Foreign Office, this was ultimately no longer its problem. The Baltic states had been sacrificed, as was shown to a certain extent by the coolness of these diplomatic dealings. The only question that remained was when Stalin would redeem the German concession.[18]

After the Soviet Union began occupying eastern Poland on 17 September, it became clear to the last skeptic what the rapprochement between the two dictatorships meant for the Baltic states. One consequence of this recognition was the immediate weakening of the Latvian government. Several ministers are said to have obtained visas so they could flee to Sweden. Ulmanis, who had bet on Great Britain and thus the wrong side, saw his image so tarnished that even Minister of War Balodis distanced himself from him and ultimately left the government in early 1940. The French ambassador in Riga assessed the situation in Latvia as hopeless, while the country's Communist movement took in the morning air. Latvia lacked the strength to accept an Estonian initiative by which the Baltic states would agree to joint action against the Soviet threat. A meeting set for 20 September was canceled for threadbare reasons.[19]

Stalin did not aim to make a direct attack, however. He opted for a policy that could be described in genteel terms as diplomatic pressure. It was in fact nothing more than blackmail. After Estonia learned from Germany that it could not count on assistance from Berlin in the event of a military conflict with the Soviet Union but, instead, the very opposite, it was left defenseless. Neither Estonia nor the Baltic states as a whole could count on the support of any other great power. The forces of France and Great Britain were tied down elsewhere. The only thing left to do was to follow Molotov's directions. Estonia and the Soviet Union signed a pact of mutual assistance, to which was added – in imitation of the Hitler-Stalin pact – a secret protocol granting Moscow basing rights for 25,000 Red Army soldiers in Estonia and the use of Tallinn harbor. After the Baltic states' united front was broken by this accord, Latvia and Lithuania had to follow the Estonian example.

First the Red Army massed on the Latvian border as a threat; then Munters was invited to Moscow for talks. There the Latvian foreign minister was more or less informed of the content of the Hitler-Stalin pact. Stalin stressed that he sought to maintain the territorial integrity of Latvia, but the Soviet Union needed access to the harbors and air bases, coastal artillery, and troops in the country. In the course of these discussions, the Kremlin leadership allowed itself to be "negotiated down" from 50,000 to 30,000 soldiers. When Munters continued to hesitate, Molotov openly threatened to occupy Latvia. On 5 October 1939, the Latvian-Soviet pact of mutual assistance, analogous to the Estonian-Soviet treaty, was signed in Moscow. By agreeing to this, Latvia hoped at least to maintain its independence. Lithuania, as the last Baltic state, signed a treaty meeting Moscow's conditions on 10 October. Shortly after the conclusion of these treaties, the Red Army's military missions, with accompanying forces, entered their respective regions and occupied the promised bases.[20]

The pessimists among the Latvian government and the public were soon to be proved correct that the stationing of Soviet troops within their country represented not the last step toward rapprochement, but the first step toward occupation. At first, the Soviets' new garrisons, especially the ports and airports, did not serve the occupation of the Baltics, but provided a basis of operations and supplies for the Soviet-Finish war. In the Winter War, which was conducted by unequal means, the Red Army was less than awe-inspiring and could only impress by fielding enormous numbers of soldiers and weapons. Its leadership and materiel were considered inferior or out-of-date. This of course applied only to the perspective of a military power such as Germany. Neither Finland – nor by comparison the Baltic states – could have held out for long against the concerted strength of the Red Army. And neither the Finns, who in their struggle were supported by France, Great Britain, and the Scandinavian countries, nor the Baltic states, who were completely left to themselves, had genuine allies. After Finland was forced to cede the Karelia Isthmus and parts of eastern Karelia to the Soviet Union in the Peace of Moscow of 12 March 1940, the Soviet impulse to expand was again directed toward the Baltic states.[21]

This impulse was seen in the boldness of the Latvian Communists, who openly agitated against the Ulmanis government. Many of them had been released from prison as a sign of the new era of cooperation when the Soviet-Latvian treaty was concluded. While the Communist Party of Latvia attempted to produce a change in mood among the population from within the country, the Kremlin complained that Latvia was secretly plotting against the Red Army forces stationed there. This transparent accusation was first articulated by Molotov to Lithuania at the end of May 1940, but as early as June, it was also directed at Latvia, which – per the accusation – was only acting more shrewdly. All three Baltic states also faced the absurd general suspicion of being allied with Finland, which a few weeks earlier had been at war with the Soviet Union.[22]

The eyes of the world were certainly not gazing on the Baltic at this time. The Wehrmacht had occupied Denmark and Norway in April 1940. Just one month later, the western campaign began, ending in the defeat of French troops and the flight of the British Expeditionary Force as well as the occupation of Belgium, the Netherlands, Luxembourg, and much of France by the end of June. The last resistance in Norway was crushed that same month. Within a few weeks, political power in Europe had been completely changed; together with its ally Italy, Germany now ruled the continent. Only Great Britain, with its back to the wall, continued to prosecute the war against the Reich with determination, but the Baltic states – which had long hosted more Red Army soldiers in their countries than agreed to by treaty – understandably played no role in London's strategic calculations.[23]

On 16 June, Molotov summoned Latvian Ambassador Fricis Kotzins and handed him a declaration of the Soviet government, which claimed that the Soviet Union felt threatened by the Baltic Entente, and that Latvia had violated its treaty of mutual assistance with the Soviet Union in the grossest terms. The Soviets demanded that Latvia immediately form a pro-Soviet government and allow the free passage of additional Red Army troops, which were to protect the Soviet garrisons in Latvia from "provocative acts." In concrete terms, this meant the country's occupation. Molotov gave Kotzins seven hours to accommodate the Soviet government's demands. That same day, Molotov had presented the Estonian ambassador with a corresponding ultimatum as well; the Lithuanian foreign minister had been confronted with nearly the same demands two days earlier. In that case, the ultimatum had already expired.

All three Baltic states complied and yielded to Moscow's demands, for Berlin had clearly signaled that they could not hope for any assistance from Germany. In Latvia's case, the Soviet Union did not even consider it necessary to wait for the seven hours to expire. On 17 June 1940, Latvia was completely occupied by the Red Army and lost its sovereignty. In the first phase of annexation, the Soviets left President Ulmanis in office. Real power, however, was exercised by Soviet Special Plenipotentiary Andrei Vyshinskii, the former prosecutor general of the Soviet Union. He appointed a new Latvian government, which was made up first and foremost of Communists or persons who had worked for the Soviet intelligence service. When Ulmanis refused to legitimate its appointment with his signature as head of state, Vyshinskii nonchalantly overrode the Latvian constitution and showed Ulmanis, who was closely guarded, that such formalities were no longer necessary. Vyshinskii appointed a presentable marionette – Augusts Kirchensteins, a professor of veterinary medicine with no party affiliation – minister president of the new "people's government," while the Interior Ministry, which was especially important for controlling the country, was placed under Communist writer Villis Lācis.[24]

The direct integration of the Baltic states via their annexation to the Soviet Union represented the final act in their takeover. The "stage directors" for Latvia envisioned the following in the process: the newly installed "people's government" was to call a new parliamentary election for 14 and 15 July. However, only candidates for the Communist unity list – to which the Social Democrats also belonged – were allowed to run, just as the election process was controlled by the Soviets. Several courageous representatives of the former democracy were forced to learn this painful lesson when they tried to introduce an alternative list of candidates. The candidates were of course banned, and the most active former parliamentarians were arrested. After it had become clear what the Soviets understood by elections, the people were allowed to go to the polls. The results, which the Soviet press agency TASS piquantly announced twelve hours before the votes were counted, showed 97.6 percent of the votes to be for the unity list. The new "people's parliament," the Tautas Saeima, convened for its first session on 21 July and declared Latvia a Soviet republic. At the same session, the Tautas Saeima sent a request to Moscow asking that Latvia be admitted to the Soviet Union.

The Supreme Soviet fulfilled Latvia's request in a resolution passed on 5 August, which formally annexed the previously independent Baltic republic. The same thing happened simultaneously to Lithuania and Estonia. Throughout the process, Germany stood squarely by the Soviet Union. The German Foreign Office may have received letters from the Latvian and Lithuanian ambassadors protesting this act of Soviet aggression, but it promptly informed them that only governments were responsible for diplomatic correspondence. The two Baltic diplomats, said the Foreign Office, had made personal statements of no consequence. The Germans, however, generously extended asylum to all three Baltic ambassadors – an offer that was gratefully accepted. After the incorporation of the Baltic states into the Soviet Union, Moscow cordially requested that the German Foreign Office close its embassies in these countries and henceforth use only the German embassy in Moscow. Ribbentrop requested that the embassies be turned into consular offices, for these were needed to maintain economic ties and to manage the resettlement of the ethnic Germans from these countries. The Soviet Union complied with this wish.[25]

In the months that followed, the two dictatorships pursued different ends in Latvia. The Kremlin sought to strengthen its position in the Baltic and to eradicate its political enemies, while the Reich sought to evacuate the Baltic Germans living there. Upon closer examination, these seemingly divergent interests were somewhat linked to one another and even contained some potential for conflict. For many of the former regime's representatives and anti-Communists, finding a place for exile was an existential matter. Germany still remained an option. But would Germany accept this group? Or would this be a violation of the Hitler-Stalin pact, something that decision-makers in Berlin would prefer to avoid? And above all: What kind of steps had the Germans taken to protect the ethnic Germans?

It should be noted for a start that the ethnic Germans in the Baltic states had probably been shocked by the announcement of the Hitler-Stalin pact in August 1939. They saw their rights as a minority and as Germans protected by the Reich against the Soviet Union. The surrender of the Baltic states also struck at the core of their existence. For this reason, German-Baltic politicians, first and foremost Alfred Intelmann, the president of the German community, and Dr. Erhard Kroeger, leader of the National Socialist movement among the Baltic Germans, made an unsuccessful effort to bring German foreign policy back to an anti-Soviet course. Kroeger had been a member of the SS since 23 October 1938 and held the rank of SS lieutenant colonel. Unlike Intelmann, he maintained the best of contacts with party agencies and of course with the Security Service, right up to *Reichsführer-SS* and Chief of the German Police Heinrich Himmler himself. At the end of September 1939, Kroeger had learned during a meeting with Himmler at Führer Headquarters in Zoppot that the arrangements between the Reich and the Soviet Union were more comprehensive than the Baltic Germans had feared. After this confidential briefing, Kroeger, who believed Baltic Germandom faced an extraordinary threat, urged Himmler to arrange by all means the evacuation and resettlement of the ethnic Germans.

Himmler apparently shared this view and went to see Hitler with this in mind. The German dictator also felt Kroeger's proposal pointed in the right direction and instructed Ribbentrop to arrange the corresponding negotiations. On 29 September, the foreign minister was able to report that this had been done. On that day, in a confidential protocol to the German-Soviet Border and Friendship Treaty, Moscow allowed all "persons of German ancestry" to depart the Soviet zone of influence, "if they wish to relocate to Germany or to the German areas of influence." After the Soviets acquiesced, Hitler announced in a speech to the Reichstag on 6 October that he intended to resettle the Baltic Germans. On 9 October, it was possible to read the first call to leave Latvia in an appeal signed by Intelmann and Kroeger and published in the newspaper *Rigasche Rundschau*. A second appeal was issued on 30 October.[26]

By the start of the new year, around 14,000 persons from Estonia and 52,500 persons from Latvia had resettled to the Reich in the first wave, while several thousand ethnic Germans declined to leave for the Reich, because they did not want to leave their homeland, did not feel threatened, or were opposed to the "Third Reich" in some way. Some 500 persons followed in April and May 1940. The Soviet leaders found themselves exposed, because many Baltic Germans assumed, correctly, that the annexation of their homeland had already been decided, and that they had better clear out quickly. At the same time, the German ethnic group was showing signs of panic: schools were closing, and doctors were abandoning their practices, while in Riga harbor at least ten ships lay at anchor to take on the settlers. The German Foreign Office calmed the People's Commissariat for Foreign Affairs, ensuring it that the evacuation of the Baltic Germans served only to avoid future tensions during the Sovietization of the Baltic countries – after all, the Reich would even then still represent the interests of the ethnic Germans – and insisting that nobody had even thought of revealing the Soviets' plans prematurely.[27]

After the responsible SS agencies – the Ethnic German Liaison Office and the office of the Reich Commissar for the Strengthening of Germandom – had whipped through the main evacuation of the Baltic Germans over a matter of months, a "posterior resettlement" followed as a consequence of the Soviet Union's takeover of the Baltic states that summer. This operation had much greater explosive potential. In addition to the last Germans, many representatives of the former Baltic elite and outspoken anti-Communists saw themselves forced to emigrate or flee. That the Soviet Union sought to eliminate its political opponents in the new Soviet Baltic republics was quickly seen in the fate of the former heads of state. Latvian President Ulmanis was deported on 22 July 1940; his counterpart from Estonia, Konstantin Päts, former Minister President Augustinas Voldemaras of Lithuania, and other leading Baltic politicians and top representatives of the military and business world shared the same fate. The start of this systematic persecution may well have been linked to the August visit of Ivan Serov to Riga. A close confidant of Lavrentii Beria, the head of the People's Commissariat for Internal Affairs (NKVD), Serov was considered an "expert on deportation" (and would himself rise to become KGB chief in the 1950s).

The NKVD proceeded to eliminate its enemies in three phases. First political opponents were registered. This category included senior civil servants of the former state, policemen, nationalists, revisionists such as Trotskyites and Mensheviks, large landowners, clergy, political émigrés, and others. Then the arrests set in, and in spring 1941 at the latest, the deportations deep into the Soviet interior got underway. Prominent victims among the Jews were Ulmanis confidant Paul Mintz, who was deported to Siberia with his family and died there in 1941, as well as Noah Maisel of the Socialist, anti-Zionist Bund party, who died in 1956 in a camp in northern Siberia. Jewish members of the Saeima who were deported included Rabbi Mordechai Nurock, who was arrested for his Zionist activities, Yerahmiel Vinnik, and Mordechai Dubin. The reason for the arrest of the latter probably lay in his religious engagement. He was the one, after all, who had motivated Rabbi Joseph Isaak Schneersohn, the rabbi of the Lubavitcher movement, to transfer his branch of Hasidic Jewry to Riga. For a short time, it seemed to many that the rabbi's residence on Briežu St. was the center of Hasidism. Rabbi Schneersohn and his family moved on to America in time. Dubin saw no reason to flee and paid dearly for his convictions. Even in the Russian interior, he was repeatedly taken into solitary confinement and ultimately locked up in an asylum. It is said he died in 1956.

The remaining Jewish population quickly learned that the repressions would hit not only representatives of the former Latvian state and traditionalists. Even if some young Jews celebrated the fall of the Ulmanis regime as the tanks of the Red Army entered Riga, they quickly experienced the growing restrictions on individual rights, the ban on the work of Jewish organizations, and the nationalization of property. The only positive thing to be noted was that all racist discrimination was banned and prosecuted, for in the wake of Sovietization the primacy of ideology was all that counted. Seen in this way, it is not astonishing to learn that, in addition to Latvian nationalists, members of Jewish organizations, such as the Zionists, were among the Soviets' main victims.[28]

The deportations from the Baltic peaked just before the German invasion of the Soviet Union. Thousands of persons were deported between 13 and 19 June 1941. Reportedly, 5,000 Latvian Jews were among them, an unusually high figure among 16,000 deportees that has yet to be subjected to scrutiny. However, it is known that, by removing this group of persons, Stalin was at the same time trying to ease the situation vis-à-vis Hitler, for he believed that the nationalists and Jews in the Baltic, as in Ukraine, could be manipulated by the Reich as a provocation that could suffice as a pretext for war. Their elimination was therefore imperative for him, if not to avoid the war, then to delay the German offensive.[29] According to Max Kaufmann, the deported Jews included many émigrés from Germany and Austria who had accepted the offer of asylum in Latvia from Member of the Saeima Mordechai Dubin. In June 1941, 21,000 people from Lithuania and 11,000 people from Estonia were sent to the Gulag. The loss of persons to deportations, secret shootings, and the conscription of young, able-bodied men into the Red Army totaled 35,000 for Latvia, 34,000 for Lithuania, and 60,000 for Estonia (where the figures for conscription were very high).[30]

Strangely enough, the posterior resettlement of Baltic Germans did not fully appeal to Himmler. He of course knew that he would be saving "German blood," but he was at the same time worried about the infiltration of political opponents, Soviet spies, and anti-Communists, fearing the Soviet Union could feel provoked by Germany's acceptance of the latter. Himmler did not stick to his position, however. In a meeting of government agencies and associations entrusted with resettlement operations, it was agreed on 15 August 1940 that the remaining 15,000 Germans (of which some 10,000 were in Latvia) would also be "posteriorly resettled." Still, Himmler insisted that a distinction be made between real "resettlers" – those who had remained in the Baltic with official permission (e.g. as economics specialists) – and "refugees" or "repatriates," i.e., Baltic Germans who had initially voted against the Reich during the main evacuation in 1939. The "refugees" were to be relocated within the borders of the prewar Reich for reasons of security and to have fewer privileges than the "resettlers." All those persons affected by the "posterior resettlement" were considered highly suspicious, which was why the Ethnic German Liaison Office and the Gestapo were instructed to monitor this group for political opponents. Vis-à-vis the Soviet government, such subtleties were dispensed with, and the entire group of people was identified as resettlers, particularly as this facilitated the transfer of their property to the Reich. Naturally, the Soviet side had to give its consent, which took until 10 January 1941.[31]

By then, the German agencies concerned had set up advisory centers in Riga and Tallinn. These had the task of "checking those willing to be resettled with respect to their politics and deciding whether permission to resettle could be given from the German side." In all, this review process involved some 14,000 persons of German origin who had submitted an application. In addition, some 4,000 other persons received resettlement papers. A precondition for this was that they be married to a spouse of German origin. Because registration was carried out under enormous time constraints and the background check carried out by the advisory centers was superficial, many Balts succeeded "in being authorized for resettlement by circumventing the preliminary test." In all, according to a report of the screening commission, 17,245 Baltic refugees were registered, of which 3,876 persons were non-Germans. Most of the latter were opponents of the Soviet Union who were thus able to flee. Prominent refugees from Latvia included Oskars Dankers (a retired general), Arturs Sigailis (a professional officer), Roberts Štiglics (a former official from the political police), Alfrēds Valdmanis (a former finance minister), Alfrēds Bērziņš (a propaganda minister), Martins Primanis (a politician active in cultural affairs), and others. The largest group was made up of former soldiers of the Latvian Army, who were not only considered suspect by the Soviets, but had also lost their posts. Other national-minded Latvians lacking familial ties to Germans, such as the police investigator Herberts Teidmanis or the Aizsargi member and administrator Alberts Eichelis, felt compelled to go underground in order to escape arrest.[32]

While the resettlers were brought to Łódź (renamed Litzmannstadt by the Germans) to be "naturalized by the Immigration Central Office like all other settlers according to regulations," the refugees were moved to special camps in Pomerania and Mecklenburg. Their supervision was turned over to the Ethnic German Liaison Office. Dr. Kroeger – now head of the Immigration Central Office in occupied Poznań (Posen) and an SS colonel – had reached an agreement with Gestapo Chief Heinrich Müller, by which the refugees had to be registered by the Security Police and their camps screened most thoroughly.[33] At the same time, particular attention was given to the search for Jews and "friends of Jews" of German origin, as two prominent examples show. Annemarie Roens, the wife of Riga textile manufacturer Karl Roens, was denounced for her "Germanophobia" and contacts with Jews. The screening commission's specialists "exposed" Dr. Erwin Meyer as a "full-Jew." Both cases were taken to Himmler for a decision. He ordered that they be confined to concentration camps.[34]

With the evacuation of the Baltic Germans, the policy of rapprochement between the dictatorships came to an end. During this phase, Latvia had been destroyed as an independent state, Sovietized, and incorporated into the Soviet Union. The German minority in Latvia no longer existed, and opponents of the new regime were threatened with deportation or murder inasmuch as they had not succeeded in fleeing. On the eve of Operation Barbarossa, when the Abwehr (German military intelligence) was recruiting specialists from among the exiles, it must have become clear to the Baltic Germans very quickly that Hitler in no way viewed the Soviet occupation of the Baltic as the status quo, and that he had merely put forward the arrangement with Stalin in order to push his drive for expansion under conditions more conducive to considerations of foreign policy and military strategy. Now this policy of conquest was aimed squarely at the Soviet Union.

Notes

1. The territory of Latvia was determined by the Latvian-Russian linguistic border, which as a consequence entailed the detachment of certain areas that had traditionally been under

Russian administration (incl. Daugavpils [Dünaburg] and Rēzekne [Rositten]) from the Vitebsk region and their cession to Latvia.
2. For details, see Sigmar Stopinski, *Das Baltikum im Patt der Mächte*, 207–254; John Hiden, *The Baltic States and Weimar Ostpolitik*, 20–35; Gregor von Rauch, *Geschichte der baltischen Staaten*, 65–80; and Gert von Pistohlkors, "Die historischen Voraussetzungen für die Entstehung der drei baltischen Staaten," in *Die baltischen Nationen*, ed. Boris Meissner, 40–44.
3. Adolfs Silde, "Die Entwicklung der Republik Lettland," in Meissner, *Die baltischen Nationen*, 64–70; Rauch, *Geschichte der baltischen Staaten*, 82–84, 92–99, 122–123, and 129–130; Max Laserson, "The Jews in the Latvian Parliament," in *The Jews in Latvia*, ed. Association of Latvian and Estonian Jews in Israel, 131–132; Hiden, *The Baltic States and Weimar Ostpolitik*, 56; Michael Garleff, "Die kulturelle Selbstverwaltung der nationalen Minderheiten in den baltischen Staaten," in Meissner, *Die baltischen Nationen*, 97–99; Bernhard Press, *Judenmord in Lettland 1941–1945*, 10–16; Max Kaufmann, *Churbn Lettland*, 40–42. Laserson himself was a member of the Saeima for the Socialist-Zionist Party.
4. The original founding took place earlier, in 1930, under the name "Fire Cross"; the first leader was Janis Greble. Only when Gustavs Celmiņš took over the group did it begin its true development.
5. Rauch, *Geschichte der baltischen Staaten*, 146–150. Drawing on remarks made by Alfreds Bērziņš, one of Ulmanis's close associates, Rauch stresses that Ulmanis did not feel drawn to either Hitler's or Mussolini's form of government. Cf. Silde, "Die Entwicklung der Republik Lettland," 70–73, who describes Ulmanis's preference for the Italian system. See also Andrew Ezergailis, *The Holocaust in Latvia 1941–1944*, 81–82, and Seppo Myllyniemi, *Die Neuordnung der baltischen Länder 1941–1944*, 31–32.
6. "Freundschaftsvertrag zwischen Deutschland und der Union der Sozialistischen Sowjetrepubliken vom 24. April 1926 und Notenaustausch vom gleichen Tage," in *Akten zur Deutschen Auswärtigen Politik (ADAP)*, Serie B, Bd. II/1, 402–403. The German ambassador in Moscow, Ulrich Graf von Brockdorff-Rantzau, knew, however, that the relationship with Soviet Russia rested "to a certain extent on bluffing," the goal of which was "to give the impression of a greater intimacy with Russia than is really existent." That the rapprochement was guided solely by tactics without substance was of course to remain concealed from other countries, including the Baltic republics. See "Der Botschafter in Moskau Graf von Brockdorff-Rantzau an Reichspräsident von Hindenburg (Entwurf)," 8 July 1926, in *ADAP*, Serie B, Bd. II/2, 98–102. Hindenburg's response is included here. See also Klaus Hildebrand, *Das vergangene Reich*, 466–474.
7. On the forced cession of the Memel territory, see "Der Reichsaußenminister an den Führer," 23 March 1939. This includes the text of the treaty between Germany and Lithuania of 22 March in footnote 2, printed in *ADAP*, Serie D, Bd. V, 440–441. With that, the Treaty of Versailles was reversed, and Lithuanian troops evacuated the Memel territory.
8. "Aufzeichnung des Vortragenden Legationsrats von Grundherr (Pol. Abt.)," 6 June 1939, in *ADAP*, Serie D, Bd. VI, 541–542; "Aufzeichnung des Legationsrats Hewel (Persönlicher Stab RAM)," 8 June 1939, ibid., 542–545.
9. Rauch, *Geschichte der baltischen Staaten*, 151–152; Silde, "Die Entwicklung der Republik Lettland," 71–72.
10. "Aufzeichnung des Staatssekretärs," 6 April 1939, in *ADAP*, Serie D, Bd. VI, 170–171; "Note der Deutschen Regierung an die Polnische Regierung," 27 April 1939, ibid., 288–291.
11. Horst Rohde, "Hitlers erster Blitzkrieg und seine Auswirkung auf Nordosteuropa," in *Das Deutsche Reich und der Zweite Weltkrieg*, ed. Militärgeschichtliches Forschungsamt,

Bd. 2, 79, 84–85, and 92–102; "Aufzeichnung des Vortragenden Legationsrates Schnurre (Witschftspol. Abt.)," 27 July 1939, in *ADAP*, Serie D, Bd. VI, S. 846–849. See also Alan Bullock, *Hitler und Stalin*, 806–807, and Philipp W. Fabry, *Der Hitler-Stalin-Pakt 1939–1941*, 12–46.

12. "Der Reichsaußenminister an die Botschaft in Moskau," 3 August 1939, in *ADAP*, Serie D, Bd. VI, 882; "Der Reichsaußenminister an die Botschaft in Moskau," 4 August 1939, ibid., 883; "Aufzeichnung des Vortragenden Legationsrates Schnurre (Wirtschaftspol. Abt.)," 10 August 1939, in *ADAP*, Serie D, Bd. VII, 14–16; "Der Reichsaußenminister an die Botschaft in Moskau," 14 August 1939, ibid., 51–52; Fabry, *Der Hitler-Stalin-Pakt 1939–1941*, 46–61; Dimitri Wolkogonow, *Stalin*, 472–473; Valentin Falin, *Zweite Front*, 87–91. Falin shows additional meetings between Astakhov and representatives of the Foreign Office and rightly stresses the initiative of Germany in these talks, but has Astakhov – who was arrested after his return in 1940 and died in the Gulag in February 1942 – appear as an independently acting diplomat who had overstepped his competences, but at the same time was one of Beria's men. See Lew Besymenski, *Stalin und Hitler*, 202–212.

13. "Der Botschafter in Moskau an das Auswärtige Amt," 16 August 1939, in *ADAP*, Serie D, Bd. VII, 63–64; "Der Reichsaußenminister an die Botschaft in Moskau," 16 August 1939, ibid., 70; "Der Reichsaußenminister an die Botschaft in Moskau," 18 August 1939, ibid., 100–102; "Der Botschafter in Moskau an das Auswärtige Amt," 16 August 1939, ibid., 111–112; "Der Reichsaußenminister an die Botschaft in Moskau," 20 August 1939, ibid., 131; "Der Botschafter in Moskau an das Auswärtige Amt," 21 August 1939, ibid., 140–141; Wolkogonow, *Stalin*, 474–475; Bullock, *Hitler und Stalin*, 808–813; Ingeborg Fleischhauer, "Die sowjetische Außenpolitik und die Genese des Hiter-Stalin-Paktes," in *Zwei Wege nach Moskau*, ed. Bernd Wegner, 32–36; Fabry, *Der Hitler-Stalin Pakt*, 62–70.

14. "Der Reichsaußenminister an das Auswärtige Amt," 23 August 1939, in *ADAP*, Serie D, Bd. VII, 184–185; "Vortragender Legationsrat Erich Kordt (Büro RAM) an die Botschaft in Moskau," 23 August 1939, ibid., 187; "Nichtangriffsvertrag zwischen Deutschland und der Union der Sozialistischen Sowjetrepubliken" and "Geheimes Zusatzprotokoll," ibid., 205–207; Besymenski, *Stalin und Hitler*, 221–229; Ingeborg Fleischhauer, *Der Pakt*, 337–339; Stefan Kley, *Hitler, Stalin, Ribbentrop und die Entfesselung des Zweiten Weltkriegs*, 298–302; Fabry, *Der Hitler-Stalin Pakt*, 71–91.

15. On the founding of the RSHA and its first conceptions of murder, see Michael Wildt, *Generation des Unbedingten*, 276–282 and 455–499. On the phase of military administration and the measures of persecution and exploitation carried out in this period: Hans Umbreit, *Deutsche Militärverwaltungen 1938–39*, 137–237; Czesław Madajczyk, *Die Okkupationspolitik Nazideutschlands in Polen 1939–1945*, 54–75; Martin Broszat, *Nationalsozialistische Polenpolitik 1939–1945*, 38–48, 85–102 and 158–163. A multifaceted overview of this first phase of German occupation and annihilation policy is offered by *Genesis des Genozids*, ed. Klaus-Michael Mallmann and Bogdan Musial; Peter Longerich, *Politik der Vernichtung*, 243–272. On the murder of the mentally ill, see Volker Rieß, *Die Anfänge der Vernichtung "lebensunwerten Lebens" in den Reichsgauen Danzig-Westpreußen und Wartheland 1939/1940*; Bruno Wasser, "Die 'Germanisierung' im Distrikt Lublin als Generalprobe und erste Realisierungsphase des 'Generalplans Ost'," in *Der "Generalplan Ost,"* ed. Mechtild Rössler and Sabine Schleiermacher, 271. According to these authors, the first studies on the politically driven demographic restructuring plans for the future, including the deportation of all Jews and 3.4 million Poles, had been prepared by Professor Konrad Meyer-Hetling by January 1940. A version of this study from February 1940 is printed in Rolf-Dieter Müller, *Hitlers Ostkrieg und die deutsche Siedlungspolitik*, 130–138.

16. In all, 2,700 men from the Gestapo and SD were deployed in the mobile commandos in Poland; this is worth nothing, because the four Einsatzgruppen in the Soviet Union in 1941 had a core personnel of 600–1,000 men each, although a disproportionately larger space was to be "worked over." On the Einsatzgruppen and the self-defense forces made up of local recruits, see Helmut Krausnick and Hans-Heinrich Wilhelm, *Die Truppe des Weltanschauungskrieges*, 32–79; Christian Jansen and Arno Weckbecker, *Der "Volksdeutsche Selbstschutz" in Polen 1939/40*, 42–79; Madajczyk, *Okkupationspolitik Nazideutschlands*, 9–18. On the plans of the RSHA, see the notes of SS Major Walter Rauff from 27 September 1939 concerning a meeting of the RSHA department chiefs and the Einsatzgruppen commanders in *Nacht über Europa: Die faschistische Okkupationspolitik in Polen (1939–1945)*, ed. Wolfgang Schumann, Ludwig Nestler et al., 119–120; Peter Longerich, *Der ungeschriebene Befehl*, 78–82. On the course of operations, see Rohde, "Hitlers erster Blitzkrieg," 111–149.
17. Hitler's speech of 6 October 1939, with commentary, is printed in Max Domarus, *Hitler: Reden und Proklomationen*, Bd. 3, 1,378–1,393. The passages concerning peace are on pages 1,388–1,393.
18. "Der Gesandte in Riga an das Auswärtige Amt," 31 August 1939, in *ADAP*, Serie D, Bd. VII, 386–387. Footnote 2 of this document provides an excerpt from Kotze's report on the mood of the Latvians. See also "Der Staatssekretär an die Botschaft in Moskau," 1 September 1939, ibid., 409, and "Der Botschafter in Moskau an das Auswärtige Amt," 2 September 1939, ibid., 434–435. These two telegrams document the arrangement between the German and the Soviet governments to keep Latvia in uncertainty with the turn of phrase concerning the existing Treaty of Non-Aggression.
19. "Note der Regierung der UdSSR an die polnische Regierung," 17 September 1939, in Gerhard Hass, *23. August 1939*, 223–224; Seppo Myllyniemi, *Die baltische Krise 1938–1941*, 54–56. On the role of the Department of Overseas Reconnaissance with the NKVD in forcing the Latvian crisis, see Pawel Sudoplatow and Anatolij Sudoplatow, *Der Handlanger der Macht*, 139–144.
20. Regarding Estonia: "Pakt über gegenseitigen Beistand zwischen der UdSSR und der Estnischen Republik," 29 September 1939, in *Schauplatz Baltikum*, ed. Michael Rosenbusch, Horst Schützler, and Sonja Streignitz, 63–67. On Latvia and Lithuania, see "Pakt über gegenseitigen Beistand zwischen der Union der Sozialistischen Sowjetrepubliken und der Lettischen Republik," 5 October 1939, in ibid., 82–86, and "Vertrag zwischen der Sowjetunion und Litauen über die Übergabe der Stadt Wilna und des Wilnagebietes an die Republik Litauen und über gegenseitigen Beistand," 10 October 1939, ibid., 90–95; Besymenski, *Stalin und Hitler*, 250–253; and Myllyniemi, *Die baltische Krise*, 58–69 and 76. In Latvia, the Soviet military mission arrived on 14 October; the Red Army followed in early November.
21. Gerhard L. Weinberg, *Eine Welt in Waffen*, 116–124; Seppo Myllyniemi, "Die Folgen der Hitler-Stalin-Paktes für die Baltischen Republiken und Finnland," in Wegner, *Zwei Wege nach Moskau*, 81–82. Myllyniemi stresses that mainly Estonia had to serve as a basis of operations for the Red Army. The violation of the principle of neutrality – especially as Finland was considered a friendly power and enjoyed the sympathy of the population and the Baltic press – openly and unmistakably highlighted the dependency of the Baltic republics on the Soviet Union. Fabry, *Hitler-Stalin-Pakt*, 195–198.
22. "Telegramm W.M. Molotows, des Volkskommissars für Auswärtige Angelegenheiten der UdSSR, an N.G. Posdnjakow, den Bevollmächtigten Vertreter der UdSSR in Litauen," 25 May 1940, in Rosenbusch et al., *Schauplatz Baltikum*, 118–119; "Telegramm Molotows, des Volkskommissars für Auswärtige Angelegenheiten der UdSSR, an die Bevollmächtigten Vertreter der UdSSR in Litauen, Lettland, Estland und Finnland," 14 June 1940, ibid., 127–129.

23. Weinberg, *Eine Welt in Waffen*, 126–162. Klaus A. Maier und Bernd Stegemann, "Die Sicherung der europäischen Nordflanke," in Militärgeschichtliches Forschungsamt, *Das Deutsche Reich und der Zweite Weltkrieg*, Bd. 2, 189–231; Hans Umbreit, "Der Kampf um die Vormachtstellung in Westeuropa," in Militärgeschichtliches Forschungsamt, *Das Deutsche Reich und der Zweite Weltkrieg*, Bd. 2, 235–237. Myllyniemi, "Die Folgen des Hitler-Stalin-Paktes," 85–86; Myllyniemi, *Die baltische Krise*, 119–121.
24. "Aufzeichnung des Gesprächs W.M. Molotows, des Volkskommissars für Auswärtige Angelegenheiten der UdSSR, mit J. Urbsys, dem Außenminister der Litauischen Republik," 14 June 1940, in Rosenbusch et al., *Schauplatz Baltikum*, 129–137; "Aufzeichnung des Gesprächs W.M. Molotows, des Volkskommissars für Auswärtige Angelegenheiten der UdSSR, mit F. Kotzins, dem Gesandten der Lettischen Republik in der UdSSR," 16 June 1940, ibid., 147–153; "Aufzeichnung des Gesprächs M.W. [sic] Molotows, des Volkskommissars für Auswärtige Angelegenheiten der UdSSR, mit A. Rei, dem Gesandten der Estnischen Republik in der UdSSR," 16 June 1940, ibid., 154–159; Egil Levits, "Lettland unter der Sowjetherrschaft und auf dem Wege zur Unabhängigkeit," in Meissner, *Die baltischen Nationen*, 139–140; Rauch, *Geschichte der baltischen Staaten*, 208–211. On the role of Andrei Vyshinskii, one of the principals in the show trials of the 1930s, in the Kremlin power structure, see Oleg W. Chlewnjuk, *Das Politbüro*.
25. Levits, "Lettland unter der Sowjetherrschaft," 140–141; Myllyniemi, *Die baltische Krise*, 133–136; "Aufzeichnungen des Leiters der Politischen Abteilung," 21 July 1940, and "Aufzeichnungen des Leiters der Politischen Abteilung," 22 July 1940, both in *ADAP*, Serie D, Bd. X, 217–221; "Aufzeichnungen des Leiters der Politischen Abteilung," 24 July 1940, in *ADAP*, Serie D, Bd. X, 235; "Der Botschafter in Moskau an das Auswärtige Amt," 12 August 1940, in *ADAP*, Serie D, Bd. X, 383–384; "Der Leiter der Politischen Abteilung an die Botschaft in Moskau," 15 August 1940, in *ADAP*, Serie D, Bd. X, 398–399. The response of 21 August is contained in footnote 6.
26. Matthias Schröder, *Deutschbaltische SS-Führer und Andrej Vlasov 1942–1945*, 51–56; Götz Aly, *Endlösung*, 38–41; "Deutsch-sowjetischer Grenz- und Freundschaftsvertrag" and "Vertrauliches deutsch-sowjetisches Protokoll," 28 September 1939, in *ADAP*, Serie D, Bd. VIII, 127–128; "Der Staatssekretär an die Gesandtschaften in Riga und Reval," 6 October 1939, in *ADAP*, Serie D, Bd. VIII, 181; "Aufrufe an die Deutsch-Balten in Lettland," 9 and 30 October 1939, in Dietrich A. Loeber, *Diktierte Option*, 163–164; Michael Garleff, "Die Deutschbalten als nationale Minderheit in den unabhängigen Staaten Estland und Lettland," in *Deutsche Geschichte im Osten Europas: Baltische Länder*, ed. Gert von Pistohlkors, 534–536. The latter contains a facsimile of the *Rigasche Rundschau* of 30 October 1939 and of the treaty concluded between Latvia and Germany on the resettlement of Latvian citizens of German origin to the German Reich. Corresponding treaties on the resettlement of the Baltic German ethnic group had been concluded by the Reich and Estonia and Lithuania on 15 and 30 October 1939.
27. "Der Botschafter in Moskau an das Auswärtige Amt," 11 October 1939, in *ADAP*, Serie D, Bd. VIII, 208. A second telegram is contained in footnote 1, here. See also "Der Reichsaußenminister an die Botschaft in Moskau," 13 October 1939, ibid., 221–222; Latvijas Valsts Vēstures Arhīvs Riga (LVVA), P 1019-1-3, 24–34, Abschlussbericht, Betrifft: Die Arbeit der Überprüfungskommandos für Baltenflüchtlinge (Kommission des SS-Oberführers Hintze).
28. Rauch, *Geschichte der baltischen Staaten*, 213–214; Myllyniemi, *Die baltische Krise*, 135–137 and 142–144; Bundesarchiv (BA) Berlin, R 58/214, Ereignismeldung Nr. 28, 20 July 1941, Anlage I, Instruktionen [Serov] zur Durchführung der Aussiedlung der antisowjetischen Elemente aus Litauen, Lettland und Estland [undated]; LVVA, P-1026-1-5, 93, [RSHA] IV A 1, [Informant] N 196034, 3 April 1941. This concerns information that

comes from a certain "Skrebers," who had reported that transfers from Riga's Central Prison for deportation had taken place at night. According to Antonov-Ovseenko, Serov had already given the order for deportation in October 1940, but unfortunately, he provides no footnotes: Anton Antonov-Ovseenko, "Der Weg nach oben," in *Berija*, ed. Vladimir F. Nekrassow, 107–108. Krausnick and Wilhelm, *Die Truppe des Weltanschauungskrieges*, 200; Ezergailis, *Holocaust in Latvia*, 69–70; (37) Ks 5/76 des LG Hamburg Urteil gegen Viktor Arajs, 31 December 1979, 8–9. On Professor Paul Mintz, see Mendel Bobe, "Riga," in Association of Latvian and Estonian Jews in Israel, *The Jews in Latvia*, 254–257. On the other persons, Menahem Beth, "Men and Deeds," in *The Jews in Latvia*, 293–294 and 299–304; Kaufmann, *Churbn Lettland*, 36–37.

29. Gabriel Gorodetsky, *Die grosse Täuschung*, 402–404, especially 403. The author here refers to a memorandum of the deputy head of the third department of the NKGB of 31 May 1941.

30. Ezergailis, *Holocaust in Latvia*, 70; the number of deported Jews is also given there. It is unclear whether this means the total number or exclusively those deported in June 1941. The weeks from the point of view of a Jewish survivor who was a victim of both dictatorships: Press, *Judenmord*, 22–24. Myllyniemi, *Die baltische Krise*, 144–145; Kaufmann, *Churbn Lettland*, 45; Gerhard Simon, *Nationalismus und Nationalitätenpolitik in der Sowjetunion*, 203. On the state of knowledge of the RSHA in the summer of 1941, see BA Berlin, R 58/216, Ereignismeldung Nr. 59, 21 August 1941, Anlage I, Das Verschickungs- und Verbannungswesen in der UdSSR. Dubin had recruited many Jews from Stettin, several of whom survived both the Soviet and the German occupations. See, for example, the story of Lidia Bobe in Prosecutor's Office Hamburg (Staatsanwaltschaft Hamburg, Staw. Hamburg), 141 Js 534/60, Bd. 33, statement by Lidia Bobe, 20 March 1963, 5,425–5,427.

31. "Der Reichsführer-SS an den Reichsaußenminister," 3 July 1940, in *ADAP*, Serie D, Bd. X, 94–95. Contained in footnote 3 of this document is the excerpt of a protocol from the meeting of government agencies involved in resettlement held on 15 August 1940. Corresponding instructions were issued to the German representative offices in Riga and Tallinn on 22 August 1940; LVVA, P 1019-1-3, 24–34, Final Report of the Screening Commando for Baltic Refugees, here 26–27; LVVA, P 1019-1-3, 73–73r, RSHA, IV A 1 – B, Betr. Umsiedlung aus Litauen, Lettland und Estland, 24 April 1941; LVVA, P 1026-1-5, 87–91, Einwanderzentralstelle an den Amtschef IV des RSHA, Betr. Nachrichtendienstliche Einwirkung russischer Dienststellen auf Umsiedler, 22 January 1941; LVVA, P 1026-1-5, 82–83, RSHA, IV A 1 - B, Betrifft: Umsiedlung von Volksdeutschen aus Litauen, Estland und Lettland, 3 February 1941. "Bericht des Landesleiters der NSDAP-Landesgruppe Lettland an den Chef der NSDAP Auslandsorganisation von etwa Februar 1940," in Loeber, *Diktierte Option*, 131–135; "Anordnung 20/II des Reichsführers-SS [als] Reichskommissar für die Festigung deutschen Volkstums vom 19. August 1940," in Loeber, *Diktierte Option*, 303–304.

32. LVVA, P 1019-1-3, 24–34, Anlagen zum Abschlussbericht mit statischem Material anhand der Einkategorisierung der Nachumsiedler. According to this document, 539 persons of Group I (positively committed to Germandom), 7,632 persons of Group II (politically indifferent but "known as upstanding people"), 1,821 of Group III (Latvians, Estonians and other "foreigners") and 189 persons of Group IV (politically compromised, suspect, or criminal) were registered. The number of Balts, however, is to be relativized, for many of them were married to Germans and categorized accordingly. LVVA, P 69-1a-21, 15–22, Der KdS Lettland an den General-Kommissar Dr. Drechsler, Betr. General a. D. Generaldirektor Oskar Dankers, 29 May 1942; Karlis Kangeris, "Kollaboration vor der Kollaboration?" in *Okkupation und Kollaboration (1938–1945)*, ed. Werner Röhr, 169–

171; Staw. Hamburg, 141 Js 534/60, Bd. 12, 1,384–1,386, letter from the World Jewish Congress, 26 February 1961, with a list of German and Latvian war criminals as well as their biographies; ibid., SB 9, 1,696–1,697, testimony of Herberts Teidmanis, 9 February 1973; ibid., SB 10, curriculum vitae of Alberts Eichelis, 6 October 1975, turned over to the Prosecutor's Office Landau; ibid., SB 11, testimony of Alberts Eichelis, 13 November 1973, 2,158.
33. LVVA, P 1026-1-5, 15–17, [RSHA] III B an SS-Brigadeführer Müller, Betr. Nachumsiedlung aus Estland und Lettland, 3 March 1941.
34. LVVA, P 1019-1-3, 1, 16–18, RFSS, 11 November 1941, as well as the appendixes 7 and 9.

– *Chapter 2* –

OPERATION BARBAROSSA

Preparations for the German Attack on the Soviet Union

On 31 July 1940, at a meeting on the overall war situation, Hitler informed representatives of the three branches of the Wehrmacht that he had decided to go to war against the Soviet Union. He had been forced to make this decision after German plans to invade Great Britain had begun to falter. The German dictator was possessed by the idée fixe that the island empire's resistance rested on a British alliance with the Soviet Union. Announcing this decision, Hitler stated: "In the course of this conflict, Russia must be knocked out," which in his view would at the same time extinguish England's last hopes for turning the tide. Germany, according to Hitler, would then have succeeded in establishing itself on the continent as the hegemonic power and would also no longer need to fear the United States' military potential.

Independent of strategic necessity, in his vision of eliminating the Soviet Union Hitler was also pursuing the long-cherished implementation of his concept of lebensraum and the racist program connected with it, which required that the Communist ideological opponent be destroyed completely. By July 1940, it was becoming clear that the Hitler-Stalin pact had not been concluded as a genuine alliance but solely for considerations of pure power politics. Now Hitler was turning to the real enemy. Even if Hitler would have preferred to attack the Soviet Union in summer 1940, he was aware that the Wehrmacht could not do so due to problems in personnel, economics, and logistics. It was not without reason that Hitler nonetheless pressed the issue; he knew that after France's defeat and the Reich's expansion, the readiness of the military and the population to widen the war was ideal. He also saw that there was "no indication of Russian activity" against Germany. Moreover, in the eyes of German military experts – such was at any rate the analysis of Foreign Armies East and the German military attaché in Moscow – the Red Army after Stalin's purges was in the poorest imaginable condition with regard to organization and personnel. That was the impression that had been gained primarily from the Winter War between

---

Notes for this chapter begin on page 50.

Soviet Russia and Finland (30 November 1939–13 March 1940). But all of this could change quickly. Hitler therefore planned the attack for spring 1941, noting that gaining space by conquering additional swaths of land alone was not enough. The operation, which Hitler estimated would take five months, only made sense if the Soviet Union were at the same time completely smashed as a state. The quicker this happened, the better. Because of the Baltic states' traditional opposition to Russia, this region was presumably viewed as a "thorn in the side" of the opponent. Such was the tenor of notes made by Army Chief of Staff Franz Halder on 22 July 1940, the day he received the assignment to "tackle the Russian problem."[1]

While the Sovietization of the Baltic states shifted into high gear and officials in Moscow were lulled into a certain sense of security, preparations for the attack on the Soviet Union got underway in the German military's planning staffs. In contrast to the struggle against Great Britain, it was clear that the Air Force and the Navy would be given only supporting roles, while the Army would carry the main burden of the attack. Operations specialists from the High Command of the Army (OKH) and the High Command of the Wehrmacht (OKW) were entrusted with planning an effective strategy, with an emphasis on the swift defeat of the Soviet opponent. Hitler, however, retained overall control; that is to say, he determined the strategic parameters. He specified that the attack had to take place in two thrusts (one aimed toward Kiev, the other – which would involve the "peripheral states," i.e., the Baltic – toward Moscow). The two offensive movements would then unite behind Moscow to form a single front and, after the collapse of the Soviet Union, seize the oil-rich area of Baku.

The German Army was organized so that other forces operating behind the combat troops would assume responsibility for occupying the conquered territories and securing the supply lines, the airports, and the transfer of prisoners of war to the west. They were also to restore the economy and civilian life. The activity of these rear area forces began in the areas of jurisdiction under each individual army within an army group. While fighting continued in the combat zone, administrative commands were to be deployed in the already conquered parts of the operations zone; these received their orders from an army rear area commandant (*Korück*), which each army had at its disposal. For the persecution of political opponents, spies, and partisans as well as opponents among the troops and deserters, the military administration commands were assigned units from the Secret Field Police and the Field Gendarmerie. As the front advanced to the east, the *Korück* formations would move out, and the area evacuated by the *Korück* would be placed under the administration of an army group rear area commander (*Berück*). In turn, every army group had at its disposal a *Berück,* who represented executive governing authority and had punitive power in military-administered areas. To exercise this authority, the *Berück* also had at his disposal high field, field, and local administration commands as well as security divisions. The *Berück* himself received specialized instructions, i.e., those tailored to each specific area, from the army group to which he was assigned, while general guidelines determining basic military policy in the occupied areas came from the Department of Wartime Administration of the OKH office of the General Quartermaster. In the south, General Karl von Roques was appointed *Berück;* in the area of Army Group Center, General Max von Schenkendorff performed this function; while General Franz von Roques served as *Berück* for Army Group North. Within their staffs, it was the task of Department VII (Wartime Administration) to set policy vis-à-vis the indigenous population in all questions of everyday life. When the war zone moved farther east, the OKH considered it opportune to turn over the areas under *Berück* command to civil administration so as not to leave too many units tied down in the rear. The civil administrations were in turn provided with a Wehrmacht territorial commander to maintain security in the occupied territories. This general, unlike his colleagues farther east, had no political authority; together with his units (mostly security divisions), he was instead responsible for protecting the territory under his command.[2]

Experience in the west (in France) and southeast (in Serbia) had shown that it was in no way a self-evident or even an incontrovertible concept of German occupation policy to install a civil administration. The concept of occupation and administration presented here for the Soviet Union was clearly designed for the implementation of political parameters, namely Hitler's wishes. In this war, the German dictator was disinclined to install a military administration for the long term – and not without reason. Unlike past campaigns, this campaign had a special character, that of a war of annihilation and ruthless exploitation. Hitler needed other instruments in addition to the Wehrmacht in order to conduct the struggle against the Soviet Union in this way.

In the "Guidelines on Special Areas for Directive 21," dated 13 March 1941 – Directive No. 21 being the order to prepare Operation Barbarossa – it was already becoming clear what was planned. According to this document, the "territory to be occupied in the course of operations" was, as soon as combat operations permitted, to be delineated anew along the lines of the army group boundaries. The political administration of these territories – the Baltic, Belarus, and Ukraine were mentioned specifically, with "Muscovy" (meaning Russia) and the Caucasus added later – was to be provided by civilian authorities subordinated to a Reich commissar. In this document, it was still stressed that the Reich commissars would receive their "guidelines from the Führer." However, at the end of March 1941 at the latest, party ideologue Alfred Rosenberg, who himself came from the Baltic region, was entrusted with the task of establishing an administrative apparatus, which was to be set up between the dictator and the Reich commissars. Rosenberg's appointment as minister, however, came only on 17 July, after a probationary period as it were, which is worth mentioning, because his rival had been *Reichsmarschall* Hermann Göring, commissioner for the four-year plan and, at the time, Hitler's designated successor. With that, Rosenberg came to head the Reich Ministry for the Occupied Eastern Territories, which grew out of his staff and was granted – at least in theory – overall control vis-à-vis the Reich commissars in all political decisions in the civil-administered territories.

Even more important than the installation of a civil administration was the role that Hitler intended for the SS: "For the preparation of political administration," *Reichsführer-SS* Heinrich Himmler received "special tasks on behalf of the Führer that will emerge from the final struggle of two diametrically opposed political systems." At the same time, Himmler was authorized to act "autonomously and on his own responsibility."[3] This sibylline passage is easier to understand if one considers that even before the Guidelines on Special Areas for Directive 21 were issued, the Reich Security Main Office (RSHA) had been negotiating with the OKH since at least early February 1941 over the use of its mobile task forces – the Einsatzgruppen and their subordinate Einsatzkommandos and Sonderkommandos – in the upcoming attack on the Soviet Union. No one in the OKH harbored any illusions about the assignment of these mobile murder units. Rather, it is to be assumed that their deployment and the policy of murder this entailed were welcomed, given the looming final conflict in the "ideological war." In any event, there is no known document in which top representatives of the Wehrmacht, or even individual generals, express any objections to having the Einsatzgruppen operate behind the lines.

If the top generals were already fully compliant in the question of reinstalling the Einsatzgruppen, then it hardly comes as a surprise that none of the Army's representatives objected when Hitler made clear to them, in an address on 30 March 1941, that combat operations against the Soviet Union would have to differ fundamentally from all previous campaigns. Halder noted the most important points from Hitler's remarks in his own words: "Conflict of two ideologies against one another. Devastating opinion of Bolshevism, same as asocial criminality. Communism is an enormous danger for the future. From this point of view, we must forget soldierly camaraderie. A Communist is no comrade, beforehand or afterward. This is a struggle of annihilation. If we do not grasp this, we will still beat the enemy, but in 30 years, the Communist enemy will confront us again. We are not waging war to preserve the enemy. Future configuration of states: Northern Russia belongs to Finland. Protectorates Baltic countries, Ukraine, Belarus. Struggle against Russia: annihilation of the Bolshevist commissars and the Communist intelligentsia."[4]

In addition, Halder also noted that the role of the courts-martial was to be curtailed, and that the troops would have to treat Soviet secret police officials and commissars as criminals, which meant nothing less than their murder. At the same time, Hitler stressed that the evaluation of the situation would ultimately depend on the "leaders," by which officers were meant. These, however, were to overcome their reservations precisely because the war in the east would differ from the war in the west. The particulars would be regulated in an order from the commander in chief of the Army.[5]

Here at the latest, it should have been clear to all of the Army generals present – provided that they did not adhere to the ideological doctrine of a war of annihilation – just what they had embarked on. The result of Hitler's speech was that the OKW and OKH formulated the infamous criminal orders now known as the Commissar Order and the Jurisdiction Decree.[6] However, even in their radical drafts, it must be noted, these orders contained few anti-Semitic passages. The Jurisdiction Decree and the Commissar Order were not directed explicitly against Jews, but against the greater part of the Soviet population – with the "bearer of the Jewish Bolshevik ideology" being labeled "an element that disrupts every form of order"[7] – and against Communist functionaries of the state, party, and army. The hunger plan developed at the same time by the Economics Staff East in turn affected entire regions – which were known as "areas to be subsidized" – not population groups categorized in advance according to racial criteria. Several weeks after the start of the war, the Wartime Economics and Armaments Office did indeed encourage "barracking" Jews and deploying them "in cohesive labor details,"[8] but this was nothing new; prior to the invasion, even the Foreign Office considered a corresponding treatment of Jews as an "immediate goal" in Latvia in order to improve "the Reich's provisioning with foodstuffs." More concretely, the following was recommended: "The Jews / some 70,000 / are – inasmuch as they have not fled – to be interned in ghettos and shut out of economic life. Moreover, the shutting out of the Jews will provide considerable political reassurance for the population."[9] And the bulletins containing the "guidelines for the conduct of the troops in Russia," which began circulating on 15 June, did not go beyond the commonplace clichés that "Bolshevism was the mortal enemy of National Socialist Germany," and that "Jewry" was "strongly represented in the USSR"; consequently, according to the guidelines, ruthless action had to be taken against "Bolshevik agitators, guerillas, saboteurs, Jews."[10] These crude efforts concerning the "treatment" of Soviet Jews in military orders on the eve of the invasion in no way meant that the Army did not recognize the racially driven ideological component of the campaign. However, these references are easily explained if one bears in mind that the OKH did not want to be actively involved in measures directed against these population groups and therefore had sought an arrangement with the SS instead.

Preparations for Himmler's apparatus, in particular the RSHA, are documented starting in early February 1941. As RSHA head Reinhard Heydrich explained at a meeting on 3 February, his agency was negotiating with the commander in chief of the Army "to ensure the deployment of the Security Police with the fighting troops." An agreement with the OKH, Heydrich said, was expected in the next few days.[11] In the following weeks and months, representatives of the both institutions met repeatedly until a lasting accord satisfactory to both parties was signed on 28 April 1941. Crucially, the Einsatzgruppen and their Einsatzkommandos and Sonderkommandos "were authorized within the framework of their assignment to take executive measures vis-à-vis the civilian population on their own responsibility." This was ultimately the same as a power of authority to carry out mass executions.[12] But Himmler did not content himself with the obvious success of having the Einsatzgruppen participate in the invasion of the Soviet Union. For the conflict with the very embodiment of Nazism's ideological enemy, the "breeding ground of Bolshevism" and "Jewry," he needed additional units that he could lead into the field for the final struggle in accordance with the "special tasks on behalf of the Führer" set forth in the guidelines.

It is not known exactly when Himmler came up with the idea of deploying Higher SS- and Police Leaders (*Höhere SS- und Polizeiführer,* HSSPF) as his personal representatives in the military-administered territories, or when he succeeded in imposing this on the OKH. It may have required little of Himmler in the way of persuasive skills, for despite the million-man army planned for the east, the Army still faced the issue of securing and controlling the rear area. In any event, in early February, the OKH Department of Wartime Administration had expressed the concern that there was a "need for police for Barbarossa." Each of the *Berück* security divisions may have had a police battalion placed at its disposal, but Himmler objected to further requests from the OKH for manpower.[13] Instead, the military's personnel constraints created an opportunity for Himmler to deploy additional SS and police formations in Army territory without having to yield control of them. Personnel changes by Himmler in early April indicate that the decision to allow a HSSPF to deploy to each army group must have been made at this time. Hans-Adolf Prützmann was foreseen for use with

Army Group North, while Erich von dem Bach-Zelewski and Friedrich Jeckeln were to be deployed with Army Group Center and Army Group South respectively.[14] In addition to Order Police battalions, the HSSPF were to have at their disposal formations of the Waffen-SS (the armed forces of the SS) from Himmler's command staff.[15] On 13 and 15 April, Himmler met with Hitler, and although we have no record of what they discussed, it should be clear that it was here that Himmler received Hitler's backing on the HSSPFs, as events over the next few days show. Right after his meeting with Hitler, whose train *Amerika* was at the time located on the Vienna Neustadt-Graz line, Himmler checked into a Graz hotel, where – together with Heydrich, Kurt Daluege (head of the Order Police Main Office), Hans Jüttner (head of the SS Operations Main Office), and Karl Wolff (SS liaison to Hitler) – he met with General Quartermaster Eduard Wagner. Given the positions of those present at the talks, it follows that the use of all SS and police formations was to be finalized here. While the integration of the Einsatzgruppen into Army structures had already been regulated in previous negotiations, these talks must have been primarily about the responsibilities of the police battalions and Waffen-SS brigades.[16]

The powers intended for the HSSPF were more clearly defined within the SS over several days. Heydrich, Daluege, and Jüttner were briefed at the end of April 1941, when they were informed of the "wartime assignments of the Higher SS- and Police Leaders," which suggests that the powerful heads of the main offices had apparently been excluded from shaping the assignment of tasks for this authority, and that the installation of the HSSPFs was coordinated at the highest level, between Himmler and Hitler. The HSSPFs had to carry out their orders pursuant to the "tasks assigned" to them by Himmler "directly" or "according to the basic instructions of the Reichsführer-SS." For this, they could have at their disposal the Einsatzgruppen, the Order Police battalions, and the Waffen-SS brigades of the Command Staff Reichsführer-SS. With regard to the latter, it was noted that these would be deployed for "similar tasks, like the troops of the Order Police, and special tasks, which they would each receive from the Reichsführer-SS." It was also stipulated that these could not involve combat missions for the Army command.[17] With the delegation of the HSSPFs to the east, Himmler had succeeded in gaining permission to deploy his units with a previously unheard-of scope of action, without having to provide a more precise definition of "special orders," and without the HSSPFs being subordinated to control by the military – and all of this was achieved before even one square inch of Russian soil had been conquered. The HSSPFs functioned in a more or less extralegal realm, free of administrative integration, having to justify themselves only to Himmler or Hitler in the event of a conflict with the

Army. Even under the Nazi regime's policies of expansion and occupation, the extent of the empowerment of the SS was up to that point a singular occurrence, the significance of which for later events cannot be overestimated. A letter by Himmler issued on 21 May 1941 regulated the use of the HSSPFs for carrying out a "special assignment of the Führer" within the organizational confines of the Army.[18] Within a few months – from February to May – Himmler and the SS had thus succeeded not only in once again installing the Einsatzgruppen as an instrument of terror for a military campaign, but in establishing a presence in the all-decisive theater of war in the form of several Order Police regiments and the Waffen-SS brigades of the Command Staff Reichsführer-SS.[19]

The personnel-related preparations for setting up the Einsatzgruppen of the Security Police and Security Service (*Sicherheitsdienst*, SD) followed in the RSHA starting in March-April 1941, after Heydrich informed the department heads within his agency of the approaching campaign. The selection of personnel was carried out by Department I (Personnel) under SS Brigadier General Bruno Streckenbach, who did this in close coordination with the other RSHA department heads, as these knew best who among their colleagues was not indispensable, and who was especially suited for the operation. In May, the men selected gathered in the baroque palace of the Border Police school in Pretzsch on the Elbe and, due to a shortage in accommodations, in neighboring Düben and Bad Schmiedeberg (near Leipzig).[20] Because the share of manpower for the Einsatzgruppen from the RSHA turned out to be thinner than initially assumed, an entire class of candidates for the executive service – as it were, an up-and-coming generation of Gestapo officers – was temporarily suspended from their studies in Berlin-Charlottenburg and ordered to Pretzsch to fill the posts of mid-level decision-makers, clerks, and detachment leaders. Only the commanders and top officials were hand-picked.

Einsatzgruppe A was designated for the Baltic region and northern Russia and assigned to Army Group North. Command of this Einsatzgruppe was given to SS Brigadier General Dr. Walther Stahlecker. Stahlecker was born the son of an assistant principal in Sternenfels (southwest Germany) on 10 October 1900. He was an exemplary pupil and graduated from gymnasium in Tübingen without any problem. He studied law at the local university and afterward took on different jobs in the service of the state. In 1929, he was appointed administrative counselor. He numbered among the first National Socialist activists, without officially joining the party, because he could work better for the party as an unsuspicious civil servant. However, his service on behalf of the National Socialists is documented as early as 1921. Hitler's party was not Stahlecker's first ideological home. Before ending up with the Nazis, he had been a member of the infamous paramilitary Brigade Ehrhardt as well as the German-Nationalist Protection and Defiance Federation. Stahlecker never relinquished his prior connections, remaining, for example, with Brigade Ehrhardt's command staff until 1928.[21] Even in the early history of the Nazi movement – despite his civil service career, which would suggest a more inconspicuous conduct – Stahlecker was not disinclined to violence. In 1921, he was "severely injured in the service of the party." As a member of a student battalion, he had taken part in the 1922 "Battle at Walfischkeller," where the Nazi movement made its first public appearance in Göppingen. In 1923, he was active as the general editor of an ethno-nationalist paper in Tübingen. He made no secret of his radical political orientation. Yet despite all this, his professional career evolved without a hitch. Stahlecker was appointed director of the Labor Office in Nagold (in the Black Forest) in 1930, and after the Nazis came to power, he became deputy chief of the political police in Stuttgart. Stahlecker then assumed leadership of the Gestapo regional office in Stuttgart in May 1934, having already joined the SS in May 1932. Thereafter, his professional advancement continued unabated. A man of action, he was transferred in rapid succession, leaving his personal mark on one post after another. In July 1938, after the annexation of Austria, he was appointed inspector of the Security Police in Vienna. In June 1939, after taking part in the occupation of the Czech lands as head of Einsatzgruppe Vienna-Brünn (Brno), he moved to Prague as the territorial commander of the Security Police and SD (*Befehlshaber der Sicherheitspolizei und SD*, BdS). While at this post, he and Adolf Eichmann organized the Nisko Project, the deportation of Viennese Jews to the General Government in October 1939. Stahlecker's next foreign deployment followed in 1940 with the German invasion of Norway, where he was named BdS Oslo at the end of hostilities.

Although Stahlecker was apparently needed, it was at the same time clear that his career had stalled; a SS senior colonel by May 1939, Stahlecker had failed to rise above the position of a BdS. Heydrich was not about to have the ambitious National Socialist posted to the Berlin central office – perhaps because he feared bringing in a competitor who had to be taken seriously. In any event, Stahlecker switched both employer and field of activity and moved to the Foreign Office, where he found use as ministerial counselor, inter alia, in the "Office of the RFM," that is to say, in close proximity to Reich Foreign Minister Joachim von Ribbentrop. However, Stahlecker did not break off contact with the RSHA.[22] In February 1941, he was promoted one last time – to brigadier general of the police and SS brigadier general. His motives for once again assuming the command of a mobile commando are unclear. Perhaps by taking on new tasks in the east he hoped to pursue a career in the RSHA instead of the Foreign Office after all. It must also be recalled that in the end Stahlecker was of a fighting nature and preferred a frontline deployment in uniform to desk-bound activity as a welcome change of pace. In this respect, Stahlecker could see himself fully in the tradition of the ethno-nationalist student he had once been. Now, however, he was no longer fighting battles on behalf of the Nazi movement in the corridors, but was to take part instead in the most crucial campaign of the war, the one against the Jews and the Communists.[23] In June 1941, he arrived in Pretzsch to organize his Einsatzgruppe. That Stahlecker – as well as the other Einsatzgruppe commanders – was allowed to recruit several old colleagues must have been an additional inducement to accept this assignment.[24]

Einsatzgruppe A was made up of a command staff, Sonderkommandos 1a and 1b (Sk 1a and Sk 1b) and Einsatzkommandos 2 and 3 (Ek 2 and Ek 3). SS Major Martin Sandberger was named commander of Sk 1a, SS Lieutenant Colonel Erich Ehrlinger commander of Sk 1b, SS Major Rudolf Batz commander of Ek 2, and SS Colonel Karl Jäger commander of Ek 3.[25] SS Major Karl Tschierschky, an aspiring career officer in the RSHA, belonged to the command staff of Einsatzgruppe A as head of Department III (SD). In May 1941, he was sent to Pretzsch from the Immigration Central Office, the agency that "classified" and "supervised" Baltic Germans and Latvian exiles. Tschierschky was considered the Einsatzgruppe's number two man, Stahlecker's deputy. Heinz Trühe, a native of Berlin and civil servant who had switched from the city administration to the Gestapo and had served in Warsaw and Prague, was assigned to run departments I and II (Personnel and Administration), while Dr. Rudolf Lange led departments IV (Gestapo) and V (Criminal Police), the latter in fact hardly existing in the field.[26]

Lange was born on 18 April 1910, in Weisswasser, Rothenburg County (Saxony). He had studied law, earning his doctorate at the end of 1933 and passing the second state law exam in summer 1936. Shortly thereafter, in September 1936, he began working for the Gestapo. Although he joined the party and the SS rather late – in May and September 1937 respectively – the ambitious junior officer advanced rapidly. That he was completely dedicated to the spirit of the corps and accepted its precepts was shown by his resignation from the church, which also took place in 1937. Even before being named administrative counsel, he held a leading position in the Gestapo in Vienna – where he served under Stahlecker – and in Stuttgart. Afterward, he temporarily took over running the Gestapo offices in Erfurt and Weimar, so he could work at the same time as the deputy head of the office of the Inspector of the Security Police in Kassel. On 17 September 1940, Lange was transferred to Berlin, where he was appointed deputy head of the city's Gestapo office. However, Lange had only been deployed on the home front and had yet to prove himself abroad. This changed on 5

June 1941, when he received his orders for Pretzsch and the command staff of Einsatzgruppe A.[27]

The personnel that Stahlecker, his staff, and the individual commando leaders had at their disposal consisted of 35 full-time SD men, 89 Gestapo officials, and 41 criminal police officers as well as several hundred drivers, interpreters, communications specialists, and additional experts who were called up on short notice. The 1st Company of Reserve Police Battalion 9 was also incorporated into Einsatzgruppe A, as company leader Theodor Clausen learned from Lange upon reporting for duty. Because the manpower available for the area to be covered was still clearly too small – a challenge facing all of the Einsatzgruppen – the 1st Company of Waffen-SS Battalion z.b.V. (for special purposes) was also turned over to Einsatzgruppe A in July and distributed by platoon to the individual commandos. According to Stahlecker's first "success report," the total strength of this formation in early autumn 1941 was exactly 990 men.[28]

In Pretzsch, weapons practice and physical fitness were the order of the day; otherwise, time was filled primarily with recreational activities. There was no ideological schooling, it being clear that all of the officers were sufficiently steadfast and less than ever in need of indoctrination.[29] This relaxed atmosphere reflected the RSHA leadership's considerable trust in the men selected. RSHA officials could take merciless action against all enemies of the Reich and state, but showed almost no end of empathy and understanding for their comrades, first and foremost those who became members of these mobile murder commandos. In mid-June, the men in Pretzsch and the neighboring towns had to report when Heydrich himself appeared at the Einsatzgruppen assembly area to give a speech limited to generalities. At this time, senior leadership personnel were also assigned individual command staffs and commandos. A flurry of activity set in, and a few days before the invasion, various talks were scheduled for senior officers. Only at this point, as Arnold Kirste of Ek 2 explained during postwar questioning, did it become clear to all that the opponent in this campaign was to be the Soviet Union, something that only the better informed among them (starting at a certain level of the RSHA hierarchy) had previously suspected. The arrival of interpreters, mostly Baltic Germans fluent in Russian, and the issuance of the "Special Wanted Persons List USSR" provided final certainty.[30] The Special Wanted Persons List USSR was a paperback handbook of dubious quality, in which the men of the Einsatzgruppen could find encyclopedia-like data about individual cities in various regions, an index of the most important press organs and institutions of higher learning, an index of abbreviations for the most important Soviet institutions, and a wanted persons list. For the latter, the various RSHA departments had produced lists of persons who were known to them and seemed either especially dangerous or came into question as possible collaborators.

The following information was available regarding Latvia's capital: Riga had 340,000 inhabitants (as of 1928) and maintained an airport, sea and river ports, several institutions of higher learning, and a university; it was home to diverse industries; and it held a certain strategic significance as a railroad junction. Particularly important buildings where material about political opponents was to be secured immediately after the city's capture were the editorial boards of the Jewish newspapers *Sewodnja* [sic] and *Idische* [sic] *Bilder,* the "Jewish Club" and a "Zionist organization" (which was not specified further, but was said to have an office at Gertrudes St. 19/21), the offices of Agudas Israel, HIAS-Emigdirect [sic], and HICEM-HIAS-ICA Emigration Association [sic] as well as Red Army installations within the Special Baltic Military District and the NKVD office located at Brīvības St. 37.[31] The wanted list contained 128 names of persons in Riga whom it was absolutely necessary to arrest or who came into question as informants, the latter being an exception.

A large part of those persons on the list were marked as "Jew" or "leading Jew," which in and of itself served to justify arrest. More specifically, those to be tracked down included: Leo Bermann, Charlotte Berner (an emigrant), the engineer Saul Fritz Berner, Dr. Moshe Glückson, Otto Isaak Goldfeld (a Hamburg-born Jew who had emigrated and risen to the rank of lieutenant colonel in the Latvian Army), A. Golender, Dr. B. Herzfeld, Dr. Michael Joffe (head of the Public Health Office), Isidor Kaplan (a physician), Jacob Kaplan (salesman and company owner), Edgar Klaus, Dimitri Knie, Krupnikow (general editor of *Proletarskaia Pravda*), Jakob Landau, Dora Leibowitz, Julia Leibsohn, the director Scholom Leibsoms, Leo Lewstein, Nachmann Moskowsky, Professor Paul Muentz, the agent Dr. Agnes Nisse, J. Noviks (commissar for internal affairs), Rabbi M. Nurok, David Rappoport (general editor of *Trudovaia Gazeta*), Rauchmann Ber Rosin (the head of Red Help in Latvia), the lawyer Rosowski, Salnajs (the commander of the political police in Latvia, codename Silbermann), the lawyer H. Samunow, Elisabeth Soloweitschik, the engineer Taubin, and Zeltins-Goldfeldt, who was marked as "half-Jew."

By contrast, the number of trustworthy informants seems limited. Only Dr. Egon Gantzkom, an agent of the former Latvian intelligence service named Rönne, and Colonel Rosenstein, chief of Latvian espionage, were mentioned. At the same time, one had to wonder whether Soviet intelligence had not long ago exposed these possible informants and eliminated them, and whether the information was at all up-to-date. In fact, this list was already considered out-of-date at the time and worthless in many respects. Heydrich was also aware of this and had therefore ordered the Einsatzgruppen to update the Special Wanted Persons List USSR as the invasion progressed.[32]

As the date of the invasion drew closer, the commanders of the Einsatzgruppen and their subordinate commandos were ordered to Berlin. There, on 17 June 1941, they met in the Prinz Albrecht Palais, where they received comprehensive instructions from Heydrich.[33] Adhering to Hitler's speech to Army generals on 30 March 1941, Heydrich stressed that this invasion was not about one nation against another, but represented the final clash of two ideologies, a life-and-death struggle for both systems. He prevailed upon those gathered to bear this responsibility in mind and stressed that intensive action against the Jewish population group was absolutely necessary, as experience in Poland had shown. Sk 1a commander Martin Sandberger said after the war that these instructions stemmed from Hitler himself, and that Heydrich was functioning merely as the German dictator's mouthpiece.[34]

More specifically, Heydrich encouraged the commanding officers – something he would later recall with reference to the Berlin meeting in a message to the Einsatzgruppen commanders on 29 June 1941 – to support by all means the "self-cleansing efforts of anti-communist or anti-Jewish circles in the territories to be occupied" and, in particular, to promote such actions, "to instigate [them] without a trace," or "to intensify [them]." Without Heydrich being more specific, his instructions could have applied only to those territories where Soviet rule had been shortest, and where the German side could still count on finding a functioning clandestine opposition. In short, eastern Galicia, Volhynia, western Belarus, and the Baltic region were meant. Heydrich stressed most clearly that the empowerment of local forces and the instigation of "national pogroms" were not to be accompanied by the installation of permanent self-defense units. The Einsatzgruppen were to make use of collaborators, but not to make concessions – everything else would sort itself out later, for the Army also had a considerable say in the political reorganization of the Soviet expanse.[35] For some commando leaders, Heydrich expressed himself too guardedly – at any rate, some statements from postwar investigations can be interpreted this way. According to Ek 3 commander Karl Jäger, there was a need for clarification. One Gestapo officer, Jäger said, asked more or less whether the Einsatzgruppen had the task of shooting the Jews; Heydrich replied that this was of course self-evident.[36]

By chance, Heydrich's instructions – although classified as "secret matter of the Reich" (the highest level of secrecy) – survived in print in at least one copy.[37] In this key document on German annihilation policy in the Soviet Union, Heydrich had been forced to put to paper his orders and considerations "in concise form," because he had overlooked a crucial factor.

Even though the senior SS leadership had met at the Wewelsburg between 11 and 15 June to discuss the impending campaign and the planned annihilation of several million Slavs, Heydrich had yet to contact the higher SS and police leaders, who, like the RSHA, could issue orders to the Einsatzgruppen. He therefore sought to make up for this omission and, on 2 July, sent his "basic instructions on the scope of operations of the Security Police and SD" to Jeckeln, Prützmann, von dem Bach, and Korsemann so that the HSSPFs could "adopt the same."[38]

In a preliminary remark, Heydrich noted that the immediate goal of their deployment overall was political pacification, the distant goal being economic pacification, for which use was also to be made of the Soviet peoples, including the Balts. The relationship of the Einsatzgruppen with the Wehrmacht was considered clarified. However, Heydrich drew attention to another point, that the Einsatzgruppen were urged to "fight all anti-Reich and anti-German elements behind the troops doing the fighting," meaning his men were to operate as close to the lines as possible. Additional paragraphs dealt with reporting as well as investigation methods, with reference being made to information in the "Special Wanted Persons List East."[39] Going beyond this list, "all methods of investigation and execution necessary for the political pacification of the occupied territories were to be taken." With that, the fate intended for those persons on the list was clearly expressed.

Under the rubric "executions," Heydrich laid out precisely which groups were to be murdered: "To execute are all officials of the Comintern (as in general professional Communist politicians per se), the higher, middle, and radical lower functionaries of the party, the Central Committee, the regional and precinct committees, people's commissars, Jews in party and state positions, other radical elements (saboteurs, propagandists, snipers, assassins, agitators, etc.), inasmuch as they in each individual case are not or are no longer needed to provide political or economic information that is especially important for additional Security Police measures or for the economic reconstruction of the occupied territories. In particular, caution is to be taken that economic, union, and trade committees are not completely liquidated so that suitable sources of information are no longer on hand."[40]

The Einsatzgruppen were also instructed to make use of local forces in carrying out murder operations in the first phase of the attack wherever possible.[41] At the same time, they had to take care that doctors and healthcare workers were not murdered, otherwise the medical care of the population could no longer be guaranteed. The Orthodox Church and religious sects were to be promoted in order to propagate the separation of church and state. By contrast, the "national question" – that is to say, primarily the reestablishment of national independence for the individual Soviet republics – was to be handled with "extreme restraint." For economic reasons, the destruction of the collectives would not be considered at first. Finally, Heydrich requested that the Einsatzgruppen establish information networks and secure political documents, above all "material from the Comintern, the party, unions, Jews, and officials."

Such were the instructions Heydrich sent to the HSSPFs on 2 July. Their content should have been identical with his remarks to the Einsatzgruppen commanders in Berlin on 17 June. With these orders from their boss, the commanders of the Einsatzgruppen, the Sonderkommandos, and Einsatzkommandos returned to Pretzsch to brief their men. In the neighboring town of Bad Schmiedeberg, two meetings were called in the large hall of the guest house, where specialists held presentations about various areas of deployment. At the first meeting, Dr. Heinz Gräfe, formerly Gestapo and SD chief in Tilsit, an East European affairs expert in the RSHA, and later a division head in Department VI, presented a general treatise on Soviet Russia, while Tilsit Mayor Dr. Hans Schindowski, also a member of the SD, followed with a talk on the Baltic states. The second gathering was about primarily Security Police matters and political issues, apparently with the goal of informing all of the officers in Einsatzgruppe A of Heydrich's basic instructions of 17 June. It concluded with a ceremonial swearing in of those present.[42] In other presentations for all Einsatzgruppen members, the Russian mentality, diseases, and partisan tactics were discussed, and the existence of the Commissar Order and the Jurisdiction Decree was made known.[43] The amount of information led to confusion among some commando leaders; even the orders regarding annihilation required interpretation. Arnold Kirste of Ek 2 observed a conversation between Batz and Jäger at their Bad Schmiedeberg quarters in the final days before the invasion. Both, according to Kirste, believed that the murder of the Jews would most probably be among their tasks, but they felt that an "incontrovertible order" had yet to be issued. Kirste reported that that the two commando leaders, given this lack of orientation, therefore decided "to let it depend on how things took shape."[44] In any event, they were not yet working from the assumption that they had been ordered to murder every Jew without exception irrespective of age or sex.[45]

The greater part of Einsatzgruppe A left Pretzsch on 21 and 22 June. There was nothing holding Stahlecker back. He had already hurried off with a small detachment to make contact with HSSPF Prützmann in Königsberg. From there, Stahlecker's group headed toward the East Prussian borderlands, where the command staff took up quarters in Gumbinnen.[46] Sk 1b, which had been allotted the 16th Army, and Sk 1a, which had been assigned to the 18th Army, established contact with their respective army high command.[47] As had been agreed, the command staff of Einsatzgruppe A, Ek 2, and Ek 3 moved on to join the staff of Rear Area Army Group North. There they waited for the order to attack.[48]

Notes

1. Franz Halder, *Kriegstagebuch*, Bd. II, entries for 22 July and 30 July, 30–34 and 46–50. According to Halder, on 22 July Colonel Hans v. Greiffenberg, the chief of the Army's operations section, and Colonel Eberhard Kienzel, the head of the General Staff of the Army's 12th Department (Foreign Armies East), were entrusted with "preparations" and "tasks" concerning Russia. Already on 3 July 1940, Greifenberg had received corresponding instructions from Halder to work out a plan of attack against the Soviet Union, see ibid., 6; Andreas Hillgruber, *Hitlers Strategie*, 207–227; Ernst Klink, "Die militärische Konzeption des Krieges gegen die Sowjetunion," in Militärgeschichtliches Forschungsamt, *Das Deutsche Reich und der zweite Weltkrieg*, Bd. 4, 191–202; Helmuth Greiner, *Die Oberste Wehrmachtführung 1939–1943*, 116–118 and 288–293; and Bundesarchiv-Militärarchiv (BA-MA), Vincenz Müller Nachlass, Mü 17. The latter contains Müller's notes on a conversation with Hitler's Wehrmacht adjutant Rudolf Schmundt in the summer of 1942, according to which Hitler had explained to Schmundt that, with the defeat of France, the ideal moment had come to commit the community of nations to military action against the Soviet Union.
2. Jürgen Förster, "Die Sicherung des Lebensraumes," in Militärgeschichtlichen Forschungsamt, *Das Deutsche Reich und der zweite Weltkrieg*, Bd. 4, 1,030–1,032; Theo Schulte, *The German Army and Nazi Policies in Occupied Russia*, 41–68; Alexander Dallin, *Deutsche Herrschaft in Russland 1941–1945*, 105–108. The deployment of Wehrmacht territorial commanders was decreed only on 13 March 1941, in the Guidelines on Special Areas for Directive 21, but Hitler had already ordered their establishment, see *Kriegstagebuch des Oberkommandos der Wehrmacht*, Bd. I, entry for 3 March 1941, 341.
3. Richtlinien auf Sondergebieten zur Weisung 21, 13 March 1941, printed in *Hitlers Weisungen für die Kriegsführung 1939–1945*, ed. Walther Hubatsch, 88–91. Cf. Halder, *Kriegstagebuch*, Bd. II, entry for 5 March 1941, 303. Halder notes that an OKW draft of the guidelines – which included a reference to the "special assignment of the Reichsführer SS" – already existed at the OKH office of the General Quartermaster. What stands out here is that this amendment to Directive No. 21 was signed by the OKW head, General Field Marshal Wilhelm Keitel. Since the "Mercy Decree," which legitimized euthanasia, Hitler had avoided signing documents that could prove his involvement in crimes. Instead, subordinate offices had to work out measures that were shared with him at oral presentations, where he could then give his blessing. The guidelines are probably to be seen as one of these documents despite the unapparent language. On the allocation of the territories for which civil administration was envisioned, see "Aufzeichnungen des Vortragenden Legationsrat Großkopf (Abt. Deutschland)," 30 May 1941, in *ADAP*, Serie D, Bd. XII/2, 772, and Lew Besymenski, *Sonderakte "Barbarossa,"* 224–227. On the Reich Ministry for the Occupied Eastern Territories, see Dieter Rebentisch, *Führerstaat und Verwaltung im Zweiten Weltkrieg*, 310–312. According to Rebentisch, Rosenberg's apparatus was initially called the "central office for work in the east." Rosenberg was appointed "com-

missioner for the central handling of questions concerning the east European expanse" on 20 April 1941, see Christian Gerlach, *Kalkulierte Morde*, 156–157.
4. Halder, *Kriegstagebuch*, Bd. II, entry for 30 March 1941, 336–337; Greiner, *Die oberste Werhmachtführung*, 370–371. Greiner stresses that Hitler argued that it was necessary to conduct war in this way, because the Soviet Union had not joined the Geneva Convention and German POWs would not be handled according to its stipulations, for which the behavior of their commissars in occupied countries such as the Baltic states stood. Cf. Case XII, German protocol, 6,416–6,417, testimony of Walter Warlimont (formerly deputy chief of the Wehrmacht Operations Staff), "On the topic that is to be discussed here, he expressed at the time [Hitler on 30 March 1941] something like the following: Commissars and GPU-men are not soldiers, rather criminals. They must also be treated as such. He would have to demand of the officers of the German Wehrmacht that they shelve their misgivings against such treatment. Above all else, these people could in no way be treated as POWs if they fell into German hands. Rather they would have to be separated immediately upon capture and were to be turned over to special commandos of the SD. These special commandos would accompany the German troops to Russia ... Such was approximately the content of his remarks on this point. They were made with the greatest emphasis, and there could be no doubt for any participant that this was to be seen as a well considered and extremely insistent order."
5. Halder, *Kriegstagebuch*, Bd. II, entry for 20 March 1941, 337. Unlike Hans-Adolf Jacobson, the editor of Halder's diary, we interpret the rubric "ObdH Befehl" not as an order to ensure discipline – i.e., the "Discipline Decree" – which does not fit with the chronology of events, but as an assignment to the OKH to realize Hitler's guidelines accordingly, something that in fact took place with regard to the commissars, cf. Nuremberg Document NOKW-209. See also Christian Hartmann, *Halder*, 241–243.
6. BA-MA, RW 4/577, 72–74, Der Führer und Oberste Befehlshaber der Wehrmacht, Erlass über die Ausübung der Kriegsgerichtsbarkeit im Gebiet "Barbarossa" und über besondere Massnahmen der Truppe, 13 May 1941. The decree was signed by Keitel. See also BA-MA, RW 4/578, 41–44, OKW, WFSt/Abt. L (IV/Qu), 6 June 1941, with the appendix "Richtlinien für die Behandlung politischer Kommissare" printed in Hans-Adolf Jacobsen, "Kommissarbefehl und Massenexekutionen sowjetischer Kriegsgefangener," in *Anatomie des SS-Staates*, Bd. 2, 182–184 and 188–191.
7. Nuremburg Document NOKW-209, OKH, Gen. z.b.V. beim Ob.d.H., 6 May 1941.
8. BA-MA, WF-01/15885, 5,882–5,887, Kriegstagebuch, Wi Rü Amt/Stab, 31 July 1941, Besprechung Amtschef.
9. Politisches Archive des Auswärtiges Amtes (PA-AA), R 105190, 84–88, Erwin von Bruemer an Generalkonsul Großkopf, 5 June 1941, including the appendix "Aufzeichnung, Betr. Die staatsrechtliche Zukunft der früher selbständigen, jetzt Sowjetrepublik Lettland." Bruemer assumed that the Jewish share of the population would be around 5 percent, including "numerous emigrants from Ostmark [Austria] and the Polish territories." His concern was that the "elimination of the Jews and the no less necessary elimination of the Latvians, who are beholden to the Soviets, will deprive the economy of leadership," which was why he argued for the timely deployment of German economics specialists.
10. Nuremburg Document NOKW-1692, Richtlinien für das Verhalten der Truppe in Rußland, printed in Jacobsen, "Kommissarbefehl und Massenexekutionen," 187–188. Cf. *Kriegstagebuch des Oberkommandos der Wehrmacht*, entry for 21 February 1941, Bd. 1, 333, where Warlimont encourages "the issuance of guidelines for the behavior of the troops toward the Bolsheviks."
11. Nuremberg Document NG-5225, Sonderkommando Auswärtiges Amt, Aufzeichnung betr.: Einbau des Sk AA in die SS, 2 February 1941. This document concerns Sonderkom-

mando Künsberg, a unit of the Foreign Office, but it also discusses the commandos of the RSHA. The German Foreign Office was informed of the negotiations between the OKH and the RSHA, because the deployment of Sk Künsberg was to take place pro forma alongside the RSHA commandos, which was also why it is mentioned in the regulations. State Secretary Martin Luther of the Foreign Office was a cautious man, however, and wanted to get hold of a copy of the OKH-RSHA agreement before he informed Ribbentrop. Interestingly, even in these early notes by Eberhard Baron von Künsberg, formulations are used that found their way into the agreements between the RSHA and the OKH in April-May 1941, Richard Breitman, *Der Architekt der 'Endlösung,'* 195–196. It should be clear that the term "negotiations" in the document hardly refers to talks within the RSHA, where Heydrich could simply decide things. However, since Sk Künsberg – and the RSHA commandos – had to be provided with pay books and weapons, these agreements concerned the OKH. Furthermore, the AA wanted to keep the Wehrmacht from drawing on its commando, "which up to now was deployed within the framework of the Army as a group of the Secret Field Police." Therefore, it was requesting Security Police uniforms. Walter Schellenberg, who apparently acted as Heydrich's liaison, must have discussed these questions with the OKH in February; his interlocutor could have been only the general quartermaster, see Nuremberg Document NG-5225, Auswärtiges Amt, Betreff: Eingliederung des Sk AA in die SS, 10 February 1941.

12. BA-MA, RH 22/155, OKH, Gen. St. d. H. / Gen. Qu., Az. Abt. Kriegsverwaltung, 28 April 1941, facsimile in *Verbrechen der Wehrmacht,* ed. Hamburger Institut für Sozialforschung, 58–60. When the agreement was put before Schellenberg during one of his later questioning sessions, he claimed that primarily "technical expressions" were to be traced back to him, see Staw. Nürnberg, KV Ankl. Interrogation, 45c: Interrogation 1979, Vernehmung Walter Schellenberg, 17 September 1947, 1. That the use of the Einsatzgruppen had been decided by April 1941 is also demonstrated in a presentation given by the commander in chief of the 18th Army, General Georg von Küchler, on 25 April (i.e., several days before they were officially confirmed). Küchler noted that "SS formations with special assignments will be deployed" in the army rear area, see Küchler's handwritten notes for a presentation to divisional commanders on 25 April 1941, printed in Hans-Heinrich Wilhelm, *Rassenpolitik und Kriegsführung,* 133–140, quote 139.

13. Halder, *Kriegstagebuch,* Bd. II, entry of 2 February 1941, 281. The higher SS and police leaders were also Himmler's representatives in the military districts within the Reich and were the highest representative of the SS in an occupied country, see Ruth Bettina Birn, *Die Höheren SS- und Polizeiführer.* A list of the security divisions assigned to the army group rear areas is given in Friedrich Wilhelm, *Die Polizei im NS-Staat,* 162–163.

14. *Der Dienstkalender Heinrich Himmlers 1941/42,* ed. Peter Witte, Michael Wildt, Martina Voigt, Dieter Pohl, Peter Klein, Christian Gerlach, Christoph Dieckmann, and Andrej Angrick, entries for 9 and 10 April 1941, 147–148, and BA Berlin, Berlin Document Center (BDC), SS Offizierakten (SSO) Prützmann and Jeckeln. According to his personnel card, Prützmann was foreseen as HSSPF for the SS Regional Sector Northeast and Ukraine on 9 April 1941. Starting 1 May, his area of operations was reduced to SS Regional Sector Northeast. Jeckeln was deployed only later; at any rate, his recall as HSSPF West took place on 1 May 1941. Afterward, he joined the RFSS Staff for Special Purposes. However, he had known since around mid April – as is seen in a letter to HSSPF Danzig and West Prussia Richard Hildebrandt dated 23 April 1941 – that he was foreseen as an HSSPF for the east. The designated HSSPF Caucasus Gerret Korsemann – who was rushed through the SS main offices for quick schooling – had been groomed to be an HSSPF and then joined Jeckeln's staff in order to familiarize himself with his duties.

15. The Kommandostab RFSS – here still labeled Einsatzstab – was formed on 7 April, see

BA Berlin, NS 22/231, 61, SS-Führungshauptamt, Betrf.: Verlegung der 8., 4., und 14. SS-Standarte, 26 March 1941. On the Kommandostab, see Yehoshua Büchler, "Kommandostab Reichsfürher SS: Himmler's Personal Murder Brigades in 1941," *Holocaust and Genocide Studies*, no. 1 (1986): 11–25, and Martin Cüppers, *Wegbereiter der Shoah*, 61–73.

16. *Dienstkalender*, entry for 16 April 1941, 150, and Franz Halder, *Kriegstagebuch*, Bd. II, entry for 17 April 1941, 371. Whether negotiations about the Waffen-SS brigades were as intensive as those surrounding the battalions of Order Police is still not known. It is possible that these were directly at Himmler's disposal without the Army being able to make a claim on them, as was the case with Waffen-SS combat divisions, see Andrej Angrick, Martina Voigt, Silke Ammerschubertand, and Peter Klein, "'Da hätte man schon ein Tagebuch führen müssen'," in *Die Normalität des Verbrechens*, ed. Helge Grabitz, Klaus Bästlein, and Johannes Tuchel, 328–329. On the planned deployment of the Order Police in the army group rear areas and security divisions, see BA-MA, RH 21-2/100, unpaginated, OKH, Gen. St. d. H. / Ausb. Abt. (1a), 21 March 1941, Richtlinien für die Ausbildung der Sicherungsdivisionen und der dem Befehlshaber des rückwärtigen Heeres-Gebietes unterstehenden Kräfte.
17. BA Berlin, NS 19/2772, 1–3, RFSS Persönlicher Stab an Daluege, Heydrich und Jüttner, 21 April 1941, with appendix. The use of the Waffen-SS regiments of the Kommandostab RFSS, which were placed at the disposal of the HSSPF, had been planned long beforehand and represented a novelty, while the use of the Einsatzgruppen and police battalions functioned as a traditional "means" of National Socialist occupation policy.
18. BA-MA, RH 22/111, unpaginated, RFSS, Betr. Sonderauftrag des Führers, 21 May 1941. This document is to be found in the Military Archive (Freiburg) in the records of numerous *Berück*s and *Korück*s. It is printed in Jacobsen, "Kommissarbefehl und Massenexekutionen," 184–185.
19. Longerich, *Politik der Vernichtung*, 308–310.
20. Staw. Hamburg, 147 Js 31/67, Anklageschrift gegen Bruno Streckenbach, 30 June 1973, 163–172. Ibid., Bd. 42, statement by Alfred Filbert, 23 September 1971, 7,565. In the process, lower- and middle-level ranks were not requested by name. The core personnel had been selected for Operation Sea Lion, the invasion of Britain. Naturally, specialists – such as interpreters – were gradually swapped out. With regard to personnel, Klaus-Michael Mallmann has noted that those delegated to the Einsatzgruppen came in large part from disbanded or downgraded SD or Gestapo field offices within Germany. As a consequence, these men had suffered a hiccup in their careers and were correspondingly motivated to accept deployment to the east; the central office was after all giving them the opportunity to prove themselves and to recommend themselves to those on high for additional tasks, see Klaus-Michael Mallmann, "Die Türöffner der Endlösung," in *Die Gestapo im Zweiten Weltkrieg*, ed. Gerhard Paul and Klaus-Michael Mallmann, 456. BA Berlin, R 58/241, 307–308, Der Chef der Sipo und des SD, 30 May 1941.
21. The free corps commanded by the right-wing radical Captain Hermann Ehrhardt took part in the 1920 Kapp Putsch against the Weimar Republic. Ehrhardt himself opposed Hitler. Nonetheless, the SA and the SS recruited selected personnel from his corps to fill out their own ranks, see Gabriele Krüger, *Die Brigade Ehrhardt*. Also, Heinz Höhne, *Der Orden unter dem Totenkopf*, 22–24 and 130–131.
22. According to the index of persons in the *ADAP*, Serie D, Bd. XII/2, 960, Stahlecker officially served at the Foreign Office until 18 June 1941. Also Staatsanwaltschaft beim Kammergericht Berlin (Staw. KG Berlin), 1 Js 4/65, Bd. VI, statement by Dr. Emil Finnberg, 11 May 1966, 284–285. According to Finnberg, Stahlecker joined Einsatzgruppe A on 18 June 1941. The rank of SS senior colonel (*SS-Oberführer*) fell between SS colonel

(*SS-Standartenführer*) and SS brigadier general (*SS-Brigadeführer*); it does not exist in the U.S. or British militaries.

23. Archive of the Interior Ministry, Prague, 114-9-95, 68-69r, Referat I A 6, 25 March 1941, excerpt from the personnel file of SS Brigadier General of the Police Dr. Walther Stahlecker; BA-MA, RH 22/12, 85–89, OKH, Gen. St. d. H. / Gen. Qu., Abt. K. Verw., 14 June 1941. In this overview, Stahlecker was already noted as acting head of Einsatzgruppe A. By contrast, the Army did not yet have the names of the commanders of Sk 1a and Sk 1b. See also Hans-Heinrich Wilhelm, *Die Einsatzgruppe A der Sicherheitspolizei und des SD 1941/42*, 489. On Stahlecker's cooperation with Eichmann, see Hans Safrian, *Die Eichmann-Männer*, 68–86.

24. Krausnick and Wilhelm, *Die Truppe der Weltanschauungskrieges*, 284–285; Staw. KG Berlin, 1 Js 4/65, Bd. VI, statement by Walter Münch, 29 September 1966, 194–195; Staw. Hamburg, 147 Js 31/67, Bd. 23, statement by Wilhelm Kaul, 14 February 1966, 4,304; ibid., Bd.43, statement by Dr. Alfred Six, 8 December 1971, 7,764; ibid., Bd. 6, evaluation by Bruno Streckenbach, Tasks and Activity as Head of Department I of the Reich Security Main Office, 921; Bd. 18, statement by Bruno Streckenbach, 8 September 1965, 3,366; Staw. Hamburg, 141 Js 534/60, Bd. 11, statement by Rudolf Batz, 26 January 1961, 1,256.

25. Staw. Hamburg, 147 Js 31/67, Anklageschrift gegen Bruno Streckenbach, 30 June 1973, 30. The ranks of the commando leaders at the time they took over their unit are also given there. Staw. KG Berlin, 1 Js 4/65, Bd. VI, statement by Erich Ehrlinger, 9 March 1966, 115–116. According to Ehrlinger, SS Major Gustav vom Felde was originally supposed to lead Sk 1b.

26. Staw. Hamburg, 141 Js 534/60, Bd. 6 [after renumeration], statement by Karl Tschierschky, 14 August 1959, 73–74; ibid., statement by Horst Eichler, 15 September 1959, 127–129; ibid., statement by Heinz Trühe, 16 October 1959, 183–184 and 188; ibid., Bd. 11, statements by Rudolf Batz, 26 January 1961 and 11 November 1960, 1,256 and 1,299. Although he had been the commander of Ek 2, Batz claimed that Stahlecker turned over command of the Einsatzgruppe to him during absences due to their long-standing mutual trust. The statements also contain characterizations of Lange, who committed suicide to avoid capture in February 1945. The organization of the Einsatzgruppen resembled that of the RSHA but in simplified form. That the Criminal Police as an organization, as opposed to its personnel, hardly played a role in the occupation of a country is clear. Its tasks were to be turned over to the indigenous administration and police, which were only supervised by the Einsatzgruppe and the regional commandos or stationary offices. This was also the case with the Dept. VI (Foreign SD) and VII (Ideological Research). Their activities – inasmuch as they came into play in pacified territory – were taken care of by either Einsatzgruppe A's Dept. III or flying commandos from the main office and received on the spot support as necessary. The RSHA jealously watched over local commanders to ensure that they did not exceed their powers. For example, Dr. Sandberger, the commander of Sk 1a and KdS Estonia, was not allowed to maintain the "opposition library" he had founded in Tartu. He had to send the material to Berlin.

27. BA Berlin, BDC, SSO Lange. With regard to his various memberships, the SSO file is not clear. A letter from the SS Personnel Main Office says Lange had joined the SS on 11 October 1936, having served in the SA since 4 November 1933. Lange, however, claimed in his SS Race and Settlement Main Office questionnaire that he had switched to the SS only in 1937. See also Wilhelm, *Die Einsatzgruppe A*, 485, and Mallmann, "Türöffner," 457–458.

28. Nuremberg Document L-180, Einsatzgruppe A, Gesamtbericht bis zum 15.10.41; Staw. Hamburg, 141 Js 534/60, Bd. 22, statement by Theodor Clausen, 30 January 1962,

3,386–3,387. The additional manpower from the Order Police and the Waffen-SS joined the Einsatzgruppe only during its advance.
29. On anti-Semitic schooling within the police apparatus, see Jürgen Matthäus, "Warum wird über das Judentum geschult?," in Paul and Mallmann, *Die Gestapo im Zweiten Weltkrieg*, 100–124, esp. 118–122.
30. Staw. Hamburg, 147 Js 31/67, Bd. 23, statement by Arnold Kirste, 31 March 1966, 4,314–4,315. Kirste describes the Special Wanted Persons List USSR as "red deployment books," which is in principle correct.
31. Although pronounced "sevodnia" (or "sewodnja" in German), the newspaper should have been transliterated here as *Segodnja*, while *Idische* should have been written *Jidische*. HIAS (the Hebrew Sheltering and Immigration Aid Society) and Emigdirect had originally been two separate organizations, the former being founded in New York in 1909, the latter in Berlin in 1921. In 1927, HIAS, Emigdirect, and the Jewish Colonization Association (ICA) merged to form HICEM.
32. *Sonderfahndungsliste UdSSR*, ed. Werner Röder, 290. This is a facsimile. All of the names mentioned, etc., are listed alphabetically. The list contains few people of prominence. Apart from Professor Julijs Auskaps, a former Latvian education minister from the Ulmanis era, or Mikhail Glinskii, the Soviet military attaché, name recognition of those listed hardly extended beyond Latvia. It is also worth nothing that officials such as Arturs Aprāns (former chief of the political police for the Riga district under Ulmanis), Jānis Friedrichsons (chief of the political police under Ulmanis), or Martins Antons (former chairman of the Latvian Rotary Club) were wanted not as informants by Department IV (Gestapo) but by Department VI (Foreign SD), which suggests a lack of coordination between the divisions and desks within the RSHA, see Krausnick and Wilhelm, *Truppe des Weltanschauungskrieges*, 170–172. Lt. Col. Rosenstein had probably been an informant for the Abwehr office in East Prussia for years. He was almost certainly no longer in office; in fact one has to wonder whether he had survived the purges, see Julius Mader, *Hitlers Spionagegenerale sagen aus*, 145. Although a semi-official publication of East Germany's Ministry for State Security, a correct accounting of the facts in Mader is not to be excluded out of hand.
33. It is possible that desk officers and other senior officials were at the gathering. In any event, Adolf Eichmann claimed that just before the invasion of the Soviet Union he and Rolf Günther, together with the entire RSHA leadership, were informed of Barbarossa in the cinema of Prinz Albrecht Str. 8 (Gestapo headquarters). (Prinz Albrecht Palais, where Heydrich had his office, was around the corner at Wilhelm Str. 102.) Eichmann even fancied volunteering for the Einsatzgruppen in the hope of being promoted to SS colonel, see interrogation of Adolf Eichmann by Avner Less, 248–250 and 1,518–1,520, here reproduced in copies in Staw. Hamburg, 147 Js 31/67, Bd. 24, 4,425–4,429.
34. Ralf Ogorreck, *Die Einsatzgruppen und die "Genesis der Endlösung,"* 67–68 and 82–83; Staw. Hamburg, 147 Js 31/67, Bd. 1, statement by Erwin Schulz, 18 October 1956, 8; ibid., statement by Martin Sandberger, 30 September 1957, 112–115; ibid., Bd. 6, statement by Martin Sandberger, 18 February 1960, 887. Other former Einsatzgruppe and Einsatzkommando commanders have circulated additional versions of the meetings in Berlin and Pretzsch, but if the statements of all of the other participants are compared with Heydrich's messages to the Einsatzgruppen on 29 June and to the HSSPF on 2 July 1941 – see below – the version given here seems most plausible. See also ibid., Anklageschrift gegen Bruno Streckenbach, 30 June 1973, 178–190; Staw. KG Berlin, Bd. VII, statement by Walter Münch, 29 September 1966, 199–200. Münch was Einsatzgruppe A's office manager and handled "secret Reich matters." He stated for the record: "From my knowledge of the reports arriving [from EG A's commandos], I know that during my

time in Riga numerous mass executions took place. In my opinion, these rested on a general order to kill. From hearsay, I learned that Hitler himself is supposed to have decreed the general order to kill. I personally, as already mentioned, saw only Heydrich's written order to kill." The order of 2 July 1941 is probably meant by the latter.
35. Heydrich an die Chefs der Einsatzgruppen, 29 June 1941, printed in *Die Einsatzgruppen in der besetzten Sowjetunion 1941/42*, ed. Peter Klein, 318–319. Heydrich introduced his message with the following words: "In reference to my verbal remarks already made in Berlin on 17 June, I remind ..." In the second part of this message, Heydrich admonished careless reporting. In a similar vein, the Berlin meeting had also addressed organizational questions regarding the duty to report and communication between the periphery and the center. Heydrich – probably for reasons of prestige – was apparently trying to keep individual Einsatzgruppe leaders from reporting directly to Himmler.
36. Statements by Karl Jäger, 15–19 June 1959, excerpted in Wilhelm, *Rassenpolitik und Kriegsführung*, 186–198, here 186–187. Jäger dated the meeting to several weeks before the start of the invasion. If the said meeting on 17 June is meant, then it must be a mistake. Otherwise, only another appointment or another meeting could be meant, but Jäger would be the only witness to it, see Peter Klein, "Die Erlaubnis zum grenzenlosen Massenmord," in *Die Wehrmacht: Mythos und Realität*, ed. Rolf-Dieter Müller and Hans-Erich Volkmann, 930–931.
37. Heydrich himself wanted to visit the HSSPFs in the field and inform them personally; beforehand, the Einsatzgruppen leaders were to inform the HSSPFs at least about "several" basic instructions, Bundesarchiv Dahlwitz-Hoppegarten, ZR 920, Akte 142, 41, Fernschreiben [der Stapo] Tilsit, 27 June 1941.
38. Der Chef der Sipo und des SD, 2 July 1941, printed in Klein, *Die Einsatzgruppen*, 323–328. This copy of the message – which was sent by Dept. IV to the command staff of the Einsatzgruppe A, Ek 1a [sic], Ek 1b [sic], Ek II and Ek III – is from Ek 3. On the meeting of senior SS generals [*Gruppenführer* and higher] at the Wewelsburg, see *Dienstkalender*, entries for 11–15 June 1941, 171–174, and the statements by Erich von dem Bach-Zelewski, 7 January 1946, in *Der Prozeß gegen die Hauptkriegsverbrecher vor dem Internationalen Militärgerichtshof (IMG)*, Bd. 4, 535–536, 539, 542, and 549. Von dem Bach recalled that, in addition to Himmler and himself, Daluege, Heydrich, Karl Wolff, Prützmann, Jeckeln, Reich Chamber of Literature President Hans Johst, Hanns Albin Rauter, and Werner Lorenz were present. The meeting addressed "questions surrounding the deployment of the Order Police and the Waffen-SS as well as Göring's basic economic problems" and did not touch on "problems of the Security Police." See also, Staw. Berlin, 1 Js 4/65 (RSHA investigation), Bd. 7, statement by Erich von dem Bach-Zelewski, 11 October 1966, 245–246, and Karl Hüser, *Wewelsburg 1933–1945, Kult- und Terrorstätte der SS*, 7.
39. The Special Wanted Persons List USSR is meant.
40. Der Chef der Sipo und des SD, 2 July 1941, printed in Klein, *Die Einsatzgruppen*, 323–328. The document addresses "cooperation with the Order Police" in detail. The rubric is misleading, however. Heydrich was trying to prove by means of argument the leading function of the Security Police over the Order Police – apparently the meeting with Order Police Chief Daluege had unsettled him – in order to preempt any encroachment on RSHA areas of responsibility by the Order Police or the HSSPFs, which drew on the police battalions. See also Alfred Streim, *Die Behandlung sowjetischer Kriegsgefangener im "Fall Barbarossa*," 88.
41. This passage in Heydrich's message of 3 July 1941 to the HSSPFs corresponds almost word for word to the corresponding passages of his message to the Einsatzgruppen commanders on 29 June 1941. In June, if the Einsatzgruppen were to "instigate [pogroms]

without a trace," to "intensify [them]" and, as the case may be, to "steer them the right way," in July these were merely to be "promoted."
42. Staw. Hamburg, 147 Js 31/67, Bd. 14, statement by Martin Sandberger, 30 November 1964, 2,492; Staw. München I, 114 Js 17/65, Bd. (V) 6, statement by Horst Eichler, 8 August 1969, 1,117; ibid., Bd. 7, statement by Gerhard Kortkampf, 15 October 1969, 1,349; Staw. Hamburg, 147 Js 31/67, Bd. 11, statement by Rudolf Batz, 27 January 1961, 1,262. On Gräfe's presentation, see Staw. München I, 22 Js 204/61, Bd. 4, statement by Albrecht Zöllner, 26 April 1962, 935. Schindowski later ran SS Special Camp Lublin and, starting in 1943, Command Russia Center for Operation Zeppelin.
43. Staw. Hamburg, 147 Js 31/67, Bd. 23, statement by Arnold Kirste, 31 March 1966, 4,315; ibid., Bd. 40, statement by Dr. Erhard Kröger, 28 June 1971, 7,364; Staw. München I, 114 Js 17/65, UR-Vernehmungen, Bd. 1, statement by Hans Discar, 4 July 1968; Wilhelm, *Einsatzgruppe A,* 17–18.
44. Staw. Hamburg, 147 Js 31/67, Bd. 23, statement by Kirste, 31 March 1966, 4,316. The conversation between Batz and Jäger revolved *solely* around Soviet Jews. Kirste's observation may also explain why – independent of all trial-related considerations – the postwar statements of those who were present in Berlin or Pretzsch vary so disparately regarding an "order of the Führer." Even then, the officials could give free rein to their imagination as to what was meant by the liquidation orders. What later seemed to one a dynamic and radical development was for the other already intended in the original distribution of orders, even if not set down in writing.
45. Streim, *Die Behandlung sowjetischer Kriegsgefangener,* 74–93; Ogorreck, *Die Einsatzgruppen,* 215–222; Longerich, *Politik der Vernichtung,* 310–320.
46. Staw. Hamburg, 147 Js 31/67, Bd. 23, statement by Johannes Feder, 2 February 1955, 4,264–4,265; statement by Kirste, 3 March 1966, 4,317. According to Feder and Kirste, the Sks moved out a day before the Eks. See also Nuremberg Document L-180, Einsatzgruppe A, Gesamtbericht bis zum 15.10.41, and Staw. KG Berlin, 1 Js 4/65, Bd. VI, statement by Emil Finnberg, 11 May 1966, 285.
47. On 13 June 1941, 18th Army High Command, which was foreseen for Riga, informed its officers "of tasks and division of authority between Wehrmacht, SS, Reichsmarschall and Staff Rosenberg." In addition, the "division of the zone of operations, Abwehr, and questions of jurisdiction" were discussed, BA-MA, RH 24-38/162, Tätigkeitsbericht Abt. Ic Gen. Kdo. XXXVIII für die Zeit v. 27.5.41 bis zum 31.3.1942, 7 July 1942, unpaginated.
48. BA-MA, RH 22/12, 85–89, OKH, Gen. St. d. H. / Gen. Qu. Abt. K., 14 June 1941; Staw. KG Berlin, 1 Js 4/65, Bd. VI, statement by Erich Ehrlinger, 9 March 1966, 115–116. It is to be deduced from Ehrlinger's statement there was much more improvisation than the strict RSHA-OKH agreements would allow one to suspect. Thus Ehrlinger maintained contact with the 16th and the 18th armies and broke with rigid adherence to assignments. Furthermore, there also existed ties on the part of Einsatzgruppe A to the 4th Armored Army, where Horst Eichler acted as liaison officer, see Staw. Hamburg, 147 Js 31/67, Bd. 11, statement by Horst Eichler, 25 January 1961, 1,250; Nuremberg Document L-180, Einsatzgruppe A, Gesamtbericht bis zum 15.10.41.

– *Chapter 3* –

FROM THE POGROMS TO
THE ESTABLISHMENT OF THE GHETTO

On the morning of 22 June, the German Wehrmacht – with forces marshaled from the Baltic to the Black seas – invaded the Soviet Union without a declaration of war. Army Group North's mission was to destroy enemy forces in the Baltic, to seize the Baltic ports, and to capture Leningrad and Kronstadt. The 4th Armored Group had to clear a giant path to the northeast, while the 18th Army advanced toward Riga on the left and the 16th Army toward Kaunas (Kauen, Kovno) on the right. Behind the armies, Rear Area Army Group North followed with the 281st, 285th, and 287th security divisions.[1] The first wave of attack – strikes on seven enemy airports launched by the 1st Air Corps – and the deployment of forces ran successfully. To the astonishment of the operations department of Army Group North, the Red Army pulled back and did not rally to fight at the border. Most bridges fell into German hands intact.[2]

That evening, Walther Stahlecker, the commander of Einsatzgruppe A (EG A), arrived in Tilsit (today Sovetsk) and informed the district Gestapo chief SS Major Hans-Joachim Böhme that he and his men, together with the district offices of the SD and police, would have to "work over" a strip of territory along the border 25 km (15.5 miles) deep. According to the guidelines issued by RSHA chief Reinhard Heydrich, this meant the murder of Jews and Communists. Use was also to be made of Lithuanian auxiliary forces. Stahlecker bellowed that this involved an "order of the Führer," which Böhme could not circumvent. Furthermore, the Tilsit Gestapo office would have to act as logistical center and field post distribution point for EG A. A skeptical Böhme asked Stahlecker to have Berlin confirm the instructions by telex. Stahlecker agreed, but had no time to wait for a response. He traveled southeast to Eydtkau (today Chernyshevskoe), where the command staff of EG A crossed into Lithuania. The following morning, 23 June, the order to obey Stahlecker's instructions arrived from the RSHA. With that, EG A could turn its attention to the advance and the unconquered towns in the east, while Einsatzkommando Tilsit covered its rear. In the

---

Notes for this chapter begin on page 82.

first days of the war, as ordered, this unit carried out mass shootings in Gargždai (Garsden), Kretinga (Krottingen), Palanga (Polangen), Tauragė (Tauroggen), Jurbarkas (Georgenburg) and several smaller places in western Lithuania. The victims were mostly male Jews, and the shootings were justified as "pre-emptive security measures." But this was merely a turn of phrase cloaked in German bureaucratese that glossed over the brutal reality.[3]

In the days that followed, the German advance in the northern sector of the eastern front continued without any difficulties worthy of mention. The military intelligence department within Army Group North even wondered whether the Red Army was only a "bluff." From the German point of view, there could be no talk of a unified conduct of operations on the part of the enemy. While Army Group Center and Army Group South were experiencing bitter fighting all along the Soviet border, retreating columns were observed on the Kaunas-Daugavpils (Dünaburg) road in the north. On 24 June there was no longer any "movement on the roads" to report along the Riga-Šiauliai (Schaulen) line and in the area south of Riga. The intelligence department noted in its war diary, incredulously: "This would be an indication of a leadership without any kind of plan." The only thing that stood out were the efforts of Russian tanks, which threatened to break the momentum of the German spearhead and did not at all look as if they were in chaotic retreat.[4] Although Commander in Chief of Army Group North Wilhelm Ritter von Leeb would soon change his estimation of Red Army resistance – now judged to be "very tough, dogged, devious" – city after city fell into German hands. In the night from 24 to 25 June, Kaunas was captured, followed on Thursday, 26 June, by Daugavpils and Šiauliai. Three days later, Liepāja (Libau) and Jelgava (Mitau) surrendered. And on 1 July, a white flag also flew over Ventspils (Windau).[5]

One factor that certainly contributed to the success of the German advance was the support provided Army Group North by nationalist Lithuanian and Latvian partisans, who sought to use the opportunity to inflict the greatest amount of damage possible on the retreating Russian occupiers. These insurgents worked in part with units from the Abwehr, the Wehrmacht's intelligence agency. Former Lithuanian diplomat Kazys Škirpa in particular proved to be a great help in the first days. Škirpa was one of the politicians who had fled to Germany when the Soviets moved to annex the Baltic, and who linked hopes for the reestablishment of Lithuanian statehood with his own return. The Abwehr successfully deployed Škirpa's "circle of activists" with the result that "his men in Lithuania destroyed what was of use to the Bolsheviks and maintained intact everything that was of use to the German troops." Ultimately, they launched a "far-reaching uprising."[6] Škirpa's expectations went unfulfilled, however. After his followers declared on Kaunas radio the formation of an autonomous Lithuanian government under Škirpa's leadership, the RSHA issued a "dictate of stay" for the nationalists, who then had to remain in Berlin under house arrest.[7] Back in Lithuania, the desired reestablishment of national independence was accompanied by the most dreadful of pogroms. During the insurgency, around 2,500 Jews were killed by the incited mob. In Fort VII, a "Jewish concentration camp" was set up with two sections, one for men, the other for women and children. Stahlecker and his staff were the first members of EG A to arrive in Kaunas. They were followed by Erich Ehrlinger and Sonderkommando 1b (Sk 1b) as well as Karl Jäger and Einsatzkommando 3 (Ek 3), which was foreseen for Lithuania. Even before Stahlecker and his men arrived, Lithuanian nationalists were murdering people on the streets. One of them beat some forty-five people to death with a steel pipe and played the Lithuanian national hymn on a harmonica afterward. He left behind a pile of corpses, without a single one of the German soldiers on hand intervening to put an end to the atrocity.[8] Sk 1b reported heavy "shooting between Lithuanian guerillas, Jews, and irregulars," noting that Lithuanian partisan groups had "in the last 3 days shot several thousand Jews already." Due to a lack of capacity in Fort VII, Fort IX was also converted to a killing site.[9] In Kaunas itself, the murdering continued systematically, but under Security Police guidance. EG A reported that in the first phase of the occupation "7,800 Jews in all have been eliminated, in part by pogrom, in part by shootings by Lithuanian commandos." The establishment of a ghetto and the marking of Jews were to be addressed next; the pogrom phase in Kaunas was considered over.[10]

Meanwhile, the 18th Army, with Sonderkommando 1a (Sk 1a) and Einsatzkommando 2 (Ek 2) in tow, continued its advance on Riga. Aside from the fact that Riga was significant as a political center, Army Group North believed that the Red Army sought to pull back behind the Daugava River in order to establish a defensive line based in the Latvian capital.[11] Would things develop as in Lithuania? Could the indigenous population be counted on as allies? Or would the Latvians have learned from the rigorous action taken against Lithuanian independence efforts and refuse to cooperate? The Abwehr in any event had taken precautions and, prior the invasion of Latvia (as well as Lithuania and Estonia), put into place "secret ethnonationalist groups of activists," giving them "missions," mostly carrying out sabotage measures or protecting important objectives. "Local RSHA agents" who "were already there in advance" would have been instructed accordingly as well.[12]

A group of Abwehr activists in Riga received orders to destroy the radio station in order to enhance confusion during operations and then to seize it.[13] However, it remained to be seen whether all of these activists would in fact let themselves be controlled. Abwehr officers noted that "it requires some effort to hold back those involved from premature attack." The activists were therefore urged "to start ... only when German troops neared the respective area during the advance."[14] Like the Abwehr, EG A also drew on exiles from the Baltic. In the entourage of EG A were several emigrants, such as the Latvian Roberts Štiglics and the Estonians Dr. Hjalmar Mäe and Dr. Alexander Massakas. These people were not active behind the lines, but were to be deployed immediately upon the occupation of Riga and Tallinn respectively in order to identify anti-German and Communist elements and to establish order. *Reichsführer-SS* and Chief of the German Police Heinrich Himmler distrusted such circles, but the RSHA ensured him that these were reliable sources of information, even – as in the case of Dr. Mäe – long-standing SD informants who could be used in good conscience.[15]

The attack on Riga initially proved difficult, even though on the evening of 28 June "strongest movements of mot.[orized]– and vehicle columns" were reported on the Riga-Pskow road, which meant that the Red Army was transferring heavy materiel to the east and would not seek a decision on the Daugava. Nonetheless, the river, which divided the city into a west and east side, remained a natural barrier and slowed the advance. Capturing Riga was the task of the 18th Army, which dispatched to Riga formations from the I and XXVI corps.[16] "Agent columns of the Abwehr Radke" had been deployed on 23 June to secure the Daugava crossings, but they had not completed their mission successfully.[17] Even if the Latvian capital and its harbor were of strategic significance, not every division could march on Riga, because this would weaken the 18th Army's right flank and risk breaking contact with the formations of Army Group North south of the Latvian capital. Such was the situation. What then happened in Riga is recorded in contradictory accounts even in the annals of the German military. After all, every unit involved in the capture of the Latvian capital sought commendation for its role, which led to a distorted depiction of events and the singling out of each unit's own heroic deeds in reports.

To capture Riga, it was vital that a crossing over the Daugava be established; therefore, it was of crucial importance for the success of German plans that the road bridge and railroad bridge located somewhat farther south were taken unscathed.[18] In storming the city, several formations found themselves in a kind of competition with one another: Advance Regiment Lasch of the 1st Division (marching on Riga's south from Bauska [Bauske]), Group Ullersperger of the 61st Division (fighting its way toward Riga from the southwest), and Advance Formation Gurran of the 291st Division (which was to occupy the city's north from the freight train station down to the Daugava bridges). The task of securing the western part of the city was given to Combat Group Brig. Gen. Burdach and Advance Formation Klar.[19] Particular importance was attached to Colonel Otto Lasch's regiment. It was supposed to take the road bridge connecting the west side with the east side and the historic old town and to prevent the enemy's retreat.[20] Strangely enough, Red Army forces stationed in Riga for the most part began withdrawing to the east and could no longer be engaged. It was different with the Soviet units streaming toward Riga from Liepāja and Jelgava in the west. These were already in retreat and could only escape as long as the Germans had not seized Riga. The Germans thus faced two opponents: one group already stationed in Riga, which was withdrawing in an orderly fashion, and the remnants of the Soviet 8th Army, which would fight fanatically to keep from falling into German hands. Between them, in Riga's cellars, were the civilians, who either looked forward to the Germans' arrival or feared the worst.[21]

Lasch's regiment managed to enter west Riga around midday on 29 June and to take the southern part of the city after heavy street fighting. The next step was to protect south Riga from the Red Army soldiers advancing from the west and at the same time to take the bridges. The operation began well enough. The Germans were able to establish a bridgehead on the east side and to put in place assault guns. They also succeeded in cutting the cables for Soviet explosives on the railroad bridge. The defenders, realizing that they could only stop the advance by taking radical measures, blew up the road bridge and a pontoon bridge. In doing so, however, they made it more difficult for their comrades on Riga's west side to flee, which was now only possible via the railroad bridge. At the same time, the German bridgehead on the east side was surrounded. For several hours, the battles on the west and east side unfolded separately from one another. Located at a safe distance, only the German artillery fired on the east side of Riga, while also directing disruptive fire at the Red Army on the west side. The wooden tower of St. Peter's Church, one of the city's trademarks, was hit by a shell and went up in flames.[22] The German soldiers cut off on the east side were forced to dig in and defended themselves courageously, but their losses mounted steadily. At the same time, fighting raged for every building on the west side. Red Army soldiers stormed the Jelgava and Sloka roads, where they met a defensive line. An attempt to send reinforcements to the Germans on the east side was made, but the infantry men were cut down on the bridge and left behind dead or wounded. The bridgehead was wiped out. Only one wounded officer, First Lieutenant Geissler, and three other soldiers were able to retreat to the west side. There, in the meantime, Soviet tanks had begun to arrive. Fighting now concentrated along Jelgava Road. Lasch's regiment received news that supplies were on the way. Lasch now had to clear the enemy from south Riga. He had no reserves left and was forced to throw everything he had forward. For this clearing operation, he also deployed a "detachment of SS (SD)," which had "reported to the regiment." Stahlecker was hoping to cross the Daugava on the morning of 1 July 1941. Beforehand, a local Latvian agent traveling with Stahlecker was to smuggle into the center of town around forty men from EG A (a few men from the command, twenty-five from Sk 1a, and fifteen from Ek 2) as well as a handful of Latvian agents under Roberts Štiglics, the former chief of the political police.

From the east side, Riga's defenders saw that their comrades would not make it to the river and, on the night of 29 to 30 June, managed to blow up a part of the railroad bridge. This in effect ensured the orderly withdrawal of the defenders on the east side and the annihilation of the Red Army units on the west side. The latter could only hold up the German forces to give their retreating comrades time. According to Jewish survivor E. Gechtman, civilians and Red Army soldiers poured into the train stations, with the military and civilian transports hampering one another, which only made evacuation more difficult. Nonetheless, around 11,000 Jews are supposed to have been evacuated. In this phase of the battle, as the chaos on the east side could no longer be contained, the 1st Battalion – one of the German support units on the west side – noticed that a pedestrian bridge across the Daugava was still passable, and that desperate Red Army soldiers were seeking to save themselves by crossing the river on rafts. These were gunned down. Because the 1st Battalion did not trust the civilian population on the west side, it began to seize all able-bodied men and to send them to the rear. Here, on the left bank of the Daugava, the Germans gradually gained the upper hand. The battles along Jelgava Road flared up now and again, but wherever resistance stirred, the buildings were set on fire. Skirmishes were soon confined to the western shoreline. At midday on 30 June, the shooting on the east side fell silent. Apparently, the defenders had almost fully evacuated the east side of Riga – as early as 11:30, German air reconnaissance had been unable to discern any enemy movement – and had withdrawn, because additional fighting had seemed futile. Now it was up to the attacker to occupy the Riga's east side with its historical old town and the administrative center.[23]

The problem of bridging the Daugava was not to be overcome by Advance Regiment Lasch, but by Group Ullersperger's combat engineers. They had also entered the city behind the advance regiment and become involved in the fighting. In the early morning hours of 1 July, Colonel Wilhelm Ullersperger and his men crossed the Daugava southeast of Riga, using assault boats and a small steamer they had requisitioned. On the other side, they set up a command in a plaster factory. Advancing from the south, Ullersperger's men had the task of fighting free the east side of the bridges "so that the work of the combat engineers on the destroyed bridges could start." Attention was first directed to the southern sector, which "represented the Jewish and Communist quarter of the city." This area was known as the Moscow Suburb (under tsarist and Soviet rule), or the Latgale Suburb (in independent Latvia), where the poorest part of Riga's population lived. This would also be the sector where the Riga ghetto would be established in a few weeks' time. All of the buildings were combed as a precautionary measure, for here the population revealed itself to be "more than reserved" vis-à-vis the invaders. Group Ullersperger then entered the heart of the city, where several Red Army soldiers left behind to cover the Soviet retreat were found in buildings and shot. Upon reaching the large road bridge, they found sixty-nine fallen German solders, shot-up assault guns, motorcycles, and autos. One of the cars bore police license plates, which indicates that members of Sk 1a had entered Riga at the very outset of the fighting and raises the question whether their goal had been to make contact with RHSA agents among the Latvian nationalists. Group Ullersperger also found several wounded men, who were evacuated by means of the assault boats.

Suddenly, German soldiers north of the two devastated bridges saw "civilians with guns." Apparently believing that these were Soviet guerillas, the Germans opened fire. It was quickly determined, however, that these people were from the Latvian self-defense force, which together with the Riga Fire Department was rushing to assist the Germans. The home defense unit was led by an unnamed former officer of the Latvian Army. Ullersperger, who did not trust the situation, ordered the Latvian officer to have the self-defense force come over unarmed. At that point, "the entire population of Riga, with women and children, suddenly appeared, while the bells began to toll." Ullersperger learned that the heart of the city was completely free of the enemy and moved on "under the cheering of the population" to the city ring. Afterward, he took up quarters in Hotel de Rome, the most luxurious address in Riga, where he was praised by a representative of the city as a "liberator." Stahlecker, who had entered the city center with his troops via Latgale Road, also arrived there. In the first issue of the newspaper *Tevija* (Fatherland), which in fact served as a gazetteer, Ullersperger on 1 July ordered that the Latvian self-defense force remain on duty, and that its members wear red-white-red armbands.[24]

This is how the capture of Riga was depicted by the German troops that took part in the fighting. The people in the city are bound to have experienced the struggle differently. Several days before Riga's capture, the deportations of Latvian nationalists to Siberia by the Soviet secret police, the NKVD, had reached their climax. EG A reported to Berlin that the entire "ruling class [had] been taken away to Siberia or murdered."[25] Even if exaggerated, the report was essentially correct. In the Central Prison, the corpses of prisoners who the NKVD had been unable to evacuate were discovered. In the logic of dictatorship, the conclusion was that these persons were not to be released but killed. Later, at Baltezers Lake, northeast of Riga, the excavation of additional graves would reveal the corpses of abducted nationalists or persons considered as such.[26] Although there was a great deal of uncertainty surrounding all of these crimes, the violence and counter-violence since the first day of fighting in and around Riga had created an atmosphere full of hatred, which was waiting to be vented.

In this respect, the RSHA's instructions to unleash pogroms fell on fertile ground here. The self-defense forces in Riga needed no encouragement to take action against their neighbors. Latvian nationalists had long cultivated an intent to do so on their own, which amounted to nothing more than putting their traditional anti-Semitism into practice. With the arrival of the German occupiers, Latvian nationalists began to transform this intent into deeds, seeing their actions "justified" as an immediate reaction to the NKVD's crimes. Years later, Hans Krauss, a Baltic German who had returned to Latvia with Sk 1b, summed up the atmosphere and the Latvian nationalists' assessment of the situation the following way: "During the occupation of Latvia by the Russians in 1940–41, the Jewish share of the population in particular sided immediately with the Russians and supported the Russians in the deportation and shooting of members of the Latvian people. At the time, horrendous acts of cruelty took place, for which the Latvians, after the expulsion of the Russians by the German troops, made the remaining Jews responsible. This explains why Jews were arrested by Latvians in many places in Latvia, locked up, and in part shot."[27] The cliché of the Jewish Bolshevik had taken hold completely and – as the above shows – even appeared in postwar trials as a stereotype used to justify the crimes against Jews that followed the German capture of Riga.

The persecution of Riga's Jews was organized by several notorious nationalists who linked the reestablishment of Latvian statehood with the staging of pogroms. On 1 July, after the radio station in Riga played the Latvian national anthem (which itself had followed the Nazi hymn "The Horst Wessel Song"), Ullersperger addressed the population in German. Afterward, Lieutenant Colonel Voldemārs Veiss, a well-known nationalist and officer of the former Latvian Army, appealed to the population to take up the struggle against the "internal enemy." The poorly organized but determined mob, which was made up of former members of the Thunder Cross and Aizsargi paramilitaries as well as other ethno-nationalist groups, had been authorized to manifest the restoration of "order" with torture and murder.

One man in particular played a crucial role in the first days of persecution, a man who had taken the lead even before German forces arrived in

Riga. Viktor Arajs, born in 1910, was a former member of the Latvian Police who had begun studying law in 1938. As a member of the student association Lettonia, he had made no secret of his anti-Semitism even during the Ulmanis era. After the Red Army occupied the Baltic states, he claimed to have hidden first in the harbor, and later, once this hideout was no longer safe, found refuge in the woods with like-minded friends. He believed that he represented the Latvian people, whose natural disposition, he said, was "in essence fully anti-Russian and anti-Communist." But, in his view, there were also "Latvians who placed themselves at the disposal of the Communists," by which he meant primarily "Jews and old Russians." With the first German attacks on Riga's east side, "a great panic broke out among the Russians." In the resulting confusion, Arajs had slipped into the east side with his men and, according to his own information, launched larger attacks on the retreating Red Army. In the process, he managed to occupy the police prefecture (a red brick building near the main train station), to plunder armories, and to secure warehouses. At the police station, everything was topsy-turvy. Amid the confusion of uniformed persons, Latvian police, and civilians – some were wearing the red and white armbands of the Thunder Cross, some the green armbands of the future auxiliary security police – a nerve-wracked activist leader was trying to bring order to the chaos and to register the opposition forces on site. Arajs quickly recognized that an organizing hand was lacking and seized the initiative. He had firearms handed out from the armory and dispatched patrols into the city.

The prefecture was one of the offices that EG A had been assigned to search for leads, and Stahlecker did not fail to take care of this himself. Heydrich after all had instructed the Einsatzgruppen to keep up with military developments and to secure "materials" as quickly as possible at especially important locations – which Riga and the police prefecture were, without a doubt. Operating alongside the command staff of EG A was Sk 1a, which had entered Riga with Ullersperger and had begun introducing immediate SD and police measures: "securing Bolshevik buildings, files, and writings, starting the arrest of all Bolsheviks, setting up the handling of Riga for Ek 2, which has in the meantime moved up."[28]

Stahlecker had been shown the way to the police prefecture by Hans Dressler, his Riga-born interpreter, who knew the town well. When they entered the building, the interpreter saw an old friend. "Viktor, you're alive!" Dressler exclaimed. Arajs and Dressler knew each other from the Jelgava gymnasium, where they had been pupils, and from the Latvian Army, where they had served. Dressler embraced Arajs and introduced him to Stahlecker. Arajs reported what had taken place on Riga's east side and explained the kind of immediate measures he had ordered. Stahlecker was apparently satisfied. Seeing in Arajs a person full of hate and thirsting for revenge, Stahlecker instructed Arajs that very day, 1 July, to set up a commando of nationalists, students, and pupils. Decades later, Arajs could not contain his admiration for Stahlecker: "I held him in high esteem. He was an enthusiastic anti-Communist and very pleased with the spontaneous Latvian support." Arajs immediately set about recruiting his people. As his right-hand man, he chose a person who enjoyed his complete trust, the former sport pilot and Thunder Cross member Herbert Cukurs. In the days that followed, Arajs spoke repeatedly on the radio and agitated in the streets, urging people to fight the Bolsheviks. He had a table set up in front of the building of the student association Lettonia, where volunteers could report by giving their name, address, profession, and – perhaps what seemed most important – time in the military. On 4 July, *Tevija* published an appeal to nationalist circles to join the Arajs Commando. Despite these recruitment efforts, the strength of the commando in July must have been around 100 men at first.[29] This was because Stahlecker's reorganization of the Latvian police was of course not in Arajs's hands. For this purpose, Stahlecker had brought Štiglics back to Riga. Štiglics sought to fill the police with "reliable persons" – people the Arajs Commando in turn had to do without – but Štiglics's men were allowed to take part, for the time being, "exclusively in the hunt for Communists and Red Army men." Lieutenant Colonel Veiss, who had appealed to Latvians to take up the fight against the "internal enemy," was assigned to take action against Soviet stragglers and red partisans. By contrast, the Arajs Commando, as its leader learned from Stahlecker on 2 July at a conference attended by German and Latvian officers and several Latvian civilians, was foreseen for another purpose. His commando had to unleash programs that looked spontaneous – inasmuch as the mob had not already taken matters into its own hands. By outward appearances, these would look like a popular uprising. In reality, they would mark the start of the systematic persecution of Jews and Communists and the organized murder of their representatives. In addition to the Arajs troops, another group of nationalists appears to have been set up especially for carrying out pogroms. This commando was under the command of the well-known athlete Arveds Dikmanis, who, like Arajs, was a member of the student association Lettonia. It must not be forgotten how important the Latvian auxiliary forces were for the Einsatzgruppe during this first phase of persecution; without their knowledge of who was considered a Jew and where that person lived, the Germans, whose paltry knowledge of leading Jewish personalities in Riga had of course been demonstrated by the Special Wanted Persons List USSR, could not have conducted their investigations. For Arajs, this order corresponded completely to his intentions. Stahlecker was therefore able to report to Berlin: "Pogroms are starting."[30] Although recruitment for the core personnel of the Arajs Commando took several days, the already existing detachments strove to fulfill their assignments.

For Latvians, 1 July 1941, was a day of liberation and revenge. By contrast, the Jews of Riga, even if they had not sympathized with the Soviets or criticized the government before 1940, expected nothing good of the change of power. These fears were quickly confirmed. The first wave of persecution was the desired staging of "the people's righteous anger." Uniformed Latvians forced their way into the homes of prominent Jewish citizens, abducted lawyers, rabbis, doctors, and other Jewish representatives, and took them away. Revealingly, the procedure corresponded to Heydrich's guidelines for the Einsatzgruppen to take action against the members of the elite first. In this context, it remains to be seen whether it was a coincidence that the nationalists vented their hatred against prominent Jews, who made for ideal objects of revenge, or whether EG A explicitly called for this.

The few survivors from this category of persons provided testimony of the kind of threat they faced from the first day of Riga's "liberation." Bernhard Press, then a medical student and later a chronicler of these events, reported a deceptive calm on the morning of 1 July. When he arrived at the independence monument, hundreds of bouquets of flowers lined the pavement, and pedestrians greeted one another, happy that the city had been captured without too much destruction. Suddenly, there appeared a group of armed young Latvians who were guarding and maltreating a group of thirty or forty Jews. The Jews were supposed to fill in the foxholes on the east side of the Daugava. This found favor with the applauding crowd, from which isolated voices called out that the time had come for Jews to do something useful for once as well. It then occurred to the young Press that his father's decision not to flee may have been a fatal mistake.[31]

Typist Ella Medalje lived with her family in a small street of Riga. Her mother was too sick to move, and after she and her husband had given up the idea of fleeing, they waited for the fighting to end. On the evening of the first day of the occupation – neither had come face to face with German soldiers – young Latvians forced their way into their apartment. They were led by a loutish young man, a neighbor who had always greeted her politely, but now demanded in no uncertain terms that her husband follow him "to work." Medalje never saw him again. Only after the war did she learn that he had not survived the first evening of the occupation – nor was he supposed to survive, in the plans of the perpetrators.[32] Max Kaufmann experienced something similar. His memoirs, which provide deep insight into these momentous events, describe how acquaintances telephoned to say that one of his brothers and his brother-in-law had been arrested by young Latvians with red-white armbands. In the process, they beat the detainees and plundered their apartment. They did not even make an "effort" to arrest some of the victims, but shot them in their homes. A day later, Max Kaufmann's turn came, as did that of his son. Armed Latvian youths plundered the apartment and drove both to the police prefecture. This took place right in front of a jeering public, which shouted: "Jews, Bolsheviks!" Some cynically added, "Stalin's unvanquished army is leaving!" As Kaufmann and his son were led past the monument to the poet Blaumanis, he caught sight of a friend, the lawyer Dr. Singel, who, although smeared in blood, was able to gesture by hand "My fate is sealed" before guards pushed him forward. Dr. Singel was murdered that same day.[33] When it came to scrutinizing at least the apartment blocks in the city center, the Soviet system of personal surveillance gave the Arajs men an ideal handle for tracking down assimilated Jews who had not been consigned to this ethnic group from the start or had not been known to be Jews. This took place as follows: The leader of a mobile commando visited the "relevant building's custodian at whose place the Jewish families living in the house as well as the apartments in which these Jews lived were determined on the basis of the house register." With that, the pursuers knew very quickly on which door to bang. There were custodians, however, who refused to divulge this information and thus saved the lives of some Jewish tenants.[34]

According to Efraim Janowski, who saw his brother-in-law for the last time during such an arrest, the Petersburg Suburb and the villa quarter Mežaparks (Kaiserwald) were also epicenters of raids, probably because Arajs's men and the militia men, frequently identified as from the Thunder Cross, hoped to find prominent victims there. When they were not looking for a specific person, the Latvian militia went from house to house and "took along every Jew known to them." The arrests spread beyond Riga's city limits. Matis Lutrinsch and his family watched their pursuers search the dachas along the coast after having failed to find victims at their permanent place of residence. Lutrinsch and his father were arrested by the self-defense force and robbed. Then they were brought back to Riga together with ten or twelve other prisoners, all of whom had been arrested close to the Melluži railroad station.[35]

One destination of the transports and internments from Riga's environs was the headquarters of the Arajs Commando. This was in a corner building on Waldemara and Elizabetes streets,[36] where the banking house owned by Aron Schmuljan had been headquartered during Latvian independence, before being nationalized by the Soviets.[37] Others were taken to the prefecture first. These places were now the main offices of terror. There Jewish prisoners, at the mercy of their tormentors, were locked up in underground cells. Some remained in these prisons. Others were transferred to the Central Prison, which was run by Franz Nakaten and Alfred Steckel, both SS first lieutenants from Ek 2's Department V (Criminal Police).[38] The city's remand prison served to admit the female victims during this phase. For the individual prisoner, it did not matter where he or she was locked up. Terror, arbitrariness, and above all sadism prevailed in all of these locations.

Dr. Herman Noim told how he and other prisoners were beaten for hours in one of the prefecture's interrogation rooms. He was thrown immediately to the floor and beaten on the head, the back, and the feet. The people he called Latvian police officers asked him no questions, accused him of nothing, and apparently expected no answer nor provided any justification. Alone the fact that Noim was a Jew constituted the "element of the offense." There was not just one interrogation room at the prefecture. Out in the corridor, the screams of tortured people could be heard from all directions.[39] Men made up a majority of the prisoners, but starting in mid July, women were also unable to elude arrest.

Several women were forced to clean the kitchen and offices of the Arajs Commando. In a special room, commando officers abused younger women.[40] Some forty years later, a survivor told a Hamburg court how she had been humiliated at the commando's headquarters; however, she considered herself lucky, because, as one of the guards said, she did not look Jewish. Other women were less lucky that day: "One evening, when we were already on the floor of our bivouac, the door opened and two Thunder Cross men with flashlights entered. They shined their light in the face of each woman and looked her over. Then they ordered the women who had been sought out to follow them, one after the other. After some time, a woman would come back in a horrible emotional state, and the Thunder Cross men would take another woman with them. In this way, they took six to seven women upstairs, where the office of their superior was located ... The next day, these six to seven women were put on a truck that was located in the courtyard and driven off somewhere. I can only assume that they were shot."[41]

Kaufmann, Press, and Gechtman also noted in their memoirs how young women were humiliated, raped, and tortured in the prefecture and at Arajs Commando headquarters. The cell block in the prefecture was not large enough to intern a large number of people for a longer period; therefore, the greater part of the male prisoners was transferred to the Central Prison, which usually amounted to a death sentence. This also applied to "older women" who had been detained at Arajs headquarters at Waldemara St. 19. On 2 August, the older women there were selected – mothers ruthlessly separated from their children – driven away, and murdered.[42]

Riga's new masters drew on another group of victims, including those Press had seen on the shore of the Daugava, to clear away debris and munitions. This, however, was no guarantee of survival. For example, of the people who had to work on the reconstruction of the bridge over the river, it is known that only 50 percent survived. For "amusement," their Latvian overseers pushed the other prisoners into the Daugava, where they drowned.[43] Driven forward by Latvians, other Jewish inhabitants – gathered in details of twenty men each – were forced to clear away the debris around Central Station. There they were beaten with fists and rifle-butts and taunted.[44]

Was it at all possible to avoid forced labor? According to Moisej Rage, an order was issued instructing all adult Jews to appear at local police stations so they could be assigned to forced labor details. Failure to comply with the order would have entailed incalculable risks. Rage himself reported and was deployed in clearing away rubble from the buildings destroyed in the siege. This did not apply to his friends Alfred Jakobson and Moisej Lat, who were "simple jurists." They were transferred to the Central Prison.[45]

There were four wings and a number of workshops in the Central Prison, but the facility was quickly overfilled, because the "arrested Communists and former members of the Soviet authorities, separated according to nationality, Latvians and Russians," were interned there alongside Jewish prisoners. Even the attic, where a large cage had been set up as a provisional cell block, was hardly able to absorb this mass of prisoners, "who made a very haggard impression." These detainees were suspected of cooperating with the Soviets during the occupation and were therefore considered traitors. Officially, a registration took place, but this was only of any significance for Russians and Latvians; the Jews "were registered in the books so they would believe that they could be released later. In reality, almost all of them were shot." Accordingly, it was not necessary to question them, because they had been condemned to die on the basis of their "Jewish nationality."[46]

It was in the Central Prison that Julius Bracs, a gymnasium director who returned to Riga on 1 July, evaluated material concerning "events in the 'year of horror'" and repeatedly scrutinized the Central Prison to that end. His work was to serve not only as propaganda for anti-Soviet agitation. He also prepared lists containing the names of Latvians who were supposed to have been "in the service of the Soviets" and was thus doing preliminary work for the Gestapo. Postwar German investigations could not confirm that he had been assigned to draw up execution lists. But it is a fact that Latvian-Soviet collaborators were sought out, and that the Gestapo needed reliable investigators with the requisite language skills.[47] In this respect, however, the occupational authorities went about their work more discreetly, while the arrests of Jews took place on the streets.

Herman Noim was also transferred, by truck, from the prefecture to the Central Prison together with some forty or fifty other Jews. The wounded and beaten men were packed tightly on the vehicle and forced to stand under the supervision of Latvian policemen as well as uniformed Germans. Upon arriving, the prisoners were subjected to a selection in the corridor of the Central Prison. Noim showed his doctor's diploma. He and a Jewish physician from Germany were allowed to step out of line and were locked in a cell, while the rest remained in the corridor. Inside the cell were other doctors who were to remain alive in order to ensure there was medical care for the city. This process corresponded exactly to Heydrich's instructions to the Einsatzgruppen. It is to be assumed that the Latvian auxiliaries were managed by EG A, which otherwise restrained itself. The doctors spent their time in prison giving lectures to one another on their specialties. Because they were still needed, they were released on 30 July.[48]

Just as Riga's Jews were to "disappear" quickly, the perpetrators sought to destroy the city's synagogues, as they were not only visible testimony to Jewish culture and religion but also centers of social life. This special task was also given to Arajs. In the first days of July, he held an inflammatory speech before his men, called the Jews "parasites," "filthy Jews," and the like and urged his men to provide proof that "the people of Riga do not desire any Jewish synagogues." Arajs divided his men into several groups, which set off that evening to Riga's various synagogues.[49]

On Friday, 4 July, Raphael Shub was on his way to the synagogue on Elijas St. There he saw local policemen, dressed in old Latvian uniforms with red-white armbands, checking passers-by in front of the prayer house. Several of the civilians were arrested, primarily inhabitants of the building at Dzirnavu St. 161, and locked in the synagogue. A little while later, the men in uniform took a barrel of gasoline into the prayer house, emptied it, and shut the doors. They then threw hand-grenades through the windows. The synagogue burst into flames. Those locked inside tried to flee, but anybody who appeared in the windows was shot at. None of the people inside survived. Some died from their burns or smoke inhalation; others were struck by bullets. They all burned together with the synagogue.[50]

The other centers of religious life, among them the Old-New Synagogue, the synagogue on Stabu St., and the smaller prayer houses of the Hasidic Jews in the Moscow Suburb, were also set on fire. That same day, a group of about fifteen Arajs men set out for the Great Synagogue on Gogol St. Taking gasoline from their own autos, the arsonists stormed the building, smashed the windows, tore up the books, and destroyed the interior. The debris was stacked up, doused in gasoline, and set alight so that the building quickly burned. Devout Jews from the vicinity ran to the prayer house and tried to do something to fight the flames. They were insulted, humiliated, and beaten back. Other Jews were inside the synagogue, among them refugees from Kaunas and other Lithuanian cities as well as from Latvia. Those who tried to escape the burning building were shot down by machine gun fire from the Arajs Commando. The bloodcurdling screams of the others pierced the flames as they burned inside the building. For a while, the Arajs Commando, together with members of EG A sitting in a nearby car, controlled the fire. The synagogue on Gogol St. burned for several hours. The "spectacle" was also attended by the Riga Fire Department, which had only been alerted in order to keep the flames from spreading to surrounding buildings.[51]

It is worth noting here the way EG A depicted these events in its reports. Berlin was correctly informed that the "self-cleansing efforts" in Latvia came up to speed "only gradually." At the same time, however, EG A stressed that it was only the "impertinence of the Jews," primarily in the cities, that had forced the "self-cleansing"; in the wake of this impertinence, the pogroms, the destruction of synagogues, and the liquidation of Jews and Communists had followed. In other words, nothing was said about the Einsatzgruppe's role in managing the excesses and its preferred instrument, Arajs and his commando. Even the select circle of recipients of the "Reports on Events USSR" within the RSHA did not learn the true background of these events and received only a vague picture of the Latvian nationalists' willingness to collaborate.[52]

Arajs's men also forced themselves into the brick building of the synagogue on Stabu St.[53] – where they had already established a collection point for arrested Jews before sending them off to the Central Prison – and "set afire everything inside that could burn." Then they broke the windows so that the ensuing draft facilitated the fire's spread. The Riga Fire Department had also rushed to the scene, but here, too, it was only to contain the flames. The Peitavas Synagogue in the Old Town escaped the arsonists. It stood among residential buildings, and the danger of unleashing a conflagration in the heart of the city proved to be too great even for the Arajs men. This prayer house, like the Jewish cemeteries, was desecrated and misused as a horse stable. According to Kaufmann, the inhabitants of the building at Kalnu St. 9 were locked in the synagogue of the Old Jewish Cemetery. At the New Jewish Cemetery, the militia imprisoned the cantor Mintz and his family in the prayer house there. Both buildings were then burned down. Everyone inside died in the flames.[54]

What happened to the prisoners of the Central Prison who were not physicians remained concealed to outsiders, although it did not require much effort to imagine the dreadful possibilities. However, at first, there was no certainty. Common sense told the family members and friends of those imprisoned that this form of detention meant nothing less than murder, but they secretly succumbed to their illusory hopes until the truth was unmistakably obvious. For EG A and its Latvian auxiliaries, it was clear from the start that the Jews held in the Central Prison, the prefecture, and Arajs Commando headquarters were not to remain alive. However, the prisoners were not to be murdered in these places of internment, simply because there were too many, and because the analogy with the NKVD would be too obvious. Instead, after a short phase of "wild executions" lasting a few days – when the Latvians possibly acted autonomously – those responsible chose a killing site outside the city center.[55] Rudolf Lange from the EG A command staff and Rudolf Batz of Ek 2 now secretly managed the Arajs Commando and continued to maintain supervision and control. The forest of Bikernieki (*Biķernieku mežs*), which is reached by taking the large arterial road to the northeast, proved better suited. Until mid July, transfers to this forest took place almost daily. The course of events in carrying out these crimes repeated itself as a matter of routine.[56]

The shooting was prepared to take place for around midnight, and the personnel divided up into groups. A convoy group drove in trucks from Arajs Commando headquarters to the Central Prison. The prisoners were handed over at the prison gate.[57] They were then forced to board the truck and to kneel, while guards stood above them to ensure that none of the victims jumped from the truck during the trip. To avoid attracting attention, a different route to Bikernieki was often chosen. Frequently used roads were also avoided. Instead, the drivers tried to head northeast by taking back roads. They were careful to reach their destination over as many different routes possible and to prevent a pattern from emerging. An outside observer who by chance saw the truck could note that it involved a transport of prisoners, but could not draw any conclusions about the regularity or frequency of the transfers. The forest was also cordoned off by Arajs's men – for one to prevent escape, but primarily to keep unauthorized persons from approaching the shooting site. During the day, a group of prisoners from the Central Prison would have to dig a grave at the site. The actual shooting commando was made up of twenty-five men, of whom twenty were to shoot at the victims with rifles, while the others stood ready at a safe distance with two machine guns in order to provide support in the event of resistance.

The trucks stopped at a distance of about 80 meters before the immediate shooting site. The people then had to get out and sit or lie down on the ground. The further course of events in the crime was arranged such that the convoy group then drove back to the Central Prison to pick up more Jewish men, while the shooting commando set about its tasks. The victims were led to the excavated pits. There ten persons were shot at a time from behind. For each victim, there were two marksmen: One fired at the base of the neck, the other at the torso. This lasted until all of the prisoners, including those who arrived during the night on other transports, were dead. At the end of the operation, men from the guards' group filled in the pit, and the entire unit returned to headquarters.

At one of the earliest operations of this kind at Bikernieki, perhaps the very first one, Arajs himself was present to address his men. He appealed to them to join the execution commando voluntarily, which some immediately did. This shooting had the character of a "show execution," because members of the SD and Gestapo from the EG A command staff and Ek 2,[58] as well as policemen from Reserve Police Battalion 9, were on hand and "demonstrated" on the first victims how an execution was to be carried out in "an ideal way." After the German marksmen had shot several groups of ten in this fashion, they stepped back from the pit and called on the execution commando of Arajs men to continue the same way. According to the depiction of the scene given by Theodor Clausen of Reserve Police Battalion 9, it was as if "one were driving pigs onto a ramp for loading or slaughter. With truncheons and kicks accompanied by a lot of noise and with pistols in hand, the Jews were driven to the shooting pit." Arno Besekow of Ek 2 described the course of events with greater distance: "The reaction of the victims to their imminent death varied considerably. Some prayed, others cried, and still others went to their deaths with composure." Some Jews were only wounded after shooting. Lying on the ground doubled over in pain, some asked for a quicker death, while others cursed their murderers. In such cases, the victims were killed by "mercy shots" delivered by the officers who stepped up to the grave after each volley. When the shooting was finished, lime was spread over the mass grave.

After the "work" was done, bread and vodka were handed out. This initiation ritual was performed at the killing site. At later shootings, members of EG A, for example, SS First Lieutenant Arno Besekow from EK 2 or SS Major Kraus from the EG A command staff, monitored the coordination and course of the murdering. Their presence, however, served first and foremost to protect the Latvian commando from unforeseen inquiries or inspections by the military authorities. The clothes of the those who had been murdered – during the first executions, the victims were allowed to keep their clothes on; later, they had to undress down to their undergarments – were collected by the commando and stacked in the halls of the factory Krasnyi Kvadrat, which was located on the edge of town; in the meantime, the number of the people murdered at each operation was reported to EK2 commander Rudolf Batz.[59]

If one adheres to the Stahlecker October 1941 report, one reason why the Arajs Commando worked so ruthlessly lay in the fact was that in assigning "Latvian forces to execution commandos" a premium was put on choosing men "whose family members and relatives had been murdered or taken away by the Russians." Here it is implied that the desire for revenge was specifically used for shootings. It must be added, however, that some men from the Order Police testified after the war that they were repulsed by the executions and had felt misemployed, assertions that cannot be disproved. Astonishingly, Arthur Rosenow, the leader of the Waffen-SS company with

EG A, is also said to have refused the enlistment of his men in executions, wishing to have them used in battle instead. Solely for these reasons, the leadership of the Einsatzgruppe was forced to fall back on more reliable Latvians.[60] Nonetheless, according to reserve policeman Bernhard Borkowski, Karl Tschierschky carried out two shootings in July 1941 using exclusively members of EG A. In these cases, men from Reserve Police Battalion 9 and the Waffen-SS had to provide the shooting commando. None of the marksmen were relieved of their duties; there "were simply too few people there" to leave the murder of thousands of people alone to one specially schooled unit, that is to say, the Arajs Commando.[61] Despite the apparent readiness to commit violence found within nationalist Latvian circles, this fraction represented a minority of the Latvian population, at least in EG A's judgment. The Einsatzgruppe had promised itself a more enduring effect from the "cleansing actions," a "comprehensive pogrom." Instead, the rapporteur for Latvian territory stated: "In fact, however, only several thousand Jews were eliminated by indigenous forces." The deception presented to the public and neutral foreign observers – that the Latvians had taken revenge on Riga's Jews completely on their own out of "righteous anger" – could not be maintained due to the lack of engagement.[62]

The number of Riga Jews killed during the first days of the occupation is known from a July report sent to Berlin describing the persecution: "Einsatzkommando 2 has viewed all of the material in Riga, searched all of the offices, arrested all of the Communists, inasmuch as identifiable, and continued to carry out the operations introduced against the Jews in an outstanding fashion under the direction of SS Maj. Barth [sic]. There are at present 600 Communists and 2,000 Jews in custody. Four hundred Jews have perished in Riga by means of pogroms, and since Ek 2 moved in, 2,300 by means of the Latvian auxiliary police, in part by means of our own forces. The prisons will be completely cleared in the coming days."[63] The summer executions continued consequently, only to be curtailed when Latvian territory was transferred from military to civil administration. By mid October, according to Stahlecker, the mass murder carried out under the aegis of EG A had claimed altogether 30,025 Jewish lives throughout Latvia, 6,378 of them from in and around Riga.[64]

Anybody from among the Jewish population who had put any hope in the German troops after Riga's occupation was quickly disappointed. On 2 July, Ullersperger himself – apparently in his capacity as head of the Field Administration Command – had issued a proclamation in the newspaper *Tevija* that forbade Jews to stand in front of grocery stores with the rest of Riga's population to acquire goods. They were only allowed to buy in stores without lines.[65] If one considers everyday life in a city that has just been conquered, this meant nothing other than the exclusion of Jews from buying food. After days of heavy fighting, most household inventories would have been exhausted; Riga's citizens had to stock up on groceries again – which is what they did – and to take precautions, because a free market without ration cards was unthinkable. A store without lines was an absurdity, a figment of somebody's imagination. If somebody from among the Jewish population joined a line, he or she had to reckon with being driven away. If the crowd responded too passively, the auxiliary police intervened, forced the person in question out of the line, and arrested him or her. In extreme cases, the price paid for this indiscretion was very high. Judif Ravdin wanted to buy some milk for her mother on 27 July. She was asked by a Latvian what she was doing in the store. After an exchange of words, the man called the police and Ravdin was arrested. Inquiries by her brother, who sought to bring his sister back home to her family, revealed that she had been shot in prison shortly after her arrest.[66] Such was the perfidy concealed in Ullersperger's ordinance. Going beyond this proclamation, Ullersperger also conferred legitimacy upon the disenfranchisement of the Jewish population for all to see by lending his authority to the Latvian auxiliary formations. On the occasion of the ordinance concerning Jews standing in shop lines, another Latvia was revealed – Latvians who were guided by thoughts of solidarity and humanity, and who provided their neighbors with groceries at personal risk to themselves, in part endangering their own lives. These upstanding inhabitants of Riga soon became the target of attacks in *Tevija,* which in July alone printed four articles aimed at "Jew lovers" and "traitors," which shows that this group was not made up of just a few individuals. Radio also agitated against the "merciful Latvians" who "day after day render services to the Jews."[67]

Ullersperger's course of action reflected in good part the anti-Semitic mentality of senior generals in Army Group North. On 8 July, the commander of Rear Area Army Group North, Franz von Roques, complained to the commander in chief of Army Group North, Ritter von Leeb, about the mass executions of Jews in Kaunas as carried out by self-defense forces under the tutelage of EG A. Leeb in turn told his subordinate that the military could not influence these measures, and that one should therefore stay clear of them. Roques judged the situation differently than Leeb. However, in this conversation, he was not criticizing the crime but the methods, which were too crude and too brutal for him. Leeb noted Roques's considerations in his diary, including an idea that seemed to the commander of Rear Area Army Group North a better way of reaching the desired end: "Roques said, probably accurately, that the Jewish question cannot be solved this way. It would be most effective to solve it by sterilizing all male Jews."[68] Thus the High Command of the Army and the Army leadership in Riga contributed considerably on their own initiative – such official assistance was never put to paper in agreements with the RSHA and the SS – to the persecution and murder and developed their own ideas as to what would constitute suitable steps for the exclusion and annihilation of Baltic Jewry. Seen this way, Ullersperger's ordinance on Jews standing in shop lines was not the result of oversight but an initial step in a series of successive decrees issued in the same spirit.

Instead of curbing the murder, the power that enforced order in Riga made use of Jews specially quartered in barracks. Max Kaufmann reported that he and his son were saved from the prefecture by soldiers from the Field Administration Command. With that, they escaped torture and other excesses committed by their Latvian guards. However, their rescue took place not out of sympathy on the part of the Wehrmacht but out of self-interest. The commandant's office, which was located across from the city opera, needed decorators and other workers and chose a few from among the detainees. For those who had been rescued and received authorization that identified them as personnel from the commandant's office, the appearance of the soldiers had been an enormous stroke of luck. But it must not be forgotten that the commandant's office otherwise gave free rein to the Latvians' sadism, and that the majority of the detainees were murdered as a result of the military authorities' conscious decision not to intervene.[69]

The military, however, wanted more: Riga, according to Nazi plans, was to become once again a metropolis, the capital and administrative center of Reich Commissariat Ostland. For the Wehrmacht, it was clear that Riga had always been a German-influenced city. The Field Administration Command hardly granted the Latvians their own "literature and art worthy of mention" – something German soldiers could read in any and every guidebook – and the Jewish element existed "only in the closed general stores and the cultural destruction of Bolshevism." Thus, as early July 1941, the reorientation of city policy got underway.[70] According to the premises of the new rulers, it was first necessary to get the economy up and running again, above all to integrate the population in the kind of labor necessary to meet the demands of the wartime economy, and to address the problem of housing space. The pogroms and mass persecution may have served the war of ideologies and acted as a manifestation of power, but they hampered production. And production had to function if Riga were to assume its role as a supply base and distribution center for the northern sector of the Soviet front. After all, ultimately, the success of Operation Barbarossa depended considerably on logistics and supplies for Army Group North, while the troops for the most part lived off the land.

According to an assessment by Economics Inspection North, Latvian agriculture suffered in mid July from a "considerable shortage of workers," which could not be eliminated by deploying Red Army POWs for reasons of security and ideology. At the same time, Economics Command Staff East had decided on 15 July that for the maintenance of the economy the use of Jewish workers was indispensable, something that was at least not seriously called into question by Einsatzgruppe A.[71] For this reason, on 21 July, Senior Wartime Administration Counselor Friedrich Ellrodt of the Labor Department of Economics Inspection North and Senior Wartime Administration Counselor Max Dorr of Economics Commando Riga met for talks to examine "the possibility of deploying the Jews" to solve the economic issues of provisioning. Both men quickly agreed on a concept and visited Ek 2 that same day. In a larger round, joined by SS Major Batz and his deputy, SS Captain Arnold Kirste, the two military men presented their thoughts:

> Our suggestion to mark the Jews, concentrate them in a ghetto, then create a Jewish Council, and, with it, pursue the comprehensive deployment of the Jews for labor met with approval. Understanding was also reached that the deployment of the Jews for labor is to be organized only by special deployment centers to be created by the Labor Office or Labor Offices in order to guarantee guidance according to the political needs of the military or state. The SS retains sole decision-making authority in political issues and the carrying out of political tasks. The marking of the Jews and their concentration in a ghetto will be organized. In addition, it was disclosed that negotiations had already taken place between the SS.-Sd. [sic] on the one hand and the Field Administration Command on the other with the result that a registration of the Jews in the police stations, a daily reporting of the Jews there, and the establishment of a special office for carrying out the deployment of labor at the Field Administration Command is to take place.

Apparently, all of the participants agreed on the procedure to follow, even if Ek 2 was to report months later that it had actually envisioned a "radical solution of the Jewish problem," which was opposed, however, by economic interests, in particular "the requirements of the Wehrmacht." In a final step, Wartime Administration Counselor Heinz Nachtigall from the Field Administration Command was visited in order to get his opinion. Here, too, the meeting led to the same results. The Field Administration Command agreed without reservation that "after the registration of the Jews, their deployment for labor will take place by means of the Labor Office." Therefore, at registration, "a special card for such deployment" was to be issued.[72]

Alongside the possibility of being able to use the ghetto as a workers depot that was easy to monitor, the forcible construction of a cohesive Jewish residential district also opened up the possibility of restructuring Riga boroughs according to the desires of the occupiers. If Riga was to assume its future function as a capital, representative buildings had to be available for assignment to the arriving civil administration organs, top functionaries, and administrators, but also for requisition by the different military offices of the OKW and the OKH as well as by the SS and police. The SS had envisioned Riga as a logistics center for the northern front with a supply command and auto workshops for the entire sector. Alone for these reasons, a strong influx from the Reich was to be expected. Longer-term planning had not fully excluded the return of the Baltic Germans, although the civil city administration pushed for a special regulation for Riga given that it was the capital of Ostland.[73] In the future, it was assumed that Riga would need around 100,000 settlers, without allowing for the strengthened presence of the police and Wehrmacht.[74]

The confiscation of homes could not of course be directed against the Jews living in the Moscow Suburb and their humble accommodations. But in the exclusive area of Kaiserwald, some 10 km (6 miles) north of Riga's center, several properties belonged to Jews or were – after nationalization by the Soviets – still inhabited by them. The SS had already confiscated many villas in this part of town. For that reason, the units from the office of the Wehrmacht Territorial Commander Ostland (WBO) that had already moved into town encountered enormous difficulties in finding suitable quarters. The advance commando assigned to search for residential areas found what it was looking for only after the Local Administration Command allocated it several streets of houses. Alone for the needs of the WBO, Jews in sixty-five buildings had to evacuate their apartments or – if no Latvians lived there – entire structures by early August 1941.[75] In seizing these dwellings, the advancing Wehrmacht agencies were only imitating what had been a part of everyday life since July. Former factory owner Samuel Gutkin reported how quickly a confiscation could take place: "On 15 July 1941, a German general in field grey uniform with red stripes on the pants and a man in brown uniform with a swastika armband came into my apartment and said they would like to look at my apartment. Afterward, the man in the brown uniform said that I, together with my family, had to leave the apartment within a quarter of an hour and could take only a towel and one piece of soap per person."[76]

In addition to the apartments themselves, the requisition process also involved an appraisal of the furnishings within, whereupon an open dispute broke out between representatives of the military already in the city and the newly arrived WBO. The position of the one side was that it would take over the buildings including their furnishings, while the other side took "pieces of furniture for the fitting of their own quarters." The responsible senior paymaster from the WBO advance commando complained that his comrades must know that "an empty or half empty apartment is of no value to us"; no mention was even made of the true owners.[77] Similar conflicts emerged between the WBO and the Security Police, where the arbitrary confiscation of apartments by SS Staff Sergeant Richard Nickel led to complaints.[78] These tensions were more than a quarrel over jurisdiction; they made it clear how scarce good, inexpensive properties were in a city that was to be built up as an administrative center.[79]

In the short period that Riga was under military administration, which lasted until the start of August 1941, an abundance of instructions that constrained the life of the Jewish population were issued. These are certain to have as their basis fundamental directives from Department VII (Wartime Administration) of Army Group North.[80] What stands out here, however, is the fact that the higher-ups were distributing instructions that Wehrmacht offices on site had in part already issued. The records of the 291st Infantry Division show that on 12 July it had ordered corresponding "immediate measures," including the marking of Jews by means of a yellow patch, the professional ban on Jewish doctors and merchants, the registration of Jews in special rolls, the entering of the notice "The bearer is a Jew" into internal passports, and the deployment of Jews for forced labor in cohesive groups.[81]

On 24 July, Rear Area Army Group North ordered that, for its entire area of responsibility, the marking of "Jews of both sexes" would be introduced. On this deadline at the latest, Jews would have to wear on the right breast of their outer garment the Star of David, a "6-point yellow star." The same order stated that – inasmuch as this had not already taken place – Jews had to evacuate their apartments as soon as Wehrmacht personnel expressed an intent to occupy them. Under the same date, *Tevija* published a call from the Field Administration Command by which all Jews had to be registered in lists. A "J" was stamped in their internal passports. This must have been an addendum to the instruction issued by Rear Area Army Group North to register all persons who had arrived after 17 June 1940 and to intern them at least temporarily.[82] Furthermore, the freedom to move and communicate was curtailed; Jews were not allowed, according to orders from Rear Area Army Group North, to change their apartments without official permission, and they were to hand in all radios. A strict curfew was imposed on them as well as other civilians.[83]

Department VII of the 281st Security Division issued its "Guidelines for Administration" for occupied Latvia on 27 July. According to these, the "formation of ghettos" was to be "prompted among the Latvian authorities." Those with whom the Wehrmacht intended to cooperate on the Latvian side were also noted. First and foremost, "personages" from the associations Lettika and Lettonia – of which Arajs and the greater part of his command staff had been members – were considered trustworthy as were old pro-German Baltic combatants from 1918–1920. "Files of all kinds, lists of persons murdered [by the NKVD], lists of Communists, etc.," which must have included lists of Jews, were to be given to the next Secret Field Police or Einsatzkommando office. For "the clearance of all kinds of war damage," "prisoners and Jews" were to be drawn on.[84] Additional orders forcing the establishment of ghettos were issued by the 281st Security Division on 30 July and Rear Area Army Group North on 28 August to their subordinate units. The field administration commands were obligated to report on "what was occasioned" in this matter.[85] Around the middle of July, Jewish businesses, offices, and practices were to cease activity. Their assets were to be confiscated. "Jews important to the economy" received special distinguishing marks that represented a certain degree of protection against excesses. Even if the dissolution of the Jewish business community was also organized by EK 2 and in cooperation with the Latvian auxiliary security police, it is clear that this measure also was enacted under the control and supervision of the Army.[86]

While the military set up house and planned the deployment of Jews as laborers, the first phase of persecution was wrapped up. A month of German occupation had brought destruction, destitution, and primarily murder, with the mass executions in the woods of Bikernieki following the pogroms. The synagogues were destroyed, Jewish shops and assets confiscated. A large part of the Jewish intelligentsia and many able-bodied men had been murdered, community life extinguished. Jewish Riga had already ceased to exist.

Notes

1. BA-MA, RH 19 III/715, 2–9, HGr. C [=North], Aufmarsch- und Kampfanweisung Barbarossa, 5 May 1941.
2. BA-MA, RH 19 III/767, 3–7, HGr. Nord, Ia, Kriegstagebuch v. 22.6.–31.8.41, entry for 22 June 1941. Army messages to Army Group North bear witness to a certain confusion; it was even thought that "the enemy had already in the last days begun a movement to the rear," which, it should be noted, hardly makes a case for proponents of the preventative war thesis. See also Wilhelm Ritter von Leeb, *Tagebuchaufzeichnungen aus zwei Weltkriegen*, 275–276.
3. *Justiz und NS-Verbrechen*, Bd. XV, Lfd. Nr. 465, 1–274, Urteil des LG Ulm v. 29.8.1958, Ks 2/57, gegen Fischer Schweder u.a. *Justiz und NS-Verbrechen*, Bd. XVII, Lfd. Nr. 509, 311–402. Urteil des LG Tübingen v. 29.8.1958, Ks 2/61, gegen Wiechert und Schulz. In addition, see Staw. KG Berlin, 1 Js 4/65, Bd. V, Statement by Werner Hersmann, 12 January 1966, 174–177; statement by Hans-Joachim Böhme, 13 January 1966, 183–192. According to Böhme, Einsatzgruppe C commander Otto Rasch, still inspector of the Security Police and SD in Königsberg, alluded to the "approaching contest between two ideologies" and noted that in its course difficult demands "surpassing all previous mea-

sures" would be made of the Security Police. See also ibid., Bd. VI, statement by Dr. Emil Finnberg, 11 May 1966, 285. BA Berlin, R 58/214, Ereignismeldung Nr. 14, 6 July 1941, and Ereignismeldung Nr. 19, 11 July 1941, provide the number of Ek Tilsit's victims at individual locations.
4. BA-MA, RH 19 III/382, 4–5, HGr. Nord, Tätikeitsberichte der Abt. Ic, here the entries for 23 and 24 June.
5. BA-MA, RH 19 III/767, 7–39, HGr. Nord, Ia, KTB 22.6.–31.8.1941, entries for 23–29 June 1941. Leeb, *Tagebuchaufzeichnungen*, 276–283, quote 280, almost same wording in war diary on page 20. With regard to chronology, Leeb's notations and those of the war diary differ slightly.
6. Tätigkeits- und Lagebericht Nr. 1, 31 July 1941, printed in Klein, *Die Einsatzgruppen in der besetzten Sowjetunion*, 112–131, here 155, and Krausnick and Wilhelm, *Die Truppe des Weltanschauungskrieges*, 349–350.
7. Myllyniemi, *Die Neuordnung der baltischen Länder 1941–1944*, 81–82, and Krausnick and Wilhelm, *Truppe des Weltanschauungskriegs*, 349–350. Apparently, a certain amount of confusion prevailed within Army Group North and EG A with regard to the Lithuanian nationalists' coup. In any event, the army group's military intelligence section (Ic) on 24 June inquired with the High Command of the Army whether the Škirpa government was to be recognized, which was answered in the negative. Instructions arrived stating that actions vis-à-vis national formations would be clarified, see BA-MA, RH 19 III/382, 5, HGr. Nord, Tätikgietsberichte der Abt. Ic, entry for 24 June 1941. Stahlecker was apparently at first uncertain about Lithuania's status. He speculated in the presence of army group staff members that the ultimate political shaping of the Baltic states had yet to be decided in Berlin, but would probably involve some mix of an autonomous form of government – as in Slovakia – and a protectorate. This was demonstrably wrong, something Leeb knew, which was why he supported Prützmann's initiative to establish civil administration quickly, Leeb, *Tagebuchaufzeichnungen*, 290, especially ft. 112. On 7 July, a notice from the OKH arrived at army group headquarters, according to which Hitler had decided that the "future political shaping of the Baltic area must not be rushed." Assistance from the "newly formed governments" was to be accepted; political recognition should not take place, however. Likewise, the raising of troops beyond self-defense forces with policing functions was to be prohibited in the Baltic states, see BA-MA, RH 19 III/767, 7–39, HGr. Nord, Ia, KTB v. 22.6.–31.8.1941, entry for 7 July 1941.
8. The Ia of Army Group North, Lieutenant Colonel Paul Herrmann, raised the "issue of the rioting of the Lithuanian guerillas" with Colonel Schmundt, Hitler's chief adjutant, during his visit to army group headquarters, which had been in Kaunas since 1 July. Herrmann did not receive an answer at first. Later, he called Schmundt at headquarters and received the following explanation: "The soldier should not be burdened by these political issues; this was a necessary 'floor cleansing,'" see BA-MA, RH 19 III/767, 52, HGr. Nord, Ia, KTB v. 22.6.–31.8.1941, entry for 3 July 1941.
9. Kaunas was surrounded by nine fortress facilities, which were used for mass shootings. According to Karl Jäger's infamous report on his commando's activity, killings were carried out in Fort IV until the end of September. At the end of November 1941, Fort IX was to be the final destination for Jews deported from Berlin, Munich, Frankfurt, Vienna, and Breslau. See BdS, Ek 3, Gesamtaufstellung der im Bereich des Ek. 3 bis zum 1.12.1941 durchgeführte Exekutionen, 1 December 1941, facsimile in Heinz Artzt, *Mörder in Uniform*, 185–193.
10. BA Berlin, R 58/214, Ereignismeldung Nr. 8, 30 June 1941; Ereignismeldung Nr. 14, 6 July 1941; and Ereignismeldung Nr. 19, 11 July 1941, quotes from Ereignismeldung Nr. 8 and 19. See also Staw. Hamburg, 141 Js 534/60, Bd. 6, statement by Horst Eichler,

15 September 1959, 129–130. Staw. KG Berlin, 1 Js 4/65, Bd. IV, statement by Erich Ehrlinger, 9 March 1966, 116, statement by Emil Finnberg, 11 May 1966, 287–288. Cf. Nuremberg Document L-180, EG A, Gesamtbericht bis zum 15.10.1941. There it is mentioned that 3,800 Jews were eliminated during the pogroms in Kaunas; Martin Broszat, "Die nationale Widerstandsbewegung in Litauen im Zweiten Weltkrieg (1941 bis 1944)," in *Gutachten des Instituts für Zeitgeschichte*, ed. Institut für Zeitgeschichte, Bd. 2, 324–328. On the man with the steel pipe, see "Bericht eines Oberst" and "Bericht eines Photographen" in *"Schöne Zeiten,"* ed. Ernst Klee, Willi Dreßen and Volker Rieß, 35–39. For the point of view of a survivor, see Alex Faitelson, *Im jüdischen Widerstand*, 19–28.

11. BA Berlin, R 58/214, Ereignismeldung Nr. 9, 1 July 1941. According to this report, an advance detachment of Sk 1a – often mistakenly identified here as "Ek 1a" – was dispatched to Riga, as was Stahlecker himself, while EG A's command staff was supposed to have been in Gumbinnen. Ibid., Ereignismeldung Nr. 12, 4 July 1941, has Stahlecker, Sk 1a, and a part of Ek 2 marching toward Riga. Ibid., Ereignismeldung Nr. 16, 8 July 1941, reports that EG A command staff, Sk 1a, and Ek 2 were in Riga.

12. BA-MA, WF 10/12769, Abschnittsstab Ostpreußen an Ic, Betr.: Entwaffnung völkischer Aktivistengruppen, 19 June 1941. In this document, strategies were developed for disarming pro-German activists after the capture of the Baltic countries. Riga was one of the centers for smuggling in agents arriving via Finland, ibid., Abschnittsstab Ostpreußen, Vortragsvermerk, Betr.: Organisation und Ausbildung der völkischen Widerstandsgruppen in den baltischen Staaten durch Abwehr II, 21 May 1941. Also, Staw. Hamburg, 141 Js 534/60, SB 6, statement by Hans Dressler, 14 November 1967, 1,090–1,092, and Kangeris, "Kollaboration vor der Kollaboration?" in Röhr, *Okkupation und Kollaboration (1938-1945)*, 172–174.

13. BA-MA, WF 10/12769, Anlage zu Abschnittsstab Ostpreußen, Aufgaben im Aufgabenbereich des V.O./Abw. II beim Abschnittsstab Ostpreußen. Three groups of activists stood ready for deployment behind enemy lines: half of one company from Batl. 800 plus 30 paratroopers, 45–90 former members of the Baltic littoral states – all of them "specialists" – and organized activist groups on enemy territory. The latter were to occupy the Riga radio station, see ibid., Abschnittsstab Ostpreußen, Betr.: Aufgabenbereich des V.O. Abw. II bei: Abschnittsstab Ostpreußen, 3 June 1941.

14. BA-MA, WF 10/12769, Abschnittsstab Ostprueßen, Ic/V.O./ Abw. II, Aktenvermerk, Betr.: Tätigkeit der Abw. II auf ruß. Gebiet. Kangeris, "Kollaboration vor der Kollaboration?" 181.

15. The incident is documented in LVVA, P 1019-1-2. See also Kangeris, "Kollaboration vor der Kollaboration?" 185–188.

16. BA-MA, RH 24-26/64, XXVI AK, Korpsbefehl, 29 June 1941.

17. BA-MA, RH 19 III/382, HGr. Nord, Tätigkeitsberichte der Abt. Ic, entries for 23 and 27 June 1941. "Radke" is most probably Lt. Col. Theo Radtke, a former desk officer at the Abwehr's Breslau office. The chief of staff of the Army Group North, Major General Kurt Brennecke, assumed at the end of June 1941 that Soviet defenses would be established on a broad front only on prewar Russian territory south of Lake Peipus. Whether members of these troops were actually deployed in Riga has not been verified, cf. Mader, *Hitlers Spionagegenerale sagen aus*, 185. Mader's comments rely on statements made by Abwehr officer Erwin Stolze in Soviet captivity. Members of the Red Army's intelligence service claimed to have unmasked around 1,500 German spies during the first half of 1941, primarily in the Baltic and Ukraine. They even provide various examples from the special section of the 8th Army in the Baltic area in June and July 1941, see A.A. Bogdanow et al., *Duell mit der Abwehr*, 12–26.

18. The road bridge from what the Nazis later called Victory Road led directly over the Daugava to the promenade of the same name. The railroad bridge ran somewhat south of Mukusalas Road, crossing a small island in the Daugava in order to reach the promenade Daugavas Krasts and Krastā St.
19. BA-MA, RH 26-1/5, 1. Division, KTB, entry for 29 June 1941; BA-MA, RH 24-26/64, XXVI AK, Ia, 30 June 1941, Korpsbefehl Nr. 1 für die Vorbereitung des Übergangs über die Düna.
20. BA-MA, RH 26-1/6, Voraus-Rgt. Lasch, Gefechtsbericht, 4 July 1941.
21. BA-MA, RH 24-26/64, XXVI AK, Ia, 29 June 1941, Korpsbefehl für den 30.6.1941. Ibid., Der OB der 18. Armee an den Kommandierenden General des XXVI AK, 1 August 1941; ibid., RH 24-26/128, XXVI AK, Ic-Abendmeldung, 30 June 1941; ibid., RH 24-26/125, 5, XXVI AK, Abt. Ic, Tätigkeitsbericht, 14 January 1942. Specifically, parts of the 10th, 90th, 48th, 125th, and 67th rifles divisions as well as the coast guard and combat engineer units were trying to withdraw to the east via the Jelgava-Riga road. On this, see the portrayal of this retreat in the official Soviet history, *Geschichte des Zweiten Weltkrieges 1939–1945*, Bd. 4, ed. A.A. Gretschko et al., 52–57. From the point of view of the Soviet Navy, N. G. Kusnezow, *Am Vorabend*, 377.
22. With regard to this national symbol, there was great debate over whether the Germans or the Soviets were responsible for the destruction of the church. From the report of the Riga Fire Department to the city administration, it is in our view easy to see that the hit must have taken place as a result of German artillery, because the fire department soberly noted that on 29 June "a heavy build up of smoke at the top of St. Peter's Church was reported," which by noon was burning fiercely. By contrast, the report accuses the Red Army of hampering efforts to extinguish fires in the city center and purposely setting fires in other places. If Red Army soldiers had been responsible for the fire in St. Peter's Church, this report would have mentioned it and provided corresponding commentary, see BA Berlin, R 91/238, 88–109, Die Berufsfeuerwehr Riga im Jahre 1941, Eine kurze Rückschau.
23. BA-MA, RH 26-1/6, 1. Division, Voraus-Rgt. Lasch, Gefechtsbericht, 4 July 1941, 74–85, quote 80; ibid., Bericht über die Straßenkämpfe des I. Btl. in Riga am 30.6./1.7.1941, 87–90; ibid., Anlage zum KTB des I. AK, 6 July 1941, Der Einsatz der zum Voraus-Regt. des I. AK gehörigen Truppen in der Zeit v. 27.6.–1.7.1941. Slightly glorifying, Otto Lasch, *So fiel Königsberg*, 18–20. See also BA Berlin, R 58/214, Ereignismeldung Nr. 9, 1 July 1941, and Ereignismeldung Nr. 12, 4 July 1941. A member of Sk 1a was wounded in combat. J. Gechtman, "Riga," in *Das Schwarzbuch*, ed., Wassili Grossman and Ilja Ehrenburg, 680. Gechtman also reports – 680–682 – that Jewish civilians with small arms, among them students led by Abraham Epstein, were involved in the battles, which in turn makes Group Ullersperger's skepticism vis-à-vis citizens on the east side of the Daugava more understandable.
24. BA-MA, RH 24-26/64, XXVI AK, Abt. 1a, Zusammenfassender Bericht über die Anordnungen des Gen. Kdo. in Riga am 30.6.41 nachmittags, 30 June 1941, unpaginated; ibid., Korpsbefehl Nr. 1 für die Vorbereitung des Übergangs über die Düna; ibid., Oberst Ullersperger, Kdr. Pi. Rgt. Stab z.b.V. 667, an den Kom. General d. XXVI AK, Betr.: Übergang des Rgts. Gruppe Ullersperger über die Düna oberstrom von Riga, 29 July 1941. Air reconnaissance also reported civilians cavorting in the streets of the east side at noon on 30 June see BA-MA, RH 24-1/260, I AK, Abtl. Ic, Betr.: Ic-Tagesmeldung, 30 June 1941. It could be that the Latvian officer mentioned in this document was Lieutenant Colonel Voldemārs Veiss. BA Berlin, R 91/238, 88–109, Die Berufsfeuerwehr Riga; Ezergailis, *Holocaust in Latvia*, 140, fn. 53, 150–151, 165–166, 180, and 197, fn. 37. Ezergailis also contains the reference to *Tevija*, which was published by Ernests Kreišmanis and for the

large part put together by editor in chief Paulis Kovaljevskis. See also, Staw. Hamburg, 141 Js 534/60, SB 44, statement by Karlis Ozols-Ozolins, 8 October 1979, 7,397.
25. BA Berlin, R 58/214, Ereignismeldung Nr. 12, 4 July 1941.
26. BA Berlin, R 58/215, Ereignismeldung Nr. 40, 1 August 1941. American journalists are supposed to have been at the exhumation; identification of the corpses – around 100 persons – turned out to be particularly difficult.
27. Staw. Hamburg, 141 Js 534/60, SB 4, statement by Hans Krauss, n.d., 757–759.
28. Ibid., SB 4, statement by Viktor Arajs, 30 July 1975, 676–682. Arajs's anti-Semitism clearly emerges from his own remarks during questioning in Hamburg. Ibid., Anklageschrift gegen Viktor Arajs, 10 May 1976, 74–75. Remarkably, Arajs's view that many Jews – above all "left-wing activists" – had acquired a "substantial mandate in the security service and in the police, offices that had been closed to them until then" is also shared by Israeli authors, see Anton Künzle and Gad Shimron, *Der Tod des Henkers von Riga*, 58–59. Empirical corroboration of this thesis has yet to be provided. The only way to clarify this issue is by gaining access to NKVD and KGB personnel records. BA-MA, RH 24-26/64, XXVI AK, Oberst Ullersperger, Kdr. Pi. Rgt. Stab z.b.V. 667, an den Kom. General d. XXVI AK, Betr.: Übergang des Rgts. Gruppe Ullersperger über die Düna oberstrom von Riga, 29 July 1941; Prosecutor's Office Tallinn 819-1-12, KdS Estland, Jahresbericht Juli 1941–30.6.1942, 1 July 1942; Sk 1a was deployed in Riga until 5 July 1941. Also, Der Chef der Sipo und des SD, Befehl Nr. 3 an die Einsatzgruppenchefs, in Klein, *Die Einsatzgruppen in der besetzten Sowjetunion*, 321–322.
29. Landgericht (LG) Hamburg, (37) Ks 5/76, Urteil gegen Viktor Arajs, December 1979, 17–19, quote 17; Staw. Hamburg, 141 Js 534/60, SB 4, statement by Arajs, 1 August 1975, 690–692 and 705, remark on Stahlecker, 705. The relatively small starting number of men in the unit suggests that, during the pogrom phase, members of other self-defense forces participated in the persecution of Riga's Jews, for the crimes of the first days could hardly have been carried out by such a small number of active members.
30. LG Hamburg, (37) Ks 5/76, Urteil gegen Viktor Arajs, December 1979, 17–18 and 21; BA Berlin, R 58/214, Ereignismeldung Nr. 12, 4 July 1941. Deputies in the Arajs Commando were the company leaders Captain Karlis Ozols and Captain Arnold Laukers. Lt. Boris Kinstlers acted as liaison to the German Security Police. Platoon leaders identified or named by Arajs himself were Lt. Diebitz, Lt. Ustups, and Lt. Kalnins. On Dikmanis, see Ezergailis, *Holocaust in Latvia*, 181–182, 189, and 198, fn. 198. According to Janson's statement, Arveds (Arwid) Dikmanis belonged at first to the Arajs Commando as "head of the administrative-operational department." In accordance with his task, he instructed the Latvian auxiliary security police to take action against the Jews. It is not known whether Dikmanis competed or cooperated with Arajs; later he left the self-defense force and took a job as a judge. Staw. Hamburg, 141 Js 534/60, SB 21, statement by Leonid Janson, 25 November 1975, 3,827 and 3,830. Janes Ustups in turn is supposed to have led a special killing commando, allegedly because the Soviets had murdered his parents and siblings and tortured him, see ibid., SB 11, statement by Karlis Kencis, 22 October 1975, 2,094–2,095.
31. Press, *Judenmord*, 33.
32. Staw. Hamburg, 141 Js 534/60, SB 17, David Zil'bermann, Recht auf Leben: Ein Dokumentarbericht, Riga 1966, 3,281–3,307. Zil'bermann put Medalje's experiences to paper. The translation is in the files of the Arajs case, here 3,282–3,284. See also ibid., SB 22, statement by Ella Medalje, 11 November 1975, 3,913.
33. Max Kaufmann, *Churbn Lettland*, 50–52.
34. Staw. Hamburg, 141 Js 534/60, SB 17, statement by Schabtai Dolgicer, 1 February 1976, 3,216; ibid., statement by Janis Brenzis, 26 November 1975, 3,783; ibid., SB 33, state-

ment by Leonid Janson, 21 June 1978, 5,809–5,810; quote from Brenzis. See also Ezergailis, *Holocaust in Latvia*, 218. Reproduced here are the reports from various police stations and watch-posts that arrested Jews in Riga in early July 1941.
35. Staw. Hamburg, 141 Js 534/60, SB 5, statement by Efraim Janowski, 18 August 1975, 981–984; ibid., SB 22, statement by Matis Lutinsch, 4 January 1976, 3,958–3,959. Janowski says the militia wore khaki uniforms with green armbands. It was clear to him that these were members of the Thunder Cross movement, which very well ought to have applied to the biographies of older perpetrators active during the Ulmanis era.
36. Later, these streets bore the names Gorkii and Kirov.
37. The younger Schmuljan had succeeded in 1940 in transferring a part of the assets to South America and bringing himself to safety. The elder Schmuljan had remained and was not affected by the deportations to Siberia in June 1941. According to David Packin, he arranged – with the assistance of a German officer – for his son to have his foreign assets placed at his disposal. The father was murdered. The son lived later in New York. See Kaufmann, *Churbn Lettland*, 42–43; Staw. Hamburg, 141 Js 534/60, SB 6, statement by David Packin, 21 April 1969, 1,150.
38. Staw. Hamburg, 141 Js 534/60, Bd. 42, statement by Alfred Steckel, 12 December 1963, 7,060–7,065; ibid., SB 16, statement by Alfred Steckel, 14 November 1975, 3,064–3,067. Nakaten was subordinated to Arnold Kirste, who led Ek 2's Dept. IV and V in personal union.
39. Staw. Hamburg, 141 Js 534/60, SB 4, statement by Herman Noim, 25 April 1974, 819–821.
40. Staw. Hamburg, 141 Js 534/60, SB 20, statement by Alexej Proschkowitsch, 16 December 1975, 3,677–3,678.
41. Staw. Hamburg, 141 Js 534/60, SB 37, statement by Ella Medalje, 15 January 1979, 6,310–6,311; ibid., statement by Janis Vabulis, 16 January 1979, 6,354; ibid., SB 41, statement by Zleda-Riwka Hait, 22 April 1979, 7,001–7,002; quote from Medalje.
42. Kaufmann, *Churbn Lettland*, 52–53; Press, *Judenmord*, 35. According to Gechtman, officers from a "Württemberg-Badischen-Grenadier-Regiment" tortured, raped, and murdered several dozen Jewish girls at Marijas St. 10; a Captain Bach was named as the man chiefly responsible. Where this information comes from is not documented, Gechtman, "Riga," 684–685.
43. On the murders that took place on the bridge over the Daugava, see Staw. Hamburg, 141 Js 534/60, Bd. 33, statement by Samuel Gutkin, 21 March 1963, 5,445.
44. Urteil des Berikgericht Postdam gegen Stanislavs Steins, 1 October 1979, in *DDR-Justiz und NS-Verbrechen*, Bd. I, 422.
45. Staw. Hamburg, 141 Js 534/60, SB 4, statement by Moisej Rage, 15 April 1974, 829–831; ibid., SB 5, statement by Dr. Jeannot Levenson, 21 May 1968, 1,124–1,125.
46. Staw. Hamburg, 141 Js 534/60, SB 3, statement by Piotr Kaukis, 23 May 1974, 653–658; BA Ludwigsburg, 207 AR 188/76, Bd. 1, statement by Julius Bracs, 14 November 1975, 31–47; quotation from Bracs.
47. BA Ludwigsburg, 207 AR 188/76, Bd. 1, statement by Laimonis Birnbaums, 25 September 1975, 3–6; statement Julius Bracs, 14 November 1975, 31–47, quotes from Bracs. Although compromised, Bracs could not be convicted of a specific crime. He claimed that he had never been a member of the Thunder Cross, but only a sympathizer, although his uncle, Professor Jakob Vitols, had held a leading position in the organization. The witness Laimonis Birnbaums was employed in the registrar's office of the prefecture and worked on lists enumerating the Jews, Latvians, and Russians who were already in prison. Every now and then, Bracs asked for information regarding the names of prisoners registered in the books. He was under the unsubstantiated suspicion of having put together lists for

shooting. A person with this same name is mentioned in connection with investigations into Jews who had gone underground, see ibid., statement Zelda Hait, 6 April 1976, 61–64. According to various statements by Janis Zirnis, a publicity-hungry poseur who had himself been a member of the auxiliary police, Bracs led a unit for identifying the internal enemy and regularly took part in shooting operations. Due to Zirnis's seemingly paranoid delusions of persecution, he was not believed in this matter (which from the prosecution's point of view was completely understandable), although his allegations at least in the first part overlapped with Bracs's own information, see Staw. Hamburg, 141 Js 534/60, SB 1, letter from Janis Zirnis to the Prosecutor's Office Hamburg, 1 March 1967, 217–224; ibid., SB 2, statement by Janis Zirnis, 2 October 1966, 236–252.
48. Staw. Hamburg, 141 Js 534/60, SB 4, statement by Herman Noim, 25 April 1974, 822,; statement by Wiktor Goldberg, 25 April 1974, 853–854; Press, *Judenmord*, 58. According to Press, there were forty-four persons, although several of them were arrested only later, when they made the mistake of inquiring at Einsatzgruppe offices about the whereabouts of relatives. Instead of receiving information, they were interned. See Press, *Judenmord*, 52–53.
49. Staw. Hamburg, 141 Js 534/60, SB 21, statement by Janson, 25 November 1975, 3,830. On the destruction of the synagogues, see Ezergailis, *Holocaust in Latvia*, 219–231, and Katrin Reichelt, "Kollaboration und Holocaust in Lettland 1941–1945," in *Täter im Vernichtungskrieg*, ed. Wolf Kaiser, 117.
50. Staw. Hamburg, 141 Js 534/60, SB 1, statement by Raphael Shub, 14 September 1965, 161; if one follows the course of events, this was probably around 4 July.
51. Ibid., SB 21, statement by Janson, 25 November 1975, 3,830–3,831; ibid., SB 27, statement by Gennadij Murnijeks, 5 May 1976, 4,682; ibid., SB 33, statement by Matis Lutrinsch, 13 June 1978, 5,682; statement by Leonid Janson, 21 June 1978, 5,810–5,811; quote from Janson's 1978 statement. Also, Press, *Judenmord*, 36 and Kaufmann, *Churbn Lettland*, 55–56. The accomplice Janson denied – probably a defensive maneuver – that anybody was murdered. According to Lutrinsch, who was forced to work in the Arajs Commando's motor pool, a commando member by the name of Runzis had procured the gasoline.
52. BA Berlin, R 58/215, Ereignismeldung Nr. 40, 1 August 1941.
53. Also known as Säulen-Str. in German, this street bore the name Friedrich Engels St. during the Socialist era.
54. Staw. Hamburg, 141 Js 534/60, SB 3, statement by Janis Brencis, 12 March 1974, 640; ibid., SB 21, statement by Brenzis, 26 November 1975, 3,784–3,785; quote from 1974 statement; Kaufmann, *Churbn Lettland*, 55–60; and idem, "The War Years in Latvia Revisited," in Association of Latvian and Estonian Jews in Israel, *The Jews in Latvia*, 353.
55. Staw. Hamburg, 141 Js 534/60, Anklageschrift gegen Viktor Arajs, 10 May 1976, 85–86.
56. Ibid., 83–84.
57. Later, the perpetrators also used the familiar "blue buses" of Swedish construction, which came from the depot of the Riga Transportation Association.
58. In statements made by participants, there was no clarity about which SS officers were actually present. Suspects in particular protested against the memory of their former colleagues. In different statements, Stahlecker, Tschierschky, Lange, Batz, Eichler, Besekow, Maywald, Wessel, and others were mentioned as present.
59. The depiction of these murders is based on the following statements, although the statements refer to killing operations in July 1941, not specific individual shootings: Staw. Hamburg, 141 Js 534/60, SB 3, statement by Edgar Jurgitis, 19 March 1974, 611–613; statement by Janis Wanders, 1 April 1975, 616–619; statement by Leonid Janson, 20

February 1974, 625–634; statement by Janis Berzinsch, 2 April 1975, 668–672; ibid., SB 4, statement by Viktor Arajs, 5 August 1975, 700–705; statement by Arno Besekow, 19 February 1965, 772–782; statement by Indrikis Punkulis, 8 May 1974, 808–818; ibid., SB 21, statement by Janis Brenzis, 24 November 1975, 3,767–3,776; statement by Edgars Jurgitis, 19 November 1975, 3,863–3,865; statement by Janis Bersinsch, 3 December 1975, 3,899–3,902; ibid., SB 28, statement by Jan-Alfred Frank-Prank, 5 April 1976, 4,738–4,743; ibid., SB 33, statement by Indrikis Punkulis, 17 June 1978, 5,748–5,750; ibid., Anklageschrift gegen Viktor Arajs, 10 May 1976, 92–93. According to Bersinsch, the factory Krasnyi Kvadrat was supposed to have been in "Jumprawmujzh" (Jumpravmuiža = Jungfernhof), but he denied ever visiting the site after participating in executions. See also, ibid., Bd. 7, statement by Hugo Saarmann, 27 April 1959, 296–297; statement by Eckhard Haack, 24 March 1963, 418–421; ibid., Bd. 29, statement by Eckhard Haack, 1 November 1962, 4,614–4,615; statement by Bernhard Borkowski, 13 December 1962, 4,621–4,627; ibid., Bd. 30, statement by Theodor Clausen, 27 March 1963, 4,846–4,850; statement by Theodor Clausen, 10 April 1964, 7,900–7,907; ibid., Bd. 44, Gegenüberstellung Clausen, Tschierschky, and Maywald, 13 February 1964, 7,246–7,258; ibid., Anklageschrift gegen Karl Tschierschky, u.a., 1 November 1973, 17–19 and 48–50; LG Hamburg, 147 Ks 3/74, Urteil gegen Heinz Trühe und Arno Besekow, 6 February 1976, 10–13. Besekow was transferred to Krasnogvardeisk at the end of July 1941; he himself admitted being in Bikernieki three times. An additional – more plausible – reason why members of Ek 2 or EG A were present at the shootings was that a Wehrmacht captain had investigated what was actually happening in Bikernieki and had inspected the killing site in order to gain information about the murders committed there. The risk of having to explain oneself had increased, since photos of shootings commissioned by members of the Order Police or the Waffen-SS began circulating in Riga. Members of EG A therefore had to be at the scene in order to confirm the "legitimacy" of the shootings vis-à-vis other agencies. According to Besekow, members of the Waffen-SS attached to EG A fired the "mercy shots." Whether this is true, or whether it is a defensive maneuver, remains to be clarified. Quotes in the text are from Clausen vis-à-vis Tschierschky and Maywald during joint questioning, 7,250, and from Besekow, 782. See also, Urteil des Beriksgericht Postdam gegen Stanislavs Steins, 1 October 1979, in *DDR-Justiz und NS-Verbrechen*, Bd. I, 424–425.

60. Nuremberg Document L-180. On the anti-Semitic mood of Latvians after the Soviet occupation, see Zenta Mauina, *Die eisernen Riegel zerbrechen*, 206–208; Staw. Hamburg, 141 Js 534/60, Bd. 6, statement by Eckhard Haack, 18 July 1959, 64–67; ibid., Bd. 8, statement by Otto Eckert, 22 September 1959, 623–625; statement by Karl Müller, 23 July 1959, 640–641; statement by Willi Göhler, 22 July 1959, 662; statement by Hans Entreß, 9 November 1959, 677; ibid., Bd. 22, statement by Theodor Clausen, 30 January 1962, 3,386–3,387; ibid., Bd. 30, statement by Theodor Clausen, 10 April 1963, 4,900–4,901; ibid., Bd. 34, statement by Arthur Rosenow, 21 May 1963, 5,539–5,540. According to Clausen's statement, he established contact with his colleague Captain Ganz from the southern sector of the front and urged that Res. Pol. Batl. 9 be replaced, something that overlaps with statements from battalion officers in other investigations and ought not be void of a certain degree of credibility. For more, see ibid., Bd. 7, statement by Eckhard Haack, 24 March 1959, 422. According to Haack, he had secretly read a letter by his superior Clausen in which another company commander – in addition to Ganz, a Captain Krumme is mentioned – complained to Clausen that the SD had gained control of the battalion. See also Staw. Munich I, 22 Js 201/61, Bd. 6, statement by Arthur Seidel, 12 December 1963, 1,322; Alfred Streim, "Das Sonderkommando 4a der Einsatzgruppe C und die mit diesem Kommando eingesetzten Verbände," 56.

61. Staw. Hamburg, 141 Js 534/60, Bd. 29, statement by Borkowski, 13 December 1962, 4,642–4,627.
62. Rossiiskii Gosudartsvennyi Voennyi Arkhiv (RGVA), 500-4-92, EG A, Tätigkeitsbericht v. 16.10.1941 bis 31.1.1942; Staw. Hamburg, 141 Js 534/60, Anklageschrift gegen Viktor Arajs, 10 May 1976, 85–86; Reichelt, "Kollaboration und Holocaust," 112–113.
63. BA Berlin, R 58/214, Ereignismeldung Nr. 24, 16 July 1941, Batz is meant by "Barth." The numbers given for victims vary even in EG A's reporting. In Stahlecker's Gesamtbericht bis zum 15.10.1941, the number of pogrom victims for Riga is given as 500 persons, see Nuremberg Document L-180.
64. Staw. Hamburg, 141 Js 534/60, Anklageschirft gegen Viktor Arajs, 10 May 1976, 96; Nuremberg Document L-180, Anhang 8, Übersicht die Zahl der bisher durchgeführten Exekutionen.
65. Ezergailis, *Holocaust in Latvia*, 118; Staw. Hamburg, 141 Js 534/60, SB 17, statement by Erma Wischniewskaja, 6 February 1976, 3,207. According to this statement, the ban on Jews standing in line at grocery stores was also broadcast over the radio. Wilhelm Ullersperger seems to have had a strong anti-Semitic streak. In British captivity, he reportedly told a fellow officer: "What do I care about Good Friday? Because an old, filthy Jew was hanged umpteen years ago?" See *Abgehört: Deutsche Generäle in britischer Kriegsgefangenschaft 1942–1945*, ed. Sönke Neitzel, 304.
66. Staw. Hamburg, 141 Js 534/60, Bd. 72, statement by David Ravdin, 29 August 1967, 11,514.
67. Margers Vestermanis, "Retter im Lande der Handlanger," in *Solidarität und Hilfe für Juden während der NS-Zeit*, ed. Wolfgang Benz and Juliane Wetzel, Bd. 2, 253–255. This includes quotes from *Tevija* and Latvian radio. Vestermanis stresses quite correctly that this order was equivalent to a general ban on purchasing groceries. This order of the Field Administration Command in Riga played a pioneering role for all of Latvia. Several people who helped Jews were forced to share the fate of the Jews. Even several Latvian auxiliary policemen interceded on behalf of Jewish women and issued them papers identifying them as "Aryans." See Staw. Hamburg, 141 Js 534/60, Bd. 60, statement by David Packin, 4 October 1965, 9,700; ibid., SB 17, statement by Erna Wischniewskaja, 6 February 1976, 3,207.
68. Leeb, *Tagebuchaufzeichnungen*, 288. The conditional tense was originally present tense in the note; the correction is entered by hand.
69. Kaufmann, *Churbn Lettland*, 54–55. See also Staw. Hamburg, 141 Js 534/60, Bd. 38, statement by Mosche Deiftz, 19 September 1963, 6,292.
70. *Riga: Ein Führer für deutsche Soldaten*, 3. Reprint of 1941 edition.
71. Margers Vestermanis, "Der lettische Anteil an der 'Endlösung'," in *Die Schatten der Vergangenheit*, ed. Uwe Backes, Eckhard Jesse, and Rainer Zittelmann, 427; BA Berlin, R 58/214, 3 July 1941. Here it is clearly noted that at least for Šiauliai the deployment of Jewish laborers was essential.
72. BA Berlin, R 92/1158, 150–151, Wi-Kdo. [für] das Gebiet des ehem. Lettland, Abtl. Arbeit, Betr. Arbeitseinsatz der Juden, 21 July 1941, Ellrodt was first mentioned as Ellroth. The author of this document was Dorr, who later took over the Riga Labor Office under civil administration and remained in the city. Ellrodt also switched from the military to the civil administration to run the Labor Department. The document's distribution list includes: Economics Inspection North – Labor Department, the [Economics] Commando, SS-SD, and the Field Administration Command. Also see Wilhelm, *Die Einsatzgruppe A der Sicherheitspolizei und des SD 1941/42*, 174–175. On the Ek 2's later position on the issue, LVVA, P 1026-1-3, 262–264, Ek 2, Lagebericht, "Judentum," unpaginated fragment of report.

73. Even if Hitler himself was to prohibit the return of Latvia's ethnic Germans in October 1941, there were indeed efforts on the part of Baltic Germans deployed in Ostland to accord to Riga a special status and to have the ban on returning to Latvia lifted – in a way analogous to the concessions made to Lithuania's ethnic Germans, see Myllyniemi, *Die Neuordnung der baltischen Länder,* 157–169; Hugo Wittrock, *Kommissarischer Oberbürgermeister von Riga 1941–1944,* 78–79; Peter Kleist, *Zwischen Hitler und Stalin,* 161–162; Gerald Reitlinger, *Ein Haus auf Sand gebaut,* 174–175; Otto Bräutigam, *Überblick über die besetzten Ostgebiete während des 2. Weltkrieges,* 79–80. It may have been that the assignment of so many agencies and supply posts to the city was one of the reasons why Himmler in May 1942 considered transferring the SS supply command from Riga to Jelgava, *Dienstkalendar,* entry for 27 May 1942. There was also a construction inspector's office from Department B (Troop Economics) of the SS Economics and Administration Main Office and a "Outpost North of the Plenipotentiary of the Reichsführer-SS for the Establishment of SS and Police Bases in the New Eastern Area," see Jan Erik Schulte, *Zwangsarbeit und Vernichtung: Das Wirschaftsimperium der SS,* 203–204, 271, 274, and 285. Likewise, the armaments manufacturer Deutsche Ausrüstungswerke, or DAW, in autumn 1941 had planned to establish factories in the greater Riga area, see Hermann Kaienburg, *Die Wirtschaft der SS,* 585. On Riga's role as a base for a Waffen-SS clothing production facility, see ibid., 936. The first complaints from the SS concerning the lack of capacity for residential and economic purposes are verified for October 1941, see BA Berlin, R 91/173, Wi.-In. Ost der Waffen-SS an den Geb.-Komm. Riga, Betr.: Zuweisung von beschlagnahmten Gebäude [sic] und Wohnungen.
74. See the June 1942 "Denkschrift Generalplan Ost. Rechtliche, wirtschaftliche und räumliche Grundlagen des Ostaufbaus," in *Vom Generalplan Ost zum Generalsiedlungsplan,* ed. Czesław Madajczyk, 91–130, 124-125. The table on pages 124-125 shows that 38,500 people were to be settled in Riga over the following five years; the surrounding countryside was to remain free initially. The number of settlers was then gradually expanded so that twenty-five years later 105,900 people would move to Riga and the surrounding countryside; the demographic developments of Riga itself and police and SS basing policy were not incorporated into these numbers. In the General Settlement Plan of December 1942, Riga was planned as a major city for the overall Baltic region, a status that only Tallinn (Reval) and Vilnius (Wilna, Wilno) enjoyed. All of the other twenty-one bases in the Baltic – with a need for a total of 811,000 settlers – were listed only as mid-sized and small-towns, see ibid., 235–255, especially 237 and 244.
75. LVVA, P 80-2-9, 9–10, Vorauskommando des WBO in Riga an den Wehrmachtsbefehlshaber Ostland, Abtl. IIa, 9 August 1941; ibid., 16–17, Vorauskommando des WBO in Riga, Aufstellung über die vom Wehrmachtsbefehlshaber Ostland beschlagnahmten Juden-Wohnungen, 11 August 1941.
76. Staw. Hamburg, 141 Js 534/60, Bd. 33, statement by Samuel Gutkin, 21 March 1963, 5,445.
77. LVVA, P 80-2-9, 18, Vorauskommando des WBO in Riga an den Führer des Vorauskommandos Major Guenter, 21 August 1941.
78. LVVA, P 80-2-13, 115, Meldung, Uffz. Hubert Brinkmann, Betr. Wohnung Vidus iela 4, 25 August 1941.
79. LVVA, P 69-1a-18, RKO, Abt. II, an den Gen.-Komm. In Reval, Riga, Minsk, Kauen, Betrifft; Ostlandeigene Haeuser (Beamtenwohnhaeuser), 20 November 1941. First and foremost, property was to be selected that was "in the possession of Jews before nationalization."
80. See Nuremberg Document NOKW-2204, Berück Nord, VII, Betr. Einrichtung von Ghettos, 3 September 1941. An "OKH order of 19 August 1941" – which remains missing to this day – is mentioned as the "basis" for this measure. From this text – as well as from

the remaining files of Berück South and the orders of local administration commandants issued within the same time frame – it is apparent that the OKH gave the order to create ghettos "in larger localities with a large Jewish population," inasmuch as "time and personnel" were sufficient. The agencies of the HSSPF were "to be called upon" in the process; however, the formation of ghettos was not seen as an urgent task.

81. BA-MA, RH 26-291/34, 75–79, 291. Infanterie-Division, Inf.-Rgt. 504, Anordnung für die Befriedung Kurland Nr. 1, 12 July 1941.
82. LVVA, P 1026-1-3, 141, Berück Nord, Abt. Ic/AO, 24 July 1941. This order remarkably annulled an EG A directive making it compulsory for Jews to wear a Star of David on the left-hand breast of the outer garment, which sheds an interesting light on the powers of the police and the Army in the "treatment" of Jews. See also ibid., EG A an die EK 1a, 1b, 2 und 3 [sowie den] Stab, 1 August 1941; Vestermanis, "Retter im Lande der Handlanger," 259; Alfred Winter, *The Ghetto of Riga and Continuance*, 6–7.
83. Vestermanis, "Der lettische Anteil an der 'Endlösung'," 427–428.
84. BA-MA, RH 26-281/25 A, Sich. Div. 281, Abt. VII, Betr.: Richtlinien für die Verwaltung, 27 July 1941.
85. Excerpt from the administrative instructions of the 281st Security Division concerning Jews from 30 July 1941 and an order of the Rear Area Army Group North concerning the establishment of ghettos, both in *Einsatz im "Reichskommissariat Ostland,"* ed. Wolfgang Benz, Konrad Kwiet, and Jürgen Matthäus, 122–123.
86. Urteil des Beriksgericht Postdam gegen Stanislavs Steins, 1 October 1979, in *DDR-Justiz und NS-Verbrechen*, Bd. I, 422–423; Staw. Hamburg, 141 Js 534/60, Bd. 60, statement by David Packin, 4 October 1965, 9,700. According to this statement, the anti-Jewish measures were issued from the Latvian side by a certain "General Weiss," which is bound to mean Voldemārs Veiss.

– Chapter 4 –

SECURING GERMAN RULE IN OCCUPIED RIGA

The Period of the Large Ghetto for Latvian Jews

The surviving records of the office of the Wehrmacht Territorial Commander Ostland show that, originally, the relocation of Riga's Jews into a ghetto created in the Moscow Suburb was to have been completed by 14 August 1941, with Jewish tenants of apartments confiscated by the Wehrmacht being granted a period of transition. The latter were "to protect our quarters … in Jewish apartments from plundering and ulterior use." To this end, the Jews in such apartments were allowed – in coordination with SS First Lieutenant Erhard Grauel of Einsatzkommando 2 (Ek 2) – to remain outside the Riga ghetto beyond the stated deadline, a gesture that, in the eyes of those in charge, was apparently a fair arrangement. The Moscow Suburb was one of the most run-down districts in Riga and, since the start of the century, had been a part of town inhabited by socially disadvantaged local Latvians and Jews as well as Jewish immigrants from Eastern Europe. Accordingly, German officials probably saw it as only consistent to establish a ghetto in a district lacking in sanitary infrastructure.[1]

While Jews were being turned out of the city's choice apartments, in late July the Labor Department within Economics Commando Riga began implementing the strategy discussed with the SD and the Field Administration Command of ghettoizing the city's Jews for the purpose of putting them to work as forced laborers. As agreed, the Field Administration Command announced on 23 July that all Jews, "the baptized as well," had to report for registration on 25 and 26 July at designated gathering places. The Jews were ordered to bring a passport or some other form of photo identification in order to confirm their identity. Children under sixteen and those who were ill or frail did not have to appear in person, but would "be registered by the head of household."[2]

The setting up of a Jewish Council, as called for by Economics Commando Riga, took place within the same time frame. As far as is known, the council included the lawyers Michail Eljaschew[3] and Grisha Minsker

---

Notes for this chapter begin on page 119.

as well as the elder Blumenau brother, who is described in the literature as an accountant or engineer. These men, all former members of the Latvian Jewish Freedom Federation, had not been subjected to the same extent of persecution as other Jewish intellectuals due to their anti-Communism.[4] Blumenau, for example, had fought for Latvian independence and received a high award, something that still earned him respect. Starting at the end of July 1941, he acted as one of the Jewish liaisons "to the Latvian and German authorities." Additional members of the Jewish Council included former city public health official Dr. Rudolf Blumenfeld, the lawyer M. Mintz, Jr., and the former director of the textile factory Zasulaiks, Ezra Kaufer. In the hope of establishing better contact with the occupational authorities, chairmanship of the council was to be given to former Austrian State Counselor Dr. Schlitter. It is unclear whether Schlitter held this position de facto or de jure (Eljaschew is usually described as the decision-maker) or whether Schlitter, who was nominated only later, took over from Eljaschew.[5]

According to Bernhard Press, this seven-member council was called to the local Gestapo headquarters, where it received its first basic instructions. The Gestapo disclosed to the council members that the creation of a ghetto was crucial, if for no other reason than to protect the Jewish population from Latvian riots. The Jews of Riga were to be resettled to the ghetto immediately, with all those able to work registered and subordinated to a special labor office. Whatever work was requested of them had to be done without objection. The council, which had to carry out these orders immediately, would be held responsible for the implementation of these instructions.[6]

In the course of registering the Jewish workforce at individual police stations, the Jewish Council's labor deployment department had to create a system of personnel records in the form of cards. All workers aged 14–65 were registered and divided by sex, with particular attention being given to urgently needed craftsmen and skilled workers. For men, the cards were made of green cardboard; for women, they were blue. The registration form was identical. Tellingly, the columns for "place of residence" and "apartment" were to be filled out only in pencil – after all, the Jews were heading to the ghetto. The same applied to "occupational limitations" and "present employment." Everything had to be recorded and checked by the local police station. These personnel cards were to be kept at the Labor Office separate from the records for other civilians. Next, every Jewish worker was to be allocated a "place of deployment," which the employer had to confirm on a three-part form that was to function as "identification." Jewish skilled workers who were already employed did not have to be turned over to other places of work, unless there existed "special instructions from the Labor Office, the Wehrmacht authorities, or the police." The Jewish Council's registration sites had to implement these instructions by

10 August and inform the council how many male and female workers aged 14–65 were "at all available," and how many were "already at work" and would no longer have to be placed. Senior Wartime Administration Counselor Max Dorr of Economics Commando Riga ordered that violations be punished accordingly.[7]

The abandonment of direct measures of annihilation at the end of July 1941 in favor of a policy of ghettoization and exploitation was linked to the transfer from military to civil rule. Accordingly, Dorr and his colleagues took steps in advance to prevent their orders on the treatment of the Jewish population from assuming a provisional quality. If anything, the installation of fixed structures was supposed to guarantee the continuation of anti-Jewish policy after the forces of Army Group North had moved on. It was also in the tradition of German occupation policy from the First World War to have the Jewish population – primarily craftsmen and skilled workers – work for German ends.[8]

On 17 July, Hitler issued a decree officially instating Alfred Rosenberg as minister for the occupied eastern territories and announcing the creation of the territorial-level Reich commissariats and the regional-level general commissariats.[9] Rosenberg had specific ideas as to who should take over the administration of his former homeland: Hinrich Lohse, a lieutenant general in the Storm Troops (*Sturmabteilung,* SA) and the Nazi party boss in Schleswig-Holstein, was appointed to run Reich Commissariat Ostland (*Reichskommissariat Ostland,* RKO) with its seat of government in Riga, while Lübeck Mayor Dr. Otto Heinrich Drechsler, who was also to reside in Riga, was chosen to run the regional-level General Commissariat Latvia. At the local level, Hugo Wittrock was to hold the office of commissarial mayor of Riga (in addition to serving as county commissar for Riga City).[10]

In Riga itself, various self-confident representatives of the Latvian elite – unaware of the plans to establish the RKO – attempted to reestablish Latvia as a state. A group around Colonel Ernests Kreišmanis, the publisher of *Tevija,* represented primarily the political interests of the old Latvian army, while another group took shape around former minister Bernards Einbergs. Einsatzgruppe A (EG A) had agreed with the German Army not to hold official talks with these two groups for the time being, but desired clarification as to which "direction [Latvia's] political development" was to be pushed solely for reasons concerning the "urgent regulation of economic questions."[11] The Army itself in turn made use of Colonel Aleksandrs Plensners and Lieutenant Colonel Viktors Deglavs, who had entered Riga with troops from the Abwehr (German military intelligence). Gustavs Celmiņš, the leader of the Thunder Cross movement, also managed to return to Riga with the Wehrmacht as a special officer (*Sonderführer*) in the hope of becoming politically active again, while the former general Oskars Dankers was tolerated at the Reich Ministry for the Occupied Eastern Territories.[12]

On 11 July, the representatives of several Latvian organizations met at the Ministry of Education. The chairman of this gathering, Alfrēds Valdmanis, was an associate of former Latvian dictator Kārlis Ulmanis and acted as an advisor to various German military agencies, primarily Rear Area Army Group North and the Economics Inspection East. Also taking part were Lieutenant Colonel Voldemārs Veiss and Archbishop Teodors Grünbergs as well as Kreišmanis, Einbergs, and Deglavs (who represented the ailing Plensners). At the conference, Valdmanis, Deglavs, and Celmiņš were empowered "to act in the name of the Latvian people and to represent, as fully entitled, Latvian interests in Berlin." A telegram to Hitler was promptly drafted, congratulating the German dictator on his triumph over the Red Army, but at the same time calling on him to integrate the Latvian nation into the new European order. The telegram amounted to a barely concealed call for independence.[13]

The German side had no other choice but to prevent such an endeavor, which General Franz von Roques, the commander of Rear Area Army Group North, immediately did. Shortly thereafter, on 18 July, Deglavs shot himself; Celmiņš was forced to leave Riga for Berlin after repeated complaints by EG A at Rear Area Army Group North headquarters.[14] Plensners was incapacitated by illness. The plan to reestablish Latvian independence, even the attempt to establish self-administration, quickly failed. Nonetheless, the German occupation authorities were dependent on cooperation with the nationalist Latvian elite, because the Nazi party functionaries and German civil servants delegated to Riga – primarily from northern Germany – accounted only for the top leadership of the RKO administration. The greater part of the accruing work had to be taken care of by local manpower.[15]

General von Roques's political advisor, Professor Wilhelm Klumberg, sought to use Valdmanis in the decision-making process as a Latvian affairs expert and representative of the Latvian population, while EG A strove to curtail the influence of this "clique" of Ulmanis associates and therefore agitated against Klumberg. Given the limited duration of military administration and the difficulties in overcoming the opposition of EG A, Roques finally named Dankers to the post of general director of internal administration and personnel on 21 August. To assist him, Dankers was assigned Dr. Visvaldis Sanders (education), Artūrs Freimanis (economics), Voldemārs Veiss (police), and, as representative of the Thunder Cross, Evalds Andersons (traffic). With that, the struggle over personnel and the running of the Latvian authorities was decided.[16]

At the lowest administrative level in Riga, an indigenous city administration – with powers analogous to those of the general director within the General Commissariat Latvia – was also established under German supervision with architect Pavils Dreijmanis at the helm.[17] This was the apparatus, from the RKO via General Commissariat Latvia to the local authorities. Working in cooperation with the local offices of the SS and police, this administrative apparatus would determine Riga's fortunes – and with them the fate of the city's Jews.

That no improvement of the situation could be expected from the civil administration was made clear shortly after Hinrich Lohse assumed office.[18] On 25 July, Lohse was officially installed as Reich Commissar Ostland at a ceremony in Kaunas (Kauen, Kovno). However, only the territory west of the Daugava River had been released by the military. This limited Lohse's authority for the time being to Lithuania and the Latvian lands around Liepāja (Libau) and Jelgava (Mitau). It had not been possible to accommodate personnel from the RKO in Riga, because the city was overfilled with diverse military facilities. Two days after his installation, Lohse, although master of a limited realm, gave a policy speech to his staff and the general and county commissars already in the RKO on how things were to proceed with regard to the Jews and announced his "preliminary guidelines" for their "treatment."[19] These were contained in an expanded and detailed list of restrictions and burdens to be imposed on the Jews.

First these guidelines defined who was considered a Jew. It was then stated that these guidelines were to apply solely to Jews from the Soviet Union, Poland, the Protectorate Bohemia and Moravia, and the German Reich as well as stateless Jews.[20] According to Lohse's will, these persons were to be registered and required to wear a six-pointed, yellow star on the left breast of their outer garment as a means of identification. Jews were forbidden to change their place of residence without permission, to use sidewalks, public transport, private automobiles, and public facilities (parks, pools, theaters, etc.), to attend school, or to own radios. Professional bans were issued within the framework of "cleansing" the flat land of Jews and driving them out of commerce. In cities such as Riga, "which already have a predominantly Jewish population," the Jews had to be concentrated in a ghetto. The Jews were forbidden to leave the ghetto; food and consumer goods were allowed into the ghetto only to the extent that "the remaining population could spare [them]." The ghetto had to set up a self-administration, with the ghetto inhabitants themselves having to "regulate" internal conditions under the city commissar's supervision. To uphold internal order, a Jewish Order Service armed with canes or truncheons and identifiable by special armbands was to be established. Jews who were able to work had to be available as needed for forced labor; such work was to be done in cohesive labor commandos whenever and wherever possible. Jews were no longer allowed to work in several legal professions or in insurance and banking; the activity of Jewish doctors and druggists was limited to the ghetto. Ultimately, all Jewish assets were to be confiscated with the exception of furniture and the minimal amount of money needed "for meager sustenance" (5 rubles per day per person). Payment of wages for Jewish forced labor was to be made to the city commissar, who, when need be, would arrange the "apportionment" of a part of the sum deposited.[21]

On 2 August, Lohse informed Higher SS and Police Leader Hans-Adolf Prützmann of these guidelines so as to guarantee "a uniform implementation also of preliminary measures against the Jews in the territory of the Reich Commissariat."[22] Naturally, Prützmann was unhappy with the apparent exclusion of his person and office as well as the simultaneous disregard of EG A. Lohse's instructions did not even mention the SS and police. In order to reassert his power to issue guidelines concerning the "Jewish question," Prützmann on 5 August entrusted SS Major Karl Tschierschky at Einsatzgruppe headquarters with a statement on "security police tasks" in the "treatment of the Jews." At the same time, Prützmann thought it necessary for EG A commander Walther Stahlecker, who was farther east in Novosel'e, to lodge a formal complaint with Lohse in order to clarify the issue. Prützmann even placed an airplane at Stahlecker's disposal to facilitate his prompt return.[23] But Stahlecker, who was hoping Leningrad would soon fall, would not be rushed into a trip to Riga. In his opinion, Lohse could not issue even preliminary measures "without our involvement," because the role of the office of the Territorial Commander of the Security Police (BdS) within the RKO administration had not yet been discussed at a higher level. For this reason, Stahlecker, who had already informed Heydrich of the situation, would wait until basic instructions arrived from Berlin. Until then, Ek 3 commander Karl Jäger, based in Kaunas, was to discuss Lohse's decree with the civil administration, but to delay its dissemination until final clarification of questions of jurisdiction.[24]

Tschierschky subsequently looked into whether EG A and Ek 2 had any objections to Lohse's instructions – aside from the evolving dispute over jurisdiction and the chain of command within the RKO – and whether these measures for "the regulation of the Jewish question" were in principle conform with those of the Security Police and SD. Ek 2 answered promptly on 6 August, emphasizing that in Riga the compulsory outward identification and registration of the Jewish population had long been a reality. There were no objections to the establishment of a ghetto – to the contrary; preparations were underway in Riga, with "a Jewish council of elders" already formed "for this purpose." Ek 2 made some critical remarks concerning the role of Jewish doctors. It was doubted that these could "be excluded from the treatment of non-Jewish patients," for medical care for the population could not be guaranteed otherwise. In any event, Jewish doctors were to be removed from public hospitals. Otherwise, Ek 2 pointed out that "the securing and confiscation of subversive, that is to say, also Jewish assets" from individuals was the task of the Gestapo, not the RKO civil authorities. Only when "a total measure" affecting the entire Jewish population was involved would there be no objections. In closing, the rapporteur reminded Tschierschky that all of the intended measures would have to be taken in closest consultation with his office.[25]

While Ek 2 put forward this description of the status quo and adhered to its own procedure, the command staff of EG A in Novosel'e – also on 6 August – suggested a more radical approach. In the General Government – the administrative designation for that part of occupied Poland not incorporated into Germany – experience had shown that it was necessary to maintain Jewish manpower. In the Baltic, by contrast, such "necessities" – save for "the question of skilled workers in some towns" – had yet to appear and would "hardly emerge later either." This was the key difference in analysis between EG A and the Economics Inspection North. In a fully incorrect assessment of the labor situation in Latvia, EG A – unlike the Economics Inspection North – assumed that non-Jewish workers could run all of the economic enterprises important to the war effort; therefore, "all aspects of labor deployment" were to be neglected "in addressing the Jewish problem in Ostland." Ghettoization was also felt to be a half-hearted measure on the part of the civil administration. EG A wanted to remove the Jewish population from the cities completely and, instead, create "districts as Jew reservation areas" as needed "in the wide expanses of Ostland." There Jewish men and women would be separated from one another and deployed "immediately in beneficial work" such as road construction, forestry, or agriculture. In this course of action, the Jewish population would gradually die off, which would "immediately and most emphatically" protect the racially high-grade part of the population "from intermingling with Jewish blood," especially in the Baltic countries.

In this proposal, EG A presented itself as the organization tackling this "problem" professionally and definitively. After all, it simultaneously criticized conditions in Berlin, where "even in 1941 Jews were still able ... to disguise themselves as Aryans" and subvert German society. In conclusion, EG A noted that the implementation of its recommendations would quickly achieve the following results: "1/ an almost 100% immediate cleansing of all of Ostland of Jews, 2/ the prevention of the Jews' reproduction, 3/ the possibility of the most intensive exploitation of Jewish labor, 4/ a considerable facilitation of the later wholesale evacuation to a Jew reservation outside Europe." This strategy was of course to be carried out only with a massive "deployment of forces from the Security [Police] and Order Police," which in turn meant that the power of the civil administration in carrying out this drastic measure would be very limited.[26]

With this recommendation, Stahlecker prevented Lohse from issuing his own guidelines for the time being. What mattered most to Stahlecker was his position as BdS within the RKO apparatus, and whether he, as a representative of *Reichsführer-SS* Heinrich Himmler, would be authorized to issue directives in matters of substance vis-à-vis the Reich commissar; after all, Himmler on 17 July had been given policing authority to secure the newly occupied eastern territories. Therefore, although he had not originally objected to the civil administration's guidelines, Stahlecker, given his staff's radical recommendations, was now using the debate over the treatment of the Jews to clarify the question of BdS authority in line with his wishes, whether it meant being promoted to political advisor to the Reich commissar or becoming able to act fully independent of him.[27] The argument was to drag on much longer than he imagined and was never clearly resolved at a higher level.[28] At the end of August 1941 – probably after the intervention of Prützmann, who had managed to gain assurances that instructions from the civil administration would not affect Security Police measures – Stahlecker accepted the Reich commissar's guidelines despite a "number of serious objections." Aware of the dynamic of the annihilation process that he himself had perhaps set in motion by having his staff make the aforementioned recommendations, Stahlecker now stressed to his commandos that anti-Jewish planning by RKO agencies would be carried out "only in closest cooperation with the Security Police," whereas EG A itself was pursuing a "definitive solution of the Jewish question by completely different means than those envisaged by the Reich commissar."[29]

In the last days of July, occupied Riga played host to many visitors seeking to be present on behalf of their agencies so as to be prepared for the city's transfer from military administration to the RKO. Even Himmler appeared in town for two days at the end of July to discuss with Lohse the regional-level SS and police leaders, the "Germanization" of the local population, police bases, and the struggle against political opponents, inter alia.[30] General Commissar Otto Drechsler had taken up quarters in Riga in advance, where he met with Otto Bräutigam of the Reich Ministry for the Occupied Eastern Territories, who was also inspecting the new realm of his boss Alfred Rosenberg. In his spare time, Bräutigam walked through the conquered city. He observed the worried faces of the Latvians, who paced earnestly through the streets, apparently no longer overjoyed by the defeat of Bolshevism, and noted the long lines in front of the grocery stores. During one walk in the city center on 11 August, he caught sight of "the Jews, all of whom wore a large yellow star on the breast."³¹ The ghettoization called for by Economics Commando Riga had yet to take full effect. The Jewish population was still able to roam around the city relatively freely. According to inspectors from the Economics and Armaments Office of the High Command of the Wehrmacht, the Jews had apparently been put to work "only" for "clearance and street work, etc."³²

Just how far along was the implementation of the plan to create a ghetto in the Moscow Suburb? On 18 August, the Field Administration Command issued a decree on the "Labor Obligation for Jews," which could be read in the newspaper *Deutsche Zeitung im Ostland,* the German counterpart to *Tevija.* By this decree, all able-bodied Jewish men and women were required "to do public and private-sector work," which would be managed by a "Bureau for the Deployment of Jews." Now anybody would be able to file "requests" for Jewish forced laborers. The Jewish Council took up headquarters in a large school building at Lāčplēša St. 141.³³ The Labor Office's Bureau for the Deployment of Jews worked several houses away across the street at Lāčplēša 145.³⁴ In these two buildings, the Germans installed a kind of "second city administration," as Bernhard Press put it, which had to organize the communal life of the ghetto's Jews, whether they were long established in Riga or newly arrived. In addition to the actual council members – who wore a white-blue armband and unlike the other Jews were entitled to take the streetcar and use the sidewalk – the leadership circle included the lawyer J. Jewelson, who headed the ghetto's Finance Office. A. Kehlman was entrusted with running the Social Office, which was also responsible for nursing homes and overnight shelters. The poorest were provided with clothing by the Riga branch of the welfare organization Malbish Arumim under Mrs. Eljaschew,³⁵ while Mrs. Blumenfeld was given the difficult task of distributing and organizing apartments. In light of the ever-growing numbers of people resettled to the Moscow Suburb, disputes in the ghetto were bound to increase. In order to cope with this internal problem, an arbitration committee was set up under a lawyer by the name of O. Finkelstein. Medical care in the ghetto was the responsibility of Dr. Rudolf Blumenfeld, who converted the Jewish women's hospital Linas Hazedek into a general hospital with departments for internal medicine, surgery, gynecology, and neurology. A pediatrics ward also existed, but was housed separately in one of the larger residential buildings. Radiologist D. I. Hasse served as hospital director. The individual stations were overseen by some of the same doctors who had been locked up in the Central Prison at the end of July.³⁶ In addition, there were two polyclinics, one led by Dr. Jakobson, the other by Dr. Oskar Press. The doctors also turned another school into a nursing home for the bedridden and invalids unable to walk.³⁷ Rabbi Mendel Zack, who had continued to preach in private after the destruction of Riga's synagogues and oversaw religious practice, acted as the community's religious leader, while Simeon Wittenberg set up a school for children.[38] Carried on the deceitful wings of hope, the Jewish Council succeeded in creating a functioning ghetto infrastructure in the Moscow Suburb within just a few weeks. For Jews, life in the heart of the city was still dangerous. Jews were subject to ambush and assault for no reason.[39] Some of the ghetto inhabitants were therefore confident that despite all of the restrictions, the ghetto represented a certain degree of protection from arbitrariness and persecution, and that once the relocation process had been completed, one could work on improving living conditions within the ghetto.

The Moscow Suburb was not some secluded place. The containment and evacuation of Riga's Jews took place for all to see. And those on Riga's streets who did not want to accept the obvious could even read about how the expansion of the ghetto was prospering in the 23 August issue of *Tevija*, the organ of Latvian collaboration. In a longer article, the ghetto terrain was described as a "large district" in the Latgale Suburb; it ran from Lāčplēša St. to the local barracks and was bordered by Jēkabpils, Katoļu, Lazdonas, Lielā, Kalnu, Lauvas, Žīdu, and Jersikas streets. In determining the borders of the ghetto, those responsible took care that the "Orthodox church with the Old Believers' Cemetery" lay outside the area, while the Jewish school on Lāčplēša St. and the Jewish cemetery near Žīdu St. became part of the ghetto. *Tevija* reported that from early morning until dusk, wagoners – meaning the evacuees – were on their way to the ghetto carrying "Jewish things." Every day, new "regiments of Jews" were arriving, giving the residential area "an increasingly Jewish character."[40] The same article contained agitation and propaganda aimed at this Jewish community of adversity: completely impoverished and barefoot women, wrote *Tevija*, stood next to "elegant Jewesses who were still wearing clothes that had been made in Parisian salons of fashion." But this, according to *Tevija*, gave Riga a character typical of foreign ghettos – which must have meant primarily the Warsaw ghetto – on the one hand wealth, on the other bitter poverty, with no solidarity to be expected from among the Jews themselves. Initiatives such as Mrs. Eljaschew's prove the opposite. It is true, however, that many people took ill – physically and psychologically – in their distress. Some committed suicide. For others, the terror, the deprivation, and the humiliation provoked anger, grief, and fear, which in some cases was bound to lead to outbreaks of aggression. In particular, Mrs. Blumenfeld, the head of the Apartment Office, had to grapple daily with hundreds of distraught and irritated people camped with their last goods and chattels in the former schoolyard in front of the Jewish Council building. Women made up the majority of them; while waiting, they talked with one another about their husbands, so many of whom had been arrested or murdered.[41]

During August, Riga's residential districts were systematically cleared of Jews. First Jews from the central districts were evacuated, then those from the outer districts.[42] The expulsion process was organized by the Resettlement Office, which was subordinated to Riga city elder Dreijmanis and headquartered at Moscow Road 68, where ten employees had been working on nothing else since 12 August. They had been instructed that the Jewish district was to offer space for just under 30,000 people, with a maximum of 4 sq. meters of living space per person. The clearing of Jewish apartments took place by street and residential blocs; at the same time, starting 1 August, Latvian, Russian, and Lithuanian families left the Moscow Suburb for other districts in Riga in order to make room for the Jews. According to a census conducted by the city administration, before the start of the relocation operation, 12,000 people lived in the ghetto district, "of which 1,700 were Jews." According to this census, "approximately 27,000 Jews" were to be settled into the ghetto area and "approximately 10,000 Christians" out of it. For substitute housing, the Christians from this part of the Moscow Suburb received an apartment that was as suitable as possible from the Resettlement Office's inventory. Resettlement alone presented a problem that was hard for the expelled Jews to overcome. In the short period between notification and relocation, they were allowed to hire only Jewish wagoners, who were of course completely overbooked. Jews had to organize transportation on their own or have the right connections. Many of those who thought they had found a place to stay were quickly disappointed, for the final borders of the ghetto had yet to be determined. Conversely, at the request of the Resettlement Office, the Jewish Council had to pay the moving costs of Christians when necessary. On the other hand, if an evacuated apartment was subsequently occupied by a Wehrmacht officer, Jewish women from the ghetto had to decorate the rooms accordingly for the new occupants. Sometimes, it happened that Latvians who lived in the Moscow Suburb swapped apartments with their Jewish friends – as was the case with the Deiftz family. Other Jews did not want to bear the strain and lost all hope. The decision of one Jewish couple, which preferred a quick death by poison to evacuation to the ghetto, stands for this group. The Latvian city administration noted that, as of 3 September, only 2,461 Jews had been resettled into the ghetto, while 2,669 Christians had left the Moscow Suburb. As of 9 September, the number of those entering the ghetto had increased to 3,142 persons, while that of the departing Christians had climbed to 3,159 persons.[43] At this rate, resettlement would have lasted another six months. This was clearly too slow for the authorities. Therefore, the Resettlement Office instructed the Jewish Council to accelerate the occupancy of space and at the same time to place more people in the already converted apartments.[44]

At the end of this first phase of what was called the "large ghetto," the final area of the ghetto was settled, with the Resettlement Office making several corrections. By order of the German administration, the Svetlanov brothers' knitwear factory, which was located on the corner of Kaṭoļu St., had to be fenced off from the ghetto. This kind of intervention for economic reasons was exceptional, however. Some thought was given to compensating the "Aryan" owners of residential buildings inside the ghetto with objects of equal value. In addition to the aforementioned factory, the Resettlement Office separated the nearby Catholic church and the adjacent cemetery from the ghetto. After clarity about the ghetto's borders had been established – sometime toward the end of August – a barbed wire fence was run along Lāčplēša St.[45] The ghetto entrance was located on the corner where Lāčplēša, Jēkabpils, and Sadovnikova streets converged. Local Latvian policemen, who had their main office at Jēkabpils St. 2, stood guard along the perimeter of the ghetto and checked those coming and going.[46]

Officially, there were sixteen grocery stores and confectionery shops inside the ghetto. Lines formed in front them in the morning and never "[grew] shorter all day long." There was no free trade in place here, but a system of provisioning a constantly growing population. Through these stores, each person received 175 g (6 oz.) of meat, 100 g (3.5 oz.) of butter, and 200 g (7 oz.) of sugar per week. Jewish Council member Blumenau organized the distribution of these items, which were diverted from the city and brought to the ghetto by Jewish wagoners. The quality of the food was often poor. Immediately after these shops were established, the Field Administration Command banned Jews from shopping in markets or "other stores no matter what kind," effective 18 August. Shop owners were forbidden under threat of punishment to deliver goods to Jews, thus making the black market the only remaining option for obtaining additional food.[47] Besides finding provisions for the ghetto, waste disposal represented the other major challenge for the ghetto's decision-makers. No longer a part of the city, the ghetto was supposed to dispose of its human waste and trash on its own. This had to take place if only to prevent the outbreak of epidemics. For the garbage, the Jewish Council had large pits dug and covered once they were filled; for human waste, the council organized the collection and dumping of human waste in other pits. As a cautionary measure, doctors had a quarantine station set up in order to be prepared for signs of an epidemic.[48] In order to limit contact between the ghetto and the city, and primarily in order to prevent any uncontrolled communication with the outside world, on 25 August, Friedrich Trampedach, the head of the RKO's Department IIa (Political Affairs), ordered all telephone connections from the ghetto capped and postal service suspended. "Infringements" on the part of Jews were to be punished by the harshest "reprisals, according to the instructions of the county commissar."[49]

As already mentioned, Lohse's guidelines also envisaged the establishment of a Jewish Order Service (*Ordnungsdienst*, OD) for each ghetto in the Reich Commissariat. This did not exist in Riga at the start of the resettlement operation, but was formed only toward the end of August. A prerequisite for being accepted into the OD was that the applicant had "served in the Latvian Army in his day and taken part in battles against the Communists on the Latgalian front." Whether the majority of later OD members could really prove this is unknown. Headquartered at Daugavpils St. 8, the OD had to see "to order and cleanliness in the Riga Ghetto." The jeweler Michael Rosenberg was entrusted with running the OD; his deputy was a former noncommissioned officer of the Latvian army and engineer known as Vozbutskii. Isidor Berel was appointed OD liaison to the German guards. These were among the ghetto's first eighty stewards. According to Max Wachtel, the OD later numbered 120 members.[50]

Max Kaufmann claimed in his memoirs that the Jews of Riga wore the yellow patch with pride despite facing the death penalty if they refused.[51] This may have been the case for some people. However, most complied more out of fear, because punishment for violating this order was not just something written on a piece of paper. Some tenaciously refused to give up their customary way of life and remain in the ghetto. Joseph Behrmann's mother Sonja was arrested, because in the night of 13–14 August she visited relatives on the west side of Riga who had not yet relocated to the ghetto – an act of defiance that was only made possible by also discarding the Star of David. On the way back to the Moscow Suburb, Mrs. Behrmann was recognized by a Latvian woman and denounced. Her case was turned over to the Jewish Council, and Blumenau had to report this "offense" to the police station on Daugavpils St. There could be no talk of release. Blumenau was issued a part of her belongings, which he had delivered to her son. After the facts of the case had been clarified, Blumenau was sent away. Mrs. Behrmann was transferred to the headquarters of the Latvian auxiliary security police for further interrogation – where her trail ends. It is rumored that she was murdered there on 17 August 1941.[52]

For the German side, the ghetto's self-organization efforts and individual violations of orders were of secondary importance. The registration of workers had priority. *Tevija* reported on 23 August that the Jewish Council was registering 200–300 persons for work daily; they were categorized by profession and set up in working groups. Already at this point in the registration phase, the Jewish Council was requested to send 200 persons to cut peat in the swamps of Babīte (Babbit) and Tirele. The background to this episode was that the production of peat – which was militarily important, because almost all of Latvia's industry depended on the fuel distilled from it – was on the brink of collapse. Only 30 percent of the workforce had returned to work after the Germans arrived. POWs could replace the missing workers only to a limited extent.[53]

On 1 September, Riga was turned over to the civil administration of the RKO, which now exercised control over all of occupied Latvia. For the Jews in the Moscow Suburb, little changed. General Commissar Drechsler's first orders reinforced the exclusionary policies and anti-Jewish decrees already in place.[54] However, the takeover by the civil administration brought to the city new police units, which were subordinated to either the territorial or the regional commander of the Order Police. Once in Riga, these units were assigned to secure the ever-expanding ghetto in addition to carrying out their customary police duties.[55] It also fell to them to oversee the ghetto's Latvian guards, who were considered unreliable. That September, Precinct-Lieutenant Friedrich Jahnke of the office of the Regional Commander of the Order Police was entrusted with the supervision of Riga's twelve Latvian police precincts as well as the smooth completion of the ghettoization process, which meant primarily intervening to prevent arbitrary acts of brutality and plundering on the part of the Latvian auxiliaries. The keys to locked apartments had to be turned over to Jahnke, who collected them and then passed them on to the county commissar's office. The ghetto's German guards were led by Lieutenant Albert Hesfehr. In addition to Hesfehr, another German policeman victims remembered particularly vividly was Otto Tuchel.[56] Although just a police corporal, Tuchel was given an incredible amount of power, which he wielded autocratically and mercilessly. The true master of the ghetto, however, was SS First Lieutenant Kurt Krause of Ek 2, who ran the unit's Jewish affairs desk and for that reason alone was already responsible ex officio for the Moscow Suburb. With the closing of the Moscow Suburb, he would preside over the ghetto as commandant where the police were concerned; the formal establishment of an office of the commandant would follow only in January 1942.[57]

While Rear Area Army Group North in mid September stressed in retrospect that the "cohesive settlement of Jews in ghettos" had been "set in motion by offices of the High. SS a. Police Leader" during the period of military administration,[58] German labor administrators had noted by contrast that the deployment of Jews and other segments of the civilian population for labor was moving too slowly. But was not the need to make up for a lack of workers – especially in agriculture – the original motive for establishing the Riga ghetto back at the end of July?

At a meeting of the economics commandos for Kaunas, Riga, Tallinn (Reval), and Görlitz one month later, the Riga-based commando boasted that its labor policy regarding the deployment of Jews as forced laborers and the desired transfer of enterprises (e.g. tailor and cobbler workshops) to the ghetto could be considered exemplary for all of Ostland. Beforehand, the Latvian Industry Department had noted just how many Jews were still working in individual enterprises. To pressure company managers, these were instructed to justify why their Jewish workers had not yet been replaced, and when it would be possible to expect their substitution with Latvians. In the process, the German officers from Riga made a crucial analytical error. The need for workers in Riga was in fact so great – the very opposite of what was desirable – that the "Jews at Wehrmacht offices did not [face] dismissal"; to the contrary, they could not be wished away from economic life for the time being. According to Economics Commando Riga, by the end of August, 25,000 Jews over age sixteen had been registered; these "were for the most part employed in clearance work and Wehrmacht offices peeling potatoes and cleaning," an assertion that hardly reflected reality.[59] Economics Commando Riga strove to substitute Latvians for these Jews, to the extent that the latter "worked at German offices or units," so as to reduce "the danger of sabotage and espionage." Given the numbers that Economics Commando Riga itself had presented, this measure could not take effect. But this may in turn explain why Jewish workers were not deployed efficiently: in those places where they were needed – e.g. in industry – security concerns prevailed; in those places where they could be used in accordance with their qualifications – e.g. as craftsmen – the required cohesive deployment in labor details could not be guaranteed. Conversely, Jews were allowed to work in the countryside only in exceptional cases – almost exclusively in the peat industry. Otherwise, the principle was maintained that their use as forced laborers was to be restricted to the city limits as much as possible.[60] In short, Economics Commando Riga become entangled in the large number of decrees it had issued during the first phase of the ghetto, with the result that Jewish workers were neither put to work on a large scale in cohesive details, nor removed from the enterprises run by the Wehrmacht, SS, police, and civil administration.[61]

A few days later, Senior Wartime Administration Counselor Dorr, who had transferred from the military to the civil administration as commissioner for labor administration, expressed the hard reality in writing. Riga now had a ghetto, he wrote, but the actual problem – the "systematic management of workers" according to the "needs of the war and the maintenance of the population" – had not been solved. Therefore, on 1 September, POWs were approved for agricultural work, as was the establishment of POW camps "under 50 persons." Nobody knew what else to do in terms of organizing workers. In addition, all unemployed persons, all males employed in construction and the wood- and metalworking industries, and all German-speaking salespersons had to be registered to ensure that their deployment was better managed – the primary aim being to force Jewish workers from commerce and industry and transfer them in cohesive labor details to road construction projects, peat works, etc.[62]

Ek 2 took note of this development, but, with regard to the ghetto, limited its activities in late summer and autumn 1941 to "purely police-related duties." It left the "demarcation and administration of the ghetto districts as well as the remuneration and provisioning of the inhabitants" to the civil authorities, although it had noticed that the crafts, in particular those of glaziers, plumbers, and stove fitters, lay "for the most part in Jewish hands."[63] The aforementioned police-related duties included the murder of some of the most vulnerable members of Latvian society. Between 30 August and 5 September, Ek 2 killed 459 persons, 237 of whom were mentally ill Jews from the "insane asylums" of Riga and Jelgava. Meanwhile, 195 Jews remained incarcerated in Riga's Central Prison.[64] During the murder of the mentally ill, Viktor Arajs's Latvian auxiliary security police was once again deployed; this time, Arajs's men only provided the guards. According to the statement of one perpetrator, the psychiatric sanatorium was located on the estate Atgāzene, near the Daugava. Patients were brought in small groups to the scene of this crime, which was located in a forest near the Jelgava Road (Mitavskaia doroga). Each victim was taken by the hand by two "escorts" and led to a pit. At that point, a member of the Security Police or the SD stepped up and shot the person in the back of the neck. In the process, a nurse was also shot by mistake; the perpetrator thought she was one of the patients.[65]

Even if Ek 2 itself had preferred such a radical solution for the entire Jewish community of Riga, one could not help but notice that in September 1941 it was above all the SS, after the Wehrmacht, that needed workers, Jews as well. To Lohse's outrage, HSSPF Russia North Prützmann alone had confiscated twelve economic enterprises at the start of August. These were administered under the trusteeship of SS Major Alwin Reemtsma, the SS economist attached to Prützmann's command staff.[66] According to SS Senior Colonel Eduard Bachl, larger contingents of Jewish forced laborers and other prisoners worked at Army Group North's clothing storeroom and cable maintenance works, AEG Riga, Ostland-Faser, the factory Meteor, the workshops of the Security Police, the SS, and the police, the Reich Railway depot, Army Group North's motor pool in Riga, and other workshops, although it is unclear whether all of these facilities were using Jews in production in autumn 1941.[67] At any rate, it is to be gathered from General Commissar Drechsler's report of 20 October 1941 that the Jewish workers were of enormous importance to the Wehrmacht, although the Labor Office had taken "preparatory measures" to substitute Latvians for

"Jews working on an individual basis" for the military. Preferably, Jews were to be employed by the Wehrmacht in such places where Latvian workers were not available "or [they] were not to be deployed" at all. However, the rigid labor market undermined the desired transfer of Jewish workers from Wehrmacht jurisdiction, although the forest administration and the supervisory agency for heating material had already filed requests for larger contingents of male Jews without success.[68]

Postwar questioning shows that in autumn 1941 Jewish forced laborers were used in Riga to assemble and to send transports of Wehrmacht uniforms. Others sorted and cleaned captured Russian uniforms in the Navy Equipment Office. According to former office manager Hermann Schmidt, 4,500 people worked at the maintenance shops and army clothing office of Army Group North. Of these, some 1,300 were Jews who the ghetto had placed at the disposal of these units. The distribution of medical supplies for the front ran through a collective medical station, where Latvian Jews also worked. Kurt Lünenschloss, who ran the local Volkswagen maintenance shop in Riga, also found Jewish forced laborers on hand there when he arrived; others worked for the Air Force, the Navy, or the Army, where they unloaded freight cars. By this point even EG A was using ghetto inhabitants for its needs. By his own account, SS First Lieutenant Gerhard Maywald set up a workshop equipped with fabrics and machines from a former menswear business. The Jewish former manager of this business, a certain Leibsohn, now had to produce his wares for the Gestapo. Maywald also had Franz Nakaten, the warden at the Central Prison, transfer Jewish tailors and craftsmen to this shop. In all of these facilities, as in "all German offices," Jews initially took care of the assignment given them "as gratis workers."[69]

If Economics Commando Riga's stated demand of deploying Jewish workers on a large scale and in a targeted manner was an illusion, the Labor Office, as of 6 September, had placed 2,638 registered Jews – 1,311 men and 1,327 women – with the Wehrmacht, the SS, and other agencies. The disorganization and the lack of management were so extreme that it came to incidents between the SS, Army, and the Navy, which made claims on each other's forced labor details. Other offices, acting on their own initiative, obtained needed workers in the Jewish Council's courtyard, "without asking the Labor Office at all." Some Jews were simply intercepted on the street, while some Jewish workers tried "in private to get a job where they would receive recompense and provisions." The Labor Office noted that in this kind of situation, the systematic placement and managed deployment of Jewish forced laborers could not be guaranteed. It therefore requested – "at a time when a large deficit of workers prevails" – that these conditions be countered with the greatest severity.[70] Dorr reacted several days later, lodging a complaint with Field Administration Command Riga that lamented the intolerable conditions and admonished the representatives of individual agencies who had "mutually insulted and threatened" one another while trying to get Jewish workers. It had also occurred to him, he noted, that there existed between members of the Wehrmacht and some Jews a tone that was too intimate. As an immediate step, Dorr recommended pushing for the ghetto to be cordoned off, because it would only be possible to manage the use of Jewish workers through the eye of the needle formed by the ghetto gate. He left off by requesting the Field Administration Command to report when the establishment of the ghetto could be expected – which, the way things stood, could have only meant the closing of the ghetto area and the completion of resettlement.[71] After a conversation with the Field Administration Command, it was considered whether to strengthen the authority of "employees entrusted with the carrying out the Jewish deployment" vis-à-vis the Wehrmacht. Such employees would be supplied with identification and armbands so that they could better assert themselves vis-à-vis those in uniform when "unjustifiable demands for Jews" were made. That this merely aggravated the problem of managing Jewish workers can be seen in the statistics: At the end of September 1941, "5,368 male and 8,357 female Jews" were working at military offices, that is to say, five times as many people as at the start of the month. The SS and SD were also informed of this increase in the recruitment of Jewish forced labor.[72]

In a sober analysis by EG A, the "process of confining the Jews to the ghetto district" was described as "rather difficult," primarily because of the task of creating living space for the Latvians to be settled outside the ghetto. This criticism aside, EG A did not intervene in the creation of the ghetto.[73] For the Latvian city administration as well, the phase of the open ghetto had lasted much too long, which was why it was the one – and not the Gestapo or SD – to insist on wrapping up the resettlement operation. At least, Dreijmanis recommended officially announcing the ghetto's borders and "setting a date by which the resettlement work is to be ended." The process of isolating Jews by means of a ghetto seemed to him a suitable instrument for enhancing control over the deployment of Jewish workers, but only when calm had returned to the city. This would definitely make it possible to eliminate once and for all the black market activity of Latvian vendors and those courageous Latvians who were still standing up for their friends. These were the only outside groups that dared enter the ghetto. The impetus for setting a deadline for sealing the ghetto thus came from the office of the Latvian mayor, although Department IIa of General Commissariat Latvia had in summer 1941 already drafted a proposal stating that the ghettoization process in Latvia's larger cities had to be completed by 10 October.[74]

By mid October 1941, there were only "80 Aryan families" still living in the ghetto. Once they had been transferred, the Moscow Suburb, now completely surrounded by barbed wire, was deemed purely Jewish.[75] With that, the process of hermetically sealing in the people living there could be completed in one last step. The date set was 25 October. In the *Deutsche Zeitung im Ostland* the day before, 24 October, the county commissar for Riga City published amended orders on the treatment of the Jews, which for the most part, however, laid out "regulations" for "non-Jews." Under threat of the "harshest punishment," non-Jews were banned from entering the ghetto, communicating through the ghetto fence, or conversing with Jews deployed outside the Moscow Suburb. This affected primarily Latvians with Jewish relatives, whom they could no longer contact. Requests for Jewish workers continued to go through Riga's Labor Office, which intended to modify the procedure of remunerating Jewish forced laborers to the detriment of employers once the ghetto was closed.[76] Effective 1 November, Jewish workers were no longer to be had at a bargain price, but would have to be paid standard wages, which were to be deposited with Riga's Finance Office. The message could not have been clearer: Either employers made an effort to find fitting replacements for Jewish "power," which would entail the desired elimination of Jews from the work force, or the city would earn a profit from the exploitation of such workers. For this reason – on orders from Werner Altemeyer, the chief of staff in the governing mayor's office – the old working papers were annulled. New yellow cardboard credentials were issued exclusively for individual workers and specialists, but the necessity of their deployment had to be verified in advance. These new papers demonstrate that the Labor Office was reasserting its monopoly on Jewish workers vis-à-vis the arbitrary acts of other agencies, which were now being forced to submit "well-grounded applications for the continued employment of Jews."[77]

According to the 8 October issue of *Tevija*, around 30,000 people were living in the ghetto before it was sealed,[78] a figure that more or less corresponds to the number of people registered by the Labor Office. According to the latter's records, the ghetto community broke down as follows:

a) Children up to age 14
    Boys   2,794
    Girls   2,858
    Total   5,652
b) Those able to work, age 14 to 65
    Men   6,143
    Women   9,507
    Total   15,650

c) Those unable to work
   Men   2,069
   Women   6,231
   Total   8,300

                         Total   **29,602**

Those are the official numbers reported to Reich Commissar Lohse.[79] Whether they were correct to such a degree of accuracy is open to doubt. In any event, it is said that the Jewish Council decided not to turn over to the Labor Office all of its data on the people living in the ghetto, which in turn made provisioning more difficult. According to the concept put forth by Department IIa of the General Commissariat Latvia, however, "the means of subsistence" for "Jews who were not working" were to be defrayed by deducting money from the working Jews' earnings. This was to force the Jewish Council "to provide as many Jews as possible for work." In other words, persons without ration cards had to be taken care of by the community. More and more Jews, "sometimes 10–12 persons in a room," lived packed together in the already tightly allocated living space. Hunger was widespread. Alone the important workers, the specialists – on whom the entire ghetto's existence depended – found themselves in a somewhat better position, because they were deployed outside the ghetto.[80]

Figure 4.1. At the ghetto fence. Undated. Courtesy of Staatsarchiv Hamburg.

In the general commissar's reports, the number of such specialists accounted for less than 10 percent of the ghetto community, which despite the strained situation on the Latvian labor market did not bode well for Riga's Jews if the ghetto was supposed to provide for itself. Thus the civil administration refused to expand Riga into a central ghetto for all of Latvia's surviving Jews – although such recommendations did exist.[81] Furthermore, on 11 October, Stahlecker had already notified Drechsler of Hitler's decision to make Riga a deportation center for German Jews – which was bound to exacerbate the situation.[82]

In the aforementioned report from the General Commissariat Latvia's Department IIa to Reich, the number of skilled craftsmen was 2,660 persons. By profession, the registration records showed 110 cobblers, 300 male and 1,300 female tailors, 120 cap makers and milliners, 200 seamsters, 50 furriers, 15 engravers, 40 makers of bags, gloves, and suitcases, 50 watchmakers, 75 plumbers, 50 glaziers, 40 upholsterers and saddlers, 15 cardboard workers, 15 bookbinders, 10 dental technicians, 25 tanners, 40 weavers, 70 carpenters, and 135 knitters. To leave the ghetto, the specialists had to show their yellow card, which also served as a form of identification, at the ghetto gate. Their employers had to fill out personnel papers for individual workers for the Bureau for the Deployment of Jews at the Labor Office. Based on these reports, the Finance Office verified correct payment of the weekly wages, which were then deposited to its accounts. A part of this was then placed at the disposal of the ghetto's self-administration. Cohesive labor details had to present a sealed pass, in which the number of workers in a group leaving the ghetto was noted. A carbon copy remained with the guards, who noted in the guard book the strength of the detail and, upon the detail's return, checked the number of persons against the guard book. Riga's Finance Office in turn made use of the guard book to calculate the payment of wages and submitted an invoice to employers for the services rendered by the group of Jews listed there.

The columns were set up as follows:

Reception:				Return			
Date Time	Collecting Formation	*Office*	Number of Jews	*Receipt*	Date Time		Place of Return
Receipt.	Note						

In the ghetto itself, each forced labor detail had a designated gathering place in order to prevent congestion at the ghetto gate and to accelerate administrative processing. The ghetto was open for these details from 7 A.M. to 6 P.M. In a clear analogy to the ghetto in Łódź (Litzmannstadt), the labor administration raised the prospect of setting up shops for cobblers and tailors, who would then work exclusively for the needs of the Wehrmacht. This would then confine the last individual workers to the ghetto as well. This idea was expressly welcomed by the military.

For the ghetto's Latvian guards, the Schutzpolizei, the German municipal police, assigned to the Moscow Suburb a detachment from Latvian Police Battalion 20, including an officer in the person of Alberts Danskops as commander, a deputy commander, a bookkeeper, and sixty men. These guards had to man twenty-eight permanent posts and reinforce patrols. To supervise them, there were always two Germans from the Schutzpolizei on duty. Guard duty assignments and the supervision of the guard posts were the responsibility of Jahnke, who was also responsible for police-related matters in the ghetto after the inner-city resettlement operation had been completed. In order to maintain a permanent presence, the Schutzpolizei set up a station in the middle of the ghetto at Ludzas St. 66. According to regulations, the guards were required "to nip in the bud" any disturbances that occurred and "to make ruthless use of their arms" in doing so. In the event that somebody climbed the fence, they were to be shot. Officially, however, there was a ban on mishandling Jews. Sealing the ghetto seemed so important that guards were not to let the Riga Fire Department into the ghetto unless a fire threatened to spread to other parts of the city. The Jewish Council had to cope with smaller fires on its own.[83] A week later, however, officials had to back off from this order, because it was not possible to establish a Jewish fire department in the ghetto.[84]

With the sealing of the ghetto, those Jews who refused to move to the ghetto could continue living in Riga only if they assumed another identity, were not well known in town, and received support from a third party. Elvira Rone hid eight people in her house, among them violinist Mark Kremer, father of the world-famous violinist Gideon Kremer. The popular athlete and businessman Arturs Monmillers first looked after Leiba Katz, goalie for the soccer team Hakoah, and then five other persons whom he had helped to elude the Gestapo's grasp. In Mežaparks (Kaiserwald), Colonel Edgars Ozols assisted Regina Frankel in evading her pursuers. A "Latvian patriot" by the name of Janis Lipke "hated the Germans and the Latvian collaborators," which was why he sided with the people in the ghetto. By profession, Lipke was "a simple dock worker." He built a bunker in his house and, shortly before the ghetto's liquidation, hid eight people there, among them the Lipchin brothers and their brother-in-law. He also looked for additional places to hide other Jews who had chosen to flee the ghetto and live in Riga illegally. According to Abram Lipchin, his indefatigable guardian saved forty-two people altogether. When life in Riga became too dangerous for his wards, Lipke found new hideouts for them in the countryside. Building custodian Alma Polis proved that those in her profession could not only denounce Jews, but were also in a position to provide them with shelter even under the most adverse conditions. Polis helped hide six Jews, but was ultimately exposed and shot. Other rescuers were arrested and sent to concentration camps, where they shared the fate of the people with whom they had tried to show solidarity. Few of those who were found to be hiding Jews survived prison.[85]

The rescue of Leo (Leib) Blech is a particularly unusual case, as it was "authorized" by the perpetrators. Blech, who was born in Aachen in 1871, had taken over directorship of the State Opera in Berlin in 1926, but in 1937 – like so many other German Jews – he had accepted the offer of asylum extended by Mordechai Dubin of the Latvian parliament and immigrated to Riga, where he was made director of the opera. The fate of such a prominent man – who had enjoyed success as a celebrated artist during the establishment of the German dictatorship and thus utterly failed to fit the stereotype of the "Bolshevik Jew" – was bound to concern world public opinion. This applied even to *Reichsmarschall* Hermann Göring and his wife Emma. Former members of the Schutzpolizei said after the war that at Göring's behest a special permit was issued for Blech.[86] Major Karl Heise, the commander of the Schutzpolizei in Riga since September 1941, summoned the "Jewish professor," who had been known to him for years "as a personage in the field of music" in Berlin. After being forced to wait for a while – Heise did not have time for him – the old man was ordered into the office. On orders from HSSPF Ostland Prützmann, Heise handed Blech a passport and exit papers for neutral Sweden. Blech left Riga and worked the next few years in Stockholm as court conductor. After the war, he returned to Germany as the general music director of the Municipal Opera Berlin (later German Opera Berlin). Blech died at an advanced age in West Berlin in 1958.[87]

Even if the occupation had divided Latvian society into one group that collaborated or sought advantage under the new regime and another that was persecuted for religious, racial, or ideological reasons and was therefore absolutely opposed to Nazi rule, there are nonetheless cases showing that the complexity of human nature cannot be reduced to tidy categories. The rescue of Alexander Ginsburg by a former fellow student who became a lieutenant at a police station under the Germans and let his friend go home may still appear ordinary in a city where it seemed that everybody knew everybody.[88] Another rescue effort, however, ran completely counter to what would be expected: the student Zelda Riwka Hait was not a native of Riga, but had studied at the local university until the German occupation. She and her family moved into the ghetto, but she suspected that this was not to be the last operation directed against the city's Jewish population. On 28 November 1941, she fled to the "Aryan" side, seeking refuge at Stalu St. 6/24, the home of Janis Aleksanders Vabulis, a former lieutenant in the Latvian Army whom she had met at a dance in February 1941. Vabulis, by then an influential man in the city administration, had rented a furnished room in the apartment of a certain Mrs. Joffe, a Jewish woman who had been forced to move into the ghetto; the agreement with her tenant, however, remained in force. Vabulis himself had come to know the ghetto before it was completely fenced in, having smuggled in groceries and placed orders with ghetto craftsmen. After Vabulis's landlord had been forced to move into the ghetto, two members of the Arajs Commando, Edgars Kraujins and Laimonis Lidums, occupied the other rooms in the apartment. Both learned from Vabulis, whom they revered as a former officer of the Latvian Army, that he had hidden Hait, but they did not betray the couple. Because Vabulis did not trust the building custodian, and because notorious Latvians such as Herbert Cukurs frequented the building, all four moved into the apartment of the widow Kaufmann at Miera St. 29/1.[89]

Also living there was Jeva Sietina, a former house servant with Hait's family, who was said to have contact with other Arajs men and "many Latvian murderers." On the other hand, Sietina also helped many Jews and

Figure 4.2. On Ludzas St. inside the ghetto. The commandant's office is on the right. Undated. Courtesy of Staatsarchiv Hamburg.

provided groceries for people in the ghetto. The contradiction between her behavior and the personal company she kept may not have occurred to this simple woman, who was described as good-natured and gullible. For all of those in hiding, however, she represented a constant threat. During a search of the apartment by the Gestapo in spring 1942 – apparently led by a German Balt and Julius Bracs – the danger of being discovered was enormous. Vabulis believed that the end had come. However, the search was directed solely at Kaufmann and her daughter. Both were transferred to the Central Prison, and the apartment was sealed. All of the others had to move back to Stalu St. The Arajs man Lidums looked into the fate of Mrs. Kaufmann and her daughter and learned that they had both been shot. Apparently, mother and daughter had not been questioned beforehand, or they had not betrayed those sharing the apartment. Using hard currency and jewelry found in the basement of the Kaufmann family's building – probably their reserve for an emergency – Vabulis and Hait managed to flee to Sweden in 1944.[90]

Olga Brüning, who was born in Tartu (Dorpat) and followed her family to Riga as a young woman, was forced to learn that the Gestapo also took care of "unsolved cases" with a certain perseverance. When her family was registered and forced to move into the ghetto, she decided not to comply with this "request." She claimed to be an Estonian and was hired as a servant in the Wehrmacht Quarters Office. This made her so secure that she felt confident enough to smuggle consumer goods into the Moscow Suburb right up until the end of October 1941. The Jewish Affairs Desk picked up her trail in mid January 1942, when the search for Jews in hiding was intensified. Brüning was lucky, though. She was not shot, but was transferred to the ghetto. She survived the war.[91]

Several weeks after the ghetto was sealed, the general board of directors of the Latvian justice administration was ordered to secure all of the available birth, marriage, and death records of the Jewish community in Latvia and send them to the Republic Archive in Riga for evaluation and storage. That the office of the Regional Commander of the Security Police was also interested in using the lists of Jewish citizens contained in these records in order to track down Jews in hiding ought to have been self-evident.[92] According to David Packin, twenty-five Riga Jews managed to remain outside the ghetto over the course of the entire occupation and survive inside the city using fictitious biographies or living in hiding.[93]

Those who had hoped to escape the terror by relocating to the ghetto soon realized that they had been deceiving themselves. Under the cover of decrees, the guards established an ever present and ominous mixture of psychological and physical violence that by no means stopped short of murder. With regard to Tuchel alone, it is documented that on 25 October, the day the ghetto was closed, he shot a girl in her mid teens who had talked to a Latvian woman on the street and dared to remove the obligatory Star of David from her clothes. After a brief interrogation, Tuchel shot the girl behind the guard house; Jewish workers then had to bury the corpse on the spot. Two days later, Latvian guards turned over to Tuchel a Czech Jew who had failed to move by the deadline; in his lack of understanding of what was expected of him, the Czech had come to the police station "in order to receive instructions." This man was also shot behind the guard house and subsequently buried in the Jewish cemetery.[94] Others died, because they had violated an order of some kind, primarily the ban on bringing foodstuffs into the ghetto illegally. As a deterrence measure, Kalman Aron's uncle was hanged for all to see, because he had smuggled eggs into the ghetto from his place of work. The body searches upon leaving the ghetto and above all upon returning were degradingly and embarrassingly thorough. If the guards found food, the consequences were clear. No consideration was given to age, gender, or even the victim's personal situation. For example, a boy was yanked from David Packin's labor detail and shot without further ado, because he had a piece of bread in his pocket. One of Tuchel's colleagues from the Schutzpolizei, Corporal Gustav Kuhn, shot a Jewish laborer during a commotion at the ghetto gate. Kuhn thought he was stopping an escape. The victim was carried away with a severe wound to the head. According to regulations, Kuhn reported the incident, which was not to bring him any merits, to the command of the Schutzpolizei. His superior looked at him scornfully and commented with the words: "Well, Kuhn, you know how to shoot Jews." Arajs is also said to have been in the ghetto on repeated occasions; witnesses charged that he shot three men behind the guard house for returning from work with hidden foodstuffs. In addition to this persistent, latent threat of being murdered for a "violation" of the rules, ghetto inhabitants always faced the "normal" terror of the guards, whose beatings and humiliations – Latvian guards were said to have groped women during body searches – were so omnipresent that many victims preferred not to recall "the particulars" during postwar questioning.[95]

There were no privileges for special cases or citizens of other states. The Abkin family, which had returned to Riga from China, did not think of themselves as Jews. Therefore, the family members refused to move into the ghetto, a decision that cost them their lives – probably after being reported by a building custodian. An American Jew who had traveled to Riga for his sister's wedding and had been surprised by the war showed his passport to Tuchel and asked whether the order to relocate to the ghetto applied to him as well. Tuchel tore up the passport, beat the man, and sent him back into the ghetto.[96] When it was to his advantage, Tuchel –and others among the

German ghetto guards – exploited the Jews' misery to his own ends. For this, he made use of a Jewish informant by the name of Aismann. Survivors depicted this man as somebody who "was capable of selling out the entire ghetto for a piece of bread or cigarettes." Aismann acted as an intermediary for Tuchel, procuring for him gold and other valuables or establishing contacts for people who needed to bribe a guard for a favor. Of greater significance, however, is another role that Aismann filled. Parallel to his services for Tuchel, Aismann served as an informant for Krause, who thus acquired a source of news not only about the ghetto community, but also about the Latvian and German guards.[97]

If everyday life was thus fraught with danger, the Jewish Council was confident that at least the worst had been averted through the creation of the ghetto, and that the threat – despite individual killings – was no longer comparable with the situation in summer 1941, when thousands were shot at Bikernieki. Eljaschew's pessimism began to wane toward the end of November 1941 after talks with various German offices. He now saw – not least due to the need for Jewish workers – prospects for the ghetto's future. The council tried to improve everyday conditions in advance of the coming winter, it being above all necessary to resolve the fuel situation. For unforeseen expenditures, a special tax was enacted, while children were schooled in the Jewish Council building so that they might be prepared for the future.[98] Eljaschew could not have suspected that this would be the moment when the HSSPF Ostland and the office of the Regional Commander of the Security Police in Riga – those institutions that strangely enough had so far left the field to the civil administration without objection – would now intervene in "Jewish policy."

Notes

1. LVVA, P 80-2-9, 14, Vorauskommando des WBO in Riga an SS Oberstrumführer Grauel, 11 August 1941; Wilhelm Lenz, *Die Entwicklung Rigas zur Großstadt*, 45–46 and 79–80. According to Lenz, a majority of the synagogues, smaller prayer houses, and Jewish schools were located in the Moscow Suburb, where two-thirds of Riga's Jews are said to have lived at the turn of the century.
2. BA Berlin, R 91/164, Bekanntmachung [des Feldkommandanten], 23 July 1941. This announcement named four places where Jews could report: on the east side of the river, at Jāņa Asara St. 13 (8th district), at Cēsu St. 13 (4th district), and Katoļu St. 8 (6th district) and, on the other side of the river, at Mārupes St. 11 (10th district). See also Staw. Hamburg, Js 534/60, SB 4, statement by Arno Besekow, 19 February 1965, 777.
3. In other sources, Michail Eljaschew (Mikhail Eliashev) is given as Michail Iljaschew (Iliashev) or Eljaschow (Eliashëv).

4. Eljaschew had been chairman of the Latvian Jewish Freedom Federation, M. Blumenau its general secretary. The association's headquarters had been at Gertrudes St. 45, a prominent address.
5. Staw. Hamburg, 141 Js 534/60, Bd. 33, statement by Samuel Gutkin, 21 March 1963, 5,445; ibid., SB 16, statement by Joseph Behrmann (Jazeps Bermanis), 23 October 1975, 3,005; Kaufmann, "The War Years in Latvia Revisited," in Association of Latvian and Esthonian Jews in Israel, *The Jews in Latvia*, 354; J. Gechtman, "Riga," in Grossman and Ehrenburg, *Das Schwarzbuch*, 690, and "Die Aufzeichnungen des Bildhauers Riwosch," in ibid., 710.
6. Press, *Judenmord*, 64–65. Unfortunately, it is not clear where Press received this information. He may well have heard it from his father, who was a confidant of Rudolf Blumenfeld. It is to be assumed that Rudolf Batz or Arnold Kirste of Ek 2 – and not Rudolf Lange's Gestapo department within the command staff of EG A – presented these demands. After all, they were the ones who, together with Economics Commando Riga, had adopted this policy of ghettoization for economic purposes.
7. BA Berlin, R 91/164, Arbeitsamt Riga, Arbeitseinsatz für Juden, Hinweise für die Anlegung von Personalkarten für jüdische Arbeitskräfte, undated. This file also contains a model for both the personal cards and the three-part working papers. Part 1 of the latter registered the holder's name and noted that these certification papers were considered "identification for the period of service," which meant that without work the person concerned no longer had papers. Parts 2 and 3 were to be filled out by the employer and included space for information concerning the start and termination of employment, customer "satisfaction," and remuneration. Staw. Hamburg, 141 Js 534/60, Bd. 65, statement by Salomon Morein, 8 November 1966, 10,466; ibid., SB 4, statement by Besekow, 19 February 1965, 778; "Aufzeichnungen des Bildhauers Riwosch," 714. Riwosch claims that several Jews refused to admit that they were skilled workers so they would not have to serve the occupiers.
8. On Jewish forced labor under German military administration in the Baltic during the First World War, see Aba Strazas, "Die Tätigkeit des Dezernats für jüdische Angelegenheiten in der 'Deutschen Militärverwaltung Ober Ost,'" in *Die baltischen Provinzen Russlands zwischen den Revolutionen von 1905 und 1917*, ed. Andrew Ezergailis and Gert von Pistolkors, 315–329, esp. 318–319.
9. "Erlaß des Führers über die Verwaltung der neubesetzten Ostgebiete vom 17. 1941," in *Kriegstagebuch des Oberkommandos der Wehrmacht*, Bd. I, 1,027–1,028.
10. County Commissar-Riga Countryside was SA Colonel Joachim Fust. During the 1917 German occupation of Riga, Wittrock had worked with the German governor as municipal affairs advisor and left Riga after Germany's defeat. He returned in 1925 for a few years, but in 1936 left once again as an open opponent of the Ulmanis regime. Like Rosenberg, he had been a member of the student association Rubonia, which is why Rosenberg turned to him in July 1941.
11. BA Berlin, R 58/214, Ereignismeldung Nr. 13, 5 July 1941; Ereignismeldung Nr. 15, 7 July 1941; Ereignismeldung Nr. 24, 16 July 1941. Quote from Ereignismeldung Nr. 24.
12. Myllyniemi, *Die Neuordnung der baltischen Länder*, 105–106.
13. LVVA, P 1018-1-2, 1–7, Zusammenkunft der Vertreter Lettischer Organisationen am 11.7.1941 in den Räumen des Bildungsministeriums, Riga Valnu iela 2. The file includes the protocol and the draft telegram.
14. BA Berlin, R 58/214, Ereignismeldung Nr. 22, 14 July 1941, General von Roques is mistakenly identified as General "von Bock."; BA Berlin, R 58/215, Ereignismeldung Nr. 40, 1 August 1941, also quote.
15. Reitlinger, *Ein Haus auf Sand gebaut*, 174; Kleist, *Zwischen Hitler und Stalin*, 161.

16. BA Berlin R 58/215, Ereignismeldung Nr. 53, 15 August 1941; ibid., R 58/216, Ereignismeldung Nr. 68, 30 August 1941; ibid., R 58/217, Ereignismeldung Nr. 93, 24 September 1941; Staw. Hamburg, 141 Js 534/60, SB 19, statement by Arthurs Freimanis, 9 March 1976, 3,378–3,379; ibid., statement by Dr. Wiswald Sanders, 6 July 1976, 4,233–4,236; LVVA, P 1018-1-2, 34, Der RmbO an RKO, 26 September 1941; Myllyniemi, *Die Neuordnung der baltischen Länder*, 106; Krausnick and Wilhelm, *Die Truppe der Weltanschauungskrieges*, 351–353. Wilhelm Klumberg was considered a Baltic expert given his former position as director of the Herder Institute in Riga. Despite his cooperation with Valdmanis, Klumberg contemplated pushing back Latvian nationalism primarily via higher education and cultural policy, see Margot Blank, *Nationalsozialistische Hochschulpolitik in Riga (1941–1944)*, 14–16; Martin Seckendorf, "Deutsche Baltikumkonzeptionen 1941–1944 im Spiegel von Dokumenten der zivilen Okkupationsverwaltung," in *1999*, 16, no. 1 (2001): 151 and 155–157.
17. Hugo Wittrock, *Kommissarischer Oberbürgermeister von Riga 1941–1944*, 26. The names of other functionaries are provided here.
18. Lohse's closer colleagues had gathered previously in the Castle of the Order Krössinsee (Pomerania), where they were also given uniforms. They were to travel from there through the military-administered territory to Kaunas as a group, see BA Ludwigsburg, 420 AR-Z 75/68, SB 13, unpaginated, statement by Dr. Willy Neuendorf, 2 March 1964.
19. BA Berlin, R 58/215, Ereignismeldung Nr. 53 from 15 August 1941; Otto Bräutigam, *So hat es sich zugetragen*, 345–351.
20. LVVA, P 1026-1-3, 310–315, RKO, IIa 4, an den HSSPF Riga, 2 August 1941. According to this document, a Jew was somebody who was "descended from at least 3 grandparents who were fully Jewish by race," or somebody who was "descended from two grandparents who were fully Jewish by race" and was of the Jewish faith or was, as of 22 June 1941, "married to a person or living in cohabitation with somebody who is a Jew in the spirit of these guidelines or who now or in the future enters into such an association." This was not the adaptation of the 1935 Nuremberg Laws but rather their intensification. In doubt, the county or city commissar was to decide who was a Jew.
21. LVVA, P 1026-1-3, 310–315, RKO, IIa 4, an den HSSPF Riga, 2 August 1941. This is printed in a slightly different form – e.g. amended with regard to the ban on butchering or the ban on foreign Jews moving – in a version dated 13 August 1941, as Nuremberg Document PS-1138, in *IMG*, Bd. 27, 18–25. The minimal sum of 5 rubles per day equaled about U.S. $0.20 per day in 1941, which in 2006 dollars would be about U.S. $2.75. These dollar figures, however, do not take into account black market exchange rates and purchasing power parity. BA Ludwigsburg, 420 AR-Z 75/68, SB 13, unpaginated, statement by Hinrich Lohse, 7 July 1960. In this statement, Lohse denied all guilt and considered his orders merely the application of the Nuremberg Laws, these being in his view a "sufficient regulation of questions concerning the Jews."
22. LVVA, P 1026-1-3, 309, RKO, IIa 4, an den HSSPF Riga, 2 August 1941. This document was signed p.p. by Ministerial Director Theodor Fründt, the head of RKO Main Department II (Political Affairs). See also Ezergailis, *Holocaust in Latvia*, 336–341.
23. LVVA, P 1026-1-3, 292–293, Tschierschky an Stahlecker, 5 August 1941.
24. Ibid., Stahlecker an Stubaf. Tschierschky, 5 August 1941.
25. Ibid., 299–300, EK 2 an EG A, z. Hd. Tschiersky [sic], 6 August 1941, Betr.: Stellungnahme zu den Richtlinien des RKO fuer das Ostland zur Regelung der Judenfrage. A few other less important reservations are raised here – apparently only to underscore the authority and jurisdiction of the Security Police and SD over the civil administration – such as the requirement that Jews wear the Star of David on inner garments, and that

these be sewed on. By contrast, Jews were to be allowed to use the sidewalks for "technical reasons concerning traffic."

26. Ibid., 296–298, EG A Stab, Betrifft: Entwurf über die Aufstellung vorläufiger Richtlinien für die Behandlung der Juden im Gebiet des RKO, 6 August 1941. In this context, it is worth noting that a general killing order apparently did not yet exist, and that the "reservation policy" was still being pursued with certain borrowings from concepts involving the use of Jews for forced labor, especially regarding road construction. According to EG A's recommendation, this was to be pursued by Jewish labor details outside the "Jew reserve" as well, an idea that reappeared in modified form during Heydrich's remarks at the Wannsee Conference. In that instance, German Jews were to be deported for "constructing roads to the east."
27. Ibid., 301, EG A an den Chef der Sipo und des SD, 16 August 1941; Staw. Hamburg, 141 Js 534/60, Bd. 4, statement by Hinrich Lohse, 19 April 1950, 384R. Lohse admitted that he had argued with Stahlecker, because the latter refused to subordinate himself to the RKO and intended to take orders only from the Reich Security Main Office (RSHA).
28. "Erlass des Führers über die polizeiliche Sicherung der neu besetzten Ostgebiete vom Juli 1941," printed in *Führer-Erlasse 1939–1945*, ed. Martin Moll, 188–189. This conflict mirrored a dispute between Rosenberg and Himmler over a key political decision, see Staw. Hamburg, 141 Js 534/60, SB 12, statement by Hinrich Lohse, 18 April 1950, 2,242–2,243; Rebentisch, *Führerstaat und Verwaltung im Zweiten Weltkrieg*, 314–316 and 322–326; *Dienstkalender*, entries for 25 May and 22 October 1941, 161 and 243–244 respectively.
29. LVVA, P 1026-1-3, 303, EG A, Stab an das EK 1a, 1b, 2, 3, Sk Grauer, 29 August 1941. This criticism of the civil administration was based on a 28 August message from Heinrich Müller, the head of RSHA Department IV (Gestapo). Müller reported that some of the newly deployed county commissars in the area of operations of EG A and EG B had sought to suspend the killing of Jews and Communists. According to Heydrich and Müller, the Einsatzgruppen were to refuse such requests and report them to Berlin, see ibid., 302, [Müller] an die EG A und B, 28 August 1941; Staw. Hamburg, 141 Js 534/60, SB 12, statement by Hinrich Lohse, 19 May 1950, 2,245–2,246. Lohse claimed that it came to an argument with Stahlecker at a meeting on the authority of the BdS. Subsequently, Lohse said, Stahlecker filed a complaint against him with the RSHA. Even if parts of Lohse's statement are to be seen as defensive maneuvering, the conflict depicted at this meeting did take place.
30. *Dienstkalender*, entries for 30 and 31 July 1941, 188–189; BA Berlin, R 58/215, Ereignismeldung Nr. 47, 9 August 1941. Here it is said that Himmler was also interested in raising non-German police formations to be deployed beyond their home country – i.e., outside the Baltic – in the struggle against partisans.
31. H. D. Heilmann, "Das Kriegstagebuch des Diplomaten Otto Bräutigam," in *Biedermann und Schreibtischtäter*, 139–141, quote 140.
32. BA-MA, RW 19/473, 100–107, Stab Ia [des Wi-Rü-Amtes], Reisebreicht über Besuch im Abschnitt der Wi.-In. Nord, 11 August 1941. This report says the "Jewish question" in Riga had "hardly been touched in any way"; by contrast, the members of this group were aware of the mass shootings in Liepāja (Libau). It is also worth pointing out that the rapporteur notes Jewish women were not being shot at this point – which was still correct in principle – but it was planned "that they would be eliminated by gassing later." On this, see the above report, 106.
33. This street is identical with what appears transliterated in some sources as Lahtschplehscha St. Under German occupation, this was Carl Schirren St., which was named for a Riga-born German historian. Today, this street is again home to a school for local Jewish

children. It is run by Rabbi Mordechai Glazman and financed by donations, including many from Jewish survivors of the Riga ghetto. A soup kitchen for the poor is also located there.
34. BA Berlin, R 91/164, "Arbeitspflicht für Juden," *Deutsche Zeitung im Ostland*, 18 August 1941 (excerpt).
35. Malbish Arumim – "clothe the naked" – is a Jewish welfare organization founded in Italy around the turn of the 17th and 18th century by Samuel David Ben Yehiel Ottolenghi, the rabbi of Venice and Padua. It was later institutionalized in the Jewish communities of Russia as well.
36. According to Press, the internal medicine department was run by Dr. V. Kretzer, the surgical department by Professor Dr. Mintz, the gynecological ward by Dr. S. Joseph (an emigrant from Berlin who had worked at the Moabit Hospital during the 1930s), and the pediatric ward by Dr. L. Blechmann and Dr. L. Rabinowitsch, while the neurology clinic was under H. Idelson and Dr. J. Krohn. Other sources report that Dr. Jawitz, Dr. Magalief, Dr. Sick of Liepāja, and the dermatologist Dr. Wassermann practiced there. See also Staw. Hamburg, Js 534/60, Bd. 14, undated report by Esra Jurmann, 5,400. Sources also state that two female doctors by the name of Brins and Kameras were held in the Central Prison, but released on orders from SS First Lieutenant Grauel. See LVVA, P 82-1-37, 48, E.K. 2, II A, 22 August 1941.
37. Press, *Judenmord*, 66–68; "Aufzeichnungen des Bildhauers Riwosch," 710; Kaufmann, *Churbn Lettland*, 71.
38. Kaufmann, "The War Years in Latvia," 354–355.
39. Staw. Hamburg, Js 534/60, Bd. 65, statement by Morein, 8 November 1966, 10,466.
40. "Das Rigaer Ghetto in der Lettgalischen Vorstadt," *Tevija*, 23 August 1941, translated in Staw. Hamburg, Js 534/60, SB 36, 6,211–6,214.
41. Ibid.; "Aufzeichnungen des Bildhauers Riwosch," 710–711; Press, *Judenmord*, 66–67.
42. The 1st and 2nd districts as well as the "forest district" (meaning Kaiserwald, i.e., Mežaparks, where the majority of the representative villas stood) were cleared first, as were the apartments confiscated on orders from the German authorities.
43. These 3,142 persons were distributed over 1,084 notices, making the average size of a family evacuated to the ghetto three.
44. BA Berlin, R 91/73, Rigaer Stadtverwaltung an den Geb.-Komm. Riga-Stadt, Betrifft: Einrichtung eines Ghettorayons in Riga, 11 September 1941; "Bereits 3200 Juden in das Ghetto verlegt," *Tevija*, 13 September 1941, translated in Staw. Hamburg, 141 Js 534/60, SB 36, 6,220; "Aufzeichnungen des Bildhauers Riwosch," 712–713; Staw. Hamburg, 141 Js 534/60, Bd. 38, statement by Mosche Dieftz, 19 September 1963, 6,292–6,923; ibid., Bd. 40, statement by Karl Heise, 23 October 1963, 6,594; ibid., Bd. 90, statement by Adele Honigwill, 24 May 1972, 14,154; ibid., statement by Max Kaufmann, 25 May 1972, 14,164.
45. A photo of the fence is in *Tevija*, 8 October 1941, see "30 000 Jews hinter Stacheldraht im Rigaer Ghetto," translated in Staw. Hamburg, 141 Js 534/60, SB 36, 6,826.
46. BA Berlin, R 91/73, Rigaer Stadtverwaltung an den Geb.-Komm. Riga-Stadt, Betrifft: Einrichtung eines Ghettorayons in Riga, 11 September 1941; ibid., Rigaer Stadtverwaltung an den Geb.-Komm. Riga-Stadt. Betrifft: Privathäuser im Ghetto-Rayon, September 1941. There were 203 residential buildings in the ghetto, according to a list dated 1 October 1941, see ibid., Verzeichnis der in den Grenzen des Gettos befindlichen unnazionalisierten [sic] Arien [sic] gehörige [sic] Grundstücke. Also, Staw. Hamburg, 147 Ks 6/71, Bd. 93, courtroom testimony by Irving Berner, 15 January 1973, 14,828. Berner said he had also been a member of the Jewish Council. See as well BA Ludwigsburg, 420 AR-Z 75/68, SB B, statement by Ego Rauch, 26 February 1964, 4 [of the statement].

47. "Rigaer Ghetto in der Lettgalischen Vorstadt," *Tevija*, 23 August 1941, translated in Staw. Hamburg, 141 Js 534/60, SB 36, 6,211–6,214; BA Berlin, R 91/164, "Arbeitspflicht für Juden," *Deutsche Zeitung im Ostland*, 18 August 1941. This article has a photograph of a poster with the ban on Jews visiting the market. On food rationing, see Press, *Judenmord*, 66.
48. Press, *Judenmord*, 68.
49. "Schreiben des Reichskommissars für das Ostland, Abt. IIa (Trampedach), an den Generalkommissar in Lettland vom 25 August 1941 mit Zwangsbestimmungen für die Ghettos," printed in Benz et al., *Einsatz im "Reichskommissariat Ostland,"* 124. The orders applied to all of the ghettos in the General Commissariat Latvia, but affected primarily the Riga ghetto due to its size. In addition to the restrictions on communication, Trampedach also ordered that all livestock be relinquished, issued a ban on tearing down sheds, etc., for firewood, and had the fences along border streets and pedestrian bridges reinforced (to the extent that these lay in the ghetto). As of 15 September 1941, the RKO was divided into main departments I (Central Department), II (Political Affairs), III (Economic Affairs), and IV (Technical Affairs). Main Department II was in turn divided into departments IIa (Political Affairs), IIb (Labor and Social Policy), IIc (Administration), IId (Health and Care of the People), IIe (Veterinarian Affairs), IIf (Legal Affairs), IIg (Finance), IIh (Culture), and IIi (Press and Propaganda). See Latvijas Valsts Arhīvs, P 1004-1-1, 1–3, Namen- und Fernsprechverzeichnis des RKO.
50. "Das Rigaer Ghetto in der Lettgalischen Vorstadt," *Tevija*, 23 August 1941, translated in Staw. Hamburg, Js 534/60, SB 36, 6,211–6,214. See also Staw. Hamburg, Js 534/60, SB 20, map of the ghetto produced by Abraham Bloch after the war, 3,686–3,687; ibid., Bd. 33, statement by Gutkin, 21 March 1963, 5,445. Vozbutskii is also spelled Wazbutzki in the literature. According to Kaufmann, OD members included: Bag, Soloweicik, Schatzow, Berner, Ginzburg, Landmann, and Gutkin. The OD wore blue caps bearing the Star of David, see Kaufmann, *Churbn Lettland*, 83–84; Staw. Hamburg, Js 534/60, Bd. 38, statement by former OD man Max Wachtel, 28 August 1963, 6,161.
51. Kaufmann, *Churbn Lettland*, 64.
52. Staw. Hamburg, Js 534/60, SB 16, statement by Behrmann (Bermanis), 23 October 1975, 3,005–3,006. It is said here that Mrs. Behrmann was murdered on 17 July 1941; this could be a typo, because all of the dates mentioned before and after this crime refer to August. Behrmann, together with his mother, had been forced to take up quarters within a large building complex that had been built for workers from the porcelain factory Kuznetsov. A lumber dealer from Danzig, who was sick with tuberculosis, also lived there. According to Kaufmann, Blumenau tried to contact the field administration command in an effort to help Mrs. Behrmann, see Kaufmann, *Churbn Lettland*, 70–71.
53. "Rigaer Ghetto in der Lettgalischen Vorstadt," *Tevija*, 23 August 1941, translated in Staw. Hamburg, 141 Js 534/60, SB 36, 6,211–6,214. According to Economics Commando Riga, around 500 Jews had been put to work in the peat industry, while Jews working in agriculture had been withdrawn (probably due to concerns that they could escape), see BA-MA, RW 30/76, Wirtschaftsaufbau Lettlands durch das Wi.-KdO. Riga, Stand 1.9.41; BA Berlin R 91/164, Industrieverwaltung Lettlands, Torfindustrie, an die Deutsche Wirtschaftsverwaltung Riga, 17 July 1941. Also Staw. Hamburg, 141 Js 534/60, Bd. 37, statement by David Fischkin, 26 May 1963, 6,058–6,059. According to Fischkin, around 200 Jews were deployed in the peat camp Sloka, which consisted of a few barracks and was guarded by Latvians. Food consisted of potatoes and water; several prisoners died of typhus. The greater part of the camp's inmates were transferred back to Riga in November 1941 and murdered during the liquidation of local Latvian Jewry, while a minority of 30 prisoners remained in Sloka.

54. BA Berlin, R 91/164, *Deutsche Zeitung im Ostland*, 1 September 1941, Judenstern auf dem Rücken, Anordnung des Gen.-Komm.s in Riga. This includes a part of Lohse's preliminary guidelines, the professional bans, compulsory outward identification, the ban on changing residence, and other restrictions.
55. Staw. Hamburg, 141 Js 534/60, Bd. 39, statement by Robert Huse, 15 September 1963, 6,303; ibid., Bd. 57, Der RFSS, Betr. Inmarschsetzung von Kräften der Gend. und Schutzpolizei der Gemeinden zu den SSPF und den KdO in Dorpat, Riga, Kowno, und Minsk, unpaginated.
56. Staw. Hamburg, 147 Js 5/71, Anklageschrift gegen Heinrich Oberwinder et al., 21 December 1971, 106–108 and 135–136; Staw. Hamburg, 141 Js 534/60, Bd. 34, statement by Friedrich Jahnke, 22 May 1963, 5,592–5,593; ibid., Bd. 75, statement by Friedrich Jahnke, 28 March 1968, 11,909–11,912.
57. Staw. Hamburg, 147 Js 5/71, Anklageschrift gegen Heinrich Oberwinder et al., 97; Staw. Hamburg, 147 Js 31/67, Bd. 23, statement by Arnold Kirste, 31 March 1966, 4,318.
58. LVVA, P 80-3-1, 2–7, Berück Nord, Abt. Ia, 18 September 1941, Richtlinien für die Tätigkeit der Feld- und Ortskommandanturen, 6r.
59. LVVA, P 80-3-28, 5–12, Protokoll über die Besprechung der Leiter der Abtl. Arbeit bei den Wi.-Kdo's, Kowno, Riga, Reval und Görlitz, 28 August 1941.
60. BA-MA, RW 30/76, Wirtschaftsaufbau Lettlands durch das Wi.-Kdo. Riga, Stand 1.9.41; Staw. Hamburg, 141 Js 534/60, Bd. 89, statement by Frida Michelson, 3 March 1971, 14,015. Michelson was initially sent to the Jelgava area, where she worked as a forced laborer among peasants. In August 1941, she was suddenly sent back to Riga for no apparent reason. This is a concrete example of efforts to implement Lohse's intention to purge the countryside of Jews.
61. Even General Commissariat Latvia, Main Department I, "urgently" needed sixteen Jewish forced laborers at the end of October 1941 for the upkeep of its building at Alfred Rosenberg Ring 9, with officials applying pro forma at the Labor Office in Riga for their continued employment. This shows that it was extraordinarily difficult even for the head of the civil administration to substitute Latvians for Jewish workers, see BA Berlin, R 92/266, 186–187, Hauptabteilung I an das Arbeitsamt Riga, Abt. Judeneinsatz, Betr. Beschäftigung von Juden, 31 October 1941.
62. BA Berlin, R 91/164, Der Gen.-Komm. in Riga, Arbeitsverwaltung v. 1.9.1941, Niederschrift über die Besprechung mit den Chefs der staatlichen- und Industrieunternehmen in Riga in Arbeitseinsatzfragen. On the absorption of personnel from the Economics Inspection into the civil administration, see BA Berlin, R 91/4, OKW/Wi Rue an Wirtschaftsstab Ost, Betr.: Uebergang von Personal in den Geschaeftsbereich des RmbO, 22 August 1941; BA Berlin, R 58/217, Ereignismeldung Nr. 93, 24 September 1941. This report says the "economic policy related activity of the Economics Inspection" had decreased due to irregularities that even led to a court martial.
63. LVVA, P 1026-1-3, 262–264, fragment of a report from Ek 2, Lagebericht "Judentum."
64. BA Berlin, R 58/217, Ereignismeldung Nr. 96, 27 September 1941. This document says Ek 2 had by this point murdered 29,246 persons, the greatest part of which must have been Jews. In the Central Prison, however, Jews were a minority. The prison was occupied primarily by 3,462 "Communists" and 108 "criminal felons," such is this remarkable formulation. The number of victims in Riga was 186 persons, but not all of them were hospital patients.
65. BA Ludwigsburg, AR-Z 101/67, Bd. 2, statement by Janis Brencis, 8 July 1968, 288–290.
66. Schulte, *Zwangsarbeit und Vernichtung: Das Wirtschaftsimperium der SS*, 284; Krausnick and Wilhelm, *Die Truppe der Weltanschauungskrieges*, 610; Kaienburg, *Die Wirtschaft*

der SS, 582–583. Prützmann and Reemtsma knew each other from their Hamburg days. With the German invasion of the Soviet Union, they had gone to Riga together and later, when the HSSPFs Ostland and Ukraine swapped commands, to Kiev. In his capacity as an SS economist, Reemtsma was sought out by EG A for an economic point of view in planning for a concentration camp. EG A envisioned – in what were quite clearly variations on its reservation solution – incarcerating all of Riga's Jews, indeed all of Latvia's surviving Jews, and separating them by sex. Reemtsma's interest in this project lay in starting up peat cutting sites and brickworks, see RGVA 504-2-4, 148–150, Der BdS – EG A, Betr.: Einrichtung eines Konzentrationslagers in Lettland, 1 October 1941.

67. Staw. Hamburg, 141 Js 534/60, Bd. 79, statement by Eduard Bachl, 22 January 1946, 12,550. Bachl came to Riga in January 1942. Bachl's statement does not say when exactly Jews were deployed at these production sites. Unfortunately, we have no official documentation for 1941. There is solid data on Jewish forced labor for the following years. This, however, does not concern the majority of Latvian Jews, as they had been murdered already by the end of 1941.

68. YIVO Institute for Jewish Research (YIVO), Occ. E-3-27, Der Gen.-Komm. in Riga, Abt. IIa, an den RKO, Abtl. IIa, Betr.: Einrichtung von Ghettos, jüdischen Arbeitslagern und Arbeitseinsatz der Juden. Anmelde- und Ablieferungspflicht des jüdischen Vermögens, 20 October 1941.

69. Staw. Hamburg, 141 Js 534/60, Bd. 6, statement by Hermann Schmidt, 9 February 1959, 13–15, meant are *Heeresinstandsetzungswerkstätten* 701 and *Heeresbekleidungsamt* 601; ibid., Bd. 20, statement by Gerhard Maywald, 13 October 1961, 2,924; ibid., Bd. 21, statement by Kurt Lünenschloss, 25 November 1961, 3,101–3,103; ibid., Bd. 25, statement by Gerhard Maywald, 3 May 1962, 3,936; ibid., Bd. 37, statement by Jehuda Feitelson, 10 April 1963, 6,032–6,033; statement by Elieser Hilmann, 23 May 1963, 6,044; statement by Schlomo Schetzen, 3 June 1963, 6,068; ibid., Bd. 38, statement by Max Wachtel, 28 August 1963, 6,160; statement by Benno Mahler, 9 September 1963, 6,273; statement by Mosche Deiftz, 19 September 1963, 6,292; ibid., Bd. 46, statement by Ernst Michelsen, 20 April 1964, 7,595–7,597; ibid., Bd. 76, Kalman Aron, 18 March 1968, 12,105; ibid., Bd. 90, statement by Leonid Pancis, 26 May 1972, 14,169; statement by Samuel Atlas, 26 May 1972, 14,176; Staw. Hamburg, 147 Ks 6/71, Bd. 93, courtroom testimony of Eugen Borkum, 8 January 1973, 14,808; ibid., courtroom testimony of Irving Berner, 15 January 1973, 14,828; Staw. Hamburg, 147 Js 5/71, Anklageschrift gegen Heinrich Oberwinder et al., 57; BA Berlin, R 58/217, Ereignismeldung Nr. 94, 25 September 1941. From the context of Schmidt's statement, it is to be inferred that the organized deployment of workers from the ghetto got underway only in the late autumn, some time before the large liquidations. Lünenschloss took over his enterprise, which was run by Army Group North's motor pool, when he was transferred from the Wehrmacht to the civil administration.

70. BA Berlin, R 91/164, Bericht [des Arbeitsamtes] über den jüdischen Arbeitseinsatz, 8 September 1941.

71. Ibid., Der Leiter des Arbeitsamtes Riga, Geb.-Komm. Riga, Abtlg. IIb: Arbeitsamt, an die Feldkommandantur Riga, Betrifft: Beschäftigung von Juden durch die Wehrmacht, 15 September 1941. Through a branch office, the Labor Office Riga managed the deployment of Jews in Ventspils (Windau), see BA Berlin, R 92/1157, [Vermerk] des Ortskommandanten Meitinger, 12 August 1941; ibid., Arbeitsamt Riga, Nebenstelle Windau, an das Arbeitsamt Riga, Betr.: Einsatz von Juden, 17 August 1941.

72. BA Berlin, R 91/164, Der Leiter des Arbeitsamtes Riga an die Feldkommandantur Riga, Betrifft: Beschäftigung von Juden durch die Wehrmacht, 30 September 1941.

73. Nuremberg Document L-180, Einsatzgruppe A, Gesamtbericht bis zum 15.10.1941.

74. BA Berlin, R 91/73, Rigaer Stadtverwaltung an den Geb.-Komm. Riga-Stadt, Betrifft: Einrichtung eines Ghettorayons in Riga, 11 September 1941; YIVO, Occ. E 3-30, Abt. IIa an die Herren Geb.-Komm. Riga-Stadt und Land, Mitau, Dünaburg, Wolmar, Welikije Luki I und II, Betr.: Einrichtung von Ghettos, jüdischen Arbeitslagern und Arbeitseinsatz der Juden, undated [probably the end of August]; Press, *Judenmord*, 73; Maurina, *Die eisernen Riegel zerbrechen*, 208–209.
75. "30 000 Jews hinter Stacheldraht im Rigaer Ghetto," *Tevija*, 8 October 1941, translated in Staw. Hamburg, Js 534/60, SB 36, 6,222; YIVO, Occ. E-3-27, Der Gen.-Komm. in Riga, Abt. IIa, an den RKO, Abtl. IIa, Betr.: Einrichtung von Ghettos, jüdische Arbeitslager und Arbeitseinsatz der Juden. Anmelde- und Ablieferungspflicht des jüdischen Vermögens, 20 October 1941. According to these two documents, the OD – described in *Tevija* as selected "overseers" – had taken up its activity, which primarily meant intervening as arbitrator at grocery stores, where the plight of provisions in the ghetto was seen most clearly – something *Tevija* cynically commented on, as was its custom.
76. BA Berlin, R 91/164, *Deutsche Zeitung im Ostland*, "Anordnung über die Bildung eines Ghettos in Riga und den Umgang mit Juden v. 23.10.1941," 24 October 1941.
77. BA Berlin, R 91/164, Arbeitseinsatz II 5431, Li./G., an die Industrie-Direktion Riga, Betrifft: Einsatz von jüdischen Arbeitskräften, 24 October 1941; ibid., Anordnung [des Arbeitsamtes Riga], Betrifft: Beschäftigung von Juden, 27 October 1941. The latter was also printed as an official proclamation in the *Deutsche Zeitung im Ostland*, 28 October 1941.
78. See "30 000 Jews hinter Stacheldraht im Rigaer Ghetto," *Tevija*, 8 October 1941, translated in Staw. Hamburg, Js 534/60, SB 36, 6,226.
79. LVVA, P 69-1a-19, 21–27, Der Gen.-Komm. in Riga, Abtl. IIa, an den RKO, Betrifft: Monatlicher Bericht über Einrichtung von Ghettos in jüdischen Arbeitslagern, Arbeitseinsatz und Behandlung der Juden, 20 November 1941. The statistics are to be found on page 22 of the file. See also Press, *Judenmord*, 65–66. Press assumes that the numbers came from the Jewish Council, which in our view is unlikely, for that would mean the council determined who was and was not able to work. It is much more likely that these numbers are from the city Labor Office's Bureau for the Deployment of Jews, which the council had to assist with registration.
80. YIVO, Occ. E 3-30, Abt. IIa an die Geb.-Komm. Riga-Stadt und Land, Mitau, Dünaburg, Wolmar, Welikije Luki I und II, Betr.: Einrichtung von Ghettos, jüdischen Arbeitslagern und Arbeitseinsatz der Juden; Staw. Hamburg, 141 Js 534/60, Bd. 60, statement by David Packin, 4 October 1965, 9,700–9,701. By his own account, Packin was president of the Jewish Community for a time after the war and therefore had greater access to information than other survivors.
81. BA Berlin, R 92/198, 21–38, Der Gen.-Komm. Riga in Riga, Niederschrift über die Besprechung v. 8.11.1941. This document says that county commissars were to "look after barracks and [the such] for the accommodation of their Jews" on their own initiative, because there would be no opportunity to accommodate Jews from the Latvian counties in the Riga Ghetto. According to the numbers of Department II of the General Commissar Latvia, as of 20 November 1941, 3,890 Jews (782 children, 3,002 adults able to work and 106 adults unable to work) were registered in Liepāja and 935 Jews (173 children, 719 adults able to work, 25 adults unable to work, and 18 over 65 years of age) were registered in Daugavpils. The Daugavpils massacre took place on 7–9 November 1941. It still appears possible that this was the savage consequence of the undesired transfer of Daugavpils's Jews to the Riga Ghetto, see Krausnick and Wilhelm, *Die Truppe der Weltanschauungskrieges*, 114–116.
82. YIVO, Occ. E-3-29, Aktenvermerk Dr. Drechslers, 21 October 1941. This note for the files concerns Drechsler's meeting with Stahlecker.

83. LVVA, P 69-1a-19, 21–27, Der Gen.-Komm. in Riga, Abtl. IIa, an den RKO, Betrifft: Monatlicher Bericht über Einrichtung von Ghettos in jüdischen Arbeitslagern, Arbeitseinsatz und Behandlung der Juden, 20 November 1941; ibid., 30–31, Kommando der Schutzpolizei, Vorläufige Wachvorschrift (2) für die Wache des Ghettos, 20 November 1941. The latter document contains the sample columns for the ghetto guard book and the quote on using fire arms. The presence of the (2) makes it clear that another set of guard instructions must have existed. See also Ezergailis, *Holocaust in Latvia*, 321–323; Staw. Hamburg, 147 Js 5/71 (141 Js 534/60), Anklageschrift gegen Heinrich Oberwinder et al., 108–109.
84. BA Berlin, R 91/237, Kommando der Schutzpolizei, 25 November 1941.
85. Vestermanis, "Retter im Lande der Handlanger," in Benz and Wetzel, *Solidarität und Hilfe für Juden während der NS-Zeit*, Bd. 2, 234–235; on Janis Lipke, see Staw. Hamburg, 141 Js 534/60, SB 7, statement by Abram Lipchin, 12 August 1975, 1,423; David Silberman, "Jan Lipke, An Unusual Man," in *Muted Voices*, ed. Gertrude Schneider, 87–111.
86. Staw. KG Berlin, 1 Ks 1/69 (RSHA), Bd. 6 (J-N), statement by Alfred Krauße, 26 July 1965, 6. Krauße was a registrar in Adolf Eichmann's office and testified that Göring successfully interceded on behalf of Blech's release.
87. Staw. Hamburg, 147 Js 5/71 (141 Js 534/60), Anklageschrift gegen Heinrich Oberwinder et al., 117; ibid., Bd. 36, statement by Friedrich Jahnke, 5 June 1963, 5,844–5,845; ibid., Bd. 41, statement by Karl Heise, 22 November 1963, 6,873–6,874; ibid., Bd. 55, statement by Herbert Furck, 17 February 1965, 8,926; ibid., Bd. 57, statement by Walter Esslinger, 27 May 1965, 9,272; Ezergailis, *Holocaust in Latvia*, 89. Heise said that the Jewish professor was a man by the name of "Klemperer." We assume that he mixed up Leo Blech with Otto Klemperer, another Jewish director who had long been in exile in the United States. All of the other information provided by Heise, in particular the reference to the professor's long career in Berlin, points to Blech. That it was Leo Blech is also to be inferred from the statements by Esslinger and Jahnke. Jahnke had to search the apartment of the prominent concert master after the arrival of the Schutzpolizei Command. The meeting with Heise was to have taken place several weeks after his arrival. We date the encounter to October 1941.
88. Staw. Hamburg, 141 Js 534/60, SB 6, statement by Alexander Ginsberg, 9 July 1968, 1,132–1,133.
89. This was a Hungarian citizen, the wife of the sock manufacturer Ernst Kaufmann, who had been murdered at the start of the German occupation. On the basis of her Hungarian passport, Mrs. Kaufmann and her daughter did not have to move into the ghetto and were allowed to keep their apartment.
90. Staw. Hamburg, 141 Js 534/60, Bd. 37, statement by Janis Vabulis, 16 January 1979, 6,348–6,355; ibid., SB 38, statement by Laimons Lidums, 4 January 1979, 6,537–6,541; ibid., SB 40, statement by Edgars Kraujins, 5 January 1979, 6,671–6,674; ibid., SB 41, statement by Zelda Riwka Hait, 22 April 1979, 6,987–7,005; BA Ludwigsburg, 207 AR 188/76, Bd. 1, statement by Zelda Riwka Hait, 6 April 1976; Vestermanis, "Retter im Lande der Handlanger," 244–245. The presentation here adheres primarily to Hait's statements. Because of their incredible experiences, Hait and Vabulis were suspected of being informants, first in Riga and later in Sweden, each time for different employers.
91. Staw. Hamburg, 141 Js 534/60, Bd. 61, statements by Olga Brüning, 8 and 12 December 1965, 9,932–9,933 and 9,937; Ezergailis, *Holocaust in Latvia*, 411–412; Vestermanis, "Retter im Lande der Handlanger," 264.
92. Use of this procedure is to be found in BA Berlin R 92/133. Although SS Major Grauel of Ek 2 had already ordered the county archive sealed for the purpose of later evaluation, the order to acquire the Jewish registers came from Einsatzstab Reichsleiter Rosenberg

and the Culture Department within General Commissariat Latvia, which both confiscated archival records as well as cultural assets of Jewish ownership. See also ibid., R 92/54.
93. Staw. Hamburg, 141 Js 534/60, Bd. 60, statement by Packin, 4 October 1965, 9,705; ibid., SB 6, statement by David Packin, 21 April 1969, 1,150. This was the number of people who reported after the Red Army took Riga for the second time. It should be clear that only a tiny part of them spent the entire occupation underground.
94. Staw. Hamburg, 141 Js 534/60, Bd. 38, statement by Wachtel, 28 August 1963, 6,160; Staw. Hamburg, 147 Js 5/71 (141 Js 534/60), Anklageschrift gegen Heinrich Oberwinder et al., 136.
95. Staw. Hamburg, 141 Js 534/60, Bd. 60, statement by Packin, 4 October 1965, 9,701; ibid., Bd. 76, statement by Aron, 18 March 1968, 12,105; ibid., Bd. 77, statement by Gustav Kuhn, 23 March 1964, 12,274–12,275; Schwurgericht Hamburg, (50) Ks 9/72, Urteil gegen Jahnke u.a., 23 February 1973, 163–164. The individual acts of homicide could not be proven beyond a reasonable doubt during the main proceedings against Tuchel, which was unnecessary anyway, since he was sentenced to life in prison for his participation in the clearance of the ghetto. We assume that the accusations made against Tuchel were true. See ibid., SB 1, statement by Ralp Shub, 14 September 1965, 161; ibid., SB 2, statement by Leonid Pancis, 11 July 1967, 438. The other murders mentioned by Shub – the killing of an older Jew by the name of Krupkin and a girl by the name of Propes – show parallels to Tuchel's crimes and could be identical. On the other hand, it is possible that these were separate crimes committed by Arajs that happened to resembled those of Tuchel. The quote is from Kuhn.
96. Press, *Judenmord*, 73–74; Staw. Hamburg, 141 Js 534/60, Bd. 38, statement by Wachtel, 28 August 1963, 6,161.
97. Schwurgericht Hamburg, (50) Ks 9/72, Urteil gegen Jahnke u.a., 23 February 1973, 168–170; Staw. Hamburg, 147 Ks 6/71, Bd. 93, courtroom testimony of Irving Berner, 15 January 1973, 14,831.
98. Kaufmann, *Churbn Lettland*, 90–91.

– *Chapter 5* –

MURDER ON A MASSIVE SCALE

The Annihilation of the Ghetto's Latvian Jews

With the installation of SS Lieutenant General Friedrich Jeckeln as the new higher SS and police leader Ostland in November 1941, a man was transferred to Riga who was not only considered as ideologically reliable as his predecessor Hans-Adolf Prützmann, but who had also pursued the persecution and murder of Soviet Jews more radically and more relentlessly than any other SS functionary.[1] Whereas Prützmann had been able to rely on Einsatzgruppe A (EG A) and Einsatzkommando 2 (Ek 2) or consciously delegated authority for this matter farther down the chain of command – such is the interpretation based on the sources available to date – Jeckeln was not about to let his personal initiative wane in this field. Jeckeln's predominance was facilitated by the fact that Walter Stahlecker, the commander of EG A, and Walther Schröder, the SS and police leader Latvia, made no effort to assume responsibility for anti-Jewish policy during the winter of 1941–1942. Stahlecker was preoccupied with the struggle against partisans – which was synonymous with the "front assignment" so desired by officials of the Reich Security Main Office (RSHA) seeking to distinguish themselves – while Schröder was thought, rightfully, to lack assertiveness.

Where the office of the Regional Commander of the Security Police and Security Service Latvia (*Kommandeur der Sicherheitspolizei und des SD*, KdS Latvia, a.k.a. Ek 2) was concerned, the ambitious Rudolf Batz, by his own account Stahlecker's deputy, had finally managed to arrange his transfer back to his old office in Hanover and had turned over official business to SS Lieutenant Colonel Eduard Strauch. Strauch in turn was to fill this position for only one month, before transferring to the same job in Minsk.[2] Among the senior officials at the office of the Territorial Commander of the Security Police and Security Service Ostland (BdS Ostland, a.k.a. EG A), only department chiefs Dr. Rudolf Lange (Dept. IV/V Gestapo/Criminal Police) and Karl Tschierschky (Dept. III SD) came into question.[3] These men were completely familiar with their duties and stood squarely behind

---

Notes for this chapter begin on page 163.

BdS policy. Logically enough, Lange was to succeed Strauch as commander of KdS Latvia in early December, but there remained, however, a clear hierarchical distance from Jeckeln and his staff officers, who enjoyed their own legitimacy through their association with the new HSSPF. That Jeckeln would transfer to Riga with his team intact had been clear since around mid October, when Reich Commissar Ostland Hinrich Lohse – more cautious as a result of his differences of opinion with Stahlecker – failed to raise any objections vis-à-vis *Reichsführer-SS* Heinrich Himmler regarding the question of personnel. By the time Alfred Rosenberg, the Reich minister for the occupied eastern territories, had been informed and the exchange of Jeckeln's and Prützmann's staffs had been realized, October had passed.[4] In early November, Jeckeln's colleagues took up their work, while the new HSSPF Ostland himself met with Himmler, who sought to acquaint Jeckeln with his future tasks. Himmler's main concern was the destruction of the Riga ghetto, which Jeckeln was to liquidate fully. Prützmann, according to Jeckeln, had failed vis-à-vis Lohse to force the ghetto's closing, but given the upcoming deportation of Jews from the Reich, a new situation had emerged.

According to Jeckeln's courtroom testimony, or interrogations conducted outside the courtroom during his trial, Himmler, on 10, 11, or 12 November 1941, ordered Jeckeln to carry out the ghetto's liquidation, which he attributed to a "wish" on the part of Hitler. Upon assuming his new office in Riga, Jeckeln was to get in touch with Lohse and convey to him this order clearly and most emphatically, because other regional options were not available: Salaspils was being built, and the agricultural complex at Jumpravmuiža (Jungfernhof) was not up for debate. Lohse did not refuse the Führer's wish. After all, Lange had already informed him of the impending arrival of the first deportation trains to Reich Commissariat Ostland (RKO), which would be heading to Minsk (planned date of arrival 10 November) and Riga (planned date of arrival 19 November).[5] Lohse – again according to Jeckeln's testimony – gave his consent to the liquidation of the Riga ghetto in the name of the civil administration.[6] However, Lohse's about-face did not mean that he had completely lost sight of economic interests. For this reason, he asked whether the needs of the Wehrmacht – which had complained in writing over and over regarding the withdrawal of desperately needed Jewish workers – should be fully ignored as well. Displaying some skill, Lohse linked this approach with his repeated criticism of the methods used in carrying out mass murder in the RKO, criticism that – something left unspoken – was aimed at watering down orders and undermining the authority of the BdS and the HSSPF. Conversely, so as to avoid being suspected of delaying these measures by dragging his heels, Lohse had to see to it that young, local non-Jews were quickly educated as skilled workers who could then have some prospect of replacing Jewish workers.[7]

By contrast, Jeckeln, who fully embraced Himmler's order, was such a murderous anti-Semite that he criticized as too lax the way things had previously been done in Riga, where "the Jews were nourished and nurtured" – words that amounted to veiled criticism of Prützmann. Jeckeln prevailed upon his confidants to go about their work in Riga as they had done in the southern Soviet Union, i.e., to carry out unmitigated mass murder with no consideration of economic interests, because the "loss of this workforce must be accepted as the lesser evil." He would "make it ruthlessly clear" to those agencies and companies that profited from Jewish forced labor what this war was all about. That these were no empty phrases must have been clear at the very least to those listeners who had accompanied Jeckeln to Riga from Ukraine.[8]

It was above all figures such as SS First Lieutenant Herbert Degenhardt, Jeckeln's specialist for partisan and Jewish affairs, and SS Private Johannes Zingler who could point to experience in implementing this state-sponsored campaign of mass murder. While Degenhardt – who later downplayed his position as nothing more than Jeckeln's personal ordnance officer – took part in planning and supervising individual massacres, Zingler was one of the "chosen" marksmen. Degenhardt had been on Jeckeln's staff since early September, and his career had been rather ordinary. It was different with Zingler, who had once risen to the rank of an SS senior colonel, but had then been convicted of misappropriating public funds, demoted, and transferred to the "lost bunch." Instead of serving a period of probation on the front, he was allowed to join Jeckeln's staff, where the HSSPF himself personally took him under his wing. In addition to the men allotted him under his budget as HSSPF, Jeckeln had managed to bring to Riga longstanding colleagues – in part from his time in Braunschweig – who would later join the marksmen in the Rumbula Forest.[9]

In implementing his intentions, Jeckeln relied less on the Gestapo and SD personnel assigned to the SS and police forces in Riga – although he did draw on them – than on the "ordinary" *Schutzpolizei* (the German municipal police) of the territorial and regional commanders of the German Order Police as well as the Latvian police. Because a crime of such magnitude could not be carried out without a certain amount of advance work, Jeckeln first set out in search of a suitable site. He undertook several excursions into the immediate environs of Riga without success. It is to be assumed, however, that from the start Bikernieki was clearly not an option. This location had already achieved a notorious "renown" among Riga's population and could no longer be used, for reasons of secrecy. Moreover, due to the ghetto's location, a southern solution was to be preferred so as to avoid marching the Jews through the heart of Riga in the process of "resettling" them.

While on an inspection tour to Salaspils, Jeckeln discovered – just off the Riga-Daugavpils road, some 10 km (6 miles) from Riga – a patch of forest that met his requirements. Not far from the Rumbula railroad station stretched a 150-meter wide field, beyond which the forest began. The ground was sandy and slightly hilly, which would make digging easier and at the same time offer a certain amount of protection from view. The trees stood far enough apart from one another that digging pits would present no great difficulties. This place was the Letbartskii Woods, a part of the Rumbula Forest.[10] After determining the site of the mass murder operation, Jeckeln began to work out a plan of action. Given the winter temperatures and the ground frost, it was advisable to dig the execution pits in advance so as not to leave thousands of corpses simply lying in the woods. SS Second Lieutenant Ernst Hemicker, the HSSPF Ostland's construction specialist, was entrusted with this task. As a first step, he calculated how much space 25,000–28,000 corpses would occupy in the ground and then determined the depth and number of pits according to the estimated volume needed. In a second step, a group of HSSPF Ostland staff members led by SS Major Heinrich Neurath – including Hemicker, Degenhardt, SS Lieutenant Colonel Robert Esser, and ten other persons – inspected the site around 20 November. The digging of the pits began this day as well. Following Hemicker's instructions, around 300 Soviet POWs from Stalag 350 (Riga), near Salaspils, also, began shoveling sand under a guard detail of Wehrmacht soldiers. It was to Hemicker's advantage that the ground did not consist of dry quicksand, but had instead a certain consistency. Furthermore, the cold prevented the sand from giving way, so the POWs were able to dig the pits as if they had used a plumb. During digging, the SS men present openly discussed with the noncommissioned officers on duty how these measures were being taken for the murder of Riga's Jews. The next day, only Hemicker returned to the site to oversee work on the pits. The plan was to force the Jews into the pits, to have them lie down, and to shoot them on the ground, i.e., not to have them fall in from the edge of the pit. Once the pits had reached a depth of three meters, Hemicker was struck by doubts as to whether this technique could be used: How were the people to climb down into the ground without stopping to make an effort? It was crucial that the flow of victims remain steady so that the killing did not come to a standstill. Hemicker solved this problem by having ramps built, to which the Jews would be led. After around three days, the pits were finished.[11]

Jeckeln's system of mass murder, which in his eyes represented the further development of the techniques practiced in Ukraine, was conceived as follows: while still in the ghetto, the victims were to be gathered into marching blocks; figures for the size of these marching blocks varied between 500 and 1,000 people per formation. At the start of the operation, these columns, staggered over a certain interval of time, were to be sent off along the country road toward Daugavpils and led to the pits in the Rumbula Forest. The aged and infirm were to be taken to Rumbula by the police motor pool. In accordance to Jeckeln's needs, successive marching blocks would – under ideal circumstances – reach the woods at the very moment when the last people from the previous column were being murdered so as not to interrupt the shooting at the pits – a concern that reflected Jeckeln's automated, factory-oriented approach. Upon arriving in the forest, the victims had to take off their clothes at one station and hand over their valuables at another – at which point they were to be forced into the pits. In this way – according to Degenhardt – one was spared having to transport corpses. Unlike the mass shootings at Bikernieki – which had involved the use of rotating firing squads shooting at rows of victims – Jeckeln relied on the mechanization of the murder process in shooting as well. This was probably intentional, if only to prove to Himmler that the "professionalization" of such techniques of mass murder was possible, an approach that would put less of a burden on the perpetrators and at the same time rob the victims of their individuality.

In the pits themselves, there were to be only a few active marksmen, each of whom used a machine pistol set on single shot. Walking over his victims, a "shooter" could fire fifty shots and then receive a new magazine from a comrade whose sole responsibility was refilling cartridges, until a row of people on the ground had been shot. After a number of magazines, the marksman would take a break. Row after row, marching block after marching block was to be killed in this manner, in accordance with Jeckeln's minutely worked out method, until there were no longer any Jews left in the Riga ghetto.[12]

While Jeckeln worked on the overall plan and Hemicker had the pits dug, it was Degenhardt's task to coordinate the operation and to instruct the police offices and units on hand in the spirit of the HSSPF at various meetings, inasmuch as Jeckeln did not do so himself. Jeckeln had already sketched out by hand the course of this crime – he intended to carry out the massacre according to the "Kiev model" (Babi Yar) – and he worked out in detail just how much manpower had to be employed. Then he summoned Lieutenant Colonel Carl Gustav Flick, the regional commander of the Order Police in Latvia, and Major Karl Heise, commander of the Riga Schutzpolizei, and disclosed to both that they had to make their men available for the ghetto's liquidation. Jeckeln had additional conversations with the chief of the Latvian police formations, Lieutenant Colonel Roberts Osis, and BdS Ostland Stahlecker. The latter, however, expressed a certain amount of skepticism about the plan. Officially, Stahlecker was of the opinion that the deportation of the Jews to Rumbula would be difficult to arrange, and given the high ground water table, there was no chance of digging mass graves in Riga itself.[13] Jeckeln, unlike his predecessor Prützmann, was to some extent in competition with Stahlecker in the "Jewish question" and refused to accept this argument. The territorial commander of the Order Police in Ostland in turn ordered Captain Richard Rehberg, the regional commander of the *Gendarmerie* (the German rural police), to keep a part of his men at the ready for the end of November, because the ghetto was to be decommissioned.[14]

After Jeckeln had provided clarity to all of the offices under his command, additional discussions with individual police units followed. More gatherings took place at offices of the Regional Commander of the Order Police Latvia (under Flick) and the Commander of the Schutzpolizei in Riga (under Heise), where the use of the Schutzpolizei commands and Latvian police officers from the police stations was determined. In addition, it was necessary to keep at the ready a sufficient number of vehicles – trucks as well as harnessed teams of horses – from the motor pools of the Latvian police stations, the Latvian police battalions, and the Schutzpolizei so that the transport of elderly and infirm Jews could be arranged.[15]

A few days before this criminal operation, a final meeting took place in the building of the Riga Schutzpolizei with around twenty-five representatives of the individual agencies involved. Among those present were HSSPF staff members, SD officers, Order Police officers, and Latvian policemen. After Major Heise had opened the conference, Neurath and Degenhardt once again reminded those present of "the technical implementation" of the operation as a whole: "This included, e.g. the question which unit at which moment with how many men and how many vehicles at which place was to be available for transporting the Jews or cordoning off the resettlement site."[16] Since all those present had been prepared accordingly, the gathering produced "nothing new in and of itself." There was a little "talking back and forth" and hypothesizing about possible difficulties. Questions as to whether panic could spread among the victims, or whether those who were unable to march or walk could cause too much of a delay in the evacuation, dominated the conversations among these "specialists." Nobody expressed any doubt about the expediency of the measure.[17]

It was Jeckeln's wish that during the shooting only a small circle of truly emotionless SS men, primarily members of his bodyguard, be deployed in the pits; the other policemen were to assume shuttle functions or to take part as observers. Moreover, according to Jeckeln's concept of morality, participation in the killing offered the marksmen the chance to redeem themselves for previous breaches of the SS codex, as Johannes Zingler learned. Jeckeln summoned the degraded SS senior colonel to his office and disclosed to him that he "would have to take part in the executions" and "in doing so could prove himself." Jeckeln's plan for how the murder of Riga's Jews was to take place was complete; the HSSPF Ostland now had to work only on the final details, for example, increasing the number of commandos that did the actual killing.[18]

With this in mind, the day before the operation, Jeckeln disclosed to the members of his motor pool, who had gathered at HSSPF Ostland headquarters in the House of the Knighthood, that the liquidation of the ghetto was imminent. Even if he intended to use primarily his "old" men – men who had "already done" something like this "in the south" – he would like to have "additional men for the relief" of the marksmen at the pits. Jeckeln added, however, that he would not hold it against anybody personally, "if he did not report, because it was a very unpleasant thing." Allegedly, nobody volunteered. However, this does not appear to have posed a fundamental problem for the HSSPF; he subsequently assigned his motor pool to help with the evacuation of the victims from the ghetto.[19]

Elsewhere, Jeckeln had problems that he could not overcome simply by issuing orders. As the date of the ghetto clearance drew nearer – it was set for 30 November – petitions from Reich Commissar Lohse as well as those from other complainants, all of whom were fighting to preserve the workforce, accumulated to the point that Jeckeln was forced to yield with regard to workers. The security concerns raised by Jeckeln and the city's "foodstuffs problem" seemed secondary in light of the looming labor shortage. A good two weeks later, the Reich Ministry for the Occupied Eastern Territories was to take Jeckeln's standpoint and decree that no consideration for economic concerns was to be made in the future. Irrespective of that order to come, in planning this crime, Jeckeln had already conceded to spare some Jewish specialists able to work.[20]

With that, the perpetrators faced two tasks: creating space in the ghetto for the Jews arriving from the Reich and finding accommodations for the Latvian Jews who were still needed and able to work. Under the circumstances, these latter Jews could not be located outside the Moscow Suburb. Therefore, a part of the ghetto in the northeast – what became the "small ghetto" – was separated from the rest and set apart by a barbed wire fence, thus creating a barrier within the ghetto as a whole. This fence served to shield the German Jews, who would take up quarters in the large ghetto from the working Latvian Jews of the small ghetto. The place envisaged for the Latvian Jews lay exactly within Kalnu St. to the north, Lauvas St. to the east, Ludzas St. to the south, and Daugavpils St. to the west.

The people in the ghetto learned of this plan when, on 27 November, the office of the HSSPF posted notices announcing far-reaching measures. The posters stated that men between 18 and 60 who were able to work had to report at the ghetto gate on Firsa Sadovnikova St. on 29 November in order to move into the new partial ghetto. All of the other ghetto inhabitants would have to leave for an outside camp that had been designated their new place of residence; there they would be drawn on for lighter forms of labor. Each person was permitted to take 20 kg (44 lbs.) of personal belongings as hand baggage. In addition, it could be inferred from the poster that the ghetto would be cleared street by street.

These instructions immediately caused a commotion and prompted intense discussions among the ghetto's inhabitants, who of course right away understood that their families would be torn apart as a result of these measures. And who could really believe that the police had arranged lighter work for elderly people? Nonetheless, the rumor was soon circulating that the elderly were to be put to work gluing paper bags, which was indeed a relatively light job. On Friday, 28 November – as prisoners hurriedly set about erecting the barbed wire fence for the small ghetto and the Jewish Order Service (OD) began evicting families living from their homes within this new perimeter – the tension and nervousness among the Jews grew steadily. They noted that ghetto commandant Kurt Krause was inspecting the streets more closely, bringing along SS men previously unknown to them. The Jewish Council tried to restore calm and to present the founding of the small ghetto as normal, although even OD members were warning their friends: "There is something in the air."[21]

On the morning of 29 November, the men who were able to work and the most prominent members of the ghetto population appeared, full of anxiety, at the appointed gate with the specified 20 kg of baggage. There they had to line up in columns alongside the existing labor commandos and wait. At the front of the columns stood, Dr. Michail Eljaschew, dressed in a black fur coat with a blue-white ribbon stretched along his arm in order to identify him as a member of the Jewish Council. It is said he projected composure and calm on those around him. Next to him stood Chief Rabbi Mendel Zack. Although the people in the columns reported in an orderly fashion, they were not readying to deploy. Those who lived on Firsa Sadovṇikova St., such as Salomon Gerstein, the Jewish Council's statistician, looked down from their windows with a mixture of apprehension and tense anticipation at what was happening. Soon prominent Germans and Latvians showed up at the ghetto gate. Among them were members of the civil administration, such as Junker of the Order Werner Altemeyer, who was Governing Mayor Hugo Wittrock's chief of staff, and the Latvian functionaries Roberts Osis and Albert Danskop as well as, possibly, Viktor Arajs and Herbert Cukurs.[22]

The deputy OD chief, a certain Vozbutskii, murmured to Samuel Gutkin that the beginning of the end had come. A rumor spread that the Germans were waiting on orders from Berlin. Others were of the opinion that the Local Administration Command had vetoed the resettlement. After a fairly long time, Vozbutskii returned, visibly calmer. He said, expressing encouragement, the sun had begun to shine somewhat after all, not least because German foremen, among them members of the Wehrmacht as well, had arrived at the entrance to the ghetto to collect "their Jews." This change probably is to be traced back primarily to the engagement of Colonel Walter Bruns, commander of the bridge command staff in Riga, who had personally intervened with Altemeyer to stop the ghetto clearance operation. Some 30–40 Jewish forced laborers alone were needed to meet the needs of the bridge command staff, something that had been arranged by Field Administration Command Riga. Army Group North's motor pool allegedly employed 1,500 Jews as well. Bruns had learned of the upcoming liquidation and, acting on his own, had sought to prevent it, since Wehrmacht Territorial Commander Ostland Walter Braemer had fallen ill and was not in the picture.[23] Although Altemeyer tried to make it clear to the colonel that this measure involved an "order of the Führer," Bruns insisted on getting a decision from a higher authority via the High Command of the Army. In a clear misjudgment of his own authority, Altemeyer assured Bruns that he would hold off on the shootings.

After several hours of delay, the individual labor details were ultimately allowed to pass the gate and move on to their place of work, as they did everyday. The employees of the Jewish self-administration were also dismissed – at least, Bernhard Press reported that his family, like that of Dr. Rudolf Blumenfeld, was back at home that afternoon, apparently without being registered for the small ghetto. All those men who may have been considered able to work but could not prove they were employed by an "Aryan" office or business remained at the ghetto entrance's barrier. They had to be evaluated by members of the civil administration, SS officers, and the Latvian police as to whether they were at all still able to perform hard labor. Those whose physical constitution passed muster under the scrutinizing eyes of an "appraiser" were allowed – after a careful identity check – to relocate to the small ghetto. The others were refused admittance.[24]

In addition to the self-serving rescue of Jewish workers, there was another reason for civil administration officials to show up in the ghetto. The start of Jeckeln's operation posed a threat to the authority of the County Commissariat Riga City where "the reported assets belonging to the Jewish Council" were concerned. The gentlemen from the county commissariat office who had appeared in the ghetto apparently feared that these funds would elude their grasp due to the HSSPF's intervention. Therefore, they confiscated the Jewish Council's money. The amount collected – RM 39,000 and 16,622.20 rubles – was to be deposited in a special account at the Reich Credit Bank, which was to be opened only with the permission of the commissar – not the SS. Furthermore, the representatives of County Commissariat Riga City also wanted to withdraw the already reported assets of individual households – 13,000 sets of completed forms existed –starting on Monday, 1 December 1941.[25] It would not come to that, however.

According to the notes of E. Gechtman, Friedrich Brasch, the civil administration employee responsible for the ghetto, disclosed to the members of the Jewish Council that a mass shooting would take place. Because the ghetto was overfilled, a part of its inhabitants would have to be killed in order to save the others. The Jewish Council was to help with the selection of the victims and to immediately draw up "lists with the names of elderly people, ill people, and criminals and other persons" whose "continued presence in the ghetto the community leadership considered undesirable." After a short time to think it over, Dr. Blumenfeld announced the committee's decision: the request was found to be incompatible with the moral principles of those on hand; furthermore, any "criminals" were more likely to be found outside the ghetto.[26]

In the meantime, the selections at the ghetto gate continued well into the evening. During the transfer of the specialists to the small ghetto, the head of the Labor Office, Standtke, stood at the gate and paid close attention to make sure that in fact only necessary workers were relocated. He pitilessly rejected all of the others.[27] Several intellectuals, such as the journalist Lev Maxim, assumed the consequences of these measures. Seeing no other way out, he hanged himself in a shed. Others, such as the world-renowned historian Professor Simon Dubnow, repressed the events taking place around them and withdrew into their work. Dubnow attempted to observe the dreadful events from the outside as a quasi-uninvolved chronicler and to bear witness to them, without succumbing to the illusion that this technique of repression could ultimately afford him any kind of real protection. Through his work, he remained true to himself right up to the end.[28]

At day's end, the male inhabitants of the ghetto were categorized into four groups: (1) elderly people, children, and infants, who were seen only as a burden; (2) men of working age who were already too exhausted or ill to be integrated in the work process any further; (3) men of working age for whom employment was to be found and who were allowed to relocate into the small ghetto; (4) men of working age who were already working in a detail or had working papers. When the labor details returned, their ranks were checked for ability to work. Latvian policemen asked the workers who felt sick or weak. Those who spoke up were to go back to the large ghetto; for them, the workday was over. They did not yet know that this concession meant that they had been selected to die. The other Jewish forced laborers had to wait a short period and were then transferred to the newly established small ghetto.[29]

In addition to these male workers, some women were to be spared as well. It is not documented whether this was the result of a sudden initiative from on high or a rescue attempt of the Jewish Council; at any rate, new posters were to be seen in the ghetto on the afternoon of 29 November. These informed readers that tailors were direly needed in the workshops and should report immediately to the Jewish Council. Around 300 Jewish workers showed up; the tailors were joined by seamstresses and furriers as well as women who as a matter of self-preservation maintained that they had learned such a profession. These women were then transferred to the Central Prison, where a guard took them into custody with the ominous words: "You are the daughters of fortune."[30]

While the selection process was underway, Jeckeln that afternoon prepared assembled SS officers and police officers in the conference hall of the House of the Knighthood for the coming day. He delivered an emphatic speech in which he raised the annihilation of Jewry to a patriotic duty, something that in turn amounted to wartime service. At the same time, the HSSPF ordered all of his staff members who had no specific task to fulfill during the murder operation, as well as SS officers stationed in Riga, to be present at the executions as "spectators." If Jeckeln breached regulations on secrecy in doing this, it was more important to him to strengthen the group's sense of cohesiveness and to celebrate the power of community. Conversely, nobody would later be able to maintain that he knew nothing about the crime and was not a part of the group. Ironically, this was precisely what most of the participants did during postwar questioning by the prosecutor's office and the criminal police.[31]

In addition to Osis's Latvian forces and those of Police Prefect Roberts Štiglics, Gendarmerie commander Rehberg's staff, the Riga Schutzpolizei, and HSSPF staff members, Jeckeln planned to use Reich Germans from BdS Ostland and KdS Latvia, but only to a limited extent. He primarily made use of drivers from the Security Police, while ordering the other members of KdS Latvia to Rumbula as "spectators." Jeckeln clearly intended to be master of this operation and to relegate BdS Ostland and KdS Latvia to a secondary role. There was also the fact that Stahlecker was not in Riga, and that Heydrich had informed BdS Ostland during a visit that "the Reich would now be made free of Jews." According to the RSHA chief, the German Jews deported to Ostland were to be integrated into the work process. Perhaps it was due to these divergent approaches in the treatment of the Jews that the Security Police and SD, according to Jeckeln's guidelines, were to appear only on the periphery during the liquidation of the Riga ghetto, something that several of their members in postwar statements correctly assessed as a kind of power struggle between the HSSPF and the BdS.[32] Instead, Jeckeln requested additional reinforcements for guard duty from Special Purposes Company Furck from the office of the Territorial Commander of the Order Police as well as the 2nd and 3rd companies of

Reserve Police Battalion 22, which were led by Captain Alfred Henze and First Lieutenant Emil Diedrich respectively. While all of the other units were stationed in and around Riga, the 3rd company of Reserve Police Battalion 22 had to be transferred at short notice from Jelgava (Mitau) to Riga on 29 November.[33] With that, Jeckeln in the end had several hundred men at his disposal for his enterprise.

After Jeckeln's speech, final meetings took place among the units under his command, e.g. at the office of the Regional Commander of the Order Police Latvia and at Security Police headquarters, where officers handed out the operational orders for the next day. It is documented that at the distribution of orders at the Schutzpolizei command – set for 9 P.M. – Heise instructed his men along the following lines. All command members – with the exception of those on desk duty and guards at a few key sites – were to arrive at the ghetto gate at 4 A.M. to supervise the evacuation of the Jews to Rumbula Station. The issuing of orders was followed by a small meeting in Heise's office; invited were officers and noncommissioned officers of the police as well as Degenhardt from the office of the HSSPF. Here, within this smaller circle, the Schutzpolizei command learned that it and the Latvian police were responsible for forcing the Jews from their apartments, gathering them in groups, and escorting them to the railroad station. The clearance was to begin in the western part of the ghetto, with Albert Hesfehr, who knew the ghetto well, in charge of the operation. Here, during Heise's and Degenhardt's reports, the uninitiated were also informed that all the official meetings that had taken place over the last few days by no means served the propagated resettlement of Riga's Jews to another camp – and that in fact the liquidation of the ghetto would begin within the next few hours.[34]

Ice from the last snowfall still lay on the streets of the ghetto in the morning hours of 30 November. It had drizzled the day before, and the temperature clearly had been below freezing. Now a wave of warmer air pushed back the chill.[35] As ordered, the members of the Schutzpolizei and their Latvian colleagues gathered at the ghetto gate early that morning; according to postwar statements, the ratio was about 1 German to 3 Latvians. There they received from Heise, who had appeared together with Degenhardt and Krause, the order to make ruthless use of their weapons if necessary in forming the marching blocks and escorting the Jews to Rumbula. Working in mixed groups, German and Latvian policemen, supported by the OD, forced their way into the buildings of the western ghetto. Other Latvians patrolled on horseback. The Jews, startled and frightened, were given exactly half an hour to be on the street. The situation became hectic. Small children began screaming. "People wept and were full of sorrow," reported a former German policeman after the war. Others yammered. Once outside on the street, the Jews, on their own, had to form into groups, which were so large that the sentries could hardly maintain an overview of what was happening. Guards with rifles loaded stood within shouting distance left and right of the marching blocks.[36] Heise – working together with Osis, diverse SS men who can no longer be identified, and several "golden pheasants" (a derisive term for brown-uniformed Nazi officials) from County Commissariat Riga City – supervised the ghetto during the morning hours. At the ghetto gate, a commotion erupted in one of the columns. Sentries had snatched the baggage of several victims – allegedly because they had surpassed the prescribed 20 kg. Heise and Osis intervened; they of course knew that the success of the endeavor depended on deceiving these "half-starved, yammering figures" and preventing panic from ensuing.[37]

Several of the victims suspected that they would be murdered, and that relocation to a camp was not planned. They therefore hid their valuables in ghetto toilets, restrooms, and outhouses so that these could perhaps help other Jews – or so that these items would not fall automatically into the hands of their executioners.[38] Over the hours, the collection of the Jews on the street did not take place as quietly as the police officers had hoped. The first warning shots fell when some Jews who were already in formation failed to follow guards' orders quickly enough. Ultimately, it made no more sense to the clearance commando led by Hesfehr to keep up the pretense. In order to adhere to the plan, the policemen – spurred on by Krause and Degenhardt and still accompanied by the OD – forced the Jews from their apartments and into the open by using the most brutal means. Once outside, they were ordered to line up single file; they had to fall into line on Ludzas St. If somebody sought to break ranks, the guards opened fire. In their distress, several Jews tried to reach the eastern part of the ghetto. Sergeant Willich killed a boy between sixteen and eighteen years of age, whose corpse the OD had to take away. Those who were gunned down were mostly men, possibly because they knew that only they had any chance at all of hiding in the small ghetto. Corporal Otto Tuchel also distinguished himself in this way. By his own account, he saw four or five severely wounded Jews lying on a sidewalk. He rolled the men over – all of them bleeding heavily and moaning – and shot them in the base of the neck. One woman turned to a member of the civil administration and asked to be exempted from resettlement, because she had to go to the hospital. The "golden pheasant" pulled his gun, shot her, and quipped, believing he was cracking a good joke, "Already operated."

By contrast, the bulk of the victims – women and children, old men and frail people – stood in their columns, lined up close to one another, until their column received its marching orders. Elderly people who had been languishing in their apartments were forced onto the street, where Latvians crammed them into waiting buses like a "transport of livestock." Other Jews – crippled and bedridden men and women – were thrown onto trucks and stacked – in the truest meaning of the word – on top of one another and evacuated to Rumbula as a crumpled "pile of people." In the Jewish nursing home, more direct action was taken; it was "shot empty" and the corpses taken to the cemetery. At a synagogue that had been converted into a quarantine station, around twenty severely ill people wasted away on stretchers and sacks of straw. The German and Latvian police were afraid of being infected and left them there. Ultimately, the OD had to enter the building and carry these sick people on stretchers out onto the street. Heise, who was giving orders there, ordered men from the Schutzpolizei – in addition to Tuchel, the colleagues Willich, Kobiella, Max Neumann, and Alfons Karassek had since arrived on the scene – to shoot these people on the ground where they lay. Then Heise took up position behind one of the sick men and fired the first shot. Inasmuch as they were still able to understand what was happening around them, the others on the ground now realized that they were about to be murdered. Some cried. Others wanted only that the end should finally come and rolled over so that they did not have to look the policemen in the eyes. One after another, the police shot them in the base of the neck, until all had been killed.[39]

Near the ghetto gate, where a crowd of people stretching as far as the eye could see had lined up in one row after another, the guards responsible for the escort to Rumbula took over the marching blocks. Around 100 Latvian policemen with rifles marched alongside each column, with the Schutzpolizei setting the pace at the head and rear of each block. In the event of questions from third parties – one thought of uninitiated German and Latvian members of the civil administration or Wehrmacht soldiers – the escorts also had to provide an official explanation for the trek, according to which the Jews of Riga were being "resettled" to Daugavpils. Between the marching blocks, motorized patrols provided reinforcement: these were to drive back and forth as additional security, should a larger group of people attempt to flee at once. Each departing group was also followed by teams of horses and several trucks, which had been allotted to pick up all those frail and elderly people who were unable to keep up the pace. A marching block was sent off in the direction of Rumbula at every half-hour interval, with the last one leaving the Moscow Suburb around noon.

To keep from forcing the Jews through the Moscow Suburb, the march took place at the southeast end of the ghetto, where an opening in the fence served as a sluice in the direction of the Škirotava railroad station. The Jews, hounded by the guards, left the Moscow Suburb through this eye of the needle and turned south onto the arterial road toward Daugavpils. The cold and ice ensured that the tempo could not be maintained. Older family members leaned on younger relatives. Stronger individuals helped carry the weaker ones. Several people fell. Others were able to drag themselves along with difficulty. Many tried to catch their breath on the side of the road. For many, their baggage of personal belongings ceased to be of any significance to them, because they had a bleak suspicion of what was coming or because they no longer wanted to carry 20 kg through the snow and ice. They let their suitcases, which they actually had packed in the vague hope of a new settlement, slip from their hands or threw them aside. The marching blocks advanced in this manner, growing slower and slower as time went by and causing Jeckeln's schedule to waver. All those who could not keep up the pace were shot by the guards. They also opened fire on "fugitives" or persons who appeared to have left the marching block. The trucks bringing up the rear were soon fully loaded, less with frail people – as had been expected – than with the discarded suitcases. The guards collected them with the intention of appraising the property, which otherwise would have lain on the road. Those among the victims who found no place on the carts were shot and left to lie where they fell. To dispose of the bodies, a labor commando was put together in the small ghetto and ordered to load up those who had been shot as quickly as possible, to transport them to the Jewish cemetery, and to bury them there. The number of those shot in the ghetto or on the road to Rumbula increased so sharply that the commando could hardly keep up. More and more corpses were left behind for all to see, especially on Ludzas St. and on the side of the road to Rumbula. The commando of prisoners from the small ghetto shouldered at least 300 dead people and took them to the Jewish cemetery. The rest of the columns that set out toward Rumbula reached the woods – according to later statements by their guards – after around two hours of an extremely exhausting marching.[40]

There were even more policemen deployed around the actual killing site. Members of the 2nd and 3rd companies of Reserve Police Battalion 22 formed a dense cordon in the field in front of the woods in order to prevent access to unauthorized personnel and to make escape from the pits impossible. The first marching block from the ghetto arrived at 9 A.M. The Jews turned off of the road to Daugavpils and walked across the field – just as Jeckeln had done several days earlier in his search for a suitable killing site. Under a barrage of yelling and screaming on the part of their murderers, they were then herded over the field through a "tube," two lines made up of members of Special Purposes Company Furck and the Latvian police. The tube grew steadily narrower and led to a path at the edge of the woods. Once there, the Jews were forced to turn over their suitcases at one station. At the next station, the perpetrators then demanded all of the clothing on their body. Nearby, around fifteen Red Army soldiers, who had been given food and drink, were waiting to be called to fill in the pits. Under the trees, the ghetto inhabitants had to undress. Stripped down to their underwear, they were then pushed forward. If things moved too slowly, they were immediately beaten. At a third station, the last one before the pits, the guards forced the Jews to remove their valuables, watches, jewelry, rings, etc., and place them in a wooden crate. SS Major Heinrich Bruns from the HSSPF command was in charge here. From the edge of the woods, the Jews had put several hundred meters behind them until they were standing in close proximity to the pits. Here, at the latest, the guards took care that a slow and steady flow of human bodies were led down the ramps constructed by Hemicker into the pits so that the marksmen could perform their "work" without interruption.[41]

Three pits were in operation at any one time. Several of them were smaller. In each of these, Jeckeln had posted one marksman, while three "shooters" – the word used in the files and statements – worked in the larger pits. Judging from the uniforms, these were members of the Schutzpolizei and SD. They did not belong to a single unit, but had been selected by Jeckeln and, over the course of the day, plied with schnapps. The "technical procedure" of the mass shooting itself took place exactly as the HSSPF had envisioned it. Having been led into the pit, the Jews lay down on the ground in rows "like sardines." At the smaller pits, the marksman fired into the pit from above, because he could not move about freely down below. In the large pits, the murderers walked over the people or past them and fired shots into the base of their necks. The victims who followed had to lie down between or on top of the warm bodies of those who had just been murdered. Frail and elderly people and children were assisted by their relatives or stronger Jews. Many people were apathetic, others fully exhausted. Some used the rest of their remaining time to embrace their loved ones, to utter a word of affection, to make a gesture of respect. Others, amid the suffering, intoned "loud songs," expressions of faith or solace. Anybody who attempted to address one of the uniformed men around them was mercilessly beaten and pushed back into the column. All of this information comes from the statements of the perpetrators, who simultaneously confirm that Jeckeln's assessment of the victims' behavior was in principal correct. There are no documented instances of resistance. Those who tried to escape had apparently already ventured to do so in the ghetto. Otherwise, the perpetrators say they witnessed no coordinated act of self-defense at Rumbula. There was of course the natural shrinking away from the pits and instinctive reaction to flee. One member of Reserve Police Battalion 22 recalled that a child began running just before one of the pits and headed for the brush. A Latvian guard shot him in the back.

With their machine pistols set for single shot, the marksmen in the pit fired one shot after another until relieved by another colleague. At the edge of the pit, a supervising officer, usually a member of the HSSPF command staff, monitored the mechanical shooting process. He watched to be sure that marksmen progressed quickly and did not "skip" a victim in the monotonous rhythm of firing. When this was the case, one of the resting marksmen – at the supervisor's command – would walk over and shoot the person discovered to be alive.[42]

On this same day, the first deportation of 1,000 Jews from Berlin arrived in the capital of the Reich Commissariat Ostland. Although the mass killing operation in progress was primarily intended to create room in the Riga ghetto for the Jews arriving from the Reich, the Berlin Jews did not reach the ghetto buildings that had been cleared for them. In Jeckeln's eyes, Himmler's order to liquidate the Latvian Jews simultaneously gave him the means to proceed just as radically against the new arrivals; from his point of view, there was no difference between German and Latvian Jews. It remains an open question whether Jeckeln misunderstood the order or consciously used it to force the dynamic behind the annihilation of the Jews. We are inclined to believe that Jeckeln's actions in Riga constituted a repetition of events as they had unfolded in late August at Kamianets-Podilsky (Kamenets-Podolsky), the site of a massacre that accelerated the killing of Soviet Jews and did indeed bring Jeckeln the accolades that he had hoped for from his superior.

Whatever Jeckeln's motives, the fact remains that the Berlin transport did not end at Šķirotava Station, where Lange, representing the Security Police, initially expected it that morning and received the escort papers. The members of the Berlin Schutzpolizei who had accompanied the transport as guards stayed put at Šķirotava and handed over the deportees to the waiting members of KdS Latvia. The transport was then routed to a siding at Rumbula Station. In the early morning hours, the policemen in the cordon at the edge of the woods were able to discern in the distance how people were chased from railcars and wavered ever closer as they moved alongside the marching blocks on the road to Daugavpils. Here members of the Security Police and SD and Latvian police, possibly forces subordinated to Štiglics, acted as guards as well.

Otherwise, these images of horror resembled one another: "I have to say that the [Berlin] Jews were allowed to keep their baggage, but that little by little they discarded this along way due to exhaustion. During the march, there were instances when the Jews were maltreated. Jews unable to march were shot; I heard shots and saw dead people. Supervision of the transport was not very heavy; I have always wondered why nobody escaped." Having arrived at the woods, the Jews from Berlin also had to line up in the "tube" and take off their clothes, which bore the yellow Star of David, before being shot together with the Jews of Riga. After several days on the train, these people were overcome by a sense of absolute incomprehension. Several asked in confusion: "Just what are you doing with us? We were supposed to be resettled!" Right up until the end, they refused to believe that they had been deceived. Some of the guards also wondered why there were suddenly Jews among the victims who spoke "immaculate German" and apparently came from Berlin and not Riga. An SS officer forbid conversation and barked at the members of the Schutzpolizei on guard duty that they were not to converse with Jews.

Among the prisoners, one young man suddenly bellowed that he was the nephew of General Field Marshall Erhard Milch, Germany's chief of aircraft procurement and supply; there had to be some kind of mistake in his case. He was not believed at first, but it was known that Milch was a "half Jew" within the scheme of National Socialist racial doctrine. Therefore, members of the Security Police took Milch's purported nephew into custody in order to check on the matter. All of the other arrivals died in the pits of Rumbula. The message that went out from the BdS Ostland teletype office after the liquidation of the Berlin transport read something like "the Jews who arrived were subjected to special treatment without exception."[43]

This message could hardly have been received with satisfaction in the RSHA. As strange as it sounds, documents and witness statements show that on 30 November, the Security Police and SD tried to prevent the Berlin transport's liquidation. Upon closer inspection, the motives for the resistance of the Security Police in Riga, in the person of Lange, become clear.[44] With his radical procedure, HSSPF Jeckeln had trespassed on the competences of the RSHA, which at this point was to some extent opposed to the ghetto operation, and had arbitrarily interpreted Himmler's order to annihilate the Riga ghetto. According to Heinz Trühe, the former chief administrative officer at BdS Ostland, Heydrich's directives were to the effect that "the Reich would now be made free of Jews," and that those Jews deported to Riga were to be integrated into the forced labor system in an area close to the front; accordingly, they were not supposed to be killed. Lange did not want to yield to Jeckeln's instructions without a fight – especially because officials from the regional Gestapo office for Berlin who had traveled to Riga in advance of the deportation had not conveyed any such orders. Lange therefore consulted the RSHA about what to do next. Lange first turned to SS Captain Emil Finnberg, chief investigator at BdS Ostland, who had excellent ties to Heydrich, in order to inform the RSHA via the BdS transmitter about developments in Riga. All other channels of communication were de facto off limits to Lange, because they ran through the office of the HSSPF or could be controlled by it. With Finnsberg's assistance, Lange succeeded in relaying his misgivings to Berlin, whereupon the gears of administrative process were set in motion. The matter appeared to be so important that nobody in the RSHA central office wanted to make a decision on his own, but rather to make everything dependent upon Heydrich, who at the time was in Prague. Repeatedly, the channels of communication were tried, costing valuable time. At 1:30 P.M., Heydrich talked on the phone with Himmler, who noted after this conversation: "Transport of Jews from Berlin. no liquidation." By the time the annoyed Himmler made this decision at the bunker Wolf's Lair, one of Hitler's headquarters, it was already too late. All of the Berlin Jews had been murdered. The radio message reporting the killing of the Berlin Jews must have gone out just hours after Himmler's instructions were issued.[45]

The intrigues within the SS surrounding the murder of the Berlin Jews on 30 November were to lead to acrimony between Himmler and Jeckeln, but in the meantime, the shooting continued at the pits. Around noon, the SS officers who were not directly involved in the operation but had been ordered by Jeckeln to view the killing began arriving. According to Georg Michalsens, there were around 100 people on hand, who, "rather equally" distributed "among the SS, the police, and the civil administration," observed the bloody events from a hilltop. HSSPF Jeckeln insisted on personally picking up antagonist Reich Commissar Lohse at Riga Castle so they could drive out to Rumbula together.[46] Jeckeln himself is said to have gazed upon his work like "Napoleon on the commanding heights."[47]

Members of various military agencies were also in the woods, although the motivation of individual officers is unknown. Several were there out of curiosity and showed up as gapers, so to speak, in order watch the mass execution as if it were a trip to the cinema or theater. A technical sergeant managed to walk up to the pits and photograph the corpses. He was immediately confronted and his camera confiscated.[48] In the postwar Hamburg criminal investigation, it was learned that a Wehrmacht officer who was not privy to the crime had suddenly appeared with his driver and approached the pits: "A general staff officer with red cords who must have had heard the noise of the shooting from the road approached. I had the impression that this officer wanted to convince himself of what was happening in the small woods. This officer did not even reach the pit. The commander, Heise, went to meet him and yelled at him loudly … In any event, in accordance with the circumstances, Heise made it clear to the officer that he was to leave the execution site."[49]

The officer was in all probability Captain Dr. Otto Schulz-Du Bois, a combat engineer and confidant of Colonel Bruns, who had dispatched him to Rumbula. A critic of the Nazi regime, Bruns had counted on avoiding the liquidation of the ghetto. He had relied on Altemeyer's word that he would wait for a decision from a higher authority. Bruns had approached

Army Group North and the High Command of the Army with corresponding petitions. He could not have known that Jeckeln was in no way inclined to take into consideration the Wehrmacht or the civil administration in the person of Altemeyer. When Bruns learned that the massacre had begun, a development that took him by surprise, he sought to have the report confirmed. He therefore sent out two courageous officers – only the name of Schulz-Du Bois is documented – whose reconnaissance was to provide the basis of a petition that claimed such barbarity jeopardized the morale of Germany's combat soldiers. It quickly became clear to both officers that an inconceivable crime was being carried out just off the road to Daugavpils. They spent about an hour on the road to get an overview and make a "rough estimate" of the number of victims en route. From their position, however, the two were unable to report more. They therefore left the crime scene to tell Bruns what was happening. Bruns then set out for Angerburg (East Prussia) in order to address the High Command of the Army directly.[50] In the meantime, the mass murder continued unabated.

Degenhardt's task during the shooting – at least according to his own testimony – was to accelerate procedures during "tie ups." When the victims took too much time disrobing, Degenhardt went to the station supervisor and ordered him to force the groups forward more quickly. What mattered for Jeckeln was "primarily the continual flow, not … that as many valuable articles of clothing as possible were saved." Only if a marching block from the ghetto failed to arrive did Degenhardt's industriousness fail, because in such moments, he could "of course do nothing."[51] Several of the perpetrators took breaks in between, as if it were a usual workday. Drivers from the Schutzpolizei filled up the trucks at their quarters, had their meals, and told their colleagues who had remained behind about the shooting.[52] Their superior was both active at the clearing of the ghetto and present in the woods. Heise admitted to shooting at least two severely wounded victims at the pits with a "mercy shot." One was a young woman, around twenty, who already had corpses on top of her. Her upper body was still visible, but she was no longer able to speak. Blood, "which apparently came from a shot to the back of the neck," was running out of her mouth. She is supposed to have waved Heise over; he then fired another shot to her head, "which led to immediate death." A few hours later, he killed a severely wounded man, around thirty years of age, who sought "to free himself from under the corpses lying on top of him." Heise added, "I also gave this man a well-aimed mercy shot to the head, after which his body jerked, stretched, and was apparently also dead. At this time, 4 SS marksmen stood on top of the corpses in the pit and kept shooting at the people who had been forced into the pit."[53]

In the meantime, the shooting was growing more hectic. Evening was approaching, and the murderers had clearly fallen behind schedule. However, the shooting could not be stopped and put off until the next day. At the very least, the marching blocks that had already reached Rumbula could no longer leave the area for reasons of secrecy. In this increasingly hectic situation, the tempo of shooting was quickened, and the marksmen urged to hurry. They shot more hastily and less precisely; consequently, the supervisors themselves were increasingly forced to deliver "mercy shots," as Heise had done. While standing at the edge of one pit, Heise was hit by a stray bullet that destroyed his left eye. He was treated provisionally by SS men who rushed to his aide and was then led away. For reasons of secrecy, the blinding of his left eye was glorified in his personnel record as a heroic act; in the official version, he had received this injury in a battle against partisans. Subsequently, Flick, the regional commander of the Order Police, ordered that the command of the Schutzpolizei at Rumbula be turned over to Rehberg, the regional commander of the Gendarmerie.[54]

In the evening, it began to snow heavily. Originally, Jeckeln had intended to carry out the liquidation of the Riga ghetto without interruption over a number of days. However, this plan was foiled by the deteriorating weather, difficulties with various desks within the civil administration regarding Jewish property, and not least of all the dispute within the SS and police apparatus unleashed by the Berlin transport. And if that was not enough, Jeckeln was forced to learn that evening that his carefully chosen legend of the "resettlement" of the Riga Jews to another location had not lasted twenty-four hours. The very night of the massacre, British and Soviet radio reported the mass shooting. The graves in Rumbula were about two-thirds full when the order was given to end the operation. The pits were then filled in with earth. The Jews assembled in marching blocks within the ghetto had already been instructed to disband around noon and told to return home. Greater difficulties were experienced in carting off the articles of clothing, which by that point in the evening were covered with a layer of snow. Together with the victims' baggage, these were forwarded in several batches to the market halls of Riga, where they were dried, sorted, and stored. What remained behind were the murdered corpses of around 14,000 Jews on this, the first day of the operation to liquidate the Riga ghetto.[55]

By this point, Himmler had also learned that the liquidation of the Berlin transport had been carried out despite his orders to the contrary, which had arrived too late. The next day, on 1 December, a clearly annoyed Reichsführer-SS (RFSS) had the following message sent to Jeckeln: "The Jews resettled to the territory Ostland are to be treated only according to guidelines issued by me or by the Reich Security Main Office on my behalf. I will punish unauthorized actions, violations. Sig. H. Himmler."[56] For Jeckeln, this could mean only that Himmler had taken the position of the RSHA – i.e., that of Lange in Riga – and had ordered a clear delineation of authority, by which Jeckeln was responsible for Latvian Jews, the RSHA for German Jews.[57] Furthermore, the HSSPF Ostland was summoned to report on the matter to Himmler on 4 December. Reports that Jeckeln, acting on his own authority, had liquidated a transport of German Jews slated for use as workers quickly circulated all the way to Kiev, where the staff of the previous HSSPF Ostland, Prützmann, discussed the "news" from Riga.[58]

Jeckeln was also in for unveiled criticism of his actions from other quarters. Ministerial Director Theodor Fründt, the chief of political affairs within the RKO, complained to Jeckeln on 3 December that "Jewish specialists had been removed from the armaments works and repair shops as a result of liquidation"; these were at the moment "not to be replaced." It is to be concluded that the man filing the complaint considered the establishment of the small ghetto to be but a half-hearted measure, and that the HSSPF was accused of murdering too many Jews able to work on 30 November despite the needs of local companies. Unlike the previous dispute with the civil administration, this complaint must have given Jeckeln pause for thought, because Fründt was arguing less on behalf of his own agency than as the mouthpiece of the office of the Wehrmacht Territorial Commander Ostland. The men in uniform sought to align themselves with the Reich Commissariat in this matter, and Fründt used the opportunity to articulate their demands vis-à-vis the HSSPF with confidence: "I most emphatically request that the liquidation of Jews who are employed in the Wehrmacht's armaments works and repair shops and are not at present to be replaced by locals be prevented. An understanding on who belongs to the irreplaceable Jewish workforce is to be reached with the county commissars (Dept. Social Administration). The accelerated schooling of suitable, new local talent as specialists is to be ensured. The same applies to Jewish specialists in enterprises that do not directly serve the Wehrmacht's purposes, but have to perform important tasks within the framework of the wartime economy."[59]

In addition to the complaint that desperately needed workers were being unnecessarily removed from the workplace, the civil administration – meaning here Governing Mayor Hugo Wittrock and Mayor Dr. Hans Windgassen on behalf of County Commissariat Riga City and Dr. Willy Neuendorff on behalf of General Commissariat Latvia – filed repeated complaints over the next few days, stating that the seizure of Jewish valuables in the ghetto was in no way the task of the SS, which "had secured certain valuable objects." This was to take place only on orders from the county commissar in Riga.[60] In just a few weeks at his new posting, Jeckeln, as a consequence of his ambitions in the "Jewish question," had quarreled with every decision-making authority in Riga, be it the civil administration, the Wehrmacht, or even parts of the police apparatus. He could survive individual conflicts without harm to his personal standing. However, the operation on 30 November had bundled complaints within a very short span of time. Jeckeln was forced to show some deference to his many adversaries, which could not help but undermine his position in the field of "Jewish policy."

On 4 December, Jeckeln met Himmler in Lötzen and reported on the first phase of the Riga ghetto liquidation. The RFSS had noted in his talking points for the meeting with his representative in Ostland: "Jewish question" and "economic enterprises."[61] Despite the mechanical methods of killing Jeckeln had developed, Himmler was dissatisfied with the technical implementation of the operation, less because of the events in Riga than owing to considerations of principle on the part of the RFSS. Himmler told Jeckeln: "shooting is too complicated an operation ... For shooting, he [Himmler] said, one needs people who can shoot, and ... this affects people poorly, therefore Himmler said further, it would be best to liquidate the people by using gassing vehicles, which had been prepared in Germany according to his instructions, and that by using these gassing vehicles the troubles connected with shooting would fall to the wayside."[62] During this private conversation, Himmler was probably unsparing in his criticism of Jeckeln for disregarding his order not to murder the Jews from Berlin. Whether the conflict between BdS Ostland and HSSPF Ostland was a topic at this meeting is not known. What stands out here, however, is that this was exactly the moment – 3 December – when Lange was appointed chief of KdS Latvia. To that extent, it seems possible that Lange's actions on 30 November facilitated his appointment. At the very least, it brought him recognition from Himmler and Heydrich. Furthermore, after the conflict over the Berlin transport, cooperation flourished between the HSSPF Ostland and KdS Latvia, whose personnel were then drawn on for subsequent operations. This could only happen, in our view, because Himmler had in no uncertain terms put Jeckeln in his place at this December meeting.

Jeckeln, on the other hand, had an ally above even Himmler, and the views of this man were identical with those of the HSSPF Ostland: Hitler, however, avoided stating his instructions too clearly even in a small circle. The German dictator may have delivered another monologue on Jewry in the night of 1 December, during which he indulged in all the usual anti-Semitic turns of phrase,[63] but this does not necessarily have to be seen as thematically connected or in response to the Rumbula operation. Hitler was by contrast less guarded when Admiral Wilhelm Canaris, the chief of the Abwehr (German military intelligence), alarmed by Bruns's complaints, showed up at Führer Headquarters to discuss what had happened in Riga. Adolf Eichmann, the Jewish affairs desk officer in the RSHA, had already noted in a letter unrelated to the killing in Riga that individual agencies or officers within the Wehrmacht were trying to intervene on behalf of Jews "in the run-up to the evacuation transports in a conspicuous manner," the

Abwehr standing out in particular in this respect. This had led to increased tensions between the Abwehr and the RSHA, which were competing intelligence services.[64] At any rate, Gerald Fleming has shown that the mass shooting in Rumbula led to a discussion between Canaris and Hitler, in which Hitler is to have taken a clear position with the following words: "You're going to go soft, sir! I have to do it, for after me nobody else will do it!"[65]

The effort made by Bruns and Canaris appears to have done absolutely nothing but prompt the *spiritus rector* of this campaign of mass killing to reveal himself. And Jeckeln probably quickly recognized that it was not the radical nature of his actions but the disregard for the chain of command, the act of leaving Himmler behind, that had created difficulties for him and weakened his position. Bruns, as it happened, quickly learned that the mass murder would go on without interruption. Upon returning to Riga from Angerburg, Bruns called on Altemeyer, the "minder for the governing mayor of the city," to reproach him for breaking his word; Wittrock's chief of staff, after all, had agreed to wait for explicit instructions from on high. Now, several days after that discussion, the two adversaries met again. During this encounter, Altemeyer confirmed that he had since received said instructions by radio. The gist of them ran: "Such mass shootings must be less conspicuous in the future."[66]

In the interim, German officials used the days after the first murder operation in Rumbula to check the identity and stated professions of the women held in the main prison. One by one, the incarcerated women had to enter a room with a door to the left and a door to the right. In the middle of the room sat two office clerks behind a table, one of whom tersely asked: "Are you a tailor and what is your specialty?" Those unable to provide a satisfactory answer were directed to the left, where the women gradually began to accumulate. These prisoners were transferred back to the large ghetto, the equivalent of a death sentence, while the others remained in prison to face an uncertain future. Sonja Bilder later recalled that Cukurs took part in the selection process in a highly compromising way. He arbitrarily whipped the women standing closest to him and announced who was to leave the prison. According to Bilder, around 150 women were sorted out by Cukurs. In exchange for the female prisoners who had been cast out, guards brought in new women whose usefulness as workers had only since come to light; these, too, were therefore spared being taken away to Rumbula. In all, some 300 women survived in prison.[67] Back in the ghetto, Tuchel also went about his business. The Jewish Council had sent to him a representative – an OD man by the name of Berel – in order to bring several selected women and children to safety no matter what before the next operation. Tuchel agreed, and around 100 people were separated from the rest and brought to a small building across from the small ghetto. In return, Tuchel received from Berel various pieces of jewelry and precious stones.[68]

The various disputes between the HSSPF, the Wehrmacht, and the civil administration hindered the continuation of the operation for several days. The German Schutzpolizei and the Latvian police secured the premises of the western part of the ghetto, which had already been cleared. They were to make it inaccessible to the occupants of the eastern ghetto so as to protect the apartments of those who had been murdered from "plundering." Similarly, they were to prevent anybody from hiding in the western ghetto. For that reason, a commando of Jewish workers was forced to erect a provisional fence along Daugavpils St. between the emptied and the inhabited streets. Other prisoners were forced to gather the corpses found in the buildings, to take them to the Jewish cemetery, and to bury them in shallow graves. Hesfehr and Tuchel had seen to it that their Jewish informant, the shady figure by the name of Aismann, also came into play, probably in order to secure objects of value for his employers. Sadovņikova St., close to the ghetto, was a restricted area. Here the perpetrators – exploiting Jewish labor – collected the victims' valuables and furnishings, over which the finance administration of County Commissariat Riga City had made such ado. The police wanted nothing more to be said about its role: Everything was sorted in good order and made available to be taken away.[69]

On 7 December, Jeckeln gave the order to continue the clearance of the ghetto despite adverse weather conditions predicted for the next day. At a short meeting at Schutzpolizei headquarters, it was made clear to the officers on hand that there would be no modifications to the strategy in the eastern ghetto. Everything was to proceed as before. In contrast to the annihilation of the western ghetto on 30 November, this time Lange's Security Police were to be used for the "emptying" of the ghetto – probably a direct consequence of Himmler's criticism of Jeckeln. Lange in turn ordered Arajs to keep his men at the ready. These were to be used primarily for cordoning off the pits at Rumbula. Instead of the injured Heise, the leadership of the Schutzpolizei, and with that the actual process of taking people from the ghetto, was now the responsibility of Rehberg, the regional commander of the Gendarmerie, who was assisted by the "experienced" Precinct-Lieutenant Friedrich Jahnke. Later, some members of the Arajs commando had to be sent to relieve the Schutzpolizei in the selection process in the ghetto.[70]

When the German Schutzpolizei and their Latvian colleagues entered the ghetto on 8 December, probably nobody among the inhabitants still believed in the ostensible resettlement, the "transfer" to another location or a factory outside Riga. There was no reason for them to cooperate. The Jews no longer followed orders to form marching blocks or did so only under enormous pressure. They barricaded themselves in their apartments, sought out hiding places, or dared to flee. The clearance commandos proceeded in correspondingly brutal fashion. As soon as they sensed any indication of resistance, they promptly opened fire. According to Jacob Nieburg, Tuchel and Neumann summoned the more prosperous Jews to the German guards' headquarters and suggested that rescue was possible. They would only have to turn over their money, jewelry, watches, etc., and they would be under the protection of the two policemen. Nonetheless, all those who accepted this offer were shot shortly thereafter at Rumbula.

The order to take away the patients in the Linas Hazedek Hospital on the corner of Ludzas and Daugavpils streets was issued in the early morning hours. Several trucks with civil service workers had been summoned to the ghetto. For all of the others who were unable to be transported, according to Rehberg, the "issue" had "to be regulated" on the spot. For reasons of expediency, these people were shot in their apartments or on the street, as they would have slowed down the tempo of the columns plodding through the snowstorm. The men confined to the small ghetto could see their companions in adversity falling dead on the snow-covered Ludzas St., while the guards forced the hastily assembled marching columns from the eastern part of the ghetto. Alongside the elderly and frail ghetto inhabitants lay children whose skulls had been smashed with rifle butts. A mother, her dead infant in her arms, was seen lying on the snow. Even if it did not come to an uprising, the ghetto inhabitants delayed the course of the operation in such a way that the Schutzpolizei was unable to stick to the "Jeckeln schedule." As a consequence, smaller units of the Arajs Commando led by Cukurs were sent into the ghetto to force the evacuation. These proceeded with no mercy whatsoever. As a result, the number of those shot in the ghetto on 8 December was several times higher than on the first day of the clearance operation. On this day alone, around 900 corpses were taken to the Jewish cemetery by the Jewish labor commandos, while scores of corpses were left lying in their apartments.[71]

Aside from the delays that arose during the emptying of the houses in the eastern part of the ghetto, the course of the crime corresponded to the scheme of things on 30 November. The Jews of the eastern part of the ghetto were forced through a hole in the fence onto the road to Daugavpils and from there over the clearing and into the forest of Rumbula. A slight modification took place at the clothing station, where young Jewish women instead of perpetrators had to sort and stack clothes. Once again, curious members of the SS and police, members of the civil administration, and soldiers arrived on the scene to watch this large-scale killing operation.[72]

Among the participants in the crime, Rehberg depicted the operation rather precisely and exhaustively despite his personal involvement:

The head of the procession had to move in the direction of the pit. A breakdown by sex or family was not carried out; there were men, women, and children. The head of each procession had to undress completely near the clothing station I pointed out. The Jews had to put their clothes down where they stood. Several selected younger Jewish women had to pick up the clothing, arrange it, and stack it in a pile. The undressed people then had to enter the pit. Two officers of the Schutzpolizei with machine pistols stood in the pit. The Jews had to kneel in the pit and were then killed with a single shot to the back of the neck. Those who followed were then forced to lie down alive on top of those who had been shot and were also killed with a single shot. The shooting, which was fired in single rounds, lasted continuously; it was an uninterrupted tak, tak, tak. The Jews' praying and singing lasted until [they descended] into the pit. It was distressing to see how calmly these people went to their deaths. The time between undressing and shooting was only about 5 minutes for individual persons. But I have to say that the people had to go to their deaths in the winter cold in a naked state. For me, it was especially stirring when mothers had to go into the pit with their children. It happened that mothers still had small children or infants in their arms. These infants and small children were shot separately in the arms of their mothers and then torn from the arms of the mother. Only then was the mother delivered [of her suffering] by death. I still remember one incident when a Jewish woman approached me and begged for her life. It was on the access road (foot path) in the woods; the woman was still clothed. She offered me a golden watch in order to buy her life. I had to explain to the woman that I had no means of saving her life. I took the golden watch and laid it down at the collection point near the clothing station… I recall yet another incident when a mother with her grown son asked for mercy. She explained loudly [that] he was a doctor after all and could help all of us. He himself just waved her off and said to his mother, "Stop it!" He then ran toward the pit, ran around it, and was finally shot.[73]

According to Rehberg, several Latvians – a trader with his wife who had to deliver goods to the ghetto and a coachman who had to transport the victims' baggage – got mixed up among the Jews and were shot.[74] Jeckeln himself was at the site several times and checked on the shooting, primarily keeping an eye on the pit where Zingler steadily shot all those brought to him. Jeckeln could depend on the "shooters" from his Braunschweig clique, among them SS Corporal Will Wedekind, SS Sergeant Johannes Lüschen, and SS First Lieutenant Herrmann Krüger.[75] They were assisted by members of KdS Latvia who had also entered the pits and by Latvian police, which can only mean members of the Arajs Commando. The marksmen were rotated out more frequently, because extremely drunk "shooters" were over time no longer able to carry out their bloody handiwork.[76]

In contrast to the first mass shooting of the ghetto liquidation on 30 November, a few people managed to escape the fate in store for them during the operation on 8 December. Matis Lutrinsch and his wife belonged to one of the first columns forced out of the ghetto. In the weeks and months before, he had worked as a mechanic in the motor pool of the Latvian auxiliary security police until its Jewish forced labor unit was disbanded due to the general liquidation order. Upon arriving in Rumbula, Lutrinsch recognized in the light of dawn vehicles that he had repaired and serviced and saw that they were loaded with articles of clothing. "I screwed up my courage and ran to this car and asked permission to get into the car and hide beneath the clothing." Amazingly, the guards took the risk and hid Lutrinsch and his wife. Their desire to have a mechanic was greater than their fear of being punished for dereliction of duty.[77]

Ella Medalje, one of the "seamstresses" sent back to the ghetto, worked in the hospital with her sister. Both were forced onto Ludzas St. only after the evacuation of the patients and were thus among the last to leave the ghetto. Before them, an endless column of people marched toward Rumbula. The snowfall had grown heavier, and evening was approaching. At the clothing station, they saw a young woman and the physician Heidenreich attempt to hide under the stacks of clothes. Both were discovered and beaten all the way to the pit by members of the Arajs Commando. Ella Medalje noticed Arajs himself among his men. She managed to push her way forward to him and threw herself on the ground, saying she was not a Jew. Arajs waved her off and said, "There are only Jews here. Today, Jewish blood must flow." In the meantime, her sister – who bore the name Sara Gutmann – had already been separated from her and shoved forward toward the pits. Medalje did not give up and appealed to an SS officer. He inquired how she, as a non-Jew, had come to Rumbula at all, to which she replied she was married to a Jew. She was allowed to step aside and get dressed again. After a period of waiting, Cukurs took her and three other women whose "racial pedigree" also seemed to be unresolved to HSSPF headquarters.[78]

Frida Michelson was collected together with a large group of women and children on ice-covered Kalnu St., where they were ordered to leave their bundles on the ground, because these would only hamper evacuation. They then set off double time, out of the ghetto and onto the road toward Daugavpils. Women who fell were simply trampled. In the woods, "not far from the railroad station Rumbula," Michelson noticed other uniformed persons, who took from them – as from the thousands before them – all of their valuables and articles of clothing after the women had reached the edge of the woods. Still dressed in only a robe, Michelson exploited a brief moment of inattentiveness on the part of the guards at the collection point and fell on the ground with her face in the snow. "I noticed then that the other candidates for death were throwing their footwear on me. Thus a hill made up of the footwear of those condemned to death formed above me, and I managed to remain lying under this hill until nightfall."[79] These are the reports of the people who were taken away to Rumbula on

8 December and survived the bloodbath by courage and luck. There are no other documented cases of rescue.

The greater part of the OD was also murdered at the end of the operation.[80] As is to be discerned from Rehberg's statement, the perpetrators harbored a premeditated desire to humiliate this group of victims one more time before putting them to death, to torture them for their own pleasure. They therefore dispensed with the mechanical killing:

> At the end of the operation, something else especially horrible was carried out. The Jewish camp police, which had driven their own companions in adversity into the woods and in doing so had hoped to save their own lives, was forced, after the shooting of the victims, to report to the clearing I pointed out at the edge of the woods. Led by an SS man, the camp police had to perform punitive drills in the clearing. The accompanying Latvians formed a path through which the Jewish police had "to run the gauntlet" at certain intervals. The Latvians vigorously beat the Jews with sticks and other implements so that the pieces just flew. Bits were beaten out of their heads, which then flew through the area in tatters. The "running of the gauntlet" was carried out right up to the pit; there the Jewish camp police was shot as well. Between the drills and the running the gauntlet, these persons also had to undress completely. Their clothing was also taken to the stacks of clothes. Here I have to slip in the fact that the female Jews who had put the clothes in order up to then had already been shot. After the shooting of the camp police, two female Jews were brought up to the pit by an SS man and an officer from the Schutzpolizei. The female Jews were surely seized after the ghetto Jews in Riga had been taken away. According to the whispering in Kaiserwald [sic], one Jewish woman must have been previously employed in the office of Jeckeln's staff. As a special "concession," it was granted to both of these Jewish women that they would be led into the pit clothed and shot.[81]

After the shooting of the OD men, there were no more Jews from the Riga ghetto to murder. Whether young or old, man or woman, erudite or day laborer, all of those who had been herded to Rumbula were dead: so many prominent names, so many more unknown people about whose lives posterity will never know anything.[82] At the end of the operation, schnapps was poured for the "shooters" as a reward; then the men were sent back to their quarters. Now it was necessary to camouflage the execution site and cover up the tracks. Again, Soviet POWs had to report. They sprinkled chlorinated lime atop the corpses and then filled in the mass graves with sand. Genuine deception, however, was impossible. A short time later, it was learned that the earth had churned and that "individual body parts [had] appeared."[83]

With the liquidation of most of the OD, the clearance operation was almost over. As a last step, it was necessary for Jeckeln to have the vacated buildings of the large ghetto combed and to order that the inmates in the small ghetto be examined for their ability to work. On the morning of 9 December, the German Schutzpolizei entered the Moscow Suburb once again to search the apartments, cellars, and attics for hide-outs or "bunkers." If they caught a Jew during the "mopping up," there were only two reactions: either they shot the victim on the spot, or they led him or her to a collection point on the street. There those who had been driven together were shoved forward to the Jewish cemetery, where they were then killed. Among the victims were Dr. Neumann's family of four, which had been able to hide until this part of the operation, as well as Dr. Friedmann's wife and child. As a member of the corpse commando, Dr. Friedmann himself was forced to bury his own family shortly after it was murdered.

While the large ghetto was being searched, the labor commandos from the small ghetto, which had been prevented from leaving for work on this day, had to report. Once again, a new inspection was held, one directed at those allegedly unable to work. The commission consisted of officials from the county commissar's administration, members of KdS Latvia, and the corresponding auxiliaries. From among the labor details, mostly older men considered expendable had to step out of line. As with the houses of

Figure 5.1. Friedrich Jeckeln in field uniform. September 1944. Courtesy of Latvijas Valsts Kinofotofonodokumentu arhīvs.

the large ghetto, the dwellings in the small ghetto were searched for hiding places. Here Cukurs and Danskop of the Latvian ghetto guards are said to have been especially active, while Tuchel and his men rampaged through the large ghetto. All those who were discovered, along with those workers who had been singled out as expendable, were taken away to the cemetery and murdered. At least 200 people were shot there alone. Others, such as the women and children from the "safe house" set up by Tuchel, were taken outside the ghetto. Then there are the undocumented number of those who were murdered in the apartments and hideouts of the vacated large ghetto. According to Max Kaufmann, around 500 people lost their lives in the ghetto on this last day of the operation.[84] At exactly 12 P.M. on 9 December, the liquidation of the large Riga ghetto was considered completed, and SS Captain Leonhardt Jäger announced to the survivors that they were lucky, for the operation was now over.[85] Several days after the end of the "clearance work," the Central Prison transferred the women it held back to the Moscow Suburb. Unlike their male counterparts, no common space had been foreseen for them in the small ghetto. Instead, their billeting took place in the "women's ghetto" – a few buildings on the corner of Ludzas and Katoļu streets within the small ghetto[86] – which could be understood as a belated and rudimentary realization of Stahlecker's idea of a "reservation strategy," by which Jewish men and women were to be separated from one another. According to a report filed by Ek 2, 27,800 people had been murdered "by means of a large-scale operation ordered and led by the higher SS and police leader" so as to make room in the Riga ghetto for the transports arriving "from the Reich in short intervals."[87]

Meanwhile, survivor Ella Medalje managed to deceive her tormentors during her interrogation at HSSPF headquarters, where Jeckeln himself was present and posed questions. Two of the other women were exposed and shot a short time later. The last two women, Medalje included, were released for the time being. Trine Harmane, a Latvian friend from Medalje's hometown of Tukums (Tuckum), interceded on behalf of Medalje and claimed under oath to be related to her. On the basis of this statement, Medalje was given a new biography, which allowed her to go on living in Riga.[88] Frida Michelson remained under the pile of shoes until nightfall. She crawled out from under it and made her way to Rumbula Station, where she hid near a farm. From there, she managed to make contact with friends who hid her until the end of the war.[89] As for Matis Lutrinsch and his wife, they were both taken to the Arajs Commando's headquarters and put to work there. When the Arajs Commando was later transferred to the building of the War Academy on Krischjan Baron St., the Lutrinsch couple was allowed to move with it as well. After some time there, Matis Lutrinsch's wife was "taken away." He never learned exactly what fate befell her.[90]

After the Jewish Council had been murdered in Rumbula, a new leadership had to be found to take orders from the German authorities and to represent the interests of the Latvian Jews in the future ghetto as a whole vis-à-vis the German Jews, who would be in the majority. Max Wandt was entrusted with this dangerous task; he was assisted by A. Nathan and Max Wachtel and some of the other remaining OD men. In the women's ghetto, several of the inmates were designated "policewomen" and took orders from Naum Goldberg. In these days, Mendel Kassel, the head of the labor service, was to function as a liaison between the "Jews in the small ghetto and the Germans."[91]

With the liquidation of the Riga ghetto, the last large massacre of Latvian Jews had been carried out. HSSPF Ostland Jeckeln passed on the final balance of the mass murder operation he had organized to Himmler in person, who received the facts with satisfaction.[92] But the event continued to make its effects felt and – relatively shortly after the 4 December meeting – was to lead yet again to a difference of opinion between Himmler and Jeckeln. This time, however, the dispute revolved not around disregarded orders or economic interests, but around leadership issues within the SS.

On 12 December, Himmler issued a basic order that was also to be understood as his commentary on the Riga massacre. He started out by confirming the general order of annihilation, according to which every source of resistance in the "territories entrusted to us" behind the front was to be eliminated and all enemies of the German people subjected to the "death sentence they deserved" in the "severest form." At the same time, Himmler exhorted all of his higher officers and commanders "to take personal care that none of our men who have to fulfill this difficult duty ever became brutal or suffer damage to their psyche or character." Rather, superiors had to assume the individual burdens, the pangs of conscience of their subordinates, to give them leave punctually, and to distract the community of perpetrators after such a difficult task by means of a "comradely get-together." At the same time, Himmler expressly forbade that the implementation of these orders and duties, which were purportedly essential to the life of the German people, later degenerate to bar-room table talk. For Himmler, the "final solution" was far too important a mission for his men to discuss "the facts and the numbers associated with them" in inappropriate terms.[93]

Based on the documentation available, it can be noted that Jeckeln probably viewed these pronouncements with a certain degree of skepticism – especially after the dispute surrounding the liquidation of the Berlin transport. Under his concept of morality, the men who had participated in such operations were by all means to be decorated openly and in full view of the national community. The "shooters" also thought nothing of the exaggerated secrecy. While conversing with members of the Wehrmacht just before the Riga massacre, they boasted of shooting untold thousands in Ukraine. Zingler in particular was able to bask in Jeckeln's goodwill; the HSSPF Ostland promoted Zingler to SS sergeant and recommended him for the Wartime Service Cross. Jeckeln regretted that he had been unable to give Zingler a medal for courage immediately. In Berlin, SS and Police Court III caught wind of this. Its members had imagined something altogether different when Zingler was transferred to the "lost bunch" for "probation." The SS judges responsible were not about to let this exceptional treatment stand, although SS Captain Hans Zentgraf, the legal affairs specialist on Jeckeln's staff, explained to them during a visit to Riga in late December 1941 that Zingler's performance was to be greatly appreciated on account of his "especially frequent enlistment in operations against Jews."

Himmler then intervened in the process and inquired via SS Lieutenant Colonel Horst Bender, the supreme SS and police judge on the personal staff of the RFSS, whether this was really the case. Jeckeln confronted the criticism by going on the offensive and used the "inquiry" as an "occasion" to take a "position on this issue." His argument ran that Zingler's actions constituted "an exceptionally harsh probationary test." He wrote: "I deployed Z. in the known operations against alien folkdom, and Z., on my orders, participated quite exceptionally in [producing] the numbers that are also known to the Reichsführer-SS. He performed this difficult and harsh duty with absolute calm and in the conviction of its necessity and remained resolute in doing so. With this, he took upon himself a heavy psychological burden and thus showed that he had earned a pardon for his one-time misdeed." Himmler initially refused to give in, deciding that "Zingler's activity up to this point" could "not be considered probation." But Jeckeln apparently also insisted on his point of view. In any event, Bender learned months later that Zingler was still parading about as a sergeant of the Waffen-SS. Later Bender was filled in by Himmler: the RFSS had reached an understanding with the HSSPF and authorized Jeckeln to use his own authority to promote Zingler to sergeant on probation.[94] Jeckeln seemed to love nothing more than showing all those in the know that even a fallen SS senior colonel could be rehabilitated by serving in the pits.

The internal SS quarrels aside, just before Christmas 1941, this act of mass murder reverberated through the "normal" administrative process in a report by SS and Police Leader Latvia Walther Schröder. Schröder for the most part had his eye on the reaction of the Latvian population, which had of course learned of this crime. According to this report, the main concern of the people of Riga – for whom the war appeared to be beyond the Latvian borders and thus played a subordinate role in everyday life – was the "return of orderly economic relations and productive reconstruction work," although the transfer of part of the ghetto site back to the state for use as living space played a significant role. More concretely, Schröder reported: "In Riga, the mass shooting of the Jews housed up to now in the ghetto is discussed in general. The greater part of the population of Riga speaks of it with gratification and hopes for a complete elimination of the Jews and thus the freeing up of the ghetto for residential purposes."[95] If the motivation for the "approval" on the part of the people of Riga regarding the mass murder truly lay in an expected improvement of their own housing-space situation, then they were quickly forced to realize that they had been deceiving themselves. The motive behind clearing the ghetto lay squarely in the use of the housing space in the Moscow Suburb for another purpose. The aim was to create additional space not for the Latvians but for the German Jews who were to be deported to the east. The cleared streets waited on the arrival "of ca. 25,000 Jews," who no longer had to be diverted to the camp at Jumpravmuiža (Jungfernhof) near Riga. Accordingly, Lange, as the head of KdS Latvia, was able to report to Berlin that "everything [was] ready in Riga" for the "reception of the transports of Jews from the Reich."[96]

Notes

1. Jeckeln and his staff were responsible for the massacre of Jews at Kam'ianets'-Podil's'kyi (Kamenets-Podolskii, with 23,600 victims) as well as those at Berdychiv (Berdichev, circa 18,000 victims) and Dnipropetrovs'k (Dniepropetrovsk, circa 11,000 victims). Furthermore, Jecklen played a significant role in the mass murders at Starokonstiantyniv (Starokonstantinov), Kremenchuk (Kremenchug), Kryvyi Rih (Krivoi Rog), and other Ukrainian towns where the victims numbered in the thousands. Likewise, he was bound to have had a key position in the largest mass shooting, which took place in the Babi Yar ravine in Kiev at the end of September 1941 (33,771 Jews). The exact extent of responsibility of Einsatzgruppe C's command staff, Sonderkommando 4a, the higher police and SS leader, and the police battalions (independent of the Wehrmacht's appalling role) has yet to be resolved clearly, BA Ludwigsburg, 204 AR-Z 13/60, Bd. 4; 2 Js 269/65, Einstellungsverfügung der Staw. Kiel gegen Herbert Degenhardt u. a., 28 July 1971; Schwurgericht Hamburg, (50) Ks 9/72, Urteil gegen Jahnke u.a., 23 February 1973, 53–54. See also: Richard Breitman, "Friedrich Jeckeln," in *Die SS*, ed. Ronald Smelser and Enrico Syring, 269–271, idem, *Der Architekt der "Endlösung"*, 279–282, Dieter Pohl, "Schauplatz Ukraine: Der Massenmord an den Juden im Militärverwaltungsgebiet und im Reichskommissariat 1941–1943," in *Ausbeutung, Vernichtung, Öffentlichkeit*, ed. Norbert Frei, Sybille Steinbacher, and Bernd C. Wagner, 139–147. On Kam'ianets'-Podil's'kyi, there exists only one essay that attempts to discuss this mass shooting in the full scope of its criminal dimensions: Klaus-Michael Mallmann, "Der qualitative Sprung im Vernichtungsprozeß: das Massaker von Kamenez-Podolsk Ende August 1941," *Jahrbuch für Antisemitismusforschung* 10 (2001): 239–264.
2. Staw. Hamburg, 141 Js 534/60, Bd. 11, statement by Rudolf Batz, 15 November 1960, 1,299–1,300, and *Fall 9*, ed. Kazimierz Leszcynski, 221–222.

3. Department I/II head Heinz Trühe is to be disregarded in this respect, for he has yet to emerge as a compromised figure and was apparently dispatched to the command of EG A around the end of June 1941 as a kind of emergency solution. Unlike Lange and Tschierschky, he did not have much of a future career and never rose above the rank of SS captain (that promotion taking place on 20 April 1940, long before his assignment in the east).
4. See *Dienstkalender,* entries for 11, 21, and 23 October, 232, 242, and 244.
5. See chapter 6.
6. Staw. Hamburg, 141 Js 534/60, Bd. 57, excerpts from a translation of the interrogation of F. Jeckeln, 26 January 1946–3 February 1946, here 9–10 of the protocol. According to this document, the ghetto had been established by Prützmann, which is correct only to some extent. It is true that Prützmann, unlike Jeckeln, had a feel for and interest in economic concerns. Here Jeckeln says 12 November was the day he was assigned the task of liquidating the Riga ghetto. See also Schwurgericht Hamburg, (50) Ks 9/72, Urteil gegen Jahnke u.a., 23 February 1973, 54–55. In addition, see Bundesarchiv Dahlwitz-Hoppegarten (BA DH), ZM 1683, Akte 1, 12, interrogation of Friedrich Jeckeln, 14 December 1945. Here Jeckeln gives 10 or 11 November as the day Himmler gave him this assignment. The academic literature has to this day always based itself on the latter statement, e.g. Gerald Fleming, *Hitler und die Endlösung,* 88. The Hamburg Prosecutor's Office also assumed that Jeckeln could have received the assignment on 10 or 11 November. However, this would contradict Himmler's office calendar, which does not mention Jeckeln on either of these days. It may have happened that a meeting was arranged on one of those days at short notice. The page for 12 November is missing.
7. YIVO, Occ. E-3-28, Reichsministerium für die besetzten Ostgebiete [RmbO] an Reichskommissariat Ostland [RKO], 31 October 1941 (Georg Leibbrandt's inquiry concerning Lohse's ban on executions in Liepāja [Libau]); ibid., RKO an RmbO, Betrifft: Judenexekution, 15 November 1941; YIVO, Occ. E-3-32, RKO, Vermerk, November 1941 (in response to a complaint concerning the murder of skilled Jewish workers in Vilnius [Wilna, Wilno] from the Wehrmacht Territorial Commander Ostland on 7 November 1941); ibid., [RKO] an HSSPF. For more information, see chapters 12 and 13.
8. This narrative follows the testimony of Degenhardt, who depicted the command's instructions upon arriving in Riga. Staw. Hamburg, 141 Js 534/60, v. 18, statement of Hermann Krüger, 11 September 1961, 2,534–2,535; ibid., v. 23, statement of Herbert Degenhardt, 28 February 1962, 3,469; ibid., v. 59, statement of Kurt Weiss, 15 September 1965, 9,535. According to Weiss, who had belonged to Prützmann's staff, the swap of HSSPF Ostland and HSSPF Ukraine took place, also because his boss was considered too "soft."
9. Staw. Hamburg, 141 Js 534/60, v. 9, statement by Friedrich Kunz, 9 March 1960, 827; ibid., v. 16, statement by Johannes Zingler, 21 April 1961, 2,136–2,141; ibid., v. 80, statement by Herbert Degenhardt, 24 March 1969, 12,766–12,769. The group from Braunschweig was made up of SS Sergeant Johannes Lüschen (Jeckeln's driver), SS Corporal Willi Wedekind, SS First Lieutenant Hermann Krüger, a certain Hermann (the head of the motor pool squadron), and several others.
10. Staw. Hamburg, 147 Js 5/71 (141 Js 534/60), Anklageschrift gegen Heinrich Oberwinder u.a., 21 December 1971, 59–60; Schwurgericht Hamburg, (50) Ks 9/72, Urteil gegen Jahnke u.a., 23 February 1973, 54–55; Ezergailis, *The Holocaust in Latvia 1941–1944,* 241–242.
11. Staw. Hamburg, 147 Js 5/71 (141 Js 534/60), Anklageschrift gegen Heinrich Oberwinder u.a., 21 December 1971, 130–131; ibid., v. 41, statement by Herbert Degenhardt, 11 November 1963, 6,746; ibid., v. 59, statement by Ernst Hemicker, 25 July 1965, 9,507–9,509; ibid., v. 79, statement by Ernst Hemicker, 9 July 1968, 12,530–12,531; ibid., v. 80,

statement by Ernst Hemicker, 11 March 1969, 12,720–12,721; Schwurgericht Hamburg, (50) Ks 9/72, Urteil gegen Jahnke u.a., 23 February 1973, 57–58.
12. Staw. Hamburg, 141 Js 534/60, v. 75, statement by Friedrich Jahnke, 28 March 1968, 11,913; statement by Herbert Degenhardt, 23 April 1968, 11,953–11,955; statement by Philipp Baumunk, 4 December 1969, 13,032–13,034. The presentation of the "Jeckeln system" with regard to preparations is taken from Degenhardt's statement; where his statement makes omissions, we use Baumunk's testimony. Baumunk depicts how the mass murder took place at the pits and was not present during planning. According a statement by Jahnke, the quartermaster (Ib staff officer) of the Riga Schutzpolizei command, it was originally intended to deport the victims to Rumbula by train, an idea that was later discarded.
13. Staw. Hamburg, 147 Js 5/71 (141 Js 534/60), Anklageschrift gegen Heinrich Oberwinder u.a., 21 December 1971, 60; ibid., v. 3, statement by Rudolf Reese, 24 January 1950, 258r; ibid., v. 41, statement by Herbert Degenhardt, 14 November 1963, 6,789–6,790; statement Herbert Degenhardt, 15 November 1963, 6,797. Jeckeln himself mentioned giving instructions to Osis, although his statement is to be considered with caution, for he also incriminated a later commander of the Order Police, Knecht, who demonstrably did not take part in the liquidation of the Riga ghetto, see BA DH, ZM 1683, Akte 1, 14, statement by F. Jeckeln, 14 December 1945.
14. Staw. Hamburg, 141 Js 534/60, v. 29, statement by Richard Rehberg, 8 January 1963, 4,652–4,653. As regional commander of the Gendarmerie, Rehberg was above all responsible for the deployment of the rural police from the Reich for duties at small posts throughout the countryside. Consequently, he had only a few men at his disposal in Riga. Apart from himself, as well as those members of his staff at his immediate disposal, there is no evidence that additional men from the Gendarmerie were deployed in the operation. On the organization of the Order Police in Riga, see Schwurgericht Hamburg, (50) Ks 9/72, Urteil gegen Jahnke u.a., 23 February 1973, 41–46.
15. Staw. Hamburg, 147 Js 5/71 (141 Js 534/60), Anklageschrift gegen Heinrich Oberwinder u.a., 21 December 1971, 63–65; ibid., v. 41, statement by Karl Heise, 22 November 1963, 6,870, statement Karl Heise, 25–26 November 1963, 6,885–6,890; ibid., v. 75, statement by Friedrich Jahnke, 28 March 1968, 11,912–11,913. Schwurgericht Hamburg, (50) Ks 9/72, Urteil gegen Jahnke u.a., 23 February 1973, 60.
16. Staw. Hamburg, 141 Js 534/60, v. 41, statement by Herbert Degenhardt, 21 November 1963, 6,857.
17. Staw. Hamburg, 141 Js 534/60, v. 75, statement by Herbert Degenhardt, 23 April 1968, 11,955–11,957; statement by Herbert Degenhardt, 25 March 1969, 12,773–12,775. The quotations come from the second statement. Schwurgericht Hamburg, (50) Ks 9/72, Urteil gegen Jahnke u.a., 23 February 1973, 61.
18. Staw. Hamburg, 141 Js 534/60, Bd. 16, statement by Johannes Zingler, 21 April 1961, 2,140. Zingler claimed – incredulously – that he objected and asked to be sent to the front.
19. Ibid., v. 47, statement by Anton Ashauer, 20 May 1964, 7,718–7,719; ibid., v. 55, statement by Alfred Jentzsch, 24 March 1965, 9,039–9,040. Quotes from Ashauer. This statement is credible in that here – contrary to many other testimonies that willfully demonized Jeckeln as part of their defense strategy – the HSSPF's concern for his subordinates comes out. Whether no one from the motor pool really volunteered for this operation, as Ashauer also claimed, may still be doubted.
20. Ibid., Bd. 80, statement by Degenhardt, 24 March 1969, 12,770–12,771. YIVO, Occ. E 3-28, Der RmbO an den RKO, Betrifft: Judenfrage. Auf das Schreiben v. 15.11.1941, 12 December 1941. In this document, it is also noted that "emerging questions are to be

resolved immediately with the higher [sic] SS and Police Leader." Thus Lohse's presentation of the arguments on the importance of the Jewish workers must have been so strong that Jeckeln gave in on this point. Whether the Economics Staff East was activated is not known and remains to be investigated.

21. Staw. Hamburg, 147 Js 5/71 (141 Js 534/60), Anklageschrift gegen Heinrich Oberwinder u.a., 21 December 1971, 70–72; ibid., v. 33, statement by Berta Jankelewicz, 24 March 1963, 5,462; ibid., v. 37, statement by Jehuda Feitelson, 10 April 1963, 6,033, statement by Elieser Karstadt, 5 June 1963, 6,070–6,071; ibid., v. 56, statement by Fred Wildauer, 3 May 1965, 9,115; ibid., SB 2, statement by Leonid Pancis, 11 July 1967, 438. Kaufmann, *Churbn Lettland*, 96–98; Press, *Judenmord in Lettland*, 89–90. Quote from the OD man is from Pancis. The view that the posters came from the HSSPF was expressed by the witness Feitelson; Karstadt was of the opinion that Lohse had signed them.

22. With regard to the latter two men, it is possible that memory is playing tricks on the witnesses, because German participants in this operation speak only of Danskop and Osis at this phase of the ghetto clearance. On the possible presence of Arajs and Curkurs, see Landgericht Hamburg, (37) Ks 5/76, Urteil gegen Viktor Arajs, 31 December 1979, 126–128.

23. Bruns possibly even used Braemer's illness to circumvent the chain of command. With Braemer, Bruns's words would have fallen on deaf ears, for the Wehrmacht territorial commander was not only an SS officer, he had long been friends with Prützmann and Jeckeln, see Krausnick and Wilhelm, *Die Truppe des Weltanschauungskrieges*, 328, and Gerald Reitlinger, *Die Endlösung*, 247.

24. Staw. Hamburg, 147 Js 5/71 (141 Js 534/60), Anklageschrift gegen Heinrich Oberwinder u.a., 21 December 1971, 71; ibid., v. 33, statement by Samuel Gutkin, 21 March 1963, 5,446; ibid., v. 37, statement by E. Karstadt, 5 June 1963, 6,071; ibid., v. 56, statement by Salomon Gerstein, 3 May 1965, 9,112; ibid., v. 58, statement by Isaak Adler, 14 December 1945, 9,353; ibid., v. 65, statement by Eugen Borkum, 11–12 November 1966, 10,477–10,478, statement by Isaak Mackel, 10 September 1965, 10,537; ibid., v. 73, statement by Alexander Ginsburg, 13 December 1967, 11,779. Many witnesses date the selection to 29 November, not 30 November – a contradiction to the actual course of events – because they witnessed the resettlement of the large ghetto in the night of 29 November to 30 November. Kaufmann, *Churbn Lettland*, 99; Press, *Judenmord in Lettland*, 89–90. On Bruns, see Subsequent Nuremberg Trials, Case 12 (High Command Case), German protocol, statement by Walter Bruns, 832–834. The information on the Jewish forced laborers of the bridge command staff and Army Group North's motor pool is also here. Also on these events, see Fleming, *Hitler und die Endlösung*, 95–96, and Bruns's account of Rumbula in Neitzel, *Abgehört: Deutsche Generäle in britischer Kriegsgefangenschaft 1942–1945*, 304-306. The latter appeared too late for consideration in this study.

25. BA Berlin, R 91/10, 39–41, Aktenvermerk [Brasch], 3 December 1941; ibid., 42, Der Geb.-Komm. Riga-Stadt an Generalkommissariat Lettland, Betr.: Beschlagnahme jüdischen Vermögens. In dollar terms, these sums were roughly U.S. $15,600 (1941) (worth about U.S. $216,700 in 2006) and U.S. $665 (1941) (worth about U.S. $9,235 in 2006) respectively.

26. J. Gechtman of Riga in Grossman and Ehrenburg, *Das Schwarzbuch*, 692–693. Even if nobody else reports this conversation, it seems to us essentially credible, for the other information from Gechtman (aside from a few phonetic errors regarding perpetrator names) is correct. Brasch's stated motive is also quite plausible: the civil administration was worried about keeping Jewish workers alive – and this is the key difference from Jeckeln's course of action – although in the history of National Socialist annihilation policy it was not unusual to seek to use the Jewish Council for selections. One recalls the examples

of Warsaw and Łódź (Litzmannstadt). In those cases, the reactions of the respective representatives, Adam Czerniaków and Chaim Mordechaj Rumkowski, were different. The members of the Jewish Council in Riga chose Czerniaków's approach without any consideration of the bitter consequences for themselves. That they were at least the first to be informed of the crime was stated for the record by Irving Berner, Staw. Hamburg, 147 Ks 6/71, Bd. 93, Protocol of the main proceedings, testimony of Irving Berner, 15 January 1973, 14,832.

27. Staw. Hamburg, 141 Js 534/60, Bd. 33, statement by B. Jankelewicz, 24 March 1963, 5,462–5,463; ibid., Bd. 65, statement by Eugen Borkum, 11 November 1966, 10,577. Based on her own experience, Jankelewicz names other members of the Labor Office, where she had to work as a forced laborer: Dralle, Fink, Thomson, and Iwanow. See also Schwurgericht Hamburg, (50) Ks 9/72, Urteil gegen Jahnke u.a., 23 February 1973, 59; Kaufmann, *Churbn Lettland*, 120, according to which Dralle was deployed the following day. According to Borkum, Dralle had gained his economic experience as the business manager of a Riga cinema before the war.
28. Staw. Hamburg, 141 Js 534/60, Bd. 71, statement by L. Pancis, 11 July 1967, 11,397; Kaufmann, *Churbn Lettland*, 259–266. Dubnow survived the first part of the clearance operation, but was murdered at Rumbula on 8 December.
29. Staw. Hamburg, 147 Js 5/71 (141 Js 534/60), Anklageschrift gegen Heinrich Oberwinder u.a., 21 December 1971, 7; ibid., SB 7, statement by Izchak Raikin, 29 August 1975, 1,417.
30. Ibid., Anklageschrift gegen Heinrich Oberwinder u.a., 21 December 1971, 71–72; Schwurgericht Hamburg, (50) Ks 9/72, Urteil gegen Jahnke u.a., 23 February 1973, 59; statement by Sonja Bilder, 10 October 1960, in Künzle and Shimron, *Der Tod des Henkers von Riga*, 72–73.
31. Staw. Hamburg, 147 Js 5/71 (141 Js 534/60), Anklageschrift gegen Heinrich Oberwinder u.a., 21December 1971; Schwurgericht Hamburg, (50) Ks 9/72, Urteil gegen Jahnke u.a., 23 February 1973, 61. Allegedly, HSSPF Jeckeln threatened to punish any refusal to carry out even insignificant orders with draconian penalties, including execution. This assertion is purely a defense tactic, devoid of any basis. To the contrary, although Jeckeln is rightly characterized as an especially strict boss, it can be shown that he also frequently revealed a streak of concern for his subordinates – e.g. with regard to Zingler (see below). But even his protégés promoted the image of a berserk Jeckeln in their postwar statements so as to play down their own role in this crime.
32. Staw. Hamburg, 141 Js 534/60, Bd. 6, statement by Heinz Trühe, 16 October 1959, 185–186; ibid., Bd. 54, statement by Paul Botor, 27 January 1965, 8,897; ibid., Bd. 63, statement by Arnold Kirste, 31 March 1966, 10,167. According to Kirste, BdS Ostland rejected such an operation, at least at *that* point in time. One may suspect that a certain division of labor prevailed, and that BdS Ostland and KdS Latvia were preoccupied more with preparing for the arrival of the deportations from Germany, while the HSSPF was responsible for measures involving annihilation. See also BA Berlin, R 58/220, Ereignismeldung Nr. 151, 5 January 1942, here twenty members of Ek 2 were assigned to Rumbula "after several hours" and only for "security purposes." Since none of the SS officers in Ek 2 were incriminated in the statements of the accused in the Hamburg investigation – assertions that would have made sense as a part of a defense strategy, since one could then accuse those among them who were already deceased without objection – we assume that these twenty men were drivers for Ek 2 and other personnel, who were then deployed at the transfer of the Berlin transport to Rumbula.
33. Staw. Hamburg, 141 Js 534/60, Bd. 55, statement by Herbert Furck, 17 February 1965, 8,918–8,920.

34. Staw. Hamburg, 147 Js 5/71 (141 Js 534/60), Anklageschrift gegen Heinrich Oberwinder u.a., 21 December 1971, 67–70; ibid., SB 1, statement by Ernst Neumann, 10 March 1964, 82. Here it is said that Jeckeln called up Štiglics's men without going through the regulation chain of command – i.e., via the BdS or KdS. See also Schwurgericht Hamburg, (50) Ks 9/72, Urteil gegen Jahnke u.a., 23 February 1973, 62–63.
35. Staw. Hamburg, 147 Js 5/71 (141 Js 534/60), Bd. 88, Deutscher Wetterdienst – Zentralamt, Amtliches Gutachten über die Wetterverhältnisse in Riga/Lettland während der Zeit v. 29. November bis 9. Dezember 1941, 8 February 1972, 13,868–13,872. According to this report, the last snow had fallen on 26 November, but the snow cover on 30 November was still 5 cm (2 inches).
36. Staw. Hamburg, 147 Js 5/71 (141 Js 534/60), Anklageschrift gegen Heinrich Oberwinder u.a., 21 December 1971, 73; ibid., Bd. 30, statement by Otto Tuchel, 19 March 1963, 4,807; ibid., Bd. 35, statement by Herbert Eilrich, 2 July 1963, 5,679; ibid., Bd. 62, statement Ewald Brüsch, 4 February 1966, 10,050, also quote. See as well "Urteil des Bezirksgericht Potsdam gegen Stanislavs Steins," 1 October 1979, in *DDR-Justiz und NS-Verbrechen*, Bd. I, 425–426.
37. Staw. Hamburg, 141 Js 534/60, Bd. 41, statement by K. Heise, 22 November 1963, 6,870–6,871.
38. Ibid., SB 2, statement by Boris Kaplan, 16 January 1967, 430.
39. Staw. Hamburg, 147 Js 5/71 (141 Js 534/60), Anklageschrift gegen Heinrich Oberwinder u.a., 21 December 1971, 73–76; ibid., Bd. 30, statement by Otto Tuchel, 19 March 1963, 4,808–4,812; ibid., Bd. 35, statement by Herbert Eilrich, 2 July 1963, 5,679–5,680; ibid., Bd. 71, statement by Leonid Panis, 11 July 1967, 11,397; ibid., Bd. 75, statement by H. Eilrich, 4 April 1968, 11,927; statement by Alfons Karrasek, 16 April 1969, 11,943–11,944; statement by Willy Dingler, 26 April 1968, 11,974; statement by O. Tuchel, 16 May 1968, 12,013–12,015 and 12,017–12,019; ibid., Bd. 77, statement by Wilhelm Mozer, 15 May 1963, 12,216–12,217. The depiction of the murder of these severely ill persons and those who were wounded stem from Tuchel. The quote "livestock transport" is taken from Eilrich's statement, while the depiction of the murder of the woman comes from Mozer's statement. See also, Schwurgericht Hamburg, (50) Ks 9/72, Urteil gegen Jahnke u.a., 23 February 1973, 64–66 and 76–77, and Press, *Judenmord in Lettland*, 91–92.
40. Staw. Hamburg, 147 Js 5/71 (141 Js 534/60), Anklageschrift gegen Heinrich Oberwinder u.a., 21 December 1971, 76–77; ibid., Bd. 32, statement by Willy Dingler, 25 April 1963, 5,288; ibid., Bd. 62, statement by Ewald Brüsch, 2 February 1966, 10,049–10,052; ibid., Bd. 75, statement by Reinhold Thaumann, 9 April 1968, 11,935–11,937; statement by W. Dingler, 26 April 1968, 11,974–11,975; ibid., statement by Albert Hesfehr, 30 May 1968, 12,143; ibid., Bd. 77., statement by Wilhelm Mozer, 15 May 1963, 12,217; ibid., Bd. 80, statement by Max Neumann, 17 March 1969, 12,731–12,734. The drivers of the patrol belonged to a company of the National Socialist Motor Vehicle Corps, possibly from Dortmund or the Ruhr region. They wore brown uniforms. Schwurgericht Hamburg, (50) Ks 9/72, Urteil gegen Jahnke u.a., 23 February 1973, 67–69.
41. Staw. Hamburg, 147 Js 5/71 (141 Js 534/60), Anklageschrift gegen Heinrich Oberwinder u.a., 21 December 1971, 76–77; ibid., Bd. 23, statement by Herbert Degenhardt, 28 February 1962, 3,471; ibid., Bd. 36, statement by Reinhold Thaumann, 16 May 1963, 5,884; ibid., Bd. 54, statement by Heinrich Bruns, 8 January 1965, 8,851–8,855; ibid., Bd. 55, statement by H. Furck, 17 February 1965, 8,921–8,923; ibid., Bd. 77, statement by Walter Parpert, 18 March 1964, 12,317; ibid., Bd. 92, statement by Ewald Sternnagel, 6 November 1972, 14,625–14,630, statement by Emil Dietrich, 4 October 1972, 14,466–14,470. On the removal of valuables in the woods, see, for example, the statement by Furck. According to Parpert, the Schutzpolizei command brought at least a part

of its own Jewish forced laborers to be shot. Special Purposes Company Furck originally belonged to the infamous Reserve Police Battalion 11, which under Major Franz Lechthaler had been responsible for mass shootings in Belarus. See also, Staw. Hamburg, 141 Js 534/60c (Furck Case), Bd. 10, statement by Johann Steffny, 17 June 1969; Schwurgericht Hamburg, (50) Ks 9/72, Urteil gegen Jahnke u.a., 23 February 1973, 69–70.

42. Staw. Hamburg, 147 Js 5/71 (141 Js 534/60), Anklageschrift gegen Heinrich Oberwinder u.a., 21 December 1971, 79–82; ibid., Bd. 32, statement by W. Dingler, 25 April 1963, 5,288; ibid., Bd. 55, statement by A. Jentzsch, 24 March 1965, 9,040–9,041; ibid., Bd. 75, statement by H. Eilrich, 4 April 1968, 11,925–11,927; statement by R. Thaumann, 9 April 1968, 11,937–11,938; statement by W. Dingler, 26 April 1968, 11,975–11,976; ibid., Bd. 78, statement by August Kossel, 18 November 1965, 12,352–12,355; ibid., Bd. 82, statement by P. Baumunk, 4 December 1969, 13,032–13,036; statement by Herbert Hering, 15 January 1970, 13,092–13,096. The comparison with sardines is taken from Dingler. See also, Staw. Hamburg, 147 Js 5/71 (141 Js 534/60), Anklageschrift gegen Viktor Arajs, 10 June 1976, 107–111; Schwurgericht Hamburg, (50) Ks 9/72, Urteil gegen Jahnke u.a., 23 February 1973, 71–76.

43. Staw. Hamburg, 147 Js 5/71 (141 Js 534/60), Anklageschrift gegen Heinrich Oberwinder u.a., 21 December 1971, 83–84; ibid., Bd. 34, statement by Jan Siem, 16 May 1963, 5,480; ibid., Bd. 42, statement by Karl Heise, 25 November 1963, 6,882–6,883; ibid., Bd. 47, statement by A. Ashauer, 20 May 1964; ibid., Bd. 57, statement by Walter Esslinger, 27 May 1965, 9,271–9,272; statement by Eugen Weinberg, 6 June 1965, 9,286–9,287; ibid., Bd. 61, statement by Adolf Bierwag, 8 November 1965, 9,841–9,843; ibid., Bd. 77, statement by W. Parpart, 18 March 1964, 12,317; ibid., Bd. 82, statement by P. Baumunk, 4 December 1969, 13,035; BA Ludwigsburg, 420 AR-Z 75/68, SB Zeugen, statement by Walter Esslinger, 16 November 1967, 138–139. Quote on the arrival of the Berlin transport is from Weinberg, the quotation on the message to Berlin, Esslinger. Esslinger, who transmitted the "execution report" to the RSHA, claims to have been at KdS Latvia. On the other hand, he "repeatedly" received instructions from Stahlecker while working the "secret teletype," which suggests that Esslinger was often assigned to BdS Ostland. This is supported by his remark that SS First Lieutenant Daiber was the head of the teletype office. Daiber was in fact head of communications at the BdS office. See also, Staw. Hamburg, 141 Js 534/60c (Furck Case); ibid., Bd. 2, statement by Willi Ziebell, 11 January 1966, 270–271; statement by Richard Dessau, 2 February 1966, 284; ibid., Bd. 3, statement by Willi Ziebell, 24 October 1967, 490–491; statement by Otto Brader, 10 November 1967, 508; ibid., Bd. 5, statement by Erwin Nagel, 9 October 1968, 782; statement by Ernst Schulz, 14 November 1967, 825–826; ibid., Bd. 9, statement by Fritz Kapischke, 20 May 1969, 1,496–1,497; ibid., Bd. 10, statement by R. Dessau, 23 May 1969, 1,551–1,553. Also, Schwurgericht Hamburg, (50) Ks 9/72, Urteil gegen Jahnke u.a., 23 February 1973, 74–75.

44. At this time, Stahlecker hardly involved himself with "Jewish affairs" and was seldom in Riga, a situation that was possibly reinforced by Jeckeln's presence there. Instead, as mentioned at the outset, he sought to prove himself as a soldier in anti-partisan operations in areas close to the front.

45. Staw. KG Berlin, 1 Js 4/65 (RSHA Case), Bd. VI, statement by Eberhard Schiele, 28 March 1966, 161–162; statement by Dr. Emil Finnberg, 11 May 1966, 289–290; Staw. Hamburg, 141 Js 534/60, Bd. 6, statement by H. Trühe, 16 October 1959, 185; ibid., Bd. 18, statement by Dr. Emil Finnberg, 26 September 1961, 2,514–2,515; *Dienstkalender*, 30 November 1941, 278; Klein, "Die Erlaubnis zum grenzenlosen Massenmord," in Müller and Volkmann, *Die Wehrmacht*, 933–935; Fleming, *Hitler und die Endlösung*, 103–104. Finnberg, according to his own statement, had been entrusted by Heydrich with checking

up on Stahlecker and the EG A staff and had already submitted reports in Berlin. According to Trühe, Heydrich had confided the RSHA's position on this issue to a "smaller circle" of his SS officers during a personal visit to Riga.

46. Staw. Hamburg, 141 Js 534/60, Bd. 6, statement by Heinz Wichmann, 26 October 1959, 215; ibid., Bd. 24, Hermann Blaas, 9 April 1962, 3,710–3,711. BA Ludwigsburg, 420 AR-Z 75/68, Bd. 1, statement by Georg Michalsen, 9 November 1967, 128. According to Michalsen, several women were also present as viewers. See also, ibid., SB Zeugen, statement by Hermann Blaas, 4 December 1967, 163; statement by Dr. Werner Feldscher, 2 July 1968, n.p.
47. Staw. Hamburg, 141 Js 534/60, Bd. 40, statement by Karl Heise, 29 November 1963, 6,600n–6,600o.
48. Ibid., Bd. 41, statement by H. Degenhardt, 21 November 1963, 6,859; ibid., Bd. 74, statement by Walter Ebermann, 8 July 1964. On the technical sergeant taking pictures, see Degenhardt.
49. Ibid., Bd. 36, statement by R. Thaumann, 16 May 1963, 5,886; ibid., Bd. 75, statement by R. Thaumann, 9 April 1968, 11,938.
50. Subsequent Nuremberg Trials, Case 12 (High Command Case), German protocol, statement by W. Bruns, 830 and 834–839. As a motive for his actions, Bruns claimed that, as a staunch Catholic, he had opposed the regime because of its "racial eccentricities" of anti-Semitism and economic fantasies, inter alia.
51. Staw. Hamburg, 141 Js 534/60, Bd. 41, statement by H. Degenhardt, 21 November 1963, 6,859.
52. Ibid., Bd. 31, statement by Norbert Müller, 9 April 1963, 5,172.
53. Ibid., Bd. 40, statement by Karl Heise, 29 October 1963, 6,599.
54. Staw. Hamburg, 147 Js 5/71 (141 Js 534/60), Anklageschrift gegen Heinrich Oberwinder u.a., 21 December 1971, 81–82; ibid., Bd. 40, statement by K. Heise, 29 October 1963, 6,600n–6,300; ibid., Bd. 75, statement by Friedrich Jahnke, 28 March 1968, 11,914; Staw. Hamburg, 141 Js 534/60c (Furck Case); ibid., Bd. 10, statement by J. Steffny, 17 June 1969, 1,616; Landgericht Hamburg, (37) Ks 5/76, Urteil gegen Viktor Arajs, 31 December 1979, 34.
55. Staw. Hamburg, 147 Js 5/71 (141 Js 534/60), Anklageschrift gegen Heinrich Oberwinder u.a., 21 December 1971, 83–84; ibid., Bd. 75, statement by F. Jahnke, 28 March 1968, 11,915; ibid., Bd. 77, statement by W. Mozer, 15 May 1963, 12,218. The reference to British and Soviet radio is from Schwurgericht Hamburg, (50) Ks 9/72, Urteil gegen Jahnke u.a., 23 February 1973, 77–78.
56. Public Records Office (PRO), London (Kew), HW 16/32, List 2 Traffic: Intercepted Radio Telegram, NR. 25, 1 December 1941, Himmler an Jeckeln; Klein, "Die Erlaubnis," 935. In the telegram itself, the RHSA's authority for guidelines concerning German Jews becomes clear. After Himmler's rebuke of Jeckeln, the HSSPF's influence on the German transports arriving in Ostland later was to be truly marginal, while KdS Latvia gained in importance overall.
57. This is also to be inferred from Jeckeln's postwar statements – which are to be considered very carefully due to possible defensive maneuvers – according to which he wanted to wait for orders from Heydrich regarding the treatment of German Jews from the Reich in January 1942. BA DH, ZM 1683, Akte 1, 15, interrogation of F. Jeckeln, 14 December 1945.
58. PRO, HW 16/32, GPD 471/4.12. 1941, German Police Decodes, 1 December 1941: Radio Telegram, Grothman to SS Lieutenant General Jeckeln, HSSPF Riga; Staw. Hamburg, 141 Js 534/60, Bd. 8, statement by Alfred Draeger, 11 January 1960, 470. Christopher Browning, Die Entfesselung der "Endlösung," 566–567.
59. BA Berlin, R 91/3, Der RKO, Abt. IIa, an den RKO – HSSPF, 3 December 1941.

60. BA Berlin, R 91/10, Aktenvermerk, signed Altemeyer, [n.d. but after 9 December 1941], 16–16r; ibid., Geb.-Komm. und kommissarischer Oberbürgermeister der Stadt Riga an den HSSPF, 13 December 1941. In the former of the two documents, it is noted that the civil administration on 3 December was relieved of the process of fiscally assessing, securing, and recording Jewish assets; the SS had taken these for itself and would do so in the future. Extensive criticism of the HSSPF and the KdS was to be heard later. For more on this, see chapter 12 in this volume.
61. *Dienstkalender*, 4 December 1941, 284. Furthermore, the talk addressed deployment of the 2nd SS Infantry Brigade. Himmler sought to give Jeckeln "instructions verbally on 4 December 1941" and exhorted Jeckeln on 2 December "for urgent response by rt. [radio-telegram]" concerning his arrival, PRO HW 16/45, German Police Decodes from 2 December 1941, Telegram, Chief of Staff [RFSS] to HSSPF Ostland; ibid., Grothmann's radio telegram to SS Lt. Gen. Jeckeln.
62. BA DH, ZM 1683, Akte 1, 24, interrogation of F. Jeckeln, 21 December 1945. At a later meeting at the end of January 1942, Jeckeln was to continue advocating shootings, for he considered them an easier and quicker means of killing; ibid., interrogation of F. Jeckeln, 14 December 1945.
63. Adolf Hitler, *Monologe im Führerhauptquartier 1941–1945*, ed. Werner Jochmann, 147–149. On this evening, Hitler formulated several objections to his hard line and admitted that "there were Jews among us who were decent in the sense that they refrained from every measure directed against Germandom." Hitler also spoke most respectfully of Otto Weininger, who, after allegedly recognizing the essence of Jewish nature, committed suicide; the dictator went on to concede that many Jews were not conscious of the "destructive character of their being." Ultimately, however, Hitler compared the Jews with a virus that the body must expel. For individuals, said the dictator, the racial legislation entailed considerable hardship, but with it, he was preventing "countless conflicts" in the future.
64. Hauptstaatsarchiv Düsseldorf, RW 58/74234, 12–12r, RSHA, IV B 4b, 2 December 1941 [letter by Eichmann]. On this and the conflict between the RSHA and Abwehr, Winfried Meyer, *Unternehmen Sieben*, 236–241.
65. Fleming, *Hitler und die Endlösung*, 96–104, quote given on 102, based on a transcript by Dr. Hans Holzamer, a close friend of Dr. Otto Schulz-Du Bois, 28 May 1980. A slightly different variation of the quote – "You're going soft, I have to do it, for after me, nobody is going to do it!" – was recorded in a statement by Erika Schulz-Du Bois, the captain's widow.
66. Subsequent Nuremberg Trials, Case 12 (High Command Case), German protocol, statement by W. Bruns, 838–839.
67. Staw. Hamburg, 147 Js 5/71 (141 Js 534/60), Anklageschrift gegen Heinrich Oberwinder u.a., 21 December 1971, 71–72; ibid., Bd. 33, statement by Lidia Bobe, 20 March 1963, 5,427; ibid., SB 37, statement by Ella Medalje, 13 January 1979, 6,313; statement by S. Bilder in Künzle and Shimron, *Tod des Henkers*, 72–73.
68. Staw. Hamburg, 141 Js 534/60, Bd. 38, statement by Max Wachtel, 28 August 1963, 6,162.
69. Staw. Hamburg, 147 Js 5/71 (141 Js 534/60), Anklageschrift gegen Heinrich Oberwinder u.a., 21 December 1971, 84–85. Aismann was shot by Hesfehr, Tuchel, and Kobiella a short time later, because they feared he would inform Krause about their misappropriations, and because an SS and police investigation was pending, Kaufmann, *Churbn Lettland*, 124; Schwurgericht Hamburg, (50) Ks 9/72, Urteil gegen Jahnke u.a., 23 February 1973, 168–170.
70. Staw. Hamburg, 141 Js 534/60, Bd. 29, statement by R. Rehberg, 8 January 1963, 4,645–4,646; ibid., Bd. 78, statement by Friedrich Jahnke, 8 November 1975, 12,404–12,405.

Rehberg's statement contains several factual errors: He mixes up Rumbula and Kaiserwald, and he disputes being in command of the Latvian police. With regard to his own responsibility, his statement is to be assessed with caution, for in previous questioning, as Rehberg himself admitted, he willfully withheld information. Jahnke, who as quartermaster of the Riga Schutzpolizei Command was one of Heise's close associates, also participated in the first clearance operation. After his boss was injured, Jahnke was more or less assigned to Rehberg. Ibid., SB 4, statement by Viktor Arajs, 5 August 1976, 706; here Arajs said that he received more precise instructions from a colonel of the Latvian municipal police [Lieutenant Colonel Osis is probably meant], who was able to sketch precisely the area to be guarded on an operational map drawn solely for the mass shooting. See also, Landgericht Hamburg, (37) Ks 5/76, Urteil gegen Viktor Arajs, 31 December 1979, 128. According to Arajs's testimony during the main court proceedings, Lange is to have passed on the order by telephone via Arnold Laukers, the chief of staff of the Arajs commando. In the courtroom, however, Arajs gave several versions of how he received his instructions.

71. Staw. Hamburg, 147 Js 5/71 (141 Js 534/60), Anklageschrift gegen Heinrich Oberwinder u.a., 21 December 1971, 85–86; ibid., Bd. 29, statement by R. Rehberg, 8 January 1963, 4,647–4,648; ibid., Bd. 37, statement by J. Feitelson, 10 April 1963, 6,034; ibid., Bd. 78, Jacob Nieburg, 31 August 1948, 12,342; ibid., SB 7, statement by I. Raikin, 29 August 1975, 1,418; statement by Alexander Lewin, 15 August 1975, 1,425–1,42; ibid., SB 11, statement by Tamara Dworkina, 23 October 1975, 2,218–2,220; ibid., Anklageschrift gegen Viktor Arajs, 10 June 1976, 111.
72. Ibid., Anklageschrift gegen Heinrich Oberwinder u.a., 21 December 1971, 87–88; ibid., Bd. 80, statement by Herbert Degenhardt, 26 March 1969, 12,783; ibid., SB 18, statement by Frida Michelson, 3 March 1971, 3,395.
73. Staw. Hamburg, 141 Js 534/60, Bd. 29, statement by R. Rehberg, 8 January 1963, 4,649–4,651; ibid., Bd. 31, statement by Johann Knöferl, 1 January 1963, 5,113–5,115.
74. Ibid., Bd. 29, statement by R. Rehberg, 8 January 1963, 4,650; ibid., SB 37, statement by Ella Medalje, 15 January 1979, 6,314. From this statement by Medalje, it is known that civilians were indeed ordered into the ghetto for the evacuation. She asked one of the drivers what was going on, whereupon the man, in tears, answered that everybody was to be taken away to be shot.
75. Ibid., Bd. 16, statement by J. Zingler, 21 April 1961, 2,143–2,145; ibid., Bd. 54, statement by H. Bruns, 8 January 1965, 8,853; ibid., Bd. 80, statement by Degenhardt, 26 March 1969, 12,769–12,770; ibid., Bd. 82, statement by P. Baumunk, 4 December 1969, 13,028 and 13,036; ibid., Bd. 85, Verfügung, 1 June 1972, 13,484–13,493; ibid., Bd. 85, Verfügung, 7 July 1972, 13,551–13,595. These documents also name additional possible marksmen from the HSSPF command staff. Despite all self-serving declarations regarding his participation, Zingler conceded that "even with the best intentions in the world" he could no longer recall the number of people he shot, but he said it was approximately 100–200 persons. Given the organization of the shooting in the pit, this clearly has to be an understatement.
76. Staw. Hamburg, 141 Js 534/60, Bd. 33, statement by S. Gutkin, 21 March 1963, 5,447; ibid., Bd. 44, statement by Benno Arthur von Witthoeft, 20 February 1964, 7,291–7,292; ibid., Bd. 77, statement by W. Mozer, 15 May 1963, 12,218; ibid., SB 28, statement by Jan-Alfred Frank-Prank, 5 April 1976, 4,743–4,744. In Witthoeft's statement, the various participants from KdS Latvia are mentioned by name.
77. Ibid., SB 22, statement by Matis Lutrinsch, 4 January 1976, 3,960–3,963, quote 3,961. Ezergailis, *The Holocaust in Latvia*, 260–261.
78. Staw. Hamburg, 141 Js 534/60, SB 22, statement by Ella Medalje, 18 January 1975,

3,919–3,921; ibid., SB 37, statement by E. Medalje, 15 January 1979, 6,314–6,316, quote 6,315; Ezergailis, *The Holocaust in Latvia*, 258–260.
79. Staw. Hamburg, 141 Js 534/60, SB 18, statement by F. Michelson, 3 March 1971, 3,393–3,394, quote 3,394. Cf. Frida Michelson, *I Survived Rumbuli*, 85–93. According to Michelson, the perpetrators enriched themselves with the property of those who were murdered, among whom were Jewish émigrés. Ezergailis, *Holocaust in Latvia*, 257–258.
80. Staw. Hamburg, 147 Js 5/71 (141 Js 534/60), Anklageschrift gegen Heinrich Oberwinder u.a., 21 December 1971, 88; ibid., Bd. 38, statement by M. Wachtel, 28 August 1963, 6,161; ibid., Bd. 77, statement by W. Mozer, 15 May 1963, 12,218; ibid., Bd. 82, statement by Anne Buvitt, 16 October 1969, 12,959. According to Buvitt, the family members of the OD found shelter in the "Jewish police station." These were taken away to Rumbula separately from the men and murdered in front of them. Otherwise, at least all those OD people who were no longer of use in the small ghetto were killed. In the eyes of the perpetrators, given the liquidation of the large ghetto, it must have appeared consistent to reduce the share of the OD for the small ghetto. According to Wachtel, thirty OD men remained at the small ghetto, which means that about ninety of them – including the entire leadership – were murdered at Rumbula.
81. Staw. Hamburg, 141 Js 534/60, Bd. 29, statement by R. Rehberg, 8 January 1963, 4,651–4,652. As noted in footnote 70, Rehberg confuses Rumbula and Kaiserwald.
82. Kaufmann, "The War Years in Latvia Revisited," in Association of Latvian and Estonian Jews in Israel, *The Jews in Latvia*, 356. According to Kaufmann, the entire leadership of the Jewish Council and a large part of the community's prominent figures fell victim to the massacre.
83. Staw. Hamburg, 141 Js 534/60, Bd. 16, statement by J. Zingler, 21 April 1961, 2,143; ibid., Bd. 77, statement by W. Mozer, 15 May 1963, 12,218; ibid., Bd. 78, statement by A. Kossel, 18 November 1965, 12,355. On covering up the mass graves, see Mozer. Kossel added that he had heard that the Russian POWs were also murdered.
84. Staw. Hamburg, 147 Js 5/71 (141 Js 534/60), Anklageschrift gegen Heinrich Oberwinder u.a., 21 December 1971, 88–89; ibid., Bd. 37, statement by J. Feitelson, 10 April 1963, 6,034; ibid., Bd. 38, statement by M. Wachtel, 28 August 1963, 6,162; ibid., Bd. 45, statement by Max Kaufmann, 29 October 1963, 7,422; ibid., Bd. 61, statement by Jechiel Kahn, 1 August 1965, 9,901; statement by Ben Hahn, 22 July 1965, 9,913; ibid., Bd. 65, statement by Eugen Borkum, 12 November 1966, 10,482; ibid., Bd. 77, statement by Salomon Morain, 4 July 1967, 11,228; ibid., Bd. 82, statement by A. Buvitt, 16 October 1969, 12,959. On Dr. Neumann's family, see Morain. See also Kaufmann, *Churbn Lettland*, 105 and 115–116. According to Kaufmann, those people murdered outside the ghetto were not killed in Rumbula but in Bikernieki, which is plausible, since the pits in Rumbula had already been covered.
85. Staw. Hamburg, 141 Js 534/60, Bd. 38, statement by M. Wachtel, 28 August 1963, 6,162; ibid., Bd. 61, statement by B. Hahn, 22 July 1965, 9,913; ibid., Bd. 82, statement by A. Buvitt, 16 October 1969, 12,960; Kaufmann, *Churbn Lettland*, 116.
86. Staw. Hamburg, 147 Js 5/71 (141 Js 534/60), Anklageschrift gegen Heinrich Oberwinder u.a., 21 December 1971, 72; Schwurgericht Hamburg, (50) Ks 9/72, Urteil gegen Jahnke u.a., 23 February 1973, 59. Here it is said the women's ghetto consisted of only one building, albeit a large one.
87. LVVA, P 1026-1-3, 262–264, fragment of a report from Ek 2, regarding "Jewry," [from the context, after December 1941], quote 263.
88. Staw. Hamburg, 141 Js 534/60, SB 22, statement by E. Medalje, 18 January 1975, 3,921–3,923; ibid., SB 37, statement by E. Medalje, 15 January 1979, 6,316–6,317. Among the two women who were shot in the HSSPF building after their interrogation was the former

wife of a well-known captain by the name of Skuja, whom she had divorced on account of a "Jew." The identity of the other woman is not documented, but she was described as a young, good-looking woman with blond hair; she had come from Liepāja, and her husband had studied Jewish Studies at Tartu (Dorpat) University. The third woman was a young girl about eighteen years of age with a Polish-sounding family name who claimed she had been adopted by a Jewish family. Medalje did not know her later fate, see Press, *Judenmord in Lettland*, 96. The event is supported by a perpetrator's statement. According to Degenhardt, Lüschen, one of the marksmen, had spared a woman who claimed to have been an ethnic German married to a rabbi. She was "separated" from her child and returned to Riga. There, said Degenhardt, she went mad and was "taken away" by staff member Neurath, Staw. Hamburg, 141 Js 534/60, Bd. 80, statement by Degenhardt, 26 March 1969, 12,783–12,784.

89. Staw. Hamburg, 141 Js 534/60, SB 18, statement by F. Michelson, 3 March 1971, 3,394.
90. Ibid., SB 22, statement by M. Lutrinsch, 4 January 1976, 3,960–3,963, quote 3,961; Ezergailis, *The Holocaust in Latvia*, 260–261.
91. Staw. Hamburg, 141 Js 534/60, Bd. 61, statement by B. Hahn, 22 July 1965, 9,912, also quote; ibid., Bd. 82, statement A. Buvitt, 16 October 1969, 12,960; Press, *Judenmord in Lettland*, 109. Wachtel remained only briefly with the ghetto police, where he no longer felt safe. Moreover, the arrival of the transports from the Reich was to alter the power structure of the ghetto society, with the Latvian Jews being in the minority – something that would not have made his work at the OD any easier.
92. Staw. Hamburg, 141 Js 534/60, Bd. 15, Der HSSPF Ostland an den SS-Richter beim RFSS SS-Obersturmbannführer Bender, Betrifft: Johannes Zingler, 9 February 1942. From this letter, it is to be inferred that Jeckeln reported to Himmler the number of those killed; what that number was exactly is not known. Also, BA DH, ZM 1683, Akte 1, 15, interrogation of F. Jeckeln, 14 December 1945. According to this protocol, Jeckeln filed his report first by telephone and later reported in person.
93. LVVA, P 83-1-80, Der RFSS, SS-Befehl, 12 December 1941, unpaginated. This order went out to all HSSPFs, SSPFs, the SS regional sectors Ostland, Ukraine, Vistula, Warta, Southeast, and Alpenland as well as the HSSPFs in the military-administrated areas of the Soviet Union. This order referred clearly to the mass annihilation in the occupied territories of Eastern and Southeastern Europe and not to the entire realm under Nazi rule, see Hans Heinrich Wilhelm, "Die Verfolgung der sowjetischen Juden," in *Gegen das Vergessen*, ed. Klaus Meyer and Wolfgang Wippermann, 63–64. In our view, given the chronological proximity between the end of the Riga operation and this order by Himmler, the order is associated causally with the events in Riga, for all of the other large-scale mass murder operations to that point had taken place weeks earlier (the last major mass shooting being the murder of 15,000 Jews in Rivne [Rovno] on 5 November) or had yet to take place (the next one being the murder of 15,000 Jews in Kharkiv [Kharkov] in early January 1942).
94. Staw. Hamburg, 141 Js 534/60, Bd. 15. All the documents on the Zingler incident are collected here: SS- u. Polizeigericht III Berlin, Der dienstälteste Richter an das HA SS-Gericht, Betr. Strafsache Johannes Zingler, 14 January 1942; Der HSSPF Ostland an den SS-Richter beim RFSS, SS-Obersturmbannführer Bender, Betrifft: Johannes Zingler, 9 February 1942; Der SS-Richter beim RFSS, Betr. Ehem. SS-Oberführer Johannes Zingler, 29 January 1942; Vermerk [Bender], Betr. Ehem. SS-Oberführer Johannes Zingler, 10 May 1942; SS-Richter beim RFSS, 25 March 1942. Jeckeln's words in Zingler's defense are from the letter of 9 February 1942. Himmler is quoted from the letter of 25 March 1942.
95. LVVA, P 70-5-44, 29–30, Der SSPF Latvia, KdO, Report of 23 December 1941.
96. BA Berlin, R 58/220, Ereignismeldung Nr. 151, 5 January 1942.

– Chapter 6 –

IN SEARCH OF TERRITORIES FOR THE "FINAL SOLUTION"

The Road to Riga as a Final Destination for Deportations

While the four Einsatzgruppen were murdering Jews behind the lines of the German Wehrmacht in the Soviet Union, deliberations were taking place back in the "Greater German Reich" as to where and how to deport not only German Jews but all Jews within the German sphere of influence. Since the invasion of Poland, forced expulsions and planned settlements had become the means of pursuing Greater Germany's population policy. In German-occupied Poland, the confinement of the Jews in ghettos had not served the purpose of their murder at a later date, as was the case in the occupied Soviet Union. The closed ghettos and "Jewish residential districts" in the annexed western Polish territories were considered giant deportation centers, whose eventual liquidation was linked to the Reich Railway's capacity to provide transport and the General Government's readiness to accept them. By the summer of 1941, however, it had been growing clear for months that a territorial solution of this kind, i.e., sending the Jews to a territory beyond the Reich's borders, was no longer feasible.[1] Neither the projected "Jew reservation" in the General Government's District Lublin, nor the Madagascar Plan had ever had a chance of being realized.

The Reich Security Main Office (RSHA), created in autumn 1939 with Reinhard Heydrich at its helm, was responsible for these failed deportations and plans. Heydrich, the chief of the Security Police and the Security Service (CdS), had always put a premium on the fact that on 24 January 1939, *Reichsmarschall* Hermann Göring had put him in charge of the Reich Central Office for Jewish Emigration in the Reich Ministry of the Interior.[2] Whenever it seemed necessary, Heydrich referred to this commission, which authorized RSHA Department IV (Gestapo) to draw up and carry out all necessary resettlement plans and expulsion measures. Heydrich had been able to expand this new array of tasks – i.e., forcing and organizing the emigration of German and Austrian Jews – beyond the turning point that followed the German invasion of Poland, because it was in autumn 1939

Notes for this chapter begin on page 192.

that the German police became an instrument of settlement planning. Hitler had assigned *Reichführer-SS* Heinrich Himmler the task of making the Reich's annexed western Polish territories purely German. Subsequently, Himmler had assumed the title of Reich commissar for the strengthening of Germandom and institutionalized executive authority for forced migration and settlement in the recently amalgamated RSHA. Thus, for the Security Police, the occupation of Poland meant not only territorial expansion through the creation of new Security Police and SD offices but also new competences.[3] At the end of 1939, Heydrich was in charge of the German central office and the Austrian and Czech central agencies for Jewish emigration. The forced migration of Poles and Jews from the western Polish territories annexed by the Reich also resided with him. Finally, the Reich Association of Jews in Germany, which had been imposed on German Jews as their legal representation, was subordinated to the Reich Ministry of the Interior, where it came under the supervision of Heydrich and Gestapo chief Heinrich Müller.[4]

It is therefore also no coincidence that the first documented strategic plan to clarify the future fate of the Jews within the German sphere of influence dates to October 1939. On 6 October, the day Hitler gave a speech to the Reichstag informing the public that the most important task was to create a new order of ethnic relations in Europe's east and southeast, Müller and Adolf Eichmann held a meeting. SS Captain Eichmann was at this point still director of the two central agencies for Jewish emigration in Vienna and Prague. The conversation between Müller and Eichmann apparently revolved around the starting point for the deportation of Jews from the Old Reich (meaning Germany in its 1937 borders), Austria, and Protectorate Bohemia-Moravia (the occupied Czech lands). To this end, the existing registration lists of the Reich Association were to be subdivided according to religious community and district representation. Special note was also to be made of Jews holding foreign citizenship, as had been done with, Jewish refugees from Poland who had recently been arrested in the region around Ostrava (Ostrau). Furthermore, Müller mentioned that the upcoming deportation of 70,000–80,000 Jews from the annexed Polish region of East Upper Silesia as well as those from the region around Ostrava would serve first and foremost to gain experience for the later deportation of "larger masses." Only a few days later in Katowice, Eichmann informed General Otto von Knobelsdorff, the chief of staff of German border troops in the region, that after this first stage of deportations a report would go to Himmler via Heydrich – and would "probably be forwarded to the Führer. There will then be some waiting until a general transport of Jews is ordered. The Führer for the moment has ordered the redeployment of 300,000 unprosperous Jews from the Old Reich and Ostmark [Austria]."[5]

It was planned here – parallel, so to speak, to the October transports of Jews from the Polish port of Gdynia (Gotenhafen) to Kielce, Radom, and Lublin – to send Jews from Katowice, Ostrava, and Vienna to Nisko (District Lublin), a fate that in the long term was to befall all of the Reich's Jews. But then, that same month, the deportation trains were stopped again, for Himmler's own first gigantic resettlement plan had priority. This order to stop, dated 30 October 1939, was a prerequisite for the settlement of foreign Germans from Latvia, Estonia, Galicia, and Volhynia. Subsequently, all short- and long-term plans for expelling Poles and Jews from the annexed territories in 1940–1941 were oriented according to Himmler's needs, with the new administrative region Wartheland under Arthur Greiser being the point of departure for the deportation trains heading to the General Government. For Eichmann, the unsuccessful Nisko operation had only positive consequences. On 21 December 1939, Heydrich informed the territorial commander of the Security Police and the SD (BdS) in the General Government as well as the regional inspectors of the Security Police and the SD in Breslau (today Wrocław), Danzig (Gdańsk), Königsberg (today Kaliningrad), and Poznań (Posen) that he had appointed Eichmann his special desk officer for evacuations in the eastern provinces.[6] With that, Desk D 4 (Evacuation Affairs) came into being in Department IV of the RSHA.

Even if the deportations of Poles and Jews were now dictated by the need to settle the "dispersed splinters of the Germandom" from Eastern Europe, creative effort was nonetheless still expended on the question of what to do with the Jews in the German sphere of influence. On 19 December 1939, the SD's Jewish Affairs Desk produced a paper on the "final solution of the Jewish problem." The original idea of no longer forcing German Jews to emigrate but deporting them instead to the General Government was maintained. What remained unclear in this paper was the question whether a "reservation" would in fact be established for the Jews, and whether there should be a Jewish self-administration:

> A Jewish administration would be more advantageous, for in this way German administration officials would be economized. Only the leading positions would be filled with Germans. In addition, it is to be decided at the same time to whom the administration would be subordinated. It would be appropriate [in my view] to leave the administration under Security Police direction until the settlement of the Jews from Reich territory, Ostmark [Austria], and Bohemia/Moravia is carried out. In this context, with regard to the creation of a reservation, a final decision would have to be made as to whether Jewish emigration will be continued. Moreover, in terms of foreign policy, a reservation would be a good means of putting pressure on the Western powers. Perhaps in this way, the question of a global solution could be raised at the end of the war.[7]

These strategic conceptions of the "final solution of the German Jewish problem" were shared by many of the Gestapo offices within the Reich. Heydrich's concept of confining the Jews of the Reich's new provinces in cities and, within them, in ghettos prior to deportation was generally known in police circles. In spring 1940, the Gestapo's district and regional offices took steps showing that there probably existed a considerable amount of anticipation that they would soon be getting rid of the Jews within their jurisdiction.

Up to this day, the deportation of Stettin's Jews on the night of 12 to 13 February 1940 has been seen in historical terms only within the context that the fate of Pomerania's Jews – like the transports to Nisko – neatly fit the overall strategy of deporting Poles and Jews from the Reich's new eastern provinces. This is correct, because Heydrich himself made this connection at a meeting on 30 January and justified the planned deportation of Stettin's Jews by citing an apartment shortage and motives related to the wartime economy.[8] But this expulsion operation led offices in the rest of the Reich to covet the same.

On 12 February, the Gestapo regional and district offices in the Reich received a letter from the RSHA stating that it – acting through Department IV – would attempt to standardize the various local measures enacted to concentrate Germany's Jews:

> In a number of districts of the Reich, various local agencies have issued orders that have limited the Jews' freedom of movement. In recent times, difficulties in accommodating the Jews have emerged as a result of such orders, because these orders take into consideration only purely local interests and were not coordinated with the needs of the remaining Reich territory. Since the Jews, on the other hand, elude necessary surveillance due to free and uncontrollable wandering, I intend to standardize this question across the Reich and to work toward the Jews being concentrated in the course of time in suitable places within a province. In these places, the Jews can be kept under surveillance and registered more easily for preparing their emigration and also for overall domestic political reasons than is possible if they live dispersed within the entire Reich territory. The cities listed in the enclosed compendium are being looked at as places of residence. For the time being, however, I request by 27 February 1940 a report on whether and for what particular reasons misgivings exist against residence in the cities named. If need be, other suitable places are to be named, although it is to be kept in mind that Jewish school facilities must be available. In addition, it is to be reported whether the Jews present in the individual provinces or states will find accommodations in the places foreseen in the enclosure. Should the occasion arise, additional recommendations are to be made in this respect. This matter is to be handled strictly confidentially for the time being; other agencies may not be approached.[9]

This letter and the fact that it carried the date of the deportation of Stettin's Jews – i.e., Jews from the Old Reich – must have had the same effect on the Gestapo offices as an order to start preparing for deportations in their districts. On top of this, it quickly became known that it had been possible to evacuate the Jews of Stettin on that fateful night only with the active assistance of the party's block managers, the SA, and a Wehrmacht motor pool.[10] On 15 March, Department IV had to take corrective action and insist in another letter to the regional and district Gestapo offices that deportation measures be suspended immediately.[11]

Through Eichmann's first deportation efforts, the SD's initial deliberations on expulsion, the fate of Stettin's Jews, and Department IV's order of 15 March, it becomes quite clear that in Berlin the original concepts of expulsion by means of a mixture of legislative pressure and physical violence aimed at the Jews in the west were now subject to renegotiation. Even if these people were to be deported only much later, their wholesale deportation into inhospitable territories had now become generally accepted. Without much trouble, a new "solution principle" – the expulsion of Jews to the east instead of their emigration – was asserting itself, an approach that was demonstrably barbaric if one only glanced at the fate of those Poles and Jews who were deported to Hans Frank's General Government at this time. The Madagascar Plan, which was seriously pursued shortly thereafter, also documents the search for a suitable territory for deportation. The prehistory of Madagascar as a place of exile for Jews is to be found in the late nineteenth century and was time and again propagated by the Nazis, primarily after 1938.[12]

As with the planning for a reservation in District Lublin, the locus of plans for the forced expulsion of the Jews to Madagascar that unfolded in summer 1940 was to be found with Hitler, Himmler, and Heydrich. If Madagascar was still the destination for the large-scale forced emigration of all (eastern) Jews to Africa in Himmler's memorandum on the "treatment of alien peoples in the East," which Hitler accepted on 25 May as "very good and correct," the desire for access to all Jews within the German sphere of influence is found once again in a 3 June paper by Franz Rademacher, who just a few weeks earlier had been appointed head of Desk D III of the Foreign Office. He wrote his superior that the foreign policy implications of individual anti-Jewish decisions in Germany had lost their significance as a result of the war with the Western powers. With regard to the Jewish question, it was now necessary to define a German war aim: "The question must be clarified, where are the Jews to go?" Rademacher suggested two possibilities, both of which named Madagascar as the destination of the expulsions. Either one sent all of the European Jews there or one sent only the West European Jews. The "Jews of the east, who represent the more virile and more Talmudic offspring for the militant Jewish intelligentsia, will remain, e.g. in the district of Lublin, as a deposit in German hands, so that the Jews of America remain paralyzed in their struggle against Germany."[13]

Just a few days later, Hitler picked up on this idea again in a conversation with Mussolini. Heydrich, referring to his commission from Göring and expressing his own preference for a "territorial solution," made the necessary contacts with the Foreign Office, and Foreign Minister Joachim von Ribbentrop gave his basic approval to the planned deportations.[14] Hitler was completely convinced that this concept could be realized when he declared at the Berghof on 3 August during the inaugural visit of Otto Abetz, the new German ambassador in occupied Paris, that "he intended to evacuate all Jews from Europe after the war."[15] Shortly beforehand, Hitler had received the support of Romanian Minister President Ion Gigurtu, who announced that although his country had taken up a solution of the Jewish question, Romania would not get very far without the help of Hitler, "who must carry out a total solution for all of Europe."[16]

After France's quick defeat in summer 1940, Hitler was at the height of his power at home and abroad. Although England was unwilling to play the role of junior European and colonial partner, Hitler was able to pursue a policy of shifting populations on the continent unconstrained by considerations of foreign policy. To expedite the process, he decided at a meeting on 25 September – present were Reich Chancellery Chief of Staff Hans Heinrich Lammers, National-Socialist Party Chancellery Chief of Staff Martin Bormann, and Interior Ministry State Secretary Wilhelm Stuckart as well as Robert Wagner and Josef Bürckel, the two heads of the civil administration in Alsace and Lorraine respectively – that his 2 August decree on the temporary administration of Alsace and Lorraine would be lifted, since Wagner and Bürckel had complained vociferously of paternalistic condescension on the part of the ministries in Berlin. In addition, both men were expressly encouraged by Hitler to make purely German territories out of these western borderlands within a decade – a formulation Bormann was to use again in a letter to Lammers that was also intended for the regional administrators in the newly annexed eastern territories. Hitler would not ask any of the *Gauleiter*, the regional party bosses, in the German borderlands about the methods they used to make their territory German, wrote Bormann; it was of no consequence to Hitler "if at some point in the future, it is noted that the methods for winning this territory were unattractive or not judicially impeccable."[17] With that, the subsequent deportation of Jews from Baden and Saarland-Palatinate on 22 and 23 October was founded on Hitler's wish that the *Gauleiter* and the *Reichsstatthalter* (regional representatives of the Reich government) along Germany's borders would also be able to seize the initiative of their own accord. Hitler gave the general final direction, and he approved the result. Bürckel and Wagner's Gurs Operation – named for the site of an internment camp for Jews in Vichy France – apparently also involved the start of deportations aimed in the long term at evacuating all Jews from "the Old Reich, the Ostmark, and the Protectorate" to Madagascar.[18]

Despite the fact that the sea lanes to Madagascar remained blocked, German leaders held on to this theoretical "solution possibility" for some time. The level of awareness of these unrealistic plans is astonishing. The abundance of remarks made by Hitler, Himmler, Heydrich, Goebbels, Frank, Bürckel, Greiser, and Wagner highlights but the higher level of political decision-makers. Only gradually did these individuals begin to realize that both a German colonial empire in Africa and a colony of Jews on an island in the middle of the Indian Ocean would remain a dream. When Himmler, toward year's end, gave a presentation on settlement activity, he mentioned in vague terms that the "final solution" had to be carried out "by resettling the Jews out of the German people's European economic space to a territory yet to be determined." At least 5.8 million people – all of the Jews of Western and Central Europe – were to be included in this program.[19]

On 8 January 1941, a planning meeting took place in the RSHA with Heydrich presiding. It was here that the third short-term plan for resettling Poles and Jews for the benefit of ethnic German settlers was outlined. In this version, 831,000 people were to be deported from western Poland, with a deportation of 60,000 Vienna Jews being addressed separately.[20] This latter issue was the result of a conversation between Hitler and Vienna Gauleiter Baldur von Schirach on 2 October 1940, during which Hitler agreed with Schirach that the Austrian metropolis should be made "free of Jews" more quickly.[21] The renewed instructions to deport Jews and Poles from the annexed eastern territories to the General Government represented in turn only the most urgent measures with regard to technical matters of settlement planning. As in October 1939, behind these orders lay a concept for the "final solution of the Jewish question" in Europe that still had to define its final destination. On 21 January 1941, Theodor Dannecker, the SD desk officer for Jewish affairs in Paris, presented to Ambassador Abetz a memorandum on the creation of a central office for Jews:

> In accordance with the will of the Führer, the Jewish question within that part of Europe controlled by Germany is to be subjected to a final solution after the war. The Chief of the Security Police and the SD has already received from the Führer via the Reichsführer-SS, and through the Reichsmarschall, the assignment to submit a final solution project. On account of the considerable experience in handling Jews available at the offices of the CdS and the SD and thanks to the preliminary

work already done over the longer term, this project was then worked out in its essentials. It is now with the Führer and the Reichsmarschall. It is certain that its implementation will involve an enormous task, whose success can be guaranteed only by the most careful of preparations. These must extend to the work preceding the complete deportation of the Jews as well as to the detailed planning of a settlement operation in a territory that has yet to be determined.[22]

When Heydrich's subordinate mentioned here at the outset that Hitler was postponing a decision on actions to be taken against Europe's Jews until after the war, it meant – at the turn of 1940–1941 – that the RHSA would be able to begin concrete deportations only after the victory over the Soviet Union. Since autumn 1940, Hitler had been determined to invade the Soviet Union the following spring and had several times predicted a short duration of the military conflict.[23] In January and February 1941, finding a destination was apparently not even the most urgent task. In a letter to Martin Luther, the head of the Foreign Office's Department III (Germany), Heydrich again mentioned an undetermined territory, whereas Bruno Streckenbach, acting on Heydrich's behalf, reported to the same address that the Jews would have to leave the mainland after a future conclusion of peace.[24] The Security Police's concrete measures at this point lay in a fully different area, however – namely, harmonizing anti-Jewish measures throughout Europe, e.g. creating a Central Office for Jews in Paris, appointing a Jewish Council in Amsterdam, and introducing the most comprehensive central registries in occupied Europe. Streckenbach's formulation was an accurate description of German strategy of persecution in early 1941: shortly after the victory over the Soviet Union, the Jews would be forcibly deported according to the most uniform guidelines possible and by a standardized procedure – where they would be deported was not yet so important.

When Eichmann on 20 March then had to appear at the office of Propaganda Minister Joseph Goebbels's state secretary to discuss Goebbels's desire for a preferential deportation of Berlin's Jews, he simply combined Heydrich's grand territorial concept and the third short-term plan, which had just failed due to the diversion of transportation capacity and materiel to the German Army: "[Party Comrade] Eichmann from the Security Main Office said that [Party Comrade] Heydrich, who has been entrusted with the final evacuation of the Jews, presented the Führer with a proposal, which is not to be carried out only because the General Government is not [at present] in a position to accept a single Jew or Pole from the Old Reich. There is in fact an order of the Führer on the evacuation of 60,000 Jews from Vienna, which the General Government still has to take in. In Vienna, however, only 45,000 Jews are available for the time being, so one could potentially remove the remaining 15,000 Jews from Berlin."[25]

But because Hitler had told Hans Frank on 17 March 1941 that the General Government would also be "de-Judaized" after the victory over the Soviet Union, resolving the territorial question was becoming more pressing for Heydrich. In these days, however, a decision was finally made. A note for the files by Heydrich on a discussion with Göring shows the CdS again presenting a concept: "Concerning the solution of the Jewish question, I briefly reported to the Reichsmarschall and submitted to him my draft, which he approved with one change concerning the jurisdiction of [future Minister for the Occupied Territories Alfred] Rosenberg and ordered its resubmission." The Soviet Jews and the Einsatzgruppen formed a separate point of discussion: "The Reichsmarschall told me inter alia that with regard to the mission in Russia we should prepare an extremely short, 3- or 4-page briefing that the troops could receive on the dangers of the GPU-organization, the political commissars, Jews, etc., so that they know in practical terms who they have to put up against the wall."[26]

As the reference to Rosenberg indicates, the large territorial solution was to take place in the occupied Soviet Union, no matter whether the Jews of Vienna were to be deported into the General Government in the short term or whether the resettlement of Poles and Jews from western Poland that had been considered so urgent in terms of population policy were suspended, because transportation capacity was tied down with the military buildup for the war against the Soviet Union. At this point, so long as Hitler put off deportations until after the war, Heydrich was dependent only on the schedule, which was linked to the defeat of the Soviet Union. In the meantime, Heydrich saw to it that work continued on creating uniform measures for the legal exclusion of Jews, for example, in the Netherlands. Hanns Albin Rauter, the higher SS and police leader in Amsterdam, noted on 18 April that Heydrich had ordered the establishment of a central agency for Jewish emigration in that country, which was "to be exemplary for the solution of the Jewish question in all European states."[27] But in the mid term, nobody was thinking of emigration any more. The only thing this projected facility had in common with the central agencies in Prague and Vienna was the name: "As in Prague, alongside the central agency, a fund subject to public law is to be established, on which the securing of the necessary monetary means for financing emigration and *the coming final solution of the Jewish question in Europe* is incumbent."[28] Four weeks later, emigration as a means of fleeing the German sphere of influence was restricted to only German, Austrian, and Czech Jews.[29] These initiatives in the occupied and allied countries were accompanied by the posting of "Jewish affairs advisors," such as SS Captain Gustav Richter, who noted shortly after taking up work in Romania in May 1941: "The road that has to be taken concerning the solution of the Jewish question in Romania was discussed with the general in its main features and accepted by him. [General Eugen] Zwidenek immediately agreed to my first recommendation 1st to consolidate Jewry in Romania organizationally and 2nd to place it under state control – as one of the most important preconditions with regard to the coming final solution."[30]

Therefore, the fact that on the evening of 31 July 1941 Heydrich again went to Göring to have him sign a letter of confirmation that had been agreed to in advance, and that once more laid out what the CdS had already been working on for some time according to previous orders is not enough to deduce a fundamental shift toward the systematic murder of all European Jews. Heydrich himself must have realized the true significance of this document only in winter 1941. Why else would he have sent a photo copy to the SS Personnel Main Office only on 25 January 1942 for the purpose of having it placed in his file?[31] It was apparently necessary for Heydrich to have Göring reconfirm his authority, because in July 1941 victory over the Soviet Union seemed within reach, and because Heydrich wanted to retain overall control of the "Jewish question" should it become necessary to involve other central authorities.[32]

It is known that in the first half of 1941 Hitler found himself repeatedly confronted with requests for the deportation of Jews. However, Schirach, Goebbels, Heydrich, and Frank were always consoled with the statement that the deportations would be set in motion only after the victory over the Soviet Union. Göring and Greiser also learned that the relocation of Jews from western Poland to the Old Reich for forced labor was not something Hitler wanted either.[33]

But Hitler changed his stance over the course of several days between 15 and 17 September 1941. On 12 September, he had already expressed his wish that, as a countermove for the internment of Germans in Iran, "ten chosen Englishmen from the Jersey Islands [be] deported to the Pripet Marshes for every deported German."[34] Two days later, Otto Bräutigam, Rosenberg's liaison with the High Command of the Army, informed Führer Headquarters that the Volga Germans had been deported to Siberia and recommended on behalf of his boss, now minister for the occupied eastern territories, "the sending of all of Central Europe's Jews to the eastern territories under our administration." A day later, Bräutigam learned by phone from Wilhelm Keitel, head of the High Command of the Wehrmacht, and Emil von Rintelen, a ranking member of Ribbentrop's personal staff, that this matter would be raised only in a later discussion between Ribbentrop and Hitler.[35] Finally, on 16 September, Hitler received a message from Hamburg Gauleiter Karl Kaufmann requesting approval for the deportation of Hamburg's Jews so that the victims of aerial bombardments could be provided with apartments and household items.[36] It was also on 16 September that Hitler, Himmler, and Abetz met for lunch at Führer Headquarters. Abetz – who had known since taking office that Hitler was pursuing a personal political goal with regard to the Jews, and who had been urged by Paris colleague Karltheo Zeitschel to insist to Himmler and Rosenberg via Ribbentrop and Göring on the deportation of Europe's Jews to the occupied Soviet Union – used the opportunity that this occasion offered him.[37]

On 17 September, Hitler finally met Ribbentrop, and Himmler later visited Ribbentrop for dinner.[38] The thrust of these talks was that Hitler had given up the link between the "de-Judaization" of Europe and the defeat of the Soviet Union that he had mentioned so often in front of domestic and foreign politicians. A day later, Himmler informed Greiser that the ghetto in Łódź (Litzmanstadt) would have to take in 60,000 German, Austrian, and Czech Jews. Whether Greiser was really surprised is open to doubt. Himmler had apparently already sounded out the two HSSPFs directly affected by such a deportation of Jews into their fiefdoms.[39] HSSPF Wartheland Wilhelm Koppe wrote Himmler about this matter in a letter of 10 September, which has not been preserved.[40] Nonetheless, the Reichsführer-SS was fully aware of the problems a mass deportation planned at short notice was bound to create. He told Greiser, "I ask you not only to understand this measure, which will certainly bring difficulties and burdens for your province, but to support it to the utmost in the interest of the entire Reich."[41]

Nevertheless, there were indeed problems at this final destination. Since its establishment, the Łódź ghetto had been expanded into a labor ghetto where textiles were produced in shifts for Wehrmacht clothing offices. It was only with great effort that Himmler and Heydrich managed to carry out the transports against the resistance of the province politicians, who had enlisted the support of the Wartime Economics and Armaments Office of the High Command of the Wehrmacht. Although the RSHA rather quickly reduced the number of people to be evacuated to 20,000 Jews and 5,000 Sinti and Roma, every German agency involved feared the collapse of the forced labor system and the outbreak of epidemics in the ghetto. The plan to deport Jews from the "Greater German Reich" by the end of 1941, first to the Łódź ghetto and then farther east in the coming spring, thus failed. Even before the first transports to Wartheland were to depart, Hitler told Brigadier General Rudolf Toussaint on 6 October, shortly before the latter assumed his post as Wehrmacht territorial commander in Bohemia and Moravia, that the Jews of the Protectorate, Berlin, and Vienna would be evacuated "farther east right away," that is to say, they would not be quartered in the Wartheland or the General Government.[42]

Reinhard Heydrich was doubly affected by this decision. As CdS, he immediately had to find new final destinations in the occupied Soviet territories. As deputy *Reichsprotektor* in Bohemia and Moravia, he still had to deport the Czech Jews. Under the telling reference that it was still necessary to defer to the authorities in Łódź, Heydrich on 10 October explained to Karl Hermann Frank (HSSPF Bohemia-Moravia), Horst Böhme (BdS Prague), Hans Günther (head of the Central Agency for the Emigration of Jews in Prague), and Eichmann that the cities of Minsk and Riga would take in 50,000 Jews. Judging from the protocol of this meeting, Heydrich had apparently learned his lesson from the difficulties encountered in Łódź. If deportations to the final destination disturbed the interests of the civil administration and the Wehrmacht, then "his" Czech Jews would initially be concentrated in one or two ghettos in the Protectorate, and these ghettos – unlike the one in Łódź – would remain under the sole control of the Security Police and the SD – and this would remain the case until a final deportation destination had been found. From the start, the Theresienstadt ghetto had been thought of as a collection camp for Czech Jews.[43] In this case, Heydrich's concept for the Jews of Bohemia and Moravia was not even kept secret. At a reception for the press after the meeting, he publicly explained that the "centralization" of the Jews of Bohemia and Moravia in – presumably – a ghetto in each region was to be only one stage on the way to the final settlement. But he did not mention Minsk and Riga by name as the next places of deportation.[44]

The next day, Einsatzgruppe A commander and BdS Ostland Walther Stahlecker visited General Commissar Latvia Dr. Otto-Heinrich Drechsler at his official residence in Riga and announced that, "in accordance with a wish of the Führer" a large concentration camp for Jews from the Reich and the Protectorate was to be set up. Stahlecker's vague reference to its location, namely that this camp was to come into being in the area around Riga, Jelgava (Mitau), and Tukums (Tuckum) is worth noting.[45] A few days earlier, Rudolf Lange, the Gestapo chief at BdS Ostland, had suggested this triangle of territory west of Riga in writing and asked Stahlecker for permission to build a concentration camp there. Lange's justification ran, inter alia, that in the long term this camp should take on the roughly 23,000 Jews living in Riga, for in this way they could be put to work more effectively as forced laborers; the Riga ghetto was to be considered an interim solution anyway.[46] Stahlecker had then turned to the RSHA, Division II C (Technical Affairs), with a written request.[47]

Now, in his meeting with Drechsler, Stahlecker again took up Lange's original concept with one important distinction: the camp was to be erected for 25,000 German, Austrian, and Czech Jews. Drechsler's reaction – also to Stahlecker's later request for assistance in finding construction materials – was one of reluctance. Nonetheless, Drechsler also said that "naturally everything had to happen to comply with the Führer's wish."[48] Heydrich's remark a few days later, on 17 October, that "agreement from Minsk and Riga for 50,000 Jews each" had already arrived could be taken to mean that, at least in the case of the Latvian capital, he was thinking of maintaining a camp for both deported and local Jews in the long run.[49] Looking back in historical terms, it should be noted that Heydrich, when confronted with the problems raised by the Łódź administration, created a concrete fallback option for the deportation of Jews from the "Greater German Reich" in a relatively short amount of time. But on the ground in Riga itself, this new, improvised decision again gave rise to anxieties, which placed additional burdens on the already swelling conflict between civil administration, on the one hand, and the SS and police, on the other.

A few days later, on 20 and 21 October – after Drechsler had reported to Reich Commissariat Ostland about Stahlecker's visit and the new camp at Salaspils and had told Lange that the Reich commissar, Hinrich Lohse, disapproved of the approaching measures due to the hurried way in which the decisions were made – a discussion took place at Lohse's office on 24 October. During the conversation, Lange was accused of creating facts without consulting the civil administration. Lange responded by invoking the need for the "greatest haste," since the first transport would arrive on 10 November. Furthermore, said Lange, Heydrich's order had of course foreseen the immediate briefing of the Reich commissar, who unfortunately had been away, which was why Drechsler had been notified. Nonetheless, Lohse and Drechsler continued to press Lange, saying that the information shared consisted merely of a briefing on accomplished facts. Softening his tone, Lange admitted that only a shed had been constructed at the site near Salaspils. Lohse called the deportations to the Reich Commissariat Ostland a measure of "preeminent political significance," which was why it had to be arranged with him.

With that, Lohse's argument was clear: the arrival and accommodation of Jews in the Reich Commissariat were to be seen as political and not as police measures and were therefore to fall under the overall control of the civil administration. Lohse threatened to have this clarified in Berlin the following day.[50] It is not known whether Lohse visited not only the Reich Ministry for the Occupied Eastern Territories (RMbO), but also took his complaints directly to the RSHA. His appointment at the former may explain, however, why RMbO racial affairs expert Dr. Erhard Wetzel merely presented his visitor with a draft letter on 25 October, instead of sending it to Riga. In his letter, Wetzel referred back to a now lost letter from Lohse of 4 October "regarding the solution of the Jewish question" and an initial response fourteen days later. In the meantime, Wetzel now wrote, it had been possible to enlist the support of Viktor Brack from the chancellery of the Führer in the production of "gassing facilities" and related "accommodations." Brack, who had played a leading role in the Nazis' euthanasia operations, would at Lohse's request send his specialists to Riga, including Dr. Helmut Kallmeyer. Eichmann also approved of this procedure. With reference to the fate of the arrivals, Wetzel wrote: "According to a message from [SS] Major Eichmann, camps for Jews are to be created in Riga and Minsk, to which Jews from the Old Reich will also go [eventually]. At present, Jews from the Old Reich are being evacuated who are to go to Litzmannstadt [Łódź] but other camps as well in order to be put to work in the east inasmuch as [they are] able to work." Given this state of affairs, there would be "no objections, if those Jews who are not able to work are eliminated by Brack-like means."[51]

This is the first open statement that Jews evacuated from the west to the Reich Commissariat Ostland could be killed with gas if they were not able to work. Nonetheless, for historians, this draft letter continues to raise more questions about the further course of action of the mass murders than it answers. It is a matter of fact that no gas chambers were ever built in the civil-administrated Reich Commissariat Ostland. Lohse and Brack testified after the war that they were unaware of the letter and its contents. The chemist Kallmeyer said he had never been to Riga. Eichmann's remarks regarding this document, which were made in Israeli custody, were different. He did not doubt the incident, but said that upon receiving the inquiry from the RMbO, he had merely passed along the position of his boss Gestapo chief Heinrich Müller. During his trial, however, Eichmann claimed that he had discussed gas chambers with regard to Riga. Wetzel in turn said he had merely taken dictation from his boss, at the time Georg Leibbrandt. These defensive statements, alongside the fact that stationary gas chambers were never built in Riga, make these negotiations on the creation of such facilities for mass murder in Riga look more like administrative contingency planning. For reasons now unknown, the idea was briefly raised but then dropped. Nonetheless – and this is what is important for the fate of the German, Austrian, and Czech Jews – this letter shows a barbaric attitude toward the evacuees that differed only slightly from the murderous operations against the Jews of the Soviet Union. On this point, the civil authorities responsible for the destinations and the Gestapo as the deportation authority were agreed. On the ground in the occupied eastern territories, the new arrivals in Riga would see those deportees who were unable to walk, usually older people, shot on the way into town.

On 8 November, the day 990 Jews from Hamburg left for Minsk, Lange informed Reich Commissariat Ostland that, according to a message from the RSHA, the deportation of 50,000 Jews into Lohse's area of responsibility had started. The Jews came from the larger cities in the Reich and the Protectorate and were divided fifty-fifty between general commissariats

Latvia and White Ruthenia. The trains would arrive in Minsk at two-day intervals, between 10 November and 16 December; the rest of the Jews would follow between 10 and 20 January. For Riga, Lange said, the first transport would arrive on 19 November, and then an additional train would arrive every other day until 17 December; the remaining Jews would also be deported between 11 and 29 January. Lange also said that he would have five transports foreseen for Riga rerouted to Kaunas (Kauen, Kovno), although it would have to be left to scheduling to decide which five.[52]

Apparently, the Security Police favored having these be the first deportation trains to leave the Reich. Lange gave no clear reason, but in the same letter, he mentioned that the construction of barracks near Salaspils would continue in the "most accelerated fashion." Nonetheless, he added, due to a lack of materials and skilled workers, the camp would not be able to take in the first transports. At the time, Lange had been trying to acquire lumber cut very close to the projected camp site. But this building material had been prepared for use by the municipal bridge construction administration and Organization Todt to reinforce the only pontoon bridge over the Daugava that could bear motor vehicles. Although Lange stressed the "utmost urgency," his request was rejected by Werner Altemeyer, the chief of staff of the county commissar for Riga City.[53] Due to such delays in construction, the first arrivals were to be taken to the former public estate Jumpravmuiža (Jungfernhof), which had empty barracks. As can be shown in witness testimony, it is clear that this site was much too small. It was not even fully fenced in. Kaunas (Kauen, Kovno) was thus certainly an alternative site. The choice of Jumpravmuiža as a site to accommodate deported Jews followed due to its proximity to the planned camp at Salaspils. After its completion, the Jews could be taken there along the Daugavpils Road or by train, more or less unnoticed by the population.[54]

Lange's 8 November message to Lohse, sent at very short notice, did not reach its recipient. Lohse was at the time once again in Berlin on official business at the RMbO, so a telex was sent to him at the Hotel Adlon. In this brief text, Friedrich Trampedach, the official responsible, asked Lohse to prevent these transports, "for the camps for Jews must be relocated considerably farther to the east."[55] Why this transfer farther east was necessary remains a mystery, but Trampedach seemed to know, at least in the case of Minsk, that the Security Police there in fact wanted to send two arriving transports to Borisov and Bobruisk. This would have meant that the civil-administered General Commissariat White Ruthenia would have merely served as another stop along the way for additional evacuations to military-administered Rear Area Army Group Center.

But the railroad situation in Army Group Center refused to permit this during the battle for Moscow. For this reason, not only did the 25,000 Jews fail to arrive there – in fact, there were just under 7,000 – but Army Group Center insisted that the trains be stopped at the border to Reich Commissariat Ostland.[56] In a letter to Lohse, the Wehrmacht territorial commander in Ostland, Major General Walter Braemer, tried to have the deportation trains on the way to General Commissariat White Ruthenia suspended. Braemer wrote that the German Jews were superior in intelligence to the local population; if they were brought into contact with White Ruthenian Jewry, they would immediately attempt to "make contact with Communist bodies, etc., and to incite."[57] On 12 November, Max von Schenkendorff, the commander of Rear Area Army Group Center, abruptly ordered the 339th Infantry Division to stop the trains headed from Minsk to Bobruisk and Borisov, "if necessary by force of arms."[58] In the case of Riga, however, there were no serious transport difficulties for Army Group North. But in Riga as well, there had briefly been some talk of interning the arriving Jews at the Salaspils or Jungfernhof camps, albeit only for a temporary period. In early December, the RMbO reported one last time that, according to a message from Heydrich, the "camp for Jews" was to be built farther east in the area around Pskov.[59]

In suggesting these proposals to deport the Jews to points east of the general commissariats, however, Heydrich was probably responding not only to the RMbO's ideas. Rather, it seems that the Security Police itself had thought about other possibilities in the long term. As early as August, Stahlecker – in a statement on Lohse's temporary guidelines for the treatment of the Jewish question – had noted that a future "Jew reservation" should be erected only farther east, and as late as February 1942, Heydrich said the "Arctic area" was an "ideal homeland for the 11 million Jews from Europe."[60] Seen in the context of these remarks, another statement by Heydrich, to the effect that the commanders of the Einsatzgruppen B and C could "take in Jews in their camps for Communist prisoners in the zone of operations," gains in significance as well.[61]

Considerable evidence has been collected that indicates that such a camp was at least temporarily planned in Mogilev, in Rear Area Army Group Center. Not only was a large crematorium ordered, but HSSPF Hamburg Rudolf Querner apparently also ordered large quantities of Zyklon-B gas from the company Tesch & Stabenow, and HSSPF Ostland in Riga expected this gas to be delivered.[62] Nothing came of these plans, however – and not just because Schenkendorff refused to allow Jews to be transported into his territory. The use of fumigation poison in the military-administered occupied eastern territories was also subject to the approval of the Army's general quartermaster.[63] It was therefore impossible to keep the use of such large amounts of Zyklon-B secret, even if Querner did in fact purchase the substance in Hamburg and have it sent to Ostland under the auspices of the SS.[64]

As in the case of Łódź, Heydrich's provisions for further deportations in the general commissariats of Latvia and White Ruthenia did not go unchallenged. The CdS was not at this point in time the chief planner of the deportations whose decisions were accepted without comment. Both the civil administration in the Reich Commissariat and the Wehrmacht tried to influence the decisions made in Berlin and Prague. If one looks beyond the first wave of deportations to Wartheland and Reich Commissariat Ostland, then it can be seen rather easily that Heydrich's position and his measures were not accepted without criticism. He therefore felt obliged to write a letter justifying his actions to the Army's general quartermaster, when the latter complained about the bombing of seven Parisian synagogues, an act Heydrich had co-organized without informing the Wehrmacht territorial commander in France. Heydrich wrote: "I was fully aware of the political consequences of the measures taken, for I have been commissioned for years to prepare the final solution of the Jewish question in Europe."[65] In the General Government as well, prevailing tendencies in autumn 1941 showed, in the opinion of HSSPF East Friedrich Wilhelm Krüger, that General Governor Frank considered the "handling of the Jewish problem" a political task of the civil administration.

With every step that he took toward the "final solution" – aside from the establishment of Theresienstadt – Heydrich had encountered difficulties. The written empowerment from Göring, dated 31 July 1941, which stated that Heydrich was to make all the necessary preparations for a "total solution of the Jewish question in the German sphere of influence within Europe," became for the CdS a document of increasing importance in order to rebuff troublesome counterproposals. Alfred Meyer (state secretary at the RMbO), Georg Leibbrandt (director of the Main Department for Political Affairs at the RMbO), and Josef Bühler (state secretary in the General Government) received copies of Göring's letter along with their invitations to the Wannsee Conference dated 29 November 1941. One day earlier, Lohse had apparently already instructed his own Main Department for Political Affairs: "[i]n the future, objections are not to be raised by us regarding any kind of transports from the Reich."[66] This was an order that would not be changed until the last transport from the west to Reich Commissariat Ostland arrived in autumn 1942. With the invitations to the Wannsee Conference, Heydrich saw to it for the first time that his commission was presented to ministers and top party and territorial leaders so that he could move forward from improvisation to the planning stage for a "total solution of the European Jewish question." Minsk, Kaunas, and Riga were the last contentious final destinations of the deportations before

Heydrich moved on to become the uncontested manager of deportation and mass murder.

Notes

1. See Götz Aly, *"Endlösung."*
2. Printed in *Archives of the Holocaust*, vol. 20, doc. 107, 297.
3. On the role of the RSHA in the "Germanization" of the western Polish territories, see Wildt, *Generation des Unbedingten*, 473–505.
4. *Reichsgesetzblatt I*, 1939, 1,097, Zehnte Verordnung zum Reichsbürgergesetz, 4 July 1939, Paragraph 4.
5. BA DH, Dok. K 324/3, Ech/L [Eichmann], Vermerk. Betrifft: Vorbereitende Tätigkeit in Berlin, 6 October 1939; Eich/L Vermerk über eine Rücksprache mit SS-Of. Müller, 6 October 1939; Vermerk G/Z. Betrifft: Besprechung mit Generalmajor v. Knobelsdorf[f] und dem Chef der Zivilverwaltung, Präsident Fitzner, in Kattowitz am Montag, den 9.10.1939, gez. G.H. Mähr. Ostrau, 28 October 1939; Wildt, *Generation des Unbedingten*, 468–469.
6. Printed in *Biuletyn Głownej Komisji Zbrodni Hitlerowskich w Polsce*, Band XII (1960), dok. 9, 32F.
7. BA Berlin, R58/544, 218, II/112, an Leiter II im Hause, Betr. Stichpunkte für das Sachgebiet Judentum zur Amtschefbesprechung, 19 December 1939.
8. Printed in *Faschismus – Ghetto – Massenmord*, ed. Jüdisches Historisches Institut Warschau, 50–52.
9. Rossiiskii Gosudartsvennyi Voennyi Arkhiv (RGVA), 503-1-385, 1, RSHA, IV-D 3c, Schnellbrief, Betr. Beschränkung der Freizügigkeit von Juden im Reichsgebiet und Zusammenfassung in größeren Orten, 12 February 1940.
10. The leaflets for these helpers, which are now available, confirm the report of Ms. G.M., who had claimed these read: "You are called upon to take part in an operation to make Stettin free of Jews." See the report of G.M. in *Lebenszeichen aus Piaski*, 23. The text of the leaflet reads: "You have been selected by your district leader to take part in an important operation. It involves making the government district of Stettin as free of Jews as possible." See RGVA, 503-1-337, 2.
11. RGVA, 503-1-385, 6, RSHA, IV A 5b, Rv. Schnellbrief an alle Staatspolizei(leit)stellen mit Ausnahme der ehemaligen polnischen Gebiete und Danzig, betr. Beschränkung der Freizügigkeit von Juden, 15 March 1939: "As has become known here, my [circular decree] of 12 February 1940 has been interpreted here and there to mean that the Jews are now to be concentrated in the places that I was looking at for this in the compilation attached to my decree. Here and there, preparations for carrying out corresponding measures are already to have been made, with it being intended, inter alia, to deport Jews to places in the area of operations. This interpretation of my [circular decree] of 12 February 1940, is incorrect, rather it was only to serve to create the basis for a later examination of the question of a general resettlement of the Jews. In order to preempt the difficulties that would inevitably emerge with regard to military-political as well as technical transport and food-related economic spheres of activity in the event of an uncontrolled handling of a general resettlement of the Jews, I therefore ask [the field offices], by way of amendment of my [circular decree] of 12 February 1940, to refrain from resettlement measures for the

Jews until the submission of express instructions so that the Jews remain at their previous places of residence for the time being. p.p. sig. Schellenberg."
12. Cf. Hans Jansen, *Der Madagaskar-Plan*, 499–506; Wildt, *Generation des Unbedingten*, 499–506.
13. Quoted from Hans-Jürgen Döscher, *SS und Auswärtiges Amt im Dritten Reich*, 215.
14. Jansen, *Der Madagaskar-Plan*, 316–360.
15. On the date of Abetz's visit, see Eberhard Jäckel, *Frankreich in Hitlers Europa*, 67. On the content of discussions, see notes by Martin Luther to Rademacher, 15 August 1940, in Döscher, *SS und Auswärtiges Amt*, 216.
16. The discussion between Hitler and Gigurtu on 26 July 1940 is described in "Aufzeichnung ohne Unterschrift," in *ADAP*, Serie D, Bd. X, 254.
17. *Akten der Parteikanzlei der NSDAP*, Fiche 101, Bormann an Lammers, 20 November 1940, 28,404–28,405.
18. The only document linking the Madagascar Plan, the Gurs Operation, the expansion of such operations to other territories, and the protest of the Vichy government is an unsigned report filed with Friedrich Gauss in the Foreign Office, see Jakob Toury, "Die Entstehungsgeschichte des Austreibungsbefehls gegen die Juden der Saarpfalz und Badens: 22./23. Oktober 1940 – Camp de Gurs," *Jahrbuch des Instituts für Deutsche Geschichte* 15 (1986): 450–457, which contains additional references. The same document is mentioned by Serge Klarsfeld, who cites BA Berlin, R22/52, 107ff. Klarsfeld identifies the handwritten remarks of Foreign Office State Secretary Ernst von Weizsäcker as follows: "I have received the same letter with the same postage stamp. 4.11. W." For more on this, see Serge Klarsfeld, *Vichy – Auschwitz*, 360–361.
19. BA Berlin, NS 19/3979, Unterlagen für den Reichsführer-SS zum Vortrag über Siedlung, undated [December 1940].
20. *Das Diensttagebuch des Generalgouverneurs in Polen 1939–1945*, ed. Werner Präg and Wolfgang Jacobmeyer, 326–328.
21. On this conversation on 2 October 1940, see the note for the files by Martin Bormann, Nuremberg Document USSR-172, in *IMG*, Bd. 39, 425–429. Written confirmation by Lammers with the formulation that Vienna's Jews were to be deported "more quickly, that is to say, still during the war" is contained in Nuremburg Document PS-1950, *IMG*, Bd. 29, 175–176.
22. Dannecker's letter of 21 January 1941 regarding a central office for Jews in Paris is printed in Klarsfeld, *Vichy – Auschwitz*, 361–363.
23. Hillgrüber, *Hitlers Strategie*, 351–377.
24. Politisches Archiv – Auswärtiges Amt (PA-AA), R 99225, Heydrich an Luther, 5 February 1941; Streckenbach an Luther, 14 February 1941. The letters involve individual cases of applications from Jews in French camps (Gurs, St. Cyprien) for release so they can go to German-occupied northern France.
25. Quoted from H.-G. Adler, *Der verwaltete Mensch*, 152.
26. RGVA, 500-3-795, 140–145, Der Chef der Sipo und des SD, Geheim. Aktenvermerk, 26 March 1941, printed in Klein, *Die Einsatzgruppen in der besetzten Sowjetunion*, 367–368.
27. Louis de Jong, *Het Koninkrijk der Nederlanden in de Tweede Wereldoorlog*, Deel 5, Helft 2, 970–971.
28. Ibid., emphasis added by the authors.
29. PA-AA, R 100862, Schellenberg an Rademacher, 20 May 1941, "In accordance with a letter of the Reichsmarschall of the Greater German Reich, the emigration of the Jews from Reich territory, including the Protectorate Bohemia and Moravia, is also to be carried out during the war, intensified within the framework of the given possibilities under

observation of the guidelines issued for the emigration of the Jews. Since only insufficient emigration possibilities are [at present] available for Jews from Reich territory, primarily via Spain and Portugal, an emigration of Jews from France and Belgium means an impairment of [emigration from Germany]. Under consideration of these facts, and in regard to the final solution of the Jewish question, which is coming without a doubt, the emigration of Jews from France and Belgium is to be prohibited."

30. *Documents Concerning the Fate of Romanian Jewry during the Holocaust,* ed. Jean Ancel, 401.
31. YIVO Institute for Jewish Research, Occ. G 197, Heydrich an Schmitt. The photo copy is to be found in Heydrich's SS personnel record, BA Berlin, BDC, SSO Reinhard Heydrich. Heydrich apparently kept the original letter.
32. Nuremberg Document NG-2586, "In addition to the task assigned you by the decree of 24 January 1939 to provide a solution to the Jewish question by emigration or evacuation in the most favorable way possible under prevailing circumstances, I herewith commission you to make all necessary preparations in regard to organizational, practical, and material matters for an overall solution of the Jewish question in the German sphere of influence within Europe.
"Inasmuch as the competences of other central authorities are affected, these are to be enlisted.
"I further commission you to submit to my office in the near future an overall draft proposal on the organizational, practical, and material preliminary measures requisite for carrying out the intended final solution of the Jewish question."
33. Dieter Maier, *Arbeitseinsatz und Deporation,* 91–93.
34. Hewel's notes on his conversation with Hitler are in "Aufzeichnung des Gesandten Hewel (Persönl. Stab RAM)," 12 September 1941, in *ADAP,* Serie D, Bd. XIII/1, 394.
35. H. D. Heilmann, "Das Kriegstagebuch des Diplomaten Otto Bräutigam," in *Biedermann und die Schreibtischtäter* (= *Beiträge zur nationalsozialistischen Gesundheits- und Sozialpolitik* 4), 144–145.
36. Peter Witte, "Zwei Entscheidungen in der 'Endlösung der Judenfrage,'" *Theresienstädter Studien und Dokumente* 2 (1995): 45.
37. Zeitschel's request to Abetz is printed in Klarsfeld, *Vichy – Auschwitz,* 367–268. Regarding Abetz's meeting with Hitler and Himmler, see *Dienstkalender,* 211. On Zeitschel's report on the success of Abetz's visit with Hitler, see *Verfolgung, Vertreibung, Vernichtung,* ed. Kurt Pätzold, 309.
38. The meeting between Hitler and Ribbentrop is mentioned in Hillgruber, *Hitlers Strategie,* 694, while the meeting between Ribbentrop and Himmler appears in *Dienstkalender,* 213.
39. *Dienstkalender,* 203 and 205–206.
40. BA Berlin, NS 19/4027, 257, Brieftagebuch, Pers. Stab RF-SS; BA Berlin, NS 19/2655, 3, Himmler an Greiser, 18 September 1941.
41. BA Berlin, NS 19/2655, 3, Himmler an Greiser, 18 September 1941.
42. BA Berlin, R 6/34a, 42–43, Koeppen-Vermerk Nr. 42, 6 October 1941, noon. Also printed in *Herbst 1941 im "Führerhauptquartier,"* ed. Martin Vogt, 63–66.
43. The notes from the Prague meeting on 10 October 1941 are printed in *Deutsche Politik im "Protektorat Böhmen und Mähren" unter Reinhard Heydrich 1941–1942,* ed. Miroslav Karný, Jaroslava Milotová, and Margita Karná, 137–141.
44. Archive of the Interior Ministry, Prague, 114-2-47, unpaginated, Presse-Empfang, 10 October 1941.
45. YIVO, Occ. E-3-29, Aktennotiz, gez. Dr. Drechsler, 20 October 1941; see also Safrian, *Die Eichmann-Männer,* 134.

46. RGVA, 504-2-8, 148–150, Der BdS – EG A – II, Vermerk, 1 October 1941.
47. Ibid., 165–166, Der BdS – EG A an RSHA, Amt II, betr. Errichtung eines erweiterten Staatspolizeigefängnisses in Riga, 7 October 1941.
48. YIVO, Occ. E-3-29, Aktennotiz, gez. Dr. Drechsler, 20 October 1941.
49. Printed in Karný et al., *Deutsche Politik im "Protektorat Böhmen und Mähren,"* 147–157.
50. YIVO, Occ. E 3-30, RKO, Vermerk zu einem Gespräch am 24.10.41 beim Reichskommissar, 27 October 1941. Cf. Safrian, *Die Eichmann-Männer,* 144.
51. Nuremberg Document, NO-365, RmbO, Sachbearbeiter Dr. Wetzel, an den RKO, betr. Lösung der Judenfrage, Geheim, 25 October 1941. See also Safrian, *Die Eichmann-Männer,* 144–145.
52. On 20 November, Lange informed the Reich Commissariat Ostland that the first twenty-five transports for Riga would be rerouted to Kaunas, YIVO, Occ. E 3-26, Der BdS, EG A – II, an den RKO, betr. Judentransporte aus dem Reich, i.A. Lange. This had apparently not made the rounds to the Gestapo field offices in the Reich, because on 3 December 1941 SS First Lieutenant Alois Brunner of the Central Agency for the Emigration of Jews in Vienna informed BdS Ostland that the second transport of Vienna Jews had been dispatched to Riga that day. The first transport, however, had gone to Kaunas, see RGVA, 504-2-1, 4, Zentralstelle for jüdische Auswanderung an den BdS, EG A, z. Hd. SS-Stubaf. Lange, betr. nach Riga abgefertigeten Judentransport aus Wien, 3 December 1941.
53. BA Berlin, R 91/95, unpaginated, Der BdS, Einsatzgruppe A – II, an den Geb.-Komm. Riga-Stadt, Brückenbauabteilung, betr. Überlassung von geschlagenem Holz im Wald Cuibe bei Kurtenhof, 7 November 1941; refusal in ibid., Altemeyer an BdS, 15 November 1951 and the written withdrawal of the request from the BdS, 23 November 1941.
54. On the departure of the Hamburg Jews for Minsk, see Gerlach, *Kalkulierte Morde,* 752. On Lange's remarks on 8 November 1941, see YIVO, Occ. E 3-31, Der BdS, EG A – II, an den RKO, betr. Judentransporte aus dem Reich in das Ostland, 8 November 1941; Safrian, *Die Eichmann-Männer,* 146.
55. YIVO, Occ. E 3-32, Der RKO, II a 4, Entwurf, sent 9 November, signature from Trampedach.
56. For more references, see Gerlach, *Kalkulierte Morde,* 751–754.
57. YIVO, Occ. E 3-34, Der WBO, Ic, an den RKO in Riga, betr. Beförderung von Juden aus Deutschland nach Minsk, 20 November 1941.
58. The relevant passage from the Ib (quartermaster) of Army Group Center reads: "In situation report of 11.11. of the [Authorized Transport Officer (Army Group) Center], it is noted on page 2 among the trains that have arrived on the regular line in Minsk. Far [?] /without/Jews?/28 [railcars]/Gestapo Minsk. An inquiry with the [Authorized Transport Officer Center] resulted in a message that, on order of the OKW, a transport of Jews will be driven to Minsk every two days (at first 2 trains everyday were intended). Inasmuch as is known here, only Minsk comes into question as end station for now. After an inquiry with the Ic, a call was made to the Ia of the [commander of Rear Area Army Group Center] (Major von Kraewel), who said that according to report of the 339th I.D. the message was passed along on the 11th [of this month] by the SD (Minsk) that 2 trains of Jews are to be driven to Bobruisk and Borisov. [The commander of Rear Area Army Group Center] ordered the 339th I.D. to prevent the entry of the trains of Jews into the zone of operations, if necessary by force of arms. Ib." Hannes Heer introduced this document into the literature, but it originates from Army Group Center, not Rear Area Army Group Center. Hannes Heer, "Killing Fields: Die Wehrmacht und der Holocaust," *Tote Zonen: Die deutsche Wehrmacht an der Ostfront,* ed. Hannes Heer, 34, ft. 90. The citation is from the Military Archive Podolsk outside Moscow, 500-12473-164.

59. YIVO, Occ. E 3-32, FS 97759 von Leibbrandt an Lohse, 13 November 1941, according to which Jews would go farther east and Riga as well as Minsk were to be considered temporary measures; YIVO, Occ. E 3-35, RmbO an RKO, betr.: Lösung der Judenfrage, i.A. Leibbrandt, 4 December 1941.
60. This speech by Heydrich in Prague on 4 February 1492 is printed in Karný et al., *Deutsche Politik im "Protektorat Böhmen und Mähren,"* 221–234, here 229.
61. This remark was made in Prague at a meeting held on 10 October 1941, printed in ibid., 137–141, here 138.
62. Christian Gerlach, "The Failure of Plans for an SS Extermination Camp in Mogilev, Belorussia," *Holocaust and Genocide Studies* 11 (1997): 60–78; on the order for Zyklon-B to HSSPF Ostland Friedrich Jeckeln, see Richard Breitman, *Staatsgeheimnisse*, 103–105.
63. Tesch & Stabenow, Hamburg, an den RKO, Abtl. IIIe, Gesundheit und Volkspflege, z. Hd. Medrat. Dr Ferdinand, 21 February 1942: "For the sake of order, we take it upon ourselves to point out that, as Dr. Tesch already informed you during his visit on 27 November 1941, we may undertake fumigation assignments in the eastern territories only with the express permission of the General Quartermaster. Perhaps, however, there exists the possibility that the intended disinfestations serve an instructional purpose for training courses that we are to carry out on behalf of the General Quartermaster for the Wehrmacht Territorial Commander Ostland in Riga and another office from the front area. For this, however, [a] precondition would be that the training could begin simultaneously with the disinfestation so that the two offices could order the training participants to Riga for this time," BA Berlin, R 90/446, 53–55. The company had learned from its fumigation director Holst [first name unknown], who worked for HSSPF Ostland Friedrich Jeckeln, that the empty part of the ghetto was to be disinfested; for that reason, the prerequisite price estimates were sent. At his trial, Bruno Tesch confirmed that he had conducted educational courses on the use of Zyklon-B for members of the SS and police in Riga, see Jürgen Kalthoff and Martin Werner, *Die Händler des Zyklon-B*, 152.
64. Breitman, *Staatsgeheimnisse*, 104.
65. Printed in Klarsfeld, *Vichy – Auschwitz*, 369–370.
66. YIVO, Occ. E 3-32, marginalia dated 28 November made on the letter, RmbO an RKO, 13 November 1941; Safrian, *Die Eichmann-Männer*, 149.

– Chapter 7 –

PLANS FOR THE SALASPILS CAMP

As already mentioned, the command staff of Einsatzgruppe A (EG A) and Einsatzkommando 2 (Ek 2) took up their Security Police duties immediately after the Latvian capital was captured. In the months that followed, the prisons, the command post of the Arajs Commando (Ek 2's local auxiliaries), and not least of all EG A's headquarters in the building of the former Latvian Ministry of Agriculture were the most feared addresses in Riga. The memoirs and witness statements by surviving Jews document the constant violent excesses committed there by the German police and Latvian self-defense forces.[1]

But during the first weeks of occupation, Latvian Jews were not the only victims of preference. According to official German records, the Latvian auxiliary police was "deployed exclusively in the search for Communists and Red Army soldiers" in early July.[2] This soon changed at the initiative of the regular auxiliary police and the Arajs men, who did not wait for German orders but instead began making arbitrary arrests on their own, spontaneously or after receiving denunciations. In addition, Ek 2 carried out a search of all offices according to lists of names, membership cards, and other materials that could prove membership in the Communist party or one of its subordinate organizations. Thus, in mid August, the Security Police discovered in the rooms of the Latvian association of commercial trade workers not only Communist propaganda material but also 624 completed questionnaires. These association members had answered the question regarding membership in a Communist organization in the affirmative.[3] Similar materials had been found in the local headquarters of the NKVD, the Soviet secret police, as well. Analysis of all this printed material had produced three wanted-persons lists naming members and informants of the NKVD and members and candidate members of the Latvian Communist Party.[4] Finally, larger and smaller police raids were continuously carried out, during which large numbers of civilians were arrested.[5]

"Clearance" of the prisons took place repeatedly by murdering Jews and Communists in the forests of Bikernieki and Jugla. They were shot in pits that had been prepared in advance.[6] On 27 September, there were 3,777

Notes for this chapter begin on page 200.

persons in Riga's internment facilities.[7] From the start, Department II of Ek 2 must have had its hands full screening prisoners.[8] If one considers that Ek 2 was made up of seventy persons, who also oversaw the screening of those in remand in provincial towns, then it can be concluded that Ek 2's personnel was overworked to a certain extent – all the more so because the Latvian auxiliary police directed most of its prisoners to various prisons.[9] The 2,973 members of the local police, who were identified by armbands, dominated Riga's cityscape. Of them, 1,219 were distributed over thirteen police stations. Some 19 officers and 381 rank-and-file policemen served in the prison system.[10]

The absence of a centralized prison system and the lack of a unified command were probably what led Stahlecker at the end of July to request permission from Dr. Rudolf Siegert, the head of the Reich Security Main Office's Department II (Organization, Administration, and Legal Affairs), to make preparations for a concentration camp in Riga. The intolerable hygienic and provisioning conditions in the detention centers – which were overcrowded despite the liquidations – took up a good part of Stahlecker's justification for a camp, but he added: "What is more, only then would the possibility arise of reviewing the prisoners systematically and separating those who are needed for further investigation and interrogation ... I consider it necessary that this concentration camp be placed exclusively under the direction of the Security Police, and that it initially draw on Latvian auxiliary police for guarding."[11]

Stahlecker also wrote that in the future the number of prisoners would be considerably higher than the capacity of the detention centers – about 4,000 – and added that Higher SS and Police Leader Ostland Hans-Adolf Prützmann would be interested in workers. Finally, he did not forget to ask that a specialist in the construction of such camps be dispatched to Riga.[12] A few days later, Stahlecker received permission from Berlin, but it was pointed out that a specialist for the camp's construction could not be provided. In this letter, and in another that followed at a later date, it was expressly called to his attention that the Security Police could establish "expanded police prisons" and "labor correctional camp," but not "concentration camps." Concentration camps were not allotted for in the budget of the Security Police and the SD. A copy of police prison regulations, the official regulations for the labor correctional camp in Watenstedt, and the decrees governing provisions for prisoners were submitted as enclosures for Stahlecker and his office.[13]

At the end of September 1941, the preparatory work for this camp began to take a more concrete shape. Writing on behalf of Department II of the office of the Territorial Commander of the Security Police and SD Ostland (BdS Ostland), SS Major Rudolf Lange drew up a comprehensive memorandum that specified the kind of place needed for the camp and the camp's greater purpose. Here there was no more talk about the need for a centralized concentration of prisoners in Riga:

> An additional aspect that speaks for the establishment of a [concentration camp] near Riga is the fact that there are about 23,000 Jews in Riga. The crowding of the Jews into a ghetto can only be a temporary solution. Soon the need will arise to clear the housing space occupied by the Jews for other purposes. Furthermore, [we] must also strive to put to work as close to 100 percent as possible of the male as well as the female Jews, who up to now have only partially been drawn on for work by Wehrmacht offices, etc. Ultimately, the ghetto does not offer any possibility of preventing the further reproduction of the Jews. Also with regard to the long run, it is necessary to maintain a concentration camp in order to accommodate those imprisoned for the long term. Transport difficulties alone make it impossible to transport prisoners to the Reich for the purpose of confining them to a concentration camp ... It can already be said that the space envisioned [for a camp] offers so many possibilities that all of the remaining Jews in Riga, and in Latvia, could be concentrated there. In the process, Jews must be accommodated separately from Jewesses in order to prevent further reproduction. Children under 14 must remain with the women.[14]

Stahlecker probably agreed to Lange's request to establish a central camp for prisoners and Jews in General Commissariat Latvia, because in Kaunas (Kauen, Kovno), Ek 3 had initially run such a concentration camp for Jews in nearby Fort VII and then in Fort IX as well.[15] But a more important factor may have been that, with the introduction of civil administration in Latvia, BdS Ostland had been forced to turn over the ghetto – still in its development stage – to County Commissariat Riga City. With that, the people confined to the ghetto were no longer solely under the power of disposal of the Security Police. Accordingly, the process of organizing the use of Jewish forced labor would be oriented toward the priorities of the general commissar and not the wishes of HSSPF Ostland Prützmann.

Lange, together with SS Major Alwin Reemtsma, the SS economist with HSSPF Ostland, had already found suitable terrain for a camp and had described the site as especially advantageous in the aforementioned memorandum to Stahlecker. This terrain, located in the triangle between Riga, Jelgava (Mitau), and Tukums (Tuckum), was, according to Lange, thinly populated, located relatively close to the Latvian capital, and suitable for the "immediate labor deployment of a larger number of prisoners." He went on to add: "It is possible, without any difficulty, to make one or several of the very small peasant farms that are in bad repair the starting point of a concentration camp. The first troops of prisoners would have to be used to build accommodations for the prisoners to be confined there later."[16] Lange recommended putting the prisoners to work cutting peat and operating the numerous small brickworks, which could be taken over as "concentration camp enterprises." Prützmann's economic affairs expert was said to be particularly interested in this. On 6 October, Stahlecker again turned to the Reich Security Main Office regarding the construction of an "expanded police prison" in the region southwest of Riga and once again repeated his request for the delegation of a specialist from the central office of the Security Police and the SD in Berlin, remarking that "the issue has become particularly urgent due to the advanced stage of the season."[17]

If one takes a closer look at the planning for the establishment of a central camp for Jews and prisoners first for Riga, then for General Commissariat Latvia as a whole, it is necessary to note that Heydrich's remarks in Prague on 10 October 1941 regarding the deportation of Jews from the west to Riga and Minsk were highly theoretical where their actual implementation was concerned. When news of Heydrich's intentions reached Riga, Stahlecker found himself confronted by a massive time problem. Stahlecker and Lange not only had to deal with objections from the civil administration regarding the proposed camp; they now had to build the camp in a hurry, because for Heydrich this undertaking represented the ideal solution for dealing with previous protests from Łódź (Litzmannstadt) concerning deportations to that city.

Apparently, the triangle of territory southwest of the occupied capital proved unsuitable for transports arriving from the west, for it has already been mentioned that Lange informed the general commissar of the camp's final location on 21 October. The camp would be established close to the town of Salaspils, some 20 km (12 miles) southeast of Riga, alongside the Riga-Daugavpils railroad; it was to hold about 25,000 people and would be under the command of the Security Police and the SD.[18] Stalag 350, which held 40,000 Soviet POWs, was already located nearby.[19] Lange entrusted Gerhard Maywald with the camp's construction after the two men had completed an inspection flight over the greater Riga area to determine the exact site. Maywald still vividly recalled the situation in November 1963, because Lange had also suggested to him the installation of workshops for Jews in Salaspils.[20]

Notes

1. Regarding this period, see chapter 3.
2. BA Berlin, R58/214, Ereignismeldung Nr. 12, 4 July 1941.
3. BA Berlin, R58/216, Ereignismeldung Nr. 67, 29 August 1941.

4. BA Berlin, R58/217, Ereignismeldung Nr. 96, 27 September 1941.
5. BA Berlin, R58/215, Ereignismeldung Nr. 40, 1 August 1941, and R58/217, Ereignismeldung Nr. 88, 19 September 1941.
6. Kaufmann, *Churbn Lettland*, 221, as well as BA Berlin, R58/217, Ereignismeldung Nr. 88, 19 September 1941: "In the prisons [of Riga], there are at present 3,857 persons, among them 3,569 Communists, 172 Jews, and 116 persons against whom various charges are being processed. Clearance of the prison takes place continuously."
7. BA Berlin, R58/217, Ereignismeldung Nr. 96, 27 September 1941.
8. A large number of Ek 2 prison release certificates dating from summer and autumn 1941 and containing a warning in German and Latvian to the person concerned are to be found in LVVA Riga, P 252-1, vol. 1–25.
9. On the make up of Ek 2, see Wilhelm, *Die Einsatzgruppe A*, 137.
10. BA-MA, RH 22/271, unpaginated, Der HSSPF Ostland an den Berück Nord, betr. Bildung von Hilfspolizeiverbänden durch Landeseinwohner, 21 August 1941. This document discusses the establishment of the local Latvian police in Riga, Madona (Modohn), Vecgulbene (Altschwaneburg), Taurupe, and Tukums (Tuckum) as of 10 August 1941.
11. RGVA, 504-2-8, 138–139, Stahlecker an das RSHA, II, z. Hd. von Ministerialrat Dr. Siegert Berlin. Dringend. Sofort vorlegen! Betrifft: Errichtung eines Konzentrationslagers in Riga, v. 23.7.1941 befördert.
12. Ibid: "In addition, I would be grateful if an experienced specialist from there could be transferred to Riga for this purpose for several weeks. I know that SS Maj. Criminal Counselor Möller, Gestapo Regional Office Berlin, was involved to a large extent and with success in the establishment of the labor correctional camp Wuhlheide. I would ask you consider delegating Criminal Counselor Möller here for four weeks to direct the construction of the camp."
13. RGVA, 504-2-8, 144, RSHA, II C 3, an EG A, SS-Brif. Stahlecker, via Tilsit, 4 August 1941, and ibid., 146, RSHA, II C 3, an Ek 2, 17 September 1941. The enclosures are not among the surviving documents.
14. Ibid., 148–150, Der BdS-Einsatzgruppe A – II, Vermerk, dated 1 October 1941. This note contains in the margins: "Agreed. Prepare request."
15. BA Berlin, R58/214, Ereignismeldung Nr. 14, 6 July 1941. On this, see also Christoph Dieckmann, "Das Ghetto und das Konzentrationslager in Kaunas 1941–1944," in *Die nationalsozialistischen Konzentrationslager*, ed. Ulrich Herbert, Karin Orth, and Christoph Dieckmann, Bd. I, 439–471.
16. RGVA, 504-2-8, 148–150, Der BdS – Einsatzgruppe A – II, Vermerk, dated 1 October 1941.
17. Ibid., 165–166, Der BdS, Einsatzgruppe A, an das RSHA, Amt II, betr. Errichtung eines erweiterten Polizeigefängnisses in Riga, sent on 7 October 1941.
18. YIVO, Occ. E 3-29, Aktennotiz, 20 October 1941, and handwritten note from 21 October 1941.
19. Staw. Hamburg, 141 Js 534/60, Bd. 29, statement by Josef Stocker, 27 September 1962, 4,464. Stocker was a former member of Home Defense Battalion 529 and guard at Stalag 350.
20. Ibid., Bd. 41, statement by Gerhard Maywald, 15 November 1963, 6,806: "We then flew around above Riga and the surrounding area in a plane from the Air Force – it was a FW Weihe – in order to search for a favorable location that had water as well as a rail connection. Dr. Lange was of the opinion that I could also set up a large enterprise after I first set up the smaller workshop. The setting up of this camp was then also carried out by me and, until my transfer to Minsk, made the most demands of my working hours."

– Chapter 8 –

THE DEPORTATION OF GERMAN JEWS TO RIGA

On 25 May 1962, Paul Salitter, a retired police major, appeared at the Düsseldorf Prosecutor's Office for questioning in connection with the deportation of 1,007 Jews from the Rhineland. This former adjutant to the commander of the Düsseldorf Schutzpolizei (the German municipal police) had been the leader of an escort commando of sixteen German policemen that had guarded the Düsseldorf transport to Riga that departed on 11 December 1941. After the investigating judge conducting the questioning had read Salitter excerpts from the confidential "Report on the evacuation of Jews to Riga," the former transport leader recoiled. He doubted that he was the report's author, for he could not have known at the time many of the details cited in it. He was sure that this was not the original report he had written; it was conceivable that back then some of his report, together with information from others, had led to this nine-page document. Some days later, Salitter sent yet another statement from the former deputy transport leader, who spoke of "mean-spirited falsifications in [Salitter's] official report." Salitter himself did not want to exclude the possibility that this "crass adulteration of my official report filed at the time" could have taken place after the war.[1]

There were reasons for Salitter's defensiveness, which came easily enough due to the lack of a handwritten signature. Even today, the report reveals the brash and overbearing tone of orders that prevailed at the slaughterhouse that served as the collection camp in Düsseldorf, on the loading ramp, and on the train. The author commented on the suicide attempt of a man who jumped in front of a streetcar on the way to boarding as follows: "However, he was caught by the tram's undercarriage trash rack and only slightly injured. He at first pretended to be dying, but soon perked up a good deal during the trip, once he noticed that he could not escape the fate of being evacuated."[2]

A day later at noon, when the train reached the small town of Konitz (today Chojnice, Poland), Salitter sought to have his team's second-class carriage switched from the end of the train to the middle in order to improve

Notes for this chapter begin on page 225.

supervision. The stationmaster, however, refused for reasons of time and suggested that the Jews from the middle of the train swap places with the policemen: "It seems appropriate that it be made clear to this railroad attendant by a position of authority that he has to treat members of the German police differently than Jews. I had the impression that, in his case, this was one of those comrades of our race who still cultivate the habit of talking about the 'poor Jews' and for whom the term 'Jew' is completely alien."[3]

Finally, the report revealed what kind of news could be taken back to Düsseldorf concerning the fate of the Jews in Riga: in the section "Stay in Riga," Salitter wrote:

> The Latvian people are, so far as I could observe, Germanophile and to a large extent speak German. However, it was in many cases discernable from the behavior of individual personages that they are still loyal to tsarist Russia. No Latvian, however, wants to have anything to do with the Bolsheviks, for there is seldom a family that survived without making a blood sacrifice during the Soviet occupation. Their hatred is directed toward the Jews in particular. Therefore, from the moment of their liberation up to now, they have also participated very extensively in the extermination of these parasites. It seems to them, however – something I was able to note among Latvian railway personnel in particular – incomprehensible why Germany is bringing Jews to Latvia and not exterminating them in their own country.[4]

Over twenty years later, Salitter remembered that the mass murder of the Jews was in fact a topic of discussion in the cafeteria of the office of the Territorial Commander of the Order Police. He certainly never forgot one important detail: the incident in which Schutzpolizei Major Karl Heise lost an eye to a stray bullet during the mass shooting of 30 November.[5]

The transport of more than 1,000 people included not only Jews from Düsseldorf. The day before, on 10 December, a transport from Mönchengladbach had arrived in Düsseldorf. In it was Hilde Sherman-Zander with her husband Kurt Winter and their family members. Her memoirs allow us to reconstruct their stay in Düsseldorf and evacuation from their point of view. The marks left by the tone of orders and physical violence resonate even decades later: "I was turning around ... when I suddenly received a blow to the back and fell down the narrow stairs into the slaughterhouse. I will never forget this moment in my life: On the stairs above stood P., a high-ranking Gestapo official ... It was as if I were stunned. It was the first time that a stranger pushed me ... This was the first time that a stranger touched me. And addressed me in the familiar form. In Düsseldorf. In Germany."[6]

During postwar criminal investigations, many surviving Jews recalled such treatment as unprovoked beatings, slaps, and kicks from men in uniform, men who did not refrain from abusing elderly people in the same way as well. Legal proceedings against former members of the local Gestapo offices were opened very early on after the war. Irrespective of the fact that the consequences were rather mild, the records of these investigations make it very clear to historians how deeply this treatment – which ranged from gruff to violent – was ingrained upon the memory of the victims as a key turning point.[7] After being evacuated to the Nuremberg collection camp Langwasser, a barracks settlement for the Nazi party rallies, Siegfried Ramsfelder, a former Würzburg salesman, was beaten several times and forced to clean latrines before being deported to Riga on 29 November 1941, along with an additional 1,000 Jews from Franconia (northern Bavaria).[8] Even more startling, however, was that the improvised collection camps became the scene of filming, for which the Gestapo sought out "Jewish types" from among the inmates. Dr. Richard Kohn, a former longstanding Nuremberg city councilor and commercial court judge, refused to step in front of the camera and protested, saying that everything going on around him was a display of mean-spiritedness. For this act of defiance, he was severely maltreated in front of more than 500 Nuremberg Jews and subsequently locked up in a small, unheated barrack until departure.[9]

This process, which finalized the Jews' "death as citizens," was highly organized along the lines of division of labor and carried out in a standardized way throughout the cities and communities affected.[10] Having already dispatched several transports to the ghetto in Łódź (Litzmannstadt) since 15 October, Adolf Eichmann on 23 October summoned to Desk IV B 4 (Jewish Affairs and Evacuation) all the administrators of the Gestapo regional and district who had to organize the deportations on site. In Berlin, they learned additional details, such as how "those to be evacuated" were to be assembled and what should be given to the deportees for the journey. At this meeting, which despite the late date was still working under the assumption that the deportations to Minsk and Riga would take place between 1 November and 4 December, Eichmann impressed upon his representatives in the field that Jews in mixed marriages, foreign Jews, and family members of Jews who had been put to work were not to be deported under any circumstances. "In addition, ill persons as well as frail persons may not be evacuated no matter their age. Exact guidelines will follow."[11]

Furthermore, each person was to be allowed a voucher for a sum of RM 50 (about U.S. $20 in 1941), marching provisions for three days, food for three weeks, bed linens, cover, bucket, broom, washbowl, and eating utensils. Moreover, Eichmann ordered that the Jews be searched prior to deportation for weapons, money, and jewelry and decreed that all personal papers be confiscated. Only identification cards and passports were to be allowed – albeit with the stamped entry "evacuated." Finally, a list of goods carried along and a transport list in duplicate were to be given to the transport leaders from the Schutzpolizei. The transport was completed by filing a report of dispatch with the Reich Security Main Office and delivering an additional transport list to Eichmann.

With the deportations underway, the Reich finance administration organized the state-sponsored robbery of the Jews. For this, on 4 November the Finance Ministry informed the subordinated senior finance executives throughout Germany that "Jews who are not employed in economically important enterprises will be deported in the next months to a city in the eastern territories. The assets of the Jews to be deported will be confiscated for the benefit of the German Reich." The basis of this confiscation procedure was having the person affected declared an enemy of the people and the state in advance. Whereas this term was left undefined, an order of confiscation had to be delivered by bailiff to every Jew in the collection camps.[12] This procedure did not last long, however. By the time of the first deportations to Riga, which took place between 27 November 1941 and 6 February 1942, the 11th ordinance of the Reich Citizenship Law was already in place. This declared, plain and simple, that all of the assets of any Jew who left Reich territory – whether forcibly or voluntarily – would be forfeited to the benefit of the Reich. This forfeiture of assets upon the crossing of the border considerably facilitated the procedure of state-sponsored theft. By collective decree, a senior finance executive could "process" a complete transport list of 1,000 persons without having to deploy additional personnel on his end.

After the Jews of Nuremberg, Fürth, Bamberg, Würzburg, and other towns in Franconia had been gathered at the collection camp on the grounds of the Nazi party rally complex, they left the city early on the morning of 30 November 1941, almost unnoticed by the local population. From the nearby freight station, they moved north for three days and two nights, reaching Riga-Škirotava, their final stop, in the morning of 2 December. Before the train departed, the Gestapo assigned Gustav Kleemann of Würzburg to serve as the person responsible for maintaining discipline during the transport. The Gestapo's organizational guidelines can only be defined as chicanery. Having been placed in third-class coaches, the Jews were forbidden to swap places during stops. A lack of space prevailed in the coupes, and since the coaches were of an older make without an aisle connecting the coupes, it was impossible to change coupe within a passenger coach. In short, it was possible to exercise one's legs only when the escort commando expressly allowed it during a longer stop. Because the coaches were heated by steam from the locomotive, the heat tapered off over the length of the train. At the end of the train, one hardly felt any warmth; toward the front, the coaches were overheated. Hardly any arrangements had been made for provisioning the Jews beyond what they had brought along. During stopovers, the Jews thus tried to convince their guards to allow them to take water into the coupes – in extreme cases, even snow.

When the transport reached Šķirotava on 2 December, the deportees immediately noticed the cold. Ordered to open the coach doors, the Jews found it difficult after days of motionlessness in close quarters to disembark as quickly as was demanded by the German Security Police and Latvian auxiliaries, who meanwhile were shouting at and beating the deportees. In addition, Šķirotava, located some 12 km from Riga, was a freight station, not a station for passenger coaches. There were no platforms or ramps. One imagines how unreal the situation must have been for the deportees. The slow process of disembarking, the awkward collection of hand baggage, the search for family members: every move was met by a torrent of blows from clubs and fists.[13] Off to the side, First Lieutenant Richard Schiebel, the transport leader from the Nuremberg Order Police, reported that he had picked up mail twice during the trip and handed over the letters.[14]

The Jews first had to assemble in rows of five, in accordance with German orders. Around 200 of these rows then left the freight station and headed toward the Daugava Road, as the Moscow Road was called once it extended beyond the Riga city limits. After almost an hour of slowly marching along this road, which ran straight out of Riga and was void of manmade structures, the procession turned sharply to the right and followed an unsurfaced path to a kind of gate, from both sides of which a fully dilapidated fence disappeared in the twilight. They had reached their destination.

After this stream of approximately 1,000 people had moved farther onto these grounds, they had to fall into formation. A small group of men from the office of the Regional Commander of the Security Police Latvia (KdS Latvia) stood before them. These men ordered the Jews to "disappear," separated by male and female, into the elongated barracks that defined the open space. After the war, numerous survivors remembered the scene and said this group was made up essentially of the following persons: SS Sergeant Rudolf Seck, who was the camp commandant, SS First Lieutenant Gerhard Maywald, who was responsible for the construction of the Salaspils camp, and SS Major Rudolf Lange, the KdS Latvia chief, who was on hand to supervise the arrival of the first transport to this site.[15]

The Jews ordered themselves anew, male and female family members keept an eye on one another in order to see where the other "disappeared," and one by one they entered either the elongated livestock stall for women or the taller, barn-like building for men. On the way, many noticed a conspicuous, unnaturally high pile of suitcases and thought others had already

Deportation of German Jews to Riga

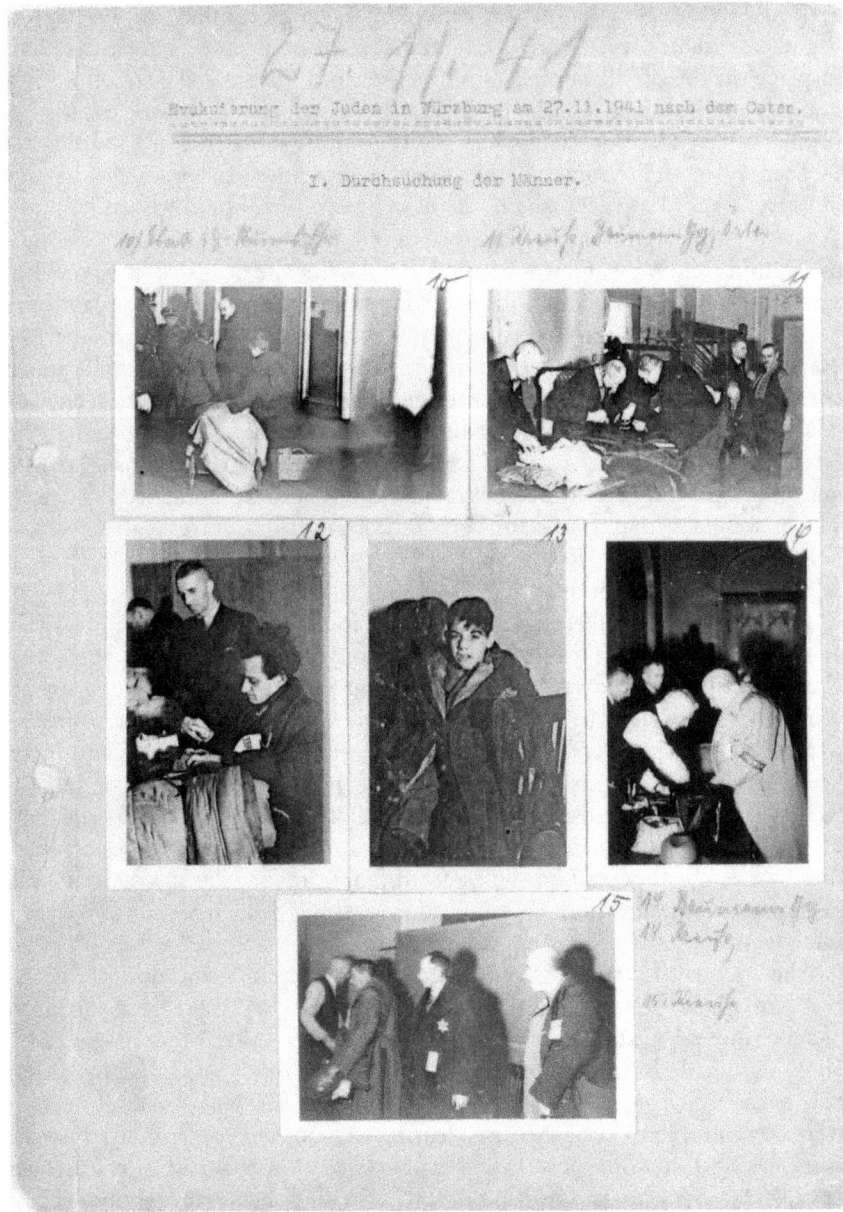

Figure 8.1. Page from an album showing the search of Jewish men in Würzburg on 27 November 1941, two days before their deportation to Riga. Courtesy of Staatsarchiv Würzburg.

arrived at this site. But in the ice-cold, drafty accommodations behind the wooden gates were merely several stacks of mattresses, which they had to place on the plank bunks. The suitcases and mattresses were without a doubt from the luggage of the Berlin transport, which had arrived on 30 November and whose passengers had been promptly murdered at Rumbula.[16]

Torn from their home surroundings a few days earlier in brutal and bureaucratically correct fashion, the Franconian Jews now apparently found themselves in a camp on an extremely windy meadow. The fence was obviously unlit, and no watchtowers were visible. But the next day, they quickly saw that there could be no talk of a camp here. The only German from the Security Police was apparently Seck, the commandant, to whom some 15–20 Latvian auxiliaries had been assigned.[17] These formed a mobile outer cordon around the grounds.[18] A full-length fence around the perimeter was missing, as were watchtowers or lights for the guards. Seck appointed the Jewish transport leader camp elder, ordered the construction of a latrine, and announced a nighttime curfew. Escape would be punished by death. The prisoners were to transform this land, some 200 hectares (ca. 494 acres) between the Daugava Road and the Daugava River, into an agricultural estate under Seck's command.

A day later, on 4 December, the first deportation train from Stuttgart arrived at Šķirotava. This group of Jews from Württemberg had been concentrated in an improvised collection camp in the park Killesberg on 28 November, subjected to expropriation, and searched before the train departed on 1 December.[19] Now, 2,000 people populated these run-down premises. To enforce his orders, Seck had a Jewish camp police of around twenty men under the leadership of Josef Levy established. After the arrival of transports from Vienna on 6 December and Hamburg on 9 December, there were 4,000 people on the estate Jumpravmuiža, the site of what was becoming the Jungfernhof camp – and everything needed for the Northeast European winter was missing.

The state of disrepair of the six to eight barracks – in addition to the two large ones the Jews had first moved into, they had since been forced to occupy one of the smaller structures as well – made itself felt on the Jews. Snow fell inside Barrack 5, the large barrack for men. The bunk beds that had been built for the inmates – with 70 cm space between each level – were comparable to bookshelves. Heating was possible only after the small wood ovens that some Jews had brought along on the transports arrived at the estate. A kitchen large enough to provide for so many thousands of inmates, as well as an infirmary, had to be built first. For the time being, the inmates had to provide for themselves with the food they had brought along. Anybody who had miscalculated and had stored a blanket in his or her large baggage was now in mortal danger.

The 800–900 fatalities lost to exhaustion and frost in Jungfernhof during the winter of 1941–42 were directly related to the fact that the most basic prerequisites for housing several thousand people of all age groups on this run-down estate were missing and had to be created by the deportees themselves.[20] In light of these conditions and the winter weather, it is hardly surprising that the Jews from Germany and Austria hardly had anything to do with agricultural chores at first. Waterproofing accommodations, finding firewood, locating luggage, constructing a medical station: in short, the struggle to guarantee their physical existence stood at the center of all their efforts. Related orders from Seck, who lived in a peasant house with solid walls and had in the meantime acquired a Jewish servant, were carried out as quickly as possible.

From Seck's perspective, the arrival of over 4,000 people was at first an irritating nuisance that he had been unable to prevent. It had not been his intention to transform himself overnight from an ambitious German estate administrator to the commandant of a "camp for Jews." An SS man and son of modest rural origins from Süderdithmarschen County in northern Germany, Seck had been transferred to Riga in August 1941 upon completing an agricultural course in order to build up an SS estate enterprise. During the era of Latvian national sovereignty, Jumpravmuiža had been government-owned. It had been given up as an integrated economic enterprise long before Soviet annexation, and the surrounding lands had been leased in part to neighboring peasants. With the Soviet occupation, plans were made for a landing strip for airplanes, but a large part of the treeless and undulating area had been abandoned years earlier. With the help of peasants and day laborers from Römershof, a new community established by the German civil administration, Seck had just begun preparatory work, when he learned from Lange – probably in the first week of November – that Jumpravmuiža would have to take on German Jews. Informed of the difficulties in building the Salaspils camp, Karl Heise, the commander of the Schutzpolizei in Riga, had directed Lange's attention to this area.[21] Jumpravmuiža was the solution to a situation that had appeared deadlocked to Lange. The site offered certain advantages. First of all, it made negotiations with the county commissar unnecessary, because it was already under lease by the SS and police; in addition, it lay outside the city and was within walking distance from Škirotava Station.[22] Furthermore, once full, it could serve as a reservoir of workers for the construction of the Salaspils camp, which was likewise being built not too far away. Faced with such prospects, Seck's counterargument that he could neither accommodate nor employ several thousand people was in vain.

But the deportees did not encounter a helpless SS estate administrator in Seck. A rather seamless transition took place from the brutal, oft murderous behavior they encountered upon their arrival at Škirotava and during their march to Jumpravmuiža, when individuals were shot for the most trifling reasons, to his demeanor on the estate grounds:[23] Seck was the "commandant."[24] Looking back, quite a few survivors described the 33-year-old SS man as megalomaniacal.[25] Seck's oft-made remarks to the effect that the deportees were modern slaves whose only justification for living was their ability to work were but one reason for this characterization. By his actions, Seck made no secret of the fact that older or heavy-set people, people who wore glasses, or academics without working skills were useless to him. If such inmates made a mistake or were caught taking a break, Seck would strike.[26] These violent outbursts were very often accompanied by death threats. The simple farmer in SS uniform took care to point out regularly that he had personally shot thousands of Jews already – which was untrue.[27] With the blows he dealt from his cane and his vile threats, Seck was ultimately compensating for his feelings of inferiority, for in a camp with over 4,000 German and Austrian Jews, he also found himself confronted with former jurists, municipal administrators, doctors, university lecturers, and salesmen whose biographical backgrounds stretched far beyond the horizons of this son of Holstein peasants. Only upon discovering that, in addition to such dignitaries, skilled craftsmen, workers, and employees were also to be found among the Jews – what is more, Jews who hailed from his native Holstein environment – was Seck sometimes able to find his way back to a normal tone. In one case, in spring 1942, he showed some young women from the Hamburg transport who were working in a field private photos from his wallet and began talking about family.[28]

The Jungfernhof camp commandant also knew how to enrich himself and lead a comfortable life. It is documented that, after having set up a sewing room, Seck selected articles of clothing from the belongings of the deportees, had monograms sewn on, and sent them home. He confiscated jewelry and wedding bands for himself and his Latvian girlfriend Olly, about whom nothing else is known but that she lived in the estate house with Seck and showed no hostility toward the Jews.[29]

If the Latvian guards reported to Seck that German Jews had been caught bartering with the local inhabitants or the fishermen from the Daugava, he often administered the punishment himself. He personally caned the victims in front of the assembled camp inmates and meted out similar humiliating penalties. The victims assumed that Seck wished to avoid filing an official report with KdS Latvia in Riga, which would have meant certain death for the "criminals."[30] By taking this approach, the commandant showed his superiors that calm prevailed at Jungfernhof. Reports to Lange about the alleged insubordination of Jews probably would have called into question Seck's authority and power.

Lucie Levi, a survivor from Hamburg, was at Jungfernhof until July 1942 as head of the sewing room. Under the title, "Seck – Terror Commandant of the Camp Jungfernhof at Riga," she wrote a three-page statement dated 6 August 1948, which was then used against Seck in court shortly thereafter.[31] According to Levi, she had to deal with the commandant everyday, for he regularly placed orders with her. One morning, still in winter 1941–42, she was looking for Seck, when she saw him coming toward her with five old men who were evidently unable to work. Seck had apparently found them lying in the barrack for men and was driving them across the yard, cursing and beating them as he went. Fully shocked, Levi sought to run away, but he shouted at her: "Stay here, otherwise, it'll be your turn." Seck then shot all five men right in front of her.[32] The Jewish "orderly" Seck had ordered to his side after the arrival of the Nuremberg Jews also survived the Holocaust. He credibly testified that Seck twice shot prisoners for trifling reasons in January 1942.[33]

If the deportees felt completely isolated at first, this view changed once the hardships of everyday camp life got underway. The Jews came into contact with the Latvian auxiliaries, who apparently seemed less trigger-happy than calculating. Later, food came from the ghetto, where there was a distribution center for Jungfernhof and Salaspils as well as both halves of the ghetto. These were delivered by SS Second Lieutenant Kurt Migge, who had a Jewish commando to unload the provisions.[34] Latvian civilians also frequented the camp to bring food, skilled workers came and went, and fishermen landed on the nearby riverbank. Moreover, commandos were assembled that took some Jewish forced laborers far away from the Jungfernhof camp. A firewood commando was able to see the Salaspils camp construction site from the outside; a quarry commando crossed the Daugava Road every day on its way toward Saurieši and thus came into contact with other civilians. In short, opportunities to barter developed to make camp life a little more bearable. If bribed successfully, the Latvian police would occasionally look the other way; otherwise, one had to reckon with the worst.[35]

Kurt Kendziorek of Lübeck arrived in Šķirotava with the Hamburg transport on 9 December 1941 and was appointed to unload the freight cars together with other men. From this episode developed Jungfernhof's "train station commando," the deployment of forced laborers for unloading freight cars attached to subsequent transports. Every morning, Kendziorek left the camp for Šķirotava with about thirty-five men. This commando had the best chance of smuggling goods for barter or even food back to the camp. If no transports arrived, Kendziorek's men had to unload other freight cars.[36] After the war, Josef Katz, a former member of the train station commando, drew on his experiences to compile a mixture of literary and documentary memoirs. Here Kendziorek is portrayed as a traitor who did not hesitate to enrich himself and to curry favor with Seck. According to Katz, it was Kendziorek's fault that he was taken away to Salaspils for construction work at that camp in December 1941.[37]

Dr. Josef Carlebach, the chief rabbi of Hamburg, along with his wife and four children, also came to Jungfernhof with the Hamburg transport. On the march from Šķirotava to the camp, Carlebach's brother died of a heart attack. Over the next three months until his death, Rabbi Carlebach came to possess great moral authority at Jungfernhof. Among the internees, it was said that he had out of principle refused any preferential treatment for his family and himself vis-à-vis the other inmates. He organized school lessons for the young and did not hesitate to visit the severely ill at their bunks. He said kaddish for the dead and held religious ceremonies:

> As we come to the camp from work [with the train station commando], we learn that a Hanukah service for the children will take place this evening in the large barrack for men. The chief rabbi has had all of the children called together in order to celebrate the festival of lights with them. Soon the bright voices of many children are heard amid the desolation and privation. The chief rabbi is standing in the center. He has two small boys by the hand. The burning candles are on the oven in front of him. The old, familiar tunes that we once had sung at home are heard. What a difference to the celebrations at home! ... People are standing pressed together around the oven, wrapped tightly in their coats. They are trying to imitate here the festival that they once celebrated under better living conditions. The singing falls silent. Doctor Carlebach begins to speak, only really softly, but we listen spellbound to each and every word ... During the chief rabbi's speech, complete calm reigns in the large barrack. Occasionally, people sob and wipe their eyes at these words of comfort. After the final prayer, he hands out small bags of sweets to the children. Their eyes are shining as they leave the large barrack for men, led by the hand by the kindergarten teachers.[38]

In January or February 1942 – the exact point in time can no longer be determined – Seck organized the first selection of those who were not at work but had stayed in the infirmary or the barracks. These people were subsequently shot in the woods of Bikernieki.[39] In January 1942, during another operation, 200 women were singled out and taken to the Riga ghetto for forced labor.[40] They had either to clear away the snow on the streets and the bridges, or to take part in the clearance work in a sealed part of the former large ghetto. During postwar questioning, Seck could not or did not want to remember the episode involving the infirmary.

The first German Jews to reach the Riga ghetto came from Cologne. Theirs was the third transport to leave the Rhine metropolis. Already on 21 and 28 October, Jews from Cologne had been deported to Łódź.[41] But now, Jews from provincial towns in the Rhineland were to be found among the deportees to Riga. The Gestapo had apparently extended its grasp beyond Cologne. In the early morning hours of 7 December 1941, the victims were brought from the trade fair halls to the railroad station Deutz-Tief, where the same inhuman journey of 1,000 people of all ages in third-class coaches of the Reich Railway was repeated. The Gestapo appointed Max Leiser, the former head of Cologne's Jewish social affairs office, transport leader. After a three-day journey, the train reached Šķirotava.

Once again, the exhausted, freezing Jews were driven from the train, assembled in rows of five, and marched along the Daugava Road to the Latvian capital. They were forbidden to take along any additional personal luggage aside from their hand baggage. The rest was taken to Jungfernhof for sorting. Later, SS Second Lieutenant Kurt Migge had the larger baggage from the arriving transports sent separately to the ghetto. Food was sent to the central office for provisions, textiles to the ghetto's clothing depot.[42] In postwar questioning, many of the survivors were no longer sure whether they had had to leave the coaches immediately upon arriving or after waiting several hours. What is certain is that the disembarking process was again supervised by members of the Latvian local police and a relatively small number of German policemen. It remains unclear whether those who were unable to walk were separated from the others and taken to the ghetto on trucks and buses or were shot along the way.[43]

Repeatedly pressed to hurry by German policemen or their Latvian collaborators, the German Jews, after two hours of marching, reached the edge of town where the Daugava Road becomes the Moscow Road. Not long after the first buildings, the rows of five took a sharp turn and crossed into the ghetto over a part of the ghetto fence that had been lowered for them. They were now in that part of the ghetto that faced away from the city center, having entered their future prison through a rear entrance, as it were. In the future, this small street, Līksnas St., was to be called Cologne St. On the left side of the street were several buildings, into which the deportees were crammed after a short address by ghetto commandant Kurt Krause. On the right-hand side was the Jewish cemetery.

The scene that met the new arrivals was shocking in every respect. Not only did these few buildings have no rooms able to accommodate around ten people each, but many of the German Jews found themselves standing on the frozen blood of the Latvian Jews who had been shot the previous day during the ghetto clearance operation.[44] Every now and then, corpses were to be seen – in some cases, in the apartments as well.[45] Günther Lippmann, who was deported from Cologne to Riga at age fourteen and later forced to work at one of the provisions distribution centers, recalled the situation very exactly even twenty years after liberation: "Our Cologne transport was the first that arrived in Riga, in the ghetto. Upon our arrival in the ghetto, we really felt upon entering our living quarters that other people had inhabited them until most recently. The apartments left a cluttered impression. Scraps of food were still on the table, and the ovens were still warm. I also saw that a large number of corpses were lying in the neighboring cemetery, which lay within the cordoned off district of the ghetto. I later learned that a short time before the arrival of our transport Latvian Jews had been shot."[46] It was also clear to Kurt Kaufmann, then twenty-one, that "something unusual must have happened here a very short time earlier."[47]

The Cologne Jews had barely adjusted to their new situation, when, on 12 December, a transport from Kassel arrived at the ghetto. This transport was comprised of Jews from several counties within the government district of the same name and had been assembled in the city of Kassel in the sports hall of a school on Schiller St.[48] The internment procedures repeated itself elsewhere. On 14 December, Jews from the Lower Rhineland, the Berg countryside, and Düsseldorf arrived at the ghetto. This transport involved 1,007 people. By year's end, these deportations had been augmented by the arrival of a transport of Jews from the regions of Münster, Osnabrück, and eastern Westphalia, which had left Bielefeld on 13 December and reached the ghetto on 16 December. Finally, on 18 December, 1,001 Jews from Hanover and its environs arrived. These people had been concentrated on the premises of the Jewish gardening school in Ahlem.[49]

After more than 4,000 people had been interned in the ghetto – several hundred persons were transferred to Salaspils upon arrival or shortly thereafter – a new self-administration had to be established, this time one run by German Jews. Structurally, it drew on the experience of the German commandant's office and resorted to those persons who had been Jewish transport leaders, that is to say, former office managers and doctors.[50] A Jewish ghetto council was formed under Leiser, the aforementioned former head of Cologne's Jewish social affairs office and transport leader during his own deportation. Leiser was given an office and a title: chairman of the Council of Elders of the Reich Jews in the Ghetto in Riga.[51] He was assigned individual group elders, who were distinguished according to each additional transport that arrived.[52] Usually, the group elders had access to a small office in their accommodations. Communications between the Council of Elders and individual persons or the various groups were organized with the help of young people who brought reports and messages as couriers. The group elders for their part kept a journal of the daily orders they received. These contained primarily working hours and preparatory minutiae for the Order Service or forced labor details.[53]

A "camp police" was also set up. It was run by Friedrich Frankenberg, who had arrived with the Düsseldorf transport. As the "leader of the camp police," Frankenberg had to convey orders to the police from each group;

he was on occasion represented by Rudolf Haar. Between him and the individual policemen of each group was an intermediary level of "foremen," Frankenberg's contact persons within the groups.[54] As a rule, the Jewish street wardens were recognizable by blue armbands.[55] A Jewish Labor Deployment Central Office was also founded in the ghetto under Herbert Schultz of Cologne: "At first, I belonged to a labor commando that was employed at the harbor. Around the start of January 1942, I was assigned to organize the deployment of labor. I received this assignment from the ghetto elder Leiser, who also came from Cologne."[56] Schultz dealt with this task by having one person from each group within the constantly growing ghetto community delegated to him. Each new transport thus had had to present an elder and deputy elder, a police foreman with 8–10 policemen, and a "group labor deployment desk person." The latter was responsible for making sure that the Labor Deployment Central Office was able to maintain a card catalogue-based overview of deployed, deployable, and sick workers.

The Labor Deployment Central Office, however, was not in a position to gain a precise overview of the ability to work or the professional qualifications of the workers within the groups until the end of March 1942. On 18 February, Schultz for the first time called on the group desk persons to provide complete registers of names, a register of men who had been taken to Salaspils, and a set of statistics showing year of birth and separated by male and female, but these instructions were handled slowly, as was his order, issued two days later, to designate the members of all groups between 14 and 65 according to one of three classes: A (meaning fully able to work / external service), B (meaning fully able to work / external service / not able to march), and C (only able to be deployed within the ghetto).[57] As of 10 March, the groups from Vienna, Cologne, Kassel, Prague, and Dortmund had still failed to comply with Schultz's requests.[58] In later inquiries concerning individuals with professional know-how, the Labor Deployment Central Office was only able to inquire with the group desk persons or the elders, as it was usually unable to ask for specific names.

As already indicated, things did not come to a stop with these five transports. About three weeks after the Hanover transport reached the ghetto, deportations from the "Greater German Reich" started again. Between 12 January and 10 February 1942, more than 10,000 Jews arrived from Prague and Brno (via Theresienstadt), Vienna, Berlin, Leipzig, and Dortmund – with the first Theresienstadt transport being at least temporarily expected at the Kaunas (Kauen, Kovno) ghetto.[59] There, on 11 January, Jewish Council Chairman Dr. Elchanan Elkes was summoned around midday to the ghetto commandant's office and ordered to evacuate a part of the ghetto by that very afternoon. Elkes immediately set about his work and – with the help of the ghetto police and fire department – began resettling inhabitants to a street in the central part of the ghetto. A settlement committee for "German Jews" was set up, but this transport of Jews from Prague and Brno did not go to Lithuania.[60]

On the other hand, in February, Lithuanian Jews from the Kaunas ghetto ended up in the Riga ghetto. To meet a request that 500 workers be sent to Riga, the German police arrested 200 Jewish workers from the Kaunas ghetto on 5 February. Although the Germans gave assurances that living conditions in Riga were bearable, and that the deployment would be only for three months, the Jews of Kaunas had long since become skeptical of such promises and went into hiding instead of reporting on their own. Consequently, Fritz Jordan and Helmut Rauca, the Germans in charge of the Kaunas ghetto, released these 200 Jews, but held a general roll call, selected 300 persons, and threatened reprisals if another 200 persons were not made available. Confronted with the possibility that such reprisal measures could be directed against the entire ghetto, the Jewish Council selected another 80 persons to provide a total of 359 persons.[61] The following day, this transport reached Riga, where its members were housed in the Latvian part of the ghetto.[62]

After the two mass killing operations on 30 November and 8 December 1941, the Riga ghetto had changed. A large part of the ghetto – the area between Lāčplēša and Daugavpils streets (see map) – remained sealed off from both the city and the rest of ghetto. Nobody lived there any more, and the buildings were at first poorly secured. This accounted for about a third of the original ghetto, whereas the remaining part had been divided into two oblong areas by a barbed wire fence along Ludzas St. The surviving Latvian Jews now lived in the smaller part, while the German, Austrian, and Czech deportees inhabited the larger part. A gate on Tulas St., which ran perpendicular to Ludzas St., connected the two areas and was guarded by German and Latvian police.

In the German ghetto, it became established practice to rename the streets. Thus the German end of Tulas St. became Prague St. and the gate was called Prague Gate. As the transports arrived, the ghetto was resettled by building or street segment. It is difficult to locate exactly the Kassel and Düsseldorf streets in retrospect, although both streets are named as roll call sites in the journal of the Dortmund Group.[63] The ghetto's main street – the site of the German commandant's office, the central office for the distribution of food to individual groups and buildings, a sick bay, and the German ghetto's central clothing storeroom – was changed from Ludzas St. to Leipzig St. Viļānu St. became Bielefeld St., and Mazā Kalna St. became Berlin St. On the Latvian side of the ghetto, the streets retained their names.

Deportation of German Jews to Riga 217

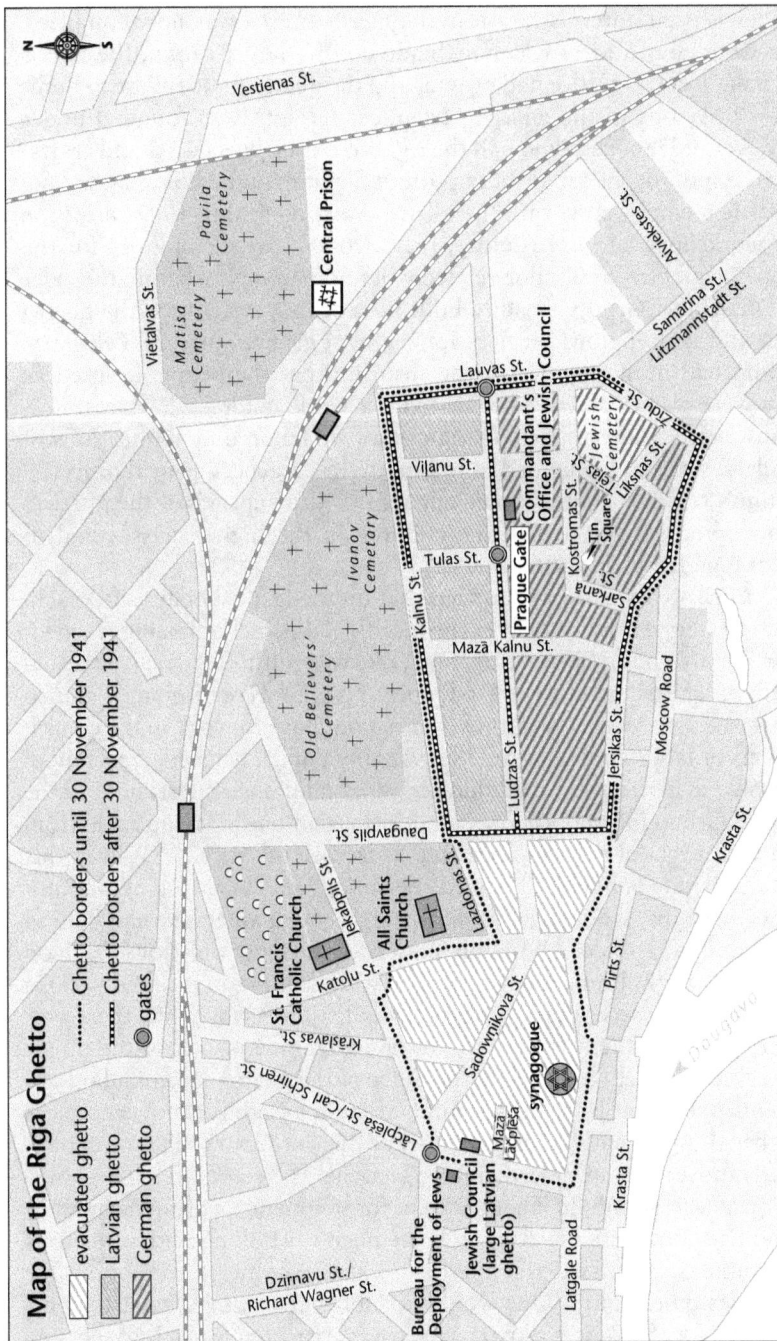

Map 2. Map of the Riga Ghetto. With the arrival of Jews from Germany, the streets were renamed: Liksnas > Cologne St.; Ludzas > Leipzig St.; Maza Kalnu > Berlin St.; Tulas > Prague St., and Vilanu > Bielefeld St. Cartographer, Peter Palm, Berlin.

The Jewish self-administration in the German area was now complete. Leiser's Council of Elders was now made up of a larger group, the Labor Deployment Central Office had grown, and the ghetto police came to number 60–70 persons in the end. A "technical service" was founded under Ernst Meyer of Hanover, who had the right to recruit specialists and craftsmen on the spot for the repair of important facilities and who oversaw Jewish craftsmen employed within the ghetto. Starting 4 May 1942, after the central workshops had been set up, these workers were employed for the most part in cobbler- and tailor-related work.[64] Benno Nussbaum, the elder of the Düsseldorf Group, steadily built up a school system for the ghetto children and led religious services for his own group. Since 25 February, Nussbaum had been responsible for ensuring that the people he used as teachers were also deployed once or twice a week as forced laborers. Lesson plans, verification of participation in forced labor, and applications to cancel classes had to be handed in to him in the "teachers central office."[65] Nussbaum's teachers central office apparently also supervised the ghetto's street sweeping service, which the children in the higher classes had to carry out together with the teachers.[66]

On 7 April, Nussbaum announced that on the last two days of Pesach, religious services would be held in the morning, with school being rescheduled for the afternoon hours; this, however, was not to jeopardize the deployment of labor. Therefore, the only persons who were ultimately able to take part in the services were those who did not have to work in the central workshops or labor commandos.[67] How many pupils, teachers, and school buildings were in the ghetto will have to remain an open question.[68] In the Dortmund Group journal, there is no information on this issue aside from the fact that a school must have existed at Düsseldorf St. 12.[69] Within this context, Gertrude Schneider recalled the sport and dance instructor Ruth Wilner of Cologne, who gave lessons once a week in an empty hall behind the commandant's office.[70] Worship service was held not only for Pesach on 8 and 9 April 1942. Immediately after the war, Kaufmann recalled various visits to the Cologne Group's synagogue hall.[71] On Leipzig St., there was also a frequently visited prayer hall in the mezzanine of one of the buildings.[72] As early as February 1942, the office of the ghetto commandant approved an application by the Dortmund Group for Catholic prayer services in the ghetto. Apparently, these were held rather often in the accommodations of Hanover Group Elder Günther Fleischel.[73]

After the war, Reinhold Thaumann, a former member of the Schutzpolizei who had transferred to Riga in September 1941 along with numerous other comrades, discussed the ghetto's food situation: "Provisioning for the Jews was quite paltry. One would not think it possible, what they offered the Jews as food. It was part garbage, part rotten food. I myself saw rabbit and cow feet. I also saw half rotten cabbage."[74] In fact, throughout the ghetto's existence, the food delivered by the Security Police was far too little and hardly amounted to a fortifying diet for hardworking laborers. For this reason, the Jews deployed within the city were forced to try and smuggle fare that was as nutritious as possible into the ghetto. Efforts to "organize" a regular supplement to their nearly inedible rations by barter determined the daily routine of every family.

How many Jews were living in the Riga ghetto in January and February 1942? This question cannot be answered on the basis of a valid number for a given day, and because the Jewish self-administration was still compiling its card catalogue, because reliable statistics are not available. The aforementioned Schultz, the head of the Labor Deployment Central Office, recalled in a March 1968 witness statement that about 18,300 Jews were housed in the ghetto "in the beginning."[75] According to a registration of workers as of 16 February 1942, a total of 4,193 men and 524 women, that is to say, 4,717 Latvian and Lithuanian Jews, were living in the Latvian ghetto.[76] In addition, there were 1,011 deportees from Cologne, 1,022 from Kassel, 1,007 from Düsseldorf, 1,031 from Bielefeld and environs, and 1,001 from Hanover by the end of 1941. In January, there followed 2,002 Jews from the Theresienstadt ghetto, three transports from Vienna with 3,207 Jews (including the last transport of 10 February), and 3,081 Jews from Berlin. Finally, there were 773 and 938 persons from Leipzig and Dortmund respectively, each group arriving on separate transports.[77] This suggests that there were 19,790 German, Austrian, Czech, Latvian, and Lithuanian Jews within the ghetto.

But this number represents merely a rough estimate, from which a number of unknowns have to be deducted. Since the 4,717 Latvian and Lithuanian Jews was the result of a registration of workers, the number ought to be certain. Things become more difficult when one tries to gain an overview of the selections that took place upon the deportees' arrival in Šķirotava, and to determine how many of the 15,073 Jews on the transport lists in fact made it to the ghetto. For this, one has to rely on witness statements. Not only were individuals shot during the march from Šķirotava to Riga, but old people and those unable to walk were also taken away in buses or trucks.[78] And it is on this point that the memories of Jewish survivors contradict one another, sometimes completely. For example, with regard to the Düsseldorf, Bielefeld, and Hanover transports, some testimonies claim that those who were driven away in advance later arrived at the ghetto, while others state that the same people disappeared. For the Vienna transport of 15 January, there is testimony to the effect that selections were carried out at Šķirotava: men who were able to work went directly to Salaspils or to Jungfernhof; all of the women who were able to work went straight to the ghetto; but no information is provided regarding old people and those unable to work.[79] Referring to an interview with survivor Vera Mausner, Gertrude Schneider writes that about 300 people from Vienna arrived in the ghetto, where they were then attached to the recently arrived Prague Group; shortly thereafter, they were assigned to the Berlin Group, because another transport with Jews from Theresienstadt had arrived.[80]

This new transport of Jews from Prague and Brno, which reached Šķirotava on 19 January, also failed to make it to the ghetto intact. With the exception of about eighty men, who were taken directly to Salaspils, the remaining members of the transport, by Schneider's account, were assigned to the first Prague Group.[81] With that, about 917 persons came to join the first group of Prague Jews.[82] But this is subject to doubt, because H.-G. Adler in his standard work on the Theresienstadt ghetto noted that almost all of those who arrived on 19 January were immediately shot.[83] It can now be deduced from Diana Schulle and Wolfgang Scheffler's work that this transport, with an average age of 44, had only seventeen male survivors, all of whom, given their age, must have belonged to the group taken away to Salaspils.[84] All of the supplemental information about this transport found in acquisition lists of the concentration camps Stutthof and Buchenwald – to which the Riga ghetto's Jews were transferred in 1944 – is for men who were between 20 and 44 years of age at the time.[85] Can it be that there was not a single survivor from the group of 917 people sent to the ghetto? If one considers that the Theresienstadt transport of 12 January also had to provide men for Salaspils, but still had 110 survivors with an average age of 45.3 years – fifty-eight of whom were women – then there is indeed reason to conclude that we still do not know whether 917 persons ever arrived in the Riga ghetto.[86]

Against this backdrop, a witness statement given in Riga as the result of an application for legal assistance filed by the Hamburg Prosecutor's Office gains in significance. On 21 November 1975, 55-year-old Arnis Upmalis testified that back then, at the age of twenty-one, he had volunteered for Viktor Arajs's auxiliary security police commando. By his own account, Upmalis had feared being conscripted for labor, possibly even being sent to Germany. He remembered the exact date he joined: 13 January 1942. Before being sent to the SD school in Fürstenberg for a three-month course with others from the Arajs Commando, Upmalis served as a guard at Jungfernhof.

Regarding his first days on the job, Upmalis said:

> Around my third day of duty with the Arajs Commando, when I was relieved from guard duty, I had to report to building 19 on Waldemar St. on orders from company leader Kjurbis. They issued us guns with live ammunition. A bus blue in color drove up. Then those who had been serving in the commando longer than me said: "We are going to Bickernieki [sic] again." We were in fact brought

to the forest of Bickernieki, which lies in the eastern environs of Riga. We drove over the Waldemar, Brivibas, Bickernieku streets and then farther on the country road that led into the forest of Bickernieki. Then the bus turned right. After we had driven about a hundred to two hundred meters on a forest path, we got out. Then we pressed deeper into the forest on the path and came to a large freshly dug pit, which was 300–400 meters from the country road. The pit was about 30–40 meters long, about 5 meters wide and about 2 meters deep. One end of the pit was sloping so that one could go down inside it. It was said that prisoners of war had had to dig the pit ... Somebody pointed out our posts on both sides of the forest path. I had to take up a post about 30 meters from the pit. From there, I could see what was happening at the pit.

The shooting site was cordoned off by police from the Latvian auxiliary security police. There were guards standing on the country road as well. Shortly thereafter, they began to transport Jews on German trucks to the shooting site. The drivers of these trucks were German soldiers and Latvians who served in the Arajs Commando. I do not remember their surnames or first names. There were several trucks. They drove back and forth the entire day. The beds of several vehicles were covered with tarpaulins. The convoy men who escorted the victims to the shooting site were police from the Latvian auxiliary police. The trucks made a practice of stopping about 60 meters from the pit. There the victims were dropped off, and they ordered them to take off their outer clothing and footwear. I did not see that they took away objects of value. I believe that they had taken them away beforehand.

After disrobing, the victims were ordered to the pit. They went to the execution site on their own in groups of several persons and went down along the sloping side into the pit ... Then one heard from the pit bursts of fire from machine pistols. That is the way the shooting process happened. The shooting lasted from about 10 A.M. until 17 P.M., until dusk fell. All day long, victims were bought to the shooting site. I probably am not wrong in saying that no fewer than 800–900 people were shot on this day ... Together with Arajs, Charij Swikeris (I don't know anything about his fate) and [SS] First Lieutenant Krause made a practice of stepping up to the pit and firing their pistols. I did not see Arajs go down into the pit.

It was said the Jews had been brought from Šķirotava Station to the shooting site and been transported from the west in mass transports to Šķirotava. The victims spoke only German. I remember that a woman asked me for help in perfect German. I answered her, also in German, that I was a soldier and could not help her whatsoever. The victims were essentially older women and men. There were hardly any children there ... In the evening, a bus came to get us, in which we returned to our quarters. Upon leaving the forest of Bickernieki, I did not see the pit with the corpses filled in. I don't know whether somebody remained behind to fill it in. I did not see anybody with shovels there or any shovels at all. I don't remember who drove the bus.

The attendant circumstances of this shooting operation have remained ingrained upon me my entire life. I went through a great deal on this day.

Two more times, I was a witness to mass shootings of Jews carried out in the forest of Bickernieki. During one of these shootings, I escorted victims on a truck to the killing site. During the second shooting action, I stood, just like the first time, in the cordon at the pit. Because so much time has passed in the interim, it is now difficult for me to remember which time I drove with the convoy people and which time I stood in the cordon at the pit. One of these shooting operations took place about ten days after the second. If the first shooting operation took place on 15 or 16 January, the second could have been on 25 or 26 January, the third on 5 or 6 February.[87]

Arnis Upmalis can be considered a credible witness, for he was able to recall a good number of details with considerable precision. He named his various quarters by house number; he was able to date the move of the Arajs Commando from Waldemar St. to Kristian Baron St.; he described his various uniforms correctly; and he gave an exact description of the crime scene and the route taken. What remains is the problem of dating. There was no shooting of 800–900 victims who had been taken straightaway from Šķirotava Station on 15 or 16 January 1942. As already mentioned, the second Vienna transport reached Šķirotava Station on 15 January, the first transport having arrived in Jungfernhof on 6 December. The second Vienna transport involved 1,002 men, women, and children, of whom thirty-one survived (as far as can be reconstructed). Thirteen of them testified in the Maywald case. None of them recalled the entire transport being driven away in trucks.[88] The only transport with such a high number of missing people is the one from Theresienstadt with the date of arrival of 19 January 1942.

A shooting on 25 or 26 January is also subject to doubt. No transport arrived at Šķirotava on either of those days. Upmalis described his contribution to this crime as follows:

> On that day, when I brought the victims in the convoy to their execution site, I drove out to the railroad station Šķirotava early that morning along with several policemen from the Arajs Commando who, like me, had been ordered to the convoy in trucks that had come to Waldemar St. 19. It [Šķirotava Station] was located on the southeast edge of Riga. I don't remember now who among the commanders had ordered us to the convoy. There were three or four trucks involved.
>
> At Šķirotava Station stood a transport that was made up of about 20 passenger coaches. The train was guarded by German soldiers. They had the Jews get out of the coaches and forced them to the vehicles. They ordered the victims to sit down on the floor of the bed. It happened that on one of the trucks I was the only guard. From Šķirotava Station, they transported the victims, as I now recall, over the following route: Moscow Road – Latschplescha St. – Brivibas St. (now Lenin St.) – Bickernieku St. and farther along the country road that forms the extension of Bickernieku St. and runs into the forest of Bickernieki. The people were shot in the same area as the first time ... I did not make a practice of staying at the

shooting site, but instead returned to Šķirotava Station. On this day, I made no fewer than 3–4 trips. With each trip, I transported about 30 people to the execution site. The other trucks made about just as many trips. Therefore, I believe that on this day no fewer than 500 people were shot. The shooting operation lasted from morning to evening ... The people who were shot all spoke German. It is not known to me exactly from where they were brought to Riga. I believe, however, that they had been brought from the west. The victims were older men and women. I did not see children among them. Young men and women were not represented among them.[89]

On 24 January 1942, the transport of Jews from Leipzig and Dresden had arrived in Šķirotava. Of these 773 deportees, forty-seven survived, sixteen of whom testified in West German investigations.[90] Although rumors about what was to come had spread anxiety and fear among the Dresden Jews on the eve of their transport, none of the witnesses said that almost two-thirds of their group had been driven off and never seen again.[91] The mass killing Upmalis dated to about ten days after the first one he witnessed must have taken place on 30 or 31 January 1942. The fourth Berlin transport arrived in Šķirotava on 30 January; in September 1967, one member of that transport, Heinz Lipowski, recalled that only several hundred of his fellow deportees entered the ghetto.[92] However, Regina Pick, who arrived with a transport from Vienna the next day, also stated that only 400–600 persons of that deportation were brought to the ghetto.[93] Else Sekules, the labor deployment desk person for this group, also survived. She testified that a selection of older persons did take place at the station – however, she was sure that this involved a maximum of eighty people at the time.[94]

Only 268 persons aged 21–50 had been deported from Vienna on that train. Most of the deportees – that is to say, 864 persons – were 51–80 years old, and 418 of these were between 61 and 70.[95] Statistical analysis of the Berlin transport reveals an age structure very similar to that of the Vienna transport. Only 177 persons were between 21 and 50 years old; by contrast, 829 people were between 51 and 80, of whom 501 were between 61 and 70.[96] It cannot be said with certainty which transport was involved during the second mass murder operation Upmalis took part in.

Upmalis's statement regarding the mass murders of Jews from the west in January 1942 not only helps to determine more exactly the fate of the Czech, Austrian, and German Jews deported to Riga. The shootings described in it also indicate that an escalation in procedures for handling deportees had taken place, and that this escalation no longer had anything to do with the individual excesses directed at exhausted stragglers during the march to Riga. If hundreds of people from these transports were driven away to prepared pits, then planning and preliminary measures would have been required.

The last operation that Upmalis mentioned was correct with regard to the date. On 5 February, a selection took place among the Berlin and Vienna Jews in the Riga ghetto in order to determine who was unable to work. Agnes Scheucher, who had been deported from Berlin on 13 January and had arrived in the Riga ghetto on 16 January, had been put in charge of labor deployment in the Berlin Group due to her engagement on behalf of transport members and her profession as work therapist. In this capacity, she was subordinated to the Labor Deployment Central Office and assigned a small office in her group's building. On 4 February, she received instructions from the chairman of the Council of Elders to draw up a list of sick and old people from the Berlin Group by the next day.[97] On the morning of 5 February, however, Maywald ordered everybody from the Berlin and Vienna groups to report for roll call. Medics and Order Service men from other groups were apparently ordered to Berlin St.[98] Scheucher remembered very clearly that the people from these two cities were the very groups with the largest numbers of old people and people unable to work. That morning, some 4,000 people stood on Berlin St., not knowing what would happen to them:

> I myself did not have to report, but instead remained in my office, from the windows of which I could follow events on the street outside. I observed Maywald going through the rows and selecting Jews. The people were all standing on the sidewalk. On the street, trucks drove up, and Maywald chose from the Jews who had reported all those who had to get onto the trucks. Those who had been chosen were overwhelmingly old people of both sexes, but there were also young people there. Other SS officers took part in the selection besides Maywald; I don't know their names ... Upon questioning, I note that the Jews on the sidewalk stood mustered along a good part of the entire length of Berlin St. That is to say, the selection took place not at a particular place, but proceeded to a certain extent along the street. The selection occurred right before the window of my work room so that I could observe events rather exactly.[99]

The selection and the search of the buildings did not take place with the brutality that had accompanied the clearance of the ghetto – to the contrary. Apparently, the German Security Police was making an effort to maintain a relatively quiet atmosphere in order not to frighten the new arrivals from the Reich. The murderers must have assumed that the German Jews had quickly learned what had happened on 30 November and 8 December.[100] Here, too, it is hard to determine the exact number of victims. Even Agnes Scheucher-Scott's information deviates considerably; she spoke of about 800 victims in 1948 and 1,500 victims in 1971. Prague Group medic Franta Winter, who had been deployed to clear the apartments, recalled around 800 victims of the selection, while Upmalis estimated that there were about 1,000 victims.[101]

Thus any attempt to answer the question posed at the outset of this section – how many people were living in the Riga ghetto after the arrival of the Vienna transport of 10 February 1942, the final transport for the time being – cannot go beyond a rough estimate. Of the 15,073 Jews from Germany, Vienna, Prague, and Brno who reached Riga, around 500 were taken away to Salaspils to build the camp there; around 900 persons from Prague (via Theresienstadt) were – with great probability – shot the day they arrived (19 January) as were about 500 persons either from Vienna or Berlin (30 or 31 January). On 5 February, an operation aimed at the "overaged" inhabitants of the ghetto's Berlin St. cost another 800 persons their lives. Thus it is to be presumed, with considerable caution, that there were about 12,400 deportees from the west in the ghetto. The search for the unknowns to be taken into consideration in arriving at this estimate leads historian and reader alike into the midst of the shocking reality of the mass murder of European Jews that was steadily unfolding.

Notes

1. Staw. Hamburg, 141 Js 534/60, Bd. 9, Vertraulich! Bericht über die Evakuierung von Juden nach Riga. Transportbegleitung in Stärke von 1/15 v. 11.12.–17.12.41, 743–751; ibid., Bd. 25, statement by Paul Salitter, 25 May 1962, 3,921–3,922; and ibid., Bd. 26, statement by the deputy transport leader with Salitter's letter of 2 July 1962, 4,109–4,110a.
2. Ibid., Bd. 9, Bericht über die Evakuierung, p. 743.
3. Ibid., 746.
4. Ibid., 748–749.
5. Ibid., Bd. 9, statement by Salitter, 25 May 1962, 3,922.
6. Hilde Sherman-Zander, *Zwischen Tag und Dunkel*, 29–30.
7. Even outside the context of criminal investigations, many survivors recall this shocking atmosphere. A then 16-year-old girl assigned by the Hamburg Jewish Community to work as an assistant in the collection camp recalled: "It is bad, you know, if you are so young and see grown-up people in such misery, people for whom you had such tremendous respect and who are now crying like small children." See Angelika Eder, "Die Deportationen im Spiegel lebensgeschichtlicher Interviews," in *Die Deportation der Hamburger Juden 1941–1945*, ed. Forschungsstelle für Zeitgeschichte in Hamburg und dem Institut für die Geschichte der deutschen Juden, 49.
8. Staw. Nürnberg, LG Nürnberg-Fürth, No. 3070/II, statement by S. Ramsfelder, 10 June 1948. This case concerned the deportation of Jews from Franconia (northern Bavaria). Among the defendants were Dr. Theodor Grafenberger, the former head of Department II at the Nuremberg Gestapo district office, and Dr. Benno Martin, the former Nuremberg police president and higher SS and police leader in Military District XIII. On these legal proceedings, see Edith Raim, "Strafverfahren wegen der Deportation der Juden aus Unter- und Mittelfranken nach 1945," in *Wege in die Vernichtung. Die Deportation der Juden aus Mainfranken 1941–1945*, ed. Albrecht Liess, 178–192.

9. Staw. Nürnberg, LG Nürnberg-Fürth, No. 3070/IV, letter of Bernhard Kolb, the last business manager of the Nuremberg Israelite Cultural Community, to the Landgericht Nürnberg-Fürth, 26 April 1949. Kolb was an eyewitness to this episode and later published a report about it, see *Schicksal jüdischer Mitbürger in Nürnberg 1933–1945*, 47–68, here 50.
10. Dirk Blasius, "'Bürgerlicher Tod'," in *Geschichte in Wissenschaft und Unterricht* 41 (1990), 3: 129–144.
11. BA Berlin, R 138/I/147, unpaginated, Besprechung in Berlin am 23.10.41 bei IV B 4 unter dem Vorsitz von SS-Sturmbannführer Eichmann. Betrifft: Führerbefehl (Evakuierung von 50.000 Juden aus dem Altreich einschliesslich Ostmark und Protektorat Böhmen und Mähren.). This document consists of the notes made by SS Captain Franz Abromeit, then the head of Department II at the Gestapo district office in Gdynia (Gotenhafen).
12. Nuremberg Document NG-4905, Der Reichsminister der Finanzen an die Oberfinanzpräsidenten, Schnellbrief, betr. Abschiebung der Juden, 4 November 1941.
13. Even decades later, survivors still considered their arrival at Riga-Šķirotava another major turning point, see, for example, Staw. Hamburg, 141 Js 534/60, Bd. 69, statement by Ernestine Spitzer, 13 February 1967, 10,935: "Our arrival there was such a grave event that it seems to me worth describing here."
14. Staw. Nürnberg, LG Nürnberg-Fürth, No. 3070/II, 230–235, statement by Richard Schiebel, 2 July 1948.
15. Staw. Hamburg, 141 Js 534/60, Bd. 3, statement by Kurt Kendziorek, 26 January 1950, 263–265r. As leader of Commando Šķirotava, Kurt Kendziorek, who arrived in Šķirotava with the Hamburg transport on 9 December 1941, and approximately thirty-five other strong men regularly had to unload the freight cars attached to the deportation transports. Kendziorek clearly remembered that the Security Police and SD men standing at the ready always included Lange and Seck as well as Maywald. In addition, Kendziorek recalled the presence of SS Second Lieutenant Migge, who ran the procurement desk at KdS Latvia.
16. Staw. Hamburg, 141 Js 534/60, Bd. 1, statement by Herbert Simon, 5 May 1949, 27. Simon, who was deported from Hamburg with his wife and son, noted: "When we arrived in the Jungfernhof camp, we found members of a transport from Würzburg there. A transport of Berliners must have been at Jungfernhof before the Würzburgers, for we found the baggage and identification cards of numerous Berliners there. However, none of the Berliners was seen by the Würzburgers nor by us, we could only speculate about what became of them. We were told by the Latvian population that the Berliners were shot." See also ibid., Bd. 36, statement by Heinrich Rosas, 20 May 1963, 5,840.
17. Rudolf Joachim Seck was born 15 July 1908, in Bunsoh, Süderdithmarschen County. After grade school and a short stint with the Leibstandarte Adolf Hitler, Seck worked on his parents' farm. He had been a member of the NSDAP and the SS since 1931. Drafted on 20 January 1941 for an agricultural course in Schmiedeberg, Seck arrived in Riga in August 1941, where he was under the command of KdS Latvia. Here he was given the assignment to administer the former estate Jumpravmuiža. See *Justiz und NS-Verbrechen*, Bd. IX, No. 307.
18. Staw. Hamburg, 141 Js 534/60, SB 27, statement by Woldemar Reinholdowitsch Rolmanis, 12 July 1976, 4,670. Rolmanis, a former Latvian auxiliary policeman, told investigators: "I was transferred several times to guard the camp for Jews in Jumprawmujzha [Jumpravmuiža]. We guarded the camp from the outside. However, I was also repeatedly inside the camp. I saw how the Jews lived in very cramped conditions. They slept on three- or four-tier bed-frames. One heard at the time that several thousand Jews were detained at this camp."
19. Among them were twenty-three Jews from Laupheim, whose evacuation to Stuttgart on 28 November 1941, was photographed by an amateur photographer. These photos are

printed in Klaus Hesse and Philipp Springer, *Vor aller Augen*, 149–152. Conditions in the Killesberg collection camp prior to evacuation were filmed on orders from the Stuttgart city administration, see "Die Lüge und der Tod. Die Deportation der Stuttgarter Juden," Stephan Hermlin, director.

20. At first, the dead were stacked behind the men's barracks. After some time, a mass grave was created in the frozen ground with the help of explosives, see Archives of the Wiener Library (AWL), Testaments to the Holocaust, Series One, reel 56, P.III.h no. 1021, Lucie Levi, "Seck – Schreckenskommandant des Lagers Jungfernhof bei Riga," 6 August 1948.

21. Staw. Hamburg, 141 Js 534/60, Bd. 41, statement by Karl Heise, 22 November 1963, 6,874–6,875: "I know Dr. Lange through the following event: He came to me one day, introduced himself, and said in effect that he was still expecting transports of Jews, whose accommodation had to be provided for. He asked me whether I knew of any buildings suitable for this. Since I had seen a closed down estate with working quarters and barns in the environs of Riga, I told Dr. Lange about it. He was of the opinion that this was a suitable site for him and asked me to drive out with him that same morning. I did so, too; I still remember that we stayed there relatively long and returned to the city only in the early afternoon."

22. BA Berlin, R 91/95, unpaginated, Der Leiter der lettischen Stadtverwaltung an Wittrock wegen rückwirkender Genehmigung von Pachtverträgen hinsichtlich Kleinjungfernhofs mit 194,06 ha mit dem Pächter "Sicherheitspolizei," 8 January 1942. A definitive arrangement, however, was reached only ten months later, when Governing Mayor Wittrock, acting on a recommendation from the municipal real estate office, declared that he was ready to lease the estate Mazjumpravmuiža/Kleinjungfernhof to KdS Latvia "for the purpose of prisoner correction by the authorities." The first three years, retroactive to autumn 1941, were to remain rent free, since "in the Bolshevik period the site's agricultural value had diminished for the purposes of military development." Starting in 1944, rent was to be RM 4,000 per annum, a year later RM 5,000, see LVVA, P 1376-1-20, 21–22, Protokoll der Rigaer Stadtverwaltung über die Sitzung am 29.10.1942 [in Latvian]. On the negotiations, see Staw. Hamburg, 141 Js 534/60, Bd. 3, statement by Rudolf Seck, 17 December 1949, 220.

23. AWL, Testaments to the Holocaust, Series One, reel 57, P.III.h no. 285, Siegfried Reinhold (Nuremberg), "Bericht über meine Leidenszeit als Häftling," 11 November 1945: "On the evening of [2 December 1941], we had to mourn the first dead and missing, who had probably been unable to follow the procession over the very icy roads and had been shot." See also Staatsanwaltschaft beim Landesgericht Berlin, 1 Js 9/65, Zeugenheft [purple], statement by Friedl Reinauer, 2 January 1969, 14–19, quote 15. Reinauer, who was from Bayreuth, said during questioning, "In addition, 4 young men were kept back to transport the baggage, and they never returned either. I know only the name of one 17-year-old boy by the name of Weinschenk from Nuremberg."

24. Staw. Hamburg, 141 Js 534/60, Bd. 1, statement by Simon, 5 May 1949, 27: "We always had to address him as 'Herr Kommandant' only, and no doubt exists for me either that Seck was the decisive man in the Jungfernhof camp."

25. Ibid., statement by Julius Ceslanski, 31 May 1949, 46–47: "As far as Seck is concerned personally, I would like to say that he was possessed by an incredible megalomania, something like a lord to serfs."

26. Ibid., statement by Siegfried Joseph, 2 June 1949, 52–53. Joseph, who was from Gelsenkirchen, came to Jungfernhof from the ghetto only in spring 1942. Seck, who was the same age, could not stand Joseph, because he wore glasses. Whenever he came close to Joseph, Seck would beat him.

27. Rudolf Seck was not a member of Einsatzgruppe A during its advance through the Baltic lands. Shortly after his arrival in Riga, he was transferred to Jungfernhof. On his bragging about the number of Jews he had allegedly killed, see AWL, Testaments to the Holocaust, Series One, reel 57, P.III.h no. 1021a, Sophie Billigs of Stuttgart, undated; No. 1021b, Bertold Kohn of Hamburg, 28 January 1948; No. 1021d, Hans W. Loszynski of Hamburg, 19 April 1949; Staw. Hamburg, 141 Js 534/60, Bd. 1 statement by Selma Weil, 1 June 1949, 47.
28. Staw. Hamburg, 141 Js 534/60, Bd. 1, statement by Gertrud Stern, 30 May 1949, 48–49: "Together with other women, I had been assigned to picking ice in a field, when Seck appeared among us and watched us work and then suddenly spoke to us, saying we were Hamburgers and since he was also from the area, we should take a look at his children. Although nothing of the sort interested us, we approached him and took a look at the pictures. That he showed such affability was due [in my opinion] to the fact that our work troop was made up only of women. For when a nearby male prisoner coming over slipped on the ice, he suddenly turned around and dealt the older prisoner, who was still on the ground, 3–4 blows to the head and back with his walking stick."
29. Ibid., statement by Hans Werner Loszynski, 20 April 1949, 37. Loszynski, a native of Hamburg, noted: "I personally have the feeling that this German-Latvian girlfriend of Seck's, by the name of Olly, exerted a very favorable influence on him; she was markedly friendly to Jews and often put in a good word for us with Seck."
30. Ibid., statement by Else Lüders, 10 May 1949, 34. Lüders was also from Hamburg.
31. AWL, Testaments to the Holocaust, Series One, no. 1021, Levi, "Seck – Schreckenskommandant."
32. "Between the individual shootings, he spoke to me. I can't remember the words anymore. The killing was carried out by shots to the back of the neck. The last man had to wait about eight to ten minutes until it was his turn. I clearly noticed that Seck took special joy and special pleasure in these killings, for he laughed and made jokes in the process," ibid. On 17 February 1950, she repeated her statement before the investigating judge, see *Justiz und NS-Verbrechen*, Bd. IX, No. 307, 186.
33. Ibid., 187, "One day in January 1942, when the accused ordered the prisoners to leave the barracks and to report to the yard in front of Barrack 5, one prisoner was late and approached those who had reported as the last one. When the prisoner came near the accused, the accused curtly ordered him to turn around. The accused then drew his pistol and killed the prisoner with a shot to the back of the neck. The prisoner died, sinking to the ground bent forward. Another time in January 1942, when the accused was in the courtyard, a Jew walked across the yard, who, because he had no suspenders, was holding up his pants with his hands. This sight irritated the accused. He drew his pistol and shot the prisoner dead from close proximity, from a distance of about 1 m."
34. Kurt R. Migge, born 1908, came from Berlin. Initially a gardener in East Prussian Angerburg, in 1935 he was an employee at an agricultural wholesaler in Königsberg. A year later, he applied successfully to the Gestapo and from 1940 until late 1941 or early 1942 was with the Gestapo in Toruń (Thorn) in the annexed Polish territories. As an official from Reich Security Main Office desk II C 3 based in Riga, Migge was responsible for procurement for the prisons and camps of KdS Latvia. Migge, one of the accused in the Hamburg investigation, admitted to being present at the arrival of transports in Šķirotava, because large amounts of goods accrued there. Regarding provisions for Jews, Migge explained: "The ghetto and the camps were provisioned according to fixed amounts set by the general commissar. As an office clerk, I was also responsible for provisions. I regularly received manpower reports from the Jewish self-administration and requested corresponding ration cards from the general commissar. I gave these to the drivers of the

motor pool, who picked up the provisions at the distribution offices and dropped them off in the ghetto. The ghetto served as a kind of central provisioning camp. Jungfernhof and Salaspils picked up their provisions there." See Staw. Hamburg, 141 Js 534/60, Bd. 3, statement by Kurt Migge, 20 January 1950, 272–274.

35. AWL, Testaments to the Holocaust, Series One, no. 285, Reinhold, "Bericht über meine Leidenszeit": "The boys, who feared nothing, not even death, walked past the cordon of guards to the Latvian peasants after the end of work in order to barter for foodstuffs. Unfortunately, very many of them were caught by the Latvian guards, who were sometimes worse than the German SS, and, after everything had been taken off them, ended up in a cold room (bunker) in which there was still water."

36. Staw. Hamburg, 141 Js 534/60, Bd. 3, statement by Kendziorek, 26 January 1950, 263–265r.

37. Josef Katz, *Erinnerungen eines Überlebenden*, 31–33, 36.

38. Miriam Gillis-Carlebach, "'Licht in der Finsternis' (Fanni)," in *Menora und Hackenkreuz*, ed. Gerhard Paul and Miriam Gillis-Carlebach, 549–563; Katz, *Erinnerungen*, 34–35, quote.

39. AWL, Testaments to the Holocaust, no. 1021, Levi, "Seck – Schreckenskommandant": "One January day in 1942 – a horrible snow storm prevailed – I observed from the window of the sewing room that the infirmary, which was about 15 meters from the sewing room, was being emptied. Seck was standing there with a truncheon and shouting at the people. On orders from Seck, the Latvian guards took the people by the legs and threw them in an unclothed state into a bus waiting outside. The people who could walk were herded into the bus." See also ibid., No. 1021a, Billigs, undated; ibid., Kohn, 28 January 1948; and Staw. Hamburg, 141 Js 534/60, Bd. 68, statement by Else Lüders, 14 March 1967, 10,901: "Solely old and sick people were carried away. These smaller selections had nothing to do with the [later] 'Dünamünde Operation.' I recall that on ca. three different days people were picked up – namely in buses. These people were never heard from again." See as well Staw. Hamburg, 141 Js 534/60, Bd. 69, statement by Hannelore Marx, 12 March 1967, 11,021: "In January/February 1942, Maywald, together with Lange, led three different operations. These involved old and sick people and people with children, who were driven away in omnibuses. These groups were smaller and involved only dozens."

40. Trudy Ullmann Schloss, "A Farm Called Jungfernhof," in *The Unfinished Road*, ed. Gertrude Schneider, 60.

41. They arrived on 23 and 31 October 1941 at the Łódź (Litzmannstadt) ghetto. The Jewish transport leader, Dr. Albert Kramer (deputy Erich Marx) and Dr. Kurt Wolf (deputy Alfred Alsberg) acted for a longer time as head of the group accommodations Cologne I and II in the Marysin section of the ghetto and on Steinmetz St. (Ceglana St.), see Archiwum Państwowe Łódź, Ghettoverwaltung Litzmannstadt (Ghetto Administration Litzmannstadt), file 124, 14 and 16, as well as the collection Przełożony Starszeństwa Żydów w Getcie Łódzkim (The Eldest of the Jews in Łódź Ghetto), file 19, 1. Kramer and Wolf contacted the synagogue community in Cologne at least once by telegram, for they needed 2,000 straw beds to set up group accommodations in the ghetto. These were sent to them in November, see Archiwum Państwowe Łódź, Ghettoverwaltung Litzmannstadt, file 124, 11.

42. Staw. Hamburg, 141 Js 534/60, Bd. 42, statement by Kurt Migge, 3 December 1963, 7,027–7,028.

43. Although numerous survivors from Cologne recalled that old people and small children were taken away by autos, nobody had such a loss to lament from their own ranks. Shots were heard again and again during the march to the ghetto, but none of the survivors

could reconstruct a shooting on the roadside, see Staw. Hamburg, 141 Js 534/60, Bd. 68, statement by Kurt W. Kaufmann, 6 March 1967, 10,910: "Upon arrival in Riga, it came to incidents with the SS guards. I would not want to say with certainty whether it came to killings in the process." Kurt Migge of KdS Latvia said, "Given the commander's [Lange's] personality, I would like to rule out the possibility that he had the sick taken away [to the ghetto] by autos from the office." See ibid., Bd. 42, statement by Migge, 3 December 1963, 7,028.

44. Ibid., Bd. 61, statement by Moritz Brünell, 30 October 1965, 9,745: "Immediately after our arrival, we had to line up in the ghetto, and they told us if we did not behave ourselves properly the same thing would happen to us that happened to the 20,000 Jews who had been shot just beforehand. By the state of the apartments into which we were directed, it could be seen that the previous residents must have been driven from the apartments in a great hurry. The lights were still on in the apartments, and there were in part still scraps of food on the tables as well. The corpses in the ghetto had to be collected by us and were taken away by truck."

45. Ibid., Bd. 70, statement by Johanna Mark, 12 July 1967, 11,337.

46. Ibid., Bd. 61, statement by Günther Lippmann, 13 November 1965, 9,800.

47. Ibid., Bd. 68, statement by Kurt W. Kaufmann, 6 March 1967, 10,910. To the list can be added statements by Frieda Eggener (29 October 1965), who said she had seen the corpses of children in the streets, ibid., Bd. 60, 9,740. Johanna Mark (12 July 1967) testified that she had seen bloody apartments, into which the Jews from Cologne had to move, ibid., Bd. 70, 11,357a.

48. On this, see Monica Kingreen "Die gewaltsame Verschleppung der Juden aus den Dörfern und Städten des Regierungsbezirks Kassel in den Jahren 1941 und 1942," in *Judaica Hassiaca* 3 (2002); AWL, Testaments to the Holocaust, Series One, reel 57, P.III.h no. 289, Letter by Sigi Zierings to her father in Holsybrunn, Sweden, 25 June 1945.

49. On the statistics as well as the dates of departure and arrival, see of late the bilingual memorial book *Buch der Erinnerung*.

50. As a result, during the next four weeks after the closing of the ghetto on 25 October, efforts to place Latvian Jews from the ghetto with various German offices were chaotic. An anonymous survivor reporting on his experiences in the ghetto wrote in summer 1942: "All of the Jews had to gather before the ghetto's inner gate, while the Germans waited for them on the gate's outer side. Since about 15,000 Jews had to go to work, there was indescribable confusion. Nobody found his place where he had to work and only gradually was a system of organization created by which the Jews who worked in various enterprises and for various SS and military services had to assemble at places designated by signs. For every workplace, a so-called 'king of the Jews' was appointed, who had to maintain order among the Jews. At the same time, a Jewish Labor Office was organized, which provided all Jews with working papers for leaving the ghetto." See AWL, Testaments to the Holocaust, Series One, reel 57, P.III.i (Latvia), no. 527.

51. LVVA, P 132-28-18, 5, Dortmund Group journal, entry for 18 February 1942.

52. Ibid., 36, Dortmund Group journal, entry for 17 March 1942, which says that Leiser asked the group elders and their deputies to report the following day to the commandant's office at 9 A.M.

53. One such journal, that of the Dortmund Group, survived the war. It contains ninety-eight pages covered with handwriting on both sides and an abundance of news pertaining to all of the ghetto groups and the ghetto police in addition to the Dortmund Group itself and individual persons. The first entry is from 15 February 1942, the last from 4 September 1942, ibid., 1–98.

54. According to entries from the Dortmund Group journal, the foremen in spring 1942 were,

for the Bielefeld Group, Mildenberg (22 February 1942); for the Berlin Group, Feldmann (17 March 1942); for the Hanover Group, Perl (17 March 1942); for the Cologne Group, van Dyck (15 March 1942); for the Kassel Group, Bibo (15 March 1942); for the Leipzig (or Saxony) Group, Haar (15 March 1942); for the Dortmund Group (sometimes Westphalia II), Flatow (4 April 1942), see ibid., 9, 35, 37, 59. All entries concern roll calls or patrols in the ghetto.

55. Staw. Hamburg, 141 Js 534/60, Bd. 36, statement by Reinhold Thaumann, 15 June 1963, 5,895. Thaumann was a former member of the Schutzpolizei.
56. Ibid., Bd. 76, statement by Herbert Schultz, 14 March 1968, 12,070.
57. LVVA, P 132-28-18, 4, entry from 18 February 1942, "Central office requests immediately a register of all people, [consecutively numbered], first name, name, [date of birth], last apartment, present apartment. In addition, names and day 1st transport Salaspils. Statistics according to age-groups, separated by men and women." Also, ibid., 7, entry for 20 February 1942, "To all groups. All groups report immediately the number of deployable men and female persons of 14–65 years, separated by classes, A-B and C. Group elders are responsible for the accuracy of this information."
58. See the notices regarding this matter from 22 February and 25 February and the last entry on this matter from 10 March 1942, ibid., 32.
59. Arrival from Theresienstadt on 12 January 1942; from Vienna, 15 January 1942; from Berlin on 16 January 1942; from Theresienstadt on 19 January 1942; from Berlin on 23 January 1942; from Leipzig on 24 January 1942; from Berlin 30 January 1942; from Vienna on 31 January 1942; from Dortmund on 1 February 1942; and from Vienna on 10 February 1942.
60. Entry for 11 January 1942, in Avraham Tory, *Surviving the Holocaust*, 66. They were mistakenly expecting the Jews to come from Vienna, ibid., 220.
61. Entries for 5 and 6 February, in ibid., 69. Ultimately, 222 male and 137 female Jewish workers were deported, see BA Berlin, R 92/1158, 154, Der Geb.-Komm. Riga, Arbeitsamt, an den RKO, Aso, durchlaufend beim Gen-Komm., betr. Judentransport aus Kauen, 10 February 1942.
62. BA Berlin, R 92/1158, 2, Abschrftl. Vermerk des RKO, Abtl. III: "Regarding: Deployment of Jews. From General Commissar Kaunas, Dept. Labor Policy and Social Administration, office clerk Palland calls and reports that the transport of Jews announced for 6 February 1942, will be dispatched 24 hours later due to difficulties that have arisen. The transport is thus expected to be dispatched from Kaunas on 7 February at 2 A.M. and to arrive in Riga on 7 February at 8 P.M. A delay in arrival in Riga of several hours is to be expected. p.p. sig. Ullrich, [Wartime Administration Secretary]."
63. For example, the entry for 22 February 1942, from the Dortmund Group journal: "To the camp police of the groups. The entire camp police of the groups, including the auxiliary police, is to stand ready this afternoon at 12:15 in front of house no. 10 on Düsseldorf St. to receive a special order. The police of the groups are to be led by the foreman to the reporting site in closed ranks. The process of assembling is to follow the order of the transports that have arrived. Conducting muster and reception of the reports of the groups: Foreman of the camp police Bielefeld – Mildenberg. The head of the camp police, signed Friedrich Israel Frankenberg." See LVVA, P 132-28-18, 9. At least in spring 1942, the reporting site for the women of the Kriegsweg and Šķirotava commandos was located on Kassel St., see ibid., 66, entry for 13 April 1942. The deportees from Dortmund lived in a building on Leipzig St./Ludzas St., most probably house number 36, Staw. Hamburg, 141 Js 534/60, Bd. 3, statement by Jeanette Wolf, 8 December 1949.
64. LVVA, P 132-28-18, 2, Dortmund Group journal, entry for 17 February 1942: "According to instructions from *Herr Kommandant*, 8 locksmiths are to report today by 2 P.M.

I ask for immediate information as to which locksmiths are in your groups who are not yet employed with me as craftsmen. Should you have not reported the locksmiths by 2 P.M., we have to communicate this to *Herr Kommandant*. You are again reminded of the immediate submission of all craftsmen (male and female), sig. Ernst Israel Meyer." See also, ibid., 18, entry for 2 March 1942, and ibid., 37, entry for 19 March 1942. Finally, ibid., 76, entry for 4 May 1942: "To all groups! Because, by order of *Herr Kommandant*, all craftsmen are subordinated to me, I ask for the following information: 1. How many shoemakers, male tailors, and female tailors are employed in your group? 2. How many sewing machines are available to these craftsmen (including the machines in the shoemaker shops)? I wish that there be a stop to accepting repair work until the 10th of this month so that the moving of the individual enterprises to the central workshops planned by me can go ahead without old orders. In the event that there are other special workers in your group aside from those named above who pursue their profession, this is also to be reported. The naming of all craftsmen by name is to have taken place by the 6th of this month. Chief of the Technical Service. sig. Meyer."

65. Concerning the deployment of teachers for work and the handing in of lesson plans, see ibid., 15, entries for 25 and 27 February 1942. On 1 April 1942, Nussbaum decreed that the following day classes would be canceled and a short worship service could be held, ibid., 55.
66. See the warning of the teachers and pupils of the Dortmund Group regarding this matter in ibid., 78, entry for 9 May 1942. Also Gertrude Schneider, *Journey into Terror*, 48.
67. LVVA, P 132-28-18, 60, Dortmund Group journal, entry for 7 April 1942. Whether, as Gertrude Schneider writes, the Jews were allowed to make matzo for the occasion, "which at another time and in another place had symbolized the end of slavery," is disputed among survivors. See Schneider, *Journey into Terror*, 17. In the notes of Karl Schneider of Euskirchen, who came to Riga with the Cologne transport, matzo for Passover in spring 1942 is also mentioned, see Hans-Dieter Arntz, "Religiöses Leben der Kölner Juden im Ghetto von Riga nach den Erinnerungen von Karl Schneider," *Jahrbuch des Kölner Geschichtsvereins* 53 (1982): 141.
68. On the teachers in the Cologne Group, see ibid., 133–134.
69. LVVA, P 132-28-18, 61 and 75, Dortmund Group journal, entries for 9 April and 3 May 1942, in which Nussbaum convened a teachers' conference.
70. Her information, which claims these classes went back to an initiative started by Hanover Group elder Günther Fleischel, cannot be proven on the basis of the sources. Ruth Wilner's classes are supposed to have been very popular with the ghetto youth, Schneider, *Journey into Terror*, 20.
71. Max Kaufmann, *Churbn Lettland*, 167–169.
72. LVVA, P 132-28-18, 27 and 55, Dortmund Group journal, entries for 6 March and 1 April 1942. For greater detail on worship services in the ghetto, see Arntz, "Religiöses Leben der Kölner Juden," 127–152.
73. LVVA, P 132-28-18, 4, Dortmund Group journal, entry for 18 February 1942, which concerns the approved application. On Fleischel's role, see Kaufmann, *Churbn Lettland*, 169; Herbert Obenaus, "Vom SA-Mann zum jüdischen Ghettoältesten in Riga," *Jahrbuch für Antisemitismusforschung* 8 (1999): 278–299. Although he was an influential man, Fleischel actually never became a ghetto elder.
74. Staw. Hamburg, 141 Js 534/60, Bd. 36, statement by Thaumann, 16 May 1963, 5,895.
75. Ibid., Bd. 76, statement by Herbert Schulz, 14 March 1968, 12,072.
76. BA Berlin, R 91/164, unpaginated, Bericht über den Einsatz der Juden, signed Standtke, 16 February 1942.

77. All of these numbers were taken from the *Buch der Erinnerung*. They were derived from data registered in deportation lists.
78. Staw. Hamburg, 141 Js 534/60, Bd. 53, statement by Helmut Grählert, 4 December 1964, 8,699. Helmut Grählert, who normally had to perform guard duty at the KdS Latvia building, recalled once being dispatched ad hoc to Šķirotava with a truck for prisoners in order to pick up about thirty older persons and children at the train station. He drove them to a shooting site. Upon driving off, he heard shooting.
79. Staw. Hamburg, 141 Js 534/60, Bd. 70, statement by Ernst Steinitz, 30 June 1967, 11,262: "On 18 December 1941, I was arrested by the Gestapo, and on 11 January 1942, I came with a transport from Vienna to Riga, where we arrived directly at the Jungfernhof camp and were unloaded. A division was made at the time in the following manner: Men between 14 and 40 came to Jungfernhof camp, women between 14 and 40 came to the Riga ghetto, the remaining Jews were finally accommodated at the Jungfernhof camp. The men between 14 and 40 came to the branch camp Salaspils." See also ibid., Bd. 38, statement by Herta Atlas, 26 August 1963, 6,228–6,230; ibid., Bd. 48, statement by Vera Mausner, 13 July 1967, 7,999; ibid., Bd. 49, statement by Herta Kisch, 23 July 1964, 8,009; ibid., statement by Otto Posament, 10 June 1964, 8,015.
80. Schneider, *Journey to Terror*, 20. Vera Mausner depicted the merger of this transport with the Prague Jews in the "sled house" and later with the Berlin Group in her article "A Child of the Ghetto," in Schneider, *Muted Voices*, 78–86.
81. Schneider, *Journey to Terror*, 21.
82. *Buch der Erinnerung*, Bd. 1, 514.
83. H.-G. Adler, *Theresienstadt 1941–1945*, 799, fn. 223c.
84. *Buch der Erinnerung*, Bd. 1, 513. In addition to the seventeen men, Josefa Zeimerová (born 1897) is named here as a survivor of this transport. She, however, belonged to the first Theresienstadt transport, according to information provided by Dr. Jana Šplíchalová of the Jewish Museum in Prague.
85. Ibid., 496–514.
86. Ibid., 495.
87. Staw. Hamburg, 141 Js 534/60, SB 22, statement by Arnis Janowitsch Upmalis, 21 November 1975, 3,991–4,003, quote 3,997–4,000. Members of the Security Police and SD were meant where Upmalis spoke of "German soldiers."
88. The number of deportees and survivors are from *Buch der Erinnerung*, Bd. 1, 426.
89. Staw. Hamburg, 141 Js 534/60, SB 22, statement by Upmalis, 21 November 1975, 4,000–4,001.
90. The number of deportees and survivors are from *Buch der Erinnerung*, Bd. 1, 831.
91. On 13 January 1942, Victor Klemperer noted in his journal, "Paul Kreidl tells us – a rumor, but it is very credible and comes from various sources – evacuated Jews were shot in Riga, in groups, as they left the train." Quoted from Victor Klemperer, *The Diaries of Victor Klemperer 1933–1945, I Shall Bear Witness to the Bitter End*, 451. On the history of the persecution of and deportation of Dresden's Jews, see Marcus Gryglewski, "Zur Geschichte der nationalsozialistischen Judenverfolgung in Dresden 1933–1945," in *Die Erinnerung hat ein Gesicht*, ed. Norbert Haase et al., 87–150.
92. Staw. Hamburg, 141 Js 534/60, Bd. 72, statement by Heinz Lipowski, 12 September 1967, 11,544.
93. Ibid., Bd. 43, statement by Regina Pick, 28 November 1963, 7,155–7,156.
94. Ibid., Bd. 47, statement by Else Sekules, 23 April 1964, 7,812–7,813.
95. Statistical information is taken from *Buch der Erinnerung*, Bd. 2, 448.
96. Ibid., 300.

97. AWL, Testaments to the Holocaust, Series One, reel 57, P.III.h no. 1035a, Agnes Scheucher, 5 February 1948; Staw. Hamburg, 141 Js 534/60, Bd. 43, statement by Suasan Taube, née Strauss, 29 October 1963, 7,094. Taube, who was deported from Berlin on 25 January 1942, lost her grandmother during this operation.
98. AWL, Testaments to the Holocaust, Series One, reel 57, P.III.h no. 1035, Franta Winter, medic of the Prague Group, 5 February 1948.
99. Staw. Hamburg, 141 Js 534/60, Bd. 82, statement by Agnes Scheucher-Scott, 3 May 1971, 12,887.
100. Schneider, *Journey into Terror,* 23.
101. AWL, Testaments to the Holocaust, Series One, no. 1035a, Scheucher; Staw. Hamburg, 141 Js 534/60, Bd. 82, statement by Scheucher-Scott, 3 May 1971, 12,887; AWL, Testaments to the Holocaust, Series One, no. 1035, Winter; Staw. Hamburg, 141 Js 534/60, SB 22, statement by Upmalis, 21 November 1975, 4,002: "To my mind, no fewer than 1,000 people were shot at the time. I didn't see children among them either. It involved older men and women."

– Chapter 9 –

THE SALASPILS CAMP
A Place of Internment with Many Functions

As already mentioned in the context of how Riga was chosen as a destination for deportations, SS Major Rudolf Lange notified Reich Commissar Ostland Hinrich Lohse on 8 November 1941 that construction of a camp of barracks near the small town of Salaspils was being "continued" at an accelerated pace.[1] Likewise, in November, it seemed clear from previous correspondence that this camp was being established for Latvian political prisoners as well as for local Jews and Jews deported from the west. But by mid December, only a construction shed had been constructed on the plot of land near the railroad, and the access road broadened.

The first German Jews to do construction work at this site came from among the deportees from Nuremberg, Stuttgart, Hamburg, and Vienna interned at Jungfernhof.[2] They initially had to camp out in the open in freezing temperatures and were not provided with food. Several of the Jews at Salaspils had been detained at the Šķirotava Station shortly after their arrival in order to sort the large pieces of baggage and had subsequently been taken away to the new camp by German members of the office of the Regional Commander of the Security Police Latvia (KdS Latvia). As a result, this group of mostly younger men had only the things they were wearing when they reached the Salaspils camp's wooded grounds. These were the first to fall victim to the inhuman weather conditions. By mid January 1942, at least 1,000 Jews, mostly recruits from the ghetto, were living and working there. The first escapees, who fled the camp on 30 December, had already been caught and executed.[3]

On 2 February 1942, a status report from the office of the Territorial Commander of the Security Police and Security Service Ostland (BdS Ostland) to the Reich Security Main Office (RSHA) optimistically stated that construction of the planned camp was moving forward: "By [telex] of 2 February 1942, it was disclosed that in Salaspils construction had gotten underway on a large camp for about 15,000 inmates, which will be completed around the end of April and is designated at the moment to take in

---

Notes for this chapter begin on page 244.

the Jews coming from the Reich. Whereas a part of the camp is to serve immediately as an enlarged police prison, the camp would be completely available as an expanded police prison and labor correctional camp after the deportation of the Jews, which is expected toward the end of the summer."[4] Thus another function had been added to Salaspils, namely that of a labor correctional camp for the work-shy and "loafers." In General Commissariat Latvia, an obligation to register for work was in force for civilians who by virtue of their unemployed status or vocational training could be enlisted for important and urgent work. The local labor offices initiated this method of compulsory mustering, and for that reason, they were severely criticized by the Latvian civilian population. Public dissatisfaction had been noted in all three of the Baltic general commissariats – Estonia, Latvia, and Lithuania – since February 1942.[5] The Labor Office in Riga at first reacted by summoning the disobedient workers, subjecting them to police interrogation, and seeking to have the county commissar – in his capacity as a police authority with order of punishment – send them to a civil-administered camp.[6] Thus, in February 1942, the Security Police and the civil administration were making preparations to deal with the problem of refusal to work independently of one another. But during the next two months, the problem became more pressing. The first complaints were beginning to arrive from those enterprises that had received "warned persons" as workers, wherein the issue of efficiently guarding such persons at the workplace – especially at construction sites – was raised.[7]

Parallel to this development, the Security Police undertook its first investigation into the causes of this problem and found:

> Strong dissatisfaction prevails in particular regarding the methods used by the Labor Office to engage the Latvians for enterprises important to the war effort on the basis of the Reich commissar's decree of 15 August 1941. This ordinance stipulates that the Labor Office can assign appropriate workers to certain places of work, also beyond their place of residence, for important and urgent work with commensurate remuneration. The Labor Office acts very recklessly in the assignment process. The Latvians also often find the working conditions to be offensive and humiliating. For example, a number of Latvians conscripted for service from professions requiring intelligence have to load freight cars at the freight station, while Jews work at the next car. Wages for those conscripted for service are very low, because all those conscripted for service are categorized independent of age and education as unskilled workers and receive an hourly wage of 27 pfennig [U.S. $0.11, 1941]. Family allowances are not paid. Appropriate footwear and work clothes are not provided either.[8]

Such shortcomings were to be found not only at the freight station. In summer 1942, during an operation to comb the local administration for workers, thirty Latvians from the harbor administration's traffic control were made available for loading work. After a short period, the jobs were abandoned, because the Latvians did not want to work together with prisoners of war and Jews.[9]

To regulate the question of how Riga's Schutzpolizei (the German municipal police) could oversee punitive measures more effectively, the officials responsible met at the office of the local commander Major Karl Heise on 25 March 1942. There Hans Donath, personal assistant to the county commissar, explained that the present methods of imprisoning the work-shy in Riga and escorting them to a place of work every morning would be abandoned in favor of a soon-to-be-completed camp under the county commissar's control. But Heise, making reference to the impossibility of delegating policemen to various places of work for individual work-shy persons, summed up the conversation with a greater emphasis on results. He recommended for the time being setting up an enclosed camp as well as a work site only for the work-shy, for "direct compulsory measures against the work-shy on site [are] almost impossible without arousing the human feelings of the good workers as well as the population and thereby causing [possible] incidents." In his conclusion, the commander of the Schutzpolizei in Riga made clear which solution he favored: "Creating and setting up the camp and the work site would be a matter of the office designated for this within the [office of the] County Commissar Riga City, if the Security Police, which is already endowed with ample experience in such correctional tasks, is not to be entrusted with this."[10]

Four weeks later, Schmutzler, the county commissar's labor deployment desk chief, Donath, and Lange inspected the Salaspils camp. After the three had gained an impression of the almost finished condition of a barrack for about 400 persons, Schmutzler recommended in a letter to County Commissar Riga City Hugo Wittrock that the Salaspils camp be used for the administration of punishment handed down for the work-shy. A day later, Max Dorr suggested during a presentation to General Commissar Otto Heinrich Drechsler that the county commissar be allowed to issue the verdict for loafers, whereas the police would be responsible for the administration of punishment. Considering the uniqueness of the penal camp, however, the degree of punishment was to remain in the hands of the police.[11]

Dorr and Schmutzler – the two officials responsible for the deployment of labor in the offices of the general commissar and the county commissar respectively – already knew at this point that Lange soon intended to withdraw around 600 Jews from the ghetto in Riga. Ghetto Commandant Krause had already informed Standtke, the head of the Labor Office's Bureau for the Deployment of Jews. This would have meant the Security Police withdrawing for its own purposes valuable workers from the civil labor administration's deployment planning. "With the extraordinary shortage of workers in this region, this loss could hardly be made up for," wrote Standtke, "particularly as the Jewish workers have been deployed almost exclusively in military-related economically important jobs and a substitute cannot be provided."[12]

With 4,391 prisoners located in Riga's four prison facilities – 801 persons were in "concentration camp custody," 2,574 Communists were detained "for further clarification," and 400 criminals were incarcerated – the city's civil administration hoped for a quick decision on behalf of Salaspils so as to avert the transfer of the 600 Jewish workers.[13] For this reason, Dorr agreed to accept Salaspils as a holding camp under the condition that the civil administration could specify the degree of punishment down to the exact number of days and weeks: "The imposition of political protective custody on the work-shy convicted by us will take place within the framework of existing laws. Here, too, I ask for a report in each individual case." Thus, because protective custody was solely a Security Police matter, Lange decided ultimately who among the "work-shy" was released and when.[14]

Dorr simultaneously told his superiors within the Reich Commissariat Ostland administration about Security Police plans to transfer 600 Jews to Salaspils and asked that this be prevented. The Security Police had justified its request by saying the Reich commissar himself had the previous autumn merely agreed to take on the German Jews temporarily and had had every intention of removing them as quickly as possible. Now, however, the labor market situation was considerably more acute, and Dorr was asking that these instructions be reconsidered.[15] As a result, a compromise was reached, by which it was agreed that, on 2 May, 300 Jews would be transferred from the ghetto to Salaspils for cutting peat.[16] In turn, some of the Jewish men who were no longer able to work would come back to the ghetto. However, the agreement on the transfer of 300 Jews to Salaspils was only provisional at first.[17] Lange continued to reserve for himself more requisitions for some time afterward until this exception also fell victim to a decision from Lohse.[18]

In the meantime, the first labor correctional and political inmates from General Commissariat Latvia had arrived in the camp.[19] When Lange drew up a two-week activity report on 24 June 1942, he was able to note that 130 men and 145 women classified as "concentration camp inmates" had been transferred to Salaspils; with that, a temporary level of 675 inmates had been achieved. Thus, within the shortest period of time, Lange had made up for the missing 300 Jews by using "concentration camp inmates."[20] Also, cases of "typical refusal to work" were now confined to Salaspils, such as sixteen persons from the Riga electricity plant VEF on 22 June.[21]

That same day, in connection with the pending approval of a labor correctional camp for KdS Lithuania, SS Colonel Dr. Robert Siegert of RSHA Department II (Administration) inquired via BdS Ostland Heinz Jost – who had replaced the deceased Walther Stahlecker in March – how far along things were at the Latvian labor correctional camp. After all, KdS Latvia had promised to have a finished camp with a capacity of 15,000 inmates for the temporary accommodation of Jews as well by April. The gulf between the expectations Riga originally raised in Berlin and the reality on the ground could no longer be kept secret. Lange had to admit that while construction at the camp had begun in September 1941, after nine months barracks for only 1,000 inmates had been built. Several work sites had also been set up, but if one were planning within the framework of what was possible, then a capacity for perhaps another 500–1,000 inmates had in fact been completed. Regarding the Jews, Lange noted merely: "Of the Jews who were evacuated from the Reich, only 400 are in the camp at present and are deployed in transportation and earthworks. The remaining Jews evacuated to Riga have been accommodated elsewhere."[22]

What Salaspils was supposed to become and what had actually been built only came to light due to an inquiry from Berlin. Nothing remained of the euphoria of being able to solve all of the problems of the Security Police in Latvia with one camp. In this respect, the history of Salaspils's conception is reminiscent of the disappointed expectations that had at first been placed in the construction of a similar camp in Lublin: Majdanek. The history of that camp's construction had also brought back down to earth all of the overblown plans regarding the role of this camp for District Lublin within the General Government. And Majdanek dwarfed Salaspils in its projected dimensions.

Starting in autumn and going into winter, Salaspils changed in character. Although it remained a camp where arbitrariness reigned, the German Jews who had built it were now gradually withdrawn. In connection with food planning for the camp, Lange made it clear that from now on a new inmate profile was in force, something he did not wish to inform the general prison administration, which was in Latvian hands. Going into detail, he explained that all of the political "concentration camp inmates" in the Central Prison had since been transferred to Salaspils; in addition, there were other political prisoners from General Commissariat Latvia's various smaller internment facilities. Finally, Lange expanded the group to include labor correctional inmates, members of the local police who had been convicted by the SS and Police Court (an office of the HSSPF), interned foreigners, and Latvians who had returned from the "old-Russian area" and had yet to be screened. This amounted to a total of 1,800 inmates in the first week of December. Among them were still twelve Jews who had been confined to Salaspils for "particular reasons" left unexplained; in fact, they were probably skilled workers. Lange also stated, however, that there were no plans to send any more Jews to Salaspils.[23]

The recent imprisonment of local policemen in Salaspils did not sit well with KdS Latvia. First of all, this meant persons were being sent to Salispils who did not fall within the Security Police's power of disposal; furthermore, persons who had been convicted by the SS and Police Court were supposed to serve their sentence in camps under the jurisdiction of the SS Economics and Administration Main Office. An inquiry asking what was actually meant by "concentration camp Salaspils" arrived from the RSHA at the instigation of the Main Office SS Court.[24] In justifying his refusal to provide information about the various groups of inmates and their numbers, Lange had previously stressed that although Salaspils bore the designation "expanded police prison and labor correctional camp," it was in reality "comparable with German concentration camps"; therefore, "like the number of inmates in German concentration camps," how many people were in Salaspils had to be considered secret. This time, he turned the argument vis-à-vis his superiors on its head: "I ask that it be reported to the Reich Security Main Office that the Salaspils camp does not involve a concentration camp ... There is no actual concentration camp in Ostland to my knowledge ... In and of itself, the camp would be suitable for admitting inmates who have been convicted by the SS and Police Court or for whom custody in a camp is ordered. If, however, a willingness is expressed to the Main Office SS Court to take in such inmates to the camp, the danger would arise that the camp could be taken from the Security Police in the course of this development and subordinated to the concentration camps administration; that must be avoided by all means."[25]

The reason for the reluctance to use the term "concentration camp" apparently lay in the fact that in the course of summer 1942 it had become known among Ostland's regional commanders of the Security Police and their top officials that the SS Economist with HSSPF Ostland Friedrich Jeckeln had been employed to monitor the concentration camps in Ostland. It was therefore to be feared, such was the opinion of KdS Estonia Martin Sandberger after talks with SS Major Josef Stüber and SS Captain Heinz Trühe in Riga, that "we are also being pushed back significantly in this field, and it is advisable that we take countermeasures in an appropriate manner." At the same time, it was pointed out to Sandberger that "labor correctional camps" were still the exclusive responsibility of the Gestapo. Adhering to terminological accuracy thus meant maintaining power vis-à-vis the HSSPF.[26] Nonetheless, from this point on, Lange was not to get rid of this problem again. In August 1943, Sandberger inquired with BdS Ostland Humbert Achamer-Pifrader, who had succeeded Jost in September

1942, as to whether it had in the meantime become possible to have Estonian policemen confined to Salaspils "so that the KdS Estonia would be relieved of this job."[27]

An additional example of Lange's bureaucratic dexterity in keeping Salaspils solely at the disposal of KdS Latvia is found in an exchange with one of his superiors in Berlin. In a decree dated 17 December 1942, SS Major General Heinrich Müller, the head of RSHA Department IV (Gestapo), had ordered that inmates able to work be released from Security Police custody for forced labor in the German Reich. Referring to reasons important to the war effort but left unspecified, Himmler had ordered this three days earlier, Müller wrote. Müller obligated the heads of the Gestapo offices in the Reich and the territorial commanders in the east to comb their labor correctional camps and prisons, according to strict guidelines, so that they could transfer as many inmates as possible to the concentration camps in Germany. "Each individual worker matters," wrote Müller. Lange subsequently confirmed that there was indeed the theoretical possibility of transferring 300 inmates from Salaspils, but he used an abundance of arguments to the effect that this German measure would ultimately lead to "comparison with the Bolshevik era" among Latvians. As a result, the inmates remained where they were.[28] Even when Himmler once more warned on 15 January 1943 that he had recently noticed a tendency among the higher SS and police leaders to set up separate concentration camps under the term "labor correctional camps," something he was banning herewith, this had no effect on Lange's camp.[29]

As a consequence of the anti-partisan operation Winter Magic, which had been underway on the Latvian-Russian borderland since January 1943, the inmate profile in Salaspils changed yet again. In a series of individual undertakings within this operation, the Security Police, Order Police battalions, and local police tried until March 1943 "to cleanse the gangsters" from the poorly secured border area of Latvia's Latgale region.[30] The measures applied resembled those that had been in use for several months in Rear Area Army Group Center and General Commissariat White Ruthenia.[31] Entire areas were plundered, villages were burned to the ground, and many civilians, as well as a few partisans, were murdered. According to a report by Lange, at least 3,951 civilians were evacuated from the area of operations in the course of these three partial actions.[32] Of these, 2,288 people, including women and children, were taken away to Salaspils, where up to this point 1,990 inmates had been accommodated.[33]

The feeding and use of these persons, however, was entrusted to the German occupation administration; in this case, the general commissar's Department I (Social Services and Welfare) was responsible. The evacuees were not inmates of the Security Police. Above all, the children in Salaspils –

around 1,100 – were to be taken to homes or orphanages as quickly as possible.³⁴ However, the civil administration's organizational preparations to this end apparently did not go quickly enough for SS Second Lieutenant Bögner, the camp's commandant. While the social department of the Latvian administration was still trying to place young people able to work at farms, Bögner had the children simply distributed among the villages. At a meeting of the German agronomists in the Riga vicinity and the agriculture chief of County Commissariat Riga Countryside, the latter was confronted with fierce complaints. Over 1,000 fully neglected children had to be accommodated, according to a directive from Salaspils, and the agriculture chief was forced to discover that his county commissariat and General Commissariat Latvia had no information about this.³⁵

Even if Lange managed to smooth over this dispute, in the wake of the first waves of refugees set in motion by Army Group Center's deteriorating situation on the front, the civil administration looked to the Salaspils camp toward the end of 1943 to help with this new challenge. In the course of planning for the stream of refugees, it was necessary to determine certain collecting points in the general commissariats. The head of Reich Commissariat Ostland's Health Department recalled Salaspils, noting: "There is a [concentration camp] located there, which with the best success has already ushered through 6,000 refugees from the areas threatened by gangs. It is to be assumed that this stream of refugees will soon dry up so that this camp will again be able to take in [refugees]. It is [partly] occupied by prisoners, but still has the possibility of taking in refugees. The prisoners were drawn on to provide for the refugees with the best success. In the event the commander of the SD-Ostland were able to decide to continue making the camp available for processing refugees, ca. 1,000 to 2,000 could be immediately taken care of and just as many every four weeks on a continuous basis. The camp offers all of the prerequisites and has also already gathered experience. The cordons are impeccable. The surrounding population is not lice-ridden."³⁶ From that point on, Salaspils served repeatedly as a temporary first port of call for "evacuees suspected of gang activity" as well as for refugees from the front area. The "gang children" were transferred from Salaspils, first to the children's section of Majdanek, then to a camp for the protection of children and young people at Konstantynów Łódzki (Tuchingen) near Łódz (Litzmannstadt), whereas the adults went to Stutthof.³⁷

In the course of setting up a concentration camp in Mežaparks (Kaiserwald), a rather fashionable residential area of the Riga city forest, Himmler must have considered, at least briefly, officially converting Salaspils into a concentration camp.³⁸ Six weeks after the announcement of a future camp near the Ganību Dambis (Weidendamm) in Riga, Himmler wrote Oswald Pohl and Ernst Kaltenbrunner, the respective heads of the SS Economics and Administration Main Office and the RSHA:

A labor correctional camp of ours is located in Salaspils, in Ostland. This camp is in practical terms a concentration camp, but is subordinated to the Regional Commander of the Security Police. The administration of punishment for Latvian, Estonian, Lithuanian local policemen and volunteers serving within the framework of the SS and police is carried out in this camp. Employment in the camp is cutting peat, mining, quarrying, chalk works, cement production, etc. Under no circumstances do I wish that a [concentration camp] be established here like a private [concentration camp] of some regional sector [SS-Oberabschnitt]. I approve this concentration camp Salaspils under two conditions: 1. If it becomes a [concentration camp], it will be subordinated to the head of the main office administration and economics. 2. If this camp receives a real and important armaments enterprise. Employment in the cement works, peat ditch, etc., may be quite nice, but it has been started only in order to employ the inmates on hand there. We cannot afford this during the war.[39]

This concept was not pursued, however: Salaspils remained a police prison and labor correctional camp, even though in mid 1943 there was brief consideration of disbanding all such places of internment under the aegis of the Security Police in favor of a central Security Police camp in Rogavka, about 50 km (33 miles) north-northwest of Novgorod.[40]

The history of the Salaspils camp and its different groups of inmates is almost unknown. But it is here, as if under a magnifying glass, that the history of German occupation and arbitrariness comes into focus. Established by deported Jews, not Soviet prisoners of war, and expanded by Latvian civilians who rejected German measures to make them work and support the war effort, the camp in the woods of Salaspils slowly grew larger.[41] Political prisoners, by no means only Communists, were added from every place of internment in the country. When Belarusian partisan resistance spilled over into Latvia, the Germans confined more civilians to Salaspils. Even local policemen and volunteers for military service were disciplined there. From the scant surviving documentation, it is possible to reconstruct only one case of coordinated resistance, which apparently involved concrete preparations for a camp uprising in the event that the Red Army drew near. In March 1943, a camp inmate betrayed the fact that the external commando at the quarry had regularly smuggled explosives into the camp. A comprehensive investigation by the Security Police revealed that pipe-bombs had been produced in the blacksmith's shop; these were to generate confusion and panic with the anticipated advance of the Red Army. Lange was able to announce proudly in his report for March 1943 that his men were able to convict seventy-six inmates for cognizance and complicity; in addition, thirty-two "ringleaders" had been executed.[42] Finally, Salaspils also served a base for Sonderkommando 1005, the special unit that came to Riga in 1944 in order to open up the mass graves in the forests around the Latvian capital and burn the corpses. At the start and the end of this camp's history, there are the Jews who worked there and who were murdered there in large numbers. Their fate will now be examined more closely.

Notes

1. See chapter 6, this volume.
2. BA Berlin, R 91/99, Der Geb.-Komm. in Riga, Arbeitsamt, an den Gen.-Komm., Abtl. Sozialverwaltung, betr. Bericht für die Zeit vom 16.11-31.12.1941, 13 January 1942: "The Jews arriving from abroad were put to work constructing a camp of barracks in Salaspils."
3. BA Berlin, R 58/220, Ereignismeldung Nr. 154, 12 January 1942.
4. RGVA, 504-2-8, 191, FS Berlin, RSHA, II C 3, an den BdS in Riga, gez. Dr. Siegert, 22 June 1942.
5. For Lithuania, BA Berlin, R 58/220, Ereignismeldung Nr. 167, 11 February 1942; for Latvia, BA Berlin R 91/30, Der Geb.-Komm. Riga, Arbeitsamt, an den Gen.-Komm., Sozialverwaltung, betr. Lage im Monat Februar 1942, 7 March 1942; for Estonia, Estonian State Archive, 819-1-12, 1-101, Jahresbericht des (Sonderkommandos 1a) KdS Estlands, 1 July 1942, here 56.
6. BA Berlin R 91/30, Der Geb.-Komm. Riga, Arbeitsamt, an den Gen.-Komm., Sozialverwaltung, betr. Lage im Monat Februar 1942, 7 March 1942
7. See, for example, BA Berlin, R 91/107, Fa. Alfons Blank, Baustelle in Mitau, 19 March 1942.
8. BA Berlin, R 58/221, Ereignismeldung Nr. 190, 8 April 1942.
9. BA Berlin, R 91/101, Aktenvermerk, betr. Stellung von Arbeitskräften für besonders wichtige Massnahmen, 26 June 1942.
10. BA Berlin, R 91/107, Kommando der Schutzpolizei S 1 a an das Arbeitsamt Riga, betr. Arbeitsverweigerer, 14 April 1942.
11. BA Berlin, R 91/107, Schreiben des Geb.-Komm. Riga, Arbeitsamt, an den Geb.-Komm. und komm. Oberbürgermeister Wittrock, betr. Errichtung eines Arbeitslagers, 24 April 1942; ibid., Vermerk, betr. Ahndung von Arbeitsverweigerung, Arbeitsvertragsbruch usw.
12. BA Berlin, R 92/1158, 6, Der Geb.-Komm. in Riga-Arbeitsamt, Fachgebiet 2 (Arbeitseinsatz), Aktenvermerk, betr. Einsatz von Juden, 23 April 1942.
13. LVVA, Riga, P 1376-1-7, 430, Tabellarischer Bericht über die Zahl der Gefangenen in den vier Rigaer Haftanstalten Zentralgefängis, Termingefängnis, Gefängnis für Minderjährige sowie der Präfektur mit Stichtag 25.4.1942, Stieglitz. There were also 409 prisoners of war, 132 Jews, 37 "Administr.[ierte]," 38 detainees, and 62 children.
14. BA Berlin, R 91/107, Dorr an das Arbeitsamt Riga, betr. Errichtung eines Arbeitslagers, 29 April 1942; also in BA Berlin, R 91/99.
15. BA Berlin, R 92/1158, 5, Der Geb.-Komm. in Riga, Arbeitsamt, an den RKO III/Aso durchlaufend beim Gen.-Komm., 29 April 1942.
16. Ibid., 7, Abtl. III/Aso an Otto Ziegenbein, 29 April 1942. Ziegenbein was Lohse's adjutant.
17. BA Berlin, R 91/63, Der Geb.-Komm. Riga-Arbeitsamt, Fachgebiet 1 (Statistik), betr. Lage im Monat April 1942, 6 May 1942: "The commander of the Security Police intended to

remove 600 Jews from the ghetto. Through negotiations, it was concluded that initially only 300 would be withdrawn."
18. BA Berlin, R 92/1158, 8, Der RKO, Abtl. III Aso, Sachgebiet Arbeitseinsatz, an den Gen.-Komm., Abtl. Aso, Fachgebiet Arbeitseinsatz, betr. Judeneinsatz, 27 May 1942.
19. Margers Vestermanis mentions two dates for the arrival of Latvian prisoners: 7 May, which involved prisoners from Madona; this was followed by a group of 200 persons on 18 May. Vestermanis, *Haftstätten und Todeslager im okkupierten Lettland*, 477 and 479.
20. United States Holocaust Memorial Museum, RG 15.007, reel 16 [RSHA-Material from Warsaw]: Der KdS Lettland, betr. Tätigkeitsbericht für die Zeit vom 23.5.-18.6.1942, Geheim.
21. LVVA, P 70-5-37, 123-124, Der BdS Ostland, Abtl. III, an den RKO, betr. Tagesmeldungen der Einsatzkommandos, 30 June 1942.
22. RGVA, 504-2-8, 191, RSHA, II C 3 an BdS Ostland, betr. Errichtung eines erweiterten Polizeigefängnisses und Arbeitserziehungslagers für den Bezirk Litauen, 22 June 1942. This telex was passed on to Lange on 25 June 1942, see ibid., 190; Lange's answer to the RSHA followed on 21 July 1942, ibid., 192.
23. LVVA, P 69-1a-10, 214–215, KdS Lettland an den Gen.-Komm., Abtl. III b Ernährung und Landwirtschaft, geheim, betr. Großbezugsscheine zur Verpflegungsbeschäftigung für die Insassen von Salaspils, 3 December 1942. In his monthly report for 1–31 January 1943, Lange noted that as of 19 January 1943, 1,857 inmates were interned in Salaspils, with 1,763 persons being political prisoners. In addition, there were 65 work-shy individuals and 29 detainees. They were watched at the time by 189 members of the Latvian security section, see in LVVA, P 82-1-39, 9–91, here 14 and 89, Stimmungs- und Lagebericht für die Zeit vom 1.-31. Januar 1943.
24. RGVA, 504-2-8, 167, RSHA, IV C 2, an den BdS in Riga, i.A. gez. Dr. Berndorff, 1 December 1942: "Urgent. Expedite quickly! According to a message from the Main Office SS Court, members of the Estonian, Latvian, and Lithuanian local police who have been convicted by the SS and Police Court are being confined to the Salaspils camp for the administration of their punishment or penal camp custody. The SS Court requests a special order and disclosure of the camp's address. Because the Salaspils camp, which is designated as a concentration camp, is not subordinated to the [SS Economics and Administration Main Office], Division D, and is not well known here either, I ask for a prompt telex-message as to whether a camp has been set up there in the area. [If so], it is to be reported on at length. [In particular] state: exact address, to whom the camp is subordinated, and what kind of prisoners are there."
25. RGVA, 504-2-8, 167-168, KdS Lettland an BdS Ostland, 8 December 1942. Lange returned the inquiry in the original with a statement on how to answer the RSHA.
26. Estonian State Archive, 819-2-3, 60, Entwurf, Sandberger an BdS Ostland, z.Hd. SS-Hauptsturmführer Jagusch, betr. Konzentrationslager, 3 December 1942.
27. Ibid., 91, Notiz für die Besprechung beim BdS Riga, 4 August 1943. In the course of the winter of 1943–44, convicted members of the Latvian Legion of the Waffen-SS were added, see Lange's report to BdS Ostland and the territorial commander of the Waffen-SS Ostland on the inspection trip by Bangerskis and Zamuelis, RGVA, 504-2-8, 178–179.
28. RGVA, 504-2-8, 23, Abschrift. Der KdS Lettland, IV C-2, "Sofort SS-Gruf. Müller vorlegen," 1 March 1943, printed in *Archives of the Holocaust*, vol. 22, Doc. 94, 202–203. Müller's decree of 17 December 1942 is mentioned in the subject line and also appears in the aforementioned collection, see *Archives of the Holocaust*, vol. 22, Doc. 93, 199–201.
29. BA Berlin, NS 19/1542, 43, Der RFSS an das RSHA zur Weitergabe an alle HSSPF und BdS, 15 January 1943.

30. On this operation, see Ruth Bettina Birn, "'Zaunkönig' an 'Uhrmacher,'" *Militärgeschichtliche Zeitschrift* 60 (2001): 99–118.
31. For a systematic study of this topic, see Gerlach, *Kalkulierte Morde*; with the focus on the civil population affected, see Peter Klein, "Zwischen den Fronten," in *"Wir sind die Herren dieses Landes*," ed. Babette Quinkert, 82–103.
32. LVVA, P 82-1-39, 92–202, Der KdS Lettland, Stimmungs- und Lagebericht für die Zeit vom 1.-31.3.1943, here 96.
33. The guard company at the camp was reinforced by 160 Latvian policemen, see ibid., 99. In a report from Schmutzler to Wittrock on the processing of legal complaints regarding refusal to work and loafing during the first six months of 1943, it can also be inferred that of 5,612 legal complaints, 449 persons (315 men and 134 women) were transferred to Salaspils to serve out their punishment, see BA Berlin, R 91/101, Der Geb.-Komm. Riga, Arbeitsverwaltung an den Geb.-Komm. und komm. Oberbürgermeister, betr. Bearbeitung der Anzeigen über Arbeitsvertragsbruch, Arbeitsbummeleien, usw., 16 August 1943, für die Zeit vom 1.1.1943-30.6.1943.
34. RGVA, 1358-4-17, 35, Der Gen.-Komm. in Riga, Abtl. I, an den RKO, betr. Bereitstellung von Mitteln zur Unterbringung evakuierter Kinder aus dem russischen Grenzraum, 20 March 1943.
35. Ibid., 99, Der Geb.-Komm. Riga-Land, Geb.-Ref. II, an den RKO, HA II, über den Gen.-Komm. in Riga, Abtl. II Verw. Betrifft: Unterbringung von Kindern russischer Evakuierter, 14 April 1943. In this source, the camp commandant is incorrectly designated as SS First Lieutenant Büchner. On the transfer of SS Second Lieutenant Bögner as camp commandant of Salaspils from his home office, Inspector of the Security Police and SD Vienna, see LVVA, P 82-1-39, 92–202, Der KdS Lettland. Stimmungs- und Lagebericht für die Zeit vom 1.-31.3.1943, 96, "Personalveränderungen."
36. RGVA, 1358-4-17, 81–82, Aktenvermerk RKO, Abtl. II Gesund., betr. Sanitäre Versorgung von Flüchtlingen aus dem Frontgebiet, Dr. v. Lilienfeldt-Toal. Additional camps were Paldiski (Baltischport) in General Commissariat Estonia; Daugavpils (Dünaburg), Stalag Rēzekne (Rositten), the nerve clinic at Strenči (Stackeln) in the General Commissariat Latvia; and Stalag Alytus (Olita) in General Commissariat Lithuania.
37. RGVA, 504-2-8, 71, Der BdS Ostland, Abtl. IV, an das RSHA, betr. Aufnahme von Frauen und Kindern in ein KL, 7 December 1943. The answer from RSHA, IV D 5, betr. Unterbringung von Bandenkindern, 23 December 1943, is in ibid., 75. The transfer of the children was delayed, however, due to cases of typhus in Salaspils, see Sipo Riga an die KdS-Außenstellen in Dünaburg, Mitau, Libau, Wolmar. Nachrichtl. an BdS Ostland, KdS Estland, KdS Litauen, betr. Aufnahme- und Entlassungssperre für das erweiterte Polizeigefängnis und Arbeitserziehungslager Salaspils, in Estonian State Archive, 819-2-2, 24 and RGVA, 504-2-8, 175.
38. RGVA, 504-2-8, 170, RSHA, IV C 2, an alle BdS, KdS, Beauftr. des Chefs Sipo/SD in Brüssel an alle Referate des Amtes IV, Referat II C 3. Nachrichtl. an alle HSSPF, IdS, an WVHA-D-Oranienburg. An Referat I B 3, Referat II A, Gst IV, betr. KL (Arbeitslager) Riga, 2 April 1943. This includes the installation of SS Major Albert Sauer as commandant of the concentration camp Riga.
39. BA Berlin, NS 19/369, 1, Der RFSS an SS-Ogruf. Pohl, an SS-Gruf. Kaltenbrunner, 18 May 1943.
40. RGVA, 504-2-8, 180, Der Chef der EG A, II A 1, an Ek 1, 2, 3, sowie die Stabsführung der EG A, z. Hd. SS-Hstuf. Höfler, betr. Errichtung eines neuen Häftlingslagers der EG A in Rogavka, 19 August 1943; ibid., 181–182, Der BdS Ostland an Abtl. I im Hause, betr. Sicherheitspolizeiliches Häftlingslager Rogavka, 27 August 1943, which contains points

of camp order. The project was not carried out due to decentralizing measures, see the marginalia in ibid.
41. Although Stalag 350 was located nearby, there was no cooperation in establishing the Security Police camp. The camp leadership under Captain Zech of Home Defense Battalion 529 did not turn over any POWs due to its own construction activities, see Staw. Hamburg, 141 Js 534/60, Bd. 29, statement by Josef Stocker, 27 September 1962, 4,464. Stocker also served among Stalag 350's guards.
42. LVVA, P 82-1-39, 92–202, Stimmungs- und Lagebericht des KdS Lettland für Zeit vom 1.-31.3.43, 176–177.

– *Chapter 10* –

GERMAN JEWS BUILD SALASPILS
December 1941–August 1942

"We are sliding more than marching. It had snowed and then frozen. The head guard says that we have to walk 15 km [9 miles]. It is the Latvian SS that is watching us, all of them brazen, burly characters. After a march of roughly 3 km, the head guard has us stop on the open road. 'Hand over your watches and rings,' he commands, 'or I will shoot you down like rabbits.' The other guards start searching our clothing, while the head guard holds his rifle level. They take everything that they can use, gold cigarette etuis, good lighters, they even pull wedding rings from our fingers."[1]

Josef Katz, from whom this memory stems, had arrived at the Jungfernhof camp with the Hamburg transport of 9 December 1941. After several days, the Jewish self-administration had assigned him to a group of young men who were being transferred to Salaspils in order to build the camp there. On orders from the camp administration, groups of men were repeatedly taken away – in part by Jewish camp personnel, in part by deportees – shortly after reaching Jungfernhof.[2] SS First Lieutenant Gerhard Maywald, who was in charge of construction at Salaspils, had also been to Jungfernhof several times to seek out and take back laborers in person.[3] Katz's experiences on this march into the forest of Salaspils are supplemented by statements from Artur Kann and Sally Simons, who recalled their groups being completely plundered during the march to Salaspils.[4]

By late 1941 and early 1942, around 1,000 younger and older men had been moved from the Jungfernhof camp and the Riga ghetto to Salaspils for construction, although the first workers still lacked accommodations. Upon arrival, they had been forced to lie down in a forest clearing, await registration, and then join the others working on the barracks. Fully soaked and half frozen from the harsh cold, those who had been taken away soon noticed that this camp was a murderous destination. Not only was there no clothing for the prisoners, but the first rations were distributed only several days after arrival.[5] The state of construction at Security Police chief Rudolf Lange's ambitious project at this point is not documented. At year's

---

Notes for this chapter begin on page 255.

end, however, there could have been only two half-finished barracks, a commandant's office building without a roof, and a fence, all of which had been erected on short notice by Soviet POWs.[6] At the start of the new year, younger and stronger men were once again selected from among the deportees arriving at the ghetto. Concrete information about occupancy above 1,000 Jews for the first days of January 1942 does not exist, however. The figures that survivors provided later diverge considerably. The most credible of these are between 1,500 and 1,800 prisoners.[7]

Working conditions were likewise murderous in Jungfernhof, but conditions in Salaspils were much worse. Water came from only one poorly functioning pump that was often rusted shut. In the winter of 1941–42, people were even less prepared for the harsh freezing temperatures, day and night, than at Jungfernhof, some 12 km (7.5 miles) away. There was initially no food for the first inmates.[8] Later, daily rations consisted of 300–400 grams of bread and just under a liter of water soup in which rhubarb leaves or old fish heads were sometimes found. Supplementary rations such as rotten potatoes or spoiled sauerkraut sometimes reached the camp.[9] The lack of opportunity to change clothes or wash brought lice into the barracks as soon as the weather got warmer.

A day's work primarily consisted of erecting barracks and watchtowers as well as finishing the fence. A lumber commando in the forest and a sawmill on the Daugava provided boards. In addition, the forest ground had to be cleared for at least forty more elongated barracks. The technical side of these matters was overseen by the Latvian construction firm of Janis Irbe, which had a long-term contract with the Security Police to provide material and professional supervision for this unusual construction site.[10] The construction firm was regularly provided with laborers from the ghetto; however, these were exclusively for the supply yard in town so that the Jews in Salaspils and their relatives in the ghetto could not make contact with one another. At the Jewish-run Labor Deployment Central Office in the ghetto, this supply yard commando was better known by the name Krause II. It was one of the first commandos under detail leader Robert Subak of Vienna, and on 4 March 1942, its members, together with those of another seventeen commandos, were the first to receive the "commando slice," as the 100-grams of additional bread ration for hard labor was called among the Jews.[11] The transports that arrived in Šķirotava between 12 January and 10 February were met by a Jewish baggage commando from Salaspils. The task of this latter commando was to haul the suitcases and goods from the transport to Salaspils or to transfer them to trucks, which then drove off in the direction of the Latvian capital. In Salaspils, the clothing storerooms and the suitcases represented the only chance prisoners had to get hold of goods for barter or additional food – always at risk of being shot or hanged.[12]

Not only did the adverse climatic, hygienic, and nutritional conditions make Salaspils a "killing center" from the point of view of survivors. Commandant Richard Nickel of Berlin and Otto Teckemeier of Pinneberg County (outside Hamburg), together with Maywald and Lange and the Latvian local police, ran a brutal and strict camp regime.[13] This was shown as early as 2 January 1942, when two young men from Hanover who had fled Salaspils on 30 December – 18-year old Erich Hanau and 16-year old Kurt Hirschkowitz – were shot in front of the assembled inmates. Lange, who had driven to the camp for this very reason, gave the order. Afterward, Lange informed the prisoners, who had been standing in the freezing air for hours and were completely shocked by the sight, that for every new escape attempt additional prisoners would be shot as well.[14] This advance notice that all of those who had been taken to Salaspils were in effect hostages came true in March 1942, when two more prisoners fled. Lange returned to Salaspils and demanded the barrack elder turn over ten hostages for execution. When he refused, Lange had the entire barrack report and demanded that all of the men from Brno (Brünn) step forward (one of the escapees apparently had come from this town). From this group, Lange then selected a victim and had him savagely beaten and hanged.[15]

Such hangings grew increasingly frequent in the course of the weeks that followed, for it was impossible to survive without barter.[16] The Latvian guards, however, were unpredictable, and the German Security Police always followed up on their reports. Commandant Nickel appears to have punished the occasional report of barter by ordering beatings, which were not registered. But his deputy, Teckemeier, put great store in filing correct reports to Riga, which always resulted in the death sentence.[17] Lange was as a rule always present at such killings: "The camp's occupants had to report. I then had to read the finding. This usually ran: 'On order of the Regional Commander of the Security Police and SD, Dr. Lange, the Jew X is condemned to death by hanging for barter.' This is the wording in spirit. The prisoner Besen and another prisoner then carried out the hanging. Besen was a professional boxer. These two were probably designated by the commandant for this task."[18]

Siegfried Kaufmann, who made this statement in March 1950, arrived in Riga from Kassel on 13 December 1941. While still in Šķirotava, he was selected for Salaspils, arriving there with about forty other men. In January, Kaufmann was given the task of establishing an Order Service of eighty-five persons with him as "Jewish police chief." A man from Stuttgart by the name of Einstein had already been appointed camp elder. In addition to the forced laborers with camp police duties, there were a good number of prisoners with specific functions, for example, in the clothing storerooms, the glazier's workshop, the plumber's workshop, the cafeteria, and in the infirmary. The best known of these, however, was Wolf Besen, the former boxer from Prague, who was called "the hangman of Salaspils."

Gertrude Schneider, who met him, twice described Besen as a friendly man and open character who had nothing ice cold or brutal about him. Besen himself justified his execution duties by explaining how, during the first days in Salaspils, a Latvian SS man had hanged another Jew from Prague so laboriously and incorrectly that the assembled prisoners were confronted with a scene of brutal torture. When it was asked of the prisoners, who had in the meantime begun grumbling, whether somebody among them could do it better, Besen said that he stepped forward and took care of the job more quickly. When he was later returned to the ghetto, many already knew of him as the "hangman of Salaspils," something that particularly bothered neither him nor his wife.[19]

Besen could not have known that he would be labeled a hangman due to this one episode. Later, he was doomed to continue this work if he wanted to save his own life. Apparently, Besen had to serve as hangman at the nearby Jungfernhof camp at least once in a case involving a man from Würzburg by the name of Kaufmann, who had been caught bartering and whom camp commandant Rudolf Seck wanted to use to set an example.[20] As survivor and historian Gertrude Schneider later wrote, only those who have never been in a situation where they were forced to make decisions about their own survival can assume the luxury of passing judgment on this man.[21] With its own coldness, the Security Police noted in this regard: "Latvia: In the last three days, three Jews brought to Riga from the Reich who had fled from the ghetto or the camps of barracks were seized. The Jews were shot or hanged in the presence of the ghetto- or camp inmates. In both of the cases handled, the hanging was done by Jews, who carried out this work without objection."[22]

From the start, the numerous dead – victims of poor nutrition, the extreme weather conditions, or Lange's spontaneous shootings – were buried in a mass grave, which due to the ground frost had to be blasted into the earth.[23] But in January 1942, a new kind of selection apparently got underway. When Nickel went on vacation, Seck was named his representative for the duration. Many of the survivors at Salaspils were able to remember these days in January 1942 quite vividly. Upon his arrival, Seck initially announced a "sick transport" back to the ghetto and had it organized. At roll call, 49-year-old Andreas Mendel was able to leave his barrack only with the help of his son Kurt and friends. Sick with dysentery and supported by two persons, he dragged himself to the reporting site, but was stopped by Seck, who addressed him with the words: "But you're not going back to

Figure 10.1. SS Technical Sergeant Otto Teckemeier in Salaspils. Third from left in the background among the camp inmates is Ernst Benjamin Freudenthal, who was deported from Cologne. March/April 1942. Courtesy of Bundesarchiv Koblenz.

your wife!" Seck had Mendel lie down on the ground and shot him right in front of the victim's son.[24] How many sick transports were organized cannot be reconstructed precisely. At first, however, the people consigned to such transports were not returned to the ghetto, but were driven instead to Bikernieki and shot in pits that had been prepared in advance by another Jewish forced labor commando. The number of those selected for execution as unable to work is unknown.[25]

But against the backdrop of plans to transfer another 600 Jews from the Riga ghetto to Salaspils to cut peat on 1 May 1942 and the subsequent need to reduce this number to 300, the Security Police changed procedure. If the ghetto could not provide the number of workers needed and Latvian political or correctional prisoners were arriving too slowly, then it seemed necessary to take care that the Jewish prisoners in Salaspils were restored to health. As word of this change in policy began to make the rounds at Salaspils, the prisoners refused to believe it. "Laughable," wrote glazier Josef Katz in his memoirs, "up until yesterday, they had annihilated Jewish life by all means available, and today, they want to send us off to recuperate."[26] The men went into hiding and could be rounded up only by use of force – but the rumors were true. Kaufmann, in his capacity as chief of the

Jewish camp police, drove the first truck into the ghetto and later returned to Salaspils safe and sound.[27] Katz wrote that on 20 April 1942 a message came back on the first vehicle, according to which all had arrived in the ghetto.[28] Herbert Hirschland later explained that it had been agreed to wipe some chalk markings off the rear of the truck if the vehicle actually reached the ghetto. The markings were missing.[29]

Figure 10.2. Siegfried Kaufmann, deported from Kassel, with armband "Supreme Jew. Camp-Policeman." March/April 1942. Courtesy of Bundesarchiv Koblenz.

Only those who have faced the fear of death can fathom how great the relief was once it became clear to the Salaspils inmates that they would not fall victim to another murder operation. In the ghetto itself, however, Jews were unsure whether they should get their hopes up. "In April 1942, an ambulance finally arrived from Salaspils. A truck stopped in front of the commandant's office. The streets were cordoned off. A Jewish ghetto policeman stepped up on the vehicle, he brought a human figure down, others did the same. They stood there, human beings, but it was impossible to recognize whether a child or an elderly person, whether a woman or man. Then the names were read out. Their relatives rushed to them and began to see to them. It took weeks until these sick persons found their balance again."[30]

Baskets for donations in kind and food were immediately set up in a courtyard so that the returning workers, who would march by in the evening, could contribute something for the returned Salaspils workers.[31] However, for many families, the return of the prisoners from Salaspils also meant receiving news that a husband or son, an in-law, an uncle, or a close friend had frozen to death, been shot or hanged, or died some other way. It should not go unmentioned that the ghetto police exploited the knowledge of the shocking living conditions in Salaspils during an inspection of all groups on 25 April, when it threatened: "In addition, it is to be announced to the groups that those persons who do not appear for roll call in order to evade inspection are to be considered as discharged to Salaspils."[32] As it was, this inspection of the entire ghetto may have been held in order to scrape together the 300 people needed for cutting peat in Salaspils, but at the time, everybody hoped to avoid being assigned to this commando. On 4 May, this new workforce left the ghetto for the feared death camp.[33]

Back in the ghetto, the survivors were very well cared for; the Jewish-run Labor Deployment Central Office made sure that they were not assigned any kind of work.[34] This group was able to recover until 29 May, for some, and 3 June, for others, before a large part of them had to return to Salaspils.[35] On 13 June, when the Labor Deployment Central Office announced that the remaining men who had returned from Salaspils would have to report for work, Hilde Schneider of Hanover noted the date and the word "Salaspils" next to Psalms 88:5–6: "I am set apart with the dead, like the slain who lie in the grave, whom you remember no more, who are cut off from your care. You have put me in the lowest pit, in the darkest depths."[36]

In the final weeks before the Jewish men assigned to Salaspils were finally taken away from the camp and replaced by Latvian prisoners, nothing changed in the barbaric everyday life of the camp. In an activity report for the period 23 May–18 June, the regional commander of the Security

Police and Security Service in Latvia reported that in the interval 675 prisoners were engaged in "beneficial work," and that within Riga twenty-nine Jews had been executed – a part of whom were almost certainly in Salaspils.[37] Starting in July and August, the camp's Jewish prisoners were gradually returned to the ghetto.[38] Upon arrival, their articles of clothing were taken away for disinfection.[39] The people were then integrated into the ghetto's forced labor system; some unlucky ones once again ended up back at the peatlands near Salaspils a short time later.[40] A few Jews ended up barracked at a completely new location, such as those who were shipped in the summer of 1942 to the Riga district Mežaparks (Kaiserwald), in order to do landscaping work as part of the Athletic Field Commando.[41] Here the former Salaspils inmates encountered ghetto Jews who worked there on a daily basis or were permanently barracked there.[42]

By September 1942, Salaspils was functioning as a police internment and labor correctional camp with fifteen of the forty-five planned barracks. It is believed that over the duration of its existence about 12,000 prisoners passed through its gates.[43] In addition to the German-Jewish victims, an additional 2,000–3,000 people perished in this camp, with the share of children and young people from the "gang areas" (i.e., partisan areas) being particularly high. The assertions put forward by the local office of the Soviet State Extraordinary Commission for Ascertaining and Investigating the Crimes Committed by the German-Fascist Invaders and Their Accomplices are to be rejected. According to its data, Salaspils, the largest "death camp" in the Baltic region, had cost at least 53,000 people their lives.[44]

At the end of November 1963, Maywald, who had been the Security Police official responsible for constructing Salaspils, wrote his own version of the truth while in investigative detention: "All of these tasks, at such a most enormous construction site, filled out [my time] completely, I was sent there for this [alone] and was not called upon for other duties. But I was constantly pressed due to the completion deadline. The Jews who were gradually called upon to assist worked cheerfully and to the best of their ability, they were glad to get their future production sites and accommodations ready to move into as soon as possible."[45]

Notes

1. Katz, *Erinnerungen eines Überlebenden*, 37.
2. Staw. Hamburg, 141 Js 534/60, Bd. 63, statement by Wolf A. M. Hirsch, 10 May 1966, 10,125–10,134. Hirsch was deported from Kiel via Hamburg; after a day in Jungfern-

hof, he was taken away to Salaspils. Ibid., Bd. 43, statement by Ludwig Gutmann, 25 February 1964, 7,311–7,311a. Deported from Würzburg, Gutmann was taken away to Salaspils after around ten days in Latvia.
3. Ibid., Bd. 42, statement by Gerhard Maywald, 28 November 1963, 6,934–6,936.
4. Ibid., Bd. 73, statement by Artur Kann, 12 December 1967, 11,769–11,777. Kann was deported from Cologne and was for a short period in the Riga ghetto before being taken away to Salaspils. Ibid., Bd. 61, Sally Simons, 15 November 1965, 9,807–9,812. Simons was also deported from Cologne, stayed initially four or five days in the Riga ghetto, and was then taken away to Salaspils.
5. Ibid., Bd. 60, statement by Artur Sachs, 11 November 1965, 9,791–9,798. Sachs had been deported from Bielefeld and after several days in the ghetto was taken away to Salaspils: "Upon arrival, we first had to lie down on a wet and snow covered meadow. Toward evening, we were driven into the half-finished barracks, which were totally covered in snow and soaked. The sacks of straw were soaked and covered with snow. There was nothing to eat that day. At night, there was a strong frost. As a result, it came to the first [cases of] frostbite, which a short time later led to a massive number of deaths. The dying was accelerated not least of all due to the fact that there were no foodstuffs."
6. Ibid., Bd. 43, statement by Heinz Trühe, 18 February 1964, 7,281. Trühe was head of Department I/II at the office of the Territorial Commander of the Security Police and Security Service Ostland. After the arrival of the deported Jewish workers, POWs were no longer used, see ibid., Bd. 29, statement by Josef Stocker, former guard with Home Defense Battalion 529 (*Landesschützenbataillon 529*), which was deployed at Stalag 350.
7. Information varies between 750 and 5,000 persons. See ibid., Bd. 4, statement by Günther Preger, 19 January 1950, 416. Preger, who was deported from Dortmund, put the figure at 750 persons. Cf. ibid., Bd. 81, statement by Henry Lucas, 27 April 1971, 12,852–12,853. Lucas said the number was 5,000 persons.
8. Ibid., Bd. 2, statement by Helmut Fürst, 23 January 1950, 250–252. Fürst, who was deported from Hanover, said: "The worst thing was the state of provisions in the period between Christmas and New Year's 1941/42, because supplying provisions was impossible due to the snow drifts. In this period, there was only water soup, no bread. After the transportation difficulties were resolved, the state of provisions improved to 300 to about 400 grams of bread per day. It was, however, still so little that those who could secure no additional foodstuffs sooner or later succumbed to death."
9. Ibid., Bd. 2, statement by Hellmut Pins, 20 January 1950, 246–247. Pins was deported to the Riga ghetto from Münster via Bielefeld. "Provisioning was very bad. It was so little that people dropped dead like flies. Several times, potatoes that had already rotted were delivered. During winter 1941/42, the mortality rate was very high, the harsh cold in particular did its part."
10. Ibid., Bd. 25, statement by Gerhard Maywald, 3 May 1962, 3,937.
11. On Commando Krause II and the construction office Irbe, see journal of Dortmund Group, entry for 24 February 1942, in LVVA, P 132-28-18, 13, as well as the entry for 29 March 1942 in ibid., 51. On column leader Subak, see the entry for 29 March 1942 in ibid., 52; on bread rations, entry for 4 March 1942 in ibid., 24. The term "commando slice" (*Kommandoscheibe*) is from Gerda Gottschalk, *Der letzte Weg*, 27.
12. Staw. Hamburg, 141 Js 534/60, Bd. 2, statement by H. Fürst, 23 January 1950, 250–252: "The acquisition of additional food was only possible through barter with the Latvian guard and the Latvian civilian population, for example, at the sawmill. I have to mention here that upon departing the train station we were allowed take along only our hand baggage, while our large baggage was not delivered to us. The large baggage apparently

went to a collection warehouse. By chance, those of us in Salaspils had access to one such collection warehouse. In light of the desperate situation we found ourselves in, it is understandable that this baggage was plundered. In this way, we secured the means to conduct barter with the Latvians. This barter, however, was forbidden, and one was always in danger of getting caught, reported, and hanged." See also ibid., Bd. 43, statement by Ludwig Gutmann, 25 February 1964, 7,311a; Gutmann was deported from Würzberg via Nuremberg; ibid., witness statement by J. Stocker, 27 September 1962, 4,464; Stocker, a former guard with Home Defense Battalion 529 at Stalag 350 (Salaspils), reported that contact between the German guards and the German Jews at the sawmill was strictly forbidden.

13. Otto Heinrich Teckemeier was born to a peasant family in 1904 and grew up in Pinneberg County. He had been a member of the NSDAP and the SS since 1933. A street sweeper in the town of Barmstedt until 1939, he was conscripted into the Waffen-SS. From late 1940 until late 1941 and early 1942, he was stationed with the Security Police in Warsaw as a guard; then around March 1942 he was transferred to the Security Police in Riga. From there, he was deployed to the Salaspils camp, ibid., Bd. 2, statement by Otto Teckemeier, 16 December 1949, 215–216.

14. Among the survivors, one version of the story that made the rounds claimed that both young men were found with their relatives in the ghetto. According to Ereignismeldung Nr. 154, 12 January 1942, the two were captured at a Riga post office, see BA Berlin, R 58/220. Of the numerous witness statements, the following are worth mentioning, because they call both of the young victims by name: Staw. Hamburg, 141 Js 534/60, Bd. 1, Kurt Rübsteck, 5 January 1949, 70, and Nuremberg Document NO-5448, statement of Alfred Winter, 15 October 1947. It should also be noted that there was indeed an escapee who fled from Salaspils to the ghetto, where he was captured and hanged. For 28 February 1942, there is an entry in the journal of the Dortmund Group, according to which a Jewish policeman had to patrol "near the executed escapee from Salaspils," see LVVA, P 132-28-18, 16–17.

15. The details concerning this case are difficult to ascertain. On the one hand, many of the survivors remember this incident, because it took place in front of the assembled camp inmates; on the other hand, the witness statements contradict one another regarding details, such as the number of those who escaped, inter alia. It seems certain that one of the escapees was named Ernst Ballon, who had arrived from Brno via Theresienstadt. The second could be Erich Kahn of Cologne, who reached the Riga ghetto on 9 December 1941.

16. It is difficult to reconstruct how many hangings took place. Although many survivors could remember numerous killings, such incidents are hard to distinguish from one another. Duplicate references are avoided when survivors remember offenders by name. The following people were murdered for barter: Luis Roseboom (Berlin), Günther Neuwald (Prague), Günther Falk (Hanover), Heinz Samuel (Hanover), Arno Zierer (Hanover), Berger (Dortmund), Kaufmann (Cologne), Neubauer (Prague), Nolting (Cologne), Löwenstein (Hanover), Margulies (Vienna).

17. Teckemeier was called "Stuka" by prisoners, because he would sneak up on workers and beat them up for the slightest violation. He himself said on this point: "I admit to beating Jews in Salaspils. Nickel pointed out to me that it was better to slap the people around the ears a few times than to report, for only so would losses in the workforce be avoided . . . In just how many cases I beat [people], I cannot say. Usually, I gave them a few slaps with my hand; sometimes, I dealt them several blows across the small of the back with my walking stick." See Staw. Hamburg, 141 Js 534/60, Bd. 3, statement by Teckemeier, 16 December 1949, 214–219, here 216.

18. Ibid., Bd. 3, statement by Siegfried Kaufmann, 3 March 1950, 338.
19. See Gertrude Schneider, "The Hangman of Camp Salaspils," in idem, *Muted Voices*, 137–144. Wolf Besen died in 1943 at Concentration Camp Kaiserwald, allegedly while trying to escape. See the comments on this by Otto Windmüller, 19 March 1952, under the title "A Part of My Life." Windmüller had to carry away Besen's corpse, see Staw. Hamburg, 141 Js 534/60, Bd. 72, 11,601–11,615, here 11,610.
20. Staw. Hamburg, 141 Js 534/60, Bd. 39, statement by Alice Wolf, born Weil, 12 September 1963, 6,347. Wolf hailed from Stuttgart. The victim was probably Henry Kaufmann, who was hanged on 13 June 1942, see ibid., Bd. 69, statement by Rosa Hausmann, 6 June 1967, 11,185. Hausmann was his fiancée.
21. Schneider, *Journey into Terror*, 64.
22. LVVA, P 70-5-37, 108–109, BdS Ostland, Abtl. III, an den RKO Gauleiter Lohse, an den HSSPF Ostland, SS-Ogruf. Jeckeln, Betr.: Aus den Tagesmeldungen der Einsatzkommandos, i. V. Stüber.
23. Whenever Lange visited Salaspils, he always left behind a bloody trail. He shot prisoners, because they worked too slowly, did not greet him, because they ate, rested, or did not stand at attention. Every witness statement concerning living conditions in Salaspils mentions some example of Lange's sadism.
24. Son Kurt dates this first transport to 16 January 1942, the date of death of his father, see Staw. Hamburg, 141 Js 534/60, Bd. 1, statement by Kurt Mendel, 23 May 1949, 41, as well as ibid., Bd. 4, statement by Kurt Mendel, 19 July 1950, 423. See also ibid., Bd. 4, statement by Jakob Dahl, 27 March 1950, 369.
25. Herbert Hirschland, deported from Hanover, remembers three transports with 120–130 victims in all, ibid., Bd. 2, statement by Herbert Hirschland, 23 January 1950, 254–255.
26. Katz, *Erinnerungen*, 54.
27. Staw. Hamburg, 141 Js 534/60, Bd. 3, statement by S. Kaufmann, 3 March 1950, 307.
28. Katz, *Erinnerungen*, 54.
29. Staw. Hamburg, 141 Js 534/60, Bd. 2, H. Hirschland, 23 January 1950, 255.
30. Gottschalk, *Der letzte Weg*, 38. Lilly Pancis, née Fischel, deported from Rimbeck-Scherfede via Bielefeld, barely recognized her cousin Alfred. Completely emaciated, covered with lice, he was unable to climb the stairs to their accommodations, Lilly Pancis, "Deportation to the East," in Schneider, *Muted Voices*, 44–45.
31. Schneider, *Journey into Terror*, 64.
32. LVVA, P 132-28-18, 72, journal of the Dortmund Group, entry for 25 April 1942, signed Friedrich Frankenberg, chief of the camp police.
33. Ibid., 75, entry for 4 May 1942: "Every group is to hand in immediately at the commandant's office a list of those men who were delivered to Salaspils today, ordered alphabetically with dates of birth, age, and commando [no signature]."
34. Ibid., 77, entry for 7 May 1942, signed Blaettner.
35. Ibid., 83, entry for 29 May 1942: "Chief of the camp police to all groups. We ask it to be arranged that those of your group who are returning to Salaspils today report without baggage at 4 o'clock in the afternoon to the 1st courtyard of the commandant's building." Ibid., 85, entry for 1 June 1942: "To all groups. You will inform the Salaspilser belonging to your group who are mentioned below that they have to report on Wednesday, 3 June 1942, in the morning before 9 A.M. in front of the commandant's building for the purpose of being transported back, signed Blaettner." These recuperation transports to the ghetto probably took place more often, see Winter, *The Ghetto of Riga and Continuance*, 121. Winter found himself on one of these transports in mid June 1942.
36. Hilde Schneider was a Protestant of Jewish origin, who in the eyes of the National Socialists was considered a "full Jew." At the time, she was in the infirmary and preoc-

cupied herself daily with a Bible, into which she occasionally entered notes in the margin. Psalms 88 struck her as fitting for the fate of the men of Salaspils. See Hartmut Schmidt, *Zwischen Riga und Locarno*, 140.
37. USHMM, RG 15.007, reel 16 [RSHA - Material from Warsaw], KdS Lettland, Tätigkeitsbericht für die Zeit vom 23.5.-18.6.1942.
38. According to a report by Lange to the RSHA, II C 3, there were still 400 Jews in the camp as of 21 July 1942.
39. LVVA, P 132-28-18, 92, journal of the Dortmund Group, entry for 11 July 1942, signed Mendel.
40. Ibid., 94, entry for 20 July 1942: "To all groups. The people who have been posted to the peat industry have to be replaced by the groups in the commandos again. We ask for a written report on this to be presented tomorrow. The people may be taken only from the reserve (including Salaspils). Labor Deployment Central office, sig. Schiff."
41. Katz, *Erinnerungen*, 55, and Staw. Hamburg, 141 Js 534/60, Bd. 29, statement by Arthur Goldschmidt, 12 October 1962, 4,512. Goldschmidt had been deported from Herne.
42. On the daily Athletic Field Commando, see LVVA, P 132-28-18, 92, journal of the Dortmund Group, entry for 27 March 1942. On barracking at the athletic field, see ibid., 82, entry for 20 May 1942.
43. Heinrihs Strods, "Salaspils koncentrācijas nometne (1941. Gada oktobris-1944. Gada septembris)," in *Latvijas Okupācijas Muzeja Gadagrāmata*, 155.
44. This is also Strods's view, ibid., 155. In one Soviet work of propaganda, it is asserted that hundreds of thousands prisoners, among them Jews from various European countries, died at Salaspils between 1942 and 1944, see *Daugavas Vanagi – Who Are They?*, ed. E. Avotins, J. Dzirkalis, and V. Petersons, 29.
45. Staw. Hamburg, 141 Js 534/60, Bd. 41, 6,900a, written statement by Maywald, 25 November 1963.

– *Excursus I* –

SS Major Rudolf Lange and the Wannsee Conference

When Rudolf Lange took his place at the meeting of state secretaries in the guesthouse of the Security Police and the SD on Am Grossen Wannsee on 20 January 1942, he was, like Adolf Eichmann, out of place in terms of protocol.[1] These two SS majors and their authority ranked far below the representatives of the ministerial and party bureaucracies.[2] But like his colleague from Desk IV B 4 (Jewish Affairs and Evacuation) of the Reich Security Main Office (RHSA), Lange had without a doubt been accorded by Reinhard Heydrich a special role at this meeting. Whereas Eichmann was able to discuss the modalities of assembling deportation transports, Lange, the regional commander of the Security Police and SD (KdS) in Latvia, was Heydrich's representative from that territory beyond the Reich that had taken in deported Jews "according to plan," so to speak.

Theoretically, it would have been possible for Heydrich to invite SS Colonel Karl Jäger, KdS Lithuania, or SS Lieutenant Colonel Erich Ehrlinger, then KdS White Ruthenia.[3] Although these two men had similar experiences in the mass murder operations directed against the Jews in their regions, in Heydrich's original concept of the deportation of Jews from the "Greater German Reich," Kaunas (Kauen, Kovno) had always been a fallback destination for the first five transports intended for Riga, while Minsk had been canceled very quickly as a destination for 25,000 Jews from the west due to "transport difficulties."[4] Furthermore, as a jurist with a doctorate, Lange was bound to have been more intellectual than Jäger, who was an organ builder, or Ehrlinger, whose behavior ranged from impulsive to choleric and whose transfer to Kiev seemed decided anyway. The question why Walther Stahlecker, the territorial commander of the Security Police and SD Ostland (BdS Ostland), was not present, but had instead sent one of his subordinates can be explained only inadequately. Stahlecker, who, save for a few short visits, had not been in the Reich Commissariat Ostland for weeks, had transferred his staff and his radius of operations to Krasnogvardeisk, where he handled Security Police matters in the four general commissariats by radio and courier while maintaining permanent

---

Notes for this chapter begin on page 263.

contact with Army Group North in anticipation of the continued advance on Leningrad. In terms of protocol, Stahlecker was Heydrich's territorial representative for all of Reich Commissariat Ostland, but in terms of actual duties, he was least familiar with the situation concerning the deportations in his territory. This was also why Lange was mentioned in the introductory list of participants in the protocol of the Wannsee Conference as the representative of BdS Ostland.[5]

Unlike all of the others on hand, Lange was a practitioner of mass murder, including the mass murder of deported Jews. In addition, he had met Heydrich's expectations despite conflicts with General Commissar Latvia Otto Heinrich Drechsler and the civil administration in planning the Salaspils camp and quartering the German Jews in the Riga ghetto. By 20 January 1942, the Latvian capital had taken on fourteen transports, and Lange's difficulties on site were in the eyes of his superior in Berlin just locally rooted attendant phenomena that had to be mastered.

As is known, there is no documentation that would make it possible to reconstruct in detail the course of discussions at the Wannsee Conference. The various conversations between the ministerial representatives and Reinhard Heydrich about the abundance of problems that had arisen are concealed behind a summarizing memorandum that stresses the chief of the Security Police and SD as the principle figure. The protocol has nothing to say about Lange. However, Heydrich's remarks that the deported Jews would be "moved [east] constructing roads, with a large part no doubt dropping off by a natural process of attrition," was as much a reference to conditions in Latvia as was the fact that the protocol said nothing about deportees who were unable to work.[6] If one considers that the average age of the deportees to Riga was just under forty-eight, then it is clear that the majority of them were not even to survive temporarily.[7] Also, if it has been noted more recently that the euphemism "moved [east] constructing roads" corresponded to reality along Thoroughfare IV in eastern Galicia, then the reference to a "natural process of attrition" was also an accurate assessment given the food and housing situation in Jungfernhof, the Riga ghetto, and Salaspils in the ice-cold Latvian winter.[8]

Because it is to be assumed that Lange knew of the problems that Higher SS and Police Leader Ostland Friedrich Jeckeln had created for himself by shooting the Jews from the first Berlin transport on 30 November 1941, it is clear that he did nothing with regard to the deportees that did not have the advance blessing of the RSHA. The murder of Jews from Prague and Brno (Brünn) outside Riga on 19 January 1942 could not have taken place without the consent of Heydrich as deputy *Reichsprotektor* for Bohemia and Moravia. This means that on 20 January 1942, Lange, as head of a Security Police regional office, was able to represent, with Heydrich's approval, all of the murders that had taken place as a result of shooting operations or hazardous living conditions. No matter how Lange's men in Riga legitimized the shooting of individuals on the way from Šķirotava, the shooting of the Czech Jews on 19 January, or the selections of those who were sick and unable to work in Salaspils on 16 January, in Jungfernhof, or later in the ghetto, it was always of the utmost importance for the Security Police chief in Latvia to act with Heydrich's consent. However, this also meant that the shooting of deported "Reich Jews" on the eve of the Wannsee Conference did not represent a radicalization that had taken place on site due to a lack of space or shortage of food, which would have required retroactive approval from the RSHA. Instead, Lange had acted within the framework of a preexisting set of orders, which reflected Heydrich's strategic planning with regard to using mass murder in the "final solution of the Jewish question." What Heydrich revealed to those present at the Wannsee Conference was already taking place. And in turn, if Lange – unlike Jeckeln in murdering the first Berlin transport – was acting completely within the spirit of Heydrich's intentions and remarks at the Wannsee Conference, then the thesis is plausible that an expansion in the scope of the "final solution" in its most murderous aspects must have taken place between 30 November 1941 and 19 January 1942.

It is uncertain what Lange might have thought during this meeting, when he was forced to infer from a set of statistics presented there that 3,500 Jews were still living in Latvia, even if it was noted as a matter of qualification that this number involved merely "Jews of faith," because a uniform definition according to "racial principles" was still lacking.[9] Back in Riga, a short time later, Lange wrote with regard to General Commissariat Latvia that 2,500 Jews were still deployed in Riga as valuable workers, along with 950 in Daugavpils and 300 in Liepāja. Concerning the German Jews, his remarks were much clearer than the euphemisms of his boss:

> Since December 1941, transports of Jews have been arriving from the Reich in short intervals. In all, 19,000 Jews from the Reich and the Protectorate have so far been deported to Riga. They have been accommodated in part in the ghetto, in part in a provisionally expanded holding camp, in part in a new camp of barracks near Riga. Of these Reich-German Jews, only a small part is able to work. Women and children and men unable to work make up about 70–80 percent. The mortality rate is constantly rising among the evacuated Jews. Primarily old and frail Jews are no longer resistant enough to survive the extraordinarily hard winter. In order to counter every risk of epidemics in the ghetto and in the two camps from the start, Jews with contagious diseases (dysentery and diphtheria) were in individual cases selected and executed. In order to avoid these measures from becoming known among the local Jews and among the Jews in the Reich, removal was camouflaged as the transfer to a Jewish home for the elderly and ill. In addi-

tion, several mentally ill Jews were selected the same way. The construction of the new camp of barracks for the Jews from the Reich is still being carried out by the deployment of all Jews able to work, who have been accommodated in the already completed barracks. In spring, the camp will have been built up so that all of the evacuated Jews who survive the winter can be admitted to this camp.[10]

This report, which is not to be surpassed in terms of clarity, is undated. However, two valuable clues regarding the date of composition are to be found there. For one, the report notes that "several mentally ill Jews" had been killed, an operation that had been carried out by members of the Security Police and Latvian auxiliaries on 29 January 1942. On 19 May, SS Major Arnold Kirste confirmed retroactively for the registrar's office in Riga that on that January day 368 incurably ill persons had "passed away."[11] In addition, Lange's report mentions that to date 19,000 deportees had arrived, which with the arrival of the Dortmund transport on 1 February 1942 was in fact the case. Since the last winter transport reached Riga from Vienna on 10 February, this is without a doubt a report from the first week of February 1942 that was supposed to give an overview of the measures taken with regard to the "Jewish question" in General Commissariat Latvia since autumn 1941.[12]

Notes

1. Since Robert M.W. Kempner's *Eichmann und Komplizen*, an abundance of studies have put this meeting of state secretaries at the center of inquiry. See, for example, Yehoshua Büchler, "A Preparatory Document for the Wannsee Conference," *Holocaust and Genocide Studies* 9 (1995): 121–129; Christian Gerlach, "Die Wannsee-Konferenz, das Schicksal der deutschen Juden und Hitlers politische Grundsatzentscheidung, alle Juden Europas zu ermorden," *WerkstattGeschichte* 6 (1997): 7–44; Eberhard Jäckel, "On the Purpose of the Wannsee Conference," in *Perspectives on the Holocaust*, ed. James A. Pacy and Alan P. Wertheimer, 39–50; Wolf Kaiser, "Die Wannsee-Konferenz: SS-Führer und Ministerialbeamte in Einvernehmen über die Ermordung der europäischen Juden," in *Täter — Opfer — Folgen*, ed. Heiner Lichtenstein and Otto R. Romberg, 24–37; Peter Klein, *Die Wannsee-Konferenz: Analyse und Dokumentation*; Peter Longerich, *Die Wannsee-Konferenz vom 20. Januar 1942: Planung und Beginn des Genozids an den europäischen Juden*; Mark Roseman, *Die Wannsee-Konferenz: Wie die NS-Bürokratie den Holocaust organisierte*; Wolfgang Scheffler and Helge Grabitz, "Die Wannsee-Konferenz: Ihre Bedeutung in der Geschichte des nationalsozialistischen Völkermords," *Studia nad Faszyzmen i Zbrodniami Hitlerowskimi* 18 (1995): 197–219. The Wannsee Conference is also duly treated in more recent surveys such as: Longerich, *Politik der Vernichtung*, 466–472; Wildt, *Generation des Unbedingten*, 627–637; Browning, *Die Entfesselung der Endlösung*, 569–592 ("Einbeziehung der Bürokratie").
2. Short biographies of all of the conference participants are to be found in Kurt Pätzold and Erika Schwarz, *Tagesordnung: Judenmord*, 201–245.

3. On Karl Jäger, see the biographical sketch by Wolfram Wette, "SS-Standartenführer Karl Jäger, Kommandeur der Sicherheitspolizei (KdS) in Kaunas," in *Holocaust in Litauen*, 77–90. On Erich Ehrlinger, see Wildt, *Generation des Unbedingten*, 92–97, 167–169, and 591–601; idem, "Erich Ehrlinger – ein Vertreter 'kämpfender Verwaltung,'" in *Karrieren der Gewalt*, ed. Klaus-Michael Mallmann and Gerhard Paul, 76–85. On the SA milieu in Berlin-Charlottenburg, to which Ehrlinger belonged starting in 1931, see Sven Reichardt, "Vergemeinschaftung durch Gewalt," in *Entgrenzte Gewalt*, ed. Herbert Diercks, 20–36.
4. On this, see chapter 6, this volume.
5. PA-AA, R 100857, 165–188, here 167.
6. "Under appropriate direction, the Jews are now to be put to work in the east in an expedient manner in the course of the final solution. In large labor details, with the sexes separated, the Jews able to work will be moved into these territories constructing roads, with a large part no doubt dropping off by a natural process of attrition. The remnant that may eventually remain will have to be treated accordingly, since this will without a doubt be the most resistant part, representing a process of natural selection, which could, upon release, become the germ cell of Jewish reconstruction. (See experience in history.)" The only known complete copy of the protocol, the sixteenth of thirty copies, is to be found in PA-AA, R 100857, 165–188, quote 172–173.
7. The average age of the all of the 20,111 deportees sent to Jungfernhof and the Riga ghetto between 30 November 1941 and 10 February 1942 was 47.7. This statistical information is based on the empirical results for the individual transports provided in *Buch der Erinnerung*.
8. On the Jewish forced labor camps along the construction sites of Thoroughfare IV, see Hermann Kaienburg, "Jüdische Arbeitslager an der 'Strasse der SS,'" *1999: Zeitschrift für Sozialgeschichte des 20. und 21. Jahrhunderts* 11 (1996): 13–39; Thomas Sandkühler, "Judenpolitik und Judenmord im Distrikt Galizien 1941–1942," in *Nationalsozialistische Vernichtungspolitik 1939–1945*, ed. Ulrich Herbert, 122–147. To verify the numerous survivor accounts of the extraordinary cold in Riga, Berlin historian Wolfgang Scheffler asked the German Weather Service to compile an expert opinion. According to this report, the following relevant temperatures are to be noted: on five days in December 1941, temperatures between -15°C and -20°C (5°F and -4°F) prevailed. Otherwise, December 1941 was relatively mild, with temperatures around freezing. From 1 to 3 January, the daytime temperature was around -15°C (5°F), but the temperature dropped below -20°C (-4°F) at night. Between 4 and 9 January, the daytime temperature rose to an average of -6°C (21°F), only to fall again to an average of -15°C (5°F) from 10 January to 13 February. Nighttime temperatures during this period ranged from -20°C (-4°F) to -32°C (-25.6°F). For more details on this, see *Buch der Erinnerung*, Bd. 1, 20, ft. 82.
9. PA-AA, R 100857, statistics, 171, quote, 172.
10. LVVA, P 1026-1-3, 262–264, undated report "Jewry" by Lange.
11. LVVA, P 132-30-27, 121, KdS Lettland, Abtl. II D, an das Rigaer Standesamt, betr. Benachrichtigung von Todesfällen, i.V. Kirste, 19 May 1942. See also Nuremberg Document USSR-397, in *IMG*, Bd. 39, 501–502.
12. For the period up to autumn 1941, see the "Stahlecker Report," Nuremberg Document L-180, with Heydrich's note asking to see the report again on 31 January 1942, in *IMG*, Bd. 37, 670–717. The undated situation report "Jewry" was then merged into a second overall report for Heydrich, which was written after 10 February 1942. The dating is clear there, because the document refers to the arrival of 20,000 German Jews, see RGVA, 500-4-92, and Nuremberg Document PS-2273, in *IMG*, Bd. 30, 72–80, here, 79.

– *Chapter 11* –

THE LATVIAN LABOR MARKET AND THE COMPULSORY DEPLOYMENT OF JEWS IN RIGA

Between the arrival of the Wehrmacht in Riga and the transfer from military administration to civil administration on 1 September 1941, the upheaval of the war had left its mark on Riga's labor market. Thousands of men had been deported on the eve of the invasion. Thousands had been killed. Thousands had fled. Two weeks after the Germans had taken Riga, the local peat industry reported to the Latvian Board of Industry its fear that the seasonal workers for cutting peat, most of whom came from the Latgale region, would not show up that summer. Of the 5,000 workers on hand in June, 1,500 at most had returned to the workplace. For that reason, the Peat Works Board asked the commander of prisoners of war in Rear Area Army Group North whether it could have captured Red Army soldiers.[1] What applied to the peat industry also pertained to agriculture. As already mentioned, one of the first initiatives for the establishment of a ghetto in Riga had been justified by the fact that, according to the agriculture group within the Wehrmacht's Economics Commando Riga, there existed a considerable shortage of workers, which at the very least was supposed to be eased by deploying Jews.[2]

In his "Preliminary Guidelines for the Treatment of Jews" of 2 August 1941, Reich Commissar Ostland Hinrich Lohse had decreed that Jews were to be called on as forced laborers as needed, though without harming the legitimate economic interests of the country's reliable inhabitants. Remuneration was supposed to cover the cost of living for all family members, including those unable to work. The private entities that profited from this were to pay a reasonable fee to the county commissar, who in turn was to make an unspecified payment to the forced laborers.[3] However, within Rear Area Army Group North, to which Riga still belonged, Wehrmacht regulations were what mattered, and here, there was no remuneration in cash whatsoever, merely rations provided in an unknown amount.[4]

Notes for this chapter begin on page 280.

At the start of August 1941, the Riga Labor Office launched a registration operation, which was supposed to be finished by 10 August. As part of the obligation to report, officials at the various reporting stations designated for Jews had to start a personnel file in the form of a card for each man and woman aged 14–65. Every Jew in Riga who later received written notification of an assignment to a workplace had to keep this document with him or her at all times. It was considered a form of identification vis-à-vis the police and all other German agencies. Upon completion of a forced labor assignment, the papers had to be turned over to the Jewish Council, where they were attached to the worker's personnel record.[5] A short time later, Field Administration Command Riga decreed that Jews were to be forcibly deployed solely through the Labor Office's Bureau for the Deployment of Jews on Carl Schirren St. (Lāčplēša St.). All requests for workers were to be directed to this bureau, which was located at the edge of ghetto across from the Jewish Council's building.[6] When Reich Commissar Lohse, then based in Kaunas (Kauen, Kovno), issued a decree regulating the general deployment of labor on 15 August, the essential registration process for mustering Jews who were able to work was already underway in Riga.

Lohse's ordinance regulating the deployment of labor can be seen as the basis for labor market policy in the territory under his rule. It was decreed here that, at the request of the Labor Office, all of Ostland's inhabitants were obliged to report for registration. The labor offices were also authorized to assign workers to certain jobs on a binding basis beyond their place of residence. For the harvest, the comprehensive deployment of entire age groups of young people was also mentioned. Layoffs involving more than ten workers had to be announced to the Labor Office in advance. Finally, violation of these regulations was subject to punishment.[7] Just one day later, Alfred Rosenberg, the Reich minister for the occupied eastern territories, introduced compulsory labor for the Jewish population in the civil-administered eastern territories. In turn, Lohse then issued the Preliminary Guidelines to his general commissars and requested that they report to him in full about anti-Jewish measures on the tenth of each month.[8]

On 1 September 1941, when General Commissar Latvia Otto Heinrich Drechsler officially took over the civil administration of all Latvia, he appointed as head of his labor administration Senior Wartime Administration Counselor Max Dorr, who had already run the labor desk within Economics Commando Riga. Dorr lost no time. That same day, he invited the heads of state and private industrial enterprises to his office. In introducing how the deployment of labor would be managed in the future, it became clear that in Dorr's view Jews should be deployed only in cohesive formations, on a temporary basis, and for certain projects, for example, cutting peat or road construction. In addition, he appealed to the "national-political duty" of those present to replace Jews in commerce and industry with "Aryan" workers as quickly as possible, and he let them know that he expected proposals to this end from them. Furthermore, he announced that there would now be a systematic general registration of all unemployed persons as well as all those employed in the construction and lumber industries; the deployment of women was also to be increased. Dorr had already noted that there seemed to be a glaring shortage of male workers in Latvia, which he hoped to ease by placing prisoners of war in cohesive details in addition to employing more women.[9]

But in the Bureau for the Deployment of Jews on Carl Schirren St., officials were still a long way from gaining an overview of the assignments already issued. After about a month, the labor administration of County Commissariat Riga City had to acknowledge that 2,638 persons had been placed with the Wehrmacht, SS, and other agencies, however: "It would be wrong to say that the entire deployment and also the regulation of Jewish labor deployments has been in the hands of the Labor Office during this period. Before the establishment of the Labor Office, the Latvian police deployed thousands of Jewish workers in large and small groups. The Labor Office has in general approved this deployment and also left the workers at their place of work after the issuing of working papers by the Labor Office."[10]

The labor administration was trying, the report went on, to get a handle on regulating supply and demand, but many employers were unwilling to cooperate. These were "poaching" workers on their own and requisitioning already formed details simply for themselves. Incidents between the Wehrmacht, SS, and the Navy had already taken place. "On the street, individual workers are also taken away, who are then reported as missing at their place of work. Only later is it possible to clarify that these had been employed in the interval at another place of work." There was no adherence to the working hours at the counter of the Bureau for the Deployment of Jews, or to its instructions. A lack of planning and chance characterized the work deployment process "at a time when an enormous shortage of workers prevailed."[11]

Thus, if Dorr, also the head of the Labor Office within County Commissariat Riga City, intended to remove the Jews from the labor market in the long term, he first and foremost had to assert sovereignty in planning. In a letter to Field Administration Command Riga, he asked all Wehrmacht offices to employ Jews only if they had a corresponding certificate from the Labor Office. Quite tellingly, he pointed out that the employment of Jews was actually allowed only if Latvian workers failed as replacements and if there was no danger of espionage or sabotage. A copy of this letter went to the SS and police as well.[12] Moreover, Dorr requested armbands from the

Wehrmacht for his employees so that they could better assert themselves against unauthorized requests. Dorr's efforts to reduce the number of 13,725 Jews placed with the Wehrmacht were at least supported rhetorically by Major General Walter Braemer, the Wehrmacht territorial commander Ostland (WBO). It was around this time that Braemer published an ordinance from the High Command of the Wehrmacht that stated:

> The struggle against Bolshevism demands ruthless and vigorous action, above all also against the Jews, the main carriers of Bolshevism. Therefore, any kind of cooperation on the part of the Wehrmacht with the Jewish population, which is openly or covertly hostile in disposition to Germandom, and the use of individual Jews for any kind of preferential auxiliary services for the Wehrmacht is [sic] to be prohibited. Under no circumstances are military offices to issue forms of identification confirming for Jews their use for Wehrmacht purposes. Excepted from this is solely the use of Jews in specially formed labor details, which are only to be deployed under German supervision. The troops are to be instructed accordingly.[13]

Dorr's efforts were reflected in an optimistic assessment by General Commissar Latvia Drechsler when he drew up a statement for the Reich Commissar. The deployment of Riga's Jews for work, wrote Drechsler, was shaping up most favorably. The Labor Office had taken preparatory measures to withdraw Jews working on an individual basis. In the long term, Jews would only come to work at Wehrmacht offices if Latvian workers could not be deployed. In addition, the forest administration and the supervisory agency for heating supplies were making efforts to get hold of larger contingents of male Jews who were then to be accommodated in labor camps and thus separated from their wives. Furthermore, the counties Riga Countryside and Jelgava (Mitau) were free of Jews. The Jews of Volmiera (Wolmar), around forty persons, had been taken to the ghetto in Daugavpils (Dünaburg), where there were now 2,185 Jews. A ghetto was be set up in Liepāja (Libau) for the roughly 5,500 Jews of the Courland region.[14]

From the perspective of Einsatzgruppe A, by October 1941 the results regarding the "Jewish question" sounded much more matter-of-fact. Making reference to the intended comprehensive elimination of the Jews in accordance with "fundamental orders," EG A commander Walther Stahlecker noted that the crafts in Lithuania and Latvia were dominated by Jews, and that many professions were completely in Jewish hands. A large part of them were deployed rebuilding destroyed towns or were indispensable to jobs important to the war effort. "Although enterprises are striving to replace the Jewish workers with Lithuanian and Latvian [ones]," wrote the commander of EG A, "immediately relieving all of the Jews deployed in the labor system is not yet possible, especially not in the larger towns."[15] On

4 October, Heydrich had warned that "in numerous cases, commerce and industry are claiming Jews as indispensable workers, and that no one is making an effort to get other workers in their stead. This, however, would render impossible the plan for a total resettlement of the Jews from the territories occupied by us."[16]

The Security Police had in Dorr a silent partner in its assessment of the "Jewish question." On the basis of his 1 September remarks, he had on 1 October urged Latvian industry to hand in registers showing how many Jews were still employed at which industrial plants.[17] A little later, the Labor Office informed the Industry Directorate that standard wages were to be paid to Jews starting 1 November. All requests for workers would be carefully examined, and only irreplaceable Jewish workers with new identity papers would continue to be sent to work.[18] When this information then appeared in the newspaper *Deutsche Zeitung im Ostland* on 28 October, it no longer applied solely to industry but to everybody – including the Wehrmacht.[19] On the other hand, Dorr was forced to make a concession when the Latvian Communal Department filed a request, explaining that it could still use Jews for clearing debris and constructing roads.[20]

The alignment of wages to the level of Latvian employees and the automatic invalidation of existing working papers did in fact have an effect. In various reports for the period from 16 October to 15 November 1941, it was repeatedly pointed out that Wehrmacht offices had cut back on deploying Jews. Making new placements subject to written application now meant a considerable reduction in the number of Jews leaving the ghetto for work, i.e., in most cases with a pass in connection with a labor detail.[21] In a comprehensive monthly report dated 20 November, which included the 25 October order calling for the establishment of a ghetto in Riga and a first set of instructions for the ghetto guards, Drechsler reported to Lohse that 29,602 Jews had been counted in the ghetto. Of those aged 14–65 and classified as able to work, 6,143 were men and 9,507 were women. There were 5,652 children and 8,300 adults unable to work.[22]

The new regulation thus led to a massive reduction of Jewish workers in November 1941, and it is to be noted with a shudder that the number of Jews placed at jobs outside the ghetto plus the Jews working inside the ghetto that month – 5,263 Latvian Jews in all – corresponds roughly to the number of non-German Jews counted in the ghetto on 16 February 1942 – 4,358 Jews (3,971 men and 387 women).[23] During the mass murder operation of 30 November and 8 and 9 December 1941, around 25,250 persons were shot in order to make room for the German Jews. The civil labor administration's new regulation had paved the way for the SS and police operation in that, in November, the bulk of Latvian Jews had been deprived of work outside the ghetto.

In the literature on the "final solution of the Jewish question" in the occupied Soviet territories, a brief written exchange between Reich Commissar Lohse and Reich Minister Rosenberg stands out. During the numerous shootings of Jews in Liepāja County during the first weeks of October – these were conducted by SS and Police Base Leader Fritz Dietrich – the mass murder operations reached such a total disregard for humanity that Liepāja County Commissar Walter Alnor felt compelled to write General Commissar Drechsler. On 11 October, Alnor reported on the recent SS and police shootings in Liepāja and Aizpute (Hasenpoth), which had been carried out despite his protests and those of the navy fortifications commandant. These murders, he wrote, contradicted Reich Commissar Lohse's orders and had produced "general consternation" due to their public nature. Even officers were said to have spoken out against them; after all, small children and pregnant women were not killed in such gruesome fashion in any civilized state. Alnor stressed his view that this approach would someday prove a great mistake.[24] Subsequently, Lohse apparently forbade additional shootings, which led the Reich Security Main Office (RSHA) to file a complaint with the Reich Ministry for the Occupied Eastern Territories.[25]

Lohse defended himself on 15 November, writing that he had "prohibited the wild executions of Jews in Liepāja, because they were unjustifiable in the way they were carried out."[26] In addition, Lohse combined the explanation for his actions with a general inquiry that reflected the difficulties he had had with similar protests from Kaunas and Vilnius (Wilna, Wilno): "I ask you to instruct me whether your query of 31 October is to be understood as a directive to liquidate all of the Jews in Ostland? Is this to happen without regard for age and sex and economic interests (e.g. the Wehrmacht's [interest] in skilled workers in armaments enterprises)? Naturally, the cleansing of Ostland is an urgent task; its solution, however, must be brought into harmony with the necessities of the wartime economy. I have so far been unable to infer such a directive either from the orders on the Jewish question from the 'brown folder,' or from other decrees."[27]

As already mentioned, Lohse – alongside Friedrich Jeckeln, the higher SS and police leader Ostland and the man in charge of the killing operations – had been at the liquidation of the Riga Jews in the Rumbula Forest, so the subsequent response from the ministry did not come as news to him. Rosenberg had Lohse informed that "clarity" in the Jewish question ought to have been provided in the meantime "by verbal discussions." The message continued: "As a rule, economic needs are to be disregarded in regulating the problem. In addition, it is asked that any ensuing questions be regulated directly with the Higher SS and Police Leader."[28] And in fact, the mass shootings – for which the HSSPF personally picked up the Reich Commissar – were not influenced by economic considerations. After all, on the eve of 30 November there had been 15,650 Jews in the Riga ghetto who were classified as able to work. Lohse had already seen with his own eyes what he was to receive in the form of a written response a few weeks later. But – given the fact that the general commissar's labor administration had already noted in a report for November that there was a glaring shortage of male workers, which would without a doubt get larger – the question arises whether this principle could remain in force after the shootings.[29]

For the labor administration of County Commissariat Riga City, the weeks leading up to spring 1942 were marked by disputes over authority in setting wages for working Jews. After Lohse had set the wage rates for workers on 21 November, the county commissar had oriented himself to the pay scale determined there. On 13 January 1942, the Riga Labor Office informed all of the local Wehrmacht units that they not only had to submit lists of names for the Jewish workers they employed by the next day. The Labor Office also referred to the wage group regulation in force for Latvians and Jews, because apparently a "lack of certainty concerning wages for Jewish workers still exists."[30] In fact, the General Quartermaster Department of the High Command of the Army had on 16 December promulgated "special orders," which then had been adopted by WBO Braemer. Braemer and Brigadier General Georg Bamberg, the local administration commandant, insisted on remunerating Jewish forced laborers according to Wehrmacht guidelines.

Due to complaints from the general quartermaster of the Army, on 21 January 1942, the Ministry for the Occupied Eastern Territories sent a telex to the RKO elaborating new daily wages for Jews. Dorr countered that the Reich Commissar had yet to issue any binding guidelines. Remuneration in accordance to the stipulations for Latvian workers was sensible, he wrote; after all, of the 30,000 Jews on hand the previous year, at most a third had been fully able to work and had had to provide for the other two thirds as well. Furthermore, it had turned out that the Jews were more efficient than the Latvians. "For this reason," Dorr added, "there existed on my part no interest in having the individual enterprise profit from a minimal payment to the Jew for his work at the general public's expense." In general, he continued, a preference for Jewish workers to the detriment of Latvian workers must be prevented. Before the publishing of the principle instruction on equality of wages, he added, a Wehrmacht representative had been invited, but had made no remonstrations. "Since the Wehrmacht offices subsequently did not let us hear anything else from them in this matter, their full understanding must be assumed ..."[31]

Many of the military offices in Riga tried to circumvent the wages, which they considered unjustifiable, by simply deciding to keep Jews at their offices. But the Local Administration Command prohibited this for reasons of security.³² On the ground, it came to a trial of strength between the civil administration and the Wehrmacht, which Dorr was able to decide in his favor. He had the option of not releasing Jews if incorrect payments were made.³³ After the RKO decreed an increase in wages for skilled and unskilled workers on 21 March 1942, the labor administration used this new regulation in May to remind the last nineteen tardy Wehrmacht and SS employers that full hourly wages were to be paid – retroactively.³⁴

But if Dorr and his deputy Schmutzler were able to book a success with regard to the remuneration of Jewish forced laborers, the Riga Labor Office's Bureau for the Deployment of Jews was undergoing a major crisis, a situation the military probably considered exploiting to its advantage. On 7 January, Edgar Dralle, a Latvian employee of the Bureau for the Deployment of Jews, appeared at the Labor Office on Aizsargu St. (Yorck St.) highly agitated and explained that the day before he had received a telephone call from SS Captain Heinrich Neurath, who had requested thirty-five Jews for the following day. Neurath had been unwilling to submit a written request, said Dralle, nor did he explain why he needed the workers. That morning, Dralle continued, Neurath had shown up in the ghetto with a group of SS officers, whipped him with his riding crop, and threatened one of his colleagues. The incident took place in front of Albert Hesfehr, the German head of the ghetto guards, as well as several members of the German municipal police and the Jewish Order Service.³⁵

As the representative of the German bureau chief Standtke, who was absent at the time, Dralle had acted exactly in accordance with the terms of the labor administration, which also intended to get its way with regard to planning authority as well as wage authority. That same day, a protocol describing the incident reached the desk of Mayor Hans Windgassen, who informed the general commissar and promptly closed the Bureau for the Deployment of Jews. Acting in his capacity as head of the Labor Office, Dorr contacted Senior Wartime Administration Counselor Friedrich Ellrodt, the RKO official responsible for labor. The two had already worked together in July 1941, when they suggested setting up the Riga ghetto at a meeting with the commander of Einsatzkommando 2 – Ellrodt as representative of Economics Inspection North and Dorr as representative of Economics Commando Riga. In a comprehensive letter justifying his actions, Dorr explained that the two Latvian employees refused to continue their official work: "I do not want to force the present employees of the Bureau for the Deployment of Jews to continue doing their work under such circumstances. However, I am also unable to acquire suitable employees for work in the ghetto. Since, however, German employees are at present not available for the deployment of Jews, I was forced to decide to close the Bureau for the Deployment of Jews. Hence, considerable difficulties will presumably arise in the orderly deployment of the Jewish workers, i.e. in the exploitation of these workers."[36]

In view of his behavior, Neurath, a member of the HSSPF Ostland's command staff, was quickly replaced. He had originally been employed as liaison between the HSSPF and the county commissar for all questions involving Jewish labor. At the same time, he had assumed the task of awarding Jewish home furnishings to the German rural police, the Gendarmerie, and other police offices. These tasks probably led Neurath into the ghetto, because around this time he had been asked to obtain individual home furnishing items for the quarters of the Gendarmerie command in County Commissariat Riga Countryside.[37] He was transferred for disciplinary reasons; his successor, SS First Lieutenant Robert Esser, gave assurances that Neurath would never again set foot in the ghetto. On 14 January, the Bureau for the Deployment of Jews reopened.[38]

The Labor Office's robust interventions, the mass murder operations, and the additional arguments over wages and planning of course had an effect on the number of Jews deployed.[39] With regard to the local Jews, Standtke reported in mid January that there were 4,092 men and 388 women registered by card index. Of them, a total of 3,253 had been deployed for work outside the ghetto as of 20 December 1941. Around 430 Jews were employed in clearance work in the uninhabited part of the ghetto. However, Standtke stressed, an exact registration was still not possible, because the guard book at the ghetto gate was kept only inadequately. Shortly after the temporary closing, only 2,876 Jews were placed by Standtke's bureau as of 16 January.[40]

In the monthly report of the county commissariat's Department of Labor and Social Policy for January, there was no longer any talk of such difficulties. Here the scope of vision was again expanded to take in the region's labor market situation as a whole. The deployment of workers was determined by the need to arrange transports for Army Group North into the zone of operations. In the process, the conscription of over 200 drivers encountered just as many difficulties as the conscription of 150 metalworkers for the maintenance of locomotives. And the need was steadily increasing. Alone in the Latvian capital, there were 8,208 open positions for male workers in metalworking, construction, traffic, and lumber. To fill them, there were 1,921 people looking for work. In a preliminary assessment for the next two months, the Labor Office calculated a need for just under 51,000 workers, above all due to springtime orders in agriculture, where almost 30,000 workers would be lacking. The peat branch needed 6,000 seasonal workers, construction 5,000 workers. In the metalworking industry, 1,000 workers would be lacking in the future to offset the transfer of contracts from the Reich to the Wehrmacht enterprises in Latvia. The workshops of Army Group North's motor pool alone needed 400 metal specialists, which would have to be provided by Jews. At the moment, said the report, 350 Jews were deployed in shoveling snow on railroads in order to guarantee transports to the east. Within the civil administration, officials were already counting on the German deportees, noting that with about another 500 Reich Jews, around 4,700 people would be available for daily deployment. Under "Deployment of Jews," the report concluded: "In accordance with the uncovered need for male workers of almost every kind, several thousand more Jews could be needed for useful work." This bottom line was a far cry from Dorr's original concept of unrelentingly replacing Jewish workers with Latvian workers.[41] In the RKO's Main Department III (Economic Affairs), where it was possible to make comparative estimates, General Commissariat Latvia was said to have the most strained labor situation of all the general commissariats in spring 1942, with Riga being affected worst of all.[42]

In the course of January, apparently no one had counted on the comprehensive deployment of the deportees from the Reich; as a result, a "loan" of Jews from the Kaunas ghetto was organized and carried out despite all the difficulties this created on the ground there.[43] On 16 February, Standtke reported that there were 4,193 men and 524 women employed with the Wehrmacht (2,632 men, 408 women), civil offices (817 men, 39, women), Organization Todt (93 men, 5 women), and the Reich Railway (281 men, 36 women). According to this report, 120 men and 5 women were with the Order Service, and 250 men and 31 women were working inside the ghetto. But Krause, the ghetto commandant, and Maywald, the man in charge of construction at Salaspils, refused to have the German, Austrian, and Czech Jews registered. The Jews from Germany were, according to them, "only temporarily accommodated here and were available only to the SS," noted Standtke. Krause was making German Jews available – "inasmuch as they are at all still able to do any kind of work" – only subject to recall, for the "needs of the SS, such as the expansion of its camps in Salaspils – Jungfernhof, ought not to be disturbed by the labor deployment of the Labor Office." Standtke expressly stated that the ability to deploy German Jews was minimal. There were many old and sick people among them, he wrote, adding that merely some 500 men and 700 women were deployed at the harbor, in bridge construction, and with the Reich Railway. He had no exact numbers for them. Of those remaining, Standtke had selected a group for shoveling snow, but "these workers had already been taken back to the ghetto on sleds, because they were falling over at work."[44]

The second large group of workers that could be deployed at discretion were the prisoners of war at Stalag 340 and Stalag 350. The civil administration could fall back on them only if the Wehrmacht agreed, however, which had been impossible since February 1942, because the commander of prisoners of war within the RKO had been presented with a set of demands from the office of the Commissioner for the Four-Year Plan, one of *Reichsmarschall* Hermann Göring's agencies. As a result, a massive pullout of POWs was about to take place, which, for example, led the county commissar in Jelgava to fear that half of the peasants in his jurisdiction would soon lose all their workers.[45]

The German Jews thus became increasingly important for meeting the demand for workers, even though they were at the disposal of the Security Police.[46] They had set up an efficient system of self-organization and had a decisive advantage vis-à-vis employers: they spoke German. The newfound importance of the German Jews was something that Lange himself was forced to take into consideration on 1 May, while seeking to transfer around 600 Jews from the ghetto to Salaspils. Dorr dared protest Lange's intention, because he knew that the prisons contained political prisoners and work-shy persons who could work at Salaspils. Dorr wrote: "I have in the meantime put these German Jews to work in Riga, so that a sensitive gap would ensue as a result of their removal. The urgent need for workers, as is known, cannot be covered even remotely." He stressed that the labor deployment process had been aggravated considerably, because he knew that Fritz Sauckel, the general plenipotentiary for the deployment of labor in Berlin, now wanted three times the originally calculated number of workers from the RKO for deployment in the Reich.[47]

Sauckel's demands were received with consternation in General Commissariat Latvia. On 2 May 1942, a meeting took place at which Ministerial Director Rachner from Sauckel's office heard a good deal about economic conditions in Latvia. When he requested 8,000 workers be transferred to the Reich over the next fourteen days and another 2,000 per week in the eleven weeks thereafter, general protest erupted. Mayor Egon Bönner responded that in the current situation, it should be the other way around; 20,000–25,000 workers should be sent to Latvia during the weeks in question. Dorr seconded: Latvia had already given up 38,000 people, 16,000 for service with the police alone. Hans-Otto von Borcke, municipal legal counselor for Riga, pointed out that Latvia had lost 233,000 people (resettlers, deportees, Jews [78,000], Work Service, Wehrmacht) since June 1941. In addition, some 44,000 workers were lacking for needs decisive for the war effort. Only a few thousand people who were unwanted for political reasons could be given up, he added.

But Rachner insisted on the May transports of 8,000 workers at the very least, even though Drechsler and Lange had drawn attention to the devastating political effects this would have on the Latvian people. In order to break the impasse, it was pointed out, for example, that the smallest enterprises in Latvia could be dissolved and the workers sent away; it was also noted that the indigenous Latvian administration was overstaffed. Finally, one could take workers from the "culturally lower areas," because there was no threat of political repercussions there. The meeting closed by recognizing Rachner's wishes and transferring the problem to the indigenous Latvian administration.[48] Against this backdrop, it was only consistent for the Riga labor administration's statistics and reporting section to report in July that the "extraordinary need for workers in all branches of the economy has again resulted in an increased demand for Jewish workers," which affected primarily the peat works, the harbor administration, and the construction group Giesler from Organization Todt.[49]

On 29 January 1942, *Reichsführer-SS* and Chief of the German Police Heinrich Himmler sent Reich Minister Rosenberg a set of draft guidelines on the handling of the Jewish question, which represented what the SS and police considered necessary. With regard to the employment of Jews for economic ends, this draft stated that economic needs were to play no role in the "elimination of Jewry." But it must be noted that this approach was impossible with regard to occupied Latvia.[50] Although all of the general commissars apparently expressed regret at a 26 March meeting with Reich Commissar Lohse that mass murder operations against the Jews were no longer taking place, this was bound to have been but lip service where Drechsler was concerned.[51] Only in General Commissariat White Ruthenia, which was administrated by General Commissar Wilhelm Kube, were mass murder operations still underway. Kube himself estimated on 31 July 1942 that the number of Jews killed in his region "in recent weeks" was 55,000, and he put a premium on the fact that this had not disrupted the work deployment process.[52] However, officials in the RKO's Main Department III (Economic Affairs) feared that exactly the opposite would be the case.[53] It therefore seems very probable that the labor market situation was the reason why the head of RSHA Department IV (Gestapo) let it be known on 18 May 1942 that Himmler had decided on a basic order stating that Jews aged 16–32 and able to work were "to be excluded from special measures until further notice."[54]

Ghetto Commandant Krause's decision to make German Jews who were able to work available to the civil administration had de facto become a permanent situation. Lange himself conceded this, but with one exception: the Security Police did not pay the Jews in Salaspils and Jungfernhof; the SS and police issued provisions without any settlement of accounts.[55] Lange also had nothing against the fact that since 1 June 1942, the placement of Jews for work had been in the hands of the Latvian self-administration – so long as a German civil servant remained in a supervisory function.[56]

However, when the civil administration tried, for example, to redeploy the Jews at Jungfernhof for its own purposes – making reference to their "garden work" as not decisive for the war effort – its efforts were coldly rejected by the Security Police.[57] After all, Lange had already allowed the Labor Office to place German Jews who were not working in his workshops or camps. When, on 22 July 1942, Lange received a complaint from the civil administration that Reich-German Jews had apparently been placed by the Security Police as orderlies at the Reich Commissar's guest house and the main railroad directorate's cafeteria, he dismissed it out of hand. All Jews, Lange responded, are now placed by the Labor Office.[58]

The shortage of skilled and semi-skilled workers was enormous, primarily in construction. For example, although German and Latvian Jews had already been employed at the Riga-Spilve airfield since April 1942, the lengthening of the airfield by the company Kieseling was making only slow progress.[59] Under these circumstances, the German Air Force's 1st Field Construction Office requested Lithuanian Jews from the Reich Commissariat. However, this was rejected, since the labor administration in Lithuania, as in Latvia, had for the time being put its Jews to work cutting peat, which was decisive for the war effort.[60] But the 1st Field Construction Office then suggested in September that the Air Force transfer the 600 Jews it already had working in Kaunas and Vilnius to Riga-Spilve. The Air Force would pay for transportation, the camp of barracks at Spilve, and the guards. Ludwig asked for a prompt, positive response, for an additional delay in construction was unacceptable in light of the military's needs.[61] This application rather quickly wound its way through the various offices to the RKO and from there to the general commissars for Latvia and Lithuania.[62] After the two regional commanders of the Security Police gave their approval, it was agreed that 300 Jewish workers would be allowed to go to Spilve, with their stay limited to mid December 1942.[63] But in early December, it became clear that the barracking of these Jews with the Air Force in Spilve would not be terminated, because the airfield urgently had to be expanded for troop transports. Not only were 100 more Jews requested, but their stay was extended until spring.[64]

The Jews of the Kaunas ghetto learned very quickly that 300 workers were to be selected for Spilve; but it took another four weeks before the Jewish Council in Kaunas called a gathering to discuss the question of how to provide the requested workers. When the German side allowed the workers to take along their families and raised the possibility of a reunion for some relatives of the group of Lithuanian Jews sent to Riga on 8 February, the Jewish Council decided to rely on volunteerism. Only a few unwanted Jews from Kaunas had to be assigned to the transport.[65]

Nothing changed in 1943 regarding the overall shortage of workers either – to the contrary.[66] Since February, the male citizens of Riga born between 1919 and 1921 had been mustered for work in the Germany. Of the 39,200 workers that Ostland had to provide, 4,000 were to come from the Latvian capital, according to one distribution key.[67] But it was difficult to come up with so many conscripts. Although 8,700 "young men" from Riga born in the years called up had appeared for mustering by the end of March, only 990 of them could be deployed. All of the others were either indispensable where they were already working, not healthy enough, free to study, serving in the Latvian SS Legion, or volunteer auxiliaries with the Wehrmacht.[68] The Riga Labor Office expressly stated that less important enterprises would now have to be closed or merged in order to meet the city's quota for workers. In addition, it was noted that agriculture was catastrophically undermanned that spring, and the specter of an approaching famine was outlined. In addition to agriculture, peat cutting had also become a center of managed work deployment. In this raw materials branch, which was essential for providing energy to the Latvian capital, there was a shortage of 5,870 male workers; according to the Labor Office, these could only be replaced by POWs or "workers from elsewhere."[69]

The Security Police in General Commissariat Latvia reached a very similar conclusion. In a report for March 1943, Lange clearly pointed out the general exacerbation of the situation and noted that mergers and closures would not free up workers on a scale worth mentioning; the reopenings of enterprises in summer 1941 had applied only to those that were important to the war effort anyway.[70] An April memorandum from the indigenous Latvian administration's General Directorate of the Economy summed up in full the quandary facing the work deployment administration. Latvia, a largely agrarian state, had always relied on roughly 50,000 seasonal workers from Lithuania, Poland, and its own Latgale region. Since 1939, the situation had changed dramatically with each year: in 1939, due to the 5,000 German landlords and landowners who had resettled to Germany; one year later, due to the "rule of the Bolsheviks" and the deportation of 4,354 families; and, at the present time, conscription for work in Germany. Some 57,000 people had been withdrawn from agriculture, while at the same time obligatory production targets had been raised. Additional tasks, such as chopping wood, improving roads, and transport services quickly brought the peasants beyond their capacity to perform.[71] Although all of the deployable Jews would have been unable to solve the problem in principle – around 10,500 people were working inside and outside the ghetto – the concentration of these workers in a single branch that was decisive for the war effort and also afforded permanent supervision seemed a promising way to relieve the situation in spring 1943.[72]

Peat cutting in General Commissariat Latvia was centralized in the hands of the German trust–run Kūdra-Torfindustrie, which administered all of the peat works in Latvia from its headquarters in Riga. A year earlier, in April 1942, this raw materials provider had struggled with the declining number of workers and applied for Jewish workers, who were withdrawn from Wehrmacht commands that seemed less important. These were also barracked outside the ghetto – in other words, the labor commandos became branches of the ghetto wherever they had been deployed.[73] During an economics inspection of Kūdra-Torfindustrie by the Riga administration in May and June 1942, the Trust Administration Department in General Commissariat Latvia noted that production for the current year would require close to 100-percent utilization of capacity of all seventeen peat works in Latvia. But an audit of capacity performance brought largely depressing results. The peat works Slamste was working at just 16 percent of capacity; the works with the best performance was Kirchholm, i.e., Salaspils, with 73.5 percent. The overall average was 37 percent of performance capacity. The main reason for this – at all of the peat cutting sites – was a lack of workers.[74] Since permission to barrack the Jews was granted only if they were kept under continuous observation at the site of deployment, it was only logical that, under the steadily worsening conditions, the Jews were one year later deployed primarily in this same raw materials branch, where they could be best supervised.

On 14 April 1943, Lange sent a standardized letter to the WBO in which he asked for understanding with regard to the pullout of Jews from Wehrmacht commands:

> The call up of male youth for the years of birth 1919–1924 has created sensitive gaps in the General District Latvia. This is all the more reason why all available workers now have to be employed in jobs that are decisive for the war effort. This applies also to the deployment of Jews. The seasonal peat cutting in General District Latvia, which is ascribed a significance that is decisive for the war effort due to the lack of sufficient amounts of other fuels, has begun. The needs of the peat works amount to several thousand persons. In other years, during the season, a part of the workers could be detached for this from industrial enterprises. With regard to the restrictions on enterprises that have already been carried out in the last half year, the combing of enterprises, and the like, an additional removal of industrial workers can at present no longer be justified considering the manufactures that are important to the war effort. Therefore, one of the last reserves of workers for peat cutting in 1943 remains the deployment of Jews. Over the next few days, the county commissar – labor administration – in Riga in cooperation with the Regional Commander of the Security Police and the SD will extract the Jewish workers suitable for peat work from the contingents made available to you up to now and deploy them for peat work until autumn 1943. Jews accommodated in the ghetto and those barracked at individual offices as well will be

affected by this. The offices that now employ Jews and are to have a part of these extracted are asked to show understanding for this measure, which lies in the interest of the overall economy. Objections cannot be taken into consideration. We ask that the offices subordinated to you that employ Jews as workers be informed accordingly.[75]

Thus, in spring 1943, the Jews were to work at Latvia's peat works in large numbers. It was planned that the first details from the ghetto would be picked up on 19 April 1943.[76] The catastrophic situation regarding workers was ultimately revealed quite plainly when the general commissariat in all seriousness approached the Security Police to ask "whether, with regard to the extraordinarily large shortage of workers of all kinds in General District Latvia, another intake of Jews from the Reich is possible."[77]

Notes

1. BA Berlin, R 91/164, Latvijas Rūpniecības Pārvalde. Torfindustrie Riga an die Deutsche Wirtschaftsverwaltung in Riga, betr. Gestellung von Kriegsgefangenenen, 17 July 1941.
2. BA Berlin, R 92/1158, 150–151, Wirschaftskdo. für das Gebiet des ehemalgen Lettland, Abteilung Arbeit. Aktenvermerk, betr. Arbeitseinsatz der Juden, 21 July 1941, also to be found in BA Berlin, R 91/164.
3. LVVA, P 1026-1-3, 310–315, Der RKO, Abtl. IIa 4, an den HSSPF, betr. Vorläufige Richtlinien für die Behandlung der Juden im Gebiet des Reichskommissariats Ostland, 2 August 1941, also printed in Benz et al., *Einsatz im "Reichskommissariat Ostland,"* doc. no. 11, 39–43.
4. Latvijas Valsts Arhīvs (LVA), P 69-5-122, 1–3, Richtlinien für Regelung der Löhne und Arbeitsbedingungen für die von Wehrmachtsdienststellen beschäftigten einheimischen gewerblichen Arbeitskräfte, gez. v. Roques, 5 August 1941.
5. BA Berlin, R 91/164, Arbeitsamt Riga, Arbeitseinsatz für Juden. Hinweise für die Anlegung von Personalkarten für jüdische Arbeitskräfte, undated. This document includes two sample cards.
6. Ibid., *Deutsche Zeitung im Osten*, 18 August 1941.
7. Staw. Hamburg, 141 Js 534/60, Bd. 57 [Beweismaterial], Der RKO, Abtl. IIb, Verordnung zur Regelung des Arbeitseinsatzes, gez. i.V. Fründt, 15 August 1941.
8. LVVA, P 70-5-7, Verordnung über die Einführung des Arbeitszwangs für die jüdische Bevölkerung, 16 August 1941, also printed in Benz et al., *Einsatz im "Reichskommissariat Ostland,"* doc. no. 10, 36–37; LVVA, P 69-1a-6, 67–70, Der RKO, Abtl. IIa 4, an die Generalkommissare in Estland, Lettland, Litauen, Weissruthenien, gez. Lohse, 18 August 1941. This includes the preliminary guidelines and the request for reports. The document was used in the Nuremberg trials as NO-4815.
9. BA Berlin, R 91/164, Der Gen.-Komm. in Riga, Arbeitsverwaltung. Niederschrift über die Besprechung mit den Chefs der staatlichen und Industrieunternehmen in Riga über Arbeitseinsatzfragen von 1.9.1941. Drechsler's order on the treatment of Jews in the territory of the former "Free State of Latvia" – which again listed compulsory identification and

bans on certain professions and movement – went into force starting 1 September 1941, see YIVO, Occ. E 3-21.
10. BA Berlin, R 91/164, Bericht über den jüdischen Arbeitseinsatz, Riga, 8 September 1941.
11. Ibid.
12. BA Berlin, R 91/164, Der Geb.-Komm. Riga. Der Leiter des Arbeitsamts an die Feldkommandantur Riga, betr. Beschäftigung von Juden durch die Wehrmacht, gez. Dorr, 15 September 1941.
13. LVVA, P 69-1a-6, 86, WBO, Ia, betr. Juden in den neu besetzten Gebieten, Bezug: OKW/WFSt/Abtl. L (IV Qu), Nr. 2041/41m, 12 September 1941. On the armbands and numbers of Jews deployed, see BA Berlin, R 91/164, Der Leiter des Arbeitsamts Riga an die Feldkommandantur Riga, betr. Beschäftigung von Juden durch die Wehrmacht, gez. Dorr, 30 September 1941.
14. YIVO, Occ. E 3-27, Der Gen.-Komm. in Riga, Abtl. IIa, an den RKO, Abtl. IIa, betr. Einrichtung von Ghettos, jüdischen Arbeitslagern und Arbeitseinsatz der Juden – Anmelde- und Ablieferungspflicht des jüdischen Vermögens.
15. Einsatzgruppe A, Gesamtbericht bis zum 15. Oktober 1941, printed in *IMG*, Bd. 37, 670–717, here 687–689.
16. Nuremberg Document NO-1020, III B El./Ma. Niederschrift über die Besprechung zwischen SS-Obergruppenführer Heydrich und Gauleiter Meyer in Anwesenheit von Min. Dir. Schlotterer, Reichsamtsleiter Dr. Leibbrandt sowie SS-Obersturmbannführer Ehlich am 4.10.1941, 11 Uhr.
17. LVA, P 69-2-14, 1. Unfortunately, only the response of the Latvian Industry Directorate, dated 21 October 1941, is documented. It emerges here that Dorr had requested the submission of such registers be filed. A referenced attachment is not among the surviving documents.
18. BA Berlin, R 91/64, Arbeitsamt Riga an die Industrie-Direktion Riga, betr. Einsatz von jüdischen Arbeitskräften, 24 October 1941.
19. BA Berlin, R 91/23, excerpt "Amtliche Bekanntmachungen," *Deutsche Zeitung im Osten*, 28 October 1941. It was specified here that all working papers would lose their validity on 31 October; applications containing justification for the continued employment of Jews were to be submitted in writing for evaluation. Standard wages for Jews would apply and were to be paid weekly to the Riga city administration's Finance Department.
20. BA Berlin, R 91/74, Kommunaldepartement Riga an die Arbeitsverwaltung des Gen.-Komm., betr. Das Beschäftigen von Arbeitslosen, Juden und Kriegsgefangenen, 4 November 1941.
21. Der Gen.-Komm. in Riga, Abtl. Sozialverwaltung, Dorr, an den RKO, Abtl. Sozialverwaltung, betr. Bericht über die Lage für die Zeit vom 16.10.-15.11.41, 27 November 1941: "The deployment of Jewish workers in Riga was subjected to new regulations starting 1 November 1941. Employers have to pay standard wages, which are to be paid to the city of Riga. Deployment takes place in groups. Jewish individuals receive individual identification papers from the Labor Office as well. The Wehrmacht offices have for the most part forgone Jewish workers. 3,373 male and 890 female workers were deployed anew by the Labor Office Riga. In the ghetto itself, 1,000 workers were employed." It is also noted in this report that the ghetto contained 24,623 registered persons considered employable, see LVVA, P 69-1a-17, 171 and BA Berlin, R 91/99. In a situation report for the same period, the Riga Labor Office provided the following figures on 18 November 1941: Jews who were able to work numbered 17,571 (5,224 men and 12,347 women). 5,030 workers (4,050 men, 980 women) had been deployed. 3,975 men and 1,571 women had been requested. "The placement of the remaining female workers was refused, instead the

offices affected were asked to employ Latvian workers. Due to the order regarding payment of Jews, which took effect on 1 November 1941, a shift in the deployment of Jews has set in, while the Wehrmacht has been the main recipient of Jews up to now, today ca. 800–1,000 Jews are employed at civil offices, harbors, construction companies, etc. The increased demand for Jewish workers is attributed to the prevailing shortage of prisoners of war ... As of 15 November, 280 identification papers for individuals have been issued, of which 115 were for military offices and 165 for civil offices. By means of passes, around 3,500 Jews and Jewesses leave the ghetto daily. Cooperation with the military offices has so far been flawless." See BA Berlin, R 91/164.

22. LVVA, P 69-1a-19, 21–27, Der Gen.-Komm. in Riga, Abtl. II, an den RKO, betr. Monatlicher Bericht über Einrichtung von Ghettos in [sic !] jüdischen Arbeitslägern, Arbeitseinsatz und Behandlung der Juden, also printed in Benz et al., *Einsatz im "Reichskommissariat Ostland,"* doc. no. 105, 139–140.
23. BA Berlin, R 91/164, Bericht über den Einsatz der Juden, 16 February 1942. 4,193 men and 524 women are counted here. Subtraction of the Lithuanian Jews from Kaunas (222 men and 137 women) leaves the 4,358 Jews (3,971 men and 387 women) given in the text, see R 92/1158, 154.
24. LVVA, P 69-1a-17, 126, Der Geb.-Komm. Libau an den Gen.-Komm. in Riga. The passages on the shootings are quoted from Wolfgang Scheffler, "Die Einsatzgruppe A," in Klein, *Die Einsatzgruppen in der besetzten Sowjetunion,* 41.
25. YIVO, Occ. E 3-28, Der RmbO an den RKO, i.A. gez. Dr. Leibbrandt, 31 October 1941, in which Leibbrandt demands an explanation from Lohse.
26. YIVO, Occ. E 3-28, Verfg. an den RmbO, betr. Judenexekutionen, gez. Lohse, 15 November 1941.
27. On Kaunas, see YIVO, Occ. E 3-30, Vermerk des Geb.-Komm. Gewecke, 3 September 1941, in which Gewecke, under reference to the economic situation, forbids SS First Lieutenant Joachim Hamann to carry out liquidations in Šiauliai (Schaulen). On Vilnius, see YIVO, Occ. E 3-32, Vermerk Trampedachs im RKO, 7 November 1941, in which the Wehrmacht official Mey informed him personally of the liquidation of Jewish specialists. The quote is from YIVO, Occ. E 3-28, Verfg. an den RmbO, betr. Judenexekutionen, gez. Lohse, 15 November 1941.
28. YIVO, Occ. E 3-28, Der RmbO an den RKO, betr. Judenfrage, i.A. Bräutigam. Also printed in *Der Krieg gegen die Sowjetunion 1941–1945,* ed. Reinhard Rürup, 91.
29. LVVA, P 69-1a-17, 166, Der Gen.-Komm. in Riga, Abtl. Sozialverwaltung, Dorr, an den RKO, Abtl. Sozialverwaltung, betr. Bericht über die Lage für die Zeit vom 16.10.-15.11.1941, 27 November 1941.
30. LVA, P 69-5-22, 4, Aktenvermerk, betr. Judeneinsatz, 12 January 1942; ibid., 5, Anweisung des Geb.-Komm., Arbeitsamt, an alle Wehrmachtseinheiten, die Juden beschäftigen, 13 January 1942. According to the latter document, unskilled workers in Wage Group I received RM 0.27/hour, Wage Group II RM 0.32/hour, Wage Group III (specialists) RM 0.38/hour, Wage Group IV (qualified specialists) RM 0.35/hour, and Wage Group V (foremen) RM 0.50/hour. A copy of this document is also in BA Berlin, R 91/142.
31. LVA, P 69-5-22, 20, RmbO, Min.Dir. Schlotterer, an den RKO, 21 January 1942, which contains reference to proposals from the general quartermaster of the Army; ibid., 11–12, Dorr's response to the RKO, 24 January 1942.
32. LVVA, P 80-3-2, 14–15, Wehrmacht-Ortskommandantur Riga. Kommandanturbefehl Nr. 2, betr. Übernachtung der Juden, Dr. Bamberg, Generalmajor und Kommandant, 20 January 1942. See also the brief remark in a monthly report from the county commissariat Labor Office, 16.11.-31.12.1941: "Individual enterprises have begun to hold back Jews taken from the ghetto and to accommodate and provision them at the enterprises."

33. On 11 February 1942, Local Administration Commandant Bamberg once again tried to circumvent the wages for Jews by means of a commandant's order, declaring them invalid for the military sphere, see LVVA, P 80-3-2, 23. But that same month, the labor administration got its way when it pointed out in a letter to all Wehrmacht offices that no Jews would be placed without receipts for the payment of wages to the Finance Office, see LVA P 69-5-122, 19, Der Geb.-Komm. Riga, Arbeitsamt, an alle Wehrmachtsdienststellen und Firmen, die Juden als Arbeitskräfte beschäftigen, 27 February 1942. A copy of this letter is also in BA Berlin, R 91/42.
34. BA Berlin, R 91/101, Finanzabtl. Riga an Arbeitsamt, betr. Stundenlohn für jüdische Arbeiter, 12 May 1942.
35. Willy Dingler, a member of the Schutzpolizei from Danzig who was sometimes deployed as deputy chief of the ghetto guards, recalled this beating in 1963, Staw. Hamburg, 141 Js 534/60, Bd. 32, statement by Willy Dingler, 25 April 1963, 5,277–5,301.
36. BA Berlin, R 91/164, Der Geb.-Komm. Riga, Arbeitsamt, Verfg. an den Reichskommissar durchlaufend beim Herrn Gen.-Komm. in Riga, betr. Judeneinsatz, hier Personal der Judeneinsatzstelle Riga. Durchschriftl. an Gen.-Komm., HA II: Gen.-Komm. Abtl. Politik; Geb.-Komm. Riga-Stadt, 8 January 1942. Another copy is available at BA Berlin, R 91/74.
37. On this, see the request from the SS and Police County Leader Riga Countryside regarding the additional equipping of Gendarmerie accommodations, 9 January 1942, in Staw. Hamburg, 141 Js 534/60, Bd. 57 [Beweismittel].
38. The entire event is documented in BA Berlin, R 91/74. In 1963, Reinhold Thaumann, a former member of the Schutzpolizei in the ghetto, also recalled this incident without prompting, Staw. Hamburg, 141 Js 534/60, Bd. 36, statement by Reinhold Thaumann, 16 May 1963, 5,891.
39. BA Berlin, R 91/99, Der Geb.-Komm. in Riga (Arbeitsamt) an den Gen.-Komm., Abtl. Sozialverwaltung, betr. Bericht für die Zeit vom 16.11-31.12.1941, "The number of Jews accommodated in the ghetto has in the period of reporting declined significantly so that [at present] only around 4,000 males and ca. 300 females are accommodated, who were completely deployed."
40. BA Berlin, R 91/164, Bericht über den Einsatz der Juden, 18 January 1942.
41. LVVA, P 69-1a-17, 386–395, Lagebericht der Abteilung Arbeits- und Sozialpolitik des Geb.-Komm. Riga-Stadt für den Januar 1942, undated. A copy dated 9 February 1942 is in BA Berlin, R 91/99.
42. BA Berlin, R 90/427, Der RKO, HA III, Lagebericht, 11 May 1942, report for March and April 1942.
43. Cf. chapter 8, this volume.
44. BA Berlin, R 91/164, Bericht über den Einsatz der Juden, 16 February 1942.
45. On the demands made on Ostland by the Four-Year Plan authority, see BA Berlin, R 91/164, RKO, Abtl. III, an die Generalkommissare in Riga, Kauen, Minsk und Reval, 16 February 1942; a written protest from County Commissariat Jelgava (Mitau) to the general commissar is in ibid.
46. The civil administration increasingly made this distinction itself in spring 1942, see, for example, the material collected by Dept. IIa of the County Commissariat for a situation report from the general commissar to the RKO for February 1942, in Staw. Hamburg, 141 Js 534/60, Bd. 57 [Beweismaterial]: "Since December [of last year], Jews from the Old Reich – their number has now reached 11,000 – have in the meantime been accommodated in the ghetto on an ongoing basis. Their supervision is a Security Police matter." Also, BA Berlin, R91/30, Aktennotiz des Geb.-Komm. Wittrock, betr. Arbeitsleistung von Juden aus Deutschland im Ghetto, 17 April 1942: "The Regional Commander of the Security Police in Riga has power of disposal over the Jews in the Riga Ghetto who

were expelled from Germany. He is also responsible for feeding them. The SD acquired the means necessary for purchasing food by having the Jews' employers pay a wage to the ghetto administration for Jewish work provided."
47. On Dorr's protest against KdS Latvia's plans, see BA Berlin, R 92/1158, 5, Geb.-Komm. Riga an den RKO, Abtl. III, durchlaufend beim Herrn Gen.-Komm. betr. Judeneinsatz, 29 April 1942. On Sauckel's intentions, see LVA, P 70-3-94, 54, Gen.-Komm. in Riga, Abtl. III e, an die Abteilungsleiter III, Propaganda und den Beauftragten für die Berufsverbände, betr. Einsatz von Arbeitskräften aus dem Ostland im Reich, 25 April 1942.
48. BA Berlin, R 91/3, Besprechung im Sitzungsaal des Justizpalastes am 2.5.42 um 9.00 Uhr unter Vorsitz des Herrn Generalkommissars, betr. Einsatz von Arbeitskräften aus dem Ostland im Reich. Those on hand were Ministerial Director Dr. Rachner, Mayor Bönner, Senior Administrative Counselor Ellrodt, Senior Administrative Counselor Dorr, Senior Administrative Counselor Dr. Dr. von Borcke, Chief of Staff Fehre, Construction Director General Weise, County Commissar Alnor, County Commissar Schwung, Wartime Administration Deputy Chief Matthiessen.
49. BA Berlin, R 91/30, Der Geb.-Komm. Riga, Arbeitsverwaltung, Fachgebiet 1 (Statistik u. Berichterstattung), an den Gen.-Komm., Fachgebiet Arbeitspolitik und Sozialverwaltung, betr. Lage im Monat Juli 1942, 7 August 1942.
50. Yad Vashem, Eichmann Document No. 1088, RFSS und Chef der Deutschen Polizei, S II A 2, an den RmbO, betr. Braune Mappe für die Reichskommissariate Ostland und Ukraine, 29 January 1942.
51. Quoted from Christian Gerlach, "Deutsche Wirtschaftsinteressen, Besatzungspolitik und der Mord an den Juden in Weißrußland 1941 bis 1944," in Herbert, *Nationalsozialistische Vernichtungspolitik*, 286.
52. YIVO, Occ. E 3-41, Der Gen.-Komm. für Weißruthenien, Abtl. Gauleiter, an den RKO, betr. Partisanenbekämpfung und Judenaktion im Generalbezirk Weißruthenien, 31 July 1942. On these murder operations, see Gerlach, *Kalkulierte Morde*, 688–709, especially 705–706.
53. BA Berlin, R 90/428, Lagebericht für Mai und Juni 1942 des RKO, HA III Wirtschaft, 16 July 1942: "It has become known that the resettlements of Jews in General District White Ruthenia are taking their course. Because the skilled workers and craftsmen in this region are mostly Jews, the problem of deployment will become especially critical with the loss of these workers, because suitable rising talent is lacking."
54. This radio message is documented only for KdS Lithuania. However, Müller mentioned here that Jews deployed in Minsk as skilled workers had been removed from an army group motor pool by liquidation. This was not relevant to the KdS in Kaunas, but all of the KdS in Ostland were supposed to have received this general instruction, see RGVA, 500-1-25, 379, printed in *Die Einsatzgruppen*, ed. Klein, 410–411. The literature has yet to give this document adequate consideration and to interpret it. Only Christian Gerlach has pointed out the similarities to the situation in the General Government, Christian Gerlach, "Die Bedeutung der deutschen Ernährungspolitik für die Beschleunigung des Mordes an den Juden 1942. Das Generalgouvernement und die Westukraine," in idem., *Krieg, Ernährung, Völkermord*, 183, fn. 44. Stahlecker's successor, Heinz Jost, claimed this order was the unsatisfactory result of his efforts to have Heydrich suspend the mass murder operations, see Staw. Hamburg, 141 Js 534/60, Bd. 3, statement by Heinz Jost, 1 March 1950, 304–305.
55. BA Berlin, R 92/1158, 39, Der KdS, Abtl. I S, an den Gen.-Komm. in Riga, Abtl. Arbeitspolitik und Sozialverwaltung, betr. Arbeitseinsatz reichsdeutscher Juden, 10 August 1942. This letter concerns the SS and police's employment of Jews in jobs that were not decisive for the war effort.

56. BA Berlin, R 92/1158, 40, Der Gen.-Komm. in Riga, Abtl. II e Aso, Fachgebiet 2, an den KdS in Riga, betr. Judeneinsatz, 12 September 1942; Lange's response is to be found in ibid., 42. The organization of labor deployments was turned over to the Latvian self-administration after a meeting of the county commissars with the general commissar on 28 May 1942. It took effect on 1 June 1942, with the divestment of the labor offices from the German administration. Schmutzler supervised this new branch of the Latvian self-administration on behalf of County Commissariat Riga City, see BA Berlin, R 91/99, Besprechungsvermerk, Riga, 29 May 1941 [sic].
57. BA Berlin, R 92/1158, 10, Der Geb.-Komm. Riga, Arbeitsverwaltung, an den RKO, Abtl. III-Aso, betr. Judeneinsatz, zweckmäßiger Ansatz der Kräfte, 14 July 1942. The rejection of any willingness to negotiate with regard to the withdrawal of Reich-German Jews, dated 22 July 1942, is contained in copy of a note signed by Eicker in the same file.
58. BA Berlin, R 92/1158, 38–39, Der Gen.-Komm. in Riga, Abtl. Aso, an den KdS, betr. Arbeitseinsatz reichsdeutscher Juden, gez. Dorr, 22 July 1942. Lange's answer followed on 10 August 1942, ibid.
59. LVVA, P 132-28-18, 66, 69, 85, and 92, Dortmund Group journal entries for 13 April, 15 May, 29 May, and 15 July 1942.
60. On the urgent peat operation, see BA Berlin, R 91/10, 79, Gen.-Komm. in Riga (Arbeitseinsatz) an den Geb.-Komm. (Abtl. Arbeitseinsatz), betr. Ernährung der beim Trofabbau beschäftigten Juden, gez. Dorr, 22 July 1942. Also BA Berlin, R 92/1158, 38, Gen.-Komm. in Riga an den KdS in Riga, betr. Arbeitseinsatz reichsdeutscher Juden, 22 July 1942.
61. BA Berlin, R 92/1158, 20, Feldbauamt 1 im Luftgau 1 – Sachgeb. 1, an den Geb.-Komm. Riga, Abtl. Arbeitseinsatz, betr. Einsatz litauischer Juden bei der Luftwaffe in Riga, 8 September 1942. Until autumn 1942, the airport in Warsaw was the Air Force's largest supply center for the eastern front. The difficulties at this logistical crossroads began in September-October 1942, when the economic enterprises of District Warsaw that were decisive for the war effort also began using the warehouses. Decentralization and transfer toward the front became unavoidable, see Monatsbericht der OFK Warschau für den 16.9.-15.10.1942, BA MA, RH 53-23/v. 16.
62. BA Berlin, R 92/1158, 21, Der Geb.-Komm. in Riga, Abtl. III e Aso, an den RKO, betr. Einsatz litauischer Juden bei der Luftwaffe in Riga, 10 September 1942; ibid., 22, Der RKO, HA III, an das Feldbauamt 1 der LW Riga, betr. Einsatz litauischer Juden, 19 September 1942; ibid., 23, Der RKO, HA III, an das Feldbauamt 1 der LW Riga, betr. Einsatz litauischer Juden, 8 October 1942.
63. The other 300 persons were assigned to the construction of the Zokniai airfield near Šiauliai, see Rose Lerer Cohen, "Deportations from Lithuania," in *The Holocaust in Lithuania 1941–1945: A Book of Remembrance*, ed. Rose Cohen and Saul Issroff, Bd. 1, 41.
64. BA Berlin, R 92/1158, 28–29, Der RKO, HA III, an das Feldbauamt im Luftgau I, betr. Umsetzung von jüdischen Arbeitskräften von der Feldbauleitung der Luftwaffe 3/1 in Kauen zum Feldbauamt 1 in Riga-Spilve, 11 December 1942.
65. Tory, *Surviving the Holocaust*, 133 [12 September 1942], 141 [12 October 1942], 144–146 [16 October 1942], 147 [21 October 1942], 148 [12 October 1942].
66. In the afternoon and evening of 11 January 1943, the local municipal gas work failed to maintain service to all of Riga due to the shortage of workers, see BA Berlin R 91/156, Städt. Betriebsamt Riga an Wittrock, betr. Aufrechterhaltung lebenswichtiger Betriebe, 12 January 1943.
67. BA Berlin, R 91/29, Sitzung beim Geb.-Komm. Riga-Stadt am 9.2.43.
68. LVVA, P 958-1-2, 62–64, Arbeitsamt Riga. Monatsbericht über die Lage im Arbeitsamt Riga, 1.-31.3.1943.

69. LVA, P 989-1-20, 40–57, Generaldirektion der Wirtschaft, Arbeitsdepartement, an den Gen.-Komm. in Riga, Betrifft: Lage im Monat März 1943, gez. Reinhards, 5 April 1943.
70. LVVA, P 82-1-39, 92–202, here 176, Der KdS Lettland. Stimmungs- und Lagebericht für den Monat März 1943, 1 April 1943, "Labor and Social Policy. In the last month as well, the problem of workers has been exacerbated. The number of unoccupied male positions rose from 22,500 to 28,000, the number of open female positions from 7,700 to 12,200. Requests for prisoners of war, especially on the part of agriculture, have increased to 16,700. In various manufacturing fields, the shortage of workers will increase considerably, whereas an easing of work deployment situation will emerge among those having a need [for laborers] who were recognized during the mustering process. In connection with the extent of the shortage of workers and in adjusting to the closure action for enterprises, which the Reich Economics Ministry announced at the start of the year, the combing, closure, and merger of enterprises that cannot be considered important to the war effort is being prepared. In Latvia, however, it is not to be expected that this action will release a greater number of workers, because in Latvia, unlike in the Reich, the German administration in general allowed only the re-opening of enterprises that were absolutely necessary for carrying out tasks important to the war effort."
71. LVA, P 989-1-4, 122–124, Abschrift. Generaldirektion der Wirtschaft, Arbeitsdepartement, Memorandum, gez. P. Reinhards, Direktor des Arbeitsdepartements, 12 April 1943.
72. On the number of working Jews, see BA Berlin, R 91/164, Der Geb.-Komm. Riga, Arbeitsverwaltung, gez. Schmutzler, 9 February 1943, with statistics as of 10 February 1943. According to this document, 10,435 Jews had been deployed, of which 2,200 were barracked at their place of work; in addition, there were 1,100 ill persons in the ghetto. Overall, 11,500 persons were living in the ghetto in spring 1943.
73. On the situation in the peat industry, see BA Berlin, R 91/63, Lagebericht des Arbeitsamtes Riga an den Geb.-Komm. für den April 1942. On the withdrawal of Jews from Wehrmacht commands, see BA Berlin, R 92/1158, 152–153, Der Geb.-Komm., Arbeitsamt, Fachgebiet 2, Aktenvermerk, betr. Judeneinsatz, Zusammenarbeit mit Wehrmachtsdienststellen, 6 July 1942. On the barracking of Jews, see BA Berlin, R 91/30, Lagebericht des Geb.-Komm. Riga, Abtl Arbeitsverwaltung, Fachgebiet 1, an den Gen.-Komm., Abtl. Aso, betr. Lage im Monat Juli 1942.
74. BA Berlin, R 92/1206, Entwurf eines Schreibens an die Hauptabteilung III, Treuhandverwaltung, des Gen.-Komm. in Riga, gez. Blumental, 11 June 1942, with appendixes on production capacity. See also BA Berlin, R 90/428, HA III/Industrie und Handel des RKO, Zweimonatsbericht Mai/Juni 1942, according to which the program's implementation depended on the full deployment of workers.
75. LVVA, P 80-2-12, 198, Der KdS Lettland an den WBO-Kommandant des Hauptquartiers, betr. Arbeitseinsatz von Juden, gez. Lange, 14 April 1943. The form letter is in BA Berlin, R 92/1157.
76. BA Berlin, R 92/1158, 45, Durchschrift. Der Gen.-Komm. in Riga, Abtl. III Aso, Vermerk, betr. Torfwirtschaft, 15 April 1943, see the section under the heading "Einsatz von Juden."
77. BA Berlin, R 92/1157, Der Gen.-Komm. in Riga, Abtl. III Aso, FG 2, an den KdS, betr. Zusammenarbeit von Dienststellen des SD und der Arbeitsverwaltung, 6 May 1943, here the heading "jüdische Arbeitskräfte."

– Chapter 12 –

THE UTILIZATION OF JEWISH ASSETS AND THE ISSUE OF GHETTO ADMINISTRATION

The securing of Jewish assets in Reich Commissariat Ostland (RKO) and the administration of ghettos had already been agreed on by Reich Commissar Hinrich Lohse in talks with his general commissars when they met in Kaunas (Kauen, Kovno) on 27 July. The result of these talks was, first of all, the draft "Preliminary Guidelines for the Treatment of Jews in the Territory of Reich Commissariat Ostland," which Higher SS and Police Leader Hans-Adolf Prützmann then received in the form of a letter. This document set forth the stipulations that, from Lohse's point of view, were necessary to guarantee a certain degree of uniformity in the general commissariats. The Jews were defined as a category of persons – "by race" and by citizenship – registered, outwardly marked, and confronted with an array of bans that resulted in total social, economic, and cultural isolation.

As to Jewish assets, it was determined that these were to be confiscated and secured. In addition, the reporting of assets was made compulsory; this also extended to all non-Jewish persons who had such assets in their safekeeping or possession. The general commissars were appointed to monitor the reporting and registration process, with the actual implementation of these steps being delegated to the county commissars. The county commissars were allowed to decide whether to pass on these tasks to non-German civil administrative offices. Jewish assets were classified as domestic and foreign currencies, securities, stocks, bonds, checks, promissory notes, bank and savings books, precious metals, precious stones, and jewelry as well as gold and silver coins that were owned by Jews. Real estate was not yet included. The Jews were to be left with essential household effects and a sum of money equal to the amount needed to support each household member under local conditions; this money was to be released at the start of each month.

According to these guidelines, the county or city commissars would merely supervise the administration of ghettos. In this document, ghetto

---

Notes for this chapter begin on page 304.

administration was still a purely internal Jewish affair, which was of course dependent on the German authorities, starting with foodstuffs. A Jewish Order Service was to take over executive authority within the Jewish residential area, whereas the ghetto walls and fences would be guarded by indigenous auxiliary policemen. Permission to enter a ghetto was to be issued by the county commissar. Finally, the county commissar was also responsible for the orderly placement of Jewish forced labor. Any regulations going beyond the guidelines were to be decreed by the general commissars, who for their part could authorize their county commissars to enact such amendments.[1]

The Preliminary Guidelines did not even mention the Security Police and the SD in the most important issues concerning the implementation of ghetto administration, the impounding of assets, and the deployment of labor. Even when Lohse later sought to have Jews from other countries included in "police measures," he applied to the Reich minister for the occupied eastern territories.[2] Moves of this kind, however, were only partially influenced by the desire of the police and civilian authorities in the occupied territories to formulate the latent disputes between *Reichsführer-SS* and Chief of the German Police Heinrich Himmler and Reich Minister for the Occupied Eastern Territories Alfred Rosenberg to their own advantage. For although the version of the guidelines that went out to the general commissariats had not changed in terms of content, the introduction did say: "For the ultimate solution of the Jewish question in the territory of the Reich Commissar Ostland, my instructions from my talk in Kaunas of 27 July 1941, are in force. To the extent additional measures are adopted in the realization of my oral instructions, in particular [those adopted] by the Security Police, they are not affected by the following temporary guidelines. The preliminary guidelines have only the task of ensuring minimal measures on the part of the general and county commissars wherever and as long as additional measures in the spirit of the ultimate solution of the Jewish question are not possible."[3] Thus, during the first fourteen days of civil administration, Lohse had clearly understood that the guidelines would take effect whenever it was still necessary to administer the limited existence of Jews beyond the actual "solution of the Jewish question" by mass murder.

From the perspective of the Security Police, this was never up for discussion anyway. Nonetheless, SS Major Rudolf Batz of Einsatzkommando 2 commented on the draft guidelines in a telex to the command staff of Einsatzgruppe A. Whereas he had no objections regarding the establishment of ghettos, the "de-Judaization" of the countryside, and other regulations, he complained as a matter of principle that securing and confiscating assets were the task of the German Security Police. The civil administration could take over only impounding, administration, and utilization. Furthermore, the compulsory reporting of Jewish assets could apply only to the Jews themselves or Latvians. German offices would by all means have to be excluded from such a regulation.[4] What is foreshadowed here was henceforth to apply in practice. Whereas Lohse saw no reason to change the guidelines in this respect, the commandos of Einsatzgruppe A did not consider it necessary to adhere to the civil administration's stipulations.

Lohse's difficulties were to start in Šiauliai (Schaulen). It was there that, on 8 September 1941, a Lithuanian captain by the name of Senulis appeared at the office of County Commissar Hans Gewecke and complained that he was unable to impound the gold and silver objects owned by Jews as the commander of Einsatzkommando 3 had ordered him to do on behalf of the Security Police. The mayors of two villages, acting on orders from the county commissar, had refused to let him. Gewecke promptly took away Senulis's confiscation permit and forbade him to take any additional action. Going through direct channels, Gewecke that same day informed the Reich commissar of this incident, writing: "This incident clearly proves that [SS] Colonel Jäger is flouting the instructions issued by the Reich commissar and county commissar on the registration of Jewish assets and is attending to things that do not concern him. If these infringements on the part of the SS do not finally stop, then I, as county commissar, will have to refuse to take responsibility for the orderly registration of Jewish assets. In addition, at every opportunity that presents itself, I will instruct the district heads and mayors in the strictest of terms not to accept instructions from any office other than the Reich commissar, the general commissar, and the county commissar."[5] Just three days later, Gewecke repeated his complaint in a second message when Joachim Hamann showed up in Šiauliai with his *Rollkommando* and demanded that the Jews there be turned over for shooting without any consideration for the deployment of labor. Gewecke remained steadfast here as well. But in these two letters to Lohse, he had reminded all concerned that a fundamental solution of the question of who was to impound, register, and utilize Jewish assets existed not only on paper, but in practice.[6]

On 20 September, Hugo Wittrock, the county commissar for Riga City, visited Hans Christian Hingst, his counterpart in Vilnius (Wilna, Wilno), where he learned that not only had the SS and police leaders shipped five transports with diverse furnishings to Kaunas, but SS Brigadier General Lucian Wysocki, the SS and police leader for Lithuania, had also confiscated a bank building that the civil administration had foreseen as the site of its branch of the Reich Credit Bank. Nobody from the SS and police would introduce himself, Hingst complained; he didn't even know who the chief of his police command was.[7] In Kaunas, the seat of the general commissar in Lithuania, the SS and police were also confiscating valuables without any consideration of the guidelines. As early as 15 August, the accounts of that town's Jewish citizens were requisitioned; a short time thereafter, a sum of 2,528,513 rubles was withdrawn. On 2 September, payouts followed in the amount of 1,240,667 rubles for the objects of value deposited there. Altogether, this corresponded to RM 376,918 or US $150,767 (1941 dollars).[8]

Such heated disputes on the ground – which can be augmented with regard to Latvia only by some general remarks from General Commissar Otto Drechsler to the effect that his county commissars repeatedly had difficulties with the "command of the German Security Service" – put Reich Commissar Lohse in a tight spot.[9] After apparently meeting with HSSPF Prützmann, Lohse wrote a formal letter of complaint insisting not only on his jurisdiction over Jewish assets but also on his sovereignty of disposal over the assets already impounded by the police, retroactive to the date when civil administration was introduced. He was the trustee responsible to the Reich for the utilization of assets that had already been confiscated, and he demanded that the HSSPF ask the police offices under his command to deliver such valuables to the county commissars.[10] The civil administration's difficulties with the SS and police regarding Jewish assets can be seen in the context of the principle dispute at the level of the Reichsführer-SS and the Reich minister for the occupied eastern territories. It may have been impossible for Rosenberg to prevent or reverse Wehrmacht confiscations, because these represented a sovereign act of the German Reich, but immediately after the attack on the Soviet Union, the SS and the police had also begun appropriating enterprises on a grand scale for their own logistical purposes. These were augmented by additional measures approved by Hitler, because they were linked to the establishment of SS and police bases in the expanses of the east. Himmler, as Reich commissar for the strengthening of Germandom, had been able to expand his authority to the civil-administered occupied territories as well.[11]

But even if it generally looked impossible for the civil administration to regain the initiative, Lohse knew that patterns of justification such as settlement planning and Waffen-SS logistics could not be applied indefinitely where Jewish assets were concerned. It was therefore a shrewd move – at least in the case of Riga, as major encroachments had not yet been reported there – for the Reich commissar to act preemptively. On 24 October 1941, one day before the Riga ghetto was to be sealed, a detailed "Order on the Handling of Jewish Assets in the RKO" dated 13 October was published in Lohse's gazetteer.[12] Not only were all of the principles in the original guidelines to be found there again, but the definition of Jewish assets now included real estate. The dating served to legitimize the compulsory reporting of Jewish assets published by the county commissar Riga City in the newspaper *Deutsche Zeitung im Ostland* on 14 October; there was no talk of movable property in this measure either, only property in general. Furthermore, in cases of doubt, "ownerless assets" were considered "Jewish assets." Nobody was excluded from this obligation. Reporting forms were handed out alphabetically between 15 and 22 October and collected between 23 and 30 October, but at first, only the Jews were required to report.[13]

Wittrock, the county commissar for Riga City and commissarial mayor, was forced to note very quickly during the establishment phase of the ghetto that the administrative guidelines, with their almost passing reference to supervisory duties, could be only rudimentary. In a big city such as Riga, the work involved in installing a ghetto did not just happen on its own. Although there was also a German expert offering his expertise, Josef Hämmerle of the Municipal Ghetto Administration in Łódź (Litzmannstadt) seemed to those responsible in Riga a commerce-minded, mid-level bureaucrat who was more likely to solidify ghetto structures than to bring about their quick demise.[14] Wittrock therefore decided to appoint his own commissioner for ghetto administration, who was to oversee in particular the organization of the forced move, the reporting of assets, and other measures affecting the city. Together with the Latvian communal authorities, which were still functioning on a provisional basis in autumn 1941, this commissioner was to resolve any emerging questions in the spirit of the top German authorities.[15] Between 17 September 1941 and 12 September 1942, Friedrich Brasch was to look after this task.[16] As there was plenty of coordinating to be done, Brasch flanked himself with Gerhard Schultz in October and Edgar Juditzky in December 1941.[17]

On 8 September, deputy city elder Pavils Dreijmanis reported to Wittrock to ask how the "Aryan" owners of buildings located inside the ghetto were to be compensated. These real estate properties, which had not been nationalized during the Sovietization of the country, were still in private hands, and many of the owners lived in their own buildings. The situation was unclear for the Latvian owners, said Dreijmanis, because it was uncertain "whether the Jews quartered there would pay rent, and who would run the buildings and bear responsibility for them."[18] But before General Commissar Drechsler would make a decision about the amount of compensation or the provision of substitute housing, he sought first to determine the number of buildings affected and to have recommendations submitted.[19] In October, it was clear that there were 203 private, developed properties, which in theory could have been compensated through a real estate swap involving the 320 previously Jewish-owned properties located outside of the ghetto. Financial compensation was considered out of the question, and as a precondition for swaps, the property relations of all private properties in the ghetto area had to be legally clarified.[20] This, however, raised the question of how to treat property nationalized by the Soviet Union. As a result, a decision on this matter was postponed.[21]

By the end of November 1941, 13,652 individual reports on Jewish assets had been counted, which, come Monday, 1 December – the day after the first mass shooting at Rumbula – would provide orientation in confiscating and securing assets in the ghetto.[22] It seemed that in the case of the Latvian capital (as opposed to Lithuania) the securing and impounding of Jewish assets would take place without any major problems. But all of the advance organization was in vain. On 28 November, Governing Mayor Wittrock, his chief of staff Werner Altemeyer, the ghetto supervisor Brasch, and Mayor Hans Windgassen learned that a large-scale operation against the Latvian Jews would take place. A day later, Wittrock informed Drechsler in writing that he would have to refuse any responsibility for the proper registration of Jewish assets. It was only possible for him to confiscate the Jewish Council's cash holdings on 28 November.[23]

Wittrock was furious with the arbitrary course of action taken by Friedrich Jeckeln, Prützmann's replacement as HSSPF Ostland. The county commissar had counted on carrying out the lion's share of the state-sponsored theft of Riga's Jews in accordance with his superiors' instructions and without being deceived by the SS and police. The governing mayor, who also had to learn from Brasch that the SS had laid claim to all objects of value in the ghetto, set out to cover himself from all sides. Because Lohse and Drechsler were not in Riga, Wittrock pressed the head of the Finance Department within General Commissariat Latvia not only to accept his refusal to take responsibility for Jewish assets, but to report the incident to the Reich commissar as well. At the same time, he forbid Brasch to release any objects and instead requested that these be collected in special rooms within the ghetto and sealed. Only when the general commissar ordered that they be unsealed, Wittrock noted, could the issue be examined further. Administrative Counselor Willy Neuendorff, the finance expert with the general commissariat, tried to clarify the situation.[24] Shortly thereafter, Ministerial Director Theodor Fründt of the RKO issued Neuendorff and Wittrock a complete discharge of liability regarding the securing of assets.[25] During these hectic hours, officials at the county commissar's office failed to give much notice to two visitors who introduced themselves as representatives of the RKO's Trust Administration Department and claimed they had been authorized to assume the administration of Jewish assets. They were simply referred to Neuendorff; the county commissariat believed that it had its discharge of liability.[26]

But the county commissar did not get rid of this responsibility so easily. Fründt had Wittrock informed a day later:

To the extent that the SS was involved in securing a part of the Jewish assets under the de facto conditions occasioned by the resettlement of the Jews, this merely concerns the SS having secured the assets, but without the SS having these objects at its disposal. *Herr Reichskommissar* wishes that the implementation of his previously issued orders regarding the handling of Jewish assets continues to take place in the manner to date. *Herr Reichskommissar* personally reserves for himself the decision regarding the future action and will make it after his return to Riga. Accordingly, the discharge of liability issued by Ministerial Director Fründt on 29 November 1941, makes reference only to the fact that the SS has secured certain assets. For the rest, however, the further registration and securing of Jewish assets is to take place through you. I therefore ask that the securing of assets is tackled immediately. As soon as other orders from *Herr Reichskommissar* have been issued, I will apprise you of them immediately.[27]

The SS and police could not have cared less about these conflicts over authority. They began shipping Jewish objects of value to one of Riga's large market halls in the slipstream, so to speak, created by the second large-scale mass murder operation.[28] One of Brasch's colleagues reported this immediately, but he could not confirm whether the county commissar's seal had been removed from the ghetto storehouses. In the meantime, Lohse had reported from Berlin and decreed that he would personally order any further course of action after his return. Mayor Windgassen now went to see Deputy General Commissar Egon Bönner, had a presentation given on conditions in the ghetto, and again refused to take any further responsibility for confiscating Jewish property. To his astonishment, Windgassen learned that Drechsler was personally of the opinion that, on the basis of an agreement between Lohse and Jeckeln, the SS was quite rightly entitled to have at its disposal the assets in the ghetto. Within the leadership of County Commissariat Riga City, it was now generally agreed: nobody wanted to have anything to do with the assets in the ghetto. Fründt's admonition was thus implicitly rejected. The two visitors from the RKO Trust Administration Department – SA Lieutenant Colonel Hermann Köster and a certain Hermann – were briefly discussed, but it was decided to wait on transfer negotiations until Lohse was back from Berlin. The Reich commissar personally wanted to reserve for himself the point in time of the transfer, at any rate that was the latest information from Fründt.[29]

After that, Brasch and his colleague Schultz received strict instructions to evict Köster and Hermann from the ghetto immediately should they attempt to remove objects of value without authorization. Confronted with a situation where his two superiors – Reich Commissar Lohse and General Commissar Drechsler – apparently believed that the assets had been awarded to the SS and the RKO trust administration, Windgassen tried in vain to receive a full discharge of liability from Fründt: "Ministerial Director Fründt replied that, nonetheless, the county commissar was still responsible for the registration of the Jewish assets."[30] In the middle of this fully deadlocked situation, the first German Jews arrived in Riga. County Commissar Riga City Wittrock did not know that Riga had been designated as a final destination for deported Jews. He learned of this only in talks with Lange on the evening of 10 December, when the first four transports had already been accommodated in the Jungfernhof camp and the Jews from Cologne had already arrived in the ghetto. Making reference to the fact that it was still unclear who was in charge of securing and registering Jewish assets, Wittrock tried without success to "prohibit the Security Police from accepting new Jews into the ghetto." Because Lange argued that everything was taking place according to an agreement and also referred to an unpublished decree stating that the HSSPF was the Reich commissar's representative during his absence anyway, Wittrock could do nothing more than give Lange his dissenting opinion in writing and have its receipt personally confirmed.[31]

In County Commissariat Riga City, an administrative nightmare was growing out of the task of ghetto administration. Whereas Wittrock's immediate superior, General Commissar Drechsler, had apparently been informed of the coming deportations since autumn and believed the power of disposal over the assets lay with the SS and police after the mass-murder operations, the regional commander of the Security Police, SS Major Lange, was acting on the basis of an unknown decree that shifted responsibility to the SS and police. At the office of the RKO, on the other hand, the only information to be had was that the county commissariat, despite all of the contradictions on the ground, was still responsible for the Jewish assets so that these could be transferred at some point to the RKO's Trust Administration Department on Lohse's orders. Wittrock now tried – this time with success – at least to have the city's present expenses determined so that this amount could be transferred to the city budget.[32]

This dispute reached its zenith on 18 December, when Köster and Hermann appeared in the ghetto and Brasch behaved precisely as he had been instructed:

> On 18 December 1941, during my inspection of the Riga ghetto, which is subordinated to me, I noticed that several gentlemen, who introduced themselves as representatives of the trust administration, were carrying off by truck furniture and carpets from the already evacuated part of the ghetto without any kind of written permission. Upon my inquiries, the gentlemen explained that they had been commissioned by SA Lieutenant Colonel Koester to carry off furniture, and that SA Lieutenant Colonel Koester had taken over the entire ghetto. I know nothing about a takeover of the ghetto, which is subordinated to me, by any other

person. The removal of things from the ghetto therefore lacks any kind of legal basis. However, in order to avoid any kind of acrimonious dispute, I proposed to the gentlemen that they submit an application retroactively and promised to grant my approval for the things already carried off. Furthermore, I asked the gentlemen in a quiet tone to leave the ghetto, because they did not have permission to enter. The ghetto, which is run by me, then ran its normal course until around 1 P.M. when a passenger car again passed the gate and the guards without permission. The gentleman who got out of the car introduced himself as [SA] Lieutenant Colonel Koester and asked me what kind of function I have here. I answered that for three months I had been the commissioner of the County Commissar Riga City for the regulation of questions concerning the ghetto, and I was not allowed to let anybody in. With that, I asked him to show some documentation and explained in addition that, after consultation with Chief of Staff Altemeyer, I was not allowed to release any items without orders from my superior. With that, Dr. Koester produced two letters: the first stating that he was assigned to take over the Jewish estate, the second from the Higher SS and Police Leader in which it was said that the police was to provide him (Dr. Koester) assistance. I cannot remember who the issuer of the first letter was. With that, I explained that I was allowed to act only according to instructions from my superior and recommended he contact my superior by phone or come with me to Governing Mayor Wittrock's for the purpose of clarifying the matter. Without going into to my recommendation at all, Dr. Koester, in a very incensed form and without consideration of my official position and uniform, subsequently ordered the German policemen on hand, in the presence of a Latvian police officer, to remove me from the ghetto in the quickest way possible.[33]

That was too much. From then on, Wittrock refused to accept any responsibility regarding the administration of the Riga ghetto. When the incident with Labor Office employee Edgar Dralle in January showed that even the orderly placement of workers would be subject to dispute, Wittrock requested a clarifying meeting with the general commissar. His goal was, with Drechsler's express consent, not to be forced to have anything to do with the ghetto. During a meeting on 13 January 1942, the governing mayor received this general discharge of liability from Drechsler – several times over even – but with one exception: the Labor Office's Bureau for the Deployment of Jews was not a function of the ghetto administration but of the labor deployment administration, because the work of the latter concerned all ethnic groups.[34] From that point on, the county commissar would have to deal with the ghetto only in individual cases, for example, when the city housing office, confronted with a tremendous need for residential space, inquired whether it was possible to take over from the RKO Trust Administration Department those buildings no longer needed within the ghetto.[35]

Conversely, Wittrock now simply forwarded to the general commissar all petitions for lost rent-related revenue filed by Latvians owning private buildings in the ghetto.[36] General Commissariat Latvia's Trust Administration Department, which had been set up in the meantime, tried unsuccessfully to stop such payments.[37] However, it was possible to reach an agreement on those buildings that lay in the evacuated and uninhabited part of the ghetto and were to be phased out. The city took control over all Jewish, ownerless, and nationalized buildings, while individual owners were to get their property back after the damage had been assessed.[38]

Until 20 April 1942, administration of the ghetto was the responsibility of the RKO's Trust Administration Department, which had selected an employee by the name of Bruns for this task. During this period, the RKO's Health and Care of the People Department made a decision that was very convenient for Köster and Bruns. After an inspection of the ghetto premises, health officials decided to quarantine the ghetto for unauthorized persons starting 6 February due to the risk of epidemics. The removal of furniture or goods of any kind was also prohibited. Only now, wrote Köster, could one concentrate – "bring order to the confusion" – because the offices of the Army and SS had been forced to clear the field.[39] "This closing was extended indefinitely on 20 February 1942, and the undersigned was granted right of disposal within the ghetto. Only from this point in time is it possible to speak of a certain responsibility on the part of the management in the ghetto. For a start, a premium was now put on creating order. The accumulating economic objects and furniture were collected and sorted in four large storehouses."[40]

Until mid March, sales of woven material to the company Ostland-Faser, bedsprings to a Latvian business, and metals were arranged, for which it was not possible to give a specific amount. The Security Police returned watches and objects of value from the shooting operations, and large amounts of white goods and linens were offered to the Wehrmacht and civil authorities. Wholesale operations got underway.[41]

On 20 April, however, the RKO delegated the "administration of the ghetto located in Riga, including Jewish personal property," to Drechsler's recently established Trust Administration Department, to which Bruns had also been assigned.[42] But this ceded to the regional authorities only the responsibility for a certain area within Riga; the comprehensive registration of Jewish furniture outside of the ghetto, for example, remained a matter for Lohse, who used it to supply his "administrative officer corps."[43] The sale of Jewish everyday items by the city and county commissars from their storehouses had to be approved by the RKO's Trust Administration Department, which then received the proceeds.[44] If "Jewish and ownerless gold, silver, and sundry objects of value" were found, then these had to be consigned via the county commissar to the depot of the Reich Credit Bank in Riga, where it would be at the disposal of the RKO's Trust Administration

Department, which at certain intervals sent such valuables to the Central Office for the Utilization of Precious Metals within the Municipal Pawn Office Berlin.[45] The German and indigenous communal administrative authorities became the executive organs of the Trust Administration Department outside the ghetto terrain.[46] With regard to nationalized Latvian and Jewish properties outside of the ghetto, a company, Grundstücksgesellschaft Lettland GmbH, was founded as the central housing administration. It also took over all those real estate objects that had previously been requisitioned by either the municipal housing office or the indigenous housing exploitation directorate.[47]

The administrative branch had hardly tackled this shuffling of responsibilities when Lohse decreed on 6 July 1942 that in the future the entire administration and utilization of movable, noncommercial Jewish, ownerless, and subversive-owned assets would no longer be handled by the trust administrations, but by his own Finance Department and those of the general commissars.[48] For the trust administration, this meant a reduction of its tasks to real estate and the temporary economic management of commercial enterprises in the general commissariat. From that point on, the head of the RKO's Finance Department, Dr. Friedrich Vialon, was to try to gain an overview of levies and sales of movable Jewish assets.[49] In this case as well, individuals working in the general commissar's trust administration were to move to its Finance Department. And once again, Bruns was caught up in the shuffle.[50]

There were two occasions in particular that made this administrative swap in Riga relevant for the ghetto. At the start of July 1942, the master carpenter Platon Sidoroff complained to the general commissar that although he was the owner of a building within the ghetto that had not been nationalized and had left his apartment and workshop without protest, the housing administration was now demanding rent from him for a small apartment in the city and threatening eviction if he refused to pay. "Payment from the Jews' income," wrote the clerk Riegel in the margins of the complaint; he could not know that only a short time later these receipts were to be withdrawn from the county commissar's power of disposal and assigned to Drechsler's Finance Department.[51] However, this money, along with all other movable Jewish objects of value, was to go directly to *Reichsmarschall* Hermann Göring, who intended to use it "for a special purpose." As of 1 July, revenue from the deployment of the Latvian Jews for forced labor amounted total of RM 928,466.58 (US $370,000 in 1941 dollars), after the city's expenses – some RM 18,000 – had been deducted. Of this, the general commissar's Finance Department diverted an initial RM 800,000 and let the county commissar know that the only other expenses that were to be subtracted were those that "arise in direct connection with the deployment of the Jews for work."⁵² By no means did this include paying rent for Latvian building owners.

The second occasion resulted from the city's constant shortage of residential space. After considerable parts of the uninhabited section of the ghetto had been returned to the city and building owners, the question arose in summer 1942 whether additional buildings on the edge of the terrain could be evacuated to the same end. Both problems had one thing in common: an appropriate administrative contact person for a solution did not exist. It was completely unclear who was authorized to pay rent on behalf of a Latvian and with which money, and who was responsible for determining which buildings in the ghetto could be phased out most easily.⁵³

When leading representatives of General Commissariat Latvia, its county commissariats, and the housing administration met on 17 August, they concluded unsurprisingly "that a general ghetto administration does not exist at all." Drechsler's representative concluded that, as a first step, a position had to be created that "occupies itself fully with the administration of the ghetto and provides the basis for a new and exclusive ghetto administration."⁵⁴ But before they could meet again to discuss a first set of recommendations on creating such an administrative office, Vialon reacted by issuing unified administrative guidelines for all of the RKO's ghettos. Quite apparently, other ghettos were also being administered differently, quasi impromptu, with the theft of assets and the deployment of forced laborers front and center. In an incomplete list, Vialon mentioned Riga, Kaunas, Vilnius, and Minsk. Vialon's "Guidelines re. the administration of Jewish ghettos" of 27 August 1942 are to be seen in the context of the disputes in Riga. When the communal and regional authorities discovered a need for action, Vialon seized the initiative in order to assert his own interests by means of basic stipulations. A full year after the RKO had decreed its first rudimentary compulsory supervision of the internal Jewish ghetto administration, there now followed a second, considerably more comprehensive set of administrative guidelines.⁵⁵

Although Vialon knew that the issues of ghetto administration and financial responsibility for the sealed Jewish districts had yet to be resolved, he stressed in the introduction to his guidelines that even though the general commissars would have to adhere to the following stipulations, "[n]ot all of the details of the guidelines will be made binding, because local conditions are simply too different."⁵⁶ Vialon then separated the two most important administrative questions. A distinction was to be made between the administration of the ghetto and the administration of the assets within the ghettos. The establishment of ghettos, wrote the future state secretary for West Germany's Federal Ministry for Economic Cooperation, falls within the realm of responsibility of the RKO's Political Affairs Department. Administration included particular measures to maintain Jewish workers and protect the structure of ghetto buildings. Security-related matters of supervision were the task of the SS and police. In the cities, administration was as a rule to be conferred on the city commissar, who had to recognize it as a sovereign function. However, Vialon also noted that he had nothing against the general commissar directly running the administration, as was the case in the Latvian capital. In terms of technical budgetary matters, administration of a ghetto was an assignment whose financial costs had to be borne by the RKO. After the city and county commissars submitted preliminary estimates, they would have to operate within the means allocated to them. However, these financial means from the RKO budget would also have to be used to settle third-party demands arising from the founding of the ghetto – such as the loss of rental payments (after deducting administrative fees and maintenance costs for non–Jewish-owned real estate used in the ghetto). After privately owned buildings had been phased out of the ghetto, damage incurred during the period of use would also have to be paid from the county commissar's financial means, though only after an estimate based on the strictest of standards. Vialon recommended placing financial supervision of the ghettos with the general commissars' finance departments, which in the case of Riga had in fact already happened. Real estate within the ghetto was no longer to be administered by the trust or the various housing administrations, but by the county commissars' ghetto administration.

In Vialon's guidelines, Jewish furnishings and above all Jewish workers were designated as assets accrued. The administration of movable assets on site was subordinated to the finance departments of the general commissars, who would preferably give up this branch of activity to their subordinate county and city commissars and merely watch over the regularity of communications. Furniture of interest was to be offered to local entities at full price. The setting up of special accounts to receive payments was prohibited; money was to be paid directly to the accounts of the RKO Finance Department at the official cashier desks. Secured goods made of silver or gold were to be made available to the RKO's Finance Department by having them sent to the Reich Credit Bank. Textiles and woven materials were, in the event of a lack of interest, to be offered to the entity Ostland-Faser GmbH.

According to Vialon, "assets accruing from the exploitation of Jewish workers" would be received in two different ways: through the placement of workers with public or private employers at standard wages set by the general commissars, and through the activity of the general commissars' own workshops. Placement of workers was to be carried out by the local Labor Office, as had already been the case for months in Riga; the presentation of invoices was to be handled by the ghetto administration – in the case of Riga, the general commissar. Regarding the workshops run by ghetto administrations, it was determined: "The ghetto administration will review whether and which workshops inside or outside the ghetto can be organized as public enterprises. Tailor, shoemaker, carpenter, locksmith, electrical installation and sundry workshops are to be considered. First and foremost, they have to cover Wehrmacht orders, second the needs of German offices and Reich Germans. The proceeds flow into the budget of the Reich Commissar just like [those] for the leasing of Jews to private companies. Already existing workshops are to be turned over to the ghetto administration unaltered."[57]

To this day, researchers know far too little about the administration of the ghettos in Liepāja (Libau), Daugavpils (Dünaburg), Šiauliai, Kaunas, Vilnius, Minsk, Slutsk, Kletsk, and other, mostly Belarusian, ghettos in Ostland. Vialon's suggestions were oriented rather precisely to conditions in Riga, because this of course was where his office was located. However, there were to be problems. Even before General Commissariat Latvia assumed control of Riga, the Wehrmacht's economics commando had, on 21 July 1941, commissioned the Latvian supervisory authority for production cooperatives to take over all privately owned Jewish crafts and small industrial enterprises. These commercial enterprises were in reality small workshops that operated with one or two employees at most. In other words, there were fewer enterprises to oversee than small workshops to be registered for their machines (sewing, knitting, looms) and tools and cleared out. However, the SS and police, the Wehrmacht, and Organization Todt had already removed and redeployed individual production machines before this order was issued.

On 9 September 1941, the Takeover Commission for Artels, which was run by Latvians working in the spirit of German interests, received permission to sell individual units from the machine park to interested local parties. In some cases, workshops were even given back to Jewish owners if the military authorities expressly wished this.[58] In the months that followed, the Takeover Commission for Artels registered 1,062 Jewish enterprises and liquidated 903 of them. The remaining 159 were either taken over by the Wehrmacht (67), given back to their Jewish owners (5), or, upon request, turned over to other authorities, primarily the trust administration (16). Twelve workshops were prematurely registered as Jewish enterprises and had to be reinstated to their Latvian owners. In 21 cases, the enterprises were found to have no value; in 3 instances, the workshops had apparently been robbed. The final 35 workshops missing from the above list were located in the ghetto, either because they were already there, or because the Jews took them along when they moved there.[59] At the request of the general commissar, these workshops were up and running in November 1941 on behalf of the Wehrmacht in order to reduce the number of Jews employed outside the ghetto. The Wehrmacht, for its part, provided articles of clothing and equipment to the ghetto and guaranteed the supply of raw materials.[60] In the course of May 1942, on orders from Ghetto Commandant Kurt Krause, the ghetto workshops were centralized at Ludzas St. 66, where clothing for Army Group North was produced on behalf of the company Ostland-Faser GmbH. At the same time, Krause also had ghetto workshops set up for the SD.[61] In addition, there were also the general commissar's workshops, which had been established by the county commissar before January 1942 and were responsible for maintaining ghetto buildings and providing clothing for the Jews.[62]

The Riga ghetto thus had three kinds of enterprises that were ultimately under two types of workshop supervision – that of the Security Police and that of the general commissar, with the latter running a large carpenter's workshop with an upholstery section, a tailor's shop with about 100 machines, a metalworker's shop, a shoemaker's workshop, and a watch shop, none of which operated for the needs of the ghetto.[63] At the start of December 1942, all of these enterprises taken together employed 1,185 Jews, including 95 craftsmen and 48 camp workers for the general commissar.[64] It is therefore interesting to see that Vialon's instructions to subordinate all of the ghetto workshops to the general commissar's ghetto administration were apparently ignored, for the majority of the Jewish workers continued to toil in SD workshops.[65]

Another important order from Vialon's guidelines for the administration of the ghetto also remained without consequence. Vialon had specified that the assets accrued through the work performed by the ghettoized Jews were a matter of the civil asset administration and involved no participation on the part of the Security Police. But the Security Police had always presumed its own right of disposal over the deported Jews and had allowed the civil authorities to deploy these Jews – subject to recall.[66] This meant that although the Labor Office placed deported Jews, the Security Police submitted the invoices and paid for the Jews' provisioning with the revenue received. On 1 June 1942, the office of the Regional Commander of the Security Police Latvia (KdS Latvia) even drew up a handout for employers that referred them to the new wages and the possibility, now in effect, of transferring remuneration on a monthly instead of weekly basis – interestingly enough, to the account of the Salaspils camp.[67] The division of the ghetto into two districts corresponded to the conventions of financial settlement for work performed; the Latvian Jews were subordinated to the civil administration, the deported Jews, to the Security Police. When the RKO Trust Administration Department paid for having the deported Jews clear out the empty part of the ghetto, the money, a far too low remuneration of RM 1,000, was paid to Krause's command by check – and only after some months.[68] Vialon's guidelines thus remained without consequence.

On 13 October, the adversaries met on the premises of the RKO's office: SS Captain Walter Jagusch and Administrative Assessor Schneider, on one side, and Ministerial Counselor Wilhelm Burmeister (acting on behalf of Lohse) and Friedrich Vialon, on the other. Jagusch went straight to the point: on the basis of a decree from Hitler, a decree unknown to the civil administration, the Security Police was in charge of "all legislative measures that are related to Jewish affairs, including asset affairs."[69] He was not interested in responsibility for the registration, administration, and utilization of Jewish assets; he was merely insisting on legislative initiative for the Security Police. The Security Police would also turn over utilization of the deported Jews as workers to the civil administration as long as they "were not held in the SD's own camps as political prisoners." But without recognition of overall control, nothing would happen. Burmeister promised to report to the minister for the eastern occupied territories.[70]

The dualism in invoicing and workshops was to change only months later. First Lohse once again announced, in a decree of 25 January 1943, that all confiscated Jewish assets were to be considered impounded. Then he distributed authority, as described previously, to the Trust Administration Department and the Finance Department.[71] A breakthrough for the civil administration was achieved when new arrangements were negotiated at a meeting of SS First Lieutenant Heyer and SS Second Lieutenant Kurt Migge as well as Administrative Counselor Willy Neuendorff and Senior Tax Inspector Bromm, which finally determined the transfer of all enterprises and financial responsibility for invoicing procedures for all working Jews to the general commissar's Finance Department.

During this round of negotiations on 8 April, Heyer and Migge accepted that the SD would deliver not only all revenues from Jewish work to date but also any additional proceeds from the utilization of Jewish property and confiscated money as well as all of the wages for German Jews that were to arrive for the previous month. The Security Police would be allowed to issue invoices to employers for the last time in March 1943 before the "card catalog of employers kept in the Wages Bureau of the SD will be transferred to the Wages Bureau of the Finance Department of the general commissar for analysis." Then, starting 1 April 1943, all invoicing was to be handled by the general commissariat alone. "The clothing stores set up by the SD for the Jews' clothing will be transferred to the general commissar's Finance Department ... The workshops run by the SD in the ghetto, along with the material, machines, tools as well as all orders, will be passed on to the general commissar's Finance Department. At the same time, the bookkeeping for the workshops' income and expenditures will be passed on to the Finance Department. The receipts for expenditures for the previous period remain with the SD."[72]

County Commissar Wittrock was again the first to feel the effects of the Security Police's sudden readiness to accommodate the civil administration in the wage and workshop questions. Just before Vialon's guidelines were decreed in August 1942, Wittrock's and Drechsler's offices had agreed to work out recommendations for a future ghetto administration run by the county commissar on behalf of the general commissar – which also took place. And when they met again on 29 August 1942, it was clear that overall control of the Riga ghetto's administration would lie in the hands of the general commissar's Main Department II (Political Affairs). The concrete handling of the ghetto-related issues would lie with Wittrock, who, according to the recommendations, would have to set up four desks to this end. Once the head of the general commissariat's Trust Administration Department had received confirmation from the RKO that his department was no longer responsible for ghetto real estate, and once it had been determined that this administrative plan was conform with Vialon's guidelines, nothing had happened at first.[73]

But now, in April 1943, the foreseen commissioning of the County Commissariat Riga City was recalled, and Wittrock was entrusted with feeding the entire ghetto population and seeing to the merger of workshops working solely for the ghetto's needs.[74] On 3 May, everything was ready. After almost a year and a half, the unloved task of ghetto administration was again one of Governing Mayor Wittrock's assignments: "I herewith transfer to you the administration of the Riga ghetto. Until December 1941, the administration of the ghetto was already among your assignments. With my consent, you then gave up this [task] for well-known reasons, which are not to be addressed again in detail here. In fact, however, you subsequently continued to administer the ghetto to this day. The present, explicit recommissioning therefore has to the greatest possible extent only formal significance and gives you the legal basis for your activity in this regard."[75]

The silence regarding Vialon's ghetto guidelines and the administration plans based on them up until spring 1943 can be explained with regard to Riga only by the fact that the Security Police was unwilling to give up its workshops and invoicing authority over deported Jews without a quid pro quo. In the files, however, it is not possible to find any written objections after the 13 October 1942 meeting between Burmeister, Vialon, Schneider, and Jagusch; only additional research into the other effects of Vialon's guidelines in the general commissariats of Lithuanian and White Ruthenia could shed light on this matter. After all, it is worth noting that these guidelines were forwarded to the county commissariats of General Commissariat White Ruthenia only in March 1943.[76]

There is no evidence to suggest that the regional commanders of the Security Police had received orders from the office of the Territorial Commander of the Security Police and Security Service Ostland or HSSPF Ostland to act in a dilatory manner. It seems fairly certain, however, that the KdS Latvia only gave up its position once it was known what further steps from on high would look like. Prior to Himmler's order of 21 June 1943 on the creation of concentration camps in the domain of HSSPF Ostland, Heinrich Müller, the head of RSHA Department IV (Gestapo), had informed all of the territorial and regional commanders of the Security Police as well as the HSSPFs that, with "the consent of the Reichsführer-SS and the Chief of the German Police," a Concentration Camp Riga was to be established effective 13 March.[77] If the civil administration was not going to accept the Security Police's overall control over the Jews, then the Jews were to be transferred to an area of jurisdiction that was within the scope of SS authority. This was almost certainly discussed in advance at a meeting between Himmler with Deputy Reich Commissar Ostland and SA Major General Günther Pröhl, HSSPF Ostland Friedrich Jeckeln, and Wehrmacht Territorial Commander Ostland Walter Braemer on 13 March 1943.[78]

Notes

1. LVVA, P 1026-1-3, 283, 310–315, Anschreiben, RKO, Abtl. IIa 4, an den HSSPF in Riga, betr. Entwurf der vorläufigen Richtlinien für die Behandlung der Juden im Gebiet des Reichskommissariats Ostland, gez. Fründt, 2 August 1941, also printed in Benz et al., *Einsatz im "Reichskommissariat Ostland,"* doc. no. 11, 38–43.
2. YIVO, Occ. E 3-17-46, Entwurf, Trampedach an den RmbO, betr. ausländische Juden, 6 August 1941. This document includes Lohse's paraph.
3. LVVA, P 69-1a-6, 67–70, 68, Der RKO, IIa 4, gez. Lohse, 18 August 1941. On 13 August 1941, the Preliminary Guidelines were sent to the Reich Ministry for the Occupied Eastern Territories (RmbO) as a matter of notification, see Nuremburg Document PS-1138, in *IMG*, Bd. 27, 18–25. See also Safrian, *Die Eichmann-Männer*, 143.
4. LVVA, P 1026-1-3, 299–300, Fernschreiben, EK 2 Riga an EG A, z. Hd. v. SS-Stubaf. Tschiersky [sic!], betr. Stellungnahme zu den Richtlinien des Reichskommissars für das Ostland zur Regelung der Judenfrage, Batz, Stubaf., 6 August 1941.
5. YIVO, Occ. E 3-30, Abschrift. Der Geb.-Komm. in Schaulen an den RKO, betr. SS-Standartenführer Jäger, gez. Gewecke, 8 September 1941.
6. YIVO, Occ. E 3-30, Abschrift, Der Geb.-Komm. in Schaulen an den RKO, Gauleiter Lohse in Riga, persönlich, 11 September 1941: "If SS Colonel Jäger sends his men through the county to confiscate the Jewish assets, for whose orderly registration and delivery I am responsible as [county commissar], then there no longer exists any guarantee that all of the Jewish assets will in fact be delivered."

   Also, YIVO, Occ. E 3-22, Abschrift an den RKO, Gauleiter Lohse, Riga, betr. SS-Standartenführer Jäger, "Subsequent to my letter of the llth of [this month], I am sending you two certificates and informing you that 7 crates of gold, silver, and valuables were picked up from Ponnewesch [sic] on behalf of [SS] Colonel Jäger. A Lithuanian was deployed as district police chief, who collected and delivered the objects of value on Jäger's behalf. It does not make the best of impressions, if I, [for example], order the assets to be delivered and I am repeatedly informed by the mayors that 'Herr Hamann' was there and took the objects of value. The impression is made by this is that we are not working with, but against one another." By Ponnewesch, Gewecke meant the town of Panevėžys, Ponewiesch in German.

7. LVVA, P 1018-1-69, 3, Vermerk zum Besuch bei Geb.-Komm. Hingst, 20 September 1941. A copy dated 23 September is located at YIVO, Occ. E 3-23.
8. YIVO, Occ. E 3-24, Abschrift, H II/F, 24 September 1941. The course at the time was 10 rubles to 1 reichsmark. One would need roughly U.S. $2.1 million in 2006 dollars to have the same purchasing power as $150,767 in 1941.
9. YIVO, Occ. E 3-37, Der Gen.-Komm. in Riga, Abtl. IIa, an den RKO, Abtl. IIa, betr. Einrichtung von Ghettos, jüdischen Arbeitslagern und Arbeitseinsatz der Juden, Anmelde- und Ablieferungspflicht des jüdischen Vermögens, 20 October 1941: "According to petitions from the county commissars, difficulties exist with the command of the German Security Service in the confiscation of Jewish assets. Before the takeover by the civil administration, large amounts of money and objects made of precious metals were secured by the Security Service. These commandos, however, now refuse to follow the county commissars' orders and release the confiscated cash and objects. An order clarifying whether the police and security organs in the county commissariats have to follow the orders of the county commissars in every respect would be needed from *Herr Reichskommissar*."
10. YIVO, Occ. E 3-25, Der RKO an den HSSPF, persönlich, gez. Lohse, 25 September 1941.
11. On this, see the individual cases in BA Berlin, R 6/9-10 and R 43 II/684a. Efforts to reach an agreement at the highest level during a meeting between Reinhard Heydrich (RSHA), Alfred Meyer (RmbO), Georg Leibbrandt (RmbO), and Gustav Schlotterer (Reich Economics Ministry) on 4 October 1941 as well as talks between Himmler and Rosenberg on 15 November 1941 were to no avail. See Leibbrandt's notes on 4 October in BA Berlin, R 6/9, 24, as well as the notes by Hans Ehlich (RSHA), Nuremburg Document NO-1020; on the 15 November meeting, for Himmler's point of view, see BA Berlin NS 19/3885, 19–21; for Rosenberg's notes, see BA Berlin, R 6/9, 31–35. For a general overview of this issue, see Diemut Majer, "Führerunmittelbare Sondergewalten in den besetzten Ostgebieten," *Verwaltung contra Menschenführung im Staat Hitlers*, ed. Dieter Rebentisch and Karl Teppe, 374–395.
12. BA Berlin, R 92/834, *Verkündungsblatt des RKO*, no. 6, 24 October 1941.
13. BA Berlin, R 91/164, *Deutsche Zeitung im Ostland*, "Anmeldung jüdischen Vermögens," 14 October 1941, excerpt. Also located at BA Berlin, R 91/23.
14. BA Berlin, R 91/10052, Josef Hämmerle an den Oberbürgermeister Wittrock, 14 September 1941. The letter contains the marginalia "no possible use"; Werner Altemeyer's letter of rejection from 16 October 1941 is in the same file.
15. At a meeting between General Commissar Drechsler and his county commissars in Riga on 8 November 1941, it was still not clear whether a German or indigenous administration should be introduced in the long term, see the notes on this meeting in BA Berlin, R 92/198. For more detail on this issue, see Werner Röhr, "System oder organisertes Chaos?" 11–45.
16. The surviving documentation sheds little light on Friedrich Brasch's role as the governing mayor's coordinator, because all of the executive decisions lay with the German authorities involved in the ghettoization process, i.e., the municipal labor office, the apartment

office, the registrar's office, and the legal office. For the most part, he was bound to have reported to Wittrock on the momentary state of affairs and to have received individual assignments from him. Brasch was assigned to the city administration on 28 August 1941, reported to Wittrock on 17 September, and was drafted into the Wehrmacht on 12 September 1942, see BA Ludwigsburg, 207 AR-Z 7/59, Bd. 39, 6,444. In February 1942, the RKO's trust administration assumed that Brasch was in charge of the records containing the reports of Jewish assets as well as the transfer of effects on loan, see BA Berlin, R 90/447, Verfg., III/Treu 6, an den Referenten Braasch [sic!], betr. Jüdisches Vermögen, 24 February 1942.

17. Whereas nothing is known about Gerhard Schultz, the records concerning Juditzky's hiring and dismissal have been preserved. Juditzky was an ethnic-German native of Riga who had joined the National Socialist movement in 1930 after training as an optician. He was invited to attend a Hitler Youth officer course in 1933 in Potsdam and resettled to Włocławek (Leslau), where, starting in April 1940, he had run an optician's shop. Married with two children, he began working as Brasch's subordinate on 1 December 1941, and was paid from the city budget, see BA Berlin, R 91/10054.

18. BA Berlin, R 91/73, Rigaer Stadtverwaltung an den Geb.-Komm. Riga-Stadt, betr. Privathäuser im Ghetto-Rayon, gez. Dreijmanis, 8 September 1941.

19. Ibid., Der Geb.-Komm. an den Gen.-Komm., 18 September 1941, and Der Gen.-Komm. an den Geb.-Komm., 20 September 1941. The latter includes the request that the buildings be counted. Wittrock noted in margin: "Brasch to determine."

20. Ibid., Rigaer Stadtverwaltung an den Geb.-Komm. Riga-Stadt, gez. Dreijmanis, 21 October 1941.

21. At the same time, the question of how to accommodate RmbO employees was becoming acute. The RKO informed his four general commissars that, in their search for suitable "Ostland-owned buildings," they were to pick out properties that had been in Jewish possession for the future trust administration. Only such properties could have been nationalized between 1940 and 1941 without raising the need for the Germans to clarify the principal question of private property, see LVVA, P 69-1a-28, 3–4, Der RKO, Abtl. IIh, an die Gen.-Komm. in Riga, Reval [Tallinn], Kaunas, Minsk, betr. Ostlandeigene Häuser (Beamtenwohnhäuser), gez. Fründt, 20 November 1941.

22. The exact number of the individual reports was only later determined, see BA Berlin, R 91/70, Bürgermeister Windgassen an die Abtl. Politik, 25 August 1942.

23. BA Berlin, R 91/10, 42, Abschrift. [Der Geb.-Komm. Riga-Stadt] an den Gen.-Komm., betr. Beschlagnahme des jüdischen Vermögens, 29 November 1941. The letter listing the itemized sums of money from the Jewish Council – RM 39,178 and 16,622.20 rubles – is in BA Berlin, R 91/70.

24. BA Berlin, R 91/10, 39–41, Aktenvermerk des Geb.-Komm., 3 December 1941.

25. Ibid., 38, Der Gen.-Komm. in Riga, Abtl. IIg, an den Geb.-Komm. Riga-Stadt, betr. Beschlagnahme des jüdischen Vermögens, i.A. Dr. Neuendorff, 3 December 1941.

26. Ibid., 39–41, Aktenvermerk des Geb.-Komm., 3 December 1941. On the trust administration in the occupied eastern territories, see 2. StS. des Beauftragten für den Vierjahresplan Neumann an den RmbO, betr. Einrichtung einer Treuhandverwaltung, 12 September 1941, as well as the notes made on a meeting between Lohse, Erich Neumann, and Ludwig Runte, 25 September 1941, contained in BA Berlin, R 6/31, 15–18.

27. BA Berlin, R 91/10, 36, Der Gen.-Komm. in Riga, Abtl. IIg, an den Geb.-Komm. Riga-Stadt, betr. Beschlagnahme jüdischen Vermögens, 4 December 1941.

28. This early registration of Jewish property was handled by a labor detail of Latvian Jews, who were supervised by Precinct-Lieutenant Albert Hesfehr. After the war, two persons testified that Otto Tuchel and Alberts Danskop in particular used the opportunity to

enrich themselves. Three Jews, among them Tolly Rosenblum, were shot by Tuchel and Danskop, because they had gone to their previous apartments to prevent the removal of personal items, see Staw. Hamburg, 141 Js 534/60, Bd. 37, statement by Israel Leschem, 6 June 1963, 6,087; ibid., Bd. 38, statement by Mosche Deiftz, 19 September 1963, 6,296. Tuchel vehemently denied the allegations, ibid., Bd. 39, statement by Otto Tuchel, 25 September 1963, 6,386.

29. BA Berlin, R 91/10, 32–35, notes for the files by Windgassen from 8 and 9 December, 1941.
30. Ibid., 16, Aktenvermerk des Stabsleiters Altemeyer, [10 December 1941].
31. Ibid., 29–30, note for files by Wittrock concerning meeting with Lange, 11 December 1941, and the confirmation of receipt.
32. BA Berlin, R 91/70, Oberstadtkämmerer Dr. Grempler an den Geb.-Komm. Riga-Stadt, betr. Ausgaben der Stadt Riga in Judenangelegenheiten, 12 December 1941. This letter shows RM 48,000 in expenses, which were transferred almost in full (RM 45,050.25) to the city's account at Latvias Banka, see ibid.
33. BA Berlin. R 91/10, 12–13, Der Referent z.b.V. Friedrich Brasch beim Geb.-Komm. und komm. Oberbürgermeister der Stadt Riga, 18 December 1941.
34. BA Berlin, R 91/74, notes on meeting with General Commissar Drechsler in the presence of his legal counsel Senior Administration Counselor Simm as well as Wittrock's deputy, Mayor Windgassen, 14 December 1942 [sic]. Later, on 5 February 1942, Edgar Juditzky applied in writing to the governing mayor for another position, because the liquidation of the city's ghetto administration on 15 February 1942 would leave him unemployed, see BA Berlin, R 91/10054, letter from E. Juditzky, 5 February 1942. A short time later, he once again took over his optician business in Wartheland, a part of western Poland annexed to the Reich, see ibid.
35. BA Berlin, R 91/10, 3, Der Geb.-Komm., Amt für Wohnungswesen, an den kommissarischen Oberbürgermeister der Stadt Riga, betr. Wohnhäuser im Ghetto, 11 March 1942. Wittrock, as head of the city community in Riga, had already pointed to the prevailing apartment shortage and the state of disrepair of the buildings located in the evacuated part of the ghetto, see BA Berlin, R 90/446, 31, Der Geb.-Komm. Riga-Stadt an den RKO durch den Gen.-Komm. in Riga, betr. Häuser im Ghetto und Wohnraumnot, 27 January 1942.
36. BA Berlin, R 91/74, Abschrift. An den Gen.-Komm. in Riga, betr. Mietentschädigungen der Hausbesitzer des Ghettobezirks, gez. Wittrock, 16 March 1942: "Because the ghetto district is no longer subordinated to me as County Commissar Riga City and I thus bear no responsibility for this part of town, I ask that the appropriate office authorize the payment of rent to the building owners."
37. Ibid., Gesuch Karline Lipperts an den Gen.-Komm. und die Weitergabe durch die Abtl. Treuhand der Hauptabteilung Wirtschaft an den Geb.-Komm., gez. Filter, 15 April 1942, and the refusal by the head of the Municipal Real Estate Office, Freiherr von Mirbach, on 28 April 1942, with reference to the outcome of the meeting between Drechsler and Wittrock on 13 January 1942.
38. BA Berlin, R 91/69, 25, results of meeting between Filter, v. Klot, and v. Mirbach in the Trust Administration Department of the General Commissariat Latvia on 11 April 1942.
39. Due to the risk of epidemics, authorization papers for entering the ghetto were no longer renewed. Even Labor Office employees Walter Lippmann and Arthur Eicker were refused, see their request in BA Berlin R 90/450, Der Geb.-Komm. Riga-Stadt, Arbeitsamt, an die Treuhandverwaltung beim RKO, z.Hd. Herrn Bruns, betr. Ausweise für Ghetto, 2 April 1942. The refusal came in the form of a letter dated 10 April 1942, see ibid.

40. BA Berlin, R 90/447, Vermerk III/Treu 44.1, betr. Bericht über den Stand der Angelegenheiten im Ghetto, 19 March 1942.
41. Ibid., The Security Police had already turned over to Köster the wedding bands collected during the shootings. At the request of the general commissar, some of them were used for the production of dental gold, which the Wehrmacht and officials from the general commissariat made available for dental care, see Gen.-Komm. in Riga, HA Wirtschaft, Referat Metalle, an die Treuhand-Ost Riga, 19 February 1942.
42. BA Berlin, R 92/382, Der RKO, Abtl. III Treu 44.1, an den Gen. Komm. in Riga.
43. BA Berlin, R 92/836, Der RKO, Abtl. I Z-B/Mz., an den Geb.-Komm. Riga-Stadt und komm. Oberbürgermeister, betr. Möbelbeschaffung, 28 April 1942. Additional examples are to be found in this file.
44. Ibid., Der Gen.-Komm. in Riga, Abtl. IIIf Treu, an den Geb.-Komm. Riga-Stadt, betr. Verkauf minderwertigen jüdischen und herrenlosen Mobiliars, i. A. Filter, 28 April 1942.
45. BA Berlin, R 91/2, Gen.-Komm. in Riga, Abtl. III, an den Geb.-Komm. Riga-Stadt, betr. Behandlung von Wertgegenständen aus jüdischem Besitz mit Weiterleitung eines diesbezugl. Schreibens des RKO, gez. Raschke, 30 April 1942. See also BA Berlin, R 92/836, Richtlinien Nr. 3 des RKO über die Behandlung von jüdischen und herrenlosen Gold-, Silber- und sonstigen Wertgegenständen, 15 May 1942.
46. On 15 May 1942, the general commissar's Department III (Trust Administration) decreed that the county commissars not only had to maintain a new account to be opened at the Reich Credit Bank in the name of the "Trust Administration with the General Commissar," they were also to render accounts for the utilization of movable Jewish assets, including cash receipts and the names of beneficiaries, see BA Berlin, R 92/836, Gen.-Komm., Abtl. IIIf Treu, an die Geb.-Komm., betr. die Erfassung des beweglichen jüdischen Vermögens, Anordunung des Reichskommissars über die Behandlung jüdischen Vermögens vom 13.10.1941, i.A. Filter, 15 May 1942. Shortly thereafter, the general commissar once again reminded officials in particular: "The desk officer in my department, Mr. Bruns, remains responsible for ghetto assets in Riga as before." See BA Berlin, R 92/836, Der Gen.-Komm. III Treu, an die Geb.-Komm., 4 June 1942. However, these holdings were ultimately offered the Reich Credit Bank in Riga, see BA Berlin, R 90/446, 33, RKO, Abtl. Treu, an die Reichskreditkasse in Riga, betr. Goldbestand aus dem Ghetto in Riga, 5 March 1942.
47. LVA, P 1492-1-12, 123–126, Der Gen.-Komm. in Riga, Abtl. IIIf Treu, IIc, IIg, an die Generaldirektion des Finanzwesens in Riga, betr. Übernahme der gesamten Wohnungsverwaltungen im Generalbezirk Lettland, 26 June 1942.
48. BA Berlin, R 92/1214, Abschrift. Der RKO, Abtl. Finanzen, an die Gen.-Komm. Riga, Kauen, Reval, Minsk, i.A. gez. Dr. Künzel, 6 July 1942.
49. BA Berlin, R 92/836, Der RKO, Abtl. II Fin-H, an die Gen.-Komm., betr. Verwaltung und Verwertung des beweglichen, nichtgewerblichen jüdischen, herrenlosen und staatsfeindlichen Vermögens, gez. Dr. Vialon, 14 July 1942. On 22 July 1942, the Finance Department of General Commissariat Latvia passed this task to the county commissars, although the letter makes it clear that work on the registration of Jewish assets in the city of Riga was still underway. See ibid., Gen.-Komm. an Geb.-Komm. Riga-Stadt, i.A. Rauch, 22 July 1942, and Gen.-Komm. an die Geb.-Komm. Riga-Land, Mitau, Wolmar, Libau, und Dünaburg, 25 July 1942.
50. BA Berlin, R 92/382, [Gen.-Komm.] Abtl. Finanzen, an die Hauptabteilung I, betr. Übergang von Gefolgschaftsmitgliedern von der Abteilung Treuhandverwaltung auf die Abteilung Finanzen, 17 August 1942.
51. BA Berlin, R 92/509, 7, Platon Sidoroff, Tischlermeister, an den Gen.-Komm. in Riga, betr. Beschwerde, 3 July 1942; BA Berlin, R 91/70, Der Gen.-Komm. in Riga, Abtl. Finan-

zen, an den Geb.-Komm. Riga-Stadt, betr. Einnahmen aus der Zwangsarbeit der Juden, i.A. Neuendorff, 7 July 1942.
52. BA Berlin, R 91/70, Der Gen.-Komm. in Riga, Abtl. Finanzen, an den Geb.-Komm. Riga-Stadt, betr. Einnahmen aus der Zwangsarbeit der Juden, i.A. Neuendorff, 7 July 1942.
53. BA Berlin, R 92/509, 10, [Der Gen.-Komm.], Abtl. IIc, Vermerk und Verfg. betr. Ghetoverwaltung [sic], 5 August 1942; BA Berlin R 92/1215, [Der Gen.-Komm.], Bericht betr. Freimachung von Wohnraum im Ghetto, 17 August 1942. U.S. $370,000 in 1941 dollars would compare with U.S. $5.2 million in 2006 dollars.
54. BA Berlin R 92/1215, [Der Gen.-Komm.], Bericht betr. Freimachung von Wohnraum im Ghetto, 17 August 1942.
55. BA Berlin R 92/509, Der RKO, Abtl. Finanzen, an die Herren Gen.-Komm. in Riga, Kauen, Minsk, betr. Verwaltung der jüdischen Ghettos, i.A. Dr. Vialon, 27 August 1942. There were no ghettos in Estonia.
56. Ibid.
57. Ibid.
58. Instructions to this effect from Field Administration Command Riga's military police during August 1941 led to protests from the Takeover Commission for Artels, which immediately after the introduction of civil administration on 1 September 1941 requested that these decisions be reviewed. RKO Department IIa (Political Affairs) subsequently decreed on 16 September 1941 that return of workshops to Jews was by all means to be prohibited, see BA Berlin, R 90/447.
59. BA Berlin, R 92/1201, Die Übernahmekommission der Artelle, an den Gen.-Komm. in Riga, betr. Übernahme der privaten jüdischen Handwerks- und Kleinindustriebetriebe, 10 June 1942. In this letter, all of the details concerning financial liquidation – i.e., revenues, own expenditures, and advance payments to the RKO – are also listed. In addition, it emerges that the Takeover Commission for Artels did not settle the enterprises' debts but compiled a list of them for a later decision. The textiles found in the Jewish enterprises were gradually sold to the Riga company Drebnieks, see BA Berlin R 90/446, 94, Übernahmekommission der Artelle, an den RKO, Abtl. II Fin., 2 February 1942.
60. Bericht des Gen.-Komm. Lettland in Riga an den RKO, 20 November 1941, here the attachment Der Arbeitseinsatz der Rigaer Juden, in Benz et al., *Einsatz im "Reichskommissariat Ostland,"* doc. no. 105, 139–140.
61. LVVA, P 132-28-18, 76, journal of the Dortmund Group, entry for 4 May 1942. On the SD workshops in the ghetto, see BA Berlin, R 92/1158, 39, KdS Lettland, Abtl. I S, an den Gen.-Komm. in Riga, Abtl. Aso, Fachgebiet 2 (Arbeitseinsatz), betr. Arbeitseinsatz reichdeutscher Juden, 10 August 1942.
62. These were "work rooms" (*Werkstuben*) in the Latvian part of the ghetto, which were supervised by H. Broders, the "economics leader of the Jewish barracking camp," see BA Berlin, R 90/446, 74–75, Broders an den Geb.-Komm. Riga-Stadt, 24 September 1942. Broders opposed the workshops being taken over by the general commissar.
63. BA Berlin, R 92/834, Monatsbericht des Gen.-Komm. für den Oktober 1942 an den RKO, Teil G: Vermögensverwaltung. This excerpt is all that survives from the original report.
64. The figure of 1,185 Jewish men and women comes from the aforementioned monthly report for October 1942. The 95 workers and the 48 male and female camp workers come from an internal report in the general commissariat for February 1943: Der Gen.-Komm. in Riga, Abtl. Finanzen – Werkstätte, an Herrn Rauch, betr. Zahl der in den Werkstätten bzw. Lagern beschäftigten Juden, 22 February 1943, see BA Berlin, R 92/836, where an exact list of the workers and their assignments is documented.
65. BA Berlin, R 91/164, Der Geb.-Komm. in Riga, betr. Judeneinsatz im Monat Dezember 1942, Stichtag 10.12.1942, 9 January 1943: "In the ghetto, there are the workshops of

the SD, which are only occupied with orders from the Army, the workshops of the general commissar, Finance Department, which work in part for the [Reich Labor Service] and for civilians, and the workshops of the ghetto, which are occupied with maintaining the buildings as well as the Jews' articles of clothing."
66. Ibid., Bericht über den Arbeitseinsatz der Juden, 16 February 1942.
67. Ibid., Der KdS Lettland, Merkblatt betr. Lohnzahlung für die als Arbeiter aus dem Ghetto zur Verfügung gestellten Juden, 1 June 1942.
68. On this see, Staw. Hamburg, 141 Js 534/60, Bd. 57 (Beweismaterial), Aktennotiz betr. Arbeitsleistung von Juden aus Deutschland im Ghetto, 17 April 1942. A cashier's check was then delivered, see BA Berlin, R 90/447, Empfangsquittung, 17 April 1942.
69. BA Berlin, R 90/446, 68, Der RKO II Fin H, Vermerk über die Besprechung v. 13.10.42 beim RKO. Besprechungsgegenstand: Zuständigkeit für die Verwaltung und Verwertung des jüdischen Vermägens, gez. Burmeister.
70. Ibid.
71. BA Berlin, R 92/836, Abschrift. Erlass betr. Einziehung des jüdischen Vermögens im Reichskommissariat Ostland: "All confiscated Jewish assets are herewith considered impounded. I entrust my Finance Department with the implementation of the required measures for non-commercial, movable assets and my Trust Administration Department with the immovable and commercial Jewish assets, sig. Lohse." The first result of this decree was a discussion between the two departments on how "commercial" and "non-commercial" were to be understood, see BA Berlin, R 92/1214, Vermerk über die Sitzung am 9.3.1943 in der Abtl. Finanzen, 11 March 1943.
72. BA Berlin, R 92/836, Abtl. Finanzen [Gen.-Komm.] an die Referate Vermögensverwaltung und Kassenwesen im Hause, betr. Lohnzahlung für Juden, die aus dem deutschen Reichsgebiet stammen, gez. Dr. Neuendorff, 27 March 1943; BA Berlin, R 92/835, Abtl. Finanzen [Gen.-Komm.], Vermerk betr. Übergang der Verwaltung des Vermögens der aus dem Reich nach hier verbrachten Juden vom SD auf den Gen.-Komm., Abtl. Finanzen, 8 April 1943.
73. BA Berlin, R 92 92/1215, Vorschläge für eine Neuorganisation der Ghettoverwaltung in Riga, gez. Fritzsche, 29 August 1942. This includes, in the form of handwritten marginalia, notes on General Commissariat Latvia trust official Filter's consultations with Administrative Counselor Sommerlatte from the RKO Trust Administration Department, 23 September 1942. It should be pointed out that another draft for the administration of the Riga ghetto, dated 8 October 1942, is supposed to have made its way to Administrative Counselor Neuendorff. It is not among the surviving documentation, see BA Berlin, R 92/509, 19, Abtl. II (Verwaltung) [beim Gen.-Komm.], Vermerk, 23 January 1943.
74. BA Berlin, R 92/836, Abschrift. Abtl. Finanzen [Gen.-Komm.] an den Geb.-Komm. und komm. Oberbürgermeister der Stadt Riga, betr. Ghettoverwaltung, 16 April 1943. At a meeting with his department chiefs, Governing Mayor Wittrock spoke out against the takeover and explained he that would reserve regulation of this matter for himself, because, "without his knowledge, this new order is supposed to have already been introduced by the general commissar effective 1 April 1943." On this, see BA Berlin, R 91/29.
75. BA Berlin, R 92/509, 22–23, Der Gen.-Komm. in Riga, I Pol./II. Fin./II. Verw., an den Geb.-Komm. und komm. Oberbürgermeister der Stadt Riga, betr. Verwaltung des Rigaer Ghettos, 3 May 1943.
76. Belorusskii Gosudarstvennyi Arkhiv (Belarusian National Archive), 391-1-9, 110, Der Gen.-Komm. in Minsk, II Fin., an die Geb.-Komm., betr. Verwaltung der jüdischen Ghettos. Eilt sehr, 17 March 1943.

77. RGVA, 504-2-8, 170, RSHA, IV C 2, an alle BdS, KdS, Beauftr. des Chefs Sipo/SD in Brüssel, an alle Referate des Amtes IV, Referat II C 3. Nachrichtl. an all HSSPF, IdS, an WVHA-D-Oranienburg. An Referat I B 3, Referat II A, Gst. IV. Betr. KL (Arbeitslager) Riga, 2 April 1943. The document also mentions the installation of SS Major Albert Sauer as commandant of Concentration Camp Riga. Also, BA Berlin NS 19/1740, 20, Feld-Kommandostelle an den HSSPF Ostland, an den Chef des SS-Wirtschafts- und Verwaltungshauptamtes, an den Chef der Sipo und des SD, gez. H. Himmler, 21 June 1943.
78. BA-DH, ZM 1457, Akte 2, 48–49, Reiseplanung des RFSS nach Riga und Reval für den 13.-16.3.1943, zusammengestellt von SS-Obersturmführer Reimers.

– Chapter 13 –

Ghetto Life and Forced Labor in Riga in Spring 1942

The Jews from Latvia and the west knew nothing of the administrative problems that their presence created. And yet every day, they felt the ramifications of the conflicts between the rivals from the Security Police and the civil administration, which were sometimes quite tangible. They knew nothing of the discussions at the Wannsee Conference, but here, too, the direct consequences were to be felt every time the Security Police carried out a selection of those unable to work for shooting, and family members and friends were murdered. They were in the ghetto in Riga's Moscow Suburb, hermetically sealed off from the rest of the district by a double barbed-wire fence and guarded by Latvian policemen. In the guardhouse on Ludzas St. (Leipzig St.), there were at least sixty men under the command of a Latvian police officer and a noncommissioned officer. They always had twenty-eight policemen on guard duty, with all of the Latvian officers supervised by the Schutzpolizei, the German municipal police. This meant in practical terms that Precinct Lieutenant Albert Hesfehr, along with Otto Tuchel and Max Neumann, were on duty on a daily basis, and that they were considered the real authority.[1]

By the time the deportations arrived at the latest, the Security Police was installed in the ghetto on a permanent basis. SS First Lieutenant Kurt Krause of the Regional Commander of the Security Police (KdS Latvia) resided in the commandant's building. He was probably the most notorious uniformed German in the ghetto. There was a member of the Schutzpolizei in the guardhouse at the end of Ludzas St. and at the gate to Lāčplēša St. (Carl Schirren St.). Generally, the outer ring of guards was reinforced by numerous men, and ultimately, the Jewish Order Service was forced to assume guard and patrol functions.[2] In addition to the announcement at the ghetto entrance forbidding access to all unauthorized persons, there were mounted all along the ghetto fence bilingual signs with the words: "Persons who cross the fence or attempt to make contact with the inhabitants of the ghetto through the fence will be shot without warning."[3]

Notes for this chapter begin on page 322.

In December and January, the ghetto remained in an indescribable state of disarray, as German agencies fought over it behind the scenes.[4] Shortly after Hermann Köster of the Reich Commissariat Ostland's Trust Administration Department assumed responsibility for ghetto property, three fires broke out in uninhabited parts of the ghetto area. On 18, 23, and 27 December, the Riga Fire Department was called upon to put out the fires, which had probably been set to cover raids by Latvian policemen or German soldiers.[5] At the time, the belongings of the Latvian Jews were gradually being stored in buildings on the ghetto premises – at first to protect them from the frost, but then to have them registered.[6] In all, 430 Latvian Jews were deployed for this.[7] These "unregulated conditions" of robbery and arson were to be traced back to the inadequate guarding of the ghetto, said the county commissar for Riga City. He was probably right.[8] On 4 February, the chief of the Latvian battalion pointed out that the Latvian guards' superiors went about their work rather carelessly. The ghetto fence had holes in it, and paths for smugglers and thieves were already well trodden.[9] The local police worked hand in hand with thieves such as Vera Minisch, who, together with the policeman Ernst Stradniek, systematically cleared out the improvised warehouses over the course of January.[10] It is also documented that Hesfehr had selected objects of value and furnishings carried directly into his apartment by members of the clearance commandos.[11]

In the process, neither the civilian population nor the local police had to commit theft themselves. It was well known that upon request one could receive an acquisition permit from Köster's colleague Hermann [first name unknown] right at the ghetto gate; afterward, Hesfehr or Tuchel would give the warehouse location.[12] Prospective buyers could thereupon seek out and purchase items right there in the ghetto.[13] Latvian policemen often processed their own requests by noting that they had been plundered by the Bolsheviks, or they commended themselves by stating that they had participated in the past "cleansing operations" against the Jews.[14] Simple furnishings, dishes, and above all baby buggies seem to have been the most sought-after objects; the chance to "pinch" something else in the warehouse itself was apparently easy enough. German agencies at the time also stocked up on the estates of the Jews who had been killed.[15] If larger items were at issue, then the goods were only turned over on the basis of a loan with the proviso that an invoice would be presented later. "Already at the crack of dawn, when we went to work, we would see long rows of Latvian women who had come to purchase blood-soaked Jewish clothes and other things. These shameless people stood in line for hours. The entire sellout in the ghetto lasted months," recalled Max Kaufmann a short time later.[16]

On 3 February 1942, a commission of medical and hygiene experts from the civil administration and the SS visited the ghetto, because items full of bugs and lice had been turned in. Above all SS Major Hans Bludau, the hygiene specialist with the office of the Higher SS and Police Leader Ostland, pressed for a solution. When he visited the ghetto, he found the following:

> At present, the ghetto is occupied by 16,000 mostly German Jews, who have been accommodated in several designated buildings and are sent to labor commandos during the day. From the remaining empty buildings, articles of linen and other still usable goods have been collected in four large warehouses and stacked there. From these warehouses, respective applicants then take the necessary materials, without these having been cleaned or disinfested beforehand. Inasmuch as furniture is requested, individual units and other applicants are directed into the ghetto where they at random take from the buildings what is needed. It is to be regretted that in these search operations more devastation and malicious destruction of the material is caused than one would absolutely have to expect from such hurried operations. Up to now, millions in value have already been destroyed in this way. The facts have been confirmed to me by Mr. Bruns, the commissioner of the trust administration with the Reich commissar. The situation in those apartments inspected is indescribable. The floors are covered up to 1 meter deep in torn out articles of linen, clothes, etc. Leftovers are lying around. Smashed up pieces of furniture are stacked high in the rooms.[17]

The situation had to be remedied. The commission decided to close the ghetto immediately and to declare it a prohibited epidemic area for the next two weeks. With that, the possibility emerged for the Trust Administration Department to have the ghetto systematically cleared. Around 300–400 Jews were put together in a new labor commando. In addition, the disinfestation of the buildings was carried out with hydrocyanic acid, and a disinfection facility was set up in the ghetto.[18] The company Tesch & Stabenow, represented in Riga by its head of fumigation, Holst, was repeatedly hired for such operations in other places and reported about them in its trade journal.[19] With introduction of this measure, which was extended beyond 20 February, the ghetto slowly changed from a "self-service shop" for all possible prospective customers to a terrain where only persons with identification papers issued by the Security Police or the Trust Administration Department could visit.[20] The process of putting together clearance commandos for cleaning, sorting, and registering the contents of the ghetto continued well into May 1942.[21]

In the Jewish-run Labor Deployment Central Office and among the Jews, this commando operated under the name "Latvian Commando": "We were called upon to perform clearance work in the uninhabited part of the ghetto. Small groups of young girls were accompanied by an older man, who pulled a sled. I joined my father-in-law's group. Under the supervision of a Latvian SS team, we were taken through the gate and the double barbed-wire into the other ghetto. The apartments looked disastrous, but we knew in the meantime what had happened. We were forced to sort, bundle, and pack on sleds all of the articles of clothing, bedding, table linen, and other items, which were then taken into the German ghetto by the men. My father-in-law Julius Winter told me that the things were stacked in enormous sheds. It was bitter cold, and we were so frozen stiff that we could hardly move."[22]

Lilly Fischel, who had been deported to Riga from a small town in Westphalia, remembered finding in one of the ravaged rooms the corpse of a baby that had been shot.[23] However, Gerda Gottschalk referred in her memoirs to the opportunities that this commando offered, mentioning firewood, clothing, and food preferred by Latvian Jews, which were smuggled into the inhabited part of the ghetto – at great risk of course.[24] Indeed, at the very outset of the clearance operation, every fourth woman in one commando was shot, because one person had been caught trying to keep a ball of wool.[25] Scrap materials such as leather, worn shoes, old rubber, rags, or even bedsprings were later taken away by the collection and manufacture company Izejviela at fixed prices for further use.[26]

Figure 13.1. Part of the evacuated and devastated half of the ghetto. Undated. Courtesy of Bundesarchiv Berlin, SAPMO.

A second ad hoc labor commando – one for clearing snow and ice – has already been mentioned [Chapter 11]. Among the Jews, it was simply called Kriegsweg; it operated outside the ghetto boundaries.

> "Kriegsweg," what would it bestow upon us? A piece of bread, a bowl of soup, wood? Up to 120 women, we marched at daybreak through the uninhabited suburb. We walked on the street – as "sub-humans," we were forbidden to walk on the sidewalks. Passing the market halls, after a good hour of the way, we reached Sand St. There a small gate opened, [and] the column entered. In the courtyard was a stone building with a smith; next to a shed stood a heated barrack that was to serve all of us as communal lounge area. But only a small part of the women found room there, the others stood freezing in the courtyard. After some time waiting, four men from the Latvian city sanitation administration came out of the stone house in upturned fur [coats] and leather boots, cigars in mouth, and scrutinized us. We were divided into groups of 10 and 20 persons, received wooden shovels or iron bars. Under the supervision of a Latvian foreman, the groups then went to their place of work. Most had to go far beyond the Daugava Bridge into uninhabited parts of town and shovel snow and hack away at the ice; it was considered quite a bit of luck to work with a small group in the inner city.[27]

The Jewish commando for clearing snow from Riga's streets, primarily along the supply line Thoroughfare XII, which ran right through the Latvian capital, served to implement a detailed municipal ordinance of 3 December 1941, by which this west-east connection had to be kept free of snow and ice at all costs. Residents, managers of tenement blocks, and owners were obliged to care for their respective section of road, whereas the bridges as well as the municipal sections – offices, parks, and parking places – were cleared by the city sanitation service and Jews.[28]

Working with Commando Kriegsweg was as much a mixed curse as working with the Latvian Commando. If one were deployed, for example, on the bridges over the Daugava, one could very quickly get lasting frostbite due to the strong winds. It was more advantageous to be deployed to one of the busy city squares. One could duck more easily into a building entrance and warm oneself. If the female forced laborers were deployed on Gertrudes St., they were close to a flourishing black market, where they could bid as well. The first infrastructure for some of the deportees also developed there: articles of clothing organized by the Latvian Commando could be turned over to the Commando Kriegsweg and exchanged for food in a public restroom on the market square. There remained, however, the risk upon returning to the ghetto entrance.[29]

Survivors were able to remember other early labor commandos, because such details were among their first occupations in Riga. One such commando was involved in clearing the iced-over Daugava of tree stumps and planks, for these would pose a threat to the pontoon bridges with the expected strong spring ice run. On order of the general commissar, all of the county commissars had to ensure that this wood was pulled from the rivers.[30] In Riga, German and local Jews saw to this.[31]

Another ad hoc commando had to work on the docks. It was later turned into a permanent labor commando for the general commissar and barracked on Pētersalas St. (Peterholmsche St.). After the general commissar, in his capacity as trust administrator of the Latvian docks, had noted that the Riga harbors still held property belonging not only to ethnic Germans from the second wave of resettlement but also to British citizens and German Jewish émigrés on their way to Asia and the Americas, the Reich commissar was asked first whether these goods should be gone through in search of usable fur goods for the Wehrmacht.[32] The former property of Baltic German resettlers was off-limits, but it was argued, also from the Latvian side, that goods impounded by Soviet customs officials were to be considered state property.[33] In early 1942, the incident was brought to Reich Commissar Lohse, who was even in favor of releasing the confiscated belongings of ethnic Germans to the Trust Administration Department.[34] All of the material stored in Warehouses 6 and 7 of the Riga customs harbor – whether it belonged to Englishmen or Jewish émigrés – was cleared out by a commando of Jews and, with the help of the transport company Gerhard & Hey, taken to a storehouse of the trust administration under General Commissar Drechsler at Pētersalas St. 6.[35] Once there, these things were opened, sorted, registered, and upon request distributed. For example, Estonian People's Aid and General Commissariat White Ruthenia received articles of clothing in large amounts.[36] One of three large warehouses was located at Pētersalas St. 6 well into 1943; nine Jews were ultimately put to work there as clerks and packers. Right next door was a flax purification plant.[37]

In general, the extensive harbor facilities of the Latvian capital offered splendid storage and transport possibilities for diverse organizations so that Jews were repeatedly assigned to the harbors.[38] Here, they worked as laborers for the harbor administration or, for example, for a branch office of the Waffen-SS Troop Economics Storehouse, which had been set up in a number of buildings belonging to a seed export company.[39] The customs harbor compound housed the Navy Equipment Office, where officials interceded in vain on behalf of barracking its Jewish forced laborers on-site. An Air Force construction warehouse occupied several work floors in the export harbor, as did the warehouses of Army provisions. All of these branches of the German Wehrmacht employed foreign and indigenous Jews.[40]

Every morning, at different times starting at 6 A.M., the labor commandos had to gather to leave the ghetto.[41] The individual detail leaders were responsible for the departure from the ghetto. These also had to account for the number of forced laborers and the number of those who had taken ill. This information was noted by an employee of the Jewish Labor Deployment Central Office and checked. One could fail to appear if one possessed a certificate from a doctor.[42] Afterward, the detail left the ghetto with a pass, as a rule accompanied by a German or Latvian company employee, who had to pick up and return the column.[43] Upon return in the evening the commandos were checked, first by Jewish employees of the labor administration to make sure all were present and accounted for and that no goods had been smuggled in.[44] This was the most precarious moment for all those forced laborers who had to care for relatives in the ghetto as well. As a rule, the detail controller might have overlooked the bulging pockets, the tied pants legs, and the hidden breast pouch. But it took only one drunk Latvian policeman or a member of the Gendarmerie (the German rural police) having a cigarette at the ghetto gate to ensure an uproar. If a person were caught for smuggling, a number of completely different scenarios could unfold. This ranged from a simple beating in the commandant's building for all concerned – the smuggler, detail leader, and the controller – to the arrest and subsequent hanging of men on Tin Square or the shooting of women at the old Jewish cemetery on the "German side" of the ghetto. The shooting of Meta Baum in the spring of 1942, which was never forgotten by all those survivors who witnessed it, makes for harrowing reading to this day.

Upon her return from a day on her forced labor commando, Baum was stopped at the ghetto gate by Tuchel and Neumann and accused of stealing the soup found in her canteen at the workplace. Baum, a Rhineland woman known to all due to her red hair, had seven children in the ghetto and needed every additional scrap of food she could find. The two German policemen nonetheless dragged her away and took her to Commandant Krause. Krause ordered her to the cemetery immediately and shot her there although the children pleaded for the life of their mother the entire way.[45] The survivor reports and witness statements made by indigenous and deported Jews after the war show an abundance of such individual acts of murder on the part of the German police in the ghetto. Murder was a part of everyday life there, something that is only sporadically reflected in the contemporary documentation. In Report on Events USSR No. 195 of 24 April 1942, it is only tersely noted that in the preceding two weeks five Jews had been arrested and an additional fourteen killed for "various infringements and crimes."[46] An activity report from KdS Latvia for the three weeks from 23 May to 18 June 1942 lists twenty-nine executed Jews, without stating why they were killed.[47]

The historical documentation on the deployment of deported and indigenous Jews as forced laborers does not allow us to trace in detail how the

Figure 13.2. Fetching water near the gallows on Tin Square. Courtesy of Bernd Haase.

use of Jews in private businesses and the civil, military, and police offices of the occupational administration developed. A general indication of the situation in early 1942 can only be gleaned from the entries in the journal of the Dortmund Group, the memoirs and recollections of survivors, and the occasional incidental contemporary correspondence regarding individual cases.

"C.[ommando] Šķirotava, 6:15 a.m., deployment of female laborers": This is the first entry in the Dortmund Group's journal, and in this case, the commando meant was based at the Riga freight station.[48] The women's work was extremely difficult, because they had been assigned to load coal and to clear the tracks of ice and snow.[49] The physical exertion required for working in commandos such as Šķirotava, Kriegsweg, Harbor Administration, or Daugava Clearance prompted Herbert Schultz, head of the Labor Deployment Central Office, to instruct the groups to replace women in such details regularly.[50] The journal provides another incomplete overview in the entry of 4 March; there the first commandos to receive 100 grams bread as a bonus – the "commando slice," as Gerda Gottschalk called it – are listed.[51]

In addition to the aforementioned deployments, more commandos are to be found there, such as Commando Richard Wagner St. That was not only where the Navy's obstacles and barriers command post had been set up for the administration and dismantling of captured munitions; it was also the site of a branch office of the Army's clothing office. Behind the designation Commando K-Werk I lay the company labor commando for Volkswagen's main garage (Army Maintenance Works). Among the other firms using Jewish forced labor, the company Bastert and Katschmarek (Army Motor Pool) as well as Halron & Co. (Aircraft Group I) were tightly bound to Wehrmacht contracts. The companies Schmidt and Irbe built bridges and provided the Salaspils camp with construction materials respectively. Commando Commandant Latvia, in which Max Kaufmann worked for a while, was employed at General Georg Bamberg's command. Nothing is known about the commandos assigned army post numbers or the commandos Streetcar, Fur Utilization, or Cloth Warehouse, although the latter cases could have involved work sorting goods and material on behalf of the Latvian company Izejviela.[52]

The worst commando, which was formed as early as February 1942, was hardly known at first and operated later under the name Special Commando Krause I or High Forest Commando. During her investigation of the former employees for labor deployment issues in the Hanover group, Gertrude Schneider met Selma Sollinger. The latter recalled that shortly before the mass shooting on 5 February 1942, around twenty Order Service members were taken to the high forest of Bikernieki and ordered to dig a large, deep pit. Afterward, they were sworn to unconditional silence by the Security Police and driven back to the ghetto. Among the men was Selma Sollinger's husband Julius, who immediately told his wife about the ominous job.[53]

In January 1950, Berlin furrier Willy Weiss recalled, as a witness in the case against Rudolf Seck, the former commandant of the Jungfernhof camp, that in the winter of 1941–1942, shortly after his arrival, he had belonged to High Forest Commando, which was what it was called at the time. The commando left in the morning and returned from Bikernieki in the evening: "Our work lay in a forest, about 8 km from the ghetto. I no longer know in which direction we went from the ghetto. It involved a large forest with tall tree trunks and undergrowth, such as one knows in Germany as well. There, we had to dig graves. It was said that these graves were fortifications. Gradually, it got around that mass graves were probably being prepared here. Each of these graves was two to three meters deep, two to three meters wide – I can't specify the length. The edges were at a right angle or sloping, each according to the quality of the soil. Sometimes, the edges were shored up by boards."[54]

Quite apparently, as early as February, these ad hoc excavation commandos were pulled together to form a permanent commando that was to remain isolated from the ghetto's remaining population, because its members witnessed shootings. Hermann Heymann, a married salesman from Duisburg who had five children and had been deported to the Riga ghetto with the Düsseldorf transport, recalled the change:

> In early 1942, a so-called High Forest Commando was put together. It was called on for only a few days and put together for only a few days, that is to say, it wasn't a standing commando. I was with this High Forest Commando for some days in Bikernieki, where we had to excavate pits. The putting together of this commando took place through the deployment of Jewish labor. On the occasion of a general roll call, Commandant Krause then personally sought out 35 people. I was also sought out by him. The purpose of this selection was not made known to us. It was said only in general terms that we were to be at Krause's personal disposition. This commando was designated Commando Krause I. One morning, we were transferred to a building adjacent Riga's Central Prison. During the next half year, we remained at the Central Prison and were deployed for work in the high forest or Bikernieki. These deployments followed at irregular intervals. It also happened that they followed in chronologically rapid succession, but it also happened that we did not leave the Central Prison for weeks. In the high forest, we had to excavate pits. These were around 8 m long, almost just as wide and three to four meters deep. The digging of a single pit usually lasted two to three days. During other deployments, we had to fill in the pits. Chlorinated lime was strewn over the corpses and earth cursorily thrown in. It also happened that, at a later time, we had to throw more earth on the pits, because the layer [of soil] had given way in the meantime. At these pits, one found large quantities of bullet casings, moreover glasses, burnt articles of clothing, sometimes watches, rings, and photographs as well. On one photograph, I recognized a young girl from Wesel who I had seen in the ghetto. I would say that, in the period from the end of February until June or August 1942, I saw around 10 pits filled with corpses, which had to have originated from ten chronologically separate mass shootings. In the early stage of my deployment, that is to say, in February, March, and April, these mass shootings were, in my opinion, most frequent.[55]

While Willy Weiss and Hermann Heymann were apparently not present at the mass murder operations, in the course of the criminal investigation against Gerhard Maywald, Ernst Metzger could testify in December 1963 that at the liquidations Krause, Lange, Nickel, and Maywald himself had given orders to shoot. Metzger, together with other Jews, had to fill in the pit even if somebody, severely wounded, was still alive inside it.[56] Although this statement had no legal consequences for Maywald, it nonetheless has considerable historical value, for during questioning Metzger wrote down unusually precise dates concerning breaks with previous practice surrounding his fate and left the piece of paper with his statement. "On 19 February 1942, Krause I. Central Prison" reads the entry, and this does in fact correspond with notes made in the Dortmund Group's journal.[57] On 21 February, it was succinctly noted under the heading "to all groups. Re. Special Commando Krause I": "The deputy camp commandant communicated the following: Special Commando Krause I, deployed since yesterday, has at present been assigned particular tasks that make its deployment to different places at any time necessary. For this reason, the men affected have been barracked [elsewhere] and will probably return in a few days. We ask the family members to be informed."[58] Three days later, the head of the Labor Deployment Central Office had it announced that mail to family members had arrived. Interestingly, this information went only to the groups Berlin, Bielefeld, Düsseldorf, Dortmund, Cologne, and Sachsen.[59] Based on the available witness statements, it is impossible to reconstruct whether Commando Krause I was later replenished with additional men from the ghetto. However, one last entry, now addressed to all of the groups, suggests this was the case. On 31 March 1942, Berthold Schiff let it be known that family members could leave clothes at the Labor Deployment Central Office, and that these would then be conveyed to the men in the commando. After assurances that the men would also be provided with extra bread and fat from the ghetto, Schultz's deputy wrote: "You can write greetings on the package, however, no message otherwise."[60]

There was in fact some news from the ghetto worth reporting: Under the rubric "Dünamünde Fish Cannery," those deported to Riga had been informed just before 31 March that transports of weak and old people no longer up to the grueling physical demands of the external and internal commandos would be departing in the next few days. This information, however, was not supposed to get through to the men of Krause I under any circumstances.

Notes

1. LVVA, 22–28, der Gen.-Komm. in Riga, Abtl. II, an den RKO, betr. Monatlicher Bericht über Einrichtung von Ghettos in [sic] jüdischen Arbeitslagern, Arbeitseinsatz und Behandlung der Juden, 20 November 1941, printed in Benz et al., *Einsatz im "Reichskommissariat Ostland,"* doc. no. 91, 126–128.
2. BA Ludwigsburg, Dokumentation UdSSR 426, 245–246, Vermerk zur Sitzung über Ghettofragen am 20.2.1942, Unterschrift Lange. The second entry in the journal of the Dort-

mund Group, dated 16 February 1942, states that the camp policemen in each group had to lead the forced laborers to roll call every morning, see LVVA, P 132-28-18, 1.
3. BA Ludwigsburg, Dokumentation UdSSR 426, 245–246, Vermerk zur Sitzung über Ghettofragen am 20.2.1942, Unterschrift Lange.
4. For a retrospective look, see BA Berlin R 92/1215, unpaginated, Aktennotiz des RKO, Abt. III-Treuhandverwaltung, 9 February 1942: "It was noted that 1. All apartments were open or broken open. 2. A hopeless mess reigned in all of the apartments, all containers had been broken open, their contents were scattered about the rooms. 3. Trucks from the Wehrmacht, motor vehicles of the SS and police formations, motor vehicles of the local Latvian police drove in and out of the ghetto without being controlled and hauled away in terms of furniture whatever was possible … Furniture was hauled out of the apartments and onto the streets and courtyards, where it was exposed to the effects of the weather and as a consequence fell victim to deterioration. Köster."
5. BA Berlin, R 91/237, unpaginated, Bericht des Chefs der Feuerwehren Riga-Stadt über die letzten Brände im Ghetto der Stadt Riga, gez. Schleicher, 30 December 1941; LVVA, P 70-5-44, 41, Bericht des KdO beim SSPF Lettland, 1 January 1942: "In many cases, it was observed by the guards from the local police that members of the Wehrmacht crawled through the fence around the ghetto during the darkness and combed the buildings and apartments in the cleared part [of the ghetto]. Two fires that broke out in this part [of the ghetto] during the evening hours suggest that unauthorized persons caused these fires by carelessness."
6. BA Berlin, R 91/10, 12–13, Referent z.b.V. Friedrich Brasch an den Geb.-Komm., 18 December 1941, concerning his ejection by Dr. Köster: "I can no longer compensate for losses incurred in the meantime through the removal of things for which I have received no accounting as well as for losses due to objects lying out in the open and damage inflicted on real estate (water pipes, etc.) by frost, etc." From the point of view of the Latvian Jews affected, see, for example, Kaufmann, *Churbn Lettland*, 124–125, as well as the memoir of Aizik Dimantstein, "From Karsava to Sweden," in Schneider, *Muted Voices*, 120–121.
7. BA Berlin, R 91/164, unpaginated, Bericht über den Einsatz der Juden für den Stichtag 20.12.41, 18 January 1942, Standtke.
8. Staw. Hamburg, 141 Js 534/60, Bd. 57 [Beweismaterial], unpaginated, Der Gen.-Komm. in Riga, HA I, an den RKO, betr. Beschlagnahme und Sicherung des jüdischen Vermögens, 31 December 1941. Wittrock's assessment is reported here.
9. LVVA, P 998-1-1, 19, translation from Latvian of file entitled "Protocol of the Commander of the XXth Riga Order Service Battalion," Protocol no. 6, 4 February 1942.
10. LVVA, P 1376-1-5, 521, R. Stiglitz, Präfekt der Stadt Riga, Tätigkeits-Bericht für den 28.1.1942, an den SS-Sturmbannführer Kirste. See also LVVA P 70-5-37, 110–111, Tagesmeldung des BdS Ostland, Abtl. III, an den RKO, 10 March 1942, with a reference to the arrest of three local policemen for plundering in the ghetto.
11. Staw. Hamburg, 141 Js 534/60, Bd. 40, 6,514, statement by William Sherman of Riga, 19 October 1963: "From Hesfehr, I often received the task to bring to his apartment select parts of things remaining in the large ghetto. Together with five, six other Latvian Jews, we broke into apartments on his orders and brought selected pieces of furniture into the apartment where he lived."
12. A large number of individual requests with marginalia by Hesfehr, Tuchel, and Hermann have survived, BA Berlin, R 90/451, unpaginated.
13. Ministerial Assistant Theodor Fründt was to be found among the prospective buyers under the date 19 March 1942. He received from assessor K. Urbans two invoices for RM 365.50 for diverse goods (watch, radio, embroidery), see BA Berlin, R 90/452, unpagi-

nated. RM 365.50 was worth about US $146 at the official exchange rates in late 1941. Adjusted for inflation, that nominal dollar figure would be worth around U.S. $2,000 as of 2006.
14. For example, the documented efforts of policeman Alfreds Oldermanis to purchase furniture on 2 January 1942, see BA Berlin, R 90/451, unpaginated.
15. On requests for household items, see the individual requests in R 90/451, unpaginated; on requests from German agencies, see, for example, Daimler-Benz, K-Werk Riga, an Dr. Köster, 7 January 1942, or the letter of the same date from the Latvian Department of Health to the Trust Administration Department in ibid. Raul Hilberg also pointed out individual cases of appropriation. However, these requests for a piano or tombstones (for their granite and marble) hardly reflected the massive demand for everyday items among Riga's population and the German authorities. See Raul Hilberg, *Die Vernichtung der europäischen Juden*, Bd. 2, 379.
16. Kaufmann, *Churbn Lettland*, 142.
17. BA Berlin, R 90/446, 28–30, Gen.-Komm. in Riga, Abtl. Gesundheit und Volkspflege II e (2), Bericht über eine Besichtigung des Judenghettos in Riga am 3.2.1942, gez. Dr. Ferdinand.
18. Ibid. Also BA Berlin R 92/1215, unpaginated, Der RKO, Abtl. Gesundheit und Volkspflege, an die Abtl. Treuhandverwaltung, betr. Seuchengefahr im Ghetto, 6 February 1942. See also BA Berlin, R 90/446, 52–55, Der RKO, Abtl. Gesundheit und Volkspflege, an die Abtl. Treuhand, betr. Gebäude- und Materialentwesung im jüdischen Ghetto; this includes an analysis by the company Tesch & Stabenow concerning prices and gas concentrations, 29 May 1942. Finally, a reminder from Tesch & Stabenow, dated 20 May 1942, regarding an invoice from 12 March 1942 for Zyklon-B fumigation, in BA Berlin, R 90/449, unpaginated. It is unclear whether the stationary disinfection facility in the ghetto really used Zyklon-B. Margot Jakob, Netti Weissglas, and Hannelore Heymann worked there initially as a Jewish "disinfesting troop," see LVVA, P-132-28-18, 2, journal of the Dortmund Group, entry for 17 February 1942.
19. See, for example, Josef Ruppert, "Gesundheitsverhältnisse und Seuchenbekämpfung im Generalgouvernement," *Der praktische Desinfektor* 6 (1941): 61; Herbert Weidner, "Die Organisation der Läusebekämpfung im Hauptkommissariat Baranowitsche, Weißruthenien," *Der praktische Desinfektor* 4 (1942): 35–36. Excerpts from these two articles are in Kalthoff and Werner, *Die Händler des Zyklon B*, 137–138.
20. Many soldiers apparently succeeded in "organizing" larger stocks of furnishings and selling them to Latvian furniture dealers in town. On this, see the verdict of the court of the Higher Commander of the Supply Troops 4, 16 November 1942, in a case involving four German soldiers who had collected in part very large sums for such furniture, BA Berlin, R 92/10,064, unpaginated.
21. BA Berlin, R 90/447, unpaginated, Vermerk III/Treu 44.1.Br/Kr. Betr. Bericht über den Stand der Angelegenheiten im Ghetto, 19 March 1942. Here it was explained that the clearance action was not yet over and would last another three to four weeks. In the journal of the Dortmund Group, the last entry for this commando is found under 28 May 1942, LVVA, P-132-28-18, 84. See also Staw. Hamburg, 141 Js 534/60, Bd. 37, statement by David Fischkin of Riga, 25 June 1963, 6,060.
22. Sherman-Zander, *Zwischen Tag und Dunkel*, 38.
23. Lilly Pancis, "Deportation to the East," in Schneider, *Muted Voices*, 43.
24. Gottschalk, *Der letzte Weg*, 27–28. From the point of view of the Latvian Jews, this was probably not so easy, as Max Kaufmann's memoir shows. See Kaufmann, *Churbn Lettland*, 124.
25. Staw. Hamburg, 141 Js 534/60, statement by Adolfine Freiberg, 22 August 1967, 11,488–11,490. Freiburg was deported from Prague via Theresienstadt; AWL, Testaments to

the Holocaust, Series One, reel 57, P.III.h. no. 1018, Malvina Reinigerová and Melanie Pragerová, who were deported from Prague, undated, 1.
26. See the agreement of 16 February 1942 between Bruns and the company Izejviela on Latgale Road, sanctioned by RKO, Dept. III, Used Materials Collection Desk, in BA Berlin, R 90/446, 49.
27. Gottschalk, *Der letzte Weg,* 28–29.
28. BA Berlin, R 91/195, unpaginated, Anordnung betreffend Instandhaltung der durch Riga führenden DG XII, gez. Dr. Windgassen, 3 December 1942. This ordinance applied to the Mitau Road (Jelgava Road), the Zemgale Bridge, von der Goltz Ring (Aspazija Boulevard), Adolf Hitler Avenue (Independence Avenue), and Dorpat Road (Tartu Road).
29. Gottschalk, *Der letzte Weg,* 30–31; Sherman-Zander, *Zwischen Tag und Dunkel,* 42–43; Staw. Hamburg, 141 Js 534/60, Bd. 49, statement by Therese Steinhardt, 27 July 1964, 8,014. Steinhardt was deported from Kassel.
30. BA Berlin, R 91 Riga-Stadt/95, unpaginated, Der Gen.-Komm. in Riga, Abtl. IV WaHä G.Nr. 64/12, an das Seedepartement Riga, betr. Eingefrorenes Holz auf Flüssen, as well as Der Gen.-Komm. in Riga, Abtl. IV WaHä, an alle Geb.-Komm. unter Hinweis auf zu stellende Arbeitskräfte, both documents dated 18 February 1942.
31. Staw. Hamburg, 141 Js 534/60, Bd. 48, statement by Erica Oppenheimer, 29 May 1964, 7,968.
32. BA Berlin, R 90/446, 156, Der Gen.-Komm. in Riga an den RKO, 31 December 1941.
33. Ibid., 155, Abschrift, Der Gen.-Komm. in Riga, Abtl. IIg, an das Zollamt Riga, betr. Rückgabe von baltischem Gut an Umsiedler, 6 January 1942; ibid., 154, and Generaldirektion des Finanzwesens, Liquidationsabteilung, an das Generalkommissariat Riga, 12 January 1942.
34. See ibid., 154, Generaldirektion des Finanzwesens, Liquidationsabteilung, an das Generalkommissariat Riga, 12 January 1942, and ibid., Vermerk Gentz, 3 February 1942. The property of the ethnic Germans, however, had already been handed out to the DUT, see ibid., RKO, Abtl. Treu, an Abtl. Fin., 4 March 1942.
35. Ibid., 152, Der RKO, Abtl. Treu, an den Bevollmächtigten der Häfen des Gen.-Bez. Lettland, betr. Umzugsgepäck der Baltendeutschen und Gepäckstücke von deutschen Juden-Emigranten, 3 March 1942. For the perspective of a Latvian Jew put to work there, see Jewgenij Salzmann, "Dieses bittere Glück, Ein lettischer Jude im Ghetto und GULAG," *Dachauer Hefte* 15, no. 14 (1998): 175–217, 186–187.
36. Ibid., 34, Der Gen.-Komm. für Weißruthenien, HA III Allwi-Inha, an den Sonderbeauftragten zur Erfassung des Judenvermögens im Ostland, Herrn Bruns, betr. Judennachlaß, 4 March 1942. Ibid., 106–107, Der RKO, Abtl. Gesundheit und Volkspflege, an Abtl. Treu im Hause, betr. Versorgung russischer Flüchtlinge in Estland mit Bekleidungsstücken, 12 March 1942.
37. BA Berlin, R 92/836, unpaginated, Verzeichnis des Gen.-Komm. Riga, Abtl. Finanzen, Nr. 102/W über eingesetzte Juden in den Materiallagern Pragerstr., Peter-Holm-Str. und Lager Matthaistr., 22 February 1943; BA Berlin, R 90/450, unpaginated, Notiz zur Flachs- und Wergreinigungsanlage, 4 April 1942.
38. BA Berlin, R 91/164, unpaginated, Arbeitsamt Riga, Lagebericht für die Zeit vom 15.10.-16.11.1941, according to which Jews were deployed in greater numbers in the harbor. On the same time period, see the summary report by Max Dorr to the Department of Labor and Social Policy at the RKO, 27 November 1941, in LVVA, P 69-1a-17, 165–172.
39. BA Berlin, R 91/73, unpaginated, Wirtschaftsinspektion der Waffen-SS an den Geb.-Komm., betr. Zuweisung von beschlagnahmten Gebäuden und Wohnungen, 4 October 1941.
40. BA Berlin, R 91/164, unpaginated, Bericht Standtkes über den Einsatz von Juden, 16 February 1942; LVVA, P 132-28-18, journal of the Dortmund Group, 24 (entry for 4 March

1942), 29 (8 March 1942), 29 (19 March 1942), 52 (29 March 1942), 66 (13 April 1942), 81 (19 May 1942), 85 (29 and 30 May 1942); BA Berlin, R 91/72, unpaginated, rejected request filed by the Navy Equipment Office Riga Customs Harbor, 22 April 1942; BA Berlin R 92/1158, 72, Heeresverpflegungsmagazin Riga, Abtl. V, an den Gen.-Komm., Abtl. Aso, betr. Arbeitseinsatz von Juden, 21 April 1943.

41. LVVA, P 132-28-18, 42, journal of the Dortmund Group, entry for 23 March 1942.
42. Ibid., 18, entry for 2 March 1943, on the examination for ability to work on the part of the group doctors.
43. This was taken care of by German soldiers as part of regular duties. At Army Group North's motor pool (*Heeres-Kraftfahr-Park* 626), this task was found in the verse of the unit song "Ha-Ka-Pe 626": "Menzel, Arno, look at that, *jubheidi* ... how he can drive the Opel. He gets the Jews every day, for him it's a downright pain, *jubheidi* ..." in a printed holiday publication by the motor pool, unpaginated. We are grateful to Martin Hözl for this reference.
44. LVVA, P 132-28-18, 29, journal of the Dortmund Group, entry for 8 March 1942, with the names of the Jewish controllers. An entry from 29 March 1942 shows that quite apparently the names of the men changed, see ibid., 52. On 1 April, the group elders were informed: "There exists once again occasion to point out that every kind of barter is strictly prohibited. We ask all detail leaders to point out to their group that, for all cases of barter on the part of members of their detail that are discovered, they will be relieved of their jobs for dereliction of their supervisory duties, possibly [for] acting as an accessory, and called to account. You will report by name all detail leaders and communicate to us that they have been instructed in the spirit of today's circular."
45. Staw. Hamburg, 141 Js 534/60, Bd. 40 statement by Hilde Sherman-Zander (deported from Düsseldorf), 15 October 1953, 6,522. See also the film, "Verschollen in Riga – Bilder einer Erinnerungsreise," directed by Jürgen Hobrecht, Federal Republic of Germany, 1992, 50 min.
46. BA Berlin, R 58/221, Ereignismeldung Nr. 195, 24 April 1942.
47. USHMM, RG 15.007, reel 16 [RSHA-Material from Warsaw], Der KdS Lettland, betr. Tätigkeitsbericht für die Zeit vom 23.5.-18.6.1942, 24 June 1942.
48. LVVA, P 132-28-18, 1, journal of the Dortmund Group, entry for 15 February 1942.
49. According to a situation report for February 1942, around 900 Jewish workers were deployed for these services (Commandos Šķirotava and Reich Railway I and II), see BA Berlin, R 91/30, Der Geb. Komm. Riga, Arbeitsamt an den Gen.-Komm., Abtl. Aso, 7 March 1942, betr. Lage im Monat Februar 1942.
50. LVVA, P 132-28-18, 10, journal of the Dortmund Group, entry for 22 February 1942: "To all groups. We would like to point out that all commandos may be provided only on the basis of a pass from Labor Office Riga. With regard to the deployment of women for labor, it is to be remembered that, in the commandos that make particular demands on the physical strength of the women and girls affected (long marches, shoveling snow, loading coal), replacements are to follow at regular intervals. It has become apparent that the non-observance of this aspect among different groups has led to an increase in cases of illness, which must be avoided under all circumstances in order not to endanger the labor deployments."
51. Gottschalk, *Der letzte Weg*, 27.
52. LVVA, P 132-28-18, 29, journal of the Dortmund Group, entry for 4 March 1942.
53. Schneider, *Journey into Terror*, 22 and note 51.
54. Staw. Hamburg, 141 Js 534/60, Bd. 3, statement by Willy Weiss, 27 January 1950, 270–271. Ibid., Bd. 20, statement Gustav Harf, 7 November 1961, 2,990.
55. Ibid., Bd. 3, statement by Hermann Heymann, 29 March 1950, 375–376.

56. Staw. Hamburg, 141 Js 534/60, Bd. 43, statement by Ernst Metzger, 6 December 1963, 7,121–7,124. Ibid., Bd. 20, statement by Gustav Harf, 7 November 1961, 2,990.
57. Ibid., Bd. 43, statement by Metzger, 6 December 1963, 7,125.
58. LVVA, P 132-28-18, 8, journal of the Dortmund Group, entry for 21 February 1942.
59. Ibid., 12, entry for 24 February 1942, "We ask the family members of the men employed by Special Commando Krause I to appear this afternoon punctually at 3:00 in the office of the Labor Deployment Central Office, Room 9, as mail from these men that can be read has arrived, and we would furthermore like to convey various wishes. Labor Deployment Central Office, sig. Schulz [sic]."
60. Ibid., 54, entry for 31 March 1942.

– *Chapter 14* –

THE TURNING POINT

Operation Dünamünde at Jungfernhof and in the "Ghetto for Reich Jews"

Operation Dünamünde, which was directed against the inhabitants of the ghetto and the Jungfernhof camp, signified the key turning point in the fate of the deportees. But although the postwar statements of survivors make clear very quickly that almost every family was affected by this operation, it is astonishing in retrospect that the dates given for the selection and evacuation of so many small children, mothers, people unable to work, and elderly persons should in part deviate so considerably from one another.

Jeanette Wolff, who had been deported from Dortmund together with her husband and her two daughters, wrote in 1947 that, after the operation aimed at the Jews from Berlin and Vienna on 5 February 1942, the work deployment desk person of each group was also forced to keep lists of old and weak Jews, who for their part were supposed to be sent to the suburb of Daugavgrīva, Dünamünde in German, for lighter jobs in canneries. Trucks shuttled back and forth between the ghetto and Daugavgrīva every half an hour, she wrote.[1] Max Kaufmann also recalled that there had been an operation against the German Jews in the large ghetto that year, during which older men and women were taken away on instructions from the group leaders to work in a cannery in Daugavgrīva. Kaufmann saw the transport and noted in his book that the returning trucks could never have managed the distance in thirty minutes.[2] Hilde Sherman reported in 1989 that the ghetto phase of Operation Dünamünde took place on 6 February 1942. According to her memoirs, it was here that gassing vans camouflaged as Red Cross vehicles were deployed for the first time. According to assurances given by Ghetto Commandant Kurt Krause, the codeword Dünamünde indicated a nearby fishing village with a cannery and light jobs.[3] Gerda Gottschalk, on the other hand, mentioned in her 1991 memoirs that transports with old people from the ghetto to a fishing village by this name took place several times, always on a Monday, and noted that the name

---

Notes for this chapter begin on page 333.

Dünamünde was a fabrication dreamt up by the SS and police – code for shootings in the Bikernieki woods.[4]

But Kaufmann was not mistaken; for a local such as himself Daugavgrīva did indeed exist. Located on the estuary of the Daugava, Daugavgrīva was founded in the twelfth century as a Cistercian monastery, but the area's original monastic character changed once the site became the location of a fortress to protect Riga's harbor. In autumn 1919, Daugavgrīva was the scene of bitter fighting between allied expeditionary forces from Britain and France, on the one hand, and Russia's Western Volunteer Army under Count Pavel Avalov-Bermondt and local German free corps, on the other.[5] The location, which was unknown to most German Jews, came to symbolize an important victory in achieving Latvian sovereignty.

Without being asked, Gerhard Maywald, who had been in charge of construction at the Salaspils camp, claimed during questioning in November 1963 that he had made up the fish cannery at Daugavgrīva. He argued that this deception had been created, for one, to lure Jews able to work away from Jungfernhof to Salaspils and, for another, to conceal the fact that a camp was being constructed at a site near Jungfernhof and thus prevent "undesirable shuttle traffic" between the two camps. When Maywald was read fifteen statements from Jewish witnesses stating that this had been a selection process for a mass murder operation, he was unable to say anything but: "The witnesses are all saying something that's untrue."[6]

Gertrude Schneider in 2002 presented a more detailed and differentiated account of the events linked to the term Dünamünde. She, too, described that every group in the ghetto had been instructed to report to the commandant's office 60–120 persons who could not be deployed. On 13 and 14 March 1942, the lists were merged by the group labor desk persons, and the individuals affected were informed by couriers and building supervisors that they would soon be transferred for work at a fish cannery. The next day, a Sunday, those who had been picked gathered outside their buildings before walking along Leipzig St. to the waiting trucks. Several relatives asked to be taken along as well; others who had been picked went into hiding. The Germans, wrote Schneider, did not bother with the lists, nor did they search the apartments for those who had remained behind. According to Schneider, on 15 March 1942, almost 1,900 people lost their lives this way. Over the next two days the evacuees' clothing was brought back to the ghetto and taken to the textile workshops, where female workers recognized personal effects. In no time, the news spread throughout the ghetto.[7]

But there are doubts about this version as well, for as already mentioned in chapter 8 of this volume, as of 10 March 1942, the Jewish-run Labor Deployment Central Office had yet to receive from all of the groups complete data on those who were unable to work; the lists drawn up by then were highly fragmentary.[8] Whether a deportation from the ghetto took place on 15 March as well is disputed; at any rate, this is the date when a general roll call for the next day was announced in writing for ghetto inhabitants who were not working.[9] This was also recalled by Erna Levie, who stressed that she had been forced to stand for hours at a roll call on her birthday, because Rudolf Lange – the regional commander of the Security Police and the SD (KdS Latvia) – and his noncommissioned officers had mustered people with an emphasis on ability to work. However, she did not mention an evacuation taking place immediately thereafter.[10]

Edith Wolff, Jeanette Wolff's daughter, told what she remembered of 16 March 1942 in a detailed statement almost eight years later:

> I remember very well the large roll call that preceded the dispatching to Dünamünde. We had to report in rows of ten. Approximately 20,000 people had reported, so it was impossible for individuals to observe what was happening. A commission of SS men, which was rather strong in numerical terms, showed up and carried out the selection. I remember the presence of [SS] Major Lange, Krause, Gimnich, Migge, Nickel, Seck, and Roschmann. These names had become known to us in part at roll calls, because these SS men loudly called their names to one another, in part I became acquainted with these names only in the course of my other experiences in Latvia. All of the SS officers carried out the selection. I don't mean to say that every SS man picked, but only the prominent people. I can't say for certain whether Migge or Seck or Nickel picked people. By the way, the people registered on the list were called out first. These lists had been compiled by our Jewish self-administration. The persons who were called out had to step forward. They were now examined once more – several were sent back again. All of the others, that is to say, those who were not on the list, were also mustered. In practical terms, this involved a correction of the lists. I can't say whether the number of those who were ultimately picked increased or decreased compared with those who had been registered on the lists. I tend to think that they were larger in the final result. The evacuations began during roll call. When the vehicles returned empty after 15–20 minutes, we became suspicious. I personally had already had an uneasy feeling after my mother and I had spoken to police lieutenant Hesfehr on behalf of my sister Juliane, who had been put on the list, and had heard from Hesfehr: My sister was to not remain on the list at any price. He did not say expressly that Dünamünde was a death commando, but one could infer from his words that it was dangerous.[11]

In addition to the 16 March deportation to the pits dug by Commando Krause I in the Bikernieki woods, there must have been two other transports from the ghetto within the framework of this operation.[12] The journal of the Dortmund Group contains an entry for 29 March stating that a day later the "first transport" would leave for Daugavgrīva, and on 2 April it was noted that the next morning two policemen from every group were to be present at the Prague Gate; these were "to be of assistance in the evacuation of the people to Dünamünde."[13] Based on a comparison of contemporary records and the memoirs of some of the survivors, it is impossible to say whether two or three transports left the ghetto during Operation Dünamünde. The statements provided by Latvian collaborators are less helpful in this case, because the majority of them speak in general terms about shooting operations against Jews in spring 1942 without explaining where the people came from.[14]

By contrast, it is much easier to reconstruct the course of Operation Dünamünde at the Jungfernhof camp. Early in the morning of 26 March 1942, a former bus driver for the Riga transit service turned auxiliary security policeman drove German members of KdS Latvia to Jungfernhof. There, Rudolf Seck had already separated from the rest of the inmates just under 450 persons whom he intended to use for the continued expansion of the agricultural estate.[15] All of the others were to be evacuated, and the trucks, buses, and auxiliary police from the Arajs Commando needed to remove them were now arriving. Seck himself freely admitted to this selection, which he carried out largely on his own, because he was seeking to stress his "naivety" with regard to the coming operation: for him, 26 March was the day of a large transport to the nearby ghetto.[16] But the abundance of credible witness statements considerably undermined the self-appointed commandant's postwar version of events. Several survivors could remember a conversation that Seck had with the daughter of Gustav Kleemann, the "elder of the Jews" in the Jungfernhof camp: Lore Kleemann asked Seck, initially in vain, for permission to accompany her father to the site of his new deployment. But after she continued to insist, Seck allowed her to go, saying she would deeply regret it that very day.[17] Seck claimed that he had sought to insinuate the adverse conditions within the ghetto, but it was too obvious that he was lying.[18]

In the meantime, the blue bus from the Riga transportation service had driven off, taking Lange, Maywald, Krause, and others from KdS Latvia to the Bikernieki woods where the pits had already been dug.[19] More than 2,000 people were subsequently driven through the middle of Riga to the scene of the crime: "When we reported that morning," said the former auxiliary security policeman Peteris Iklaws,

> I was appointed to escort the Jews to the shooting. I myself and the other policemen who had to escort the Jews left by truck ... Later, I saw that the Jews were also escorted to the shooting in buses ... When we arrived in the ghetto, which was located in Jumprawmujzha [Jumpravmuiža, Jungfernhof], a group of Jews

who were to be shot was already standing there ready ... The trucks with the victims drove through the city, that is via the Moscow, Brīvības (now Lenin St.), and Bikernieku road. Then we drove on to the Bikernieku woods. Here, we drove several hundred meters along a country road, then we turned right. Not far from the country road, we unloaded the Jews from the trucks. Here, there was a group of policemen from the Arajs Commando who took over the victims from us. The shooting site was about 100 meters from the place where we unloaded. The victims went to the pit between a cordon of two rows [of men] from the Arajs Commando. They stood several steps apart from one another, and they were armed with rifles.

On the trucks, we escorted men and women of various ages, young and old Jews, and children. Apparently, they were being transported in entire families. On the way, they asked in German (I understood German) where they were being transported. We answered that we did not know, although it was known to us what awaited them. In the course of the day, I made no fewer than 4–5 trips. The shooting of the Jews lasted from morning to evening. On this day, around 2,000 Jews were murdered.

After the Jews had been unloaded from the truck, they were ordered in German to strip ... The Jews grasped what would happen to them. For that reason, out of panic, several of them did not undress. The policemen from the Arajs Commando violently tore their clothes off of them, and they were stripped down to their undergarments ... After I, together with other policemen, had taken the Jews to the shooting site, I left the truck several times and [went] over to the pit, because I was interested in seeing what was actually happening. There I saw the Jews being driven into the pit and policemen from the Arajs Commando shooting at them with machine pistols ... Furthermore, the head of the Security Police and the SD in Latvia, Lange, was at the pit, in addition, several German officers from the SD whose family names I did not know. Arajs and several officers from his command – who concretely, I no longer remember – were standing there with them. I saw Arajs, Lange, and other German officers walking back and forth next to the pit and shooting into the pit with pistols.[20]

The overall number of victims from Operation Dünamünde at Jungfernhof and in the ghetto is difficult to reconstruct. A very imprecise rough number, more interesting due to the justification given for the operation, is found in Report on Events USSR No. 195 of 24 April 1942, where it is said that 983 Jews "who had contagious diseases or were so old and frail that they no longer came into question for deployment for work" were shot.[21] However, realistic estimates based on witness statements from survivors and marksmen from the ranks of the perpetrators speak of around 1,800 victims from Jungfernhof and 3,000 from the ghetto.[22]

For the deportees, these appalling days when families were torn apart and the murder of relatives was slowly confirmed were a major turning point. At Jungfernhof, the Jews realized that only one in eight of those who had originally arrived at the once overfilled farmyard was still alive. In the ghetto, the deportees now realized that the fate of the Latvian Jews had been no exception, but instead seemed to be the rule. In historical perspective, however, Operation Dünamünde is better understood as the continued intensification of the mass murder operations directed at the deportees, which must have started, strictly taken, a few days before the Wannsee Conference. During his stay at the SD guest house on Am Grossen Wannsee, Lange must have found that his views were in line with the planning of his boss Reinhard Heydrich. After Lange returned to Riga, the murder of Jews unable to work continued. Not even the death of Territorial Commander of the Security Police and SD Walther Stahlecker on 23 March 1942 seems to have slowed the pace of this local wave of killings.[23]

For Lange, implementing Heydrich's vision of the "final solution" resulted in a number of positive local effects on the periphery: He was able to yield to Seck's insistence on relief for Jungfernhof; he could demonstrate to the civil administration that it was not necessary to enlarge the ghetto to accommodate the Jews from the west; and he was able to show that he still intended to exercise power of disposal over the deportees – at any rate over those who were unable to work. It has already been shown that with regard to workers, the situation on the Latvian labor market had deteriorated to the point that Lange was in fact forced to refrain from seizing the working Jews for shooting. But when new transports arrived later that year, would he make the new arrivals who were able to work available to the general commissar as forced laborers?

Questions regarding the further shape of the Holocaust in Latvia are bound up not only in the events that took place in Riga in January and the following two months. If, since the start of 1942, Lange had been having German Jews who were unable to work – as well as two of the January transports – shot in accordance with orders, why was it necessary for Himmler to visit Łódź (Litzmannstadt) at the end of April 1942, when he apparently ordered the expansion of the mass murder operations at Chełmno (Kulmhof) to include deportees from the west who were unable to work?[24] And if – as the historian Peter Witte recognized quite early on, and as Himmler's official calendar confirms most impressively – Himmler preferred to make decisions in talks with his subordinates on the ground, what moved him to change his opinion so radically between the arrival of the Berlin transport on 30 November 1941 – a shooting he sought to prevent – and the arrival of the Theresienstadt transport on 19 January 1942?[25]

Notes

1. Jeanette Wolff, *Sadismus oder Wahnsinn*, 11–12. Wolff puts the number of those sent off at 5,000 persons.

2. Kaufmann, *Churbn Lettland*, 140–141, Kaufmann puts the number of victims at 1,000 people.
3. Sherman-Zander, *Zwischen Tag und Dunkel*, 48–50. The deployment of gas vans in this operation is not documented. Latvian policemen from Victor Arajs's auxiliary security police who were deployed during Operation Dünamünde spoke exclusively of shooting operations. Because a good many of them were transferred to Minsk in spring 1942 in order to guard the arrival of Viennese Jews at the extermination camp Maly Trostenez (Maly Tras'tsianets, Malyi Trostenets), where gas vans were used, the difference in their actions was quite apparent to them, see Staw. Hamburg, 141 Js 534/60, SB 23, statement by Ilgonis Leonardowitsch Wajnkowskis, 28 November 1975, 4,077; ibid., statement by Karlis Janowitsch Strazds, 26 December 1975, 4,138; ibid., statement by Paulis Awgustowitsch Mikajns, 8 January 1976, 4,284.
4. Gottschalk, *Der letzte Weg*, 36.
5. Sigmar Stopinski, *Das Baltikum im Patt der Mächte*, 243–245.
6. Staw. Hamburg 141 Js 534/60, Bd. 24, statement by Gerhard Maywald, 28 November 1963, 6,939–6,940.
7. Schneider, *Journey into Terror*, 34–36.
8. See chapter 8, this volume.
9. LVVA, P 132-28-18, 35, journal of the Dortmund Group, entry for 15 March 1942: "To all groups. I ask the following order be observed exactly: For the roll call that is to take place tomorrow, the camp police of the groups is to place at the disposal of the work deployment 2 policemen each at 9:00 in the morning. Report to Mr. Baum through the foreman of the Cologne Group van Dyck. In addition, the foreman of the Cassel Group, Mr. Bibo, is to join this commando. The daily patrol is not to report [to] Cologne Camp tomorrow morning at 8:00, but is to be at my disposal at 9:15 on the corner of Düsseldorf and Kassel streets. Mr. Haar, the foreman of the Leipzig Group is to join this [commando]. Signs of respect such as standing will be shown only through military bearing. Sig. Frankenberg."
10. AWL, Testaments to the Holocaust, Series One, reel 57, P.III.h. no. 1011a, response of Erna Levie, deported from Gelsenkirchen via Dortmund, to a written inquiry of the Committee for the Investigation of Nazi Crimes in the Baltic Countries, 14 November 1947.
11. Staw. Hamburg 141 Js 534/60, Bd. 3, statement by Edith Sophia Wolff, 9 December 1949, 206–207.
12. That Jews from Commando Krause I were deployed is documented by a statement of one of the Latvian guards, see ibid., SB 23, statement by Wajnkowskis, 28 November 1975, 4,076.
13. LVVA, P 132-28-18, 50–51, journal of the Dortmund Group, entry for 29 March 1942: "Allotted from the group to the first transport to Dünamünde are the medics: Ferdinand Sternberg, Nathan Michel, Ernst Levy. Nurse Johanne Szulmann. The aforementioned have to appear in the barrack yard punctually at 7:00 A.M. on Monday, 30 March, without luggage for transport to Dünamünde. Sig. Dr. Herzberg." Also from the entry for the same day: "Nurse Anne Wolff of the Dortmund Group was belatedly allotted for Dünamünde. I informed Nurse Anne Wolff of this fact personally on behalf of Dr. Aufrecht on 29 March. The date of departure has yet to be made known. Dr. Herzberg." Also, ibid., 58, entry for 2 April 1942, "At 6:45 A.M., on 3 April 1942, the groups are to place at my disposal two strong policemen at the Prague Gate. The Dortmund Group will stand ready with the group for deployment (behind Vienna, Berlin). The requested policemen are to be of assistance in the evacuation of the people to Dünamünde and must be available to me at the appointed hour. Labor Deployment Central Office."

14. For example, the witness statement given on 28 November 1975 by auxiliary policeman Ilgonis Wajnkowskis, who was assigned to the cordon: "This essentially involved older men and women. There were no children among the victims, as far as I can remember. I don't know from whence they were brought to the shooting site. I did not hear the Jews speak Latvian. They spoke German or Hebrew." See Staw. Hamburg, 141 Js 534/60, SB 23, statement by Wajnkowskis, 28 November 1975, 4,075; ibid., SB 27, statement by Woldemar Reinholdis Rolmanis, 12 July 1976, 4,671: "I didn't know and was not interested in where the victims to be shot were brought from."
15. Ibid., Bd. 1, statement by Herbert Simon, 5 May 1949, 27. Simon, who was from Hamburg, said: "The picking of these 1,500 victims was done primarily by Seck. It may be that a certain Maiwald [sic] also assisted." Seck confirmed that he was solely responsible for selection, see ibid. Bd. 2, statements by Rudolf Seck on 23 December 1949 and 3 January 1950, 222–224.
16. Ibid., Bd. 1, statement by Rudolf Seck, 6 May 1949, 29: "However, it was not known to me at the time, and to this day, I don't believe that these people were shot in the high forest or anywhere else. In my view, these people went on living in the ghetto. That their relatives have received no sign of life from the evacuation from the Jungfernhof camp to this day is something I can't explain ... I received the order from the regional commander of the Sipo and the SD in Riga, SS Major Lange, to pick as many people as I needed to run of the Jungfernhof estate. He would have the rest picked up in trucks and taken to the ghetto in Riga." In the public session of the courtroom proceedings in his case at a Bergedorf court on 7 July 1949, Seck said, "My Jews never told me that their relatives had never arrived in the ghetto." See ibid., 59.
17. Seck's sentence became known throughout Jungfernhof quite quickly. Artur Herz, deported from Gelsenkirchen via Dortmund and initially confined to Salaspils, learned of the story in August 1942, when he came to Jungfernhof from the ghetto, see Staw. Hamburg, 141 Js 534/60, Bd. 1, statement by Artur Herz, 4 June 1949, 54; ibid., statement by Lucie Levi, 6 May 1949, 32; ibid., statement by Henny Jünger (née Herz), 25 May 1949, 45; ibid., statement by Kurt Kendziorek, 22 June 1949, 57. Levi and Kendziorek were deported from Hamburg, Jünger from Stuttgart.
18. Ibid. Bd. 2, statement by Seck, 3 January 1950, 224–225.
19. Ibid., SB 29, statement by Jan-Alfred Frank-Prank, 5 April 1976, 4,742. Frank-Prank, a former driver for the Riga municipal bus depot who had come to work for the German Security Police, participated in carrying out the operation.
20. Staw. Hamburg, 141 Js 534/60, SB 22, statement by Peteris Petrowitsch Iklaws, 13 January 1976, 4,042–4,044.
21. BA Berlin, R 58/221, Ereignismeldung Nr. 195, 24 April 1942.
22. On this, see *Buch der Erinnerung*, Bd. 1, 12 and 27.
23. On Stahlecker's death after a partisan attack near Saniki on 19 March 1942, see Klein, "Die Erlaubnis zum grenzenlosen Massenmord," in *Die Wehrmacht*, ed. Müller and Volkmann, 938.
24. Witte, "Zwei Entscheidungen in der 'Endlösung der Judenfrage'," *Theresienstädter Studien und Dokumente* 2 (1995): 38–68.
25. Ibid., 57–58.

– Chapter 15 –

Forced Labor and Annihilation in County Commissariat Riga City

The survivors of the operations against those unable to work were given no time to come to terms with their experience. At the same time, astonishingly enough, conditions in Jungfernhof changed completely after 26 March. It seemed as if the megalomaniacal commandant, Rudolf Seck, had been turned into an initiative-friendly estate administrator, who with the beginning of spring had thrown himself into concrete structural plans for the Jungfernhof camp. Numerous survivors recalled that after Operation Dünamünde conditions in Jungfernhof generally improved.[1] That is not surprising, for in addition to the advent of warmer weather, additional articles of clothing were made available to everybody, and in the weeks that followed, the first harvests were brought in. It was characteristic of local conditions that Jungfernhof still lacked fencing in spring and summer 1942. Any German Jew attempting to flee would have had to trust in the existence of a latent infrastructure of solidarity and assistance on the part of the Latvians. Understandably, such trust had not developed at Jungfernhof given the presence of Latvian auxiliary policemen from the Arajs Commando. Besides, in spring 1942, the inmates at Jungfernhof were increasingly in a position to assess their situation. Compared to the Riga ghetto inhabitants and the Salaspils camp inmates, the Jews at Jungfernhof had fortune in their misfortune.[2]

In addition, almost all of the agricultural chores and the construction of additional barracks at Jungfernhof served to improve the Jews' situation. From time to time, Seck set aside the trappings of his status as camp commandant when he saw how the performance of "his" Jews advanced the estate's development. The Jews could occasionally allow themselves a lapse in discipline, such as bathing in the Daugava. Brought before survivor Else Lüders on 10 May 1949, Seck reluctantly admitted to abusing the woman – she had been in her early thirties while in Riga – but defended himself by saying he had never reported anybody to Riga and thus avoided the imposition of death sentences. "The witness admits this without qualification," according to the protocol, "and stresses that after 26 March 1942, Seck

---

Notes for this chapter begin on page 346.

treated the inmates of the camp so well that she actually could have felt like a [German youth] training service conscript [at camp]." Seck also elicited from Lüders that some fifteen dances had been held between summer 1942 and spring 1943, where Seck was not only on hand but also possibly played music.[3]

Käthe Friess, however, left no doubt in her personal reminiscences that such "amusements" were compulsory and ultimately served to distract the commandant. Friess, who was deported from Würzburg at the age of twenty, also assessed the period after Operation Dünamünde as considerably more pleasant than before: "The day after began with the construction of a new barrack. We all helped build our new home. It became a fairytale palace vis-à-vis the previous accommodations. It was a large wooden construction with heating. Yes sir, we didn't freeze anymore! The bunks were only two stories high, large and comfortable, and the entire room was bright and friendly. In front of the men's and women's sleeping quarters was one toilet each, a lovely washroom, and a lounge with long wooden tables and benches. It looked like 'in a third class waiting room.' It was all so luxurious and unfamiliar that we felt out of place and awkward in this warmth and cleanliness. But did all those dear people have to leave us so that we should have it so good?"[4]

In the ghetto, there could be no talk of such improvements. Nothing changed for the better there, even as the character of forced labor through the daily routine of being sent to work was increasingly being augmented by the "barracking" of Jews at their place of work. Whereas the labor administration had complained in December 1941 about some enterprises housing and feeding Jewish workers on company premises without prior consultation, it now accepted such actions on the part of employers in "urgent cases justified by the wartime economy" if the Security Police raised no objections.[5] To this end, the Security Police drafted a bulletin in which, alongside the regulations for handling labor commandos and details, it was pointed out that barracking absolutely had to be applied for.[6]

Administrative Counselor Schmutzler of County Commissariat Riga City's Labor Department was receiving a growing number of petitions from military offices and private enterprises, which were then being permitted to barrack Jews when assignments were important to the war effort.[7] In April 1942, 300 workers had already been deployed outside the ghetto on a sustained basis, and in the labor administration, officials were trying in vain to stop the trend.[8] But construction measures important to the war effort, such as those of the Königsberg-based company Wolf and Döring, were not to be thwarted; its application to barrack 200 Jewish workers near the prisoner of war camp at Salaspils was also approved, as was, for example, a request from the Wehrmacht Quarters Office to take on an initial forty-two men.[9] A little later, this bureau, which was subordinated to the office of the Wehrmacht Territorial Commander Ostland, once again applied for ninety workers, because it was responsible for maintenance and construction of collective quarters for soldiers passing through Riga; this was also immediately accepted as important to the war effort.[10] Since September 1941, a work commando of several hundred Jewish men had been placed with this employer.[11] This wave of barrackings is also reflected in the journal of the Dortmund Group: for example, the women who were designated for Commando Athletic Field were instructed prior to departure to take along brooms, scrub brushes, and buckets.[12] The German women for the barracking known as "Reich Commissar" were ordered to depart on 27 May.[13]

For Jews, barracking resembled the daily commandos inasmuch as they first had to find out how difficult the work was, and whether it was possible to barter for additional foodstuffs. It was of course much harder to get out of an inhumane barracking or to be transferred to a more auspicious barracking than it had been with the daily commandos. Furthermore, Kurt Krause, the ghetto commandant, prohibited improvised mail to the ghetto under threat of death, which made many of the deportees reluctant to participate in the barracking experiment.[14] In fact, a 20-year-old man from Kassel, a detail leader in a barracking camp, was hanged on 10 August 1942, because he "had regularly conveyed letters and small packages to the ghetto and other camps."[15]

What lay behind the Reich Commissar Ostland's request of 22 May 1942, for fifty-four Jewish women? It was possible to learn from the Latvian Jews that for a long time the barracking Reich Commissar meant tailoring work.[16] But this time, the women passed the workshops on Valnu St., headed to the harbors, and were taken from there to Bulduri (Bilderlingshof). "At 48 10th Line, we moved into an empty building ... The building had to be thoroughly cleaned and furnished for the Reich Commissar's coming vacation guests in the palace. For weeks, it was up and down the stairs with bucket, scrub brush, and later furniture as well."[17] The women had landed at the beach near Riga in a well-known resort close to Jūrmala (Riga-Strand), and they apparently worked so well that on 3 June the local technical inspector managed to have their barracking extended until the end of the month. As this was not important to the war effort, the labor administration pointed out that there was no possibility of granting a longer extension.[18]

From Bulduri, the road soon led to neighboring Dzintari, not far from Majori (Majorenhof), where German men from the ghetto had been employed in maintenance work since 6 July.[19] The women were at the mercy of an easy-going German inspector by the name of Dähne and a Latvian policeman, a situation that could have its pleasant sides. The women were often allowed to take walks on the beach and to bathe in the sea. "Finally, both homes were ready to receive guests; they were to be opened with a large gala in the women's home ... We scrubbing women and furniture movers turned into cooks and waitresses. Dähne ordered us to take off the star. The guests were free of suspicion, chatted with us, they were delighted with their vacation stay and gave large tips. The gala lasted the entire night. We ordered some portions of food that had not been ordered, carried them into an empty room, and ate hastily. In the following week, we didn't wear the star either."[20]

But this life, which was rather idyllic compared with all of the other deployments, was not to last long. On 22 July, Senior Administrative Counselor Max Dorr, the head of General Commissariat Latvia's Labor Department, complained to the Security Police that German Jews were being deployed in jobs that were not important to the war effort and pointed to Jungfernhof as well as to conditions near Jūrmala: "Thus, for example, the German guests of the cafeteria of Herr Reichskommissar for Ostland in Riga Beach and also the cafeteria of the Main Railroad Directorate in Riga Beach are being served by Jewesses, who also prepare the fare they dispensed [sic]. Three days ago, the undersigned himself encountered Jews preparing a tennis court. Jews and Jewesses are said to be employed in considerable number in garden and gardening jobs, for which an urgent need is not discernible. This apparently involves Reich-German Jews who have not yet been transferred to me for labor deployment."[21]

Shortly thereafter, Schmutzler, the head of the Riga Labor Office, visited Jungfernhof to convince himself that the site included a blacksmith and wash salon for the maintenance of SS equipment and clothing in addition to its core agricultural activities.[22] The labor administration did not make another push to seize the Jews of the Security Police, in part because the response from Rudolf Lange, the regional commander of the Security Police (KdS Latvia), was most clear:

> With the exception of the Jews who I need for my workshops and for the construction plans of the Security Police, the deployment for labor of all Jews who are able to work is regulated via the ghetto Labor Office, which is subordinate to the county commissar. The Labor Office issues the passes for all work details. Therefore, the Labor Office is most accurately informed with regard to deployment for labor and the number of Jews assigned to external jobs and [it] plans the assignments itself. My ghetto commandant supports the Labor Office insofar as he – by means of strict inspections and checks – immediately detects persons sick with laziness and numerous shirkers and brings them to their labor deployment. In order to exploit for the wartime economy workers no longer suitable for exter-

nal deployment, I recently set up workshops in the ghetto and have articles of clothing that are important to the Army manufactured for the company Ostland-Faser. Otherwise, it is correct that the Jews requested by the Reich Commissariat were in part employed in housecleaning and kitchen jobs at the Reich Commissariat's beach resort. This office has already pointed out to the director of the rest home, Inspector Dähne, that Jews may be used only for truly urgent jobs.[23]

Such barrackings, for example, those at the beach of the Riga vicinity resort area, were considered islands for recuperating from the daily hard labor and the fear of inspections at the ghetto gate. However, the actual goal of accommodating Jewish workers outside the Moscow Suburb was to exhaust them thoroughly on the job. The first external barrackings at the peat camps Schlock (Sloka), Salaspils, and Priedaine as well as at the Air Force's construction camp or the Railroad Station Commandant's Office were much more in line with the German goal of physical exploitation. The Jews had to perform hard labor, which the Air Force Construction Technical Procurement Office, for example, admitted when it sent the County Commissariat Riga a written reminder for the regular allocation of food rations.[24] It was no different for the mostly Latvian Jews who were lent to the sugar factory in Liepāja (Libau) and Jelgava (Mitau) in the course of 1942.[25] The eighty Jewish men barracked with the Office of the SS Economist in summer 1942 labored so strenuously that even the Riga Labor Office mentioned it.[26]

Because there are no numbers available to shed light on the development of barrackings, very little empirical data on the course of this kind of forced labor distribution can be derived. Toward the end of 1942, County Commissariat Riga City determined that around 10,500 Jews had been deployed for labor. Just under 6,500 men and about 4,000 women pursued a daily job inside or outside the ghetto, but the number of Jews who were unemployed, sick, or otherwise unable to work for an extended period remained Krause's secret. This information was not released, for "Security Police-related reasons." The Riga civil administration put the overall number of ghetto inhabitants at approximately 12,000 persons. Of these, some 2,000, about one-sixth of the ghetto population, were barracked outside the ghetto. Around 1,190 people worked in the ghetto workshops, meaning that every morning more than 7,300 persons had to leave the ghetto for their place of work.[27]

Like the Security Police at the Jungfernhof estate, the construction site Salaspils, and the mass graves of Bikernieki, other SS and police offices profited from the deployment of forced laborers. In response to a query, KdS Latvia reported that as of November 1942, there were 598 Jews working in twelve SS and police camps in General Commissariat Latvia and another 793 Jews at various SS and police offices.[28] Because most of the work done in Liepāja, Jelgava, and Daugavpils in late autumn 1942 was for the Kūdra peat works and the Wehrmacht, almost all of the above 1,391 Jews were bound to have worked in the offices, construction camps, infirmaries, workshops, and lodgings of the Security Police, the Order Police, and the Waffen-SS in and around Riga.[29]

One of the daily commandos that worked for the Security Police had existed since spring 1942. Every morning, at least fifty Jewish men under the supervision of a certain Salomon left the ghetto and walked to where Reimersa St. (Moltke St.) meets Raina Blvd. (Alfred Rosenberg Ring). On either side of Reimersa St. were the buildings where the Security Police had its various offices. These two buildings also contained a food storeroom, a cafeteria, a weapons depot, and, until spring 1943, a clothing store for items belonging to the deportees but considered by KdS Latvia to be of value and useful for work. Behind one of the buildings was an inner courtyard, which was dominated by the garages of the motor pool. The German and Latvian Jews who worked there were spread out over most of the offices. In this respect, this commando of Jewish workers was located at a source of news and rumors. They learned when weapons were handed out in large numbers, when trucks or buses were readied for departure, and when large amounts of used clothing arrived.

But for daily survival, access to the clothing store and the food storeroom was key. Although they were working in the central office of their tormenters, the Jewish forced laborers had to try and organize what was important for the survival of their families in the ghetto. One evening in summer 1942, the entire detail was stopped on the premises and randomly searched. Within minutes, the garage courtyard was littered with food discarded in panic. In a rage, Lange summoned the building administrator, SS Second Lieutenant Rudolf Reese, showered him with criticism, and ordered him to conduct a thorough search of the Jews. In the end, around fifteen men, among them several adolescents, were confined to the garages and taken to Salaspils the next day. There, after a "verdict" had been read aloud, they were shot by auxiliary policemen from the Arajs Commando.[30]

The German labor administration under Schmutzler and Arthur Eicker, at one point the former's chief advisor at the Bureau for the Deployment of Jews, along with the Jewish-run Labor Deployment Central Office, worked feverishly in summer 1942 on regrouping workers primarily for cutting peat, which was now in great demand. When Herbert Schultz, the head of the Labor Deployment Central Office, announced on 18 July that the first details for the peat works were to report the next day for roll call in the presence of Commandant Krause, he expressly pointed out that attempts to obtain certificates of illness from Dr. Hans Aufrecht would be futile. A day later, Schultz declared that failure to show up for this barracking would be considered sabotage and would have to be reported. Schultz then ordered that incomplete commandos be filled out. On 28 July, he threatened that all those who were able to work and had yet to be allocated would be transferred to the clothing depot for Army Group North, namely to Department IV in Milgrāvis (Mühlgraben).[31] Work there was considered particularly revolting, because blood-soaked scraps of uniforms and battle dress arrived there by the wagonload for disinfection, cleaning, and mending. However, rapid placement and the internal ghetto registration process could not alleviate the general problem confronting the German labor administration in General Commissariat Latvia. Agriculture aside, there were thousands of job openings in the lumber, metal, and construction industries, primarily for semi-skilled workers. Furthermore, Latvian conscript laborers regularly attempted to flee those camps where the heaviest labor had to be done – especially those associated with Organization Todt and its Construction Group Giesler.

This was the background to the arrival of two new transports with Jews from Berlin and Theresienstadt. The transport from Berlin departed on 15 August with 938 persons; the train from Theresienstadt left Bohemia five days later with 1,000 people. Despite the glaring shortage of workers, these Jews were not even taken to the ghetto, but were instead led straight to Bikernieki and shot. If KdS Latvia had adhered to "the carrying out of a general order of the Reichsführer-SS and chief of the German police" to exempt from "special measures" those deportees "aged 16–32" who were able to work, then at least 194 people would have been selected from these two transports. Whereas the Jewish-run Labor Deployment Central Office instructed the group labor desk persons to call up 14–16-year-old youths for daily deployment, the members of this same age group from the newly arrived Berlin and Theresienstadt transports were murdered in Bikernieki on 18 and 23 August 1942.[32]

One of these murder operations was attended by visitors from Estonia. SS Technical Sergeant Karl Geese, his driver Willi Bartsch, and two members of the Estonian Security Police, Alexander Laak and Ralf Gerrets, had come from Tallinn in order to follow the arrival of one of the two transports and the subsequent shooting operation. Laak and Gerrets were to run KdS Estonia's recently established labor correctional camp Jägala and were to familiarize themselves in advance with handling the arrival of transports. Both were informed in Riga that they would receive a transport in Estonia in a few days. While in Riga, Laak himself is supposed to have joined the shooting in the Bikernieki forest.[33] A few days later, another transport from Theresienstadt reached Riga, but continued on to Estonia and the agreed point of unloading at Raasiku, where the Jägala camp and the shooting pits of Kalevi Liiva had already been prepared.[34] After a selec-

Figure 15.1. Detail of Jewish forced laborers on the way to the workplace. Undated. Courtesy of Staatsarchiv Hamburg.

tion of about 200 young people, almost all women, the other 800 victims were driven to the pits in city buses.³⁵

On 8 September, another transport arrived in Šķirotava. It brought 797 people, average age 49.6 years, from Berlin to the Latvian capital; in addition, there were another 250 people from East Prussia whose passenger coaches had been attached to the same train in the course of the transport. Six men survived this transport. One of them, Georg Netler, described the arrival in Šķirotava in a 1949 statement: "The order was given that the men between 20 and 40 should step forward. There were about 80 ... All of the transport train's other passengers, that is to say, over 900 persons, were immediately loaded into blue buses. We heard nothing more of them. They were not allowed to take along any luggage. The luggage was loaded on smaller vehicles. The 80 of us went immediately to an OT camp in Mitau and were fully subordinated to the OT. We were employed in railroad construction (laying rails). The deployment lasted about 6 months until February 1943. 42 of us survived it. The rest died from diseases like abscesses and fluid build up, a consequence of the poor provisions and accommodations."³⁶

Later, on 29 September, another train from Berlin, this time with 1,049 people, including more than 200 Jews from Frankfurt am Main, reached the Raasiku station. SS Technical Sergeant Geese had already informed Gerrets that a transport would arrive in Estonia due to difficulties in Riga.³⁷ On the train itself, the Jews noticed that they were in Riga; shortly thereafter, it was said that Riga was unable to take them on, and the occupants of the passenger coaches feared the worst.³⁸ Upon arriving in Raasiku, this transport was also divided up according to ability to work. About 140 young girls went to Jägala; a few young men met this same fate.³⁹ About fifty young men who had previously unloaded the luggage and taken it to Jägala were then returned to the Raasiku station and taken to Jaunjelgava (Friedrichstadt) in County Commissariat Jelgava. There the young men spent several months in exhausting road construction work.⁴⁰

On 22 October, the next Berlin transport, which must have left the Reich capital three days earlier, reached the Šķirotava Station with 959 persons. The average age of this transport was 36.7 years.⁴¹ There were 264 people between 16 and 40 on this train; nonetheless, only some eighty persons were selected for labor, apparently only men. They were immediately put to work unloading the coal cars attached to their transport. Shortly thereafter, they were sent to the Security Police athletic field in Mežaparks (Kaiserwald), where they relieved the Jews barracked there and continued with the leveling work.⁴² Individual survivors were taken to the barracking at the Security Police auto workshop on Pētersalas St. (Peterholmsche St.)⁴³ The final transport to come to Riga left Berlin on 26 October 1942, reaching Riga three days later. All 798 people, including 201 potential workers aged 16–40, were shot upon arrival.[44]

These transports between mid August and the end of October 1942 were carried out in the wake of a large wave of transports from the "Greater German Reich," during which several trains from Vienna and Theresienstadt left for the camp Maly Trostenez (Maly Tras'tsianets, Malyi Trostenets) near Minsk, while large transports left German cities for Theresienstadt.[45] Many of these transports, which were organized by the Reich Security Main Office, were agreed to at a conference in Frankfurt am Main on 6 August 1942. Among these transports were two trains that had already been scheduled for Raasiku. Thus the impression made on Gerrets and the deportees that the decision to send the Berlin transport farther north was made on-site on 26 September is inaccurate. Riga was a planned stopover. While the first transport, Da 404, left Theresienstadt on schedule on 1 September, the second transport of 26 September, with Jews from Berlin and Frankfurt, was actually slated for 10 September. However, it should still be noted that despite individual postponements the seven deportation operations to Riga and beyond were an integral part of the planning session that had taken place two weeks earlier.[46]

The fate of these deportees makes clear that the acute shortage of workers in General Commissariat Latvia was not what guided the actions of the Security Police. Lange did not intend to provide the German or indigenous civil labor administrations with Jewish workers over whom he apparently would no longer have uncontested power of disposal. This would also mean that Himmler's basic instruction of May 1942 to exempt Jews between 16 and 32 from "special measures" either no longer applied, or did not apply to new arrivals.[47] As has already been mentioned, in September and October 1942 there had been negotiations on transferring Lithuanian Jews from Kaunas (Kauen, Kovno) to Spilve.[48] Such a solution for the urgent construction tasks of the German Air Force's Field Construction Office was preferred to using new workers from the recent transports. Furthermore, it is characteristic of the situation on the ground that the few selected Jews were placed with Organization Todt in County Commissariat Jelgava, while bypassing the civil administration in the process. The county commissar there wrote in his monthly report for September that Jews had been deployed with Construction Group Giesler "without activating the labor administration." The Jewish women and handful of men in Estonia disappeared for several months at the labor correctional camp Jägala, while the survivors of the transport of 22 October were accommodated at the Kaiserwald athletic field and a Security Police auto workshop.[49] The Security Police left behind no more evidence than was absolutely necessary. In the reports of the general commissar and governing mayor for Riga, there is not the slightest indication that these offices had been officially informed of the arrival of the transports, or that they sought to intervene when those transports arrived. Such an omission says nothing about the civil administration's state of knowledge; there was no reason for officials from the Main Railroad Directorate in Riga to consider such transports secret.

As is known, the situation was completely different in General Commissariat White Ruthenia. There, at the end of the July, Wilhelm Kube tried to intervene with Reich Commissar Hinrich Lohse against any further transports from the Reich and the General Government, pointing out that the few people working at KdS White Ruthenia were urgently needed in the struggle against the partisans.[50] But higher up, it had been clear for months that the civil administration would not interfere in transports, and this still applied – for Kube as well.[51] This situation shows very clearly that nobody had thought about trying to influence the transports to Reich Commissariat Ostland in such a way as to alleviate the strained labor situation.[52] The transports to Maly Trostenez that so troubled Kube also included people who were still able to work and could have been deployed in General Commissariat Latvia. In the tension between economic exploitation and the ideologically driven process of annihilation, "weltanschauung" had long since gained the upper hand.[53]

Notes

1. Staw. Hamburg, 141 Js 534/60, Bd. 1, statement by Carola Israel, 25 May 1949, 39; Trudy Ullmann Schloss, "A Farm Called Jungfernhof," in *The Unfinished Road*, 61.
2. Every two weeks, Jews were allowed to go to the ghetto and visit relatives, see Staw. Hamburg, 141 Js 534/60, Bd. 1, statement by Mascha Katz, 10 May 1948, 36; Schloss, who was deported from Stuttgart, recalled: "Our external commandos told us that we looked healthier than the ghetto people; fieldwork was evidently beneficial!" See Schloss, "Farm Called Jungfernhof," 61.
3. Staw. Hamburg, 141 Js 534/60, Bd. 1, Gegenüberstellung Else Lüders, Jahrgang 1909, mit Rudolf Seck am 10.5.1949, 34–35.
4. AWL, Testaments to the Holocaust, Series One, reel 56, P.III.h, no. 268, Käte Frieß, "Meinem Gori gewidmet," 1945, 25 (of report).
5. BA Berlin, R 91/99, Der Geb.-Komm. in Riga, Arbeitsamt, an den Gen.-Komm., Abtl. Sozialverwaltung, 1 January 1942, Bericht für die Zeit vom 16.11.-31-12.1941; LVVA, P 69-1a-17, 401, materials of the county commissar's Political Affairs Department collected for the February 1942 monthly report to the Reich commissar. These are also available in BA Berlin, R 91/30.
6. BA Berlin, R 91/72, Der KdS Lettland, Abtl. II D, an den Geb.-Komm. Riga-Stadt, 17 April 1942, along with the attachment entitled "Richtlinien für die Dienststellen, denen jüdische Arbeitskräfte zugeteilt sind."

7. Approval followed by means of a standardized letter stating that, in consultation with the regional commander of the Security Police in Latvia, a recall of the workers at any time remained open. The payment of standardized wages was made obligatory, see BA Berlin, R 91/10, 203.
8. Several individual barracking applications from *Heereskraftwagenpark* 642 (Workshop 3), the Local Administration Command, the hygiene institute of the SS and Police Leader Latvia, and the Navy Equipment Office are documented for April 1942 in BA Berlin, R 91/72. The monthly report for April 1942 from Department IIa of County Commissariat Riga City noted: "The approval of additional applications for barracking is being refrained from as a matter of principle." See BA Berlin R 91/30. The Labor Office's monthly report for April 1942 stated: "In addition, 25 workers who had been barracked at the place where they were needed without approval were brought back to the ghetto again." See BA Berlin, R 91/63. An application from Large Army Construction Office 1, dated 14 April 1942, was refused on 1 May with reference to the fact that the obligatory return of Jewish details had been extended to 8 p.m.: "It is not at all compatible with our stance on the Jewish question, when a ghetto exists in the city, to have innumerable smaller ghettos come into being at present." See BA Berlin, R 91/10, 253.
9. Ibid. 254, Der Geb.-Komm., IIa, an Wolf und Döring, 1 May 1942. Permission for an extension followed on 12 May 1942, BA Berlin, R 91/72, and on 18 June 1942, BA Berlin, R 91/10, 109. Finally, on 24 June 1942, the Air Force received approval for 350 workers for construction measures that were decisive for the war effort, see ibid., 76–77. On the Wehrmacht Quarters Office, see BA Berlin, R 91/72, Geb.-Komm. IIa an Wehrmacht-Quartieramt, 30 April 1942.
10. BA Berlin, R 91/10, 203–206, Wehrmacht-Quartieramt an den Geb.-Komm., 23 May 1942, which includes a list of the names of the Jews deployed.
11. On this see the detailed memoirs of Abrams Kits, "Zwangsarbeit in Riga, Stutthof, Gotendorf," *Dachauer Hefte* 16 (2000): 18–35, here 23–25.
12. LVVA, P 132-28-18, 82, journal of the Dortmund Group, entry for 20 May 1942.
13. Ibid., 82–83, entries for 20, 23, and 26 May 1942.
14. Ibid., 96, entry for 31 July 1942: "Order of the Commandant's Office No. 6. For a given reason, I expressly point out once again that any exchange of letters (packages) with the camps Salaspils or Jungfernhof as well as the barracked external commandos is likewise strictly forbidden. In the future, the death sentence will be applied upon such violations. Sig. Krause, SS First Lt."
15. LVVA, P 70-5-37, 149, Der BdS Ostland, Abtl. III, an den RKO, betr. Ereignismeldungen, 25 August 1942. This source contains the name Horst Israel Kassel of Kassel, on whose person an inflammatory poem was also found. Horst Israel Kassel is not on any of the deportation lists.
16. Kaufmann, *Churbn Lettland*, 412. In a letter dated 25 November 1963, Maywald, writing from prison, tried to convince the investigating judge that he had been concerned about the Latvian Jews, saying that he, together with Leibsohn, the Jewish owner of the fashionable tailor atelier Jockey Club, had set up a custom clothing shop for leading German officials, which functioned as a Security Police enterprise until taken over by the civil administration: "The Jews felt very at ease with me, I took good care of them, and they were very attached to me." See Staw. Hamburg, 141 Js 534/60, Bd. 41, Maywald an den Untersuchungsrichter, 25 November 1963, 6,898–6,899.
17. Gottschalk, *Der letzte Weg*, 46–48.
18. BA Berlin, R 91/10, 141–142, Der RKO, Abtl. I Z (B), an die Kommandantur der Ghettoverwaltung in Riga [sic], betr. Instandhaltung der Häuser des Reichskommissars am Strand, 3 June 1942.

19. LVVA, P 132-28-18, 90, journal of the Dortmund Group, entry for 3 July 1942; see also Staw. Hamburg, 141 Js 534/60, Bd. 1, statement by Wolf Hirsch, 6 May 1949, 30–31. Hirsch had the good fortune to leave Salaspils for the ghetto in a recuperation transport; from there, he went to Majori (Majorenhof).
20. Gottschalk, *Der letzte Weg*, 46–48. Katie Gutenstein (née Selling) of Stuttgart confirmed that the Star of David was not worn at this time, see Staw. Hamburg, 141 Js 534/60, Bd. 47, statement by Katie Gutenstein, 21 April 1964, 7,732–7,733.
21. BA Berlin, R 92/1158, 38, Gen.-Komm., Abtl. Aso, an den KdS Riga, betr. Arbeitseinsatz reichsdeutscher Juden, 22 July 1942. The main railroad directorate referred to here is Main Railroad Directorate North. It is noted in the margins of a draft of this letter that the Jews were withdrawn on 6 August 1942, ibid., 15–16.
22. Ibid., 11, Der Geb.-Komm., Abtl. III (Aso), an den Gen.-Komm. sowie RKO, betr. Judeneinsatz, hier Jungfernhof, gez. Schmutzler, 29 July 1942, printed in Benz et al., *Einsatz im "Reichskommissariat Ostland,"* doc. no. 116, 151. Schmutzler's special desk officer for Jewish affairs, Arthur Eicker, had previously visited the estate and reached the same conclusion, see the copy of the report "Judeneinsatz im Kasernierungslager Junfgernhof," 22 July 1942, in BA Berlin, R 92/1158, 12. There was also a sewing room for shirts for the SS, which was run by a certified laundry seamstress from Vienna, see Staw. Hamburg, 141 Js 534/60, Bd. 1, statement by Mascha Katz, 10 May 1949, 36. Katz was originally from Hanover.
23. BA Berlin, R 92/1158, 39, KdS, I S, an den Gen.-Komm., Abtl. Aso, betr. Arbeitseinsatz reichsdeutscher Juden, 10 August 1942.
24. BA Berlin, R 91/10, 160–162, Bautechnisches Beschaffungsamt, Luftgau I, Beschaffungsstelle Riga, an den Geb.-Komm. Riga, betr. Judenverpflegung, 6 June 1942. This involved the daily provisioning of 190 female Reich-German Jews and 40 Latvian Jews, who had to carry out construction work as well as load and unload cargo "outside protected premises."
25. BA Berlin, R 92/1158, 24, Das Geb.-Komm. Libau an Gen.-Komm. in Riga, betr. Rückführung von 50 jüdischen Arbeitskräften nach Riga, 2 November 1942.
26. BA Berlin, R 91/164, Bericht des Geb.-Komm., Abtl. Aso, betr. Judeneinsatz im Monat Dezember 1942, 9 January 1943. This report, which depicts the situation as of 10 December 1942, states: "Likewise, the unit SS-Economist barracked around 80 Jews in summer. The [work of the] commando is so difficult – 40 railway cars are to be loaded and unloaded daily – that of the 80 Jews only ca. 35 are still able to work. The inability to work is the result of poor nutrition."
27. The numbers given are from ibid.
28. LVVA, P 1026-1-3, 341, Der KdS Lettland, Abtl. I S, betr. Beschäftigung von Juden und deren Unterbringung, 16 November 1942.
29. According to its monthly report for September 1942, County Commissariat Daugavpils reported 458 Jews working at Army Group North's local accommodations administration (*Heeresunterkunftverwaltung* 322) and construction office (*Heeresbaudienststelle* 100), see LVA, P 69-2-80, 57–62. For the same month, 256 Jews were reported deployed in Jelgava with Construction Group Giesler and in the peat works, see ibid., 50–56. The same goes for the Jews of Liepāja, who in December 1942 were reported to be working either with Construction Group Giesler or in enterprises that were important to the war effort, see ibid., 66–75.
30. On this incident, see Staw. Hamburg, 141 Js 534/60, Bd. 2, statement by Rudolf Reese, 22 December 1949, 213–214; ibid., Bd. 5b, statement by Ewald Aul, 13 December 1951, 718–720; ibid., Bd. 20, statement by Siegfried Joseph (deported from Dortmund), 16

October 1961, 2,853–2,855; ibid., Bd. 39, statement by Elliot Welles (deported from Vienna under his previous name Kurt Sauerquell), 24 September 1963, 6,460–6,464; and ibid., Bd. 39, statement by Joseph Behrmann of Ventspils (Windau), 24 September 1963, 6,360–6,371; ibid., Bd. 3, statement by Joseph Behrmann, 21 January 1950, 248–249. On the verdict and shooting, see ibid., Bd. 3, statement by Siegfried Kaufmann, 3 March 1950, 307–310. Kaufmann, who was deported from Kassel, had served as chief of the Jewish camp police in Salaspils. Rudolf Reese, born 1909, was originally an insurance agent and came to the Security Police relatively late. The administration of KdS real estate in Riga was subordinated to him. The abuse and selection of the ca. fifteen persons was the subject of a criminal investigation against Reese; he was found not guilty, see the verdict in 14 Js 210/49 (case against Seck et al.), printed in *Justiz und NS-Verbrechen*, Bd. IX, Lfd. Nr. 307, 181–182, 203–207.

31. LVVA, P 132-28-18, journal of the Dortmund Group, entries for 18 July (92–93), 19 July (93–94), 20 July (94), 27 July (94–95), and 28 July 1942 (95).
32. On the departure, arrival, and age structure of the two transports, see *Buch der Erinnerung*, Bd. 1, 17, 321, 532. The "general order" refers to a radio message from Gestapo Chief Heinrich Müller to KdS Lithuania via Riga, 18 May 1942, in RGVA, 500-1-25, 379, printed in Klein, *Die Einsatzgruppen in der besetzten Sowjetunion*, 410–411. Cf. also chapter 11, this volume. Berthold Schiff's instructions concerning 14–16-year-old youths are in the journal of the Dortmund Group, LVVA, P 132-28-18, entry for 28 August 1942, 98.
33. Lukás Pribyl, "Die Geschichte des Theresienstädter Transports 'Be' nach Estland," *Theresienstädter Studien und Dokumente* 8 (2001): 148–229, here 149–152. Pribyl analyzed the criminal case against Ralf Gerrets in the Dept. KGB of the Estonian Prosecutor's Office, Tallinn (129-28653-1 to 19).
34. Apparently, some of the deportees had learned in Theresienstadt that the transport was to go to Riga, see ibid., 148–149. On the shooting pits at Kalevi Liiva, see ibid., 152–154. The train left Theresienstadt on 1 September 1942 and arrived in Raasiku on either 4 or 5 September.
35. Ibid., 164.
36. Staw. Hamburg, 141 Js 534/60, Bd. 2, statement by Werner Georg Netler, 7 December 1949, 200. Netler incorrectly dates his transport by several days, but the statistics show that there were 91 persons between 21 and 40 on the transport, see *Buch der Erinnerung*, Bd. 1, 339–340.
37. Ibid., Bd. 1, 17–19 and Bd. 2, 914; Pribyl, "Die Geschichte des Theresienstädter Transports," 162 and 219, fn. 27.
38. Staw. Kassel, 3 Js 59/66, Bd. 7, statement by Helga Verleger (nee Drexler), 19 February 1968, 1,228: "After a train journey of several days and nights, I can't say the exact number anymore, we read the signs 'Riga' outside. In the compartments, people had cried and prayed during the trip. We younger ones by contrast were still being silly and giggled about everything. As I recall, the train stayed in Riga for one night. Then the train all of sudden moved again. Then some 'hearsay' [*Mundfunk*] went through the compartment, the ghetto in Riga was full. The people in the compartment said, now they don't know where to send us, and now we are going to be shot for sure. I personally didn't believe this at the time and said they shouldn't talk like that and should wait and see."
39. Ibid., Bd. 5, statement by Fanny Lederer (Frankfurt am Main), 17 January 1967, as well her report "Meine Deportierung von Anfang bis Ende" also ibid.
40. Ibid., Bd. 5, statement by Sally Ismar Herlitz of Frankurt, 17 January 1967, 1,086–1,089; ibid., Bd. 7, statement by Erich Neter of Frankfurt, 4 March 1968, 1,257–1,258.

41. *Buch der Erinnerung,* Bd. 1, 17; ibid., Bd. 2, 361–362.
42. Staw. Berlin, 1 Js 9/65, ZH 171 [lila], statement by Joachim Wind, 10 March 1970. Regarding the athletic field in Kaiserwald, see also chapter 10, this volume. On relieving the Jews barracked at the athletic field, but with incorrect dates, see Katz, *Erinnerungen eines Überlebenden,* 64: "Transports with Berlin Jews reach Riga. At the train station, selections take place. Usually, 90 percent of all arrivals are led into the high forest and thus to their deaths. Those designated to live are sent to the camp we have left so that they can get used to the new conditions."
43. Staw. Hamburg, 141 Js 534/60, Bd. 2, statement by Herbert Kurt Kallmann, 7 December 1949, 202–204.
44. *Buch der Erinnerung,* Bd. 1, 17, 363, 380.
45. On the transports to Maly Trostenez, see Gerlach, *Kalkulierte Mord,* 756–761.
46. Belorusskii Gosudarstvennyi Archiv, 378-1-784, 28–30, Deutsche Reichsbahn, Generalbetriebsleitung Ost, an die Reichsbahndirektionen, Generaldirektion der Ostbahn in Krakau, RBD Mitte in Minsk, HBD Nord in Riga, betr. Sonderzüge für Umsiedler, Erntehelfer und Juden in der Zeit v. 8.8.-30.10.1942, 8 August 1942.
47. See fn. 32, this chapter.
48. See chapter 11, this volume.
49. LVA, P 69-2-80, 50–56, Der Geb.-Komm. in Mitau, Abtl. Arbeitsverwaltung, an den Gen.-Komm., Abtl. IIIe, betr. Monatsbericht für den September 1942, 55.
50. YIVO, Occ. E 3-41, Der Gen.-Komm. für Weißruthenien, Abtl. Gauleiter, an den RKO, betr. Partisanenbekämpfung und Judenaktion in Weißruthenien, 31 July 1942. Referring back to this report, Kube also inquired "to what extent do I also have to consider basic decisions about taking on additional Jews in White Ruthenia a police matter, or to what extent can I reserve a decision for myself." See YIVO, Occ. E 3-43, Der Gen.-Komm. für Weißruthenien, Abtl. IIa, an den RKO, 18 August 1942.
51. See the internal instructions on this matter from 28 November 1941 and 17 January 1942, occasioned by the expected arrival of 50,000 deportees in Minsk, in YIVO, Occ. E 3-37, RKO, Abtl. IIa, 13 January 1942. As a final step, see the internal ordinance in YIVO, Occ. E 3-43, RKO, II Politik, an die Abtl. II Verwaltung, 21 August 1942.
52. This also applies to the two transports to Estonia. The current state of the research leaves open the possibility that these transports stemmed from an initiative of HSSPF Ostland Friedrich Jeckeln, because he had considered establishing a camp near Tallinn, see Ruth Bettina Birn, "Heinrich Bergmann – eine deutsche Kriminalistenkarriere," in Mallmann and Paul, *Karrieren der Gewalt,* 49.
53. See the convincing examples regarding the General Government and the "Greater German Reich" in Ulrich Herbert, "Arbeit und Vernichtung," in *Ist der Nationalsozialismus Geschichte?* ed. Dan Diner, 198–236. For a focus on Jewish inmates, see Falk Pingel, *Häftlinge unter SS-Herrschaft,* 139–144.

– Chapter 16 –

FAILED RESISTANCE
The Tin Square Operation, October 1942

After the large massacres at Rumbula at the end of 1941, the remaining members of the Jewish Order Service (OD) in Riga were forced to come to the painful conclusion that the policy of cooperation it and the Jewish Council had pursued with the SS had failed as a strategy to guarantee the survival of the Latvian ghetto community until liberation. The OD men at Rumbula had been granted no concessions either; instead the German marksmen, as depicted in chapter 5 of this volume, had directed the full fury of their hatred against the "Jewish police" in particular. Among the thirty OD members who remained in the ghetto, Max Wachtel, for example, faced up to the consequences for himself "after all these events." He left the Jewish police and reported to a work commando as a locksmith. The risk of being murdered as an officeholder in another operation was simply too great for him.[1] Other OD men must have been aware of the danger of staying in the police, but made the exact opposite decision.

The members of the Latvian OD were all natives of Riga. Since most of them had lost their families at Rumbula, they no longer had to take into consideration personal ties. They could now plan with some degree of freedom, because they were only responsible for themselves and their actions. The OD was subordinated initially to Yitzchag Bag, who had to work with Max Wand, the head of the small ghetto, and was later relieved by Anatoly Nathan. Bag and his men continued to perform their duties, because they saw in their official activities the chance to act – not to derive personal gain but to work in secret against the occupation. That the OD men were allowed to move about relatively freely in the ghetto and the city – after all, they escorted commandos to their respective workplaces – was an advantage not to be underestimated. And the ghetto – narrow and full of nooks and crannies, occupied solely by Jewish inhabitants, and cut off from the outside world – made it possible to hold conspiratorial meetings and hide individuals from the Gestapo.

In the opinion of survivor Israel Kaplan, the idea to put up armed resistance did not originate with the OD. Rather, the possibility became ap-

---

Notes for this chapter begin on page 361.

parent only after talks with the engineer Ovsei Okun, who was deployed with a work commando outside the ghetto, and the lawyer Jevelson. The OD men were confirmed in their intent by respected persons of ghetto life, such as the Hebrew teachers Eliyahu Latt and Michelson as well as the blacksmith Botwinik. Young men from Zionist circles as well as adherents of left-wing ideologies soon joined the movement as well. In addition, the Latvian OD men – Gertrude Schneider correctly calls them the elite within the small ghetto – expressly tried to win over German Jews for such an endeavor. The group also debated whether the conspirators should flee to the partisans and take action against the occupiers in targeted fashion or stay in the ghetto and fight until the end. This discussion may well have taken place, because their mentor Jevelson was captured and shot after an escape attempt (he had wanted to flee to Sweden by ship). But no matter which option was chosen, weapons were absolutely necessary. With the help of contacts in the work commando assigned to the Powder Tower, it was possible to smuggle pistols and ammunition into the Latvian ghetto.[2]

Events took a dramatic turn on 5 September 1942, when a group of Red Army soldiers escaped from a prisoner of war subcamp located at the Wehrmacht communications center at Citadeles St. 1a.[3] The group of escapees was made up of two captains, Vasilii Yariomka and Sergei Yakovlev, Lieutenant Boris Pismanov-Kravchenko, and a Ukrainian named Anatolii Maklash. Yariomka had originally been the leader, probably in part because he had established contact with a Communist cell in Riga. This cell, led by the teacher Alexii Makarov, had already enabled several POWs to escape and was part of a larger network with contacts all the way to Moscow. Makarov's aim, however, was not just to free POWs. Instead, he chose men who seemed suitable for taking part in active resistance, such as gathering information and relaying it to the east or carrying out acts of sabotage. For this reason, Yariomka was given a counterfeit passport and smuggled to a hideout in the countryside, some 70 km (43.5 miles) from Riga, leaving the rest of the group in Riga.[4]

Among those who remained behind, Pismanov determined what had to happen next. More than the others, Pismanov had good reason to fight the occupiers. Although he claimed to be Ukrainian, he was in fact a Jew and, on top of that, a lieutenant in the NKVD border troops, two facts that he apparently had kept to himself in the POW camp, because both were, in the eyes of the Germans, offenses "deserving the death penalty." After leaving the camp, Pismanov went into hiding with Viacheslav Shapiro; from there, he planned his subsequent activity. Some time earlier, Pismanov had become acquainted with an inhabitant of the Riga ghetto by the name of Russ, to whom he sent a letter telling of his successful escape. From the letter, it is clear that Russ was to get hold of money and papers to help Pismanov and other ghetto inhabitants escape.⁵ As quid pro quo, they would be then be smuggled farther and hidden by Pismanov's "people," by which the Makarov group may have been meant.⁶ Preparations and discussions lasted until mid October 1942. On 13 October, Pismanov met with Russ, who revealed that "there existed in the ghetto an organization of Jews who by all means now" wanted to break out "in order to join the partisans." Enough money and weapons were available as well. However, they needed contacts on the outside, persons who were trustworthy so that they could "be accommodated in safety the first few days." Russ's intent was to smuggle out of the ghetto those who were considered "less Jewish looking" and "most courageous."⁷

According to the results of the investigation conducted by German military intelligence, the Abwehr, Pismanov (a.k.a. "Borka") now had contact with "an organization of Jews in the ghetto" that was seeking to break out and join the partisans. Russ, his confidant on the Jewish side, was allegedly a member of the camp police. Actual control of this "organization of Jews" was in the hands of three men who kept "in the shadows" and maintained contact with a resistance group in the Lettgale Suburb via a confidant. This confidant was a Jewish detail leader by the name of Sandel, who was deployed for work at Matīsa St. 37/39. Pismanov knew of his position and used this contact to sneak into the ghetto, for this was the only way to come "into direct contact with the members of the ghetto organization." Once within the ghetto, the fugitive NKVD officer was well received and taken care of. However, the weapons store, which even included a submachine gun, was bound to have been more important to him. According to the Abwehr, the organization had obtained these after bribing "18 Jewish policemen in the ghetto" and buying "weapons for RM 9,000 in Mühlgraben [Mīlgrāvis]."

From Israel Kaplan, we know that Mischka Fischer, the detail leader for the Powder Tower commando, procured the weapons, and that the OD men Paik, Hlaser, and Schatz trained with the pistols in a cellar hideout. In retrospect, it seems likely that Russ acted as intermediary between the OD men and the Jewish buyers. Pismanov, who was now hiding in the Moscow Suburb, also received four fake passports. The Gestapo's network of control had holes in it. But from what has just been depicted, it must be clear by now that the resistance had failed to insulate itself completely and conceal its plans. The Abwehr had placed at least one informant amid these multiple layers of personal bonds of trust and mutual dependencies, and this person had not aroused the suspicion of those under observation. This would prove to be a fatal oversight, as things turned out.⁸

Pismanov's plan was "to meet suitable Jews" via the work commandos' detail leaders and "to flee to the partisans with them." He therefore met repeatedly with Sandel, who was for his part looking around the ghetto for people willing to flee.[9] On 19 October, another meeting of the conspirators took place at Avotu St. 23 (Sprenk St.), at which Bronislav Linenev (codename "Leinikov") joined Pismanov, Russ, and Sandel. Linenev was responsible for the fake passports and for finding safe quarters in the countryside. All of those present agreed to implement the escape plan in the next few days, the intent being to smuggle the "members of the ghetto organization" out of the ghetto gradually. Pismanov assumed that this would take place at an interval of about five days. The first trip was to take place on Wednesday, 28 October, and was to lead to a small place with the name Abrene (today Russian Pytalovo), which lay on the Daugavpils-Pskov road several kilometers northwest of Augšpils (today Russian Vyshgorodok).[10]

All of this was revealed to the Abwehr office in Riga, which kept its Gestapo colleagues informed as to the state of affairs. On 21 October, Captain Link of the Abwehr and SS First Lieutenant Rudolf Lange of the Gestapo's desk for Communism and espionage agreed on how to prevent the planned escape and to break up the illegal organization.[11] Shortly after this meeting, the Abwehr's source conveyed the exact time of departure and the destination of the transport; with that, the decisive phase of the operation was launched. The two officers met again on 24 October and developed a concrete plan: They intended to let the escapees flee the ghetto and start the trip to Abrene. KdS Latvia was then to overtake the escapees' truck with its own vehicle – camouflaged as a Wehrmacht vehicle – and to arrest the Jews. The Abwehr was to make available its source (so he could identify the escapees), some material (for example, uniforms), and a Latvian policeman (probably more to keep an eye on the informant than to participate in the arrest). Everything else was in the hands of the Security Police, with Ghetto Commandant Kurt Krause keeping "the Jew Russ" under surveillance within the Moscow Suburb.

The Abwehr was in charge of things in Abrene, where the Germans intended to arrest the Jews' contact person to the partisans. The Latvian police would carry out the arrest, but they were to be let in on the matter only at short notice. In addition, it was considered necessary to send a fake message from there to the ghetto – via the "source," who was also to go to Abrene – stating that the flight of the first group had been successful. The text was to read "We arrived safely" and would be signed "Grisha." When Pismanov and the remaining members of the resistance organization were convinced of the first undertaking's success, it was believed that they then would "set the next transports in motion."[12] Behind all of this lurked the idea that the Germans could thus gradually catch all of the members of the organization – including the Latvians outside the Moscow Suburb – without having to comb the ghetto.

On 27 October, SS First Lieutenant Lange noted that the transport was to depart from Sadovnikova St. 26/24 at 5 A.M. This was the address of an apartment that served as both meeting point and hideout, but it had been under German surveillance the entire time. Four Jews who had already fled the ghetto believed the location was safe and spent the night there. Another six Jews from the ghetto were to join them the night before the escape, once they had bribed their way through the surrounding fence. All of them had dispensed with their Stars of David. Altogether, "10 Jews, among them a prisoner of war," wanted to start their journey on the morning of 28 October. The man who was to guide them to safety was a ghetto inhabitant by the name of Schorschik, who issued weapons to those at the apartment who did not have a gun. Schorschik prevailed upon them to use the revolvers in an emergency and, in particular, "if the truck should be stopped, to shoot immediately."[13] Because Lange was also aware of this, he felt that the standard issue of arms to his men was no longer sufficient. The Abwehr therefore issued a submachine gun to the SS commando that was to overtake the truck.[14]

The Abwehr and Gestapo's plan was successful only to the extent that the truck with the escapees was stopped on the road. Whether either agency had contemplated a bloody outcome from the start cannot be inferred from the files, but it seems unlikely, because the escapees were needed for interrogation. The truck's occupants followed Schorschik's instructions and opened fire on their pursuers, but they didn't have a chance. Seven of them were killed in an exchange of fire lasting an hour and a half. In addition to Sandel, who had left the ghetto without organizing any additional transports, the dead included Marzinski, Rybak, Bilacki, Josef Blankenfeld, and Maczijewski. The Gestapo was unable to clarify the identity of one person. Two survived – Hirsch Bank and Chaim Eljaschewitsch – and were transferred to Gestapo headquarters in Riga. Among the attackers, only one was wounded, and none was killed, although the literature sometimes refers to three dead SS men.[15] After the fighting, Lange's men collected various gold and silver articles, watches, gold jewelry (some of which had precious stones), and other objects of value (fifty-eight pieces in all) and paid them according to regulations for "the benefit of the state."[16] The weapons cache was also considerable. In addition to the submachine gun, two German Army pistols and five revolvers were secured.[17]

At the Abrene-Augšpils crossroad, the Abwehr did not achieve the desired success. It had waited in vain for the partisans' contact man. Perhaps the contact had been too skeptical or had even been warned. More likely, however, is that the partisan contact insinuated by the escapees never existed. In any event, Pismanov later stated for the protocol that, using the money Sandel had procured, he had intended to push forward to the front and find a partisan group there or break through the German lines.[18] Absent the contact person, the Gestapo dispensed with the reserve needed for intelligence gathering purposes. Without trying to explore additional secret structures in the city or the ghetto in accordance with tried and true methods, it began arresting all of the known members of the conspiratorial group.

Pismanov, whom KdS Latvia had known up to now only by his alias Borka, was arrested on Matīsa St., as were his comrades Sergei Yakovlev and Anatolii Maklash. Of the cell around Aleksii Makarov, the ringleader himself and four other members of his organization – all Latvians – were apprehended. Arrest warrants were issued for persons outside the ghetto. People were picked up in the ghetto as well. Ghetto Commandant Krause was authorized to arrest Russ as well as two other ghetto occupants by the name of Kuklja and Judelis.[19] In a report to the Reich Security Main Office, KdS Latvia wrote that sixteen persons had been seized and the resistance group rolled up.[20] According to Israel Kaplan – whose dates are not particularly reliable – the weapons smugglers on the Powder Tower work detail were exposed around mid October 1942, with the arrest of detail leader Mischka Fischer being a particularly painful loss, because it made the procurement of additional weapons unthinkable.[21]

In breaking up the organization outside Riga and prosecuting the contact persons in the ghetto, KdS Latvia had achieved only a part of its covert aims. From the statements by Pismanov and the two survivors of the shootout, SS lieutenants Lange and Krause knew that there was still one person in the ghetto with access to weapons. Furthermore, it was obvious that the entire escape attempt could not have gotten so far without the support of the Latvian OD. SS Major Dr. Rudolf Lange, the chief of KdS Latvia, must have decided to eradicate the OD in the Latvian ghetto some time after learning of the shootout at the latest.

After the group around Pismanov and Makarov had been rolled up, it was above all necessary for SS Major Lange to crush the secret Jewish organization within the ghetto. Besides killing the Latvian OD members, he wanted to have all of the storage sites where weapons, money, or jewelry may have been hidden raided so as to deprive any new movement of the means for future resistance. Therefore, on 30 October, an operational order was issued to Krause to prepare five commandos – forty-eight men plus commando leaders – for 5:30 A.M. the next day.[22] Their main task was to search the residential blocks of the Latvian ghetto, while Gestapo officials seized forced laborers from the departing work details and subjected them to a spot check. Lange also ordered that all of the ghetto inhabitants who had not gone to work be forced to line up on the street during the search of the buildings. The greater part of the German police would then storm the apartments in order to seize the weapons and objects of value assumed to be there. Lange urged his men to be careful, because "resistance on the part of the Jews was to be expected." Lange's primary goal was to isolate the thirty OD men, but after the buildings had been searched, the Jews gathered in front of the buildings would be registered, and "another 50 male Jews" would then be singled out, all of whom were to be rated "no longer particularly able to work." Lange gave Krause decision-making authority for selecting the victims. In his view, it would be about 9:00 A.M. by that point, and the operation involving the shooting of eighty Jewish men – to be killed in groups of eight persons each – would be over. A "Jewish burial commando" was to carry away the corpses. Such were the stipulations of Lange's order.[23]

Shortly before the start of the operation, Krause went about making preparations. This is at any rate what is reported by Frieda Marx, who handled Krause's correspondence and was on hand when Krause took the elder of the German Jews, Max Leiser, and the chief of the German-Jewish ghetto police, Rudolf (Rudi) Haar, into his confidence: "One evening[24] in the office, Krause told Leiser, the ghetto policeman Haar, and me that in a few days the Latvian order people would be shot, along with 70 Latvian and 30 German Jews as hostages. He committed us to discretion and threatened us with a walk to the cemetery should we violate this confidentiality."[25] It was not without reason that Krause informed Leiser and Haar of what was about to happen – an act that violated his official duties and put SS Major Lange's measures at risk.[26] This was instead almost certainly connected with the specific concern of finding German Jews to replace the Latvian OD men.

In the end, the ghetto would continue to function, and for that, the Germans needed the Order Service, which, however, would now be given a purely German character. When the work details returned to the ghetto on the evening of 30 October, a group of German Jews were called to the commandant's office, where thirty of them were designated new ghetto policemen for the Order Service. It also happened that members of the German-Jewish OD named additional candidates. The new members were given an emblem, a cap, and an armband as symbols of their authority. They were to report for duty the following morning. At least some of the German OD men suspected the origins of their appointment. Years later, Kurt Rübsteck, a survivor of the Düsseldorf transport, recalled the tense atmosphere: "The commandant of the Jewish camp police, a Herr Frankenberg, who later died in Buchenwald, said to me that the next day would probably be the hardest in our life."[27]

When dawn broke on 31 October, the raid on the ghetto began as foreseen. The people who had not left with the work commandos were driven into the streets, where they had to fall into formation. The sick and frail were also not allowed to remain indoors, but were forced to leave their buildings. Because the policemen were carrying weapons and wearing helmets, their threats were all the more ominous. Then one building after another was searched from cellar to attic for hiding places. Meanwhile, Kurt Migge, Max Gymnich, and other well-known German perpetrators carried out an "assessment" of the departing work commandos.[28] Those who seemed too old had to step to the side and were not allowed to leave.[29] At the same time, the Latvian OD was summoned to the commandant's office, where the young policemen had to report to the courtyard. They were frisked for weapons, and some of them were found to be carrying "unapproved clubs" but no pistols or revolvers. The OD men then had to take off their boots. After a body search, the guards on hand then ordered them to Tin Square. There they were met by SS Staff Sergeant Karl Tollkühn and his men,[30] all of whom were armed with submachine guns.[31]

Having arrived at Tin Square, the OD men who had been caught with the clubs were told to line up with faces against the wall. The other OD men were ordered to wait. But Tollkühn lost control of the situation. Just as he ordered "ready,"[32] Anatoly Nathan grasped what was to happen and ordered his men to flee. The OD men scattered in all directions, followed by German policemen. Gymnich and his unit, the reserve commando, quickly appeared on Tin Square to chase down the OD men. Krause himself was also there. The OD man Seligsohn, allegedly Nathan's right-hand man, could only curse Krause before being shot. As for Nathan, he was cornered at a fence, where Gymnich shot him. Amid the chaos, one of the KdS Latvia men, a certain Haase, was struck by a stray bullet; he collapsed and bled to death on the ground.[33] Almost all of the members of the Latvian OD men died on Tin Square. Their bodies lay scattered over the killing site. Later, the corpses were removed by horse-drawn wagon.[34]

Although wounded, the OD man Genkin managed to escape briefly. He found shelter in a potato cellar, where German Jews protected him. Krause, however, tracked him down in his hideout, led him out onto the street, and shot him.[35] Another ghetto policeman by the name of Israelowitsch managed to flee to Washington Square and the tailoring and shoemaking workshops overseen by SS Technical Sergeant Fritz Scherwitz, who must have protected him (See Excursus II). Later, Israelowitsch's cover was blown, and with that, the last member of the Latvian OD captured.[36] It is said that Israelowitsch then worked for the Gestapo and passed on secret information to the Germans. Whether he survived could not be determined.[37] In addition to the OD men, the Jews selected from the work commandos were also killed. They were taken to a forested area outside Riga and shot, something the ghetto inhabitants later suspected when the murdered men's clothing was transferred back to the ghetto for further use.[38]

In accordance with SS Major Lange's order of 30 October, after the operation in the ghetto a poster stating the "reason" for the massacre and announcing new rules of conduct was put on display. The operation against the Jewish OD men was carried out, the poster said, because they had not reported the escape of other Jews, meaning the Pismanov-Makarov group. Another factor was that the escapees had carried weapons and had put up resistance on the country road. The two survivors would be "soon be hanged," whereas additional "necessary measures" had already been taken against the OD. Consequences for the ghetto inhabitants who had not taken part in the escape attempt were also revealed on 31 October. SS Major Lange used the occasion of the Tin Square Operations to restrict their already scant freedoms even more. From now on, the Jews were forbidden to go out on the street between 7 P.M. and 5 A.M. Work details returning to the ghetto later than the given time were instructed to "to take the shortest way possible to their accommodations." Anybody who was seen on the street during curfew could be shot without warning, just as "Jews who in the future violate the orders issued" had to reckon with severe punishment. The curfew did not apply to the Jewish elders and the newly deployed OD, because their members had to be available to the Gestapo on a continuous basis. Jewish doctors were also excepted from this regulation.[39]

According to the memoirs of Esra Jurmann, Krause informed the ghetto inhabitants on his own about the execution of the Latvian OD, saying the ghetto police had provided the escapees with weapons and money. At the same time, Krause designated Friedrich Frankenberg chief of the entire, reorganized OD, Rudolf Haar OD chief in the German ghetto, and Herbert Perl OD chief in the Latvian ghetto,[40] which simultaneously meant – as Migge stressed in postwar testimony – that the administrative division of the OD into two separate entities was ended.[41] Likewise, the self-administration of the Latvian ghetto was disbanded and integrated into that of the German ghetto. However, Leiser is said to have made it possible for the Latvians to preserve a certain amount of autonomy despite the change. This was also seen in the fact that Max Wand, the chairman of the Latvian ghetto, was not simply pushed out but instead became a part of the Jewish Council. It must be noted, however, that the Tin Square massacre inflicted lasting damage on relations between the two groups. Many of the Latvian Jews held various German Jews indirectly responsible for what had happened. This applied in particular to the German girlfriends of the murdered Latvian OD men; the girlfriends had allegedly been unable to keep quiet when confronted by the SS. Thus, for some Latvian Jews, the ghetto community's new hierarchal direction also seemed an expression of trust, a kind of reward on the part of the SS for "their" German Jews.[42]

On the part of the perpetrators, probably nobody gave any consideration to such thoughts. Internally, KdS Latvia brought the affair to an end in administrative terms. All the ghetto inhabitants had long since been registered in a card index in the office of the ghetto commandant. Now the personnel cards of the Latvian OD men as well as the other victims from the small ghetto were marked to indicate that they were dead. In addition, Krause dictated a "death sentence" listing the names of Anatoly Nathan's men so as to give the "decommissioning" of the Latvian OD an official appearance.[43]

Several days later, Krause dealt another blow to the resistance movement and future escape attempts. Although the Gestapo had arrested "9 male and 5 female Jews" seeking to flee to Sweden, Krause had yet to unmask the secret connection behind the operation.[44] After a long investigation, in early November 1942 Krause learned who was helping the Jews. In order to eliminate these persons, however, he needed the help of the Local Administration Command and thus turned to Lieutenant Colonel Hampe. At Krause's request, Wehrmacht military police, on 4 November, arrested three soldiers of the 16th Composite Company:[45] Corporal Kurt Wanschaff, Corporal Paul Koehler, and Sergeant Erwin Brodt. According to the records, all three men had "associated with the Jews" of the ghetto "beyond the framework of what was otherwise usual." Wanschaff was especially incriminated, because he had "taken Jews from the ghetto and brought them to the harbor." He had also provided them with new civilian clothing. After the three men were picked up by the military police, a Latvian Jew by the name of Donde was captured in the soldiers' quarters.

Ultimately, a search of offices at Waldemara St. 57/59 (Hermann Göring St.) led to the seizure of papers and materials that were to be used for the escape. Krause had the Jewish women working there screened because of the special relationship between them and the soldiers and arrested one of them, Lia Müller, as an accomplice. The local administration commandant, Brigadier General Georg Bamberg, was then informed of the security breach. Under pressure from Krause, courts-martial were initiated against Wannschaff, Koehler, and Brodt. Their immediate superior, Captain Rudolf Hennewig, was also called to account for dereliction of duty, because the Jews "employed" at his office enjoyed "great liberties."[46] The outcome of the proceedings is not documented in the relevant files, but one can hardly have any illusions about the fate of the three men.

In the course of further investigations, the engineer Ovsei Okun, one of the initiators of the resistance movement, was also arrested.[47] When the weapons cache in the ghetto was finally found – allegedly due to information provided by Israelowitsch – Krause's victory seemed complete.[48] But despite the risks, not every escape attempt failed. A German Army technical sergeant with the codename Smigula, together with six other persons – a German noncommissioned officer, a Soviet POW, and four Jews – left Riga in early September 1942. Their journey led them through Königsberg, Leipzig, Cologne, Aachen, Paris, Bordeaux, and Hendaye, where they managed to reach safety. One of them, Arnost Jakubovic, who was questioned by the British secret service in 1943, testified about the mass murder operations in the woods near Riga and the living conditions in the ghetto. The names of some of the main figures responsible were at the time noted for the files: Jeckeln, Krause, and Danskop.[49]

Thus the history of Riga escape attempts is not one of failure alone. In fact, the Allies learned very early on who would have to be held accountable after the war for crimes committed in Riga. More important, not all of the witness accounts given by escapees disappeared into the files of the British and American intelligence services. In October 1942, representatives of the Jewish Agency received even more detailed information about events in Riga – primarily from Gabriel Ziwian, who left the Riga ghetto in December 1941 and found refuge in Geneva in September 1942 – thus making it possible to publicize these crimes. The *Palestine Post* of 23 November 1942 contained a long article on the massacre of 24,000 Riga Jews – meaning the large-scale killings in Rumbula – which informed readers in detail about the gruesome events. In autumn 1942, the genocide, which for many people – even for Jews in countries that were neutral or at war with Germany – was unimaginable in its scope, seemed the figment of a destructive imagination. Recognition that the annihilation of the Jews of Europe was a part of the German Reich's realpolitik came to be accepted only slowly.[50] That the world learned of what had happened in Riga and came to believe the reports of mass suffering and death was not least of all owed to escapees from the Riga ghetto.

Notes

1. Staw. Hamburg, 141 Js 534/60, Bd. 38, statement by Max Wachtel, 28 August 1963, 6,162.
2. Israel Kaplan, "Weapons in the Riga Ghetto," in Schneider, *Muted Voices*, 26–27; Schneider, *Journey into Terror*, 68–69; Press, *Judenmord in Lettland 1941-1945*, 107; Staw. Hamburg, 141 Js 534/60, Bd. 1, 14 Js 210/49 Anklageschrift gegen Seck u.a, 1 June 1951, 25–26.
3. Given the location, this site must have been a part of Stalag 350, which was located in an old barracks facility on Pernavas St., but had at its disposal numerous subcamps in the

city and surrounding area – e.g. at Salaspils, Stalag 350-S – see Margers Vestermanis, "Die nationalsozialistischen Haftstätten und Todeslager im okkupierten Lettland 1941–1945," in Herbert et al., *Die nationalsozialistischen Konzentrationslager*, Bd. 1, 480–481.
4. Bundesarchiv Ludwigsburg, Dokumentation, UdSSR 426, 394–396, Abschrift, n.d. [between 19 and 28 October 1942]. These pages consist of reports by Abwehr informants.
5. Named are "Breslaw" and "Boris." The former had established the contact between Pismanov and Russ. The latter must have been considerably well-to-do and faced extreme danger. Pismanov had Boris informed "that he could be completely saved" and no longer need despair, because the intent was to get him out "any day."
6. BA Ludwigsburg, Dokumentation, UdSSR 426, 427–428, [Abwehr Dossier], Russ, wohnh. Riga. Ghetto. The document in question includes a translation of a letter from Pismanov to Russ, ibid., 408–410, IIa Verhandelt. [Vernehmung des] Pismanov, genannt Borka, 28 October 1942.
7. Ibid., 427–428, [Abwehr Dossier], Russ, wohnh. Riga. Ghetto. Here, a note for the files dated 13 October 1942.
8. Ibid., 394–396, Abschrift, n.d. [between 19 and 28 October 1942]; ibid., 408–410, IIa Verhandelt. [Vernehmung des] Pismanov, genannt Borka, 28 October 1942; Kaplan, "Weapons in the Riga Ghetto," 27.
9. Ibid., Vermerk, 2 November 1942; ibid., 384–385, IIa Weiterverhandelt. [Vernehmung des] Pismanov, genannt Borka, 29 October 1942. According to these records, Pismanov maintained no direct contact with any detail leader other than Sandel. However, the statements of Chaim Eljaschewitsch and Hirsch Bank suggest that their detail leaders aroused the suspicion of KdS Latvia. These were the detail leaders Koppl (Latvian Jews) and Sommer (German Jews) from the Slaughterhouse Commando and the detail leader Mischka Fischer (Latvian Jews) with Wehrmachtsdienststelle A at the Powder Tower. In any event, their names appear in the protocol, see ibid., 401–404, IIa, Verhandelt, [Vernehmung] des Chaim Eljaschewitsch and ibid, 411–413, IIa, Verhandelt am 28.10.1942, [Vernehmung] des Hirsch Bank.
10. Ibid., 394–396, Abschrift, n.d. [between 19 and 28 October 1942].
11. Known as "Little Lange" due to his lower rank, this Rudolf Lange was no relation to his boss SS Major Dr. Rudolf Lange.
12. BA Ludwigsburg, Dokumentation, UdSSR 426, 389–391, IIA, Meldung, 24 October 1942; ibid., 384–385, IIa Weiterverhandelt. [Vernehmung des] Pismanov, genannt Borka, 29 October 1942.
13. Possibly a cover name.
14. BA Ludwigsburg, Dokumentation, UdSSR 426, 389–391, IIA, Meldung, 24 October 1942; ibid., 411–413, IIa, Verhandelt am 28.10.1942, [Vernehmung] des Hirsch Bank. The name of the informant is not mentioned anywhere. Without being able to say with 100 percent certainty who it in fact was, it is striking that the files say nothing about the driver of the getaway vehicle or about how and where the truck was arranged or borrowed in the first place. The informant was very mobile and provided very exact information about the meeting places, including those outside the ghetto. All of this leads to the conclusion that the betrayal did not take place within the ghetto, and that it involved a Latvian – possibly a member of the Makarov group – who may have driven the getaway vehicle. This suspicion is also articulated in Press, *Judenmord in Lettland*, 109.
15. BA Ludwigsburg, Dokumentation, UdSSR 426, 386–388, II A, Vermerk, 2 November 1942. On the basis of the material available, it could not be determined whether the persons mentioned in the files for the first time were associates of Sandel or Russ. Nor can it be said whether they belonged to the inner circle of the "Jewish Organization," that is to say, to the three men "in the shadows." From the existing records, it seems

rather doubtful that there could have been such a tightly organized secret organization in the ghetto. At any rate, the Gestapo investigation did not get beyond Pismanov, which suggests – assuming the methods of interrogation used – he had no knowledge of other Jews working clandestinely. Press expressly stated that the resistance organization in the ghetto was decentralized, and that it had lost its initiators early on, Press, *Judenmord in Lettland*, 107–108. In addition, Pismanov and his people were ultimately Communists. It is doubtful that they were suitable partners for all would-be members of an opposition. Some may have wanted to take action without such an alliance. For more on the events depicted here, see BA Berlin, R 58/699, Meldungen aus den besetzten Ostgebieten Nr. 33, 11 December 1942; Landgericht Hamburg, (89) 1/83 Ks, Urteil gegen Karl Tollkühn, 9 May 1983, 26–28.

16. BA Ludwigsburg, Dokumentation, UdSSR 426, 437, KdS Lettland, I S, an Abt. I W 4, 28 October 1942.
17. BA Berlin, R 58/699, Meldungen aus den besetzten Ostgebieten Nr. 33, 11 December 1942. Furthermore, it was noted with some degree of astonishment that the group was well prepared for the winter and wore quilted clothing.
18. BA Ludwigsburg, Dokumentation, UdSSR 426, 390, excerpts from one of Pismanov's interrogations [derived from context of contents]. It could not be determined whether the original document survived in this form or Ludwigsburg investigators were given only a partial copy from the Soviet repository.
19. Ibid., 405, IIa, Vermerk, 28 October 1942,; ibid., II A, Vermerk, Dem Kommandeur über Leiter II m.d.B. Kenntnisnahme vorgelegt, 2 November 1942. At the time of the arrest, Makarov's daughter was on the way to Valmiera (Wolmar) with two other escaped POWs. Krause was also ordered to arrest the "detail leader" in the ghetto. At the point when the order was issued, it was not known that Sandel had been killed during the firefight. The source here says Matthäikirchstr. and Matthäistr., but the latter is bound to be meant.
20. BA Berlin, R 58/699, Meldungen aus den besetzten Ostgebieten Nr. 33, 11 December 1942. It is not apparent whether the number of arrested persons refers solely to the number of those arrested outside the ghetto or includes Krause's prisoners in the count.
21. Kaplan, "Weapons in the Riga Ghetto," 27–28. Kaplan dates the escape attempt to 4 October 1942, much earlier than was actually the case. Furthermore, by his account, the wounded survivors were able to return to the ghetto. By contrast, documents from Ludwigsburg show that the two survivors were arrested and interrogated. Nonetheless, Fischer was certainly arrested, but only – in accordance with the rules of undercover investigations – after such an arrest no longer risked interfering with measures directed against the Pismanov-Makarov group, and the informant was no longer in danger of being exposed.
22. Commando I (SS First Lieutenant Träger), Commando II (SS Master Sergeant Neumann), Commando III (SS Master Sergeant Mauritz), Commando IV – which was held in reserve – (SS Staff Sergeant Gymnich) and Commando V – which was the execution commando (SS Staff Sergeant Tollkühn).
23. BA Ludwigsburg, Dokumentation, UdSSR 426, 420–423, Der KdS Lettland, Einsatzbefehl für den 31.10.1942, 30 October 1942.
24. This could only have been between 28 and 30 October, because the decision to liquidate the Latvian ghetto's OD was a consequence of the firefight on 28 October. Because Lange's order was carried out on the morning of 31 October, the period in which this gathering could have occurred is very small.
25. Staw. Hamburg 141, Js 534/60, Bd. 3, statement by Frieda Marx, 28 March 1950, 372–373. Marx had worked for Leiser as a secretary at the Jewish Welfare Office in Cologne

and was bound to have had a special relationship to him. Krause himself was also from Cologne. A seizure of German Jews as hostages is not recorded in any other documents or the postwar statements. According to Ezergailis, the tense relationship between the leaders of the Latvian and the German Jews stemmed from these events as well as the prehistory of the Tin Square Operation. He also raises the question whether the mysterious deaths of Max Wand (the overseer of the small Jewish ghetto) and Rudolf Haar (the OD chief for the German Jews) in Concentration Camp Kaiserwald involved an act of revenge for the Tin Square Operation, see Ezergailis, *The Holocaust in Latvia 1941–1944*, 360 and 370, ft. 53; Press, *Judenmord in Lettland*, 109–110.

26. Staw. Hamburg, 141 Js 534/60, Bd. 3, statement by Kurt Migge, 5 April 1950, 379–379r. Migge rightly pointed out: "Krause would not have been so foolish as to tell Leiser and the witness [Marx] several days before this operation that such an operation was impending, not even if the Jews at Krause's [office] are supposed to have enjoyed a good deal of trust otherwise."

27. Ibid., Bd. 2, statement by Siegfried Goldenberg, 20 January 1950, 245; ibid., Bd. 3, statement by Alfred Kaufmann, 3 March 1950, 311; ibid., 53, statement by Kurt Rübsteck, 5 November 1964, 8,677; ibid., Bd. 69, statement by Julius Oppenheimer, 3 April 1967, 11,053.

28. The selection followed in two steps. Migge and his men carried out the first selection in the Latvian ghetto – 200 men were singled out – whereas Gymnich's reserve commando, which was stationed at the Prague Gate, then screened the group again, releasing several individuals in the process, ibid., Bd. 2, statement by Siegfried Goldenberg, 20 January 1950, 245r; ibid., Bd. 3, statement by Nathan Rohloff, 26 January 1950, 266–266r. Gymnich sent Rohloff back with the words: "What are you doing here?"

29. Kaufmann, *Churbn Lettland*, 174–175; Press, *Judenmord in Lettland*, 110; Staw. Hamburg 141 Js 534/60, Bd. 3, statement by Alfred Kaufmann, 3 March 1950, 311r; statement by Alexander Ginsburg, 29 March 1950, 377r; ibid., Bd. 4, statement by Adolf Kahn, 13 June 1950, 417.

30. The following KdS Latvia personnel belonged to the firing squad: Matauschek, von Sivers, Haase, Grählert, Kirschey, Winzker, and Oswald.

31. Staw. Hamburg, Js 534/60, Bd. 14, undated typewritten report by Esra Jurmann, 5,550; Landgericht Hamburg, (89) 1/83 Ks, Urteil gegen Karl Tollkühn, 9 May 1983, 34–36 and 67–68.

32. Staw. Hamburg, Js 534/60, Bd. 14, report by Jurmann, 5,550; Landgericht Hamburg, (89) 1/83 Ks, Urteil gegen Karl Tollkühn, 9 May 1983, 68–69.

33. Kaplan, "Weapons in the Riga Ghetto," 28–29; Staw. Hamburg 141 Js 534/60, Bd. 3, statement by Rohloff, 26 January 1950, 266r; ibid., statement by Hans Baermann, 27 March 1950, 368r; ibid., Bd. 4, statement by Nathan Rohloff, 25 May 1950, 413; ibid., Bd. 5b, statement by Siegfried Kaufmann, 18 December 1951, 736–737r; ibid., Bd. 60, statement by Horst Golnik, 28 September 1965, 9,654; ibid., SB 2, statement by Boris Kaplan, 16 January 1967, 431–432; statement by Leonid Pancis, 11 July 1967, 442. Prior to the operation, according to Kaplan, Krause had already shot one of the ghetto policemen, a certain Borowski, who had also wanted to escape. Anatoly Nathan's words (e.g. "Every man for himself!" or "Run, boys, let's try to save ourselves.") are described differently in the literature and witness statements, but are clear in meaning. According to Kaufmann, Jewish Council elder Fleischel also witnessed the crime. They observed the shooting from Fleischel's office and noted with surprise that SS men such as Migge, "who had otherwise never stood out" as marksmen, "took part in this operation."

34. Ibid., Bd. 60, statement by Golnik, 28 September 1965, 9,654; with incorrect dates, Sherman, *Zwischen Tag und Dunkel*, 82.

35. Kaplan, "Weapons in the Riga Ghetto," 29; Schneider, *Journey into Terror,* 70; with a different emphasis, Sherman, *Zwischen Tag und Dunkel,* 82–83.
36. Staw. München, STAnW 17434/1, statement by Abraham Schapiro, 4 May 1948; ibid., statement by Josef Wysokotworsky, 5 May 1948. According to Scherwitz, who was later promoted to SS second lieutenant, Lange ordered his workshop commando watched more closely after the escape attempt, see ibid., statement by Eleke Scherwitz, 27 April 1948. Some survivors suspected that Israelowitsch was ultimately found, because his girlfriend stopped protecting him.
37. Yad Vashem, O. 33/4126m 72–73, memoirs of Werner Sauer; Sherman, *Zwischen Tag und Dunkel,* 83.
38. Landgericht Hamburg, (89) 1/83 Ks, Urteil gegen Karl Tollkühn, 9 May 1983, 34, 37–38, 73–75, and 78. The exact number of dead cannot be determined. There were at least fifty persons, as Lange ordered, but witnesses remembered as many as 300 persons, see ibid., 74. Before their shooting, the victims were interned briefly in the Central Prison.
39. BA Ludwigsburg, Dokumentation, UdSSR 426, 420–423, Der KdS Lettland, Einsatzbefehl für den 31.10.1942, 30 October 1942; Kaplan, "Weapons in the Riga Ghetto," 30–31.
40. Staw. Hamburg, 141 Js 534/60, Bd. 14, report by Jurmann, n.d., 5,550.
41. Ibid., Bd. 3, statement by Kurt Migge, 5 April 1950, 379; Wolfgang Scheffler, "Das Schicksal der in die baltischen Staaten deportierten deutschen, österreichischen und tschechoslowakischen Juden 1941–1945," *Buch der Erinnerung,* Bd. 1, 36.
42. Kaplan, "Weapons in the Riga Ghetto," 31–32.
43. Staw. Hamburg, 141 Js 534/60, Bd. 3, statement by Marx, 28 March 1950, 372–373; Scheffler, "Das Schicksal," 36.
44. It is possible that Jevelson, the lawyer who inspired the resistance movement, was a part of this group.
45. In the original, *Sammelkompagnie.*
46. BA Ludwigsburg, Dokumentation, UdSSR 426, 431–432, KdS Lettland, I S-Ghetto, Vermerk, 5 November 1942; ibid., an die Wehrmachts-Ortskommandantur, betr. Vorfälle in der Sammelkompagnie 16, n.d.; see also BA Berlin, R 91/10, 147–147r, Sammelkomp. 16 an Lagerkommandantur der Reichsjuden im Ghetto, 6 May 1942. According to this letter, Captain Hennewig had applied months before the arrests to have the Jews from his commando (Faiwisch Jofe, Israel Jofe, Isac Gluckin, and Chaim Done) barracked at the composite company's office. He also asked for similar privileges for Nachmann Wulfson, Philipp Israelson, and Jakob Barner.
47. Kaplan, "Weapons in the Riga Ghetto," 31–32 and 36.
48. Staw. Hamburg, 141 Js 534/60, Bd. 3, statement by A. Kaufmann, 3 March 1950, 311; ibid., SB 2, statement by L. Pancis, 11 July 1967, 442. According to these witnesses, the weapons cache of the Latvian OD was in a bunker that could only be reached through an oven. The cache was, said Pancis, discovered, because one of the OD men (who had attempted to flee earlier, meaning a person from the Pismanov group) was captured by the Gestapo and tortured. See also Sherman, *Zwischen Tag und Dunkel,* 83. Sherman writes that the cache was revealed by the girlfriend of an OD member. On the role of Israelowitsch, see Yad Vashem, O. 33/4126m 72–73, memoirs of Werner Sauer.
49. Public Record Office, WO 208-3710, M.I. 19 (R.P.S.), Report Riga, Interrogation Arnost Jakubovic, 23 August 1943. We thank Stephen Tyas for providing us with this report.
50. Martin Gilbert, *Auschwitz und die Alliierten,* 93–94, 103, 409, fn. 1. According to Gilbert, Gabriel Ziwian fled the ghetto in October 1941 and remained in the "Aryan" part of Riga until March 1942. He then fled to Stettin (today, Szczecin) before ultimately making his way to Switzerland.

– Chapter 17 –

ANNIHILATION INSTEAD OF FORCED LABOR

Himmler's Struggle against Production Constraints and Armaments Interests in General Commissariat Latvia

Reinhard Heydrich, the head of the Reich Security Main Office, was right when he expressed a fear some eight months before his death that commerce and industry could wreck his plans for a "total resettlement of the Jews" by claiming Jewish forced laborers "as indispensable workers."[1] The second wave of mass murder directed at the Jews of General Commissariat White Ruthenia ran almost exactly the way the SS and police envisioned it, because General Commissar Wilhelm Kube also approved of the strict mustering of Jewish skilled workers for indispensability and agreed with the identification of Jews as "adherents of gangs," meaning of course partisans.[2] In Reich Commissariat Ukraine, annihilation operations were likewise stepped up over the course of summer 1942, because Reich Commissar Erich Koch had ceded authority in the "Jewish question" to Higher SS and Police Leader Ukraine Hans-Adolf Prützmann.[3] But in the General Government the desired total extermination of the Jews threatened to lead to an impasse, for after *Reichsführer-SS* and Chief of the German Police Heinrich Himmler had issued his order of 19 July 1942 to murder the General Government's entire Jewish population by year's end – save for the forced laborers in the "collection camps" of Warsaw, Cracow, Częstochowa, Radom, and Lublin – his men there began to encounter difficulties.[4]

In the course of spring 1942, Himmler had managed to wrest control over the "Jewish question" from General Governor Hans Frank, but the practical implementation of his "final solution order" by 31 December 1942 had to take into consideration the deployment of Jews important to the war effort. Independent of the back-and-forth between Himmler and Frank, the SS and police leaders in the districts of Galicia and Lublin, Fritz Katzmann and Odilo Globocnik respectively, had been able to assert their

---

Notes for this chapter begin on page 375.

own interests to the greatest extent possible. On the other hand, the mass murder of the Warsaw ghetto's Jews, which was underway at the killing center Treblinka, could only be carried out if the Wehrmacht's interests were guaranteed.

The office of the High Field Administration Commandant in Warsaw (OFK Warsaw) reacted to the deportations, which began on 22 July, by closely monitoring Wehrmacht workplaces and armaments enterprises within the ghetto. The Jewish forced laborers in Warsaw were barracked on-site like those who had to work at military offices outside the ghetto.[5] During later deportations, when the SS and police seized Jews who were deployed on behalf of armaments enterprises but not registered as such, OFK Warsaw tried unsuccessfully to intervene with Friedrich-Wilhelm Krüger, the higher SS and police leader in the General Government. After filing a request at the Main Labor Office Warsaw, local OFK officials learned that it was impossible to use Polish workers as substitutes due to the demand for workers for the Reich. The labor administration itself claimed to be surprised by the sudden "resettlement" of the Jewish workers in question.[6] This situation was the tangible outcome of a unilateral announcement by Krüger made on the eve of Himmler's "final solution order" for the General Government. According to Krüger's decree, all prior agreements with the Wehrmacht concerning Jewish forced laborers were null and void; in the future, armaments enterprises would be provided with Jewish workers from the camps of the HSSPF.[7]

The deportation operations, however, interfered so much in the running of wartime production that the office of the Military District Territorial Commander in the General Government (WiG) turned to the High Command of the Wehrmacht with his complaints:

> The resettlement of the Jews, which is taking place without notification of most Wehrmacht offices, brought serious difficulties in supplies and delays in immediate production for the wartime economy. Jobs at the SS-level, urgency level "winter," cannot not be taken care of on time ... Immediate removal of the Jews would have as a consequence a considerable reduction in the military potential of the Reich and at least a momentary hold up in provisioning the front as well as the troops of the General Government ... As has now been discovered, orders important to the war effort of the highest level of urgency, above all for winter needs, are being processed in the General Government on behalf of various Reich Wehrmacht offices without the knowledge of the Armaments Inspection and the WiG. The timely completion of these jobs has been made impossible by the resettlement of the Jews. A systematic registration of all such enterprises requires some time. It is asked that the resettlement of the Jews active in commercial enterprises be suspended.[8]

If these jobs important to the war effort were not to suffer, wrote WiG Kurt Freiherr von Gienanth, then either the 140,000 Polish workers promised to the general plenipotentiary for the deployment of labor would have to stay in Poland so as to replace the Jews, or only a gradual extraction of Jews after the training of qualified replacements would have to be considered.[9] Himmler's answer was clear. First he dismissed all those Jews deployed in clothing enterprises as "so-called" armaments workers and explained that he had ordered these people in Warsaw and Lublin to be collected in concentration camps. He would guarantee the continuation of deliveries to the Wehrmacht. On the other hand, Jews who worked in real armaments enterprises, such as weapons and auto workshops, would initially be collected in various enterprises. Afterward, these workers would be transferred to isolated enterprises and, as a last step, their substitution with Polish workers would follow. The last such large concentration workshops with Jews would be located "as far to the east of the General Government as possible." Himmler added: "However, there, too, the Jews are to disappear in accordance with the Führer's wish."[10]

The Reichsführer-SS did not even try to address Gienanth's complaints or show any readiness to compromise; he merely explained how he intended to maintain complete power of disposal over the Jews who were still living, despite the needs of enterprises important to the war effort and without allowing difficulties in orders to arise.[11] When Himmler registered the continued presence of 35,000–40,000 Jews during a visit to the occupied Polish capital on 9 January 1943, he had the chief of the local armaments command report to him and issued him an ultimatum: by 15 February, all working Jews were to be transferred to concentration camps in District Lublin.[12] When this proved to be completely impractical, Himmler founded Concentration Camp Warsaw – one day after his deadline had elapsed.[13]

Without elaborating on the history of various ghettos in the districts of the General Government, Białystok District, or Reich Commissariat Ukraine, it can be said in short that in autumn 1942, Himmler, with Hitler's approval, was pursuing a program covering entire regions of Eastern Europe in order to prevent Heydrich's fear from coming true. Although Concentration Camp Warsaw existed merely on paper – the ghetto terrain was in part merely "rededicated" – that was not what really mattered. What was important was that the ghetto inhabitants working as forced laborers had been turned into concentration camp inmates – and as such they were formally subordinated to Division D of the SS Economics and Administration Main Office. In practical terms, however, they were under the control of the office of the SS Economist attached to the HSSPF.[14]

Given the comparably low number of Jews still living in General Commissariat Latvia, this former Baltic republic was not a focal point of Himmler's struggle against economic interests. Even after the murder operations that swept General Commissariat White Ruthenia, 30,000 Jews were still living and working there at the end of 1942.[15] In General Commissariat Latvia, by contrast, there were still 12,000–13,200 Jews in Riga, 841 in County Commissariat Courland, 289 in County Commissariat Jelgava, 454 in County Commissariat Daugavpils – that is to say, not even half the number of those in General Commissariat White Ruthenia.[16] Nonetheless, their existence still served to aggravate Himmler. Unlike General Commissar White Ruthenia Kube, Reich Commissar Ukraine Koch, or General Governor Frank, who had in the course of 1942 turned over authority for handling the "Jewish question" to the police or had coordinated with the police, decision makers in Latvia had yet to create clarity. On the one hand, it had become obvious even to officials in the Reich Commissariat Ostland (RKO) that Himmler alone could lay claim to the solution of the "Jewish question"; on the other hand, the SS and police had the impression that Reich Commissar Ostland Hinrich Lohse was working toward subordinating the police to the civil administration.[17]

On top of that, Wilhelm Burmeister, Lohse's representative at talks with SS Captain Walter Jagusch on 13 October 1942, had been reluctant to recognize the Security Police's control over all legislative measures concerning the Jews, but had instead referred the matter to Reich Minister for the Eastern Territories Alfred Rosenberg.[18] For Riga, the actual placement of laborers with enterprises lay firmly in the hands of the civil administration, and for the Security Police, its practice of loaning deported Jews to the civil administration created only problems whenever it sought to recall them.[19] The SS and police were unable to take action against the ghetto by arguing that the Jews presented a partisan danger; General Commissariat Latvia had few guerilla attacks to report.[20] Plans for armed resistance in the Riga ghetto, which had been ruthlessly crushed by the Tin Square Operation, could hardly be considered a pretext.

Therefore, on 2 April 1943, Himmler established Concentration Camp Riga, effective 13 March, with the backdating referring to a conversation with Deputy Reich Commissar Ostland Günther Pröhl, HSSPF Ostland Friedrich Jecklen, and Wehrmacht Territorial Commander Ostland Walter Braemer.[21] Having found an unresolved situation on site in the occupied territories, Himmler had once again deployed this new instrument. But unlike the case in Warsaw, there are clear differences here that cannot yet be fully explained given the current state of the research The address – Ganību dambis 31 (Weidendamm 31) – was far away from the Moscow Suburb, probably the address of a part of the office of the SS Economist. Whereas Himmler had intentionally set up the new concentration camp in the Polish capital on the ghetto terrain, he refrained from doing so in the case of

Riga. Furthermore, the decree establishing Concentration Camp Riga made no mention of Jewish inmates, whereas this had been the stated aim behind setting up Concentration Camp Warsaw. Finally, the establishment of Concentration Camp Riga took place "with the approval of the Reichsführer-SS," whereas Himmler had personally ordered the establishment of Concentration Camp Warsaw.[22]

Jeckeln probably suggested to Himmler the idea of setting up a concentration camp in Riga, because this not only offered a certain advantage for Jeckeln vis-à-vis the civil administration, but also increased his own power. The HSSPF Ostland was able to forgo the ghetto premises, because using them would have entailed an abundance of legal questions concerning the ownership of nationalized and private non-Jewish properties. But why the order establishing Concentration Camp Riga did not define the inmates more precisely remains a mystery. At any rate, none of this bothered the general commissar enough to keep him from once again entrusting County Commissar Riga City and Commissarial Mayor Hugo Wittrock with the administration of the ghetto on 3 May, an endeavor that was to prove completely unrealistic in the weeks to come.[23]

For the time being, however, it was up to the county commissar to produce a prospective ghetto budget, for which 13,200 Jews were assumed as the basis for the estimate. In the future, the county commissar was supposed to feed 8,000 hard laborers and 5,000 laborers, there being 600 people unable to work among the 5,000 "normal rations." The breakdown of this budget item shows that the administration intended to make do with RM 126.44 per person annually. In addition, each person was to be allocated 600 grams of washing powder per year.[24] Wittrock's field of responsibility had seemed clearly defined since the meeting between the general commissar's office and the Security Police on 8 April 1943. The county commissar had to look after the ghetto's internal needs, such as food and housing maintenance, as well as see to labor deployment. All invoicing for Jewish forced laborers would be processed by the Finance Department, whereas the Security Police would turn over to the general commissar the ghetto workshops and all of the Jews who were not working. The SD employer card index was also to be transferred to the general commissar.[25]

However, this division of duties to the civil administration's advantage was to exist solely on paper, for just as Himmler had striven to gain power of disposal over the working Jews, the local Security Police now began to intervene in the deployment of labor. In early May 1943, the general commissar was forced to complain to Rudolf Lange, the chief of the Regional Command of the Security Police and SD Latvia (KdS Latvia), because the HSSPF had ordered the Security Police to have the civil labor administration provide Jewish workers for construction work on behalf of the Waffen-SS

Latvian Legion. Jeckeln refused to detach Jews from the Security Police's contingents for this purpose. However, after the requested Jewish workers had been mustered from other commands, they were not picked up, which produced considerable disgruntlement on the part of Paul Seeliger of the Labor Office's Bureau for the Deployment of Jews. Despite prior approval, the Security Police also blocked a barracking of Jewish workers at the AEG peat works in Olaine (Olai), because officials at the site had not deployed the workers during the Easter holidays, but had let them rest between Good Friday and Easter Monday.[26]

That same month, it became clear that the Security Police intended to have a decisive say in all new allocations. After the captured munitions center in Riga-Cekule and the Army Clothing Office (*Armeebekleidungsamt*, ABA) reported their need for workers to the Bureau for the Deployment of Jews and 216 Jews had to be placed with these two Wehrmacht offices, the new ghetto commandant, SS First Sergeant Eduard Roschmann, announced that the new request for Cekule had been rejected, and that the ABA was requesting an "old unit" once again. On the other hand, there were no objections. Seeliger's report on this incident was clear: "SS Sergeant [sic] Roschmann declared that he was in agreement with the placement of 93 female and 23 male workers for the ABA by explaining that this was an old unit and stressed again that another placement of Jewish workers, no matter what kind or to which office, would not be considered. Likewise, SS Sergeant [sic] Roschmann is asking that my papers for new allocations be submitted, for whatever reason is unknown to me. With this, I have been placed under ward and ask my superior to clarify the matter with the SD and to give me additional instructions."[27] For its part, the Wehrmacht's Armaments Commando Riga accepted the changes being initiated at this time – apparently without much objection; faced with the threat of having its Jewish workers withdrawn, it immediately entered into direct negotiations with KdS Latvia.[28]

As already mentioned, these new forms of intervention took place against the backdrop of a massive restructuring of worker distribution in favor of the peat industry so that Schmutzler, the head of County Commissariat Riga City's Labor Department, immediately seconded them and then met with Lange a short time later.[29] This conversation, however, unfolded along the lines of Lange's aims, because Schmutzler was forced to recognize that despite the strained labor situation, Security Police–related concerns could also lead to a situation in which a circular swap of civilian workers would have to be made possible. Schmutzler's only success in these negotiations was that Lange agreed to direct all future allocation applications only to the Labor Office on Aizsargu St. (Yorck St.), where decisions were supposed to be made. However, the Security Police had negotiated with the Wehrmacht and commerce and industry for more than a year and was most familiar with the assignments and the location of manufactures important to the war effort. The police could always raise objections if it did not approve of a work detail or barracking. It did not matter where a decision was made, whether it was at the Bureau for the Deployment of Jews in the ghetto or at the Labor Office in the city center. Finally, Lange and Schmutzler agreed that inspections concerning the expediency of deployments should be carried out on site.[30]

When officials within General Commissariat Latvia debated how far the restitution of private property should go, and whether ghetto property was to be included, Dr. Willy Neuendorff of the Finance Department voted against the reprivatization of property in the ghetto. He argued that the ordinance on the reestablishment of private property made an exception where reprivatization ran counter to the public interest. The ghetto, however, had been founded in the public interest and was not expected to be dissolved any time soon. KdS Latvia, Neuendorff added, had also reported its unwillingness to approve the reprivatization of this property due to Security Police–related considerations.[31] Thus, with regard to the ghetto, the civil administration completely failed to see what was happening; the imminent withdrawal of workers, as had occurred in Warsaw, was not recognized as such.

On 21 June 1943, however, Himmler intervened again:[32] "1) I order all Jews who are still on-hand in the territory Ostland to be collected in concentration camps. 2) I forbid any Jews being taken outside concentration camps to work, effective 1 August 1943. 3) A concentration camp is to be established near Riga, to which all of the clothing and equipment manufactures that the Wehrmacht today has outside the camp are to be transferred. All private companies are to be shut down. The enterprises are to be purely concentration camp enterprises. The head of the SS Economics-Administration Main Office is to see to it that no reduction in the necessary manufactures for the Wehrmacht takes place as a result of the reorganization. 4) As large a share of the male Jews as possible is to be taken to the concentration camp in the oil shale area for the exploitation of oil shale. 5.) The unneeded members of the Jewish ghettos are to be evacuated to the east. The deadline for the reorganization of the concentration camps is 1 August 1943."[33]

The Security Police immediately began withdrawing those commandos made up of Jewish concentration camp inmates whose deployment it did not view as important to the war effort and whose departure would not produce widespread protests. When the Security Police tried to withdraw six Jews working for the company Kopperschmidt & Söhne, a Wehrmacht enterprise, an agreement was quickly reached. Kopperschmidt & Söhne received twenty-one instead of six Jews, and negotiations with the Wartime

Economics and Armaments Commando Riga ensued on the "deployment of Jewish workers ordered by the Reichsführer-SS in a [concentration] camp or the establishment of a [concentration] camp in manufacturing shops."[34] Now, County Commissar Wittrock was simply pushed aside. Likewise, the Security Police inmates from the labor correctional camp Salaspils at the airport construction site Spilve were promptly replaced by 200 male and female Jews – a large part of whom were craftsmen – from circa 160 various details. In the Security Police workshops on Washington Square and Pētersalas St. (Peterholmsche St.), fifty-one Jewish craftsmen were barracked without the labor administration being informed.[35] Whenever Seeliger protested, it was said the Jews were being used for a "Security Police deployment."[36]

From the perspective of the Security Police, this phase of the uncompromising implementation of its prerogatives vis-à-vis the civil administration was to force the latter to recognize the new conditions. This would best happen if the Reich Commissariat would move beyond the stage of silently acknowledging its impotence to itself and inform its subordinate offices of the new state of affairs. On 7 July 1943, on invitation from Lange, a representative of the RKO, two department chiefs from General Commissariat Latvia, Schmutzler of County Commissariat Riga City, and SS Second Lieutenant Kurt Migge met at the headquarters of KdS Latvia. The unsigned, highly confidential report for the files drawn up by the labor administration of County Commissariat Riga City clearly shows that circumstances had changed completely. After Lange explained the dispute over the 160 disbanded details by referring to Himmler's concentration camp order, he declared that in the future he would be setting up concentration camps with an occupancy of no fewer than 1,000 people each. Lange and Hans-Otto von Borcke, the RKO's representative, urged the lower-ranking offices present to quickly locate enterprises that were in a position to establish barracking camps on such a scale. However, Lange understood that this would not be possible by Himmler's deadline of 1 August. During the meeting, the Army Clothing Office, the general commissar's workshops, the captured munitions center in Riga-Cekule, and the Spilve airport were all mentioned. Lange declared that he was willing to have the craftsmen in Spilve placed again elsewhere, but according to the protocol, he ordered that these workers not be transferred back to their previous workplace. Finally, County Commissariat Riga City asked that the representatives of the senior offices on hand make recommendations for large-scale barrackings in the shortest possible time.[37]

At this meeting, the civil administration essentially recognized the new planning authority of the Security Police in General Commissariat Latvia. In historical retrospect, all further disputes are to be seen merely as the usual conflicts over interpretation that arise between government agencies, with the civil administration having nothing more in the hand than its promises to keep armaments production constant.[38] On this point, however, it was first and foremost the Wartime Economics and Armaments Commando that supervised the maintenance of Wehrmacht production in Riga, and since 14 July, it had been part of a joint commission with the Security Police and the Labor Office.[39] The remarks made by General Commissar White Ruthenia Wilhelm Kube, RKO Main Department Economic Affairs head Martin Matthiessen, and Deputy Reich Minister for the Occupied Eastern Territories Alfred Meyer at a large meeting on labor deployment in Berlin on 13 July 1943 are to be understood in this context. But Fritz Sauckel, the general plenipotentiary for the deployment of labor, refused to provide the workers needed to replace the 50,000 Jews who were to be resettled to concentration camps. The civil administration had lost the initiative at every level.[40]

If one looks closely at the surviving monthly reports for July 1943 from the Security Police and the civil administration in General Commissariat Latvia, one sees that the question that had been left open since autumn 1941 – namely, whether the "final solution of the Jewish question" was a economic-political issue or a Security Police matter – had clearly been resolved in favor of the Security Police. In his report, Lange was able to note with satisfaction that immediately after the arrival of Himmler's concentration camp order KdS Latvia had promptly introduced all of the necessary measures. All of the Jews employed in 312 enterprises had been withdrawn without exception in the course of the month; at 153 enterprises, employers had carried out job cuts affecting 50–70 percent of the Jewish workforce. All of the measures had taken place in coordination with "a representative of the Wartime Economics Commando," and there had also been cooperation with the "Labor Office with the County Commissariat Riga City." In July, wrote Lange, almost 3,000 Jews had been confined to concentration camps or accommodated in a similar fashion.[41]

By contrast, Schmutzler could only document in his situation report that he did not know how things could continue. In an unchanged economic situation, an enormous strain on the labor situation had emerged, because the "SD" had recalled the Jews, a loss that was not to be made up for by placing indigenous, non-Jewish workers. He could not exactly say whether the Security Police approved barrackings and under which circumstances. It was only clear that the Jews were to remain under the permanent control of the Security Police.[42]

As if to test one more time whether it was really impossible for the civil administration to intervene in any meaningful way, Lohse, on 10 August 1943 instructed the general commissars to see to it that Jewish work details in large or small concentration camps really "are disappearing from the streets of the cities of Ostland."[43] Shortly thereafter, the general commissar for Latvia sent these instructions to Lange, making reference to the latter's July situation report, in which it had been noted that 153 offices had merely reduced the number of Jews in work details, and asking for a statement on this matter. Lange promptly presented both letters to Friedrich Panzinger, the new territorial commander of the Security Police and SD for Ostland, who in turn demanded that Lohse withdraw the decree. On 14 October, Friedrich Trampedach, the head of Lohse's Department IIa (Political Affairs), informed the general commissars that this decree was "only to be regarded as an informational briefing" and added: "The Security Police is exclusively responsible for the concentration [of Jews]. The implementation of this measure, which was ordered by the Reichsführer-SS, is also monitored by the central office in Berlin," by which the SS Economics and Administration Main Office was meant.[44]

Although the changeover to concentration camp administration in General Commissariat Latvia did not run as smoothly as Raul Hilberg believed, it was successful.[45] When Himmler addressed the top national and provincial party leaders – the *Reichsleiter* and *Gauleiter* – in Posen on 6 October 1943, he was able to note, despite the Warsaw Ghetto Uprising: "You will believe me [when I say] that I had enormous difficulties with many economic establishments. I have cleaned out large Jewish ghettos in the rear-area territories."[46]

Notes

1. Nuremberg Document NO-1020, Abschrift. III B. Niederschrift über Besprechung zwischen SS Obergruppenfürher Heydrich und Gauleiter Meyer in Anwesenheit von Min. Dir. Schlotterer, Reichsamtsleiter Dr. Leibbrandt sowie SS-Oberstummmbannführer Dr. Ehlich am 4. Oktober 1941, 11 Uhr.
2. YIVO, Occ. E 3-40, Der Gen.-Komm. für Weißruthenien, Abtl. II a, an den RKO, betr. Jüdische Facharbeiter, 10 July 1942; YIVO, Occ. E 3-41, Der Gen.-Komm. für Weißruthenien, Abtl. Gauleiter, an den RKO, betr. Partisanenbekämpfung und Judenaktion im Generalbezirk Weißruthenien, 31 July 1942; RGVA, 504-1-7, 1, Der Gen.-Komm. für Weißruthenien, Abtl. IIA, an den RKO sowie den HSSPF, 8 September 1942. For an overview, see Jürgen Matthäus, "'Reibungslos und planmäßig': Die zweite Welle der Judenvernichtung im Generalkommissariat Weißruthenien (1942–1944)," *Jahrbuch für Antisemitismusforschung* 4 (1995): 254–274. For an overview that includes the involvement of Rear Area Army Group Center, see Gerlach, *Kalkulierte Morde*, 683–774.
3. On Ukraine, see Pohl, "Schauplatz Ukraine, Der Massenmord an den Juden im Militärverwaltungsgebiet und im Reichskommissariat 1941–1943," 135–173, in particular 157.

4. BA Berlin, NS 19/1757, 1, printed in *Faschismus – Ghetto – Massenmord*, doc. no. 229, 303.
5. BA-MA, RH 53-23/16, Monatsbericht der OFK Warschau v. 16.7.-15.8.1942.
6. Ibid., Monatsbericht der OFK Warschau v. 16.8.-15.9.1942.
7. See the commentary in *Dienstkalendar*, entry for 9 July 1942, when Himmler at a meeting with HSSPF Krüger and SSPF Globocnik agreed on the further course of action in the General Government, 483, fn. 35.
8. BA-MA, RH 53-23/66, Wehrkreisbefehlshaber im Generalgouvernement, O.Q./ Qu. 2, an das OKW-W.F.St. betr. Ersatz der jüdischen Arbeitskräfte durch Polen, 18 September 1942. Also in BA Berlin, NS 19/352, 2–4, and in *Faschismus – Ghetto – Massenmord*, doc. no. 354, 444–446.
9. Ibid.
10. BA Berlin, NS 19/352, 11–12, RFSS, 9 October 1942; also printed in *Faschismus – Ghetto – Massenmord*, doc. no. 355, 446–447.
11. For a detailed examination of this episode, Helge Grabitz and Wolfgang Scheffler, *Letzte Spuren*, 290–333.
12. On this conversation from Himmler's point of view, BA Berlin, NS 19/352, 20–21, Reichsführer-SS an den HSSPF Krüger, 11 January 1943. Also printed in Grabitz and Scheffler, *Letzte Spuren*, 180–181. The conversation from Colonel Freter's point of view is in "Rüstungskommando Warschau an den Rüstungsinspekteur der Rü.In. im GG, Krakau," printed in ibid., 315–316.
13. BA Berlin, NS 19/1740, 8, Der Reichsführer-SS an den Chef des WVHA, SS-Obergruppenführer Pohl, 16 February 1943.
14. On Division D of the Economics and Administration Main Office, see Johannes Tuchel, *Die Inspektion der Konzentrationslager 1938–1945*. On the tasks of the SS Economist with the HSSPF in General Government and the occupied eastern territories, see BA Berlin, NS 19/3909, 33, Der Reichsführer-SS und Chef der Deutschen Polizei, betr. Neugliederung der Wirtschafts- und Verwaltungsdienststellen bei den Höheren SS- und Polizeiführern in den besetzten Gebieten einschl. GG, 18 June 1942. Also printed in *Archives of the Holocaust*, v. 22, doc. no. 95, 204.
15. In response to an inquiry from the Reich Ministry for the Occupied Eastern Territories (RmbO) dated 23 October 1942, Kube wrote a month later: "In the course of the first year of civil administration, Jewry in the general district has been reduced to about 30,000 in the entire general district." See Der Gen.-Komm. in Weißruthenien an das RmbO, betr. Judenfrage. Bezug: Ihr Erlaß I/20/710 v. 23.10.1942. Both documents – the RmbO inquiry and Kube's answer – are in YIVO, Occ. E 3-45. See also LVVA, P 1026-1-3, 331, KdS Strauch an den BdS Riga, 6 November 1942: "There are 27,660 Jews in the overall, White Ruthenian deployment of labor."
16. On Riga, see BA Berlin, R 91/164, Bericht des Geb.Komm., Abtl. Aso, betr. Judeneinsatz im Monat Dezember 1942, 9 January 1943. For the number 13,200, see below. On County Commissariat Liepaja (Libau) / Kurland, see BA Berlin, R 92/1157, Geb.-Komm. Libau, Arbeitsverwaltung, II a, an den Gen.-Komm., betr. Einsatz jüdischer Arbeitskräfte im Gebiet Kurland. On Gen.-Komm. Mitau, see ibid., Statistik v. 5.1.1943. On Gen.-Komm. Daugavpils/Dünaburg, see ibid., Statistik v. 9.1.1943.
17. YIVO, Occ. E 3-45, Der RKO, Abtl. Politik, Vermerk: "The solution of the Jewish question in Reich Commissariat Ostland has been transferred exclusively to the Security Police. Alone questions of belonging to Jewry and the treatment of half-breeds are worked on in the Political Affairs Department at the Reich Commissar's office or at the general commissars' offices [paraph of RKO Political Affairs Department chief Friedrich Trampedach]. For the files, Political Affairs (Racial Policy, Jewry)." After a meeting with Rosenberg on 22 October 1942, Gottlob Berger, Himmler's liaison to the RmbO, conveyed his impres-

sion that Lohse might seek to raise with Hitler the possibility of subordinating the police to the RKO, see BA Berlin, NS 19/1976, 1–4, Berger an Himmler, 22 October 1942.
18. Cf. chapter 12, this volume.
19. Cf. chapter 9, this volume.
20. On this, see the daily reports from the office of the Wehrmacht Territorial Commander Ostland on the partisan situation in the RKO for November and December 1942, LVVA, P 70-5-42.
21. RGVA, 504-2-8, 170, Erlaß, RSHA, IV C 2, 2 April 1943: "Regarding: Concentration Camp (Labor Camp) Riga. With the approval of the Reichsführers-SS and the Chief of the German Police, the Concentration Camp (Labor Camp) Riga has been established. For the time being, the camp will not be considered a camp for confinement. The address is: To the Commandant of the Concentration Camp Riga in Riga, Weidendamm 31. It is to be reached by telex via the Regional Commander of the Security Police and SD in Riga. A telephone connection is not yet available and will be announced later. SS Major Sauer has been deployed as camp commandant. As soon as the aforementioned camp is considered a camp for confinement, additional information will follow. This decree is not meant for the county and local police authorities."
22. The transformation of the POW camp Lublin into a concentration camp on 9 April 1943 also took place "by order of the Reichsführer-SS and the chief of the German police," see *Archives of the Holocaust*, vol. 22, doc. 102, 218.
23. See chapter 12, this volume.
24. BA Berlin, R 91/30, Budgetanschlag über die Ausgaben für den Lebensunterhalt der Insassen des jüdischen Ghettos zu Riga für ein Jahr. For the figure of 13,200 Jews, see BA Berlin, R 91/2, Lagebericht des Geb.-Komm., 3 June 1943.
25. See Chapter 12, this volume.
26. BA Berlin, R 92/1157, Der Gen.-Komm. in Riga, Abtl. II Aso, an den KdS, betr. Zusammenarbeit der Dienststellen des SD und der Arbeitseinsatzverwaltung, hier: jüdische Arbeitskräfe (2 Anlagen), 6 May 1943. Lange had approved the allocation of Jews to the AEG peat camp on 14 April, because the camp was secure, see BA Berlin R 92/1158, 45, Der Gen.-Komm. in Riga, III Aso, Vermerk betr. Torfwirtschaft, hier Einsatz von Juden.
27. Ibid., 68, Bericht 2 2 e 2/a, Judeneinsatz, Betr. Gestellung jüdischer Arbeitskräfte für die Munitionsanstalt Cekule und für das ABA, 21 May 1943. On the labor commando in Cekule, see ibid., 62, Feldzeugdienststelle A, Abwicklungs.-Kdo, an den WBO/O.Qu., Betrifft: Jüdisches Arbeitskommando in der Beute-Munitions-Anstalt Cekule, 28 April 1943.
28. BA-MA, RW 30/69, 20, entry for 23 April 1943.
29. BA Berlin, R 92/1158, 59, Schmutzler an den Gen.-Komm. in Riga, 21 May 1943: "I consider it intolerable that at certain intervals subordinate offices of the SD repeatedly try to thwart the agreements made and go their maverick ways. I would welcome it if a corresponding change were brought about for once and for all." On the relevance of the Jewish workers in the peat industry, see chapter 11, this volume, and BA Berlin, R 92/1158, 57, Gen.-Komm an den Geb.-Komm, betr. Einsatz von jüdischen Arbeitskräften – Torfwirtschaft, 30 April 1943. In April 1943, 942 workers were withdrawn from the work details, see BA Berlin, R 91/101, Der Geb.-Komm. - Arbeitsverwaltung, Fachgebiet 2, an den Gen.-Komm., Arbeitsverwaltung, betr. Arbeitslagebericht für den Monat April 1942. Over 400 Jews were subsequently employed in the peat works of County Commissariat Liepāja, see LVA, P 69-2-81, 73–80, Der Geb.-Komm. Libau, Arbeitsverwaltung. Monatsbericht für den Mai 1943.
30. BA Berlin, R 92/1157, Der Gen.-Komm. in Riga, Abtl. III e Aso, Vermerk über Besprechung zwischen KdS Dr. Lange und Reg. Rat Schmutzler, gez. Droysen, 26 May 1943.
31. BA Berlin R 92/509, 26–27, Abteilung Finanzen an die Abteilung III Treu. im Hause, betrifft: Reprivatisierung der im Ghetto befindlichen Grundstücke, gez. Dr. Neuendorff.

A copy of this letter with marginalia from the Trust Administration Department is in BA Berlin, R 92/1215.

32. Two days earlier, during a visit with Hitler at Obersalzberg, Himmler had given a presentation on the Jewish question. Hitler had made clear "that the evacuation of the Jews is to be carried out in a radical manner over the next 3–4 months despite the turmoil that will arise and will have to be endured," see BA Berlin NS 19/1432, 2, Aktenvermerk, Himmler regarding his presentation to Hitler on 19 June 1943.
33. BA Berlin, R 91/3, Abschrift. Tgb.-Nr. Kdo.-Stab RFSS, Ia Nr. 1754/43.
34. BA-MA, RW 30/70, 8 and 24, entry in war diary for 5 July 1943.
35. BA Berlin, R 92/1157, Seeliger an den Geb.-Komm., Abtl. Arbeitsverwaltung, betr. Liquidierung von 160 Marschkolonnen, 6 July 1943.
36. BA Berlin, R 91/164, Vfg. Der Geb.-Komm. Riga, Arbeitsverwaltung, an den Gen.-Komm. Betr.: Einsatz jüdischer Arbeitskräfte, 6 July 1943. A copy is also in BA Berlin, R 92/1158, 80.
37. BA Berlin, R 91/164, Der Geb.-Komm. in Riga – Judeneinsatz. Bericht (streng vertraulich), Betr.: Umsetzung der Juden in Lager nicht unter 1,000 Mann. Vorgang: Verhandlung am 7.7.43 von 10.00 bis 12.30 bei dem Herrn Sturmbannführer Dr. Lange im Beisein des Herrn Dr. Dr. von Borcke (Reichskommissar), ORR Wurthmann vom Generalkommissar-Arbeitseinsatz, RR Droysen vom Generalkommissar-Arbeitseinsatz und Ustuf. Migge. Hans von Borcke was actually the head of the general commissar's Main Department Economic Affairs, but he is referred to in this report as well as in a draft as the RKO's representative.
38. After another meeting between the Security Police and the civil administration on 13 July 1943, the general commissar's labor administration tried to initiate at least a joint informational flyer for employers. Not long thereafter, however, this was "outdated," see BA Berlin, R 92/1158, 81, Gen.-Komm. in Riga, Vermerk betr. Judeneinsatz.
39. BA-MA, RW 30/70, 10, Gruppe Z. Beitrag zum KTB für 11.-17.7.1943.
40. Nuremberg Document NO-1831, Sitzungsvermerk v. 20 August 1943 des ORR Hermann über eine Tagung am 13.7.43 im RmbO zum Thema: Arbeitseinsatzfragen des Reiches unter besonderer Berücksichtigung der Verhältnisse in den besetzten Ostgebieten. During the meeting, Meyer pointed out the 22,000 Jews "to be resettled" and the 50,000 Jews to be registered in concentration camps. For an approximate breakdown of these numbers for the RKO, see Yitzhak Arad, *Ghetto in Flames*, 402 (Vilnius: 20,000; Kaunas: 17,000; Šiauliai: 5,000, Riga/Latvia: 15,000; Minsk: 8,500; Lida: 7,500). The meeting with regard to Kube and conditions in General Commissariat White Ruthenia is covered in Gerlach, *Kalkulierte Morde*, 736–737.
41. YIVO, Occ. E 3-b -29, excerpt from the monthly report of the KdS Latvia for July 1943. According to marginalia, BdS Ostland Friedrich Panzinger presented this document to RKO Lohse personally. See section "Gegnerkreise," item "Juden."
42. BA Berlin, R 91/1001, Der Geb.-Komm. in Riga, Arbeitsverwaltung, an den Gen.-Komm. Abtl. Aso, betr. Arbeitslagebericht für den Monat Juli 1943, 3 August 1943.
43. LVVA, P 69-1a-6, 29, Der RKO, Abtl. I Politik, an den Gen.-Komm. in Reval, Riga, Kauen, Minsk, 10 August 1943, betr. Zusammenfassung von Juden in Konzentrationslagern.
44. Lange's response to the general commissar: Der KdS Lettland, Abtl. IV B 3, an den Gen.-Komm., betr. Zusammenfassung von Juden in KZ-Lagern, 15 September 1943, in LVVA P 69-1a-6, 130. Trampedach's memorandum: Der RKO, I Politik, an die Gen.-Komm. in Reval, Riga, Kauen, Minsk. Betrifft: Zusammenfassung von Juden in Konzentrationslagern. Bezug: Mein Erlass vom 10.8.43, in LVVA P 69-1a-6, 127. A copy is also contained in BA-DH, ZA I 12045, Akte 4.
45. Hilberg, *Die Vernichtung der europäischen Juden*, Bd. 2, 407.
46. Heinrich Himmler, *Geheimreden 1933 bis 1945 und andere Ansprachen*, 163–183, 170.

– Chapter 18 –

CONCENTRATION CAMP KAISERWALD AND THE BARRACKINGS

Heinrich Himmler's aforementioned strategy to make concentration camp inmates out of ghetto inhabitants did in fact work, but the required move of the Jewish forced laborers together with the production sites where they worked to a camp was hardly practical. If the *Reichsführer-SS* really believed that the transfer of the private companies Többens and Schulz from the Warsaw ghetto to Trawniki constituted a model, this option was not possible in Riga. By way of anticipation: not a single enterprise was to transfer full production to Concentration Camp Kaiserwald before the evacuation of the Latvian capital. It was not even tried.

No more than three weeks after Himmler's concentration camp order, Rudolf Lange adopted its key provisions to conditions in Riga, remarking that he intended to set up several concentration camp barrackings at the enterprises. According to Lange, Himmler's deadline for moving was "technically not feasible" and would be delayed by several weeks.[1] The regional commander of the Security Police and SD in Latvia was reacting to the fact that a large number of the Jewish forced laborers were, for example, working in construction with Organization Todt or being exploited at jobs involving the loading and unloading of cargo at the harbor, the freight stations, or the lumberyards of the SS, police, and Wehrmacht. Furthermore, Lange had learned from the construction of Salaspils that, given a lack of building materials and an enormous waste of workers, only small camps came of big plans. And who in summer 1943 was going to build this camp, which was supposed to be set up by the office of the SS Economist attached to the Higher SS and Police Leader Ostland? In General Commissariat Latvia itself, there was a crass shortage of workers; the POWs had for the most part long since been withdrawn for deployment in the Reich, and the surviving Jews could not be withdrawn from manufactures important for the war effort for very long. In the meantime, German officials, with the help of the local police, had introduced systematic arrest and deportation operations in Latvia's Latgale region in order to meet the demand for workers for the Reich from Fritz Sauckel, the general plenipotentiary for the de-

---

Notes for this chapter begin on page 390.

ployment of labor.² Apparently, not even the Security Police inmates from Salaspils could be used, although in January 1943 Himmler had remarked that he had noted a tendency toward establishing labor correctional camps, which he forbade: "In the overall interest of armaments [production], I have taken over large assignments in the concentration camps. That is where the workers belong."³

The start of construction on a camp in the Riga villa suburb of Mežaparks (Kaiserwald) can be dated only imprecisely to March 1943, probably after Himmler's 13 March meeting with top Ostland officials. To this end, Concentration Camp Sachsenhausen sent Riga around 500 convicted criminals and political prisoners, who had to overnight at the construction site. A group of Jews that had been barracked at the company Wolf & Döring for several days was probably also deployed there.⁴ In June 1943, the camp consisted of at most four barracks apiece for men and women, which were separated by barbed wire within the camp premises. There was an area for the commandant's office, which included an office for registering inmates, an office for managing the deployment of labor, a clothing store, separate kitchens for the SS and inmates, a small dental station, and a work barrack. An infirmary was located in a fenced-off section of the men's camp. After summer 1943, the structure of Concentration Camp Kaiserwald was not expanded in any essential way, and the SS never made an effort to set up a central camp, for example, for General Commissariat Latvia, let alone for Reich Commissariat Ostland.⁵

The admission and treatment of the Jews who were continuously confined to the camp or barracked again outside the camp corresponded to a standardized process; from the point of view of the SS, the new registration of the ghetto inhabitants as inmates was the most important stage. The survivors depict the process as another major turning point, one that made unmistakably clear that from that moment on they were only an inmate number. Upon entering the camp, the details were received by function-serving inmates from Sachsenhausen, who wore striped drill and blue caps. Before registration, the Jews had to practice falling in and lining up; in the process, they met the zebra-uniformed convicts and non-Jewish political prisoners from Sachsenhausen, who subjected the Jews to beatings. Among them were numerous Ukrainians and Poles who gave free rein to their anti-Semitism. First the new arrivals were registered on cards and assigned numbers in the commandant's office area. This was then followed by "disinfection": the shearing of body hair and a thorough physical examination. Afterward, the new arrivals were forced into the showers, where they hardly had time to wash. In the clothing store, they were then randomly tossed articles of street clothing with which they had to make do. With that, the Jews lost their last personal belongings, including the clothing on which the yellow Star of David had been sewn. This was replaced by a yellow triangle, next to which stood the inmate's number in indelible ink. A large cross and a white stripe were then painted onto the back and legs of the clothing to round off the inmates' new attire.

Before they were herded into the men's or women's camp, the new arrivals had already met many of their tormentors. "Iron Gustav," a member of the SS rank and file from Sachsenhausen by the name of Gustav Sorge, was considered one of the most ruthless thugs. SS Technical Sergeant Hermann Wurz was first in charge of the clothing store, but was replaced by SS Sergeant Karl Hirsch, who for his part was a notoriously ill-tempered and violent man. The office holding the labor deployment card file, where Jews also later worked as inmate-clerks, was run by an inmate-overseer (*Kapo*) named Willy Schlüter. Xaver Abel, Hans "Hannes" Bruhn, and Reinhold Rosemeyer were three of the other responsible inmate-functionaries who for the most part saw to the people entering the camp. After the war, these inmate-functionaries were also depicted as brutal sadists. Details of Jewish women arriving at Kaiserwald were received by SS overseer Emilie Kowa and female inmate-functionaries, who were in no way second to their male

Figure 18.1. A flogging carried out in front of the assembled inmates of Concentration Camp Kaiserwald. Courtesy of Bernd Haase.

colleagues in brutality. When the inmates reached their barracks, they then found themselves at the mercy of the barrack elder and the report leader, who lived in separate rooms and maintained daily camp order with their batons and their fists.

Medical supervision was subordinated to SS Major Dr. Eduard Krebsbach and the medic Heinz Günter Wisner. They were deployed in the infirmary and the bed-rest bloc in the women's camp, which was set up later. Until October 1944, both carried out numerous selections of persons unable to work. Finally, the inmates met the German camp leadership. Albert Sauer, who had been transferred to Kaiserwald from Concentration Camp Mauthausen, was camp commandant.[6] SS First Lieutenant Eberhard von Bonin was responsible for camp administration until he swapped places with SS Captain Wilhelm Vogler from Concentration Camp Stutthof, effective 1 June 1944. SS Captain Hans Brüner ran the labor deployment office.[7]

If it had still been possible to retreat into private family life in the ghetto, at Jungfernhof, or at some of the barrackings, the Jews in and around the Latvian capital now came into contact with the brutal, isolated world of concentration camp life, which denied them any means of psychological and physical recuperation. For the survivors, the humiliations experienced upon arrival at the camp, the loss of togetherness imposed on them by the separation of the sexes, and the constant threat of bodily harm at roll call and work were a shock that made them forget the trials of the previous two years. Clothed in lice-ridden, unfamiliar clothes, shaved bald, and constantly malnourished, the Jewish inmates were forced to endure the extremes of the day-in, day-out routine of camp life and not give up on themselves. Faced with the daily terror of the Kapos and SS men, the Jews learned very quickly to remain on constant alert. For all of the survivors, Kaiserwald was a form of hell, which one tried by means of luck or a guardian's protection to get out of as fast as possible.[8]

Among the first people who were forced to endure this new experience were 286 men and 125 women whose detail was stopped by the Security Police on 5 July 1943, before it left the ghetto.[9] That day, 125 employers waited in vain for their workers. The head of the Jewish-run Labor Deployment Central Office told the waiting forced laborers on Prague St. to return to their quarters, pack their things, and wait until the next day for a roll call on Tin Square so that they could then be taken to a new labor camp. This sudden announcement alone caused panic, because the last such registration for the deployment of workers to an unknown camp had been Operation Dünamünde. Nonetheless, the following day, a large group of heavily packed people left the ghetto for a 10-km (6-mile) walk through the heart of Riga to the new camp in the northeastern part of the city. Having arrived in Kaiserwald and gone through the admission process, some 200 of these Jews were then transferred to the airport Spilve. With this transfer, the decommissioning of the Riga ghetto had gotten underway.[10]

At the end of July 1943, there were at least 700 Jews registered and accommodated at Kaiserwald on a lasting basis.[11] Details were disbanded one after another, while the affected employers depicted the loss of services and the stop in production in letters to the civil administration and the Security Police.[12] Other interested parties, such as the Reich Traffic Directorate Riga, filed requests for the new concentration camp inmates, explaining that other workers could then be released for transfer elsewhere: "Our railroad improvements works in Riga has submitted an application to the Regional Commander of the Security Service for the allocation of 520 Jews by 1 August 1943. Accommodation of the Jewish workers on the premises of the works is guaranteed. We ask this application be supported by all means. The cohesive deployment of Jews would free 140 prisoners of war, which we urgently need at other offices due to the overall withdrawal of Jewish workers. We ask for prompt notification, if need be by telephone, so that further orders concerning accommodations can be implemented."[13]

In mid August 1943, the first concrete planning began to take shape as to who would benefit from the far-reaching restructuring measures. Some employers, such as the clothing depot for Army Group North or Einsatzstab Nord, a unit for collecting scrap and old metal, were to be provided labor details from Concentration Camp Kaiserwald on a daily basis, but

Figure 18.2. Roll call in Concentration Camp Kaiserwald. Courtesy of Bernd Haase.

the emphasis of the deployment of camp inmates was to be on additional large barrackings.[14] In talks between Paul Seeliger of the Labor Office's Bureau for the Deployment of Jews and SS First Lieutenant Fritz Blaschek and SS Captain Willi Barth of the office of the SS Economist, the first short- and long-term large barrackings were discussed. These were to be provided in part with Jews returning from the peat works but also with Jews from Ostland's other ghettos, which were to be closed down as well.[15] The efforts made to compare the reports on the need for manpower arriving at the offices of the county commissar, the Security Police, and the SS Economist and to coordinate the further course of action bear witness to the complete chaos caused by Himmler's order of 21 June 1943.[16]

With 1,950 Jews already partly distributed among daily commandos, Barth explained, Kaiserwald was to be seen first and foremost as a transit camp that had to supply ten large barrackings in the long term and therefore had to be provided with additional Jews. A deadline for the end of the operation, he wrote, was uncertain, but the target was 30 September. Twelve entities had been provided with 2,763 workers, and another ten entities were to receive a total of 4,605 Jews over the next few weeks. What was not calculated in these figures but had already been planned were two other large barrackings, but neither had been established. The general commissar's ghetto workshops were to continue operating with a barracking of 700 workers, but it was unclear where this would take place.[17] As a consequence, these Jews were at first not withdrawn from the ghetto workshops and camps outside the ghetto and sent to Kaiserwald for registration.

Another concentration camp was to be set up in a part of town known as Jugla (Strasdenhof), on the site of a former thread manufacturer. The Wehrmacht had already considered storage halls found there for itself in July, but had agreed with the Security Police to forgo them. This enterprise belonged to the Latvian textile enterprise Lenta, and the Security Police underscored the fact that it was already running another facility of the same company on the Jelgava Road on the far side of the Daugava.[18] The camp envisioned for Jugla was to be allocated 3,000 Jews in the future.

In mid August, the camp planners at their disposal over 13,000 Jews for their number games, that is to say, almost all of the registered Jewish forced laborers still in Riga. This, however, also meant that any additional reports on the need for manpower for an undertaking decisive for the war effort would have to be satisfied by Jewish workers from Liepāja (Libau), Jelgava (Mitau), and Daugavpils (Dünaburg) as well as from the concentration camps at Kaunas (Kauen, Kovno) and Vilnius (Wilno, Wilna). During the talks between Seeliger and Barth, planners were already reckoning with about 250 workers from Kaunas; in addition, the ghettos in the Latvian provinces were to be decommissioned soon as well.[19]

A further necessary measure to be introduced straight away so as to implement such large-scale projects was the immediate return of all of the Jews deployed in the peat works of Kūdra GmbH. Because the peat cutting season was supposed to end in the autumn, the SS was already counting on the circa 1,300 Jews the Security Police had loaned out. But there were also temporary difficulties here as well, because in County Commissariat Liepāja planners were already expecting to employ around 700 of these Jews at Kūdra in the winter as well, while the others were needed in sugar beet processing. Only after weeks of negotiations was clarity created on 27 September: SS Captain Wilhelm Schitli of the office of the SS Economist rejected both the transfer of Jews from Kūdra to the sugar beet drive as well as their retention in the peat works. Schitli blamed this on the "current situation" in Riga and a "renewed order concerning this matter" from Himmler.[20]

Whether Himmler had in fact intervened in the affairs of the Latvian capital is unclear. However, in September, new SS projects had come along that could very well have been submitted to the Reichsführer-SS during planning. Seelager, a large training center located at Dundaga (Dondangen), near a rail crossroad linking Ventspils (Windau), Mazirbe (Klein-Irben), and Dundaga close to the entrance of the Gulf of Riga, was one of these new large construction measures.[21] In addition, the SS training staff needed to enlarge the camp for foreign units at the old estate Suzi (Suschenhof) on Ķīšezers Lake.[22] Both facilities were to be built by Jews. These unrealistic projects were rounded out by demands from the military. AEG Ostlandwerk had established its own camp for Jews and, like the Wehrmacht-affiliated enterprise Hellmann, was requesting new Jewish workers.[23] Finally, the company Dünawerke Gerätebau GmbH reported that it was now ready to host a barracking as well.[24]

Throughout autumn 1943, the ghetto was steadily emptied. In September, the SS Economist decreed the decommissioning of twenty-seven details and eight barrackings with altogether 450 people, who were to be transferred to Kaiserwald on 4 and 8 September.[25] A short time later, another 245 Jews from seven barrackings and seven details were to be transferred to Kaiserwald so that they could be transported to the training center near Dundaga on 16 September.[26] Independently gathered information from two summaries attempting to provide an overview of the situation for the general commissar's Labor Department makes it possible to reconstruct a few facts about mid September 1943. That month, the ghetto definitely played an important role as a reservoir of workers. There were still 2,371 Jews leaving the ghetto every day for work in one of thirty-three details and circa 3,900 Jews still considered "old barracked," meaning they had yet to be registered as concentration camp inmates. The two largest details were designated for the workshops of the general commissar (787 Jews) and the 701st Army Clothing Office (931 Jews). The largest "old barracking" was that of the Security Police workshops (910 Jews), which had been concentrated at the factory Lenta. Finally, 3,789 Jews were considered "newly barracked," 2,681 of whom had been accommodated in Kaiserwald for the short term.[27] Two months later, on 15 November, there were only 320 persons in old barrackings, and the number of day workers from the ghetto had decreased to 810 Jews.[28]

When a transport of Jews from the decommissioned Vilnius ghetto reached Kaiserwald on 26 September 1943, a large number of those who were able to work were distributed to various barrackings.[29] At the outset of the decommissioning of the Vilnius ghetto, a transport of young male Jews was directed to the shale oil camp in Estonian Kiviöli.[30] A second transport to this site is to have left Kaiserwald on 17 November. These operations should have satisfied Himmler's demand for more laborers in shale oil production.

Figure 18.3. At the fence surrounding the site of the Concentration Camp Kaiserwald. The sign reads "Anybody entering the neutral zone will be shot without warning." Undated. Courtesy of Staatsarchiv Hamburg.

The general commissar's workshops, both inside and outside the ghetto, continued to function well into November, because a centralized barracking site could not be established. As early as August, Barth had recommended to Willy Neuendorff, the head of the Finance Department, that these enterprises be integrated into Concentration Camp Strasdenhof. At the time, Neuendorff had refused, because the general commissar had wanted to establish his own concentration camp.[31] But when winter came, there was still no solution in sight, and these barrackings were moved to the Strasdenhof camp after all.[32]

These decisions were not the only steps taken to reduce the ghetto population. On 2 November, the Security Police exploited the fact that families with small children had on the whole managed to remain assigned to daily work details and thus avoided Kaiserwald and the unknown barrackings. Those responsible for children or sick persons had sought to maintain a life together in what was by then a familiar setting and, in many cases, had apparently succeeded. But after the workers left the ghetto on this particular day, the children and sick persons were forced out of their buildings and deported from the nearby Šķirotava Station to Auschwitz. When the forced laborers, fully unaware of what had happened, returned home that evening, the ghetto became the site of indescribable scenes of despair.[33]

At almost all of the barrackings, everyday life was marked by long hours of work. The only thing that varied in these different places of internment were the conditions under which the forced labor had to be carried out. In the late Baltic autumn of 1943, it made a difference whether one was forced to work in relatively sturdy and spacious premises or in the open air. Moreover, there were still the almost routine subversive activities to attend to, such as "sounding out" opportunities for barter, searching for auxiliary policemen and soldiers receptive to bribery, and making contact with other barrackings.

Among the Jews who had to work in the open autumn air – for example, in the peat bogs and at the Spilve airfield – those who were exploited for the establishment of the training center Seelager had it worst. They lived in "Finnish tents," small wooden and straw-filled accommodations, which were not able to keep out the cold.[34] The construction of Seelager included erecting power poles, laying artificial barriers, and working at the Waffen-SS lumberyard. The commandant of the branch camp at Dundaga was SS Technical Sergeant Max Groeschel, who was later succeeded by Gustav Sorge from Kaiserwald. The mortality rate at this barracking was very high, because the Jews here were constantly exposed to the elements, and because there was always a shortage of drinking water, but no numbers are known to have survived the war. One document shows that this barracking was founded with 220 men and 25 women.[35] Those who were exhausted and unable to work were replaced by new forced laborers from Kaiserwald.³⁶ In spring 1944, 2,000 Hungarian Jews were transferred to Seelager from Auschwitz; they were forced to camp out in the open. Because men such as Groeschel and Sorge – not only merciless overseers but also outright sadists – were made commandants at Dundaga, the Jews in Riga soon referred to this camp as a "killing center."³⁷

Unlike this new SS project, the large-scale barracking Mühlgraben (Mīlgrāvis) was already a well-known employer under the direct supervision of the Wehrmacht. Since spring 1942, the 701st Army Clothing Office (ABA 701) had maintained five different entities throughout Riga where daily commandos from the ghetto reported for forced labor.³⁸ Mīlgrāvis was actually the name of an arterial road from the Latvian capital to the north where the Daugava River and Ķīšezers Lake meet. There, on the outmost edge of town, the Wehrmacht had requisitioned the premises of a former chemical factory (Leverkuzi Ultramarina Fabriks) and expanded it into a collection point for used Wehrmacht clothing. As has already been mentioned, work at Mühlgraben was especially filthy and disgusting, because blood-caked uniforms arrived there from the front for initial disinfection. Work was comparatively better at Commando Infantry Barracks, because by that point the vermin in the clothing had already been done away with.³⁹

The ABA was one of the first potential large-scale barrackings mentioned during talks between Lange and representatives of the civil administration on 7 July 1943.⁴⁰ Some five weeks later, after plans had been made for a barracking of about 1,000–3,000 persons, there were only 737 persons in details employed at the ABA and its affiliated entities.⁴¹ As of 27 September 1943, 931 Jews, the majority deported women, were leaving the ghetto every day for one of what were now six branch entities of the ABA.⁴² Only after the "children operation" on 2 November did Mühlgraben become a place of internment for 1,500 Jews.⁴³ Survivor Käthe Friess wrote later: "So on 6 November – we had to spend another four nights in the deserted, ghastly ghetto – we were barracked to Mühlgraben ... Early in the morning, I then reported alone [without her loved ones] to the roll-call grounds at 6 A.M., wandered full of fear and terror through Kaiserwald, which we all had to pass in order to be registered there and once again receive a number ... They fleeced us ably in Kaiserwald, and we had on only what was most necessary."⁴⁴

It was precisely the arrival process that was supposed to show the inmates that with their registration as concentration camp inmates a new era of repression had begun. On the one hand, the greater part of the Jews who came to the ABA from the ghetto via Kaiserwald succeeded, with the help of German soldiers, in having their personal effects delivered to

Mühlgraben without these having to go through the concentration camp. But Franz Schwellenbach, the noncommissioned officer responsible for the deployment of the inmates at Mühlgraben, confiscated and examined the baggage to see, for example, whether stolen military textiles could be found among the "thieves." Schwellenbach and a colleague named Müller did find some things. And for those they considered guilty of theft, what followed was a week of rough treatment at the hands of the two noncommissioned officers.[45] Three brothers, natives of Riga by the name of Galanter who had previously worked in the detail assigned to the Wehrmacht's Local Administration Command and who had made an unsuccessful attempt to flee just before the barracking, were constantly subjected to Schwellenbach and Müller's cruelty.[46] Only those who did not stand out and thus avoided such excesses were able to lead a tolerable existence at Mühlgraben. In the accommodations for inmates at the entity Ultra, there were two spacious sleeping halls, a cafeteria where food was dispensed, and relatively modern sanitation facilities. Because the other branch entities continued to exist, some inmates were able to leave the premises as part of a detail, for example, in order to work with Commando Infantry Barracks. This also entailed the chance to barter and make contact with other barrackings – activities the inmates in Dundaga could only dream of.

The surviving records do not enable us to gain a complete picture of all of the barrackings that existed toward the end of 1943. If one examines the memoirs and witness statements of surviving Jews, one finds alongside Spilve, Dundaga, ABA, Suschenhof, Strasdenhof, and Lenta references to Ostland-Werke, the rubber factory Meteor, Dünawerke, the Waffen-SS Troop Economics Storehouse on Balasta dambis (Ballastdamm), and the Army Group North motor pool. Although the conditions of exploitation differed slightly from camp to camp, it is necessary to note that German managers and noncommissioned officers from the Wehrmacht and the SS ruled in all of them. Hardly one of them treated Jews humanely. To the contrary, the reading provided by witness accounts – whether they were made against the backdrop of a criminal investigation or as part of a personal process of coming to terms with the injustices suffered – makes clear that the genocide in occupied Riga consisted of an enormous number of individual murders in addition to the large-scale operations. The image of the Holocaust in Latvia conveyed in these reports is not that of a gigantic, impersonal killing machine, even if the plans for shooting the Jews of Riga in winter 1941 conjure up a process of mass murder based on division of labor. The overall pattern in these accounts is dominated by individual murders committed out of a desire to kill, punish, or deter. It was people such as Kurt Krause and Otto Tuchel, Rudolf Seck and Otto "Stuka" Teckemeier, Eduard Roschmann, Eduard Krebsbach, Max Groeschel, Gustav

Sorge, and Franz Schwellenbach, who, alongside Rudolf Lange, determined the murderous course of the Jews' everyday life. But within the office of the Regional Commander of the Security Police and SD, of all places, there was one camp commandant – first in the "SD workshops" on Washington Square and later in the thread factory Lenta – who, although unable to revise this picture, nonetheless stands out, because, despite his eagerness to enrich himself, he apparently had no interest in the murder and ruthless exploitation of his oppressed fellow human beings.

Notes

1. BA Berlin, R 91/164, Der Geb.-Komm. in Riga – Judeneinsatz. Bericht (streng vertraulich), betr.: Umsetzung der Juden in Lager nicht unter 1,000 Mann, 8 July 1943.
2. The events of the arrest operation, which was led by Lange on 25 August 1943 under the codename Operation Summer Trip (*Sommerreise*), are described in BA Berlin, Berlin Document Center, SL 47 D, 34–54.
3. BA Berlin, NS 19/1542, 43, Der Reichsführer-SS an das RSHA zur Weitergabe an alle HSSPF und BdS, 15 January 1943.
4. Staw. Hamburg, 141 Js 534/60, Bd. 19, statement by Hans Bruhn, 2 October 1961, 2,699–2,700. Bruhn had been the second elder among the inmates who came from Sachsenhausen. On Wolf & Döring, see Kaufmann, *Churbn Lettland*, 317–318.
5. BA Ludwigsburg, Sammelakte Nr. 580, Urteil des LG Düsseldorf XV-8/84 = 130 Js 2/78(Z) gegen Heinz Günter Wisner, 14 August 1985, 27–29.
6. For more on Sauer's background, see BA Berlin, BDC, SSO Albert Sauer (17 August 1898–3 May 1945), NSDAP no. 862,698, SS no. 19,180; French MacLean, *The Camp Men*, 197 and 322.
7. On the admittance process and the camp personnel, see BA Berlin, NS 3/403, 1, 9, and 10, Stellenbesetzungspläne und Personalveränderungen in der Verwaltung des KL Riga, 1 January 1944 and 1 June 1944; AWL, Testaments to the Holocaust, Series One, reel 57, P.III.h. no. 286, Herman Voosen, "Report on the Criminals of Riga," 28 July 1945; ibid., P.III.h. no. 289, Sigi Ziering, "Brief an den Vater," June 1945; ibid., P.III.h. no. 367, Erna Valk (geb. Stern), "Meine Erlebnisse in der Zeit vom 10. Dezember 1941 bis 30. Juni 1945"; ibid., reel 56, P.III.h. no. 1024, Fanny Gurwitz and Frieda Schmuschkowitsch, "Emilie Kowa – a most cruel SS-Woman Supervisor," 20 July 1948 and 11 November 1948 respectively; ibid., P.III.h. no. 1024a, Basia Kurz, "Emilie Kowa, Hirsch & Sauer at Kaiserwald," 23 November 1948; Wolff, *Sadismus oder Wahnsinn*, 19–23; Katz, *Erinnerungen eines Überlebenden*, 130–148; Meir Levenstein, "Du sollst sterben und nicht leben," 67–70; Winter, *The Ghetto of Riga and Continuance*, 126–131.
8. On this turning point in all of the vitae of the Jews, see also Schneider, *Journey into Terror*, 90, as well as all of the aforementioned accounts and published memoirs.
9. BA Berlin, R 92/1157, Verzeichnis der Einheiten, die am 4.7.1943 liquidiert wurden. This list includes the previous pass numbers, place of work, and information about the workers separated by sex. The largest groups concerned here were a detail of thirteen persons for the sawmill Latvijas Koks, a detail of twelve persons for the Zentralhandelsgesellschaft Ost, and a detail of ten persons for the Reich commissar's cafeteria. The company Kop-

perschmidt & Söhne was listed as having seven Jews. On 4 July 1943, the Security Police also withdrew two Jewish cleaning women from the Labor Office.
10. Such marches were soon given up in favor of transportation by truck, see Schneider, *Journey into Terror*, 85–86. On deployment to Spilve, BA Berlin, R 92/1158, 80, Der Geb.-Komm. in Riga, Arbeitsverwaltung, an den Gen.-Komm. Abtl. III Aso, betr. Einsatz jüdischer Arbeitskräfte, 6 July 1943.
11. BA MA, RW 30/70, 27, KTB Eintrag der Gruppe Rü. beim Wirtschafts- und Rüstungskommando Riga, 29 July 1943.
12. On the full process of withdrawing Jewish plumbers and electricians from service with the county commissar, BA Berlin, R 92/1158, 94–102, Der Geb.-Komm. an den Gen.-Komm., betr. Judeneinsatz, 14 July 1943; on the planned replacement of labor correctional inmates by Jews at the company Rigaer Baustoffwerke, the sudden diversion of those Jews to Kaiserwald, and the catastrophic lag in production expected by the company as a result, see ibid., 85–86, Treuhänder der Fa. "Rigaer Baustoffwerke" an das Arbeitsamt, 17 July 1943; for a letter of protest from the head of the Army Provisions Magazine Riga with a request for new allocations of workers and the subsequent letter of rejection from the Labor Office, see ibid., 87–88, HVM Riga, der Leiter, Abtl. I 2b, an den Gen.-Komm. Abtl. Aso, betr. Gestellung von Ersatz-Arbeitskräften für entzogene jüdische Arbeitskräfte, 27 July 1943; message reporting that the Security Police did not consider the deployment of Jews in the brick industry decisive for the war effort despite the reported need, ibid., 92, Geb.-Komm., Arbeitsverwaltung, an Gen.-Komm., Abtl. Aso, betr. Zuweisung jüdischer Arbeitskräfte für die Ziegelindustrie, 6 August 1943; letter of protest from the Wehrmacht Beschaffungsamt, Zweigstelle 22, 18 August 1943, according to which the withdrawal of Jews had led to a standstill in the sorting of old cloth, while the transfer of sorting operations to a concentration camp was considered impossible to due to a lack of space, see ibid., 141.
13. Ibid., 89–90, RVD Riga an den RKO, Abtl. III, betr. Einsatz von Juden, gez. Stoltenhoff. It is telling that the Reich Traffic Directorate was asking only the RKO for support in this letter. Accordingly, the marginalia reads: "The SD already informed, therefore nothing more to arrange here." Additional examples are provided by the railcar factory Vairogs and the 592nd Medical Evacuation Section, which both applied to host barrackings, BA Berlin, R 91/64, Der Geb.-Komm., Arbeitsverwaltung, an den Gen.-Komm. Abtl. Aso, betr. Einsatz von jüdischen Arbeitskräften, 13 August 1943.
14. On the expansion of the clothing depot for Army Group North, see BA Berlin, R 91/164, Der Geb.-Komm., Arbeitsverwaltung, an den Gen.-Komm., Abtl. Aso, betr. Einsatz von jüdischen Arbeitskräfte, 13 August 1943. On Einsatzstab Nord, which was responsible for the collection of scrap iron and metal east of the Reich in its 1937 borders, BA Berlin, R 92/1158, 135–138, Einsatzstab Nord, Major Schu an den Gen.-Komm., betr. Arbeitseinsatz, 24 August 1943, and the subsequent action taken.
15. SS First Lieutenant Fritz Blaschek was the head of Group C (Construction) in the office of the SS Economist, which was responsible, inter alia, for planning bases in Reich Commissariat Ostland, see Schulte, *Zwangsarbeit und Vernichtung*, 317–318.
16. BA Berlin, R 91/164, Der Geb.-Komm., Arbeitsverwaltung, an den Gen.-Komm., Abtl. Aso, betr. Einsatz von jüdischen Arbeitskräften, 13 August 1943; BA Berlin, R 92/1158, 103–114, Der Geb.-Komm., Arbeitsverwaltung, an den Gen.-Komm., Abtl. III Aso, betr. Abzug jüdischer Arbeitskräfte aus Wehrmachtsdienststellen und Rüstungsbetrieben zwecks Umsetzungen in KL, 18 August 1943.
17. Ibid.
18. BA MA, RW 30/70, 9, Rüstungskommando Riga, Gruppe Z, war diary entry for 7 July 1943: "Occupancy of the decommissioned thread manufacturer Strasdenhof has been

contemplated by the Wehrmacht Local Administration Commandant Riga for purposes of the Wehrmacht (storeroom and the like). The evacuation of the still usable machines by Ostland-Faser has already been planned. The other machines are to be scrapped." Later, ibid., 10r, war diary entry for 16 July 1943: "For the purpose of concentrated employment of Jews, the SS, Dept. SD, intends to resume operating the decommissioned enterprise Ostland-Faser, thread manufacturing works Strasdenhof, Livonia Road, as purely Jewish enterprise, as has already been the case for months at the enterprise Ostland-Faser GmbH, Lenta II works, Jelgava Rd."

19. On the 250 Jewish workers from Kaunas, see BA Berlin, R 92/1158, 113–114, Der Geb.-Komm., Abtl. Arbeitsverwaltung, an den Gen.-Komm., Abtl. III Aso, betr. Abzug jüdischer Arbeitskräfte aus Wehrmachtsdienststellen und Rüstungsbetrieben zwecks Umsetzungen in KL, 18 August 1943. On the decommissioning of the ghettos in Liepāja and Daugavpils, see ibid., 117, Der Gen.-Komm., Abtl. III Aso, an die Geb.-Komm., Arbeitsverwaltung in Libau und Dünaburg, betr. Einsatz jüdischer Arbeitskräfte, 15 September 1943. The entry of the war diary of the SS and Police Base Leader Liepāja notes for 8 October 1943, the complete withdrawal of all Jews to Riga, LVVA, P 83-1-21, 148r, KTB Nr. 1, SSuPolStaOf. Libau (20.9.41-30.11.43). On 30 October 1943, the labor administration of County Commissariat Daugavpils noted the total withdrawal of Jews (27 October 1943), which had a catastrophic impact on the labor deployment situation, LVA, P 69-2-82, 25–28. This assessment was shared in Liepāja, see LVA, P 69-2-81, 191–199, Monatsbericht der Verwaltung des Geb.-Komm. Libau für den Oktober 1943.

20. BA Berlin, R 92/1158, 128–131, Der Gen.-Komm., Abtl. III Aso, an den SS-Wirtschafter, z. Hd. SS-Hstuf. Barth, betr. Bereitstellung von Juden für die Winterarbeit in den Torfwerken, 28 August 1943; Barth an den Gen.-Komm., 3 September 1943; Gen.-Komm., Abtl III Aso, an den SS-Wirtschafter, betr. Bereitstellung von Juden für die Winterarbeit in den Torfwerken und für die Zuckercampagne, 17 September 1943; and Schitli an den Gen.-Komm., 27 September 1943. Schitli was the head of Group D (Concentration Camps) within the office of the SS Economist. His authority was to be extended to include later concentration camps in Kaunas (Lithuania) and Vaivara (Estonia), see Schulte, *Zwangsarbeit*, 319.

21. On Seelager, see BA Berlin R 92/1004, undated report on the planned establishment of the training center, Schulte, *Zwangsarbeit*, 318–319.

22. According to a list of barracked Jews, the first thirty-seven workers were assigned the training staff at Suschenhof, BA Berlin, R 92/865, Stand der Kasernierten am 27.9.43. Suschenhof was run first by SS First Lieutenant Rudolf Reese, then, starting in 1944, SS Captain Dr. Robert Klatt, cf. LVVA, P 1026-1-3, 204, Beauftragter des Chefs der Sicherheitspolizei und SD bei der H.-Gr. Nord-Ausbildungsstab an den BdS Ostland und KdS Lettland, betr. Hetzarbeit von Juden und Aufwiegelung zum Widerstand, 18 January 1944. For more on Suschenhof from the victims' point of view, see Staw. Hamburg, 141 Js 534/60, Bd. 28, statement by Alex Salm, 8 December 1961, 3,333–3,337, here 3,336. Salm had been deported from Cologne.

23. Regarding the company Ingenieurbau Hellmann, which worked for the Wehrmacht, see BA-MA, RW 30/70, 18–19, Rüstungskommando Riga, Gruppe Z, war diary entries for 6, 8, and 13 September 1943. On AEG Ostlandwerk, see ibid., 36, war diary entry of 25 September 1943, which noted that the construction done by inmates on the works' premises had been completed. A month later, 350 Jews were barracked there, BA MA, RW 30/71, 65–71, Rü.-Kdo. Riga, Abtl. Z, Lagebericht für die Zeit vom 1.10.43-28.10.43.

24. On the progress of construction at Dünawerke, see BA-MA, RW 30/70, 71–75, Rü.-Kdo. Riga, Ia, betr. Lagebricht für die Zeit vom 1.-31.8.1943. On long-term labor deployment planning, see BA Berlin, R 91/158, Der Gen.-Komm., Abtl. III Aso, an den Geb.-Komm.,

Arbeitsverwaltung, betr. Arbeitseinsatz bei den Dünawerken in Riga, 14 September 1943, and BA-MA, RW 30/70, 80–85, Rü.-Kdo. Riga, betr. Lagebericht für die Zeit vom 1.9.43-30.9.43. The latter contains notes regarding the SS Economics and Administration Main Office's assignment of 1,000 Jews to Dünawerke and the planned start of production on 1 December 1943.

25. BA Berlin, R 91/164, Der HSSPF für das Ostland. Der SS-Wirtschafter an den KdS Lettland, betr. Abziehung von jüdischen Arbeitskräften, 3 September 1943.
26. Ibid. Der HSSPF für das Ostland. Der SS-Wirtschafter, Gruppe D, an den KdS Lettland, betr. Abziehung von jüdischen Arbeitskräften, 12 September 1943.
27. BA Berlin, R 92/865, Der Gen.-Komm., Abtl. II Fin., Lohnbüro im Ghetto, an Gen.-Komm., Herrn Dr. Neuendorff, betr. Stand der Kasernierten und Marschkolonnen am 27.9.1943, 30 September 1943. Here it emerges that 559 deported Jews and 228 indigenous Jews had to work in the general commissar's workshops. There were 729 deported Jews and 202 indigenous Jews working in the Army Clothing Office. The "old barracking Lenta" consisted of 253 deported and 656 indigenous Jews. On the number of "newly barracked" Jews, see ibid., [Liste] Riga, Stand der Neukasernierten am 15.9.43, 16 September 1943. The number of Jews in Concentration Camp Kaiserwald broke down into 1,656 deported and 1,025 indigenous Jews.
28. Ibid., Der Gen.-Komm., Abtl. II Fin, Lohnbüro im Ghetto, betr. Auszug aus dem Kontrollbuch über die in Marschkolonnen und Sprungkommandos im Monat Oktober herausgegangenen einschl. der in den Werkstätten des Gen.-Komm. beschäftigten Juden sowie der Kasernierten am 15.11.1943.
29. Cohen, "Deportations from Lithuania," 43; Staw. Hamburg, 141 Js 534/60, Beiheft 1, sworn affidavit of Chaja Portnoi, née Krecmer, 30 June 1950. Portnoi tells how she was sent to Strasdenhof two days after her arrival at Kaiserwald on 26 September 1943. Also, ibid., Bd. 73, statement by Miriam Feldmann, 23 October 1967, 11,738–11,739. Feldmann relates that she was taken to Dundaga after arriving in Kaiserwald; on arrival in Kaiserwald, cf. the memoirs of Schoschana Rabinovici, *Dank meiner Mutter,* 107–130.
30. Grigorij Schur, *Die Juden von Wilna,* 166–172.
31. BA Berlin, R 91/164, Der Geb.-Komm., Arbeitsverwaltung, an den Gen.Komm., Abtl. III Aso, betr. Abzug jüdischer Arbeitskräfte aus Wehrmachtsdienststellen und Rüstungsbetrieben, 18 August 1943.
32. On the relocation of the workshops, see Kaufmann, *Churbn Lettland,* 408.
33. AWL, Testaments to the Holocaust, Series One, reel 57, P.III.h. no. 287, Anonymous, "Ein Überlebender Rigas": "The blackest day of our time of suffering was 2 November 1943. Upon returning from work, we found our apartments devastated and plundered. Parents looked for their children, men and women, relatives. Heart-rending scenes took place. The SS had deported 2,216 [persons], primarily children, allegedly to Auschwitz, and that says everything." See also ibid., P.III.h. no. 288, Heinz Samuel, "Kurzer Bericht von unserem Leidensweg," 1945. Samuel, deported from Krefeld with his parents and siblings, reported: "When I came from work that evening, I found the ghetto deathly quiet, where happy children otherwise ran up to their parents and siblings returning from work. Here and there, one saw a light on and heard horrendous crying and screaming. When I entered our apartment, I found it in the same condition as we found it in December 1941, but mother and sister were not there anymore. I ran around the entire building, but searched in vain." Cf. ibid., P.III.h. no. 290, Anni Reisler, "Aktion! Der 2. November 1943 im Rigaer Ghetto," 24 August 1945, and ibid., P.III.h. no. 1030f., Karl Schneider, Eidesstattliche Erklärung, February 1948. Reisler had been deported from Cologne. Schneider, who had been deported from Cologne with his wife and children, lost his entire family on this day.

34. Staw. Hamburg, 141 Js 534/60, Bd. 26, statement by Ludwig Schön, 4,469. Schön, the former chief of construction, was trying to claim this "act of consideration" as his own.
35. BA Berlin, R 91/164, Der HSSPF Ostland. Der SS-Wirtschafter an den KdS Riga, betr. Abziehung von jüdischen Arbeitskräften, 12 September 1943.
36. Staw. Hamburg, 141 Js 534/60, Bd. 20, statement by Kurt Warner, 25 October 1961, 2,874–2,876. Warner, a former SS sergeant and medic, called the mortality rate among the Jewish inmates "rather high."
37. AWL, Testaments to the Holocaust, Series One, reel 55, P.III.h. no. 1029, Joseph Berman "Concentration Camp Dondangen," 1 January 1949; Kaufmann, *Churbn Lettland* 419–421. From among the small number of women in Dundaga, see Staw. Hamburg, 141 Js 534/60, Bd. 3, statement by Else Lüders, 1 November 1949, 164–165; ibid., Bd. 40, statement by Rachel Senor, 17 September 1963, 6,484–6,486. Lüders was from Hamburg, Senor from the Vilnius ghetto. See also ibid., Bd. 3, statement by Arthur Sachs, 3 November 1949, 177; ibid., statement by Heinz Rosenthal, 8 December 1949, 205; ibid., Bd. 73, statement by Kurt Scheurenberg, 1 December 1967, 11,767. Sachs had been deported from Bielefeld, while Scheurenberg had come from neighboring Frille; Rosenthal had been deported from Berlin.
38. These were the commandos Moscow Road, Dünaburg Road (Daugavpils Road), Richard Wagner St. (Dzirnavu St.), Infantry Barracks, and Mühlgraben (Mīlgrāvis).
39. AWL, Testaments to the Holocaust, Series One, no. 268, Frieß, "Meinem Gori gewidmet," 71.
40. BA Berlin, R 91/164, Der Geb.-Komm. in Riga, Judeneinsatz, Bericht betr. Umsetzung der Juden in Lager nicht unter 1,000 Mann, 8 July 1943.
41. On planning for a large-scale barracking of 1,000 persons here, see BA Berlin, R 91/164, Der Geb.-Komm. in Riga-Arbeitsverwaltung, Arbeitseinsatz, an den Gen.-Komm. in Riga, Abtl. Aso, betr. Einsatz von jüdischen Arbeitskräften. The information contained in this document came from SS First Lieutenant Blaschek. See also BA Berlin, R 92/1158, 103–113, Der Geb.-Komm. in Riga-Arbeitsverwaltung, Arbeitseinsatz, an den Gen.-Komm. in Riga, Abtl. Aso, betr. Abzug jüdischer Arbeitskräfte aus Wehrmachtsdienststellen und Rüstungsbetrieben. The need for 563 Jews for the ABA is noted here; 737 Jews were working in part in small-scale barrackings.
42. BA Berlin, R 92/865, Der Gen.-Komm., Ablt. II Fin, Lohnbüro Ghetto, an Dr. Neuendorff. Stand der Kasernierten und Marschkolonnen am 27.9,1943, 30 September 1943.
43. BA Berlin, R 91/164, Personenstand, Riga, 15 November 1943.
44. AWL, Testaments to the Holocaust, Series One, no. 268, Frieß, "Meinem Gori gewidmet," 82.
45. Ibid., reel 57, P.III.h. no. 1034, Erwin Sekules, 17 August 1947.
46. Ibid., P.III.h. no. 1034a, Jakob Galanter, 3 September 1947.

– *Excursus II* –

SS Second Lieutenant Fritz Scherwitz, the Commander at Lenta

A Biographical Sketch

By his own account, Fritz Scherwitz arrived in Riga for the first time in September or October 1941 as a driver for the Gestapo.[1] Starting around the end of 1940, he had previously served in the Air Defense Police in Berlin as well as in Warsaw and Łódź (Litzmannstadt). After suffering a case of frostbite during a supply run to a post in Tallinn (Reval) in winter 1941–1942, he was no longer able to perform his assigned duties. His superiors therefore found another area of activity for him in Riga. They surely knew that Scherwitz had certain shortcomings. His reading and writing skills were modest, which was why he had attended a school for people with learning disabilities in the early 1930s – with modest success, as his postwar statements would show. Nonetheless, the SS made allowances for the fact that he had spent his youth in the Lithuanian town of "Buscheruniai" and had therefore never mastered certain cultural skills.

What is less known about this restless SS man is that at the start of the 1930s he ran a small laundry in Berlin-Lichtenrade and, after that business failed, worked as a toolmaker at Firtz Werner AG in Berlin-Marienfelde. In 1938, after another job change, Scherwitz made it to manager of the cement company Westphal Hartbeton. This kind of professional experience carried more weight than his lack of formal education. At any rate, in Riga, Scherwitz was initially assigned a small Jewish work commando that produced mostly textile goods but also household items exclusively for the Security Service, even though – at least according to Scherwitz – the workshops were subordinated to the office of the Higher SS and Police Leader Ostland in January 1942. This was also where the textiles and articles of clothing of murdered Jews were reprocessed. HSSPF Ostland Friedrich Jeckeln himself is supposed to have entrusted Scherwitz with the technical management of the operation.[2]

Notes for this chapter begin on page 402.

No matter which office oversaw this commando, there were, in addition to Scherwitz, only two Berlin municipal policemen (Lorenz and Deling) and a Latvian SS man (Szilliensiet) assigned to the Washington Square workshops. These were the "authorities" who for the most part determined everyday life and the daily routine of the Jews there. It did not take long for the Jewish forced laborers to notice that their commando differed considerably from the others. For example, they learned that the workshop master craftsman, a man by the name of Boris Rudow, was in fact a "full Jew." Nonetheless, Scherwitz, who apparently needed Rudow's specialized knowledge – indeed, conferred on him actual decision-making authority in technical matters – had simply declared Rudow an "Aryan." He decreed that Rudow no longer needed to wear a Star of David and put him in charge of the workers. He also dreamed up a legend that claimed Rudow had been raised by Jews as a foundling, but did not descend from them.[3]

Scherwitz ordered something similar for his mistress Tamara, who suddenly became an "Aryan Pole." The inmates wondered whether he did this solely for his own benefit and knowingly ignored the SS codex. For example, Rudow is said to have set aside jewelry and objects of value for Scherwitz. However, it was obvious that Scherwitz was not a humanist or someone who could simply be called a "good person." Even if he did fulfill many requests for "his Jews," he did not intervene on behalf of the forced laborers out of empathy. Rather, he let things slide so that work commando members could use the resulting leeway as they saw fit; this went so far that some Jews used their deployment to explore Riga's Old Town and take a look at "the magnificent city in detail," as survivor Werner Sauer put it. In return, Scherwitz tried to adopt the skills of his craftsmen, to improve himself, and then, turning the facts on their head, to declare what he had just learned as his own profession, a part of his own wealth of experience. Furthermore, it was important to him to take on well-to-do Jews and have these pay for his protection and other favors. However, because production also had to show presentable results, he had to recruit Jewish skilled laborers. These were necessary in order to handle the accumulating jobs and to provide guidance and training for the Jews he was protecting.[4]

Given their field of activity, Scherwitz and his command also had access to the clothing store on Pētersalas St. (Peterholmsche St.), where articles of clothing belonging to the Jews who had been confined to the ghetto or murdered were collected. Under the supervision of Lorenz and Deling, Scherwitz commando members were allowed to go through the clothing and pick out items for themselves; it even happened that they sold the textiles received there to Latvians or exchanged them for basic everyday goods. All of this was in-line with Scherwitz's profit instinct; for reasons of self-interest, he fostered this system to the best of his ability. If Scherwitz's business dealings made him seem predictable, and if the Jews in his commando were reasonably well-off, the forced laborers under his supervision nonetheless could not figure him out. Was he a murderer? They did not know what kind of tasks he had attended to during his external assignments. It was said that these had once taken him to Minsk but also to other towns in order to fight the partisans.[5] In this, Scherwitz may not have differed considerably from other SS men who for the most part performed their duties not in order to indulge in excesses but to carry out their orders. There was, however, something mysterious about Scherwitz, something that clearly made him differ from the others.[6]

Sauer characterized Scherwitz as follows:

> He spoke perfect Polish, even knew "Jewish songs," and even sang them when he was drunk. Nobody knew anything about his prior life. Perhaps taxi driver, perhaps some kind of unskilled laborer? Who could have known that? He was himself a horrible braggart who "spoke" in turn of a laundry or tannery or weaving mill according to the trade of the respective master craftsman with whom he was conversing. For example, to me, he was the "inventor" of a particular construction material, "Westfall hard concrete," the "builder," in his own words, of a good half of the autobahns. However, the fact was that he could just barely write, better said paint, his name correctly. Brutal and inconsiderate, like all SS men, on the one hand, on the other, so long as he needed the Jews, he exploited them and was in turn good to them at the time.[7]

This applied not only to the commandant's treatment of the Jews but to the general living conditions as well. The forced laborers in Scherwitz's commando had the luxury of being able to cook for themselves separately instead of being supplied by a central kitchen; in addition to the standard fare, there were also "delicacies" of which the Jews "in the ghetto had previously only dreamed." There was a shower with cold and warm water for washing, and the beds and clothing were considered "excellent." There was also something like free time, which young Latvian Jews used in order to get to know the women deported from Germany. All of this together made the Scherwitz commando – "compared with the ghetto and other barrackings" – a small "paradise" for the inmates.[8] On the other hand, Scherwitz was apparently liked by his superiors; it was even said that he had good contacts to Jeckeln. Nonetheless, Scherwitz's commando was repeatedly screened – primarily due to the suspicions of Ghetto Commandant Kurt Krause, who probably harbored doubts about his colleague's explanations concerning Rudow.[9]

At any rate, Scherwitz was able to pursue a career within the framework of what was possible; he was promoted in rapid succession from precinct corporal to precinct sergeant, then to SS first sergeant and SS second lieutenant.¹⁰ He undertook trips to the Reich – to Berlin, where he had furs transferred, and even to Paris, where he purchased fabrics and cloth.¹¹ Apparently, this small, somewhat corpulent, dark-haired man managed to pull off whatever he set out to do. He was even able to reverse his mistress's arrest, which had taken place while he was in France, after filing a complaint. She was allowed to leave Riga for the Reich.¹²

But Scherwitz managed to do much more. If the previous examples have demonstrated how a cunning SS man could optimally use his position for his own benefit as well as that of his prisoners, Scherwitz showed in summer 1943 that he in no way intended to leave it at that. It was around this time that the factory Lenta ("ribbon" in Latvian), a large weaving and spinning works on the other side of the Daugava, was converted to meet the needs of the office of the Regional Commander of the Security Police Latvia (KdS Latvia) and Concentration Camp Kaiserwald. Management was assigned to Scherwitz, with his Washington Square commando being integrated into the new undertaking.¹³ Scherwitz was said to have received considerable support for this move from KdS Latvia Rudolf Lange and – by Scherwitz's own account – from HSSPF Ostland Friedrich Jeckeln.¹⁴

By mid September 1943, the number of Jews under Scherwitz's command had grown from the original 120 inmates at Washington Square to 927 inmates at Lenta.¹⁵ In part due to Scherwitz's efforts, this was numerically the largest of all the barracked commandos – even larger than the ones involving the peat commando at Slok (Schlock), the harbor commando, or the commando for Army Group North's motor pool.¹⁶ In addition to the previous weaving works on Washington Square, Lenta now produced everyday items in almost every sector. It had a printing press, a book binder, a photo lab, a knitting floor (mainly for silk stockings), a glover, silversmiths, goldsmiths, auto workshops, and even a garden center with greenhouses. In addition to the actual production sites, Scherwitz's complex also included a wing for the Jews with the facilities that they needed – a large kitchen, laundry center, etc.¹⁷

The statements and memoirs of survivors are contradictory where Scherwitz's deployment of personnel is concerned. On the one hand, he was accused of employing "doctors and technicians" not according to their professions but "as shoemakers and tailors," and transferring slow workers "to base 1005 without any consideration," the equivalent of a death sentence.¹⁸ On the other hand, Scherwitz was given credit for pushing through special rations for the hardest-working laborers and for preventing various Gestapo operations by raising "material arguments." It was considered an achievement that he kept Lenta open until August 1944. Through his "intervention," Scherwitz saved the lives of scores of Jews, because their jobs at Lenta prevented them from being transferred to Concentration Camp Kaiserwald, "which would have meant certain death."[19]

Scherwitz did clearly better in direct comparison with his intermittent successor Eduard Roschmann. Not a single survivor took up for the latter or provided an exonerating incident on his behalf. From time to time, Roschmann took over management of Lenta, because, as a result of his expanding enterprise, Scherwitz repeatedly had to make distant journeys to procure material. It may be that Roschmann also acted as controller, because the success of this external camp brought onto the scene suspicious competitors and envious rivals. Under Roschmann, conditions for the inmates deteriorated dramatically: Sunday work was reintroduced, while Latvian guards and Roschmann's own informants and protégés caused the atmosphere to tip ominously. Solitary confinement was ordered for alleged violations, and torture was employed. Roschmann transferred those who tried to escape to the "base."[20] In this SS internal power struggle, Scherwitz, who drew on support from Richard Nickel as well, was able to assert himself vis-à-vis Roschmann. He again assumed management of the enterprise on site and retained it until the evacuation of Riga. As an immediate step, he had Roschmann's informants transferred to Kaiserwald and reintroduced his own high-handed style, which for most inmates was for the better, although "it was never again life as it was before Roschmann's rule."[21]

But even if various survivors had positive things to say about Scherwitz in their memoirs and interceded on his behalf after the war, the Munich investigators entrusted with his case in 1948 nonetheless filed charges against him. Scherwitz was responsible for the 1942 hanging of the Jewish prisoner Psawka on Washington Square and for various killings at Lenta, for example, the shooting of the inmates Elchonon "Moishe" Glaser, Harry Schenker, and a certain Haid (possibly Edgar Heidt) in August 1944. Furthermore, there were the general allegations that he had taken part in the evacuation of the ghetto in 1941, participated in missions outside of Riga, and selected people for the "base."[22]

However, during the investigation, Bavarian police officials were to find themselves confronted with a completely different person. His biography consisted of a string of fantastic defensive maneuvers thought up by a brazen imposter who had successfully and skillfully concealed his wartime activities. The investigation brought to light astonishing things. Even if he was not a highly compromised SS perpetrator, Scherwitz had been tracked down just like any other member of the terror and annihilation apparatus deployed in Riga.[23] His arrest followed in Munich on 27 April 1948. While providing his personal information to the police, Scherwitz claimed that he had most recently served as representative of the state commissariat for the racially, religiously, and politically persecuted in the County Schwaben and had handled trust-related assignments in the administration of economic enterprises.[24] He had received this post after telling the Bavarian Relief Organization that he was a full-blooded Jew and a victim of Gestapo and SS persecution. His name, he said, was Eleke Scherwitz.

Scherwitz went on to say that he had been born in 1909 in the Lithuanian town of "Buscherani," held a doctorate in mechanical engineering, was of the Mosaic faith, and had been widowed by the war. Moreover, he had been active as a Communist in Berlin between 1938 and 1941. During his imprisonment, he claimed that he had spent four weeks in the "Jewish Camp Litzmannstadt," but had been interned for the longest period, from 1941 to 1945, at "Concentration Camp Riga." The Germans had gassed his immediate family in 1943, he said. Going into greater detail, he added that family members had died in Dachau, Auschwitz, and Stutthof. Furthermore, he stated that he had had to perform forced labor under SS First Sergeant Nickel and had been poorly treated by him, while the camp as such had been subordinated to an SS Major Sauer. He incriminated former SS Second Lieutenant Roschmann, who had maltreated inmates by beating them. Just before the war's end, he managed to flee with twelve other prisoners; he was the only member of his family to survive. His closest living relative was an adopted sister named Bela, who was in the Displaced Persons Camp Feldafing. In front of some officials, he embellished his tale of woe even more. For example, he claimed that his wife and child had been shot right in front of him in Riga.

Apparently, Scherwitz was so convincing that he had indeed been able to get the job at the Bavarian Relief Organization, and he had previously been active in the assets administration of the U.S. military government. He had lived in Emersacker since July 1945.[25] After his arrest, Scherwitz was confined to Dachau by a U.S. judge for suspicion of involvement in war crimes and then transferred to Nuremburg in June 1948. In addition to the investigation into crimes in Riga, the police was by this point also investigating Scherwitz for fraud and perjury. Gradually, law enforcement officials determined that much of his story was based on lies. Scherwitz was by no means an engineer and certainly had not earned a doctorate. Likewise, his wife, who had ostensibly been sent to the gas chambers at Auschwitz or shot in Riga due to her Jewish origins, was in fact German and in the best health. She did not know her husband as a Jew, but as an SS man who had "always" spoken out "against Jewish operations."[26]

SS personnel records sent from Berlin, among them a curriculum vitae of December 1939, identified Scherwitz as a member of Freikorps Diebitsch (a post–First World War irregular formation), a Nazi party member, and an

SS man.²⁷ Making things even more difficult for Scherwitz was the fact that during a search of his home officials had secured diverse valuable pieces of jewelry, which he claimed to have purchased from various persons shortly after the war.²⁸ That he was circumcised meant nothing to investigators, because this could be traced back to a medical procedure that had been necessary or performed to provide cover. Even if the police had been inclined to believe Scherwitz, where then did he get the money to purchase such valuables? Hardly from his time as a prisoner. Fritz Scherwitz could twist and turn any which way he wanted, but he had entrapped himself in a net of prevarications, contradictions, and personally motivated boasts that left everything that exonerated him with a taint of lie as well.²⁹

Scherwitz made another effort: this time, he really wanted to tell the truth about his life. He told those questioning him that his name was in fact Elias (Eleken) Sirewitz, and that he had been born in Vilnius (Wilna, Wilno). Until age ten, he had lived in his parents' house together with his four sisters. His father had owned a furniture company. Due to the political changes after the First World War and Russian Civil War – Vilnius ended up in Poland – his parents resettled to Šiauliai, Lithuania, but were without means. Therefore, he moved in with a friend of the family, an estate owner who could afford to take on the adolescent. After another four years, Sirewitz was drawn to Berlin, where he was trained at Siemens as a tool maker and precision mechanic. Through the mediation of a baker in Berlin-Lichtenrad, he joined the SS around 1934 in order to avoid further upheaval in his life. The rest of his life unfolded on its own as a result of this decision, which ultimately saved his life, because his family really was killed by the Nazis.³⁰ To the surprise of investigators, the family's adopted daughter, whom the accused had named, confirmed his story and stated for the record that she had been confined to the Šiauliai ghetto with his mother and four sisters. None of his relatives had survived.³¹

None of this protected Sirewitz – as investigators now called him – from prosecution. On 3 March 1949, the first criminal division of the State Court Munich I sentenced him to six years imprisonment for his criminal actions.³² Due to a formal error, the sentence was annulled on 13 July 1949, and his case retried in December. Sirewitz was once again found guilty of second-degree murder, and on 1 August 1950, he was again sentenced to six years in prison.³³ Sirewitz spent almost four years of this sentence in prison before being released on parole by the State Court Munich II on 23 June 1954. His sentence was considered served as of the end of November 1957. Sirewitz and his lawyers later attempted to obtain a new court ruling on his actions, but failed. The former "lord of Lenta" was unable to save his honor and remained a convicted criminal.³⁴ He died in Munich on 4 December 1962.

Scherwitz's role in Riga defies neat categorization within a coordinate system of good and evil. For some, he was a profiteer who craved recognition, a half-silk bon vivant who, using gold and jewelry from other Jews – actually his companions in misfortune – sought wealth and respect without any consideration of the losses. In doing so, he did not shy away from violence, which was why survivors called for "a just punishment."[35] For others, he was a skillful tactician who not only succeeded in concealing his Jewish origins, but assisted the people entrusted to him within the framework of what was humanly possible. The Lenta Commando was a place of refuge at a time when death could come to any Jew on any given day. Scherwitz had to commit acts of violence – such as transferring informants to fatal assignments – in order to maintain his cover, while he accumulated wealth not only to line his own pockets, but to use it as a means to bribe or to curry favor with other SS members. Through this wittingly cultivated network of corruption and enrichment, it was possible to save many lives.[36]

Understandably, one can hardly reconcile these positions with one another. For the historian, however, it is not absolutely necessary to do so. The historian does not have to reach a final judgment about the person Scherwitz/Sirewitz and his actions. The outsider can accept that his outstanding quality was that of pretense. Just as an actor can slip into various roles, Sirewitz could assume other identities and fill them out most convincingly. It could be that behind all of these roles the person Sirewitz was no longer available, and that even in the face of court proceedings, the power of his imagination so completely suppressed his real life simply because for him his real life had in fact ceased to exist.

Notes

1. Fritz Scherwitz's life story is marked by such inconsistencies and contradictions that no one among those who met him seems to have come close to providing an assessment of his character as a whole. His unbelievable career, where elements of truth and lies exist next to one another unchecked to this day, has rightly earned a monograph, which appeared only during the production phase of this book, see Anita Kugler, *Scherwitz*.
2. Staw. München, STAnW 17434/1, statement by Eugen Borkum, 27 April 1948, 13r; ibid., statement by Fritz Scherwitz, 2 June 1948, 64–64r. A locality by the name of Buscheruniai has yet to be found in East Prussia, Poland, or Lithuania.
3. According to Max Kaufmann, Scherwitz relieved the "senior Jew" Arnow and replaced him with the prisoner Schönberger in order to eliminate a possible informant. Kaufmann stressed that despite his privileged status Rudow continued to intervene on behalf of his family – he found work for his father and brother under aliases on Washington Square – and for the Jewish community, see Kaufmann, *Churbn Lettland*, 366–368.

4. Yad Vashem, O.33/4126, 54–58, memoirs by Werner Sauer; on sightseeing in Riga, 56.
5. Scherwitz was suspected of enriching himself at mass killings in Minsk, Staw. München, STAnW 17434/1, Vermerk Landaus, 12 May 1948, 67; ibid., statement by Antoine Landau, 1 June 1948, 76–76b.
6. Yad Vashem, O. 33/4126, 54–58, memoirs by Sauer; Staw. München, STAnW 17434/1, statement by Max Kaufmann, 30 April 1948, 15–16.
7. Yad Vashem, O. 33/4126, 57, memoirs by Sauer.
8. However, if a woman got pregnant, she faced a life-threatening situation, according to Sauer, who described the fate of one such female prisoner. She was forced to abort the child and was immediately transferred – in poor physical condition – to another commando. On everyday life on Washington Square, see ibid., 58–59.
9. Ibid., 63.
10. Staw. München, STAnW 17434/1, statement by Ephraim Magram, 7 June 1948, 76. Scherwitz's career in the SS cannot be reconstructed exactly. Sometimes, Scherwitz is listed as SS captain, which is incorrect, but it gives an idea of what people apparently thought this careerist was capable of, see Ezergailis, *The Holocaust in Latvia 1941–1944,* 382.
11. Scherwitz is said to have set up a depot of valuables for the postwar era with friends in Paris. He wanted to transfer this to the United States, see Staw. München, STAnW 17434/1, statement by John Schabel, 8 May 1948, 30–30r; statement by Abe Karelitz, 1 June 1948, 70b; statement by Werner Sauer, 27 May 1948, 80i; Schlußbericht der Kripo München, 18 August 1948, 94.
12. Kaufmann, *Churbn Lettland,* 368–369; Staw. München, Generalstanw. beim Oberlandgericht München, Nr. 207, statement by Chaim Garb, 23 November 1950. According to this account, the mistress survived the war and emigrated to the United States.
13. There are hardly any contemporary sources on Lenta, which is why it receives so little attention in the literature, see Gudrun Schwarz, *Die nationalsozialistischen Lager,* 223. According to Schwarz, Lenta officially went into operation on 18 August 1943, but her dating may be due to new barrackings for Lenta from Concentration Camp Kaiserwald, which opened in August 1943. According to the statement by Robert Matjukov, who had to work there throughout his internment in Riga, the founding of Lenta took place in March 1943; he dates its decomissioning to September 1944, see Staw. München, STAnW 17434/3, statement by Robert Matjukov, 6 November 1949, 219r.
14. Staw. München, STAnW 17434/1, statement by Eleke Scherwitz, 2 June 1948, 64r; statement by Abe Karelitz, 1 June 1948, 70.
15. Yad Vashem, O. 33/4126, 58, memoirs by Sauer.
16. BA Berlin, R 92/865, Lohnbüro für das Ghetto, Stand der Kasernierten und Altkasernierten v. 15.9.1943, 16 September 1943.
17. Yad Vashem, O. 33/4126, 74–78, memoirs by Sauer.
18. Staw. München, STAnW 17434/1, statement by Jehoschua Wainer, 19 May 1948, 51–52.
19. Ibid., statement by Karelitz, 1 June 1948, 70–70r.
20. Yad Vashem, O. 33/4126, 77–78, 92–99, memoirs by Sauer.
21. Ibid., 99–120; Staw. München, STAnW 17434/1, statement by Abraham Schapiro, 4 May 1948, 17–17r; statement by Karelitz, 70b.
22. Ibid., Schlußbericht der Kripo München, 18 August 1948, 92r–94.
23. Ibid., Association of Baltic Jews in Great Britain an den Staatskommissar Dr. Phillipp Auerbach, 15 April 1948, 4–4r.
24. Ibid., Münchner Polizeipräsidium an das Polizeipräsidium Berlin, 29 April 1948, 80.
25. Ibid., copies of various questionnaires filled out by Scherwitz between 1947 and 1948, 34–37r; statement by Bernhard Ehrenreich, 31 May 1948, 54r. As with Buscheruniai,

a locality by the name of Buscherani could not be found in East Prussia, Poland, or Lithuania.
26. Ibid., Bayerisches Staatsministerium des Inneren an das Polizeipräsidium München, 21 May 1948, 44; statement by Erna Scherwitz, 26 May 1948, 46 (quote); Schlußbericht der Kripo München, 18 August 1948, 92–94r.
27. Ibid., copies of various documents concerning Scherwitz from the Registrar's Office Berlin-Tempelhof, 80c–80h. According to these records, Scherwitz also served for a time with the Secret Field Police. Because his family background was a mystery – he claimed he had lost his parents in the First World War – the Reich Office for Family Research (Reichsstelle für Sippenforschung) conducted its own tests. After a racial examination, the Kaiser Wilhelm Institute for Anthropology certified that Scherwitz's appearance showed Dinaric traits, while Jewish traits could not be determined, see ibid., 80f.
28. Staw. München, STAnW 17434/2, Landespolizei Bayern, 14 December 1948, 113–114.
29. Staw. München, STAnW 17434/1, statement by Eleke Scherwitz, 27 April 1948, 7–8r and 10–11; Staw. München, STAnW 17434/2, statement by Elke Sirewitz, 18 November 1948, 111–111r.
30. Staw. München, STAnW 17434/1, statement by Fritz Scherwitz, 2 and 3 June 1948, 64–65r.
31. Ibid., statement by Bela Fuchsbrummer, 15 May 1948, 33.
32. Staw. München, STAnW 17434/2, 12 K.Ls.18/49, Urteil gegen Elke Sirewitz, 3 March 1949, 160–165.
33. Staw. München, Generalstanw. beim Oberlandgericht München, Nr. 207, 1 Ks 26/49, Urteil des LG München I, v. 1.8.1950 gegen Elke Sirewitz.
34. Staw. München, STAnW 17434/3, BVerwG, Urteil v. 30.8.1962.
35. Staw. München, STAnW 17434/1, statement by Cic Nisch, 29 April 1948, 14–14r; statement by Hirsch Danziger, 4 May 1948, 14r; statement by Max Weiner, 19 May 1948, 52; statement by Max Leib, 26 May 1948, 80j.
36. Ibid., Josche Wysokodworsk an Dr. Auerbach, 2 February 1948, 6–6r; War Crimes Group an den Public Safety Officer, 18 June 1948, 72–73.

– Chapter 19 –

THE DECOMMISSIONING OF CONCENTRATION CAMP KAISERWALD, EVACUATION, AND LIBERATION

In January 1944, SS Colonel Paul Blobel arrived in Riga to inform Higher SS and Police Leader Ostland Friedrich Jeckeln of a special assignment that he had been given. Blobel had received the "very serious" to open all of the graves in the east where victims of mass shootings lay buried and to destroy the evidence of the crimes committed there. If the conquered territories could no longer be held, the Reich leadership sought at least to cover up the genocide so as to avoid being accused of crimes against humanity on the propaganda front. With German troops falling back to the west, Blobel now felt it necessary to take up work in Riga and the surrounding area. To do so, he needed from Jeckeln the exact location of the mass graves in and around Riga, by which he meant primarily those places where the corpses of Jews from the Riga ghetto lay.[1]

Jeckeln readily provided Blobel with the information needed and asked how he intended to carry out this plan in technical terms: "Plobel [Blobel] said the corpses would be dug up and stacked in piles. One row of corpses, the other wood, etc. The piles would be doused with fuel and set on fire. This process would go on until there no were no longer any traces of human corpses left."[2] In addition, Jeckeln learned that Blobel's activity was so secret that his unit had not been given a designation, but only a numeric code for correspondence. The actual work – the excavation, stacking, and cremation of corpses – was to be carried out by Jewish concentration camp inmates as much as possible. The Jews would be overseen by particularly trustworthy members of Blobel's commando and then eliminated after the "unearthing process."[3] In addition to Jeckeln, the office of the Territorial Commander of the Security Police and Security Service Ostland (BdS Ostland) and its then head, SS Colonel Friedrich Panzinger, were told of the operation; in fact, BdS Ostland had probably been aware of Blobel's activity for some months already. At any rate, on Panziger's instructions, Jewish inmates from nearby camps were detached to Blobel's unit for its work in

---

Notes for this chapter begin on page 427.

and around Riga.[4] Since late October or early November 1943, prisoners from BdS Ostland's jurisdiction – most of whom were Jews from the Red Army – had been employed at the notorious Fort IX in Kaunas (Kauen, Kovno), unearthing the mass graves of General Commissariat Lithuania's principle killing site,[5] while the gruesome work in General Commissariat Latvia and its capital, Riga, although located farther northeast and closer to the front, did not start until the new year.

In January 1944, the Red Army launched a large-scale offensive that broke the ring around Leningrad and pushed Army Group North under General Walter Model onto the defensive. German troops were forced back along the Narva-Lake Peipus-Pskov line, as the Red Army cleared out Leningrad Oblast. The eastern front's northern sector, which for years had seemed static, had been set in motion by Soviet thrusts north and south of Luga and was not to come to a prolonged standstill again. To that extent, the events of spring and summer 1944 resembled those of the German attack in summer 1941, only the roles of attacker and defender were reversed. For Latvia, this meant not only the replacement of civil administration by military administration but also the imminent return of the war to Latvian territory and the repeated destruction of the towns and countryside. Before this happened, however, the Red Army would first deal several blows to Finland, which had rejected Soviet demands for a separate peace, and to Army Group Center.[6]

The special formation announced by Blobel was unofficially called Sonderkommando 1005 (Sk 1005), a designation taken from its Reich Security Main Office reference number (*Geheime Reichssache 1005*). A detachment from this unit, Sonderkommando 1005-B (Sk 1005-B), had transferred to Riga from L'viv (Lemberg) by rail via Toruń (Thorn) at the end of March 1944 in order to begin the unearthing process. Because the search for a new commander for Sk 1005-B was still underway, the well-informed Rudolf Lange, regional commander of the Security Police and SD in Latvia (KdS Latvia), assigned the leaderless commando quarters at the labor correctional camp Salaspils. A few days later, SS First Lieutenant Walter Helfsgott, the newly appointed head of Sk 1005-B, arrived in Riga and met with Lange to discuss what would happen next. Lange assured Helfsgott that he could make available a sufficient number of Jewish prisoners for the necessary work; these Jews would be deployed and accommodated at Rumbula near the first "construction site" – to use the perpetrators' idiom. At the same time, the two agreed that the Jews detached to Sk 1005-B, as "bearers of secrets," were to be shot as soon as the evidence of the massacre in this sector had been eliminated. Because the number of mass graves near Riga bore no relation to the size of similar "facilities" in Latvia, Sk 1005-B was reinforced with local personnel from KdS Latvia under the command of Eduard Roschmann.

In the meantime, inmates at Concentration Camp Kaiserwald were offered the prospect of working for a new commando that needed volunteers. The perpetrators recruited laborers by promising better food and clothing, and even the possibility of release if the employer was satisfied with their work. Without suspecting what kind of work they were reporting for, 40–50 prisoners ended up at Rumbula. Earth bunkers located near the worksite served as housing. After the escape of a Sk 1005 work detail in Kiev in September 1943, it had been ordered that all future inmates assigned to the commando be chained at the ankles. Therefore, all of the prisoners in Riga had to lug around a 75 cm (29.5 inch) iron chain. In their work, the Jews were spurred on by "specialists" from Sk 1005, while regular German policemen from Riga acted as guards. The latter were, for one, to prevent the Jews from escaping and, for another, to secure the gravesites from uninvited guests.

The manpower of the maltreated Jews was not enough to do all of the work. They were expected to dig up the pits with shovels, to stack the extremely decomposed bodies over prepared layers of wood by using hooks, to sift the remnants for gold teeth and jewelry, to use a ball mill to crush the bones that did not burn, and to scatter the ashes near the gravesite. In order to speed up the digging, an excavator operated by SS Staff Sergeant Fiedler was at work at the site; the excavator's bucket tore upon the soil and scooped out layers of "matter" from below. Despite this technical support, work at the Rumbula "construction site" lasted until early June 1944. With the murder of the group of Jewish forced laborers and the burning of their corpses, Sk 1005's first mission in Riga came to an end.[7]

Lange and the administration of the Salaspils camp were interested not only in having Sk 1005 use the camp's barracks as quarters, they also wanted it to unearth the surrounding graves of murdered inmates as well as those of the prisoners of war from the nearby Stalag. For this purpose, Lange had 125 shackled Jews transferred from Salaspils to Helfsgott's unit.[8]

In addition to Salaspils, the mass graves at Bikernieki were also on Sk 1005-B's agenda. There were two "construction sites" to eliminate in Bikernieki, because the mass graves there were located far apart from one another. According to a postwar investigation by the Stuttgart Prosecutor's Office, the two complexes were about the same size. One was made up of six or seven mass graves with 10,000-12,000 corpses; the other was somewhat larger, with seven or eight pits, although the estimated number of unearthed corpses also ranged between 10,000 and 20,000. However, one must keep in mind that this is a minimal figure based on the testimony of former Sk 1005 members, which is another reason for the imprecise estimates; the actual figure is to be set somewhat higher. We are of the opinion that the pits of the first killing site contained the victims of the selections and shootings of summer 1941, whereas the corpses of those selected during Operation Dünamünde and the Jews deported from Germany and elsewhere were buried at the second site. Sk 1005-B, which had by this point given up its quarters at Salaspils and moved to an improvised camp of barracks about 250 m (230 yards) from the diggings, was deployed at the smaller complex from mid June until the end of July 1944. The prisoners deployed there – some fifty Jewish forced laborers – carried out the work described above and were then shot at the end of the unearthing operation.

In these weeks, as Helfsgott's men opened one mass grave after another and burned the corpses, Army Group North managed to fend off attacks by the Red Army (1st, 2nd, and 3rd Baltic fronts) and to reestablish contact with Army Group Center. Riga no longer served as the capital of Ostland, but as a control center for the military – the command staff of Army Group North had taken up quarters at Sigulda (Segewold), some 50 km (31 miles) east of Riga – and logistics center for supplies. This was urgently necessary, for the losses of German officers, noncommissioned officers, rank-and-file soldiers, and local volunteer helpers were enormous. Because Hitler did not intend to give up the Baltic and allow Army Group North to withdraw and align the front, the German generals in the field were preparing a defensive strategy toward the end of August 1944.[9]

By contrast, the Red Army's summer offensive had made it clear to the office of the Inspection of Concentration Camps within the Economics and Administration Main Office that Kaiserwald, with all of its subcamps and labor commandos, could not go on operating as it had been, but was on the brink of collapse. Originally conceived for Riga and Latvia, Kaiserwald had grown in size and by this point maintained barrackings of Jewish inmates in, inter alia, Spilve (Spilwe), Jugla (Strasdenhof), Dundaga (Dondangen), and Eleja-Meitene (Elley-Meiten) near Jelgava (Mitau), in addition to all those in Riga such as the Army Group North's motor pool, the Army Clothing Office, the Waffen-SS Troop Economics Storehouse, the Reich Railway, and AEG. Kaiserwald itself also had at its disposal workshops for electricians and roofers. A blacksmith's shop had been added, and a pigsty was in operation. In the front part of the camp complex – outside the actual premises – the inmates of Commando Anode had to dismantle worn-out batteries and sort out the parts that were still usable.[10]

The increasingly severe and perilous conditions were reflected in the high mortality rate at the main camp, where death certificates were issued for 484 prisoners from among at most 3,000 inmates between 15 December 1943 and 8 August 1944.[11] Whether those persons whom the camp's commandant, SS Major Albert Sauer, had ordered executed in the "blue barrack" – the camp's execution site – as politically intolerable or "superfluous" were registered among them is not known due to the lack of contemporary sources. Other, exhausted and sick inmates were driven by truck into the surrounding woods to "High Forest Commando," that is to say, to the "base," and shot there.[12] Conditions in the external camps, the permanent fear of a possible selection, and the miserable provisions were characteristic of the situation that prevailed in the main camp. Shortages of workers were mitigated by the arrival of Jews from Lithuania, the General Government, and above all Hungary. The latter group involved Jewish women who were transferred from Auschwitz and distributed among several subcamps. At the subcamp Dundaga – run by Gustav Sorge – there were around 2,000 female Hungarian inmates.[13]

Children and sick persons were not among those considered indispensable. Hilde Sherman-Zander describes in her memoirs how the SS stormed the inmates' hospital run by Dr. Joseph at the subcamp Mühlgraben (Milgrāvis) and selected thirty-five patients. A week later, a selection team seized sixty-four children and sent them to Kaiserwald. Sherman-Zander wrote that, according to a Kapo, one of the camp's inmate-overseers, the little ones were locked up in a cattle car and shunted off on a sidetrack. For three days, the children could be heard crying, screaming, and whimpering; then they fell silent. After another six days, prisoners were allowed to open up the wagon. They saw the corpses of

Figure 19.1. Selecting children for extermination in Riga woods. Courtesy of Bernd Haase.

up the wagon. They saw the corpses of the children, from which worms crawled "upright like snakes." Other witnesses said that the children were killed by means of a gassing van.[14] Even if the version of events provided by Sherman-Zander is implausible, exaggerated to the point of fantasy by her legitimate and understandable fears, the crime itself, the targeted selection and murder of children, is itself beyond dispute.

Rita Wassermann, who was born in 1930 and robbed of her childhood by the murderous events of the war, was no longer a child and thus survived the March 1944 "children operation" at Kaiserwald. She was allowed to join the adults. Her friends Ilse Ullmann and Günter Kaufmann had no such luck. With the cynical words "Faster, faster, can't you pick up your feet?" medic Heinz Wisner forced them onto the trucks that then took the children to a secret killing site.[15] In addition to singling out of children, SS Major Dr. Eduard Krebsbach, with a flick of the hand, chose which adults were slated for death; this took place during degrading examinations, the women naked or half-naked, the men naked. Anybody who refused to accept the doctor's decision, such as Louis Roseboom, who wanted to stay with his selected parents, was slapped by Krebsbach and sent back to the line. Jews were not allowed to go their death on their own volition.[16]

It was primarily Krebsbach who determined the course of fate within the infirmary. However, for everyday operations, he readily turned over his authority to Wisner, only showing up when he considered it necessary. Krebsbach seemed to prefer acting as a sinister threat in the background, which served to reinforce the inmates' fear of him. Various inmate-doctors were on duty in the infirmary itself. First among them was Dr. Boleslaw Luczak (called Dr. Bolek), a political prisoner from Poland. There were also the Latvian Jews Dr. Weinreich, Dr. Max Zik, Dr. Elsass, and Dr. Javetz[17] as well as a barber named Weinstein. In addition to them, the non-Jewish political prisoners Dr. Jindrich Sik and Dr. Ostry were employed in the sick bay. In the women's camp, Dr. Nadia Reznik, a survivor from the Vilnius (Wilna, Wilno) ghetto who had been sent to Kaiserwald at the end of September 1943, looked after the female inmates.[18]

Everything needed for adequate medical treatment was lacking. Medications were in short supply, bandages seldom to be had. Because disinfectants were also lacking, hygiene was poor. Operations were carried out only in extreme cases, usually with no chance of success. It therefore comes as no surprise that a seriously ill inmate had only the slightest chance of leaving the infirmary alive. Prisoners did their best to avoid being admitted to the infirmary, because they were all too aware of the peril there. When Erika Oppenheimer was forcibly brought before Wisner in February 1944 due to a high temperature, he claimed to have "no time" for her, words that could only be understood as a threat. Despite the dedicated support of the inmate-nurses, it was impossible to give Oppenheimer adequate medical attention. Unsure of her prospects of surviving in the sick bay, Oppenheimer managed to be released despite her condition through the intervention of her labor detail, Commando Meteor. She was lucky that Wisner was not too active in the sick bay at the time. On another occasion, Trudy Schloss witnessed how the feared medic beat inmates, carried out selections, and forced them onto a truck that was to take them to the "base."[19]

Roll calls repeatedly took place in the final months of German occupation. According to Solomon Gerstein, who was deployed and barracked in the infirmary, during Wisner's orders to assemble, the inmates had to report to the camp square and walk past the medic. With a simple hand gesture, he let it be known whether an inmate would go on working with his colleagues or was to be taken away and shot. In the infirmary itself, Wisner, always accompanied by the inmate-physician Dr. Bolek and sometimes by members of the SS, sought out additional victims by means of inspections: "The defendant [Wisner] went from bed to bed during his selections and determined those who were to be taken away. At every selection, ca. 20–30 or even more rather sick patients were singled out. The selected persons were loaded onto a truck that same day. I myself had to help load onto the truck those selected persons who were no longer able to walk so well. Among those selected in sick bay were some acquaintances of mine."[20] Finally, inmates were sometimes given lethal injections. Within the camp, there were also persistent rumors that "experiments" on human beings were being carried out, and that none of the "subjects" survived.[21]

The murdering also continued at the Salaspils camp. In mid August 1944, Stalag 350-S transferred wounded Red Army soldiers to the nearby Salaspils labor correctional camp. These soldiers' wounds had healed, but they were unable to walk as a result of their amputations. Considered a hindrance to the Stalag, they were to be left behind and murdered by Salaspils personnel under Commandant Kurt Krause. The prisoners themselves were told that they were being taken to a hospital. Krause promptly seized the opportunity to go through his "stock" of prisoners and drew up lists of persons – for the most part older prisoners, those who were physically weak, ill persons, and those who were unable to work – all of whom were to be liquidated as "superfluous." Lange confirmed these lists with his own signature. A shooting squad made up of Lange as well as Krause, Albert Widusch, and the censor Arkadii Schmutow drove the victims to the killing site, a place in the woods near the Salaspils railroad station. Waiting for them there was a group from Sk 1005, including Helfsgott and Roschmann, which had prepared a pyre for the subsequent cremation of the victims. "The execution of the 500 captured Red Army soldiers took at least four hours. When the entire 20-meter-long layer of wood had been covered by the corpses of those who had been shot, these were covered with wood and doused with oil. Then the next prisoners were shot in the same way, and the next layer of corpses was laid. Together with the captured Red Army soldiers, 70–80 older and physically run-down prisoners from the camp [Salaspils] were shot that day." In an orderly fashion, the head of administration at Salaspils, Erich Brauer, noted for the books the "losses" among the camp's inmates, while the Red Army soldiers had to be registered anonymously and summarily, because "we had not received their personnel records."[22]

The example of Army Technical Sergeant Willi Hühnerbein shows that not all of those in uniform who were granted power over inmates during the Soviet campaign mutated into perpetrators. Given a corresponding predisposition of character, a few men were instead able to maintain a sense of morality and decency amid conditions that encouraged the opposite. Hühnerbein looked after the inmates of Commando Ordnance Park in such exemplary fashion that after the war the Jewish community of Dortmund successfully campaigned for his early release from Soviet captivity.[23] But Hühnerbein's treatment of the Jews under his purview was an extraordinarily rare case.

Unlike the Wehrmacht, the Economics and Administration Main Office (WVHA) was not required to hold every position until the end. And although Economics Commando Riga stressed the performance of the workshops "occupied by Jews" even at the end of March 1944,[24] the WVHA made sure that, as a first step, several labor commandos from the branch camps were returned to Kaiserwald starting at the end of May in order to be sent to the Reich. Exceptions were the inmates from camps at Popervale (Poperwahlen), Lenta, and Milgrāvis (Mühlgraben), who for most part ended up in Liepāja (Libau) prison and were killed there "as a result of military operations," according to historian Alfred Streim. Armaments enterprises also made plans to send Jewish prisoners to the west, at least in the course of the partial transfer of manufactures. For example, at the end of June 1944, the company AEG Ostlandwerk sought to transfer around 500 Jewish women from Riga to Toruń so that it could go on using their labor in production (e.g. making antennas). As a next step, the WVHA began closing the branch camps at Dundaga, Kurben (Kurbe), and Krottingen (Kretinga, Lithuania) as well as the barrackings in the Riga vicinity (Army Group North's motor pool, the Waffen-SS Troop Economics Storehouse, Dünawerke, Strasdenhof, Spilve, etc.).

Starting in July and increasingly throughout August 1944, Kaiserwald's inmates had to be transferred back to the main camp in the course of preparations for the evacuation of Riga, with "useless" prisoners being separated out and murdered. At Strasdenhof, a commando led by SS First Sergeant Meisel selected all those persons who were either over fifty years old or considered children. At Kaiserwald itself, Dr. Krebsbach made selections according to the aforementioned categories during a large roll call in late July 1944[25] that achieved infamy and remains forever linked to his name as the "Krebsbach operation." The selection of the prisoners lasted almost the entire day. Krebsbach and Wisner walked between the rows of prisoners and with a flick of the hand indicated those who were not to go on living. The selected persons were dragged to trucks and taken to Bikernieki,[26] where Sk 1005 was in the process of burning the final corpses it had exhumed. Even the inmate-doctors were not spared if they had themselves taken ill as a result of their regular contact with patients.[27]

Parallel to the selection operations in early August, ships began leaving Riga with former prisoners from Mühlgraben, Army Group North's motor pool, Lenta, and the freight train commandos of the Waffen-SS Troop Economics Storehouse. The journey led over the Baltic to Danzig (Gdańsk), where the inmates were transferred to Concentration Camp Stutthof. Those who remained behind were put to work unloading cargo in the Riga harbor, where provisions and munitions were brought up for the German Army.[28] Even if the overall evacuation order was not issued until late August, the sea route represented the only possibility of flight, because the Soviet occupation of Jelgava, Tukums (Tuckum), and Šiauliai (Schaulen, Lithuania) had cut rail links to the Reich. Every transport that left the Riga harbor had to be reported to Lieutenant Colonel Vester from the office of the High Quartermaster North; he decided the order of loading on the basis of priority. In addition to valuable freight, such as tools and machines, it was necessary to get slave-workers – Jewish inmates and prisoners of war – specialized Latvian craftsmen, wounded men, and officials from Ostland out of Riga. The first inmate transport left on 6 August 1944, with the greater part of the Jewish inmates being evacuated on the steamship Bremerhaven.[29] It should come as no surprise that the most senior members of the civil administration, Reich Commissar Hinrich Lohse and General Commissar Otto Heinrich Drechsler, had sought the wide open as soon as possible during the evacuation of Riga, and that their subordinates had quickly followed. The exercise of power once again lay completely in the hands of the Army and the SS.[30]

In the meantime, Sk 1005 had begun with the excavation of the second grave complex within Bikernieki. For this, it had requested another work detail – assumed to be at least forty persons – whose inmates pulled the corpses from the ground and burned them between early August and mid September. After the unearthing operation was completed, these prisoners were murdered as well. Although there was by this point a danger of being surrounded by the Soviet troops, Sk 1005 then began exhumation work in the northern part of Riga, where the mass graves of those murdered at Kaiserwald were located. For this, the commando helped itself to a new group of inmates from the camp, another 40–60 persons, whom the commandant dispatched to Sk 1005 and thus condemned to death.[31]

With all signs increasingly pointing to a major Soviet attack, the commandant for combat operations within Riga itself had all troops in the city placed under his command. The First Baltic Front marched west of the city to Jelgava, while the Second and Third Baltic fronts approached from the east and southeast toward Riga's defenses, thus making the surrounding of the city probable. On 19 September, Soviet forces managed to advance via Baldone (Baldohn) to the Daugava within 20 km of Riga.[32] It could not be any clearer that the city would soon fall.

Toward the end of September, Lange gave the order to stop the unearthing operations in the Riga area. Due to the advances of the Red Army, additional excavation work no longer made sense. Furthermore, in the eyes of those who had commissioned it, Sk 1005 had surely been a success. It had managed to destroy the greater part of the evidence and kill all of those forced laborers who were "bearers of secrets." In fact, it was now necessary to protect the German commando members from capture and interrogation in order to prevent the Soviet Union from gaining the opportunity to use "secret matter of the Reich 1005" and the crimes of the "Third Reich" for propaganda purposes in a show trial.[33] In the event of such a trial, the "success" of the exhumations would have been quickly relativized by reports in the world press. It was just as necessary to get Helfsgott and his men to the west as it was to evacuate Kaiserwald's inmates. They, too, were to sail to Danzig.

Just before boarding, another large killing took place near the mass grave complex at Kaiserwald. Using trucks, members of KdS Latvia drove the circa 300–400 men, women, and children to the site, where a pyre had already been prepared, and forced them to line up in columns. From a postwar statement, it is known that the victims came from a camp near Riga. The operation involved mostly Hungarian Jewish women and their children, but this group also included some German Jews from the Reich, e.g. from Hamburg. The first column had to lie down on the logs; then SD-men walked past the row and killed each individual with a shot to the back of the neck. The victims of the second column were forced to lie down on top of the people who had just been shot before their very eyes. Then they were shot as well. And so it went, one column after another, until none of the prisoners was left alive. Before the members of KdS Latvia and Sk 1005 departed for the Riga harbor, they lit the pyre and burned the corpses. Max Kaufmann mentioned in his book that the fate of the Hungarian women transferred from Kaiserwald to Spilve was unknown to survivors, because the women's trail had been lost. From information gathered by West German investigators after the war, it may be concluded that these women and their children were among the victims of the crime depicted here, one of the last during the German occupation of Riga.[34]

With the Second Baltic Front's advance on Riga, the evacuation order for Salaspils was issued at the end of September 1944. Camp Commandant Kurt Krause had all of the inmates able to work report for departure. He judged twenty of them to be too weak and shot them on the spot. The barracks were then set on fire, and the camp was abandoned.[35] At Strasdenhof, the course of events was similar. Camp personnel under SS Sergeant Gustav Döring, the camp's commandant, went in search of people who had gone into hiding and had been missing when marching orders were received. A group made up mostly of forced laborers from the general commissar's workshops who had not shown up on the assembly grounds. Anybody tracked down during the combing of the barracks – such as Egon Hamburger of Vienna, who had hidden in the fur storehouse, or an inmate named Buchbinder, who had tried to flee over a roof – had forfeited his life, just like a group of inmates from the external commandos that had recently tried to flee. As a deterrent to others, the would-be escapees were drowned in the nearby lake by means of a beastly practice called "coercive diving." The terror came to an end at Strasdenhof only on 26 September, when the last inmates were evacuated.[36]

The systematic destruction of the camps – which was carried out less to destroy evidence than to prevent the Red Army from using the buildings – was not a specialty of the SS. The SS was instead following established practice. During the withdrawal from Riga, combat engineers from the 16th Army systematically destroyed industrial and economic facilities as well as the harbor premises, including many of the buildings where Jewish labor details had worked for months to meet their production quotas. The last prisoner transport set sail toward Danzig on 10 October 1944. With the end of ship traffic, the harbor was mined. Artillery fire and air raids brought the war back to Riga, as the German divisions made an orderly retreat over the Daugava bridges and left through the western part of the city. The population hid as best it could in the burning city's cellars and sheds. Three days later, the bridges, which Jewish forced laborers had repaired in 1941, were destroyed once again, as the Red Army moved into the city center. One may expect that KdS Latvia was decommissioned at the same time Riga was given up, but this was not the case. Instead, it resumed work in Liepāja as the "Administration of the SD Latvia" – until Soviet forces put an end to its beggarly existence there as well.[37]

Packed into the bowels of the ships and steamers, many of the inmates may have succumbed to the illusion that with the retreat the worst was over, and that things could only get better. The journey over the Baltic was evidence that such expectations could end in bitter disappointment. According to Fanny Kopolowitz, her transfer from Riga to Stutthof lasted eight days, during which she spent most of her time struggling for a seat among the several thousand inmates below deck. In the stifling atmosphere and August heat, her worries were justifiably directed at another danger: Soviet attacks on the transport ship, a legitimate military target in the eyes of the Red Navy. That this was not the product of a tortured imagination is seen in a statement by former SS guard Johann Roppelt, who confirmed that transport ships were sunk by Soviet submarines. This could have applied to transport ships with prisoners on board – one direct hit and the ship would have been lost in the Baltic Sea.[38]

The final destination of this odyssey was Concentration Camp Stutthof, near Danzig, which had been established in early September 1939 as a camp for Higher SS and Police Leader Vistula Richard Hildebrandt, the notorious Guard Battalion Eimann, and the Danzig Gestapo. It had not been constructed at the outset as a concentration camp in the sense of the SS system of classification. Instead, it had originally served as a regional internment site, where primarily Poles but also Jews and German critics of the Nazi regime were held after the seizure of the interwar Free City. The camp would not be subordinated to the office of the Inspection of Concentration Camps until January 1942. Only then did Stutthof's incorporation into the apparatus under Oswald Pohl's responsibility take place, thus putting an end to the phase of improvisation at the camp, which in the internal correspondence of the SS had sometimes been called a "civil internment camp," a "labor correctional camp," or a "special camp." In addition to Stutthof's role as an internment center, a crucial element in determining the camp's status was that the systematic exploitation of inmate labor had gained in importance as a factor of consideration. In this, *Reichsführer-SS* Heinrich Himmler followed the established practice of the Danzig Gestapo, which since October 1941 had forcibly deployed inmates as laborers, even leasing them to private companies and thus turning a profit for the SS. In Himmler's longer-term view, this "success" was to be built on and Stutthof expanded by adding larger camp workshops. In accordance with these guidelines – which were also owed to the wartime economic situation in Germany and the shortage of workers after the failed siege of Moscow in December 1941 – the camp's change in function began to unfold, with the SS leadership entrusting SS Captain Max Pauli, the commandant, with the carrying out of this assignment.

The expansion of Stutthof therefore seemed imperative, so that, right next to the "old camp,"[39] work was begun on the construction of another complex – the "new camp"[40] – where 20,000–25,000 inmates were to be accommodated. It was not possible to expand the camp to this extent by the war's end. Nonetheless, workshops for the company Deutsche Ausrüstungswerke GmbH, storerooms, ateliers, stalls, and kitchen facilities were built. East of the original camp, a crematorium was also completed in autumn 1942.[41] This was augmented by a brick gas chamber in spring 1944. A sidetrack of the Danzig-Steegen line led past this site and came to an end at the Deutsche Ausrüstungswerke complex. This represented Stutthof's link to the railroad network. Otherwise the camp, which was located in the woods, was connected to the outside world only by a country road leading from the village Stutthof (today Sztutowo) to Danzig. Altogether, the camp encompassed 741 acres (300 hectares) and was surrounded by barbed-wire fences and watchtowers for the guards, who were armed with machine guns.

Himmler's new orders primarily served to internationalize the inmate community. From this regional internment center, which had originally been foreseen for 1,000 inmates and held about double that number in late autumn 1942, emerged a branch of the network of the Inspection of Concentration Camps. And just as leading camp personnel swapped places with one another, there took place an exchange of inmates – Stutthof increasingly being an exception – who were transferred according to the needs of the forced labor market. It was mainly the share of inmates from Germany and the Soviet Union that increased with the camp's new orientation, but Poles still accounted for the majority of inmates. The camp had originally been laid out for men, but starting in summer 1940, women were also confined there, with a separate area being allocated for them in January 1941. This development only underscored Stutthof's later official classification as a concentration camp.

As a result of the approaching front and the implementation of the "final solution" in Hungary, the array of tasks at Stutthof changed once again in summer 1944. In only a few weeks, camp occupancy grew extraordinarily quickly as a result of the enormous number of Jewish inmates transferred to Stutthof. Between 29 June and 14 October 1944, 47,109 Jews arrived in 26 transports and were confined there. By comparison, according to Karin Orth, during Stutthof's early phase – from September 1939 to late 1940 – around 10,400 inmates had passed through the camp, that is to say, had been forced to spend a relatively short part their imprisonment there before being deported to other internment sites. By contrast, analysis of the available documents shows that between 8 August and 1 October 1944, 14,395 inmates shipped from Riga and Liepāja arrived in Stutthof and were registered as belonging to the camp. Likewise, Kaiserwald's SS guards, who had gone on land in Danzig together with the camp's inmates in October, were integrated into the SS Death's Head Battalion Stutthof. This influx of prisoners in summer 1944 left a deep mark on the structure of the camp and, in our view, had murderous consequences for the Jews deported from Riga.

First all of the inmates had to perform forced labor, but there was a lack of tools and machines. Making matters worse for the Jews from Riga was that there were plenty of workers in Stutthof – a crucial difference when compared with their situation in the Riga ghetto and Kaiserwald. To that extent, there was no genuine interest on the part of those in charge at Stutthof to show any kind of consideration for exhausted or sick inmates. Furthermore, most of the Kapos came from the "greens" – the professional criminals – who dominated camp life as if they were an extension of the SS.[42]

Second, overcrowding at Stutthof led to the establishment of various branch camps and labor details, which were more or less attached to the main camp in an improvised fashion and were to exist only temporarily. This impeded the systematic management of inmate deployment, which thus became more arbitrary and more unpredictable. Third, within a few weeks in summer 1944, Stutthof had been transformed from a camp primarily for political prisoners from Poland, Germany, and the Soviet Union into a camp for Jews. Moreover, with the deportations from Hungary, women were no longer a minority in the camp. This new diversity of language, "race," and sex led to a breakdown in homogeneous structures and complicated the unified management of the prisoners as well as communication. With that, the Jews from Latvia who were unable to articulate themselves were relegated to the periphery of a community of scarcity in which an individual prisoner or Kapo could decide life and death. Fourth, even in times of peace, such an expansion would have presented enormous logistical demands on the camp leadership. Given the approaching front, Paul-Werner Hoppe, who had taken over as commandant in autumn 1942, could only manage the deficits, as provisions and medicines could not be found in the quantities needed.

What was primarily an organizational problem for the camp leadership resulted in untold suffering among the prisoners. As frequently stated by survivors, even after the years of scarcity and degradation as well as all the murders and selections in Riga, Stutthof seemed the worst camp. Here, the fear-ridden imagination of the inmates was unable to match the brutal reality. Progress in barrack construction was in general so inadequate that camp officials and prisoners had to resort to replacement housing that made a mockery of all hygienic standards, whether it was through the occupation of casemates or raising of tents. At the main camp, a "camp for Jews" – the designation given to ten hastily constructed barracks on the northern edge of the "new camp" – was established for the Jewish inmates considered able to work. These barracks were primarily for Jewish women. Several people were assigned to each bed, but for many, even next to the emaciated bodies of their companions in adversity, there was no space – they had to sleep on the bare floor. There were no water mains and therefore no washing and showering facilities or sewage. The "dispensing of meals" was an inhumane humiliation. The women were often forced to wait for hours before being permitted to eat. By the time the soup was ladled out, it had turned cold or, in winter, even frozen. The wind blew sand into the vats of soup on the way from the kitchen to the dining hall. Making matters worse, the community of solidarity from Kaiserwald was torn apart. Meanwhile, women frequently looked for relatives, unaware that these were no longer alive, because they had been among the victims of the selections prior to evacuation from Riga.

Male Jews were considered more valuable, to the extent that they were considered able to work. They were therefore not accommodated as a group within the main camp, but were dispersed among Stutthof's branch camps or deported farther west to other concentration camps as specialists. According to one survivor's assessment, of roughly 33,000 Jews deported to Stutthof during the second half of 1944, some 25,000 were sent to other camps, while the smaller part remained behind. In light of these extensive problems, it was not surprising that even the camp leadership at Stutthof insisted on forwarding as many inmates as possible farther west to less overcrowded camps, because they knew of no other way to bring the situation under control. To this end, the WVHA granted Hoppe the permission he had sought so that as early as August 1944 some of the Jews from Riga had reached Buchenwald near Weimar. In the weeks and months that followed, others were deported to Mauthausen, Dachau, and Sachsenhausen.[43]

From the departure lists, it can be seen that transports from Stutthof sometimes took place separated by sex or under the rubric "Jewish inmates." Selection officially took place according to the criterion of ability to work, which was determined by SS physician Dr. Otto Heidl and the head of the labor deployment in coordination with SS Captain Theodor Meier, the senior leader of the protective custody camp. This explains why many inmates born between 1919 and 1924 were sent farther west.[44] As a precaution, Heidl told receiving camps that prisoners from Stutthof were not to be integrated into the work process immediately, but were to be quarantined instead, because typhus, paratyphoid fever, diphtheria, and scarlet fever were rampant at Stutthof.[45] Another motive behind the transfer of female inmates was that in Stutthof the women usually could not be assigned an activity useful to the war effort, while need for female workers existed elsewhere. Originally, it was planned to use the women for the manufacture of airplane parts within the framework of a plan to boost aircraft production. When this proved impractical, they were deployed in building tank traps, digging entrenchment works, and tending to the fields. However, after several escaped, transporting the female inmates to other camps seemed a suitable way of disposing of them, insofar as the physically exhausted and psychologically broken women had not already succumbed to the conditions of their internment, malnourishment, or disease.[46]

In addition to the structurally rooted shortages of the inhumane camp system, there were two reasons for the sharp increase in mortality during the second half of 1944. One lay in the overcrowded nature of the camp. Not least for this reason, amid the summer temperatures and inadequate hygienic conditions, was it possible for a typhus epidemic to break out. The death rate was so high that the crematorium's capacity soon proved inadequate, and a large number of the corpses had to be burnt on pyres. Quarantine was imposed on the camp, which simultaneously meant the reduction of provisions to a minimum. However, the second reason for the sharp increase in mortality lay in German plans to systematically kill all of the Jewish inmates.

In late July or early August 1944, Hoppe – according to his own testimony – was ordered to Oranienburg to SS Major General Richard Glücks, the head of Department D of the WVHA, who first informed him of the "final solution of the Jewish question." After Hoppe had been let in on the totality of the annihilation measures, and after he had been sworn to secrecy, Glücks ordered him to murder all of the Jewish inmates at Stutthof by 31 December. Because Stutthof – like other camps – had no gas chambers for this purpose, Glücks and Hoppe discussed how this killing order could be implemented. Glücks proposed mass shootings. Hoppe countered that he did not know how to get rid of so many corpses using such a procedure. He was dismissed by Glücks with instructions to come up with ideas as to how he could efficiently implement the murder program for Stutthof.

A short time after returning to Stutthof, Hoppe received a written inquiry from Glücks asking whether there was a clothing disinfection facility in the camp. Hoppe answered that this was the case, but that it was still under construction. Several weeks later, he was again summoned to Oranienburg. At this second meeting, it was decided that the inmates were to be gassed with Zyklon-B in the clothing disinfection facility, and that Hoppe would have to implement the respective guidelines. Back at Stutthof, Hoppe informed camp doctor Dr. Heidl and protective custody chief Meier that they were initially to select Jews who were old, sick, or unable to work, as it was intended to murder them first. The canisters containing the deadly gas were ordered by WVHA Division D III (Sanitation and Camp Hygiene) and sent to Dr. Heidl. In addition, Rudolf Höss, the former commandant at Auschwitz and now head of WVHA Division D I (Central Office), showed up in Stutthof in order to school the camp personnel in the professional handling of Zyklon-B, to the extent that this had not already taken place in the disinfection training courses in Oranienburg held by SS Colonel Dr. Enno Lolling, the head of WVHA Division D III.[47] In September 1944, the preparations had been completed, and gassing in the clothing disinfection facility could begin.

In addition to Dr. Heidl and Meier, the roll call leaders Arno Chemnitz (who was responsible for the men's camp) and Ewald Foth (who was responsible for the women's camp) selected people unable to work from among the Jewish inmates housed in the northernmost row of barracks of the "new camp." After a superficial examination and a degrading set of physical exercises – the victims had to show their tormentors how well they could jump and run – female inmates were taken aside and led to a special barrack or directly to the clothing disinfection facility. Just how exhausted the people were – independent of bullying during the selection process – is clear from one survivor's statement: "In Stutthof, selections were carried out several times per week. We inmates had to report. Then several members of the SS, male and female, came along. They always singled out the sick and the weak inmates, who then went to the crematorium. That was just known. Those of us who were not singled out had been lucky once again. What does sick and weak mean anyway? I had only 35 kg [77 lbs.] to show for myself. With those 35 kg, I still survived. Try to imagine what those who were singled out looked like."[48]

During the singling out process and the waiting in front of the gas chamber, scenes unfolded that could suspend belief in any higher moral law or man's capacity for compassion. Inmates threw themselves on the ground in front of their tormentors, begged for their life, and insisted that they were able to work. Others were only able to scream or cry, while many lay silently and apathetically in front of this place of horror. Some found something to hold onto in religion and sang songs to manifest their faith, which they hoped would be able to offer consolation.[49] Members of the camp personnel forced the selected people toward the gas chamber in groups of 25–35 persons, which sometimes included inmates who had survived Kaiserwald. Those who were so weak that the body had given out were dragged by other inmates on wagons to the murder site. Several refused to enter and had to be shoved in by the SS guards. Once the people were in the gas chamber, the door was shut from the outside. Then, a member of the SS climbed on the roof and put on a gas mask fitted with a special filter against hydrocyanic acid.[50] On the roof, the cans of Zyklon-B – issued in advance from the camp stores by a clerk named Hinrichs – were opened with a can opener and their contents poured down a shaft.[51] The shaft was quickly shut again, while below the effect of the gas from the "poison bombs" – as one former SS guard described the Zyklon-B cans – began to take effect. The perpetrator on the roof, said defendant Otto Karl Knott in court after the war, then heard a "rumbling" through the closed shaft. After a short time, the rumbling stopped.

After about two hours, the door to the gas chamber was opened in order to "ventilate" the facility and to remove the corpses. The sight was horrific. In their panic, the people had torn out their hair and clawed their bodies. Those standing closest to the shaft may have died more quickly; others may have briefly watched their companions in adversity struggle with death. Before dying, the bodies had gone into convulsions and frequently entwined with one another. The sight of the discolored and clawed corpses was so appalling as to be unbearable even to the perpetrators themselves.[52] A detail of inmates dragged the corpses over a wooden path from the gas chamber to the crematorium, where the bodies were then stacked with the help of a large two-pronged fork and then burned.[53]

That was how it worked in a "normal case." But as soon as disease and deprivation began to influence the mortality rate more than the arbitrariness of the camp's personnel, the burning of bodies could no longer be carried out in the crematorium. One of the guards who had transferred from Death's Head Battalion Riga to Stutthof described the process of getting rid of the corpses: "The most terrible thing that I experienced in Stutthof was the burning of corpses on pyres. These were inmates who just could not survive. They literally dropped dead. Burning in the crematorium was just no longer possible due to the large number of inmates who had passed away. I would like to say that almost every night about 1,000 – one thousand – inmates were burned.[54] As a result, I also came to do sentry duty at a burning several times. It always lasted from 4 A.M. to 5 A.M. The corpses were driven out of the [concentration camp] in a truck. Inmates now had the task of stacking the corpses in layers. The corpses were laid heads outward, that is to say, with the legs toward the center of the pyre. After this was finished, something was poured over it. I can't say what it was. When it was ignited, there was immediately a blazing flame."[55]

Once the secret of the converted disinfection facility could no longer be maintained and inmates began putting up more resistance when being forced into the gas chamber, the camp leadership came up with the idea of starting up another killing site. This involved a modified freight car on a sidetrack of the Danzig-Steegen line. The railway car was made airtight and a pipe for pouring Zyklon B was built in. For reasons of camouflage, a fully normal freight car was placed next to it, sometimes a locomotive as well so that the victims would believe that this short train really was in service. An SS man wearing a railway man's uniform and holding a whistle stood in view nearby. The victims were to believe that the train would take them to a potato harvest outside the camp. After they had entered the railway car, the door was secured. Another SS man, also dressed in a railway man's uniform and protected by a gas mask, climbed on the roof of the wagon and shook the Zyklon B down the pipe. After the people had asphyxiated, their corpses were taken to the crematorium as well.[56]

Parallel to the gassings, some inmates, mostly Jewish women, were killed by a shot to the back of the neck in the rooms next to the crematorium. Such killings had a certain tradition in Stutthof, and in spring 1944, the Germans began using this method on the camp's Jewish women, apparently because the gas chamber was still inoperable. In such cases, examinations were feigned. During the measurement of height, when the victim was standing still, she was shot from behind.[57] Even after the completion of the gas chamber, the camp leadership continued to use this killing method.[58] In addition to the systematic killing in the gas chamber and crematorium as well as the converted railway car, inmates were exposed to murderous acts of arbitrariness on the part of Dr. Heidl, senior medic SS Technical Sergeant Otto Haupt, and other SS medics in sick bay, who carried out "lethal injections" using syringes full of benzene or administered shots of phenol directly into the heart. Jewish women were selected from the women's camp in groups of up to fifty persons and brought one by one to a room at the crematorium, where members of the camp personnel dressed in white gowns feigned an examination. In the process, the fatal procedure took place. According to the findings of the Hamburg Prosecutor's Office, such selections took place three times a week in summer 1944.[59]

It also happened that on "suitable occasions" inmates were torn to pieces by specially trained German shepherds. Even former SS members openly admitted that, "for the fun of it," the dog handlers would sic their animals on members of external details returning to the main camp from work in order "to liven up the inmates a bit." Apparently, the monotonous workday of the dog handlers every now and then justified such distractions, which wounded or even killed an unknown number of prisoners.[60] Nonetheless, for the starving inmates, feeding the German shepherds was among one of the more coveted jobs, "a particularly good post": Whoever fed the dogs "could always take something from their feeding bowls."[61] Finally, as a means of deterrence, hangings – whether to punish alleged violations of camp orders or to execute prisoners of the Reich Security Main Office – were carried out in front of the camp's inmates.[62]

Why it happened that, despite orders from the WVHA, the number of people murdered in the Stutthof gas chambers was in the end relatively low compared with other National Socialist camps was obvious to former SS medic Knott: "I would say a figure of 3,000–4,000 at most as the number of inmates killed [by gas], without wanting to commit myself, however. Because most of the camp's inmates died of typhus, a continuous gassing operation was not at all necessary."[63]

During winter 1944–1945, as the bottlenecks in supplies made themselves felt more acutely,[64] more and more people died of hunger, dehydration, and exposure, even if epidemics were contained. The inmates' bodies failed as a result of the deprivation, and the spirits of many must have been broken by these torturous conditions. Nothing describes the situation better than the fact that many inmates [carried] human bones in their pockets, "which they sucked on like candy."[65] In the camp's accounting department, the cause of death of a victim was usually given as "heart - general asthenia"; sometimes, however, the true cause of death – such as "dysentery," "edema," or "pneumonia and cerebral hemorrhage" – was named. The SS clerks meticulously drew up lists, noting the victims' last place of residence and citizenship before they had been swept up by occupation and terror and delivered into the camp system, where their lives ultimately came to an end at Stutthof. Joseph Denemark from Paris did not survive Stutthof, nor did Abram Lewenstein of Riga, Erich Herzenberg of Liepāja, Jonas Schwart of Amsterdam, Georg Israel of Cologne (deported to Riga on 7 December 1941), Henri Glaube of Budapest, Benjamin Dyn of Cracow, or Josef Lauer of Suceava, Romania.[66] Although Stutthof was located close to Danzig, the lists of those who died there make clear that many of the inmates had been deported there from far away, and that the camp had long ceased to function as a camp for the administrative region of Danzig-West Prussia.

Toward the end of 1944, railroad transports began leaving for the west, such as one with 500 male and 300 female inmates in November,[67] until Hoppe, acting on instructions from HSSPF Vistula Friedrich Katzmann, ordered Stutthof's partial evacuation on 25 January 1945.[68] That day, the first eleven columns of around 1,000 inmates, each separated by sex, left the camp for Lauenburg (Lębork), Pomerania, some 75 miles (120 km) away. It was planned to send forty-one such columns west. In reality, no more columns were set in motion due to the icy temperatures and short daylight hours. According to Hoppe's stipulations, Lauenburg was to be reached in seven days, but only two days' worth of provisions was issued. Accordingly, stopovers were planned for rest. "Only inmates who were sick as well as unable to march and the workers who were needed to dismantle the camp" had to stay behind at Stutthof.[69]

But it is a fact that, after the departure of the first eleven columns, the others did not leave. Only on 15 February 1945 was a group – not a column – sent to the branch camp Burggraben (today Kokoszki, a part of Gdańsk). Back in the main camp, chaos prevailed, with apocalyptic consequences for the inmates. There was a lack of drinking water, supplies were no longer being sent to Stutthof, and a new typhus epidemic was claiming 50–200 victims per day, primarily among the Jewish inmates. The number of inmates was drastically reduced. On 1 February, there were 10,506; on 15 February, 9,061; and on 21 March, 3,906 persons. At the end of March, inmates from the subcamps were transferred back to the main camp. As a result, occupancy rose to 5,148 inmates, only to drop to 4,938 people by 4 April. That day, the bulk of the camp's SS personnel, in particular Hoppe, was evacuated from Stutthof and directed to Schleswig-Holstein. In the final report concerning camp occupancy, Stutthof had over 4,508 inmates (1,976 women and 2,532 men).

As Stutthof's last commandant, SS Captain Paul Ehle was to carry out the decommissioning of the camp, which in the meantime had been cut off by the Red Army. Therefore, the sea was the route chosen for the evacuation, which began on 25 April 1945. After all of the inmates who were able to march had left the camp and boarded ship, Ehle set the buildings on fire. A few women who were already near death and whom the Germans did not intend to evacuate were left behind in their barracks and burned alive. Finally, the crematorium was blown up, and the premises turned over to the Wehrmacht for its defense against the approaching Soviet 2nd and 48th armies. Ehle and the rest of the camp personnel then headed west. When the Red Army entered Stutthoff on 8 May, they found only 100 inmates and several thousand civilian refugees from East and West Prussia whose flight had ended there.[70]

In Stutthof's branch camps, there were 22,521 inmates as of 24 January. The evacuation of these sites took place separately from that of the main camp, to the extent that this was possible. During these death marches, crimes took place that lacked none of the brutality of the marches from Stutthof. Guards forced one group of mostly female Jewish prisoners from the East Prussian camps of Jessau (today Yuzhnyi), Heiligenbeil (today Mamonovo), and Seerappen (today Liublino), which were close to the front, to march to Königsburg (today Kaliningrad). There, they were combined with the inmates of the branch camp at the railway car factory Steinfurth and marched west. They marched all day in the wind, snow, and cold – those who could no longer go on were shot mercilessly – until they reached the town Palmnicken (today Yantaryi). They were locked up in the defunct factory Stadthalle and given inadequate provisions. After five days, a selection took place; all those who were unable to march were shot on the spot. The rest was forced to march along the Baltic shore toward Pillau (today Baltisk). When evening fell, the guards forced the rest of the inmates onto the iced-over sea and shot them. Only a few survived the massacre; the number of victims was over 3,000 persons.

Of the originally 3,300 female inmates of the construction commando Weichsel from Brodnica (Strasburg) and Toruń, the surviving 1,700 were transferred to Groden (today Grodno). In January, they had to report and were examined for their ability to march. Around 900 survived this test; the others were beaten to death with truncheons and buried in a mass grave. Those who were sent off marched ten days until Soviet troops freed them in Tczew (Dirschau). Around 300 women survived the strain. Other columns – such as 500 women of the AEG branch camp Toruń, 1,200 women from the branch camp Bydgoszcz (Bromberg), or inmates from the branch camp Pölitz (Police) – were overtaken by the Red Army during the retreat. Among the survivors were several Jewish women who had been sent from Riga-Kaiserwald to Stutthof, and from there to Chinow (today Chynowie) via the camp Sophienwalde in Brusy (Bruss). Others had less luck. There were several evacuation marches that did not have any survivors – for example, the commandos at Gutowo (Guttau), Gwiździny (Quesendorf), Krzemieniewo (Krumau), and Naguszewo (Nagelstal), all in occupied West Prussia. It is not even known how and where these people were killed.[71]

As the German reign of terror neared its end, the exhausted Jews were still far from safe. Many were shot during the evacuation to the west, if they could not keep up. Others drowned in the hectic process of boarding the landing boats or in the rowboats that departed for Rügen, Lübeck, Flensburg, and Neustadt. The only fortunate ones were those who ended up in a boat supervised by the Red Cross, such as the inmates of the rowboat that landed in Klintholm. Once there, the former inmates were tended to by members of the Danish Red Cross. Similarly, those who survived the deadly odyssey of the dinghy Knut were given proper treatment after being evacuated from Flensburg to Malmö on the steamer Rheinfels, which had been chartered by the Swedish Red Cross.[72]

According to estimates by Janina Grabowska, 47,000 registered inmates died in Stutthof and its branch camps during the camp's existence. Another 10,000–20,000 persons were not in the camp statistics, because they were murdered immediately upon arrival. During the 1945 evacuation over the Baltic, 2,000 people succumbed to the strain or were murdered by the guards. The toll in human life during the death marches was clearly higher: circa 16,500 victims, of whom 12,000 were from the branch camps. Overall, the last year of Stutthof's existence is bound to have taken the most lives; in the period from 25 January to 9 May 1945 alone, the death toll exceeded 25,000.[73] According to calculations by Diana Schülle and Wolfgang Scheffler, just over 1,100 of the 31,000 German, Austrian, and Czech Jews deported to the Baltic lands survived the horrors of the National Socialist camps.[74] Of the Latvian Jews, a generous estimate – based largely on Max Kaufmann and Bernhard Press – suggests that about 1,000 of them survived the occupation, circa 1.25 percent of Latvia's Jewish prewar population.[75] All of the others were murdered by the self-appointed executors and compliant accomplices of a state-organized mass crime that was so monstrous words can hardly be found, a crime still unequaled in the history of mankind.

Notes

1. Aside from the fact that Blobel had to report to Jeckeln for reasons of hierarchy and cooperation, it also seemed expedient to do so in practical terms. Blobel usually turned to the offices of the territorial or regional commanders of the Security Police, which had at their disposal the records he needed. However, because the HSSPF had been responsible for planning the massacres at Rumbula in late 1941, it appears only logical for Blobel to call on Jeckeln as well in this matter.
2. BA DH, ZM 1683, Akte 1, 19, statement by Jeckeln, 14 December 1945. Blobel and Jeckeln already knew each other from the massacre at Babi Yar at the end of September 1941 at the latest. There Blobel's Sonderkommando 4a and other police formations carried out the murder of Kiev's Jews in accordance with Jeckeln's instructions.
3. Ibid. Jeckeln incorrectly gave the code as "II89."
4. Archiv des Beauftragen zum Stasiunterlagengesetz (Federal Commissioner for the Records of the Ministry for State Security of the German Democratic Republic), FV 6/74, Bd. 73, 118, statement by Friedrich Panzinger, 12 February 1947.
5. M. Jelin, "Die Todesforts bei Kaunas," in Grossmann and Ehrenburg, *Das Schwarzbuch*, 582–604, here 592–593.
6. *Geschichte des Zweiten Weltkriegs 1939–1945*, ed. H. Hoffmann et al., Bd. 8, 153–174; Boris Semjonowitsch Telpuchowski, *Die sowjetische Geschichte des Großen Vaterländischen Krieges 1941–1945*, 323–334.
7. Staw. Stuttgart, 17 Js 270/64, Anklageschrift gegen Hans Sohns u.a., 11 December 1967, 21–22 and 40–43; BA Ludwigsburg, 204 AR-Z 419/62, Bd. 5, statement by Erich Brauer, 10 February 1949, 989; Katz, *Erinnerungen eines Überlebenden*, 160.
8. BA Ludwigsburg, 204 AR-Z 419/62, Bd. 5, statement by Brauer, 10 February 1949, 985.
9. Helmuth Forwick, "Der Rückzug der Heeresgruppe Nord nach Kurland," in Hans Meier-Welcker, ed., *Abwehrkämpfe am Nordflügel der Ostfront 1944–1945*, 102–109.
10. BA Ludwigsburg, Sammelakte Nr. 580: XV – 8/84 S = 130 Js 2/78 (Z), Urteil des LG Düsseldorf gegen Heinz Günther Wisner, 14 August 1985, 24–29.
11. LVVA, P 132-30-43 a, 2–44, Totenscheine KL Kaiserwald. These were regularly signed by Wisner.
12. In our view, there was at this time no forced labor detail designated "High Forest Commando" or "the base." It was instead a euphemism for annihilation. Starting in 1944, shootings are bound to have taken place at graves prepared by Sk 1005 in order to immediately cremate those who had just been shot. Some of the victims' clothing – smeared with blood and perforated by bullet holes – was returned to Kaiserwald, see BA Ludwigsburg, Sammelakte Nr. 580: XV – 8/84 S = 130 Js 2/78 (Z), Urteil des LG Düsseldorf gegen Heinz Günther Wisner, 14 August 1985, 39–49.
13. Vestermanis, "Haftstätten und Todeslager im okkupierten Lettland," in Herbert et al., *Die nationalsozialistischen Konzentrationslager*, Bd. 1, 487–488; Winter, *The Ghetto of Riga and Continuance*, 174–176; Krausnick and Wilhelm, *Die Truppe des Weltan-*

schauungskrieges, 612; Staw. Hamburg, 141 Js 534/60, Bd. 2, statement by Else Lüders, 1 November 1949, 164r; statement by Heinz Rosenthal, 8 December 1949, 205r; ibid., Beiakte [Altverfahren, unpaged], protocol of statement by Egon Klein, 30 November 1948, 3, this also contains the reference to the "blue barrack." The statement by Lüders also includes information on Dundaga. The selections in the camp at Jugla (Strasdenhof) are vividly described in Mascha Rolnikaite, *Ich muss erzählen*, 211–231.

14. Sherman-Zander, *Zwischen Tag und Dunkel*, 91–98; Winter, *The Ghetto of Riga*, 182; Wolff, *Sadismus oder Wahnsinn*, 35–36; Staw. Hamburg, 141 Js 534/60, Bd. 2, statement by Feige Harms, 25 November 1949, 189; statement by Gertrud Stern, 25 November 1949, 190; statement by Rosalie Hansen, 28 November 1949, 193; statement by Elias Spielmann, 7 December 1949, 199r. According to Stern and Hansen, a "children operation" was to take place at AEG as well, but because there were only three children under fourteen years of age at this barracking, it was possible – with the help of the overseer Kowa, who is depicted as willing to help on this occasion – to send them to work on the appointed day so that the selection commando found nobody in the accommodations but an old lady. The lady was taken away and shot. A version of this episode involving a gas van is in Spielmann's statement, which sounds credible as well.
15. BA Ludwigsburg, 207 AR-Z 128/78, Bd. 1, statement by Rita Wassermann, 8 May 1980, 190–191.
16. Ibid., statement by Ruth Roseboom, 22 April 1980, 222–223; for more on the selections, see BA Ludwigsburg, Sammelakte Nr. 580, XV-8/84 S = 130 Js 2/78(Z), Urteil des LG Düsseldorf gegen Heinz Günther Wisner, 14 August 1985, 54–55, 80–81, 83–84.
17. The name Javetz is not 100 percent certain. He is sometimes referred to as Javisch.
18. BA Ludwigsburg, 207 AR-Z 128/78, Bd. 1, statement by Solomon Gerstein, 2 May 1980, 160–161; ibid., statement by Nadia Reznik, 30 April 1980, 194. The doctors Minsk worked at the sick bay of Army Group North's motor pool. The younger of the two died on a ship during the evacuation. A certain Dr. Jacobi was used at the branch camp Freight Station-Reich Railway, where his daughter was also an inmate. It is said that he had to remove gold crowns from corpses. The gynecologist Dr. David Klebanow and his wife were deployed at Spilve. Placed at Krebsbach's disposal, they tried to pursue their profession as best they could, given the circumstances. Klebanow's wife died in July 1945. Ibid., statement by Ingeborg Berner, 18 April 1980; statement by Dr. David Klebanow, 16 April 1980, 239–241; statement by Grigori Golin, 21 April 1980. On Weinreich and Sik, see also Press, *Judenmord in Lettland*, 102.
19. BA Ludwigsburg, Sammelakte Nr. 580, XV-8/84 S = 130 Js 2/78(Z), Urteil des LG Düsseldorf gegen Heinz Günther Wisner, 14 August 1985, 75–76.
20. BA Ludwigsburg, 207 AR-Z 128/78, Bd. 1, statement by Gerstein, 2 May 1980, 162; BA Ludwigsburg, Sammelakte Nr. 580, XV-8/84 S = 130 Js 2/78(Z), Urteil des LG Düsseldorf gegen Heinz Günther Wisner, 14 August 1985, 52–53 and 56–57.
21. Ibid., 55, 73–78, and 85–92. In addition to Wisner, SS Sergeant Huck and SS Corporal Grelack were deployed in the sick bay.
22. BA Ludwigsburg, 204 AR-Z 419/62, Bd. 5, statement by Brauer, 10 February 1949, 985–988. On the background of this shooting, see Vestermanis, "Haftstätten und Todeslager," 481–482.
23. Staw. Hamburg, 141 Js 534/60, Bd. 2, statement by Else Isaak, 19 January 1950, 243.
24. BA-MA, RW 30/72, 52–54, Wehrwirtschaftskommando Riga, Lagebericht für die Zeit v. 1.3. bis. 31.3.1944, 31 March 1944.
25. Postwar investigations showed that this took place on 28 or 29 July. At this time, as depicted, a selection was carried out at Mühlgraben as well. The last selection at the branch camp Freight Station-Reich Railway took place on 6 August 1944, that is to say,

prior to the retreat, see BA Ludwigsburg, 207 AR-Z 128/78, Bd. 1, statement by Golin, 21 April 1980, 274–275.
26. BA Ludwigsburg, 207 AR-Z 128/78, Bd. 1, statement by Wassermann, 8 May 1980, 191; BA Ludwigsburg, Sammelakte Nr. 580, XV–8/84 S = 130 Js 2/78(Z), Urteil des LG Düsseldorf gegen Heinz Günther Wisner, 14 August 1985, 82.
27. BA Ludwigsburg, 207 AR-Z 128/78, Bd. 1, statement by Reznik, 30 April 1980, 197. Reznik reports that an eye specialist from Germany was abruptly sent to her death.
28. Alfred Streim, "Konzentrationslager auf dem Gebiet der Sowjetunion," in *Dachauer Hefte 5* (1989): 183; Schwarz, *Die nationalsozialistischen Lager*, 223–224; Karin Orth, *Das System der nationalsozialistischen Konzentrationslager*, 271; Wolfgang Scheffler, "Das Schicksal," in *Buch der Erinnerung*, Bd. 1, 39–40; Staw. Hamburg, 141 Js 534/60, Bd. 33, statement by Helena Harpak, 21 March 1963, 5,457; ibid., Bd. 34, Bericht zur Aussage von Esra Jurmann, 29 April 1963, 5,504; ibid., Beiakte [Altverfahren], statement by Egon Klein, 30 November 1948, 3. On the shipping out of inmates from individual camps, see Sherman-Zander, *Zwischen Tag und Dunkel*, 98–100; BA Ludwigsburg, 407 AR 3680/65, Bd. 2, statement by Helmut Wendriner, 13 December 1968, 298–301; Katz, *Erinnerungen*, 195–197. On the transfer of Ostlandwerk GmbH, see BA-MA, RW 30/73, 53–54, Wehrwirtschaftskommando Riga, Rü-Gruppe, 30 June 1944, Bericht für das KTB, Rückblick über das 2. Quartal 1944. On the fate of this group as well as the transfer of other commandos, see Winter, *Ghetto of Riga*, 177, 183, 191–192, and 202.
29. BA-MA, RW 30/74, 43–44, Wehrwirtschaftskommando Riga, 23 August 1944, Bericht für das KTB für die Zeit v. 1.7. bis 23.8.1944; Vestermanis, "Haftstätten und Todeslager," 488–489; Schneider, *Journey into Terror*, 97; Staw. Hamburg, 141 Js 534/60, Bd. 34, Bericht zur Aussage von Esra Jurmann, 29 April 1963, 5,504; ibid., Bd. 51, statement by Oskar Waller, 14 August 1964, 8,331; ibid., SB 12, statement by Zalman Gawartin, 14 November 1975, 2,294. According to Waller, members of KdS Latvia also left Riga together with transports of wounded persons and Latvian refugees.
30. Wittrock, *Kommissarischer Oberbürgermeister von Riga*, 92–97; Hans Umbreit, "Die deutsche Herrschaft in den besetzten Gebieten 1942–1945," in *Das Deutsche Reich und der Zweite Weltkrieg*, ed. Militärgeschichtlichen Forschungsamt, Bd. 5/2, 48–49. Lohse was replaced by Reich Commissar Ukraine and Gauleiter East Prussia Erich Koch.
31. Staw. Stuttgart, 17 Js 270/64, Anklageschrift gegen Hans Sohns u.a., 11 December 1967, 43–45. In September, just before the decommissioning of Kaiserwald, twenty-five female patients (who had for the most part been treated for broken arms or legs) simply disappeared. It appears that they were also murdered, see BA Ludwigsburg, 207 AR-Z 128/78, Bd. 1, statement by Gerstein, 2 May 1980, 160–161; ibid., statement by Reznik, 30 April 1980, 195–196.
32. Forwick, "Der Rückzug," 110–118.
33. A show trial had already been carried out in Kharkiv (Kharkov), Ukraine, without Sk 1005 being a topic. According to an assessment of the Foreign Office and the Reich Security Main Office, this was a propaganda offensive designed to counter the Germans' own efforts to denounce the crimes at Katyn, where the Soviets had murdered thousands of Polish prisoners of war in 1940. See Andreas Hilger, Nikita Petrov, and Günther Wagenlehner, "Der Ukas 43: Entstehung und Problematik des Dekrets das Präsidiums des Obersten Sowjets vom 19. April 1943," in *Sowjetische Militärtribunale*, ed. Andreas Hilger, Ute Schmidt, and Günther Wagenlehner, Bd. 1, 204–206. In a closed military tribunal in the area of the Third Baltic Front, three defendants accused of war crimes were condemned to death on 10 October 1944, just a few days before the Red Army took Riga, see ibid., 204. The members of Sk 1005, who were incomparably more incriminated, were well advised to flee west.

34. BA Ludwigsburg, 204 AR-Z 419/62, Bd. 10, statement by Hermann Kappen, 11 July 1967, 168–169; BA Ludwigsburg, 207 AR-Z 128/78, Bd. 1, statement by Klebanow, 16 April 1980, 241–242; Staw. Stuttgart, 17 Js 270/64, Anklageschrift gegen Hans Sohns u.a., 11 December 1967, 43; Kaufmann, *Churbn Lettland*, 339–340. Kaufmann also mentions that in August 1944 inmates from Spilve were deployed for clearance work and then sent, via Kaiserwald, to Sk 1005 – which Kaufmann identified as the Potato Commando due to the prisoners' erroneous belief that they would receive higher rations – where they were then murdered, see ibid., 400–401.
35. BA Ludwigsburg, 204 AR-Z 419/62, Bd. 5, statement by Brauer, 10 February 1949, 988. For more background, see Vestermanis, "Haftstätten und Todeslager," According to Brauer, the evacuation followed several days later, around the start of October 1944.
36. Staw. Hamburg, 141 Js 534/60, Bd. 43, Bericht zur Aussage von Esra Jurmann, 29 April 1963, 5,504–5,506. Several of the corpses were stacked in the camp garden in the months before evacuation. Prisoners who were recaptured were sometimes sent to "High Forest Commando" of Sk 1005.
37. Aufstellung des Pionierführers der 16. Armee v. 13.10.1944 über Zerstörungen bei der Räumung Rigas, printed in *Europa unterm Hakenkreuz, Die faschistische Okkupationspolitik in den zeitweilig besetzten Gebieten der Sowjetunion (1941–1944)*, ed. Norbert Müller, 584–585; Forwick, "Der Rückzug," 163–165; BA Ludwigsburg, 204 AR-Z 419/62, Bd. 5, statement by Brauer, 10 February 1949, 985 and 989. According to Brauer, a rump formation of KdS Latvia maintained a camp in Liepāja with 700 inmates under the command of SS Captain Heck. See also Vestermanis, "Haftstätten und Todeslager," 489. Vestermanis writes that the camp in Liepāja served only as a transit camp for the greater part of the Riga inmates before they were deported farther to the west to the camp Hamburg-Fuhlsbüttel.
38. The assessment of the situation below deck is based on Christian Gerlach and Götz Aly, *Das letzte Kapitel*, 381. On the sinking of freighters and transport ships during the evacuation of Riga, see BA Ludwigsburg, 407 AR 91/65, Bd. 6, statement by Johann Roppelt, 13 July 1976, 1,417. Roppelt's statement is supported by the literature, see N.A. Piterskij, *Die Sowjet-Flotte im Zweiten Weltkrieg*, 279–280, and Rabinovici, *Dank meiner Mutter*, 186. Rabinovici says the inmate transports were not attacked, because they flew the Red Cross flag.
39. In addition to the prisoners' barracks, the "old camp" consisted of the two-story brick commandant's office as well as utility buildings for storage and administration, a garden shop with a greenhouse, garages, kennels, stalls for small animals, space for guards and clerks, a coal storage facility, and later a house for the commandant, which Pauli's successor, Paul-Werner Hoppe, had built. The prisoners' sick bay was also set up in the "old camp" and outfitted with sickrooms, a pharmacy, an x-ray room, office space, and an isolation barrack. Accommodations for the camp's civilian employees and the guards, as well as a training camp for volunteer helpers and storage sites for construction materials and fuels, were to be found about 1.5 km (ca. 1 mile) from the "old camp."
40. The completed part of the "new camp" involved four rows of barracks with ten buildings each. These primarily served as accommodations for the inmates, but were also used in part by Deutsche Ausrüstungswerke as well as the kitchen, the dining hall, and the clothing store. The north and west parts of these premises remained a construction site. Even farther west stood storehouses and several other fenced-in barracks, which formed the "special camp" (*Speziallager*), where prominent persons and their families were held, e.g. members of the resistance movement that tried to assassinate Hitler on 20 July 1944. East of the new camp, factory halls and office buildings housing the SS construction management, inter alia, had already been established.

41. The precise date could not be determined. We follow the findings of the Tübingen State Court, see *Justiz und NS-Verbrechen*, Bd. XXII, Lfd. Nr. 584, Urteil des LG Tübingen v. 22.12.1964, Ks 5/63, gegen Otto Haupt u.a., 600. Before the construction of the crematorium, the inmates who had died or been murdered were buried outside the camp in the community cemetery.
42. *Justiz und NS-Verbrechen*, Bd. VII, Lfd. Nr. 240, Urteil des LG Hamburg v. 21.9.1950, (50)26/50, gegen die ehemaligen Kapos S. und K., 435–451.
43. *Justiz und NS-Verbrechen*, Bd. XIV, Lfd. Nr. 446, Urteile des LG Bochum v. 4.6.1957 und 16.12.1955, 17 Ks 1/55, gegen Hoppe und Knott, 154–156, 181–187, and 191. The abbreviated sketch of the history of Stutthof is otherwise based on Marek Orski, "Organisation und Ordnungsprinzipien des Lagers Stutthof," in Herbert et al., *Die nationalsozialistischen Konzentrationslager*, Bd. 1, 283–308; Janina Grabowska, "K.L. Stutthof: Ein historischer Abriß," in *Stutthof*, ed. Hermann Kuhn, 8–93; Orth, *Das System*, 69–76 and 228–230; Kaienburg, *Die Wirtschaft der SS*, 516–525; Scheffler, "Das Schicksal," 40–41; Schwarz, *Die nationalsozialistischen Lager*, 226–231, which also contains an accurate list of all known subcamps or forced labor details with the date of each commissioning and decommissioning. On the "dispensing of food," see BA Ludwigsburg, 407 AR 3680/65, Bd. 2, statement by Erich Nagel, 10 December 1968, 292. On the women's camp, see BA Ludwigsburg, 407 AR 91/65, Bd. 7, statement by Witold Zbroja, 28 March 1968, 1,666–1,667; Kaufmann, *Churbn Lettland*, 495–499 and 513–519. On the search for relatives, BA Ludwigsburg, 207 AR-Z 128/78, Bd. 1, statement by Reznik, 30 April 1980, 196.
44. As examples, the following lists are mentioned: BA DH, R 479, KL Stutthof – Einsatz v. 15.7.1944, Transportliste/Jüdinnen/Kommando Bromberg; ibid., Transportliste (Jüdinnen) Kommando Langhorn-Hamburg (Neuengamme), 2 September 1944; ibid., Fernschreiben, Maurer an die Kommandanten der KL Stutthof und Flossenbuerg, 23 November 1944; ibid., Kommandantur des Konzentrationslagers Stutthof, Betr. Häftlingsüberstellung zum KL Flossenbürg, 24 November 1944.
45. Ibid., Bescheinigung des SS-Standortarztes [for Flossenbürg], 24 November 1944.
46. *Justiz und NS-Verbrechen*, Bd. XIV, Lfd. Nr. 446, Urteile gegen Hoppe und Knott, 155–156. On the entrenchment works, see, for example, BA Ludwigsburg, Dokumentation, Polen 365 A 8, 168–169, Kommandantur des Konzentrationslagers Stutthof, Sonderbefehl über die Aufstellung des Baukommandos "Weichsel," 24 August 1944.
47. *Justiz und NS-Verbrechen*, Bd. XIV, Lfd. Nr. 446, Urteile gegen Hoppe und Knott, 153, 156–158, and 191–192; Tom Segev, *Die Soldaten des Bösen*, 209–211; Kalthoff and Werner, *Die Händler des Zyklon B*, 191.
48. BA Ludwigsburg, 407 AR 91/65, Bd. 5, statement by Klara Bender, 2 September 1975, 1,210.
49. *Justiz und NS-Verbrechen*, Bd. XIV, Lfd. Nr. 446, Urteile gegen Hoppe und Knott, 159–160.
50. For example, Otto Karl Knott, SS Staff Sergeant Hans Rach, and SS Technical Sergeant Ewald Foth, possibly others. Willi Knott was also suspected of being involved in gassings on a stand-in basis.
51. On Zyklon-B's effects and history, including the steps taken to deceive victims, see Kalthoff and Werner, *Die Händler des Zyklon B*, 28–60, 77–78, 85–88, 96–97, 110–111, 120, and 135–136.
52. *Justiz und NS-Verbrechen*, Bd. XIV, Lfd. Nr. 446, Urteile gegen Hoppe und Knott, 158 and 160–161. This also contains a precise description of the course of the murder. See also BA Ludwigsburg, 407 AR 91/65, Bd. 5, statement by Hubert Lange, 24 September 1975, 1,146. According to Lange, a prisoner was even forced to direct the gas into the

chamber. Lange is also the source of the term "poison bomb." That Jews from Riga were also among the victims can be deduced from, for example, the statement by Edith Marx, whose sister was gassed in Stutthof. See also BA Ludwigsburg, 407 AR 3680/65, Bd. 2, statement by Walter Hahnenberg, 18 January 1969, 384; statement by Edith Marx, 5 February 1969, 396; Grabowska, "K.L. Stutthof," 64–66.

53. BA Ludwigsburg, 407 AR 91/65, Bd. 4, statement by Max Carl Grabe, 19 November 1973, 966; ibid., Bd. 8, statement by Alfons Wojewski, 7 November 1972, 1,984–1,986. According to Grabe, the inmates deployed at the crematorium were themselves killed and burned there as a consequence of their activity.

54. Even if this number is too high, it gives a certain impression of the extent of these burnings. The two ovens of the crematorium could burn 400 persons per day, Grabowska, "K.L. Stutthof," 60. The corpses exceeding this number would have been cremated on the pyres accordingly.

55. BA Ludwigsburg, 407 AR 91/65, Bd. 6, statement by Roppelt, 13 July 1976, 1,418–1,419; ibid., Bd. 8, statement by Grzegorz Smyk, 12 November 1973, 1,922.

56. BA Ludwigsburg, 407 AR 3680/65, Bd. 4, Einstellungsverfügung der Staw. Hamburg gegen Alfred Bublitz v. 12.2.1973, 918–925. In addition to Theodor Meier, Arno Chemnitz, Ewald Foth, Peters, Otto Haupt, and Alfred Bublitz, as well as the head of the crematorium Hans Rach and his colleagues Schwaiger and Nordmann, it was primarily Otto Knott who poured the gas granules into the shaft. As was already mentioned, the suspicion also arose during investigation that inmates were misused to this end. It was not possible to identify which inmates were used to this end due to the gas mask, see ibid. as well as BA Ludwigsburg, 407 AR 91/65, Bd. 7, statement by Zbroja, 28 March 1968, 1,666; Grabowska, "K.L. Stutthof," 66.

57. The measuring process took place against a yardstick that had slot in the middle and a crossbar that could be moved up and down in order to precisely determine height. The measuring stick itself was mounted on the wall. The slot at the same time formed an opening to the adjoining room. When the crossbar was set, a SS man in the adjoining room pulled a pistol with a silencer and shot the victim through the opening in the back of the neck. Haupt, Chemnitz, Foth, Meier, Bernhard Luedtke, and others were said to have been marksmen. The room was then cleaned, the corpse burned in one of the crematorium's ovens, and the examination room prepared for the next victim.

58. *Justiz und NS-Verbrechen,* Bd. XXII, Lfd. Nr. 584, Urteil gegen Haupt, 600–601 and 611–613; BA Ludwigsburg, 407 AR 3680/65, Bd. 4, Einstellungsverfügung, 912–913.

59. *Justiz und NS-Verbrechen,* Bd. XIV, Lfd. Nr. 446, Urteile gegen Hoppe und Knott, 208. According to this case, lethal injections were no longer carried out in Stutthof due to instructions from the WVHA. Acting on his own initiative, Dr. Heidl is said to have ordered the murder of about 10–15 women sick with typhus using this method. In doing so, Heidl sought to get around reporting the outbreak of typhus and to avoid quarantine for the camp. According to the findings of Hamburg investigators, Haupt was suspected of independently and arbitrarily arranging lethal injections, see BA Ludwigsburg, 407 AR 3680/65, Bd. 4, Einstellungsverfügung, 912–913.

60. BA Ludwigsburg, 407 AR 91/65, Bd. 6, statement by Albert Petlikau, 13 October 1976, 1,495. For more extensive information, see *Justiz und NS-Verbrechen,* Bd. XIV, Lfd. Nr. 446, Urteile gegen Hoppe und Knott, 214–222. This includes details on the use of guard dogs and an evaluation of survivor statements. Here, recollections diverge even among many survivors. This may be because the guard dog – alongside the guards' whips – is a topos in the system of terror and thus represents a synonym for a threat that in retrospect is expressed more strongly in memory than was endured in reality. There is no doubt, however, that killings by dog took place.

61. BA Ludwigsburg, 407/ AR 91/65, Bd. 6, statement by Abram Karelitz, 17 December 1974, 985.
62. The public killings, which had to be carried out by the camp elders Lehmann, Selonke, and Klierforth or the block elder Koslowski, were preceded by a "reading of the verdict." There were, however, secret hangings as well. In 1942–1944, around thirty people were murdered by hanging, see BA Ludwigsburg, 407 AR 3680/65, Bd. 4, Einstellungsverfügung, 906–911.
63. BA Ludwigsburg, 407 AR 91/65, Bd. 6, statement by Otto Knott, 24 September 1975, 985.
64. Concentration Camp Stutthof had its own garden, which produced food for the camp. Otherwise, food was issued by the SS Provisions Office Danzig according to allocations for camp inmates stipulated by the Reich Food Ministry. In 1942, Commandant Hoppe had requested supplemental allowances and in exceptional cases even received them. Given the overcrowded camp and the weather conditions in the winter of 1944–1945, such measures (inasmuch as the hard laborers' supplements were at all approved) had no effect. See *Justiz und NS-Verbrechen*, Bd. XIV, Lfd. Nr. 446, Urteile gegen Hoppe und Knott, 155.
65. BA Ludwigsburg, 407 AR 91/65, Bd. 7, statement by Zbroja, 28 March 1968, 1,665.
66. BA DH, R 479, Todesfälle von Transportjuden in [sic] Konzentrationslager Stutthof in der Zeit v. 1.1. bis 31.1.1945 und der noch nicht gemeldeten restlichen von den Außenkommandos im Monat Dezember 1944. Remarkably, Jewish prisoners are not identified as such, but are shown under their respective citizenship, e.g. "German Reich" or "Latvia," which in light of the categories applied otherwise – also in the registration of victims – was an unusual procedure.
67. BA Ludwigsburg, 407 AR 91/65, Bd. 5, statement by Abraham Abramowicz, 1 October 1975, 1,192; statement by Bender, 2 September 1975, 1,210.
68. This represents a certain reversal of Glücks's maxim for the total annihilation of Jewish inmates, but it reflects Himmler's reorientation, which culminated in his negotiations with Count Folke Bernadotte and representatives of the Jewish International Congress in Stockholm on 25 April 1945. At the same time, it is to be kept in mind that the RFSS in no way wanted inmates to fall into the hands of the enemy – above all the Red Army – because he needed them as negotiating leverage (in particular vis-à-vis the Western powers), see Stanislav Zamecnik, "Kein Häftling darf lebend in die Hände des Feindes fallen," *Dachauer Hefte* 1 (1993): 230–231.
69. BA Ludwigsburg, 407 AR 3680/65, Bd. 1, Der Kommandant des KL Stutthof, Einsatzbefehl Nr. 3, 25 January 1945, 26–29; Der Kommandant des KL Stutthof, Ablaufplan, 25 January 1945, 30–31; ibid., Bd. 8, statement by Smyk, 12 November 1973, 1,922–1,923; statement by Wojewski, 7 November 1972, 1,979–1,980; BA Ludwigsburg, Dokumentation, Polen 195, Bericht von Paul-Werner Hoppe v. 24.8.1946 über die Vorbereitungen und die Durchführung der Verlegung der Häftlinge des Konzentrationslagers Stutthof in den Raum Lauenburg/Pommern im Januar und Februar 1945, 636–639; Kaienburg, *Die Wirtschaft der SS*, 525. A stirring description of one of the eleven marches is in Rabinovici, *Dank meiner Mutter*, 210–230.
70. Grabowska, "K.L. Stutthof," 73–76 and 89–90; BA Ludwigsburg, 407 AR 91/65, Bd. 7, statement by Zbroja, 28 March 1968, 1,668–1,669; BA Ludwigsburg, 407 AR 3680/65, Bd. 2, statement by Walter Englert, 8 January 1969, 348; *Justiz und NS-Verbrechen*, Bd. XIV, Lfd. Nr. 446, Urteile gegen Hoppe und Knott, 183.
71. Grabowska, "K.L. Stutthof," 81–84; Orth, *Das System*, 282–283. On Chinow, BA Ludwigsburg, 207 AR-Z 128/78, Bd. 1, statement by Wassermann, 8 May 1980, 188–189; statement by Dr. Gertrude Schneider, 25 April 1980, 211; ibid., BA Ludwigsburg, 407 AR

91/65, Bd. 4, statement by Käthe Hoffmann, 28 November 1974, 967–970; statement by Eva Weisz, 18 April 1975, 1,028. According to Weisz, the guards for this march were shot by the Soviets and laid out on the market square in Chinow.
72. Grabowska, "K.L. Stutthof," 83 and 86–89. This includes a detailed description of the fate of individual evacuations by sea. The evacuation of the branch camp Gotenhafen, which was similar to that of Stutthof, is also described. Of 618 prisoners, only 239 reached Hamburg alive. These were then sent to Stalag X-B via Neuengamme. Few lived to see liberation. See also BA Ludwigsburg, 407 AR 3680/65, Bd. 2, statement by Erich Nagel, 10 December 1968, 292–293. Others from Riga had managed to escape the National Socialist terror to Denmark or Sweden via Bergen-Belsen, Hamburg, and finally (in grueling marches) Kiel, or had been liberated by the advancing Red Army as early as March 1945, see Scheffler, "Das Schicksal," 41–43; Katz, *Erinnerungen*, 252–257; Sherman-Zander, *Zwischen Tag und Dunkel*, 115–140.
73. Grabowska, "K.L. Stutthof," 66 and 90.
74. Scheffler, "Das Schicksal," 43.
75. Press, *Judenmord in Lettland*, 141–142; Kaufmann, *Churbn Lettland*, 528.

– Chapter 20 –

A New Start and the Search for Justice

With the defeat of the National Socialist regime, the survivors of the Riga ghetto regained their freedom, whether they had been among the vast majority liberated in the camps and on the death marches, or a part of the tiny minority that had experienced the German retreat from the Latvian capital in hiding. After all they had been through, there could hardly be any talk of a return to normality. The ghetto, the selections, and the camps had changed everything; the survivors were marked for the rest of their lives with the memory of what had happened ingrained indelibly upon them. There was hardly a family that had not lost at least one member; more frequently, the opposite was the case, and one family member at most was still alive. Where were these people to turn? Could Latvia or Riga serve as a home for the survivors who had lived there before 22 June 1941?

These were the questions that the handful of survivors in Riga, now organized as a community of fate, was asking itself, just as the Latvian Jews who had been deported west, now designated "displaced persons," were considering whether to return east.[1] As ghetto inhabitants and camp inmates, they had longed for the Red Army to recapture Riga. However, they soon realized that anti-Semitism had by no means been eradicated with the return of the Soviets; rather, it had been given another shade within the framework of Stalin's cult of personality, which was to assume increasingly ominous traits. Moreover, many of the survivors among Riga's Jews still saw themselves primarily as patriots, not as Jews but as Latvians who had by no means forgotten 1940 and the destruction of their country's national sovereignty. For this group, the dictatorship under hammer and sickle was not an option for the future.

German Jews returning from Riga faced a similar dilemma. To the extent that they returned to the cities from which they had been deported, they were forced to note that, despite all the democratization efforts, they were still in the land of the perpetrators, where their "Aryan" neighbors, full of indifference to others and pity for themselves, expressed more regret for their own fate than for the victims of the crimes committed in the

---

Notes for this chapter begin on page 458.

faraway east, while local officials went about business as usual, as if the deportations and murders had never taken place. The hypocrisy went so far that some returnees even had to explain where they had been. Josef Katz of Lübeck was asked by the same policeman who had taken away the keys to his apartment why he had not reported his departure. It was a world turned inside out. These impressions were reinforced by anti-Semitic agitation that accused the displaced persons of profiteering within the military governments of the western zones of occupation. With the memory of their experiences in Riga still fresh, the survivors had to make a personal decision about their future. Did they want to try again in their hometown – whether Kassel, Hanover, Hamburg, Nuremberg, or Vienna – or was it now necessary to leave Europe?

Among those who decided for the second option, and they were not few in number, Palestine and the United States beckoned as alluring countries and New York as a promising city. Encouraged by the failure of de-Nazification and overt signs of anti-Semitism – almost 40 percent of the 500 Jewish cemeteries in the western zones of occupation were desecrated between 1945 and 1950 – survivors inevitably reorientated themselves. Above all non-German Jews, who made up a majority of Jews in the U.S. zone of occupation, began leaving Germany in growing numbers starting in 1949. But many returning German Jews also saw no future in a country where the deep-seated anti-Semitism of broad parts of the population had merely been given a democratic whitewash.

It should also be kept in mind that there were not enough spiritual leaders available for the reconstruction of community life. When Rabbi Alexander Carlebach visited Düsseldorf's synagogue community on behalf of the Jewish Relief Unit, he had to note that personnel for regular religious services, religious education, and holidays and family festivals were not available in desired measure, and that local Jews therefore had to fall back on rabbis from elsewhere for religious guidance. The situation in the Düsseldorf community was typical in the postwar era, when it was not always possible to have a rabbi on hand even for bar mitzvah ceremonies. It was even worse in northern Rhineland, where the shortage of rabbis made circumcisions, weddings, conversions, etc., de facto impossible. Religious life there was in danger of dying out or degenerating into conflicts between various factions. Thus only a minority of survivors remained in the occupation zones of West Germany, while the history of European Jews was now written in the United States, Palestine or Israel, South America, and other places that were in principal more open to the new arrivals.[2]

Even if identities were torn and many religious communities had been wiped out, even if differences existed between deeply religious East European Jews and assimilated German Jews, all of the victims were united on one point: the perpetrators responsible had to be apprehended and brought to court. Efforts here were understandably focused on investigations into those criminals whose names had become synonymous with the everyday terror of the National Socialist system. Furthermore, it was clear that the Latvian Jews had collected information not only on the German commanders and perpetrators renowned for their excessive brutality, but also on collaborators in positions of responsibility. Lists of war criminals were drawn up, and the streams of emigrants from Europe to the United States were kept under observation in order to see whether any known perpetrators or "persons who had appropriated Jewish property" were among them.[3]

Although the survivors from the Baltic and those from the West were active in separate associations, it was nonetheless difficult to obtain reliable information. There were two reasons for this. For one, due to the onset of the Cold War and the integration of intelligence services into that conflict, there was a lack of communication and transparency between individual organizations and authorities. Facts that had long been known to one side represented a novelty to the other. Also, the memories of survivors, together with the desire to make the murderers atone, sometimes encumbered rather than facilitated investigations. Nonetheless, by cooperating with prosecutors, it was possible to learn a great deal about the whereabouts of the men who had to answer for so many people.

The world public knew a lot from press reports about the fate of Nazi eminences such as Adolf Hitler, Heinrich Himmler, and Reinhold Heydrich, the main perpetrators whose names would later be repeated ad infinitum in the verdicts of West German courts. By war's end, Heydrich had been dead for almost three years. The "Führer" had not left Berlin but had committed suicide in his bunker, and "loyal Heinrich" – who in the end had been dismissed from his post as *Reichsführer-SS* and disowned by Hitler – poisoned himself after being captured by British soldiers. It was less well-known that the first higher SS and police leader responsible for Riga, Hans-Adolf Prützmann, had done the same. The funeral oration for Walther Stahlecker had been delivered by Heydrich himself. Stahlecker, an exemplary careerist, had swapped his desk in the Foreign Office for the command of Einsatzgruppe A (EG A). This posting as head of the northernmost of the four mobile murder formations in the Soviet Union was supposed to bring about his glorious return to the Reich Security Main Office (RSHA) and at the same time bestow upon him the reputation of a hardened front-line soldier, a quality that so many functionaries among the ideological elite considered an indispensable attribute of leadership strength.

This striving had cost Stahlecker his life in a forward skirmish in Saniki, Russia. His wounds – to the posterior and one of his hands – were relatively unspectacular. He lay in the snow in shock, but there was no external bleeding. His men brought him by sled to a base, at which point he was in "good spirits." Stahlecker was given additional treatment and then transferred to Pskov; the doctor of EG A, SS Lieutenant Colonel Dr. Hans Meixner, made a favorable diagnosis. Nonetheless, the RSHA wanted Stahlecker to be flown home for further treatment. The commander of EG A remained cheerful and had some tea and red wine, but suddenly his pulse disappeared. All Meixner's efforts to handle Stahlecker's circulatory collapse were in vain. His boss's breathing grew steadily weaker, until he slipped "gently and painlessly into death." By the time the plane landed, Stahlecker was dead, and his corpse had been laid out. Only his lifeless body could be transferred to Prague. The man who with his "Stahlecker report" gave the "performance records" of the genocide against the Jews a name died of an infection on 23 March 1942. Heydrich, fully unaware that he would meet a similar fate, held funeral services for the deceased in the Prague Castle on 26 March.[4]

Albert Sauer, the former Kaiserwald camp commandant, also did not live to see the war's end. He succumbed to wounds on 3 May 1945, a few days before the Wehrmacht's unconditional surrender. He allegedly fell in battle as a member of the last contingent of Sonderkommando Dirlewanger.[5] It was rumored that SS First Lieutenant Eberhard von Bonin, who had been in charge of administration at Kaiserwald, had killed himself in the final days of the war.[6] Kurt Krause, whose term as commandant of the Riga ghetto had given terror a face, and whose name was indelibly stuck in the victims' memory alongside the horror of the Salaspils camp, met a grim fate. After the transfer of his office from Riga to Liepāja, he was captured by Soviet partisans – another version says that they were Jews – and executed. Rumors of Krause's end and his corpse, which had allegedly been mutilated – the tongue, for example, had been cut out – soon made the rounds,[7] as if this version of his demise amounted to a just punishment for all of his deeds. It was as if a sentence had been pronounced, which to many among the Gestapo, SD, and Order Police seemed like a threat and therefore spurred them on in their efforts to elude the grasp of the Soviets, better yet of all victors. These efforts would prove only partially successful, as the highest representative of the SS in the Baltic was to learn firsthand.

That Friedrich Jeckeln, one of the greatest mass murderers in the history of mankind, had faced a Soviet military court in the capital of Latvia was something that the Jews who had returned to Germany or emigrated could learn only if they had access to contacts in Riga or knew how to interpret properly the sparse information found in the western press, for example, in the newspaper *Kieler Nachrichtenblatt* in January 1946. This official organ of the British occupying forces reported in two short items that eight former generals had been indicted in Riga, among them the "previous commander of the Waffen-SS Ekkelen, chief of the German police in district 'Ostland'," who was charged with murdering of tens of thousands of Baltic citizens, including Metropolitan Sergius of Vilnius (Wilna, Wilno), and deporting thousands of others and confining them to concentration camps.[8] Nothing was said of the fact that "Ekkelen" was identical with Jeckeln, and that most of his victims had been the Jews of Riga – and the Jews of Ukraine during his stint as HSSPF Russia South. In order to know who in fact was on trial in Riga at the end of January, the interested reader first had to find information of this kind and then know how to interpret it correctly – and this at a time when the world was talking about Hitler, Himmler, and Heydrich as well as the Nuremberg trials. At any rate, Jeckeln's trial did not last long, from 26 January to 3 February 1946. Jeckeln was convicted and promptly hanged on the same day.[9]

Alongside Ghetto Commandant Krause, it was "Lange" or "Dr. Lange" or "Major Lange" who was seared upon the memory of the victims, the Gestapo official whose name stood for absolute power and constant danger. If there was a perpetrator who had to be apprehended and brought to account, then he was the one. In a letter to the municipal council of Greater Berlin, Willy Weiss, a survivor of the Berlin transport of 19 January 1942, expressed what must have been a view shared by many others: "You can be assured that the acts of cruelty of this criminal are monstrous. I myself would tear the flesh from his bones with pliers."[10] Given Lange's importance, everything was done to find him. British investigators initially concentrated on Hans Lange, who had belonged to Prützmann's staff in Riga and was thus suspected of being the wanted man in question. In an elaborate case before a Hamburg court, Hans Lange was able to prove that a mix-up had occurred.[11] The search for the wanted Lange was by no means over.

After an examination of records from the Berlin Document Center, where the United States kept captured SS records and other Nazi documents, it was learned that in early 1945 Dr. Rudolf Lange had taken up his post as regional commander of the Security Police and the SD in Poznań (KdS Poznań), where his "achievements" lay primarily in seizing deserters and saboteurs. Furthermore, the following was also established: attacking the forces of Army Group Vistula, the Red Army at the end of January 1945 was advancing on the city in a massive push. On 1 February, Himmler, in his capacity as commander of the Replacement Army, appointed Colonel Ernst Gonell commandant of Poznań and declared the city a "fortress." Gonell was ordered to halt the Russians' advance on this strategically important crossroads. Poznań, along with the forces stationed there – including many wounded soldiers – was quickly surrounded. With each day, the situation of the besieged German forces deteriorated. Lange was forced to give up his office premises and to cease working as KdS.

Together with a small group of employees from KdS Poznań, Lange withdrew to the "core," the inner ring of the German defenses, where he is said to have placed himself at the disposal of Hans Kurt Moser, the city commandant's chief intelligence officer, who then assigned him to the core's gate. It is reported – this should not be withheld either – that Lange fought courageously. Nonetheless, the defenders were unable to hold the core. In the night of 22–23 February 1945, soldiers of the Soviet 8th Guard Army and the 69th Army broke though the lines, and Lange was wounded. Although his KdS colleagues had already assumed new identities and donned Wehrmacht uniforms, this was not a practicable course of action for Lange. He took his own life around 6 A.M. on 23 February so as to avoid being captured by the Soviets. A few days before Lange's death, Hitler, acting on a recommendation from RSHA chief Ernst Kaltenbrunner, had awarded Lange the German Cross in Gold, one of the Reich's highest military awards, for his loyal services in Riga among other things.[12]

The prosecutor's offices in Frankenthal and Hamburg reached identical conclusions in 1947 after questioning Lange's relatives – although they did not reconstruct Lange's final days to the same extent.[13] Even if individual survivors – among them even the renowned historian Gertrude Schneider – expressed doubts about Lange's death in Poznań and interpreted reports of his death as a large-scale act of deception so he could assume a new identity, there are no compelling arguments for such a theory.[14] The former KdS Latvia and Wannsee Conference participant did not live to see the end of the "Third Reich," but died in Poznań. His death was certified at the Registrar's Office in Berlin-Charlottenberg on 5 June 1951.

Even if some of the most wanted SS officials from Riga – Lange, Krause, and Sauer – had been killed during the war, the greater part of the perpetrators emerged from the war unscathed. Rudolf Seck, the former Jungfernhof commandant, was released from a military hospital at war's end, but was soon in the sights of British military police, who arrested him and transferred him to an internment camp. The same happened to Kurt Migge, who was arrested in Hamburg by British military police on 5 July 1945. Together with Otto Teckemeier, who was arrested in 1948, and Rudolf Reese, who had fled the Soviet zone of occupation to Frankfurt am Main, Migge was tried in Hamburg in 1951 after British efforts to prosecute the accused in a military court were curbed due to the return of judicial authority to Germany. Seck was sentenced to life in prison mainly for crimes at the Jungfernhof camp, as was Migge for his involvement in Operation Dünamünde and the shootings on Tin Square – but not for shootings in the peat camps Olaine (Olai) and Sloka (Schlock). Teckemeier, who was considered by most survivors to have been a greater horror at Salaspils than the real commandant Richard Nickel (who was missing after the war),[15] was given a sentence of six years' imprisonment, because no autonomous acts of killing could be proven.

Various survivors charged that Reese had beaten up and tormented members of the ghetto's labor commandos, whereas the prosecution's charge read "bodily injury inflicted by a public official" and "grievous bodily injury." However, there was not enough evidence to convict Reese; he was the only one of the four defendants to be acquitted in the verdict issued on 29 December 1951.[16] Proceedings could not be launched against Max Gymnich, Krause's former driver and an alleged participant in individual killings. After being taken into custody, he had committed suicide in a remand prison in Braunschweig.[17]

In the wake of this trial as well as preliminary investigations by the British prosecution authorities, the acts of felonious homicide committed in and around Riga were further investigated by the Hamburg Prosecutor's Office, which soon systematically investigated the former personnel of the offices of the Territorial Commander of the Security Police and SD Ostland (BdS Ostland), KdS Latvia, and HSSPF Ostland with the aim of filing indictments whenever sufficient evidence was found. However, it was to be many years before investigations could be considered exhaustive. This was above all because the role of the HSSPF offices and the Order Police in implementing the genocide had been neglected by postwar German historians and could only be clarified by the prosecution authorities' own systematic research efforts.

The mills of justice turned very slowly, and not a few of the most incriminated persons – such as Herbert Degenhardt, who had been Jeckeln's chief of staff, or Johannes Zingler, who had "proved himself" as a marksman in the pits at Rumbula – died during investigation, without ever having to stand trial.[18] Karl Heise, who had lost an eye to an errant bullet while supervising the mass shooting at Rumbula, died in an automobile accident; it was assumed that he killed himself so as to avoid prosecution.[19] At the end of December 1971, however, indictments were filed against Heinrich Oberwinder, Friedrich Jahnke, Paul Draeger, and Max Neumann for their active participation in the clearance of the Riga ghetto. Ernst Hemicker – the seemingly harmless head of the construction department within the HSSPF Ostland staff, who had "only" supervised the digging of the pits in order to provide the best possible mass graves for one of the largest massacres in history – was almost certainly not a "prominent name" during the period of the Latvian ghetto. Nonetheless, he was indicted, because investigators from the Hamburg Prosecutor's Office had discovered his role in the crime. First and foremost, the indictment was directed at Otto Tuchel, who also had to account for numerous individual crimes in addition to his involvement in the large-scale operation in late 1941.[20]

By the time of the proceedings, Hemicker, like Oberwinder and Jahnke, was already an old man.[21] He was declared permanently unfit to stand trial. In his case, this was not a variation on a particular kind of defense strategy that was successfully applied in other trials of much younger defendants accused of National Socialist crimes, but represented a justified application by his lawyer. Hemicker really was so sick that his passing was soon to be expected.[22] Obwerwinder was not to take part in the trial either, because the chances of convicting him were rather slight. Although he was the man who had organized the mass shooting on 29 November 1941 and then, on 9 December, assigned subordinates to the killing site, he had been indicted primarily for his official position as chief of operations within the office of the Regional Commander of the Order Police Latvia. This alone did not substantiate reasonable suspicion, according to the Hamburg State Court. On 13 March 1972, the court refused to admit Oberwinder's indictment and thus stopped his prosecution; Draeger did not take part in the main proceedings for similar reasons.[23] On 23 February 1973, a verdict was issued against the remaining defendants: Jahnke was sentenced to three years in prison, and Tuchel was given a life sentence. In the case of Neumann, the court refrained from punishment, because it considered his complicity "modest."[24]

Jahnke successfully appealed his verdict. The Federal Court of Justice returned his case to the Hamburg court. There was no subsequent trial against him, because his lawyers succeeded in having him certified unfit to stand trial. No other suspect members of the Order Police and the office of the HSSPF – inasmuch as they were still alive by the 1970s – had to appear before court. The prosecutors gradually filed stays of legal proceedings and refrained from criminal prosecution, because guilt was considered minimal, involvement in a crime could not be proven with certainty, or "necessity" was allowed – that is to say, the existence of a threat to the suspect if a criminal order was not carried out. Older suspects, such as the former head of the Riga ghetto guards, Albert Hesfehr, were dropped from proceedings, because the suspects were considered permanently unfit to stand trial. A number of persons could not be identified or located.[25]

Otto Tuchel was therefore the only member of all the Order Police units and offices of HSSPF Ostland who had to atone for his crimes. This verdict has a certain symbolic character where German criminal law is concerned: thousands of people were murdered at Rumbula in late 1941, but only one person was sentenced to prison in West Germany. This clearly shows how inadequate West German criminal law was for punishing crimes of genocide. Convicting an individual for murder under West German criminal law – a carryover from the Bismarck era – required prosecutors prove a premeditated act, exceptional brutality and cruelty, or base motives. A premeditated act was all but impossible to prove, because suspects could claim they had acted on the order of the day, not with premeditation. Proving exceptional brutality and cruelty or base motives – especially in a case such as Rumbula, for which the only living witnesses who could name names were the perpetrators themselves – meant that the investigations, which were carried out in good faith, required a great deal of time. By the time an indictment could be filed, the older, ranking officers – for whom the evidence was usually greatest – had either died or were unfit to stand trial. Collecting enough evidence to indict and convict the rank-and-file and junior officers was even more difficult; these men, for example, did not issue the written orders or submit the final reports. The West German parliament first extended the statute of limitations for murder in 1965, but all of the other possible charges for which perpetrators could have been prosecuted – e.g. bodily injury, illegal restraint, criminally negligent homicide, accessory to murder, etc. – had already fallen under the statute of limitations or were close to doing so. Among the active members of the office of the Regional Commander of the Order Police Latvia and its subordinate units, proof of guilt for murder in the letter of West German law could be produced only against Otto Tuchel, who was indeed an everyday source of terror for the Riga ghetto's inhabitants. Given the large number of men from the Order Police involved in the genocide, doubts as to the suitability of West German law for punishing National Socialist crimes seem all too justified.[26]

This is also clearly seen in the prosecution of personnel from the very agency that was ex officio institutionally responsible for the persecution, torture, and killing of Jews. The Hamburg Prosecutor's Office carried out a systematic investigation of officials from the Gestapo and the SD, not only Rudolf Lange and his aide Kurt Krause. Rudolf Batz, the first commander of Einsatzkommando 2 (Ek 2) and the first chief of KdS Latvia, had been tracked down by the West German criminal police in Bielefeld, where he was living under the false name Rolf Kohl. Like other incriminated former officials after the war, Batz had found employment at the company Informator für Wirtschaftsangelegenheiten und Wirtschaftswerbung GmbH, which had enabled him to draw on an informal network of old Nazis and thus facilitated his return to a middle-class existence. However, a larger circle of people also knew of his survival, and gaps in security made it possible to unmask him.

Having been an especially dedicated Gestapo official, Batz found himself in an awkward situation, because he was at the same time wanted by several prosecutor's offices for his involvement in other Nazi crimes in addition to the killings carried out in Latvia in summer 1941. He was confronted with his deployments as deputy BdS Netherlands as well as KdS Cracow in the General Government, where he was deployed in late summer

1943. It must have been clear to Batz that on the basis of his official position alone, he bore a great deal of responsibility. He did not withstand the pressure very long. Vis-à-vis investigators from Hamburg and Dortmund, he gave detailed statements about his career, while making cautious remarks about the crimes in question. In January 1961, when the first protocols of his testimony had been submitted, he saw how hopeless his situation appeared. He committed suicide in remand.[27]

Batz's deputy, Arnold Kirste, never considered such an option. He testified willingly in various proceedings and skillfully talked his way out of all confrontations with the authorities. Referring to Kirste, who by 1970 was almost 70 years old, a court official familiar with the investigations noted with resignation: "K. is a suspect in various cases. It has not been possible up to now to prosecute him. Questioning seems only sensible, when concrete evidence is submitted."[28] That is also the way it remained. The case of Eduard Roschmann involves another one of the most wanted Nazi officials from Riga. After the war, the second commandant of the Riga ghetto managed – with the support of Alois Hudal, titular bishop of Aela and rector of Rome's Collegio Teutonico, and his entourage – to get hold of a fake passport that enabled his flight to South America.[29] Nonetheless, many years later, and ultimately owing to the initiative and publications of Simon Wiesenthal, the public began to take an interest in the problem of the "rat lines" and secret organizations of Nazis who were fugitives or living incognito. This newfound interest hit Roschmann particularly hard, because Wiesenthal had provided thriller author Frederick Forsyth with details about Roschmann's career, and on the basis of this information, the British novelist had developed the evil protagonist of his bestseller *The Odessa File*. Wiesenthal had urged Forsyth to chose a real perpetrator, one "who is relatively unknown but abominable." Thus no pseudonym was given Roschmann; instead, he was left with his given name. The British original appeared in 1972; the German translation followed shortly thereafter.

From then on, Roschmann was no longer just any wanted SS criminal but a prominent figure in the same category as Heinrich Müller (the Gestapo chief), Franz Stangl (the first commandant at Sobibór and the second commandant at Treblinka), and Josef Mengele (the notorious Auschwitz doctor). In 1973, when Forsyth's book was filmed with a cast of stars, including Oscar-winning actor Maximilian Schell in the role of Roschmann, the international public, which got to see the film the following year, wanted to believe that this man had been a mass murderer and, even worse, posed a real threat to the State of Israel. The Hamburg Prosecutor's Office desperately tried to have Roschmann extradited from Argentina to Germany, although the success of the film and the book went one step further in increasing the pressure on investigators as well as the German Foreign Office. Roschmann tried to go underground. He may have been able to resist extradition from Argentina, where the film was shown in 1977, but he was nonetheless forced to leave the country that had generously granted him and other Nazi perpetrators asylum. Roschmann spent the last weeks of his life on the run and died of heart failure on 19 August 1977, in Asuncion, Paraguay.[30]

Roschmann was also strongly suspected of having committed crimes as part of Operation 1005, the unearthing and cremation of the Jewish bodies in the woods near Riga.[31] Walter Helfsgott, the head of the special commando in Riga, was indicted for these crimes in the Stuttgart State Court. On 13 March 1969, when the verdict was announced, he was able to leave court a free man, although he "objectively and subjectively made a significant contribution to the death of the Jewish inmate-workers who were shot by Sonderkommando 1005 B in the vicinity of Riga." The judges, however, allowed his plea of an act of necessity. This meant the judges gave credence to his assertion that he had acted in the belief that he faced a threat to his own life, in particular from Rudolf Lange. The consequence of this legal opinion was that ultimately the suspect in such a case could be incriminated only by himself – namely by more or less openly elaborating on his true motives during questioning, which for reasons of self-protection was only possible in cases involving especially witless persons or convinced fanatics. By providing a few explanations about their inner turmoil during the war, other perpetrators facing prosecution could hope to be "excused" for their acts of murder – as in Helfsgott's case.[32]

Among other former members of the Gestapo and SD – officials from EG A / BdS Ostland and Ek 2 / KdS Lettland – living in the Federal Republic of Germany and under investigation for crimes committed in Riga, Hamburg investigators concentrated their efforts on Karl Tschierschky, Heinz Trühe, Arno Besekow, and Gerhard Maywald. On this occasion, the Hamburg Prosecutor's Office was certain that the evidence gathered would have to lead to conviction. In the separate case against Maywald, the judges characterized the defendant in their verdict as a confidant of Rudolf Lange and a key figure within Department IV of KdS Latvia. The verdict, dated 2 August 1977, noted that Maywald had also been actively involved in the construction of Salaspils. Moreover, the indictment maintained that it was there, on 2 January 1942, that Maywald had overseen the killing of Hirschland and Hanau, the young inmates who, having allegedly fled to the ghetto to look for their parents, were then seized in a post office and sent back to the camp. Latvians had been deployed in the firing squad, whereas Maywald had read the "verdict." However, because witness testimonies during the main proceedings were contradictory – some recalled Lange, but not Maywald at the execution, while others depicted another course of execution – Maywald could not be convicted on this count. The same applied for the individual shootings of exhausted inmates at Salaspils, with which Maywald had also been charged. It also could not be proven that, on 30 January 1942, Maywald, acting of his own accord during the arrival of a transport at Šķirotava, had shot a deaf-mute man who, owing to his disability, had not followed guards' orders quickly enough.

Although Maywald was unmistakably identified as present in the ghetto during the operation in late March 1942 (Dünamünde Ghetto II) and as active in the selections, he was also acquitted of this charge. Again, witness statements were contradictory, and it appeared that what had been experienced was no longer distinguishable from knowledge of hearsay. Even credible information from survivors was called into question; in the back and forth of questions and answers, pro and con, other witnesses began to doubt their own memory. Maywald was also acquitted of another count in the indictment, namely participation in the operation at the SS estate Jungfernhof on 26 March 1942, which also involved the transfer of inmates unable to work to an alleged fish cannery in Dünamünde. Here at least, the court expressed no doubt in the crime itself and admitted that there was a good deal of evidence pointing to Maywald's participation. Nonetheless, none of the survivor statements were able to substantiate the charge, because in the eyes of the court they had to be considered "unreliable."

By contrast the court saw it as proven – primarily due to statements by two of the plaintiffs, Ervin Sekules and Elliot Welles – that Maywald had singled out people from the ghetto's Vienna and Berlin groups in February 1942 and thus bore some guilt for their murder in the surrounding forests. At the same time, however, an independent intent to kill was disallowed in Maywald's case; instead, he was considered a recipient of orders who conscientiously carried out Lange's instructions without "making the racial hatred of the commander his own and acting on (his own) base motives." Under "consideration of all the circumstances," the Hamburg State Court saw the four-year prison sentence given Maywald as appropriate, because during sentencing allowances were made for "the particular psychological burden" caused by "the extra long investigation" – a clear criticism of the Prosecutor's Office. The court also deducted the circa sixteen months of pretrial detention that Maywald had "suffered," thus once again reducing the punishment (which according to the verdict was already "in the lower realm of a possible assessment of imprisonment").[33]

In the case against Tschierschky, Trühe, and Besekow, it was the actions of the mobile units EG A and Ek 2 that were in the foreground and not, as in the case against Maywald, their stationary counterparts BdS Ostland and KdS Latvia. With its indictment of 1 November 1974, the Hamburg

Prosecutor's Office filed for the main proceedings to be held before the Hamburg State Court. In the persons of Tschierschky, head of Department III (SD), and Trühe, head of Department I/II (Administration and Personnel), those members of EG A who had held leading positions were tried, as was the former lower-ranking officer Besekow, who had been the leader of a detachment of Ek 2 deployed at Bikernieki and elsewhere. Specifically, all three were brought to court for their participation in killings "in or near Riga" in July 1941. Besekow was also charged with other killings in Krasnogvardeisk, namely the murder of fifteen inmates of an asylum for the mentally ill and two persons suspected of being partisans.

On 11 March 1975, the verdict was announced. In the view of the court, Trühe was "to be acquitted of premeditated aiding and abetting murder." The prosecution had failed to refute Trühe's assertion that he had believed a killing operation in which he had participated, and in which fifty people had been shot, had involved "the lawful shooting of partisans who had been condemned to death." It was also granted that he had not acted with excessive brutality or cruelty, or had at least been unaware of doing so, because the operation in question was the first time he had taken part in a shooting, and he was therefore so nervous that he was unable to judge the situation objectively. Although Trühe was said to have shot five people, he left court a free man. It was nearly the same for Besekow. The court saw it as proven that he had violated the law, but at the same time, it assessed his guilt as minimal. The court expressed understanding for his then situation, that of an individual policeman who, despite being an officer, could "distinguish between right and wrong according to today's standards" only with difficulty, "because the state in this case was itself the lawbreaker." Because Besekow's aiding and abetting in the murders in Riga and Krasnogvardeisk was deemed minimal, and because he had been in a "conflict situation," the court refrained from punishment. Karl Tschierschky, the man who in August 1941 had struggled with the newly installed civil administration over his office's authority to issue guidelines regarding the "Jewish question," was not on hand at the reading of the verdict. He had died during the trial.[34]

From among the personnel of Concentration Camp Kaiserwald, only two men and one woman had to answer to justice. Dr. Eberhard Krebsbach, who had ended up in American captivity, was tried and sentenced to death by a U.S. military court for his complicity in crimes at Concentration Camp Sachsenhausen, without his murderous acts in Kaiserwald being broached. He was executed in Landsberg am Lech on 28 May 1947.[35] The senior overseer Emmy Kuppinger, better known as Emmy Kowa, had to answer to a tribunal of the military government in the French occupation zone. It could not be proven that she had beaten inmates to death in Kaiserwald, or even that she had knowingly committed murder. But Emmy Kowa had severely maltreated many prisoners and had at least indirectly participated in selections. She also was suspected of having enriched herself. The French General Tribunal, in its verdict of 20 February 1948, therefore handed down a punishment of twenty years of prison and forced labor. Furthermore, it ordered that all of her assets be confiscated.[36]

With Dr. Krebsbach already dead, investigations of the Central Office in North Rhine-Westphalia for the Processing of National Socialist Crimes of Violence at the Cologne Prosecutor's Office, which in 1978 picked up on investigations into the Nazi crimes committed at Kaiserwald, concentrated on the other levels of leadership within the camp administration. Suspicion hardened primarily around Krebsbach's assistant, the medic Heinz Wisner. It took months of questioning survivors and witnesses before Wisner could be indicted on 3 November 1980.[37] Just over two years later, on 21 January 1983, the Düsseldorf State Court sentenced Wisner to a total of six years imprisonment for aiding and abetting murder. After an appeal and a retrial, the sentence was reduced to five years on 14 August 1985, because, in the eyes of the court, Wisner's independence of action in the crime was "very minimal," although the judges had to admit that he certainly "had acted premeditatedly as well."[38] Because it was not possible to prove that other staff members had committed specific acts of killing, the Wisner verdict concluded the investigations into the crimes at Kaiserwald, without the vast majority of the camp's personnel ever being called to account for their actions.[39] One former official – Wilhelm Vogler, the last head of administration at Kaiserwald – briefly caught the attention of investigators, because he had been questioned regarding something else and, after his career had been revealed, was asked about events in Kaiserwald on the periphery.[40]

The Polish state was much more aggressive in prosecuting Nazi crimes than was West Germany, as is seen in the case of Concentration Camp Stutthof. After a large trial at the Gdansk District Court running from 8 October to 31 October 1946, guilty verdicts were returned without exception; in addition to long prison terms, death sentences were issued to ten of the defendants, including Theodor Meyer, Ewald Foth, and Hans Rach. The punishments were carried out without exception.[41] It was not possible to bring other incriminated persons such as Commandant Paul-Werner Hoppe, camp doctor Dr. Otto Heidl, and medic Otto Karl Knott before Polish courts. After escaping from the Fallingbostel internment camp in 1948, Hoppe had lived under a false name in various places. Once he believed he was safe and would no longer be extradited to Poland as a war criminal, he assumed his proper name again and settled in Witten. He also summoned his family to join him. In 1953, Hoppe was found there and called in for questioning. He was arrested in April 1954. Together with Otto Karl Knott, he was tried before the Bochum State Court. Heidl, who had also been tracked down, committed suicide in remand after it had become clear to him that he was among one of the most incriminated officials from Stutthof. In December 1955, Hoppe was given a sentence of five years and three months' imprisonment, while Knott received three years and three months. However, the proceedings were taken up again on appeal. The Bochum State Court confirmed the verdict against Knott in June 1957; Hoppe, however, was given nine years in prison.[42] Other trials against members of the Stutthof camp personnel also ended in guilty verdicts, but the greater part of the officials and guards deployed there – especially in the branch camps – went without punishment despite extensive investigations.

In addition to the members of the SS and police, officials and functionaries from the civil administration of Reich Commissariat Ostland as well as Army officers from the military administration bore no small amount of guilt for the crimes committed in the Baltic. As the decision-makers and top representatives of these occupation regimes, their powers placed them, at least nominally, above Himmler's apparatus, even if everyday rule had shown that fierce arguments had taken place precisely over authority regarding the "Jewish question." It meant little that at the Trial of the Major War Criminals in Nuremberg the verdict against defendant Alfred Rosenberg, the former Reich minister for the occupied eastern territories, also passed judgment on the agencies subordinated to his ministry. None of the other top officials responsible for occupation policy in the Baltic stood trial at Nuremberg. It was similar with regard to military officials.

In Subsequent Nuremberg Trial No. 12, the High Command Trial, General Field Marshal Wilhelm von Leeb, who had been entrusted with the leadership of Army Group North until 16 January 1942, was sentenced by a U.S. military court to three years' imprisonment on 28 October 1948, with the judges finding him complicit only in the dissemination of the Jurisdiction Decree. All of the other matters contained in the indictment, among them crimes against civilians, were assigned to the Security Police and SD, not the supreme commander for the northern zone of operations.[43] Former Commander of Rear Area Army Group North Franz von Roques – unlike his cousin who had had the same job in the southern sector of the eastern front – was not even tried, although during the period of military rule he had signed and transmitted various anti-Jewish administrative measures ranging from the mandatory marking of the Jews' outer garments to ghettoization. He had also debated with Leeb whether the sterilization of Jewish families would be a suitable alternative to mass murder, which in the form of pogroms was not something he had sought to stop. Franz von Roques did not have to answer for any of this. The biggest problem he faced was whether he would testify against his former superiors or against his cousin during the High Command Trial, since the two had built up contradictory defense strategies regarding the responsibility of the commander of the army group rear areas in the question of "executive power."[44]

Otto Lasch, once celebrated as the conqueror of Riga, had less luck. In 1945, Lasch, by then a general, had been deployed to Königsberg (today Kaliningrad) as fortress commandant, where he ended up a Soviet prisoner of war. According to his own testimony, he was sentenced to twenty-five years' imprisonment in a corrective labor camp for crimes committed by the division under his command. Only in 1955 was he allowed to leave the Soviet Union, without being pardoned.[45] Whether a hard but just verdict had befallen returnees such as Lasch, or whether they had been overtaken by vengeful Stalinist tyranny was left to opinion-makers within the two German states to decide in their polemics for newspapers and "discussions."[46] At any rate, neither side seriously examined the matter. Other military personnel – such as Senior Wartime Administration Counselor Friedrich Ellrodt, who was very involved in the establishment of the ghetto,[47] or Colonel Wilhelm Ullersperger, who had sought to close ranks with Riga's anti-Semitic-inclined self-defense force – were mentioned only on the periphery of investigations. Apparently, West German prosecutors were unable to assess the significance of these officers' actions within the framework of the postwar investigations.

Even worse, former Reich Commissar Ostland Hinrich Lohse also got off relatively lightly. Unlike his colleague to the south – Reich Commissar Ukraine Erich Koch had been extradited to Poland in 1950, where he was sentenced to death by a Warsaw court on 9 March 1958[48] – a court in Bielefeld sentenced Lohse to ten years in prison and ordered the simultaneous confiscation of his assets. By 1951, Lohse was already at large again; he had been granted a reprieve for reasons of health. He later testified against members of the SS and police, without going into his own role in the system and incriminating himself. When the systematic investigation into the members of the Reich Commissariat Ostland got underway, Lohse – who had died in Mühlenbarbek, outside of Hamburg, on 25 February 1964 – could no longer be prosecuted.[49]

With regard to other employees of the civil administration apparatus, there was initial suspicion surrounding the heads of the RKO's four main departments, Theodor Fründt (Political Affairs), Wilhelm Burmeister (Central Department), Martin Matthiessen (Economic Affairs), and Johann Lorenzen (Technical Affairs) as well as the Reich commissar's personal advisor, Karl Egger. The Kiel Prosecutor's Office quickly viewed it as proven that the suspects had ex officio received news of the systematic annihilation of the Jews within their sphere of influence. But their defense that they had not been involved, even the assertion that Lohse and his office had tried to resist Jeckeln's radical action, could not be refuted in the assessment of the Kiel investigators. Proceedings against suspect former members of the civil administration were therefore stopped.[50]

In reconstructing the RKO's administrative hierarchy and the areas of responsibility of individual top civil servants, Kiel investigators came across the person of Administrative Counselor Friedrich Trampedach, who as head of Department IIa (Political Affairs) had occupied a key position below Fründt. The Kiel Prosecutor's Office could not come up with any solid findings about his career; it was assumed that Trampedach was killed during the war.[51] Hermann Alletag, who ran the desk for the administration of "accrued enemy assets" within the RKO, could not be questioned either. He had died in Starnberg in August 1950, without justice officials being able to confront him with his past.[52] Former General Commissar Latvia Dr. Otto-Heinrich Drechsler decided to perish along with the "Third Reich." He followed the example set by Germany's surrender and took his own life.[53]

The fate of the heavily incriminated desk officer for Jews within the mayor's office, Junker of the Order Werner Altemeyer, who was transferred to the front in 1942, could not be clarified with absolute certainty. It is said that he fell in battle on 17 February 1944; this was in any event the date recorded in a decision issued by a court in Lingen.[54] The commissarial governing mayor of Riga, Hugo Wittrock, returned to Germany in 1945 and began writing his memoirs under the working title "An Eventful Life: Recollections of a German Balt." The manuscript was finished in 1950. Eight years later, Wittrock died in the aftermath of a traffic accident; he was never questioned by Hamburg investigators.[55]

Other members of the various civil offices who were indirectly entrusted with the "solution of the Jewish question" ex officio but who had handled "only" the deployment of Jewish forced laborers, ghettoization, provisions, or the collection of assets, were also located by prosecutors. Years after the crimes in question, they were summoned from their middle-class idyll for questioning – no matter whether they were still active as top civil servants and successful managers or were highly respected pensioners. They ultimately provided witness statements, knowing full well that that they were not to be prosecuted. All the things for which these notabilities had borne at least some authority and responsibility – theft, forced labor, and other arbitrary measures – had long since exceeded the statute of limitations. If they confessed ignorance, could not remember, told half-truths, or sloughed everything off on the SS, they could be sure that the opposite had to be proved first. Accordingly, given their experience in dealing with official judicial business, they acted with self-confidence.[56]

In 1967, the Koblenz Prosecutor's Office attempted to prosecute a prominent witness for knowingly providing false statements. Dr. Karl Friedrich

Vialon, the man who in mid 1942 had tried to unify ghetto administration in Reich Commissariat Ostland, had been state secretary in the Federal Ministry for Economic Cooperation. During an investigation concerning General Commissariat White Ruthenia, Vialon had represented his function in the RKO in a trivializing manner and – despite the overwhelming record to the contrary – depicted himself as a civil servant serving the good of the state. Nothing happened to Vialon – at first. Only when East Germany denounced him in its *Braunbuch,* an effort to play up the personnel continuities between the "Third Reich" and West Germany for polemical purposes, was there any movement in the matter. Due to the ensuing debate and public pressure, Vialon was forced to resign from his post in 1966, because he was politically no longer tenable. Commenting on the affair, Gerhard Maunz of the magazine *Der Spiegel* wrote that this kind of political decision meant that the West German justice system was impotent. It was a system that was not in a position to prosecute officials such as Vialon and was either taken in by their self-serving explanations, or could not refute them. Maunz saw in this a clear signal that the West German establishment – right up to Chancellor Kurt Georg Kiesinger – had lost all moral credibility, and that others like Vialon at the top of West German society were able to exculpate themselves on their own at no risk to themselves. The case against Vialon – which ended inconclusively – brought to a close a public debate that in the end concerned the person Vialon and the role of top civil servants of the RKO only to a limited extent.[57]

Friedrich Brasch – formerly tasked by Riga's occupation authorities with administering the ghetto – preferred not to appear before court. He was so sure of his invulnerability that he refused to make any kind of statement to the police or the Hamburg Prosecutor's Office. The tactic worked. He was left alone.[58] The investigations also failed to touch Paul Seelinger, the former head of labor deployment in the ghetto, and Hermann Bruns, the former head of the Central Office for the Collection of Jewish Assets. Seeliger had died in Wesseling just before Christmas in 1955.[59] Bruns lived only a few months longer; his death is registered as 1 March 1956.[60] The justice system contributed a great deal to the reconstruction of the course of events in these crimes, and historians have much to thank it for. Unfortunately, investigators were not equipped with the proper tools to prosecute those members of the civil offices who had helped ex officio to plan and implement the mass murder of the Jews although they were seemingly far-removed from the scene of these terrible events, and who were indispensable in making it possible to carry out this genocide.

By contrast, those who stood at the pits, those who performed the "work" on site, could not hope that they had been forgotten. The survivors remembered their tormentors all too well. The pain, the torments, and the loss of so many family members were seared into their memory.[61] These ruminations also concerned those Latvians who – for whatever motives – had made common cause with the Germans and served with them.[62] After the Soviets had reconquered the Baltic lands, the second phase of Sovietization set in for the collaborators and nationalists, picking up seamlessly on the terror prior to the German invasion. Because the central authorities in Moscow harbored a deep-seated distrust of the remaining local population – independent of this situation, as many as 280,000 Latvians are said to have fled west – officers and soldiers from Baltic units of the Red Army were stationed in the country. These included in particular Estonians and Latvians who had been living in Russia since the end of nineteenth century as well as their descendents, who now were ordered to resettle to Latvia. Next, those in power resumed the deportations that had been interrupted in June 1941. These expulsions to the Soviet interior still seemed to the Soviets a suitable means of eliminating potential opponents to the regime. By the turn of 1944–1945, some 38,000 Latvians had been deported in a first wave; most of these men had served with the Wehrmacht. A second wave between summer 1945 and spring 1946 resulted in the relocation of 60,000 people to the east; this time, women and children were also included.[63]

Above all, members of the Latvian self-defense force and the Latvian police formations could hardly count on leniency. Those who fell into the hands of Red Army soldiers from the 3rd Baltic Front were interrogated by either the counter-espionage agency SMERSH or the KGB. Sentencing usually followed in a closed trial. A less incriminated perpetrator usually received a sentence of twenty-five years in a labor camp – with the mere fact that the accused had worked for the Germans at all sufficing for conviction. More incriminated persons had to reckon with a death sentence. In July 1945, Soviet intelligence issued a wanted list that included 2,822 names of alleged war criminals, most of whom were Latvian. Altogether, the KGB launched about 30,000 investigations in this connection.[64]

However, the most incriminated Latvians, such as Viktor Arajs, his deputy Herbert Cukurs, and many members of their special commando, had left Latvia, as had various Latvian police chiefs from the smaller towns and a large number of the rank-and-file. The chances of tracking down Arajs and bringing him before a court were quite favorable at the end of the war. After Germany's capitulation, he wound up in British captivity, passed through numerous camps, and was finally taken into detention, which he spent in Camp 3CI Fallingbostel. Although he had been exposed quickly enough, no further steps were authorized.[65] On 1 October 1948, he was separated from the others, because attention had again fallen upon him during a screening of prisoners. He was transferred to a remand center in Braunschweig, but the British military officials there could not find any-

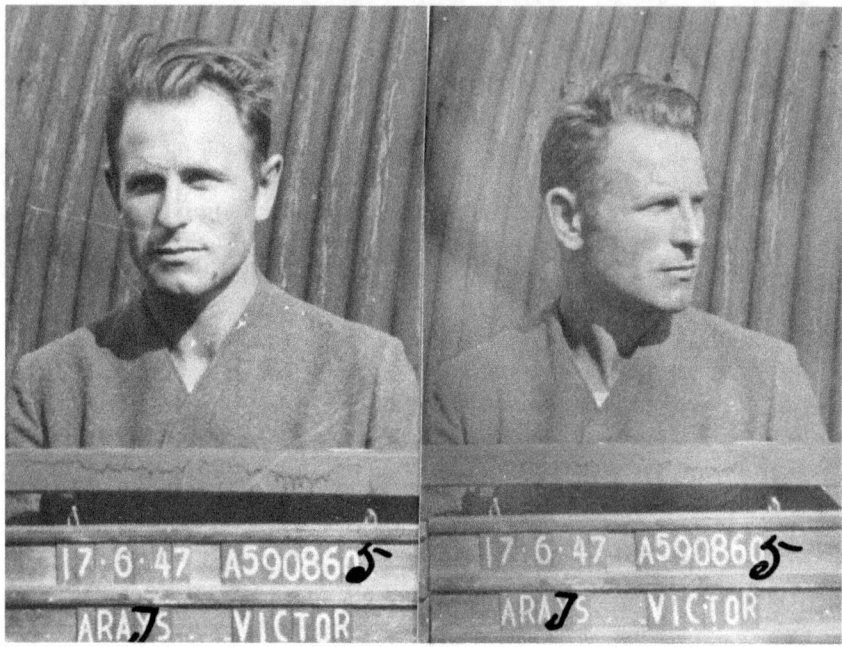

Figure 20.1. Viktor Arajs in a mug shot taken by the British military authorities in June 1947. Courtesy of the National Archives of the United Kingdom.

thing to prosecute him for, so he we was released on 1 February 1949. Arajs searched for a job and worked four or five months as a driver for a military office in Delmenhorst. Afraid his past would soon catch up to him, he assumed a new identity with the help of Latvian friends. When Hamburg investigators appeared in Delmenhorst to carry out an arrest warrant made out in the name of Arajs, they were forced to learn that he was on vacation. Arajs never returned. He had begun a new life under the name Viktor Zeibots and had settled in Frankfurt, where he found a steady job at the publishing house Neue Presse GmbH.[66]

Nothing could keep Cukurs in Germany. Together with his family, he had made his way to Marseille. Like Roschmann, he had received support from certain Catholic organizers and managed to flee to South America, where he had settled in Brazil.[67] There is a certain irony in the fact that – for completely different motives – survivors seeking a new homeland had also chosen Brazil. In Rio, the perpetrator crossed paths with a survivor, who then reported at length about the wanted man to the London-based Committee for the Investigation of Nazi Crimes in the Baltic Countries. After that, Cukurs was unable to go on living in Brazil anonymously. To the contrary, the prominent pilot also ran a floating bar on a lake and a boat dealership. A local newspaper called the owners by name and described them as an "unfortunate family that had fled the Russian terror in Latvia" and had found a new home in Rio.

Cukurs was kept under surveillance by the Committee for the Investigation of Nazi Crimes in the Baltic Countries; his address, his conduct of business, and his habits were noted, and a representative of the critical press set upon him. That Brazil could agree to extradition of the war criminal was considered unlikely. At first, it was simply important that Cukurs had been located and was under observation.[68] He stayed in Rio for years despite applications from West Germany and the Soviet Union, because as the father of a child born in Brazil – the official reason given – he could not be extradited. Moreover, he enjoyed the sympathy and protection of the domestic intelligence service DOPS. However, after a group of young Jews destroyed his boat dealership, he was forced to move to São Paulo.

Much more dangerous was the threat that emanated from the Israeli intelligence service Mossad, which had sought out Cukurs as a target for retaliatory action. On 1 September 1964, one of its agents was assigned to have the fugitive war criminal executed in a way that would be highly media-effective. The plan was to gain his trust surreptitiously, to take him out of the country – preferably to Uruguay – and to carry out the retaliatory action there. Acting as an Austrian businessman by the name of Anton Künzle, the Mossad agent flew to Brazil. Cukurs had built up a new business – boat rental, air taxi, and restaurant – on an artificial lake. Künzle quickly succeeded in establishing professional and personal contacts with Cukurs. A relationship of trust was soon established – which was to seal Cukurs's fate. Künzle succeeded in convincing Cukurs to organize a business trip that would take the two "friends" to Montevideo. Having arrived there, Künzle escorted his target to a villa located in the Carrasco quarter on 23 February 1965. A special commando from Mossad was waiting for them. Originally, it had been planned to execute Cukurs in a kind of court proceeding after the reading of an indictment in the name of Riga's murdered Jews and a verdict. However, Cukurs resisted and was killed by two shots to the head in the course of the row. The agents left behind a copy of the verdict in the name "of those who never forget." After the corpse was found by the police, the text of the verdict set off the desired reverberations in the media.[69]

Arajs, however, remained missing. With Cukurs's fate in all the papers, he did well not to attract attention to himself. For Latvian émigrés in Germany, a good deal of their conversation turned on the war and the loss of their homeland; it was therefore natural that somebody like Arajs was still a good topic. Rumors circulated that he was living under a false name in

West Germany, and that he had been seen at cultural events and meetings of exile Latvians, with like-minded nationalist Latvians providing protection for him. Even his cover name Victor Zeibots was apparently known to the initiated, such as the publisher Zanis Umans, who had also seen him in Frankfurt.[70] Partly due to the commotion that Cukurs's execution had unleashed in the German press the police, in March 1965, began receiving additional clues concerning Arajs, but the female informant was considered untrustworthy due to her "pro-Communist inclination." Making things more difficult was the fact that in the sessions of questioning that followed, the wanted man's assumed name – Zeibots, the maiden name of his wife, from whom Arajs had long since separated – was only noted phonetically as "Zeiboth" or "Zeibold."[71] After the appearance of the Soviet propaganda tract *Daugavas Vanagi – Who Are They?*, which attracted considerable attention among nationalist Latvian émigrés, the Central Office of the State Justice Administration for the Investigation of National Socialist Crimes in Ludwigsburg, Germany's primary agency for investigating war crimes, again intensified its efforts to find Arajs, but still lacked even a usable photograph of the man.[72]

The fact remained that Arajs could not be located, and interest in his person soon dried up again. Some years later, the Baden-Württemberg State Criminal Police informed the Ludwigsburg agency that Viktor Arajs was living under the name Viktors Abele in Mönchengladbach[73] or as Albert Arajs in Cologne.[74] The affair was again picked up in 1972, when rumors began circulating that the Soviet intelligence service had liquidated Arajs in secret.[75] In an extensive statement on the facts of the case, the Stuttgart Prosecutor's Office summed up the situation by saying that there had "hardly" been a "systematic investigation into Arajs" since 1964.[76] The hypothesis that he was dead could not be maintained. Instead, it was necessary to pick up his trail and to carry out the arrest warrant issued by the Hamburg Prosecutor's Office. On 10 July 1975, Viktor Zeibots of Frankfurt was arrested. Brought before the investigating judge that night, the man at first insisted that he was not Viktor Arajs. But after about twenty minutes of questioning, his evasions were to no avail; the suspect finally admitted to being the "man wanted for 30 years."[77]

After all the decades of searching for the chief of the Latvian murder commando, the proceedings before the Hamburg State Court proved relatively easy compared with other Nazi trials in the Hanseatic city. On 10 May 1976, Arajs was indicted. The burden of proof was so great – the defendant's inept tactics only made things worse – that he was sentenced to life in prison on 21 December 1979.[78] The trial itself took several years, primarily because witnesses in Israel, North America, and the Soviet Union had to be questioned. With the questioning of other members of the Arajs

Commando at the latest, it became clear that the cases of Cukurs and Arajs, beyond their personal involvement in the crimes, did not for stand for themselves alone. Instead, they had directed the attention of prosecutors in West Germany as well as the United States and Canada to the careers of other exiles in the west. Investigators there now began systematically tracking down offenders who, without being recognized, had succeeded in portraying themselves as political refugees and building up a middle-class existence in their host countries.

In the wake of the Arajs case, Albert Eichelis – in 1941 a member of the Latvian self-defense force in Riga, later Latvian district police chief in Rēzekne (Rositten) and Kuldīga (Goldingen) – was tried in the Landau State Court. Eichelis died before the verdict was announced.[79] Boleslavs Maikovskis, a former member of the prewar Aiszargi, which at the outset of German occupation had organized the self-defense force in Rēzekne, was also tried. After the war, he had managed to enter the United States, where he was allowed to settle and eventually held leading positions in exile Latvian organizations. Once his wartime activity had been examined in detail, he was forced to leave the United States. Maikovskis fled to Germany in autumn 1987 and applied for asylum. Instead of approving his application, the German authorities screened the reasons for his entry more closely. In the meantime, the Anti-Defamation League as well as Riga survivor Elliot Welles had tracked down the asylum seeker in Münster. An article about Maikovskis in the *New York Times* did the rest. Once suspicion hardened, the Central Office in North Rhine-Westphalia for the Processing of National Socialist Crimes of Violence at the Dortmund Prosecutor's Office, on 2 August 1989, indicted Maikovskis as a former member of the Latvian police for his involvement in various annihilation operations in the Rēzekne district.[80]

On 18 January 1990, when the trial against the 86-year-old defendant got underway in the Münster State Court, there were some people who asked whether such trials still made sense, as the era of National Socialism had long since passed into history and no longer concerned the present. The only people who can make that argument are those who were too young to remember the war or were born after it. People who – fortunately – played no role in the crimes and were not among the victims may have called for forgiveness and the mercy of forgetting. For the others, what mattered – and still matters – are the criminal code and the call for the aggrieved individual's vested right to see that murder does not fall under the statute of limitations, but is prosecuted. The proceedings against Maikovskis lasted for months. During this time, an era was quickly coming to an end in the Baltic, as had already happened in Germany with the fall of the Berlin Wall and reunification.

The former tsarist provinces, later Soviet republics, then German general commissariats, and once again Soviet republics left Russia's sphere of influence to proclaim independence. Lithuania acted as the outrider on 11 March 1990, with Estonia and Latvia following on 20 and 21 August 1991. Latvia remembered its past in such a way that it considered the phase of Soviet and German rule as an interruption of state sovereignty and consequently adopted the "suspended" constitution of 1922 anew in 1993. The greater part of Soviet or Russian troops had left the country by April 1997; the last group departed in October 1999. With that, Latvia lost its status as an occupied country. If the recurrence of important family names symbolizes continuity of political ideals, then this is the case Latvia as well. From 1993 to 1999, Guntis Ulmanis, a great nephew of Karlis Ulmanis, served as the reestablished country's head of state.[81]

Jewish life also returned to Riga. The former building of the Jewish Council now houses a school as well as a kitchen for the poor. These and other facilities to ease the life of Riga's Jewish minority are supported not least of all by families living abroad or the descendents of those for whom Riga was once a home or place of deportation. Maybe it will be possible to reverse the disappearance of Jewish life, which is influenced chiefly by emigration and mortality.[82]

To what extent the new state will confront its history and in particular the judicial review of its darkest chapter remains to be seen – despite the raising of a monument in the forest of Bikernieki. An end to the criminal cases is not to be reckoned with yet. In Germany, the last investigation against a former Latvian guard, Juris Kauls, who was charged with participating in crimes in the Riga ghetto, came to a close in May 2000. Faced with a pending trial in the United States, Kauls had fled to West Germany and applied for citizenship in Münster in 1995.[83] Nonetheless, there still exists the possibility that a suspect from Canada or the United States will be extradited to Latvia. Only then will it be clear whether this new member of the European Union is as capable of setting standards in addressing the country's past, above all in researching collaboration, as it has been in restructuring its economy.[84]

Notes

1. Among the organizations that looked after the needs of the Latvian Jews deported to Germany were the Union of Baltic Jews in London, the Munich-based Federation of Liberated Latvian Jews in the U.S. zone of occupation, the Central Committee of Liberated Jews in the British zone, headquartered at Bergen-Belsen, and the Central Committee of Liberated

Jews in the American-occupied Zone in Germany, also headquartered in Munich, see Staw. Hamburg, 141 Js 534/60, Beiakte 1, Staw. Mannheim an den Untersuchungsrichter 2a, LG Hamburg, 2 November 1949, 46–46r.
2. This section draws from Josef Foschepoth, *Im Schatten der Vergangenheit*, 29–41; Donate Strathmann, *Auswandern oder hierbleiben?*, 33–49 and 262–263; Katz, *Erinnerungen eines Überlebenden*, 262–263. On the difficulty of choosing between homeland and emigration, see Sasha Semenoff, "After the Liberation," in Schneider, *Muted Voices*, 231–237. On the return of the former officials and incriminated policemen, see Stefan Noethen, *Alte Kameraden und neue Kollegen*, especially 380–408. Noethen's is the first study to investigate the problem of returning National Socialist functionaries – in this case the police in North Rhine-Westphalia – using a broad empirical sample.
3. Staw. Hamburg, 141 Js 534/60, SB 7, circular from the Federation of the Liberated Latvian Jews, Munich, May 1948, 1,408–1,412. This letter to Latvian Jews in Germany contains various lists: two lists of suspects who had been located or gone underground, a list of suspect Latvians who had received an entry visa for the United States, a list summarizing inquiries about various victims whose fate was unknown, and a list of Latvian Jews who now found themselves in the U.S. zone.
4. Archive of the Interior Ministry, Prague, 114-9-95, which contains an extensively documented account of the events surrounding Stahlecker's death. The quote comes from Gruppenarzt der EG A, SS-O'Stbaf. Meixner v. 25.3.1942, Bericht über Verwundung und Tod des Brigadeführers Dr. Walter Stahlecker, 30 (of file).
5. Maclean, *The Camp Men*, 197; Staw. Hamburg, 141 Js 534/60, Bd. 2, statement by Georg Netler, 7 December 1949, 200r.
6. BA Ludwigsburg, 202 AR-Z 12/66, Bd. 3, statement by Wilhelm Vogler, 4 May 1971, 899.
7. Staw. Hamburg, 141 Js 534/60, Bd. 2, statement by Helmut Fürst, 23 January 1950, 252; ibid., Bd. 6, statement by Hildegard Reinecke, 22 October 1959, 204; ibid., Bd. 33, statement by Samuel Gutkin, 21 March 1963, 5,448. Fürst, a survivor of the December 1941 Hanover-Riga transport, claimed that he had seen Krause's funeral procession. The dates given for Krause's death diverge. Some sources say February 1945. In the late 1990s, the Central Office in North Rhine-Westphalia for the Processing of National Socialist Crimes of Violence at the Dortmund Prosecutor's Office concluded that Krause had probably been killed by partisans in the vicinity of Liepāja on 8 December 1944, see BA Ludwigsburg 207 AR-Z 9/98 [= Zentralstelle im Lande Nordrhein-Westfalen für die Bearbeitung von nationalsozialistischen Gewaltverbrechen bei der Staatsanwaltschaft Dortmund 45 Js 2/99], Bd. 5, Schlußvermerk der Zentralen Stelle Ludwigsburg, 15 March 1999, 1,122.
8. *Kieler Nachrichtenblatt*, "Anklage gegen Generale," 29 January 1946, and "12 Hinrichtungen in Kiew," 31 January 1946, located in Staw. Hamburg, 141 Js 534/60, Bd. 57 (Beweismittelordner). The analysis of the contemporary press, carried out by the Institute for the World Economy on behalf of the Hamburg Prosecutor's Office, claimed that no other indication of "military court trials against Germans in Riga" were to be found in the institute's holdings, see ibid., Institut für Weltwirtschaft an die Staw. Hamburg, 3 June 1970.
9. The trial against Jeckeln, as well as other trials, is available at BA DH, ZM 1683. The last volume contains the verdict, see Birn, *Die Höheren SS- und Polizeiführer*, 337.
10. Staw. Hamburg, 141 Js 534/60, Beiakte (Überstücke), Willy Weiss an den Magistrat von Groß-Berlin, Hauptamt Opfer des Faschismus, 18 July 1949.
11. Staw. Hamburg, 141 Js 534/60, Bd. 3, statement by Hans Lange, 21 October 1949, 155r–156; ibid., Beiakte 35, copies from Spruchkammerverfahren 12 Sp Js 14/49 Hamburg Bergedorf, 17–28.

12. This section is based on Staw. beim LG Berlin, 1 Js. 9/65, Dossier Lange = 1 AR (Stapoleit) 172/67. This contains Lange's SS officer file from the Berlin Document Center, witness statements, and sworn affidavits. The account of his activity in Poznań (Posen) is given according to the recommendation for the German Cross in Gold, dated 5 February 1945, as well as the sworn affidavits of Hans-Kurt Moser, 21 April 1948, and 15 March 1951. The military course of events from the German view are from the *Kriegstagebuch des Oberkommandos der Wehrmacht*, Bd. IV, entries for 20 January –23 February 1945, 1,057–1,119, quote 1,062. From the Soviet point of view, see Gretschko et al., *Geschichte des zweiten Weltkrieges*, Bd. 10, 95–101.
13. The confusion was complicated by the fact that Lange's first name was abbreviated to Rolf in the protocols, see Staw. Hamburg, 141 Js 534/60, Beiakte 1, statement by Hermann and Hilde Schmitt, 31 January 1947, 49r–51. This part of the investigation actually resulted from a family argument, because a cousin of Lange's mother-in-law had told officials that Mrs. Lange or her parents possessed Jewish property that Lange had sent his wife from Riga.
14. Schneider, *Journey into Terror*, 163, ft. 31. Schneider and her mother visited Lange's wife in 1971. According to Schneider, Lange's wife did not make the impression of a widow to either visitor, because she blushed during the conversation. Also, in Schneider's opinion, Lange's wounding in Poznań was not proof of his death. Even if Schnieder's line of argument regarding Lange's state of health in Poznań were followed, the logical consequence would be Soviet captivity, with Lange getting rid of the SS uniform in advance. Suggesting that he managed to do so and keep his true identity secret throughout years of captivity – all of which implies Schneider's criticism of confirmed facts – seems rather far-fetched.
15. Some survivors testified positively about Nickel. For example, Siegfried Kaufmann of Kassel said, "Our permanent overseer in the camp Salaspils was SS Technical Sergeant Nickel of Berlin, to whom a guard commando of about 50 Latvian SS men was subordinated. I can say that this man was a very decent person, whom I tried to contact again after the war. I wanted to help him to the extent that he might have needed it. Unfortunately, I didn't meet him again or hear anything from him." See Staw. Hamburg, 141 Js 534/60, Bd. 11, statement by Siegfried Kaufmann, 23 November 1960, 1,148. Nickel himself was never located and is considered missing in action, see BA Ludwigsburg 207 AR-Z 9/98, Bd. 5, Schlußvermerk der Zentralen Stelle Ludwigsburg, 15 March 1999, 1,121.
16. Staw. Hamburg, 141 Js 534/60, Bd. 1, 14 Js 210/49, Anklageschrift der Staw. Hamburg gegen Seck u.a., 1 June 1951, (50) 14/51 and 14 Js 210/49 Urteil des Schwurgerichts Hamburg, 29 December 1951, 127–156r. We rely on a draft version of the indictment here, because it contains even more comprehensive passages – later omitted – on the objective course of the crime, which is of more benefit to the historian. See also Helge Grabitz, *Täter und Gehilfen des Endlösungswahns*, 73–74.
17. Staw. Hamburg, 141 Js 534/60, Bd. 1, Anlage 1, Aktenübersicht, 5 December 1950, Liste der Angeschuldigten; Schneider, *Journey into Terror*, 75.
18. Staw. Hamburg, 141 Js 534/60, Bd. 32, Vermerk des Leitenden Oberstaatsanwalt beim LG Hamburg, 26 April 1963, on Johannes Zingler's death on 18 April 1963, 5,266; ibid., Bd. 85, Die Landespolizei Schleswig Holstein an das LG Hamburg, 25 June 1971, and the death certificate for Herbert Degenhardt, 24 June 1971, 13,462–13,463.
19. Staw. Hamburg, 141 Js 534/60 [Teilkomplex A], Bd. 85, Verfügung der Staw., 12 January 1971, 13,402.
20. Staw. Hamburg, 147 Js 5/71 (141 Js 534/60), Anklageschrift gegen Heinrich Oberwinder u.a., 21 December 1971.
21. Oberwinder and Jahnke were born in 1895, Hemicker in 1896.

22. Staw. Hamburg, 141 Js 534/60 [Teilkomplex A], Bd. 86, Vermerk der Staw., 13 December 1971, 13,625. In this document, a doctor's expert opinion was ordered, which later confirmed that Hemicker was unfit to stand trial.
23. Ibid., Bd. 89, Beschluß des LG Hamburg in der Strafsache gegen Heinrich Oberwinder, 13 March 1972, 13,996–14,001. The decision of the Hamburg State Court was to some extent understandable, because Oberwinder had been primarily incriminated by former Commander of the Gendarmerie Latvia Richard Rehberg, who had repeatedly and knowingly made false statements, and who apparently harbored a dislike of Oberwinder. As a result, Oberwinder's indictment was shaky.
24. Ibid., Bd. 94, (50)9/72 Urteil des Schwurgerichts Hamburg gegen Jahnke u.a., 23 February 1972, 14,910–15,123. On sentencing see ibid., 15,117–15,123 (214–220 of the verdict). During the proceedings, the indictment of Emil Diedrich, the former commander of the 3rd Company, Police Battalion 22, which was deployed in the evacuation of the ghetto, was linked "to a joint hearing and decision." See ibid., Bd. 92, Beschluß in der Hauptverhandlung des Schwurgerichts, 4 October 1972, 14,466. In Diedrich's case as well, the court refrained from punishment due to his "marginal guilt."
25. The most important stays of legal proceedings are: Staw. Hamburg, 141 Js 534/60 [Teilkomplex A], Bd. 85, Einstellungsverfügung v. 1.6.1972 hinsichtlich verstorbener und nicht zu ermittelnder Beschuldigter der Dienststelle HSSPF Ostland bzw. der Ordnungspolizei, 13,484–13,493; Einstellungsverfügung betreffend die Angehörigen des Kommandos der Schutzpolizei, 8 June 1972, 13,504–13,542; ibid., Bd. 86, Einstellungsverfügung betreffend ehemalige Angehörige der Dienststellen des HSSPF Ostland, SSPF Riga, KdO Lettland und des KdG Lettland, 7 July 1972, 13,551–13,595; Einstellungsverfügung betreffend ehemalige Angehörige der Dienststelle des Kommandeurs der Schutzpolizei Riga, 10 July 1972, 13,596–13,602; Einstellungsverfügung weitere ehemalige Angehörige besagter Dienststellen betreffend, 2 March 1973, 13,621–13,626; Einstellungsverfügung in gleicher Sache, 8 June 1973, 13,653–13,688; ibid., Bd. 87, Abschlußverfügung in gleicher Sache, 11 February 1974, 13,763–13,778; Abschlußverfügung in gleicher Sache, 27 August 1976. With this last stay of legal proceedings, the investigation into Rumbula – Sachkomplex A within the Riga investigation – was closed.
26. For a longer discussion on the difficulties of convicting perpetrators, see, for example, Adalbert Rückerl, *NS-Verbrechen vor Gericht*, especially 124–139.
27. Staw. Hamburg, 141 Js 534/60, Bd. 11, statement by Rudolf Batz, 26 January 1961, 1,255–1,258; statements by Rudolf Batz, 11, 14, and 15 November 1960, 1,286–1,300a. According to his own statements, Batz ran Dept. II at BdS Netherlands, whereas in Cracow he also acted as deputy to the BdS East [i.e. General Government], SS Senior Colonel Walther Bierkamp. In Germany, he had temporarily belonged to the Gestapo regional office in Breslau as deputy chief. Formally, he spent the longest stint of his career, from January 1940 until September 1943, running the Gestapo regional office in Hanover, with his activity in Latvia being recorded as only a short-term deployment outside the Reich. In the wake of Germany's annexation of Austria, Batz organized the Gestapo district office in Linz. Solely on the basis of this list of postings, it must have been clear to Batz that he risked being questioned regarding numerous crimes, if not incriminated, on top of proceedings that had already been launched. On his biography, see Wilhelm, *Die Einsatzgruppe*, 476. The position of KdS Estonia mentioned in Wilhelm is incorrect; a mix-up occurred with Bernhard Baatz.
28. BA Ludwigsburg, 207 AR-Z 101/67, Bd. 2, Schlußbericht der Zentralen Stelle Ludwigsburg, 27 August 1970, 349.
29. On Hudal's efforts in obtaining passports and facilitating escapes, see Ernst Klee, *Persilscheine und falsche Pässe*, 32–50.

30. Holger M. Meding, *Flucht vor Nürnberg?*, 127–128 and 148–149; Hella Pick, *Simon Wiesenthal*, 333–337 and 480–481, quote 336, according to an interview with Forsyth; BA Ludwigsburg, 207 AR-Z 9/98, Bd. 5, Schlußvermerk der Zentralen Stelle Ludwigsburg, 15 March 1999, 1,122. In Staw. Hamburg, 141 Js 534/60, there were constant inquiries regarding Roschmann. After the death certificate arrived, the corpse was examined and – due to a deformity of his feet – its identity unmistakably confirmed.
31. Schneider, *Journey into Terror*, 75–76. Schneider quite rightly stresses that Roschmann's criminal acts were more evident in connection with Sk 1005 – also called the "base" starting in mid 1944 – than with the ghetto.
32. BA Ludwigsburg, 204 AR-Z 419/62, Bd. 6, Ks 22/67 Urteil des Schwurgerichts Stuttgart gegen Hans Sohns u.a., 13 March 1969, 1,068–1,265. The quotes regarding Helfsgott are on 1,253 and 1,259. On "necessity," see Rückerl, *NS-Verbrechen vor Gericht*, 285–286.
33. BA Ludwigsburg, 207 AR-Z 7/59, Bd. 13, (37) 3/76, Urteil des LG Hamburg gegen Gerhard Maywald, 2 August 1977, 3,011–3,072, quotes 3,064 and 3,072. With this verdict, Teilbereich C (KdS Latvia) was closed.
34. Staw. Hamburg, 141 Js 534/60 [Teilkomplex B, Einsatzgruppe A], Bd. 85, Anklageschrift gegen Tschierschky u.a., 13,310–12,368; ibid., Bd. 87 (50) 44/74, 147 Ks 3/74 Urteil des LG Hamburg, 11 March 1975, 13,782–13,857. Quotes regarding Trühe, 13,842 and 13,843; quotes on Besekow, 13,856.
35. BA Ludwigsburg, 207 AR 128/78, Bd. 1, Verfügung der Staw. Hamburg, 31 October 1977, on the separation of the case against Heinz Wisner, 6. It is stated here that Hans Brüner, the deputy commandant and head of the main labor deployment office, had lived in Cologne and had died before the case against the camp leadership was opened.
36. BA Ludwigsburg, Dokumentation, Verschiedenes 301 En, 226, General Tribunal der Militärregierung der französischen Besatzungs-Zone in Deutschland, Bestätiges Urteil, 17 April 1948 (after the reading of the verdict on 20 February 1948), 171–175. The full protocol of this session, with the statements of the witnesses and the defendant, is preserved in BA Ludwigsburg AR-Z 7/59, Bd. 9, 1,788a–1803.
37. The quick and efficient work of the Central Office Cologne this time may lie in the fact that the charges were aimed at an individual, and that the Prosecutor's Office Hamburg had provided a large part of the evidence. Cologne investigators were therefore able to concentrate on questioning the relevant witnesses and former officials.
38. BA Ludwigsburg, Sammelakte Nr. 580 XV – 8/84 S, 130 Js 2/78 (Z), Urteil des LG Düsseldorf, 14 August 1985. On the facts of the case and the sentencing, see 95–117, quotes from 101 and 104.
39. Only a part of the commandant's office could be reconstructed and located. It is known that labor deployment was run by an SS man named Kauffeld, who had replaced the aforementioned SS Technical Sergeant Hans Brüner. The clothing store was run by SS Technical Sergeant Karl Hirsch, who also had administrative tasks. SS Technical Sergeant Patzack had been assigned to him.
40. Bundesarchiv Ludwigsburg, 202 AR-Z 12/66, Bd. 3, statement by Vogler, 4 May 1971, 892–893. Vogler had been the administrative chief for the Waffen-SS supply command in Army Group Center, to which the infamous forest camp (a camp for Jews) Bobruisk had belonged. Starting in September 1943, he was deployed to Concentration Camp Stutthof and served as administrative head at Kaiserwald from May 1944 until evacuation. His subsequent postings were again Stutthof and finally Bergen-Belsen, which is where he was when the war ended. In May 1947 – according to his own information – he was convicted by a Polish court for his deployment in Stutthof, but was released early, because a punishable act could not be proven. The possible responsibility of labor deployment chief Brüner

and one of Vogler's predecessors, SS Captain Michl, remains unexamined. On the most incriminated SS men at Kaiserwald, see Kaufmann, *Churbn Lettland,* 317–318.
41. Grabowska, "K.L. Stutthof," 91–92. In addition to the persons named above, Albert Paulitz, Fritz Peters, Karl Zurell, Kurt Dietrich, Karl Eggert, Paul Wellnitz, and the Kapo Alfred Nikolaysen were sentenced to death. Grabowska discusses the other cases against members of Stutthof's personnel, the political department officials, and Kapos.
42. *Justiz und NS-Verbrechen,* Bd. XIV, Lfd. Nr. 446, Urteile des LG Bochum v. 4.6.1957 und 16.12.1955, 17 Ks 1/55, gegen Hoppe und Knott, 151–226. The verdict of the Federal Court of Justice of 8 November 1956, which allowed an appeal by the Prosecutor's Office and thus made possible the resumption of proceedings, is also printed here on pages 227–234. It is known that Hoppe led an inconspicuous, middle-class life after being pardoned just before Christmas 1960. Nonetheless, his wartime experiences did not let go of him. He felt threatened by an "Eastern Bloc" conspiracy and – just before his death in July 1974 – suspected his son of being an Israeli spy who was seeking to kidnap him so that he could be tried in Israel, see Segev, *Die Soldaten des Bösen,* 12–17; Karin Orth, *Die Konzentrationslager-SS,* 293–295.
43. *Fall 12,* 133–144 and 291; Jörg Friedrich, *Das Gesetz des Krieges,* 920–924.
44. See the memoirs of Franz von Roques, BA-MA, N 153/1, Berück Nord, 31.
45. Lasch, *So fiel Königsberg,* 118–119.
46. Ute Schmidt, "Spätheimkehrer oder 'Schwerstkriegsverbrecher'?" in Hilger et al., *Sowjetische Militärtribunale,* Bd. 1, 274–350. Lasch belonged to the group of 749 soldiers who were not pardoned upon their release. Of these soldiers, 177 were generals or admirals, see also 297–299.
47. This Friedrich Ellrodt is most probably the same Friedrich Ellrodt who served as director of the Labor Office in Weiden, Oberpfalz, at the end of the 1950s. He was mentioned repeatedly by witnesses in cases concerning not only Riga. We could not find any statement from him in the files that we examined, cf. BA Ludwigsburg, 420 AR-Z 75/68, SB(A) Zeugen, statement by Theodor Fründt, 18 April 1968.
48. Reitlinger, *Die Endlösung,* 585. Because Koch was already very sick and mentally deranged, his sentence was commuted to life in prison. Koch died in a Polish prison in 1986.
49. Wilhelm, *Einsatzgruppe A,* 486. The Bielefeld trial is registered as Bielefeld 2 Sp Ls 179/47. On the investigations into Lohse and others among the RKO leadership, see BA Ludwigsburg, 207 AR-Z 497/67, Bd. 4, Einstellungsverfügung der Staw. Kiel, 15 August 1972, 549–568, here 554. The object of this investigation was the extent to which members of the RKO administration bore responsibility for the annihilation of the Roma (gypsies) within their jurisdiction as a consequence of centrally managed measures issued by their agencies. See also BA Ludwigsburg, 420 AR-Z 75/68, Bd. 2, Einstellungsverfügung der Staw. Kiel, 17 May 1971, 421–476, here 422. The issue under investigation here was the extent to which more or less the same group of persons was involved in measures involving the annihilation of the Jews in Ostland. In Lohse's case, it is clear that in the 1950s the sources – which were either still in the United States or had to be viewed and copied in Moscow's archives by prosecutors from the Central Office Ludwigsburg within the framework of legal assistance – were not yet available, which was why it was hard to confront Lohse with his crimes.
50. BA Ludwigsburg, 420 AR-Z 75/68, Bd. 2, Einstellungsverfügung der Staw. Kiel, 17 May 1971, 421–476, especially 422–424, 434, 437–440, 458–461, and 471.
51. BA Ludwigsburg, 207 AR-Z 497/67, Bd. 4, Einstellungsverfügung der Staw. Kiel, 15 August 1972, 564–565.

52. Regarding the search for Alletag, see Staw. Hamburg, 141 Js 534/60, Bd. 86, Linden Polizei an StAnw. Hamburg, 27 November 1973, 13,715–13,716.
53. Staw. Hamburg, 141 Js 534/60, Bd. 54, statement by Walther Schröder, 10 December 1964, 8,814. Drechsler thus avoided the fate of his colleague General Commissar Lithuania Adrian von Renteln, who was executed in 1946.
54. BA Ludwigsburg, 207 AR-Z 9/98, Bd. 5, Schlußvermerk der Zentralen Stelle Ludwigsburg, 15 March 1999, 1,126; Wittrock, *Kommissarischer Oberbürgermeister*, 57.
55. Wittrock, *Kommissarischer Oberbürgermeister*, 7–8, from the introduction by Wilhelm Lenz, the memoirs' editor.
56. A few examples – in addition to the already named officials – are the following statements: Staw. Hamburg, 141 Js 534/60, Bd. 86, statement by Egon Rauch, 26 February 1964, 13,634–13,639; BA Ludwigsburg, 7 AR-Z 75/68, SB(A) Zeugen, statement by Kurt Köster, 23 June 1965; ibid., SB (B) Zeugen, statement by Willy Neuendorff, 2 March 1964; ibid., statement by Egon Rauch, 26 February 1964.
57. See Staw. Koblenz, 9 Js 298/63; *Braunbuch*, ed. Nationalrat der Nationalen Front des Demokratischen Deutschland and Dokumentationszentrum der staatlichen Archivverwaltung der DDR, 42–43; Annette Weinke, *Die Verfolgung von NS-Tätern im geteilten Deutschland*, 285–286.
58. Staw. Hamburg, 141 Js 534/60, Bd. 86, Vermerk [on Brasch's refusal to make a statement], 13 April 1973, 13,650; ibid., Sonderkommission des LKA an die Staw. Hamburg, 3 July 1973, 13,693.
59. Ibid., Bd. 87, Sonderkommission des LKA an die Staw. Hamburg, 26 September 1973, 13,761.
60. Ibid., Bd. 86, Staw. Hamburg an die Staw. Kiel, 10 April 1973, 13,641.
61. Jules R. Lippert, "The Return to Riga," in *Muted Voices*, 261–262.
62. Reichelt, "Kollaboration und Holocaust in Lettland 1941–1945," 119–120.
63. Levits, "Lettland under der Sowjetherrschaft," in Meissner, *Die baltischen Nationen*, 145. Based on Levits's figures, the number of those who fled west amounted to 20 percent of the ethnic Latvian population. All of the other figures are according to Simon, *Nationalismus und Nationalitätenpolitik in der Sowjetunion*, 251–252.
64. Robert G. Waite, "Kollaboration und deutsche Besatzungspolitik in Lettland 1941 bis 1945," in *Okkupation und Kollaboration (1938–1945)*, ed. Werner Röhr, 236–237. The information on the interrogations and sentences comes from translations of Latvian criminal cases excerpted in the files of the Hamburg Prosecutor's Office or the Central Office Ludwigsburg. The KGB cases mentioned by Waite were at the time inaccessible to scholars, but are now housed at LVA and can be analyzed by researchers.
65. PRO Kew, WO 308-1707, Dossier Arajs. According to these records, the former SS major and lawyer Viktor Arajs – who was wanted according to Crowcass lists and Special List 7 – was in 2227 PW. Camp in Schleswig. On 17 June 1947, the authorities had photos of Arajs made – perhaps to show witnesses – and placed in the file. We thank Stephen Tyas of St. Albans for the reference to this document.
66. Staw. Hamburg, 141 Js 534/60, Anklageschrift against Viktor Arajs, 10 May 1976, 9–11; LG Hamburg, (37) Ks 5/76, Urteil gegen Viktor Arajs, 31 December 1979, 6–7.
67. Künzle and Shimron, *Der Tod des Henkers von Riga*, 79–80. A survivor by the name of Myriam Kaicner also arrived in Rio with the Cukurs family. Cukurs had hidden her in Riga and seen to her survival – even after her transfer to Reich territory. For reasons never fully explained, she accompanied the family and defended the man others called the "hangman of Riga" before a Jewish investigating committee, see ibid.
68. Staw. Hamburg, 141 Js 534/60, Beiakte 14, Committee for the Investigation of Nazi Crimes in the Baltic Countries an den Untersuchungsrichter Vogt in Hamburg,

15 February 1950, with appendix, 73–75. The committee refrained from passing on to the Hamburg officials the name of its informant and submitted only excerpts from his report.
69. Künzle and Shimron, *Der Tod des Henkers*, 81–83, 205–216, and 226–233. The full text of the verdict against Cukurs is in Staw. Hamburg, 141 Js 534/60, SB 2, Das Verfahren gegen den Kriegsverbrecher Herberts Cukurs und dessen Hinrichtung, 356–357.
70. Ibid., SB 1, LKA Niedersachsen an die Zentralle Stelle, 31 March 1965, 123. Here the wanted man is correctly identified as Viktor Zeibots. It is said that in particular a certain Urdse, a Latvian pastor in Oldenburg, was one of Arajs's confidants. See also ibid., SB 2, statement by Zanis Unams, 11 February 1974, 336–337.
71. Ibid., SB 1, Polizeidirektion Hannover an die Sonderkommission Z des LKA Niedersachsen, 10 March 1965, 124; Bericht der Sonderkommission Z, 31 March 1965, 125–126.
72. Ibid., Stellvertretender Leiter der Zentralen Stelle, Dr. Artzt, an den lettischen Staatsverlag, Riga, 30 June 155. Apparently, Ludwigsburg did not know – at least at this point – about the photographs made of Arajs in British custody. The Latvian State Publishing House later placed photos from their collection at the disposal of the Germans.
73. Ibid., LKA Baden-Württemberg an die Zentrale Stelle, 29 August 1972, 154.
74. Ibid., SB 2, Staw. Stuttgart an die Staw. Hamburg, 22 February 1974, 343–344, 345–346, which contains information concerning the screening of Albert Arajs. What was rather piquant was that Albert Arajs was working on behalf of the Office for the Protection of the Constitution in Cologne and may have even entered into a similar arrangement with British intelligence. This ultimately incorrect trail hampered progress immensely, because it became necessary to expect obstruction in the investigations. Albert Arajs's activities had been known to authorities for a long time, however.
75. Ibid., SB 3, Aktenvermerk des Landeskriminalamts Baden-Württemberg zur Festnahme des staatenlosen Letten Zeibots, 11 July 1975, 515–521. On the alleged attempted murder on the part of the Soviet secret service, see 516.
76. Ibid., SB 2, Sachverhaltsdarstellung, Staw. Stuttgart, 22 January 1974, 388–296, quote 394. The "correct cover name" of Arajs alias Zeibots was noted here.
77. Ibid., SB 3, Vermerk, Staw. Hamburg, 10 July 1975; LKA Stuttgart, Fernschreiben, Nr. 3188 and Nr. 3286, 11 July 1975, 509–510, quote on 510; statement by Viktor Zeibots, 11 July 1975, 526–531; statement by Viktor Arajs, 11 July 1975, 587–587r.
78. Ibid., Anklageschrift gegen Viktor Arajs, 10 May 1976, 9–11; LG Hamburg, (37) Ks 5/76, Urteil gegen Viktor Arajs, 31 December 1979, 177.
79. BA Ludwigsburg, 207 AR 751/64, Bd. 5, Staw. Landau, 7 Js 585/76, Anklageschrift gegen Albert Eichelis, 27 June 1977, 780–891; Staw. Landau an die Zentrale Stelle, 13 June 1985, 916.
80. Ibid., Anklageschrift der Zentralstelle im Lande Nordrehein-Westfalen für die Bearbeitung von nationalsozialistischen Gewaltverbrechen bei der Staatsanwaltschaft Dortmund gegen Boleslavs Maikovskis, 2 August 1989, 952–1,043.
81. Michael Garleff, *Die Baltischen Länder*, 189–190 and 201.
82. Wilfried Schlau, "Der Wandel in der sozialen Struktur der baltischen Länder," in Meissner, *Die baltischen Nationen*, 376. Accordingly, from 1959 to 1989, the share of Jews as a part of Latvia's population declined as a percentage (from 1.7 percent to 0.9 percent) and in absolute numbers (from 36,592 to 22,897 persons). This trend could not be stopped; in fact, the opposite took place. In 2001, the number of Jews in Latvia declined to 9,992 persons (of whom 5,770 have Latvian citizenship) and accounted for only 0.4 percent of Latvia's total population, see Eva-Clarita Onken, *Demokratisierung der Geschichte in Lettland*, 95.

83. BA Ludwigsburg 207 AR-Z 9/98, Bd. 5, 45 Js 2/99, Zentralstelle im Lande Nordrehein-Westfalen für die Bearbeitung von nationalsozialistischen Gewaltverbrechen bei der Staatsanwaltschaft Dortmund, 2 May 2002, 1,162–1,168. In his curriculum vitae, Kauls claimed that he had been deployed at Concentration Camp Riga. According to the findings of the Central Office Dortmund, neither the ghetto nor Kaiserwald is meant, but a prison on Samarin St. that people called "Concentration Camp Riga." Because no criminal action could be proven in Kauls's case, the investigation had to be closed.
84. Onken, *Demokratiserung*, 179–208.

– Chapter 21 –

Conclusion

The murder of tens of thousands of indigenous and deported Jews in Riga between 1941 and 1944 makes up just one part of the "final solution of the Jewish question" in German-occupied Europe. Nonetheless, the example of the Latvian capital raises a good number of historical issues and questions that are of particular importance for the study of the Holocaust. For instance, the question of the extent of Latvian collaboration, a topic of discussion to this day, cannot be limited to, say, the number of men who served in the Arajs Commando and the student associations from which they were recruited. This may well lead to clear conclusions about the size of that particular group of local murderers and accomplices, but such assessments will continue to provide only a patchwork overview so long as the field lacks more detailed studies on the Latvian auxiliary police formations deployed under German command outside Latvia in the struggle against real and ostensible partisans.

Moreover, this survey has made clear that the German-supervised Latvian administration, acting on its own initiative, fulfilled indispensable empirical tasks in certain sectors such as the registration of Jewish workshops, enterprises, and apartments. With that, the field of willful cooperation with the German authorities expands into broad areas of communal economic policy, where Latvian-supervised enterprises important to the war effort as well as the indigenous civilian population figure into the equation. Although there is no evidence that an absolute majority of Riga's non-Jewish population approved of the mass shootings, in the first weeks of 1942 there was certainly a great deal of interest in purchasing on the cheap everyday household items from that part of the ghetto whose inhabitants had been murdered.

Furthermore, if 60 percent of the ghetto inhabitants able to work left the ghetto every day in order to go to their jobs, which were spread out over 200 enterprises throughout Riga, then the work details of persons outwardly marked as Jews were a familiar feature of the cityscape. The citizens of Riga did not have to witness what had happened at Bikernieki and Rumbula; it was enough for them to note that thousands of Latvian-Jewish forced laborers were apparently missing and a lot of Jews from the west had taken over their jobs. Although the occupiers were already coming under increasing criticism by autumn 1941, due, for example, to their robust labor deployment policies vis-à-vis Riga's ethnic Latvian civilians, it remains an open question as to whether the mass murder of Jews was among those first events that made Riga's non-Jewish population come around to seeing the Germans, whom they had initially greeted as liberators, as despots instead.

In spring 1942, the ghetto developed into a labor reservoir for the fully understaffed metropolis. If the Wehrmacht had been the initiator in the ghetto's founding for economic considerations, it remained the primary beneficiary of the physical exploitation of the Jews. This addresses the significant involvement of the Army and Air Force's logistics offices in that exploitation, which by no means was to be observed in Riga alone. Because the present focus of research on the Wehrmacht's role in the Holocaust and the war of annihilation against the Soviet Union is mostly on the reconstruction of specific criminal actions and the German military's contributions to those crimes, analysis of the competition of interests between the Wehrmacht and the Security Police over the "final solution of the Jewish question" and the resulting withdrawal of much-needed workers will have to await additional regional studies. In the case of Riga, however, it can be shown that the local Wehrmacht offices also worked smoothly with the Security Police when the latter seized responsibility for the distribution of Jewish workers. For the military, it did not matter whether a Jewish forced laborer was a ghetto inhabitant or a concentration camp inmate.

After the local civil administration's first plodding steps to register Riga's Jews as workers and its unsuccessful attempt to exclude them from the labor market in autumn 1941, the unannounced murder operations carried out by the office of the Higher SS and Police Leader Ostland initially destroyed those administrative structures that had been established. Soon thereafter, there followed the arrival of the German Jews, who for their part first had to be withdrawn from the Security Police's power of disposal. The Security Police may have always insisted on maintaining decision-making authority over the fate of the deportees, but given the shortage of replacement workers, it could not undermine the deployment of the German Jews as forced laborers on behalf of manufactures decisive for the war effort. The Security Police reacted to this by resorting to an approach based on weltanschauung, murdering, with few exceptions, all of the Jews from the autumn 1942 transports and thus keeping them from ever coming under the civil labor administration's planning authority. These killings produced a paradigm shift that ultimately led to the establishment of Concentration Camp Kaiserwald. The founding of this concentration camp completed the civil administration's loss of power in planning the deployment of the Riga ghetto's inhabitants.

There are numerous indications to suggest that the transformation of ghetto Jews into prisoners of the SS Economics and Administration Main Office was an overarching strategy on Himmler's part to assert the primacy of ideology over Wehrmacht production interests everywhere. One of the peculiarities of Holocaust historiography is that, in the historical analysis of summer 1942 and the implementation of the "final solution," the deportations from France and Holland as well as German diplomatic efforts elsewhere to expand the pool of victims stand at the center of events in chronological terms. While this territorial change of direction – from eastern to western Europe – often leads to the central role of the labor and killing facility Auschwitz, the mass murder beyond Auschwitz-Birkenau and the camps of Operation Reinhardt (Sobibór, Treblinka, and Bełżec) is – with few exceptions – lost from view. The study of Riga-Kaiserwald presented here is able to offer some initial explanations for Himmler's strategy in the last years of the war, which of course need to be verified with regard to other cases where concentration camps were established during this period.

Regarding the still almost completely ignored question of how the communal civil authorities administrated "closed residential areas" for Jews, the case of Riga shows several peculiarities characteristic of ghettos elsewhere. Much like the establishment of ghettos in occupied Poland, the Germans in Riga did not think that the ghetto in the Moscow Suburb would exist for a long time. If, in the case of occupied Poland, the Germans had reckoned with quick deportations to the "reservations" District Lublin or Madagascar, in the case of Riga the limited duration of the ghetto's existence was already reflected in the preliminary guidelines issued by Reich Commissar Ostland Hinrich Lohse on 18 August 1941. These were seen as "minimal measures" that were to be in force until the Jews could be murdered by the Security Police. As was already the case in occupied Poland, the decommissioning of the Riga ghetto was delayed as well.

But the integration of a desk or department in the internal administration of the county commissar did not follow ghettoization. The deployment of labor was organized in the Labor Department through an external office of the Labor Office, whereas all questions concerning Jewish property were located either in the Trust Administration Department or the Finance Department of the county or general commissariats. A glance at the ghetto administration in Warsaw or Łódź (Litzmannstadt) clearly shows that the respective civil authorities there made preparations in advance to set up an administrative office. A year after the preliminary guidelines went into effect in Riga, when the Reich Commissariat Ostland sent out new instructions for the standardized configuration of ghetto administrations, it became clear that no prior thought had been given to a uniform organization of such communal offices.

As a microcosm of the perpetrators, occupied Riga is also worthy of attention. Here, the major killing operations in winter 1941–1942 and Operation Dünamünde are emphasized less than the large-scale barrackings and camps. If Fritz Scherwitz at the production center Lenta managed to create a camp largely free of murder and abuse, or Inspector Dähne at the beach resort Jurmala could show a benevolent indifference toward the Jewish women assigned him, then this could have applied in theory at Jungfernhof or Salaspils as well. Both camps lay outside the city, and both internment facilities were rarely inspected during the cold winter of 1941–1942. But under Rudolf Seck and Otto Teckemeier, the Jews in those camps found themselves confronted with ruthless SS noncommissioned officers whose behavior has been described at length in this volume. When questioned by investigators and confronted by survivors just a few years after the war, Seck and Teckemeier tried in vain to portray a normal camp life. While Seck pointed to dances with the Jews at Jungfernhof, Teckemeier relativized his maltreatment of the Jews in Salaspils as the occasional slap in the face for violations that were actually subject to reporting to Riga headquarters – and thus subject to the death penalty. Both men, whom survivors considered violent and homicidal, vehemently protested their reputation as "bad people." Their self-perception that "history" had dropped them in some faraway place where they had done their duty in a "hard but just fashion" does not always have to be a defensive maneuver employed only to avoid prosecution. Gerhard Maywald wrote years later in investigatory detention that the Jews considered themselves well-off under his management of construction at Salaspils.

Even if the question of the perpetrators' self-perception during or close to the time of the events analyzed in this study could not be addressed, an important corrective to such myth-making was nonetheless regularly cited: the statements in criminal investigations and published memoirs of the survivors. It is their accounts and books that tell the real story of the Holocaust as carried out by the lower-ranking German personnel in Riga. Without the survivors' testimony, this book could not have been written.

Glossary

The following glossary contains translations used in the text on the left and the German original on the right. A few words untranslated in the text are described in the left-hand column as well.

administrative assistant	Regierungsassessor
administrative counselor	Regierungsrat
administrative director general	Regierungsdirektor
administrator	Assessor
Bureau for the Deployment of Jews	Abteilung Judeneinsatz
department	Amt (within the RSHA and SS-WVHA)
Department VII (Wartime Administration)	Abteilung VII (Kriegsverwaltung)
desk	Referat
division	Amtsgruppe
Ethnic German Liaison Office	Volksdeutsche Mittelstelle
field administration command	Feldkommandantur
Gauleiter	regional-level party boss
German-Nationalist Protection and Defiance Federation	Deutschvölkischer Schutz- und Trutzbund
Gestapo District Office	Stapostelle
Gestapo Regional Office	Stapoleitstelle
high field administration command	Oberfeldkommandantur
Immigration Central Office	Einwanderzentralstelle
Labor Deployment Central Office	Arbeitseinsatz-Zentrale
local administration command	Ortskommandantur
ministerial counselor	Ministerialrat
ministerial director	Ministerialdirigent
ministerial director general	Ministerialdirektor
regional commander of the Security Police and the SD	Kommandeur der Sicherheitspolizei und des SD

Reich Association of Jews in Germany	Reichsvereinigung der Juden in Deutschland
Reich Central Office Jewish Emigration	Reichszentralle für jüdische Auswanderung
Reich commissar for the strengthening of Germandom	Reichskommissar für die Festigung deutschen Volkstums
Reich Security Main Office	Reichssicherheitshauptamt
Reichsleiter	national-level party functionary
Reichsstatthalter	regional-level representative of the Reich
Schutzpolizei	German municipal police
SD regional sector	SD Leitabschnitt
SD sector	SD Abschnitt
senior administrative counselor	Oberregierungsrat
senior finance executive	Oberfinanzpräsident
SS Economics and Administration Main Office	SS Wirtschafts- und Verwaltungshauptamt
SS Operations Main Office	SS Führungshauptamt
SS regional sector	SS Oberabschnitt
SS sector	SS Abschnitt
state secretary	Staatssekretär
Storm Troops	Sturmabteilung (SA)
territorial commander of the Security Police and the SD	Befehlshaber der Sicherheitspolizei und des SD
Wehrmacht territorial commander	Wehrmachtsbefehlshaber

Organizational Chart 473

The SS and Police and Civil Administration Organization for Riga, 1942–1944

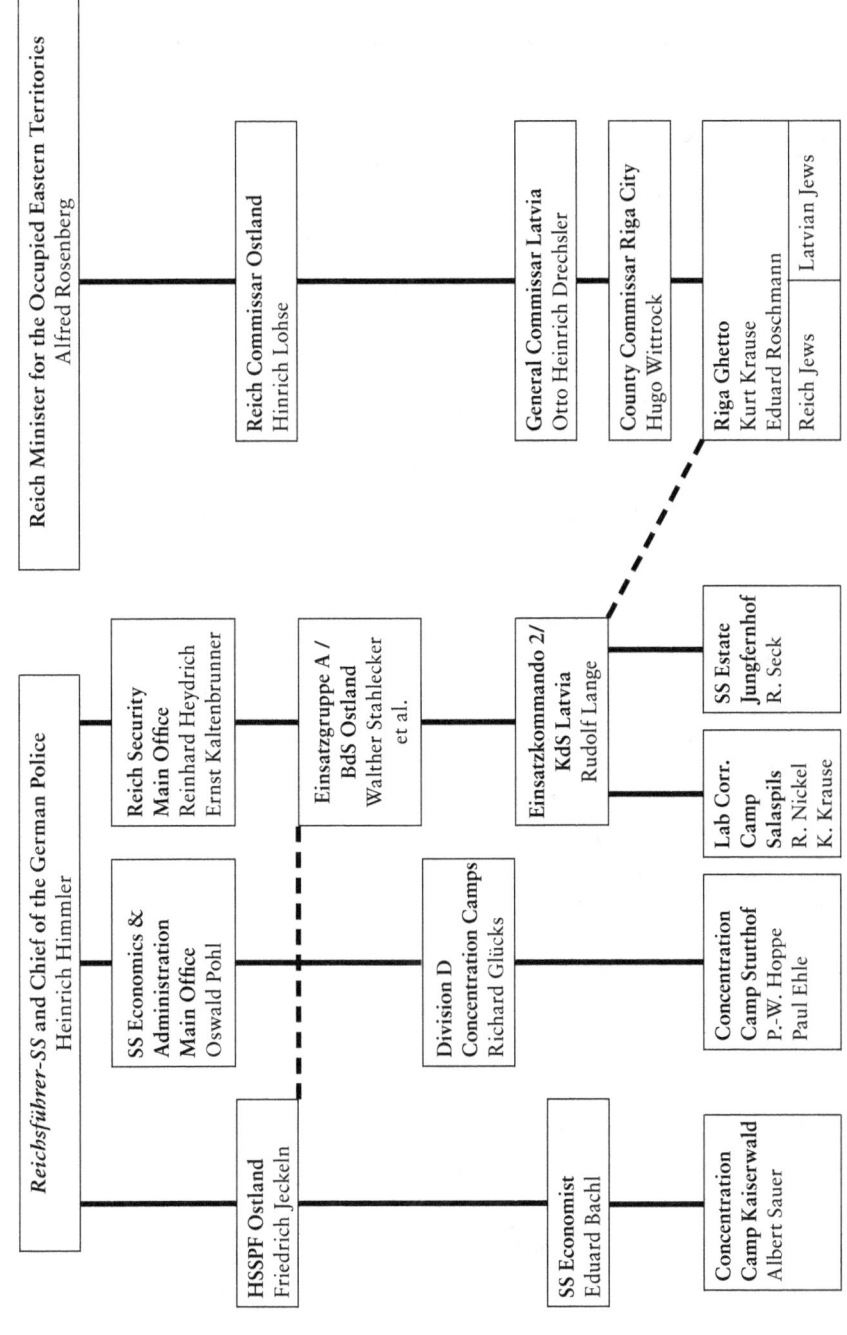

Comparative Table of Ranks

U.S. Army	SS	Order Police	Wehrmacht
Private	SS-Mann	Unterwachtmeister	Soldat
Private First Class	Sturmmann	Rottwachtmeister	Obersoldat
Corporal	Rottenführer	Wachtmeister	Gefreiter
—	—	Oberwachtmeister	Obergefreiter
—	—	—	Stabsgefreiter
Sergeant	Unterscharführer	Revieroberwachtmeister / Zugwachtmeister	Unteroffizier
Staff Sergeant	Scharführer	Hauptwachtmeister	Unterfeldwebel
Technical Sergeant	Oberscharführer	Meister	Feldwebel
First Sergeant	Hauptscharführer	—	Oberfeldwebel
Master Sergeant	Sturmscharführer	—	Stabsoberfeldwebel
Second Lieutenant	Untersturmführer	Leutnant	Leutnant
First Lieutenant	Obersturmführer	Oberleutnant	Oberleutnant
Captain	Hauptsturmführer	Hauptmann	Hauptmann
Major	Sturmbannführer	Major	Major
Lieutenant Colonel	Obersturmbannführer	Oberstleutnant	Oberstleutnant
Colonel	Standartenführer	Oberst	Oberst
—	Oberführer	—	—
Brigadier General	Brigadeführer	Generalmajor	Generalmajor
Major General	Gruppenführer	Generalleutnant	Generalleutnant
Lieutenant General	Obergruppenführer	General der Polizei	General
General	Oberstgruppenführer	Generaloberst	Generaloberst
General of the Army	Reichsführer-SS and Chief of the German Police		Generalfeldmarschall

Source: *The Holdings of the Berlin Document Center* (Berlin 1994), pp. 276–277.

Biographical Appendix

Arajs, Viktor (13 January 1910–13 January 1988) born in Baldone; law student; member of student association Lettonia; policeman; July 1941 founder of Latvian commando of volunteer auxiliary security police; July 1941–October 1944 involvement in mass murder operations in Latvia; 1945 British POW; February 1949 released from British custody; shortly thereafter assumed new identity and disappeared; July 1975 arrested in Frankfurt am Main; December 1979 convicted by a Hamburg court and sentenced to life; died in prison in Kassau.

Batz, Rudolf (10 November 1903–8 February 1961) born in Langensalza (Thuringia); son of railway maintenance engineer; Protestant upbringing; law student; May 1933 NSDAP; December 1935 SS; June 1936 deputy Gestapo chief in Breslau; June 1938 Gestapo chief in Linz; April 1940 SS major; October 1940–January 1941 at office of territorial commander of the Security Police and SD Holland; spring 1941 Gestapo chief in Hanover; June 1941–November 1941 commander Einsatzkommando 2; November 1942 SS lieutenant colonel; August 1943 head of KdS Cracow; January 1945 SS colonel; after the war life under false name in West Germany; January 1961 arrested and questioned; suicide in custody.

Drechsler, Otto-Heinrich (1 April 1895–5 May 1945) born in Lübz (northern Germany); Protestant upbringing; 1914 First World War; 1922 dentist; July 1925 NSDAP, rises to rank of SA brigadier general; August 1932–May 1933 deputy *Gauleiter* Mecklenburg-Lübeck; June 1933–March 1937 mayor in Lübeck; April 1937 governing mayor of Lübeck; 17 July 1941 general commissar Latvia; suicide.

Ehle, Paul (22 October 1897–14 August 1965) born in Danzig (today Gdańsk, Poland); grade school education; farmer; March 1916–November 1918 First World War; May 1932 NSDAP; March 1933 SS; January 1938 SS second lieutenant; 1939 various small camps in the Danzig area, including Westerplatte, Neufahrwasser, and Guteherberge; November 1941 SS first lieutenant and transfer to Stutthof; June 1944 SS captain; April 1945 commandant at Concentration Camp Stutthof.

Helfsgott, Walter Ernst (11 January 1911–22 July 1980) born in Barschdorf (today Bartoszów, Poland); son of farmer; Protestant upbringing; law student; November 1934–October 1935 military service; May 1937 NSDAP; December 1937 SS; July 1939 SS second lieutenant; February 1940 Criminal Police Executive Field Office Breslau; April 1941 SS first lieutenant; August 1942 Ek 6 in Ukraine and Russia; March 1943 anti-partisan operations in Pripiat marshes; April 1944 Sk 1005-B and destruction of evidence of mass murders in and around Riga; November 1944 SS captain and transfer to Special Purposes Group Iltis in Yugoslavia; post-1945 work for Criminal Police in Düsseldorf; December 1965 convicted by Wuppertal court for crimes committed by Ek 6 and sentenced to four years and three months imprisonment; March 1969 acquitted by Stuttgart court for crimes committed by Sk 1005.

Heydrich, Reinhard (7 March 1904–4 June 1942) born in Halle an der Saale; son of music school director; Catholic upbringing; 1920 German-Nationalist Protection and Defiance Federation and paramilitary activity; March 1922–May 1931 navy officer; May 1931 SA; June 1931 NSDAP; July 1931 SS; August 1931 intelligence service, staff of Reichsführer-SS; July 1932 chief of staff of SD; November 1933 chief of SD Main Office; March 1936 member of the Reichstag; June 1936 chief of the Security Police; September 1939 chief of the Reich Security Main Office; September 1941 SS lieutenant general and general of the police; September 1941 deputy Reichsprotektor Bohemia-Moravia; 27 May 1942 fatally wounded in assassination attempt in Prague.

Himmler, Heinrich (7 October 1900–23 May 1945) born in Munich; son of teacher; Catholic upbringing; December 1917 army training; December 1918 discharged; April–August 1919 paramilitary activity; agricultural studies; August 1923 NSDAP; November 1923 Hitler putsch; August 1925 SS; September 1926–April 1930 deputy propaganda chief of the NSDAP; 1927–1929 deputy Reichsführer-SS; January 1929 Reichsführer-SS; September 1930 member of the Reichstag; January 1933 SA lieutenant general; April 1934 commander of the political police in Bavaria, thereafter gradual accumulation of similar offices throughout Germany; October 1934–April 1936 police president in München; June 1936 Reichsführer-SS and chief of the German police; October 1939 Reich commissar for the strengthening of Germandom; July 1944 commander of Replacement Army; January–March 1945 commander of Army Group Vistula; 29 April 1945 declared a traitor by Hitler and stripped of all his offices; 23 May 1945 capture by British and suicide.

Hoppe, Paul-Werner (28 February 1910–15 July 1974) born in Berlin; son of architect; agricultural technical school; gardener; February 1932 NSDAP and SS; SS career; 1938 staff Concentration Camp Oranienburg; September 1938 SS captain; 16 March 1942 wounded on front while serving with SS Division Death's Head; September 1942 SS major and commandant at Concentration Camp Stutthof; 1948 escape from Fallingbostel internment camp; assumed new identity; April 1954 arrested; June 1957 convicted by a Bochum court and sentenced to five years and three months; verdict confirmed on appeal in June 1957, with the sentence extended to nine years in prison; died in Bochum.

Jeckeln, Friedrich (2 February 1895–3 February 1946) born in Hornberg (southwest Germany); son of factory owner; Protestant upbringing; engineering student; August 1914–November 1918 First World War; 1919–1925 farmer near Danzig; 1925–1929 engineer in Braunschweig; October 1929 NSDAP; December 1930 SS, thereafter SS careerist; July 1932 member of the Reichstag; February 1933 SS major general; June 1933 Braunschweig police; September 1936 SS lieutenant general; June 1938 HSSPF Center (Braunschweig); July 1940 HSSPF West (Düsseldorf); April 1941 general of the police; June 1941 HSSPF Russia South; November 1941 HSSPF Russia North; July 1944 general of the Waffen-SS; February 1945 commanding general Breslau area; May 1945 captured by the Soviets south of Berlin; 26 January–3 February 1946 trial; sentenced to death and hanged on the same day in Riga.

Krause, Kurt (27 February 1904–8 December 1944) born in Liegnitz (today Legnica, Poland); medic with German Red Cross; customs official; Jewish affairs desk EG A and KdS Latvia; January 1942 formally installed as ghetto commandant; participant in murder of Jews deported from Germany upon arrival and in Operation Dünamünde; 1943 SS first lieutenant; commandant at Salaspils; captured by Soviet partisans and executed.

Lange, Rudolf (18 April 1910–23 February 1945) born in Weisswasser (Saxony); son of Reich Railway construction inspector; Protestant upbringing; doctorate in law; November 1933–October 1936 SA; September 1936 Gestapo; May 1937 NSDAP; September 1937 SS; August 1938 SS second lieutenant, while working in Vienna; November 1938 SS first lieutenant, while based in Stuttgart; April 1940 SS captain; Erfurt and Weimar as well as deputy inspector of the Security Police and SD in Kassel; September 1940, deputy chief of Gestapo regional office Berlin; March 1941 SS major; June 1941, head of Gestapo department within Einsatzgruppe A; December 1941 head of KdS Latvia; November 1943 SS lieutenant colonel; January 1945 SS colonel and head of KdS Poznań; committed suicide to avoid capture by Soviets.

Lohse, Hinrich (2 September 1896–25 February 1964) born in Mühlenbarbek (north Germany); son of a farmer; Protestant upbringing; 1913–1915 salesman; September 1915–November 1916 service in First World War, severely wounded; 1916–1918 wharf industry; 1919–April 1920 and November 1922–March 1924 bank employee; spring 1923 NSDAP (first time); 1924–1928 city councilor in Altona; March 1925–July 1932 *Gauleiter* in Schleswig-Holstein; June 1925 NSDAP (second time); 1928–1933 member of the Prussian State Parliament; July–September 1932 and November 1933–1945 member of Reichstag; November 1933 SA major general; January 1937 SA lieutenant general; July 1941–July 1944 Reich commissar Ostland; May 1945 arrested by British Army; 1948 sentenced to ten years in prison and confiscation of assets; February 1951 released for reasons of health.

Maywald, Gerhard Kurt (16 April 1913– ?) born in Karlsruhe (southwest Germany); Protestant upbringing; teacher turned policeman; May 1937 NSDAP; July 1941 SS second lieutenant; member of Department IV of KdS Latvia until spring 1942 and supervisor of construction of responsible for construction at Labor Correctional Camp Salaspils; implicated in Operation Dünamünde in the Riga ghetto and at Jungfernhof; from May until October 1942 commandant at Maly Trostenez; 1970 investigation of activity at Maly Trostenez suspended; 1977 convicted by a Hamburg court for actions in Riga and sentenced to four years minus sixteen months for time served in pretrial detention.

Prützmann, Hans-Adolf (31 August 1901–21 May 1945) born in Tolkemit (today Tolmicko, Poland); Protestant upbringing; agriculture student; November 1918–autumn 1924 paramilitary activity; 1929 NSDAP; 1930 SS, thereafter SS careerist; July 1932 member of the Reichstag; November 1933 SS brigadier general; February 1934 SS major general; June 1936–May 1941 HSSPF Northwest (Hamburg); April 1941 major general of the police; May 1941–February 1944 HSSPF Northeast (Königsburg); June–October 1941 HSSPF Russia North; November 1941 HSSPF Russian South, SS lieutenant general and general of the police; October 1943 highest SS and police leader in Reich Commissariat Ukraine; June 1944 Himmler's liaison to High Command of the Wehrmacht; November 1944 commander of Werwolf resistance movement; 21 May 1945 capture by British and suicide.

Roques, Franz von (1 September 1877–7 August 1967) born in Treysa (north Hesse); career officer; 1911 assigned to Great General Staff; 1914–1918 various general staff posts during First World War; 1919 retained in the Army; February 1931 brigadier general; January 1933 major general; 30 September 1933 retired from active duty; November 1939 commander

177th Division; June 1940 general z.b.V. (for special purposes) I; March 1941 commander of Rear Area Army Group 101 (= North); July 1941 general of the infantry; March 1942 commanding general of security troops and commander in Army Group Area North; April 1943 relieved of command, assigned to officer reserve; 31 July 1943 retired from service; witness during Nuremberg trials.

Roschmann, Eduard (25 November 1908–10 August 1977) born in Graz, Austria; son of brewery official; 1927–1934 Steyer Homeland Protection Force; six semesters at university; 1931 brewery employee; 1935 civil service; 1938 NSDAP and SS; 1939 Waffen-SS; 1940 SS first sergeant; January 1941 Security Police; temporarily in charge of workshops at Lenta; second commandant of the Riga ghetto; participation in Sonderkommando 1005 and efforts to destroy the evidence of the mass shootings in and around Riga; 1947–1948 arrest and flight to Latin America; 1977 forced to leave Argentina; died of heart failure in Asuncion, Paraguay.

Rosenberg, Alfred (12 January 1893–16 October 1946) born in Tallinn (Reval), Estonia; son of salesman; Protestant upbringing; studied architecture in Riga and engineering in Moscow; student association Rubonia; November 1918 in exile in Germany; January 1919 member of precursor to National Socialist German Workers Party; 1921 editor at Nazi party newspaper *Völkischer Beobachter*; November 1923 participation in Munich putsch; September 1930 member of the Reichstag; April 1933 head of the Foreign Policy Office of NSDAP; June 1933 title of *Reichsleiter*; 1934 Plenipotentiary of the Führer for the Supervision of the Entire Intellectual and Ideological Training and Education of the NSDAP; July 1941 Reich minister for the occupied eastern territories; 1945–1946 defendant at the Trial of the Major War Criminals before the International Military Tribunal; found guilty and sentenced to death.

Sauer, Albert (17 August 1898–3 May 1945) born in Misdroy (today Międzyzdroje, Poland); Protestant upbringing; grade school education; January 1917–November 1918 First World War; paramilitary activity; carpenter; September 1931 SS; December 1931 NSDAP; July 1937 Concentration Camp Sachsenhausen; August 1938–August 1939 commandant at Concentration Camp Mauthausen; September 1938 SS major; October 1941–April 1942 Wartheland office of Reich Commissar for the Strengthening of Germandom; May 1942 SS Economics and Administration Main Office; August 1942 Division D, SS Economics and Administration Main Office; summer 1943 commandant at Concentration Camp Kaiserwald; died of wounds in Falkensee.

Seck, Rudolf Joachim (15 July 1908– ?) in Bunsoh (north Germany); peasant family; farmer; May 1931 member of the NSDAP and the SS; May–August 1940 western front; January 1941 sent to Schmiedeberg for an agricultural course; arrived in Riga in August 1941 and assigned to KdS Latvia; commandant at Jungfernhof (Jumpravmuiža); May 1945 arrested by British military police; January 1949 released from British custody; May 1949 arrested again; July 1949 sentenced to ten years in prison for SS membership; December 1951 sentenced by a Hamburg court to life in prison.

Stahlecker, Walther (10 October 1900–23 March 1942) born in Sternenfels (southwest Germany); son of vice-principal school; law student; German-Nationalist Protection and Defiance Federation and paramilitary activity; professional civil servant; 1921 first activity on behalf of NSDAP; 1923 editor of ethno-nationalist paper in Tübingen; 1930 director of Labor Office in Nagold (Black Forest); May 1932 SS; 1933 deputy head of political police in Stuttgart; May 1934 head of Gestapo office in Stuttgart; July 1938 inspector of the Security Police and SD Vienna; June 1939 territorial commander of the Security Police and SD (BdS) Prague; 1940 BdS Oslo; November 1940 Foreign Office; February 1941 brigadier general of the police and SS brigadier general; June 1941 Einsatzgruppe A; August 1941 BdS Ostland; died of wounds received in anti-partisan operation in Russia.

Wittrock, Hugo (19 July 1873–25 August 1958) born on island Ösel in Estonia; son of estate administrator; studied mechanical engineering; student association Rubonia; insurance officer; 1917 advisor for German military administration; 1919 exile in Germany; 1925 return to Riga, activity on behalf of National Socialist politics; 1936 resettled to Königsberg; 1939 German citizenship and translator for German military intelligence in Königsberg; July 1941 commissarial governing mayor and county commissar Riga City; died in Lübeck in the aftermath of a traffic accident.

Archival Sources

Archives in the Federal Republic of Germany

Bundesarchiv (BA) Berlin
NS 3 SS-Wirtschafts-Verwaltungshauptamt
NS 19 Persönlicher Stab RFSS
NS 22 Reichsorganisationsleiter der NSDAP
NS 33 SS-Führungshauptamt
R 6 Reichsministerium für die besetzten Ostgebiete
R 58 Reichssicherheitshauptamt
R 70/SU Polizeidienststellen in eingegliederten und besetzten Gebieten – Sowjetunion
R 90 Reichskommissar für das Ostland
R 91 Gebietskommissare im Geschäftsbereich des Reichskommissars für das Ostland
R 92 Generalkommissar Riga
R 138 Behörden der allgemeinen inneren Verwaltung und Selbstverwaltung im Reichsgau Danzig-Westpreußen

Berlin Document Center (BDC) Collection

Bundesarchiv-Militärarchiv (BA-MA) Freiburg
Mü 17 Nachlaß Vincenz Müller
N 153 Nachlaß Franz von Roques
RH 19 Oberkommandos der Heeresgruppen
RH 20–11 Armeeoberkommando 11
RH 21–2 Panzer-Armeeoberkommando 2
RH 22 Befehlshaber der rückwärtigen Heeresgebiete
RH 24–26 Generalkommando XXVI. Armeekorps
RH 24–38 Generalkommando XXXVIII. Armeekorps
RH 26–1 1. Infanteriedivision
RH 26–281 281. Sicherungsdivision
RH 26–291 291. Sicherungsdivision
RH 53–23 OFK Warschau
RS 4 Brigaden, Kampfgruppen und Einheiten der Waffen-SS
RW 4 OKW/Wehrmachtführungsstab
RW 5 OKW/Amt Ausland/Abwehr
RW 19 OKW/Wehrwirtschafts- und Rüstungsamt
RW 30 Rüstungsdienststellen in den Reichskommissariaten Ostland und Ukraine
RW 31 Wirtschaftsstab Ost

Microfilm series:
WF-01 Höchste Befehlsstellen des Heeres
WF-03 Kommandobehörden des Heeres
WF-10 Abwehrorgane

Bundesarchiv-Zwischenarchiv Dahlwitz Hoppegarten (BA DH)
Dok. K Unterlagen des ehemaligen Dokumentationszentrums der DDR
R 479 Unterlagen zum KL Stutthof
ZA I Mischbestand
ZM 1457 Unterlagen des Persönlichen Stabes RFSS
ZM 1683 Prozeß gegen Friedrich Jeckeln u. a.
ZR 920 Mischbestand – hauptsächlich Aktenkopien zum RSHA

Politisches Archiv des Auswärtigen Amtes (PA-AA)
R 27341
R 99225
R 100857
R 100862
R 105190

Archiv der Bundesbeauftragten für die Unterlagen des Staatssicherheitsdienstes der ehemaligen Deutschen Demokratischen Republik
FV 6/74 Unternehmen Zeppelin

Hauptstaatsarchiv Düsseldorf
RW 58 Geheime Staatspolizei – Personenakten

Staatsarchiv München
StAnW 17434 Scherwitz-Verfahren
Generalstanw. B. OLG München Nr. 207 Scherwitz-Revisionsverfahren

Staatsarchiv Nürnberg
KV Ankl. Interrogation

Case 9 The Einsatzgruppen Case
Case 12 The High Command Case

Nuremberg Documents L, NG, NO, NOKW, PS

LG Nürnberg-Fürth, Nr. 3070/II Verfahren gegen Benno Martin u. a.

Non-German Archives

Latvijas Valsts Vēstures Arhīvs (LVVA) Riga
P 69 Generalkommissariat Lettland
P 70 Reichskommissariat Ostland
P 80 Wehrmachtbefehlshaber Ostland
P 82 SS- und Polizeiführer Lettland
P 83 SS- und Polizeistandortführer Libau
P 132 Materialien der Außerordentlichen Kommission – Bezirk Lettland
P 252 KdS Lettland und Einsatzkommando 2

P 958 Arbeitsdepartement, Stadt Riga
P 1018 Reichsministerium für die besetzten Ostgebiete
P 1019 Geheime Staatspolizei
P 1026 BdS Ostland und Chef der Einsatzgruppe A
P 1376 Mischbestand Polizeibehörden Riga

Latvijas Valsts Arhīvs (LVA) Riga

P 69 Generalkommissariat Lettland
P 70 Reichskommissariat Ostland
P 989 Generaldirektion der Wirtschaft/Arbeitsdepartement
P 1004 Gebietskommissar Riga Stadt
P 1492 lett. Stadtrat Riga

Rossiiskii Gosudartsvennyi Voennyi Arkhiv (RGVA) Moscow

500 Reichssicherheitshauptamt
503 Gestapoleitstelle Stettin
504 Befehlshaber der Sicherheitspolizei und des SD Ostland
1301 Militärische und militärbauliche Einrichtungen
1358 Reichsministerium für die besetzten Ostgebiete

Estonian State Archive Tallinn

819 KdS Estland

Public Record Office (PRO) Kew

HD Ultra Decodes
WO War Office

Archiv Ministerstva Vnitra Prague

114 Reichsprotektor Böhmen und Mähren

Belorusskii Gosudarstvennyi Arkhiv Minsk

378 Tages- und Kommandobefehle der Haupteisenbahndirektion Mitte in Minsk
391 Gebietskommissar Borisow

Archiwum Państwowe w Łodzi

Ghettoverwaltung Litzmannstadt (Ghetto Administration Litzmannstadt)
Przełożony Starszeństwa Żydów w Getcie Łódzkim (The Eldest of the Jews in Łódź
  Ghetto)

YIVO New York

RG 215 Berlin Collection – Occ E. and Occ G.

United States Holocaust Memorial Museum, Washington (USHMM)

15.007 Selected Records – RSHA Material from Warsaw

Yad Vashem, Jerusalem
Eichmann Documentation
O. 33 Erinnerungsberichte

Criminal Investigations and Trials

Bundesarchiv Ludwigsburg (formerly Zentrale Stelle der Landesjustizverwaltungen)

AR-Z Cases
207 AR-Z 7/59 Ludwigsburger Überlieferung des Hamburger Riga-Verfahrens
7 AR-Z 233/59 Verfahren gegen Angehörige des KdS Reval
204 AR-Z 13/60 Verfahren gegen Degenhardt u.a. vom Stab HSSPF Jeckeln
204 AR-Z 419/62 Verfahren gegen Sohns u.a. vom Sk 1005
202 AR-Z 12/66 Verfahren gegen Pannier von der Nachschubkommandantur der Waffen-SS Bobruisk
207 AR-Z 101/67 Verfahren gegen Angehörige des KdS-Außendienststelle Wolmar
207 AR-Z 497/67 Verfahren gegen Angehörige des RKO
420 AR-Z 75/68 Verfahren gegen Angehörige des RKO
207 AR-Z 9/98 Ermittlungen gegen Kauls u. a. zum Wachpersonal des Ghettos Riga

AR Cases
207 AR 751/64 Verfahren gegen Eichelis u. a. zu NSG in Rositten
407 AR 91/65 Verfahren zu NSG im KL Stutthof
407 AR 3680/65 Verfahren zu NSG im KL Stutthof
207 AR 188/76 Verfahren gegen Dr. Bracs wegen NSG in Riga
207 AR 128/78 Verfahren gegen Wisner wegen NSG im KL Kaiserwald
207 AR 86/83 Verfahren gegen Tollkühn wegen NSG in Riga

Dokumentation Collection

Zentralstelle im Lande Nordrhein-Westfalen bei der Staatsanwalt Köln
130 Js 2/78 Z Verfahren gegen Wisner wegen NSG im KL Kaiserwald

Staatsanwaltschaft beim Landgericht der Freien und Hansestadt Hamburg
141 Js 534/60 Riga Hauptverfahren: This case is divided into four sections and contains various sections as well as old cases conducted by the British military authorities, including:
= 14 Js 210/49 Altverfahren gegen Seck u.a. = Beiakten
= 147 Js 5/71 Oberwinder u.a.
= 147 Ks 6/71 Jahnke u.a. = 147 Js 5/71
= 147 Ks 3/74 Trühe und Besekow
147 Js 31/67 Verfahren gegen den ehemaligen Amtchef I des RSHA Bruno Streckenbach
Landgericht Hamburg, 37 Ks 5/76, Urteil gegen Viktor Arajs
Landgericht Hamburg, 89 1/83, Urteil gegen Karl Tollkühn
Schwurgericht Hamburg, 50 Ks 9/72, Urteil gegen Jahnke u. a.

Staatsanwaltschaft Berlin
1 Js 4/65 der Staatsanwaltschaft beim Kammergericht Berlin Verfahren zum Kommandostab Einsatzgruppen

1 Ks 1/69 der Staatsanwaltschaft beim Kammergericht Berlin Verfahren gegen Angehörige des Referates IV B 4
1 Js 9/65 der Staatsanwaltschaft beim Landgericht Berlin Verfahren zur Stapo-Leitstelle Berlin

Staatsanwaltschaft München I
22 Js 255/61 der Staatsanwaltschaft München I Verfahren gegen Gabel vom Stab des RPB 9
114 Js 17/65 der Staatsanwaltschaft München I Verfahren gegen Angehörige des Sk 10a

BIBLIOGRAPHY

Published Sources and Editions

Abgehört: Deutsche Generäle in britischer Kriegsgefangenschaft 1942–1945. Ed. Sönke Neitzel. Berlin, 2005.

Akten zur Deutschen Auswärtigen Politik 1918–1945 (ADAP), Serie B, Bd. II, Göttingen, 1967. Serie D, Bd. V, Baden-Baden, 1953; Bd. VI, Baden-Baden, 1956; Bd. VII, Baden-Baden, 1956; Bd. VIII, Frankfurt am Main, 1961; Bd. X, Frankfurt am Main, 1963.

Akten der Parteikanzlei der NSDAP: Rekonstruktion eines verlorengegangenen Bestandes. Munich, 1983–1992.

Anatomie des Krieges: Neue Dokumente über die Rolle des deutschen Monokapitals bei der Vorbereitung und Durchführung des zweiten Weltkriegs. Ed. Dietrich Eichholtz and Wolfgang Schumann. Berlin (East), 1969.

Archives of the Holocaust: An International Collection of Selected Documents. Ed. Henry Friedlander and Sybil Milton. New York and London, 1993.

Biuletyn Głownej Komisji Badania Zbrodni Hitlerowskich w Polsce, Bd. XII (1960).

Braunbuch: Kriegs- und Naziverbrecher in der Bundesrepublik. Ed. Nationalrat der Nationalen Front des Demokratischen Deutschland Dokumentationszentrum der Staatlichen Archivverwaltung der DDR. Berlin (East), 1965.

Cohen, Nathan. "The Last Days of the Vilna Ghetto – Pages from a Diary." In *Yad Vashem Studies* 31 (2003): 15–59.

DDR-Justiz und NS-Verbrechen. Ed. Christian Frederik Rüter et al., Amsterdam and Munich, 2002–2004.

Deutsche Politik im "Protektorat Böhmen und Mähren" unter Reinhard Heydrich 1941–1942: Eine Dokumentation. Ed. Miroslav Kárný, Jaroslava Milotová, and Margita Kárná. Berlin, 1997.

Der Dienstkalender Heinrich Himmlers 1941/42. Ed. Peter Witte, Michael Wildt, Martina Voigt, Dieter Pohl, Peter Klein, Christian Gerlach, Christoph Dieckmann, and Andrej Angrick. Hamburg, 1999.

Das Diensttagebuch des Generalgouverneurs in Polen 1939–1945. Ed. Werner Präg and Wolfgang Jacobmeyer. Stuttgart, 1975.

Die Einsatzgruppen in der besetzten Sowjetunion 1941/42: Die Tätigkeits- und Lageberichte des Chefs der Sicherheitspolizei und des SD. Ed. Peter Klein. Berlin, 1997.

Documents Concerning the Fate of Romanian Jewry during the Holocaust. Ed. Jean Ancel. New York and Paris, 1986.

Documents Concerning the Destruction of the Jews of Grodno. Ed. Serge Klarsfeld. New York and Paris, 1987–1992.

Domarus, Max. *Hitler: Reden und Proklamationen 1932–1945*. Leonberg, 1988.

Einsatz im "Reichskommissariat Ostland": Dokumente zum Völkermord im Baltikum und in Weißrußland 1941–1944. Ed. Wolfgang Benz, Konrad Kwiet, and Jürgen Matthäus. Berlin, 1998.

Europa unterm Hakenkreuz, Bd. 8: Die faschistische Okkupationspolitik in den zeitweilig besetzten Gebieten der Sowjetunion (1941–1944). Ed. Norbert Müller. Berlin, 1991.

Fall 9: Das Urteil im SS-Einsatzgruppenprozeß, gefällt am 10. April 1948 in Nürnberg

vom Militärgerichtshof II der Vereinigten Staaten von Amerika. Ed. Kazimierz Leszcynski. Berlin (East), 1963.
Fall 12: Das Urteil gegen das Oberkommando der Wehrmacht, gefällt am 28. Oktober in Nürnberg vom Militärgerichtshof V der Vereinigten Staaten von Amerika. Berlin (East), 1960.
Faschismus-Ghetto-Massenmord. Dokumentation über Ausrottung und Widerstand der Juden in Polen während des zweiten Weltkrieges. Ed. Jüdisches Historisches Institut. Warsaw, Berlin (East), 1960.
Führer durch Riga. Ed. Wehrmacht-Ortskommandantur Riga. Riga, 1942.
Führer-Erlasse" 1939–1945. Ed. Moll, Martin. Stuttgart, 1997.
Halder, Franz. *Kriegstagebuch: Tägliche Aufzeichnungen des Chefs des Generalstabes des Heeres 1939–1942*. Ed. Arbeitskreis für Wehrforschung and Hans-Adolf Jacobsen, 3 volumes. Stuttgart, 1962–1964.
Hass, Gerhard. *23. August 1939: Der Hitler-Stalin-Pakt. Eine Dokumentation*. Berlin, 1990.
Heilmann, H. D. "Das Kriegstagebuch des Diplomaten Otto Bräutigam." In *Biedermann und die Schreibtischtäter. Materialien zur deutschen Täterbiographie*. (= Beiträge zur nationalsozialistischen Gesundheits- und Sozialpolitik 4). Berlin, 1987, pp. 123–187.
Herbst 1941 im "Führerhauptquartier": Berichte Werner Koeppens an seinen Minister Alfred Rosenberg. Ed. Martin Vogt. Koblenz, 2002.
Himmler, Heinrich. *Geheimreden 1933 bis 1945 und andere Ansprachen*. Berlin, 1974.
Hitler, Adolf. *Monologe im Führerhauptquartier 1941–1944: Die Aufzeichnungen Heinrich Heims*. Ed. Werner Jochmann. Bindlach, 1988.
Hitlers Weisungen für die Kriegsführung 1939–1945: Dokumente des Oberkommandos der Wehrmacht. Ed. Walther Hubatsch, Koblenz, 1983.
Justiz und NS-Verbrechen: Sammlung deutscher Strafurteile wegen nationalsozialistischer Tötungsverbrechen 1945–1999. Ed. Christian Frederik Rüter et al. Amsterdam und Munich, 1968–2004.
Klemperer, Victor. *The Diaries of Victor Klemperer 1933–1945, I Shall Bear Witness to the Bitter End*. London, 2000.
Kriegstagebuch des Oberkommandos der Wehrmacht (Wehrmachtführungsstab) 1940–1945: Geführt von Helmuth Greiner and Percy Ernst Schramm. Ed. Percy Ernst Schramm. Frankfurt am Main, 1961–1965.
Lebenszeichen aus Piaski: Briefe Deportierter aus dem Distrikt Lublin 1940–1943. Ed. Else Behrend-Rosenfeld and Gertrud Luckner. Munich, 1970.
Leeb, Wilhelm Ritter von. *Tagebuchaufzeichnungen und Lagebeurteilungen aus zwei Weltkriegen*. Ed. Georg Meyer. Stuttgart, 1976.
Loeber, Dietrich A. *Diktierte Option: Die Umsiedlung der Deutsch-Balten aus Estland und Lettland 1939–1941*. Neumünster, 1972.
Der Prozeß gegen die Hauptkriegsverbrecher vor dem Internationalen Militärgerichtshof: Nürnberg, 14. November 1945–1. Oktober 1946. Nuremberg, 1947–1949.
Reichsgesetzblatt Riga. Ein Führer für deutsche Soldaten: Im Auftrage der Feldkommandantur. Riga, 1941.
Schauplatz Baltikum. Szenarium einer Okkupation und Angliederung: Dokumente 1939/1940. Ed. Michael Rosenbusch, Horst Schützler, and Sonja Striegnitz. Berlin, 1991.
"Schöne Zeiten": Judenmord aus der Sicht der Täter und Gaffer. Ed. Ernst Klee, Willi Dressen, and Volker Rieß. Frankfurt am Main, 1988.
Schumann, Wolfgang et al., *Nacht über Europa: Die faschistische Okkupationspolitik in Polen (1939–1945)*. Cologne, 1989.

Seckendorf, Martin. "Deutsche Baltikumkonzeptionen 1941–1944 im Spiegel von Dokumenten der zivilen Okkupationsverwaltung: Eine Dokumentation." 1999, *Zeitschrift für Sozialgeschichte des 20. und 21. Jahrhunderts* 16 (2001), 1: 140–172.

"*Sonderfahndungsliste UdSSR" des Chefs der Sicherheitspolizei und des SD: Das Fahndungsbuch der deutschen Einsatzgruppen in Rußland. Faksimile des Originals.* Ed. Werner Röder. Erlangen, 1976.

Tory, Avraham. *Surviving the Holocaust: The Kovno Ghetto Diary.* Cambridge, MA, and London, 1999.

Die Ukraine und das Baltenland: Tornisterschrift des Oberkommandos der Wehrmacht. Berlin, 1941.

Verbrechen der Wehrmacht: Dimensionen des Vernichtungskrieges 1941–1944. Ed. Hamburger Institut für Sozialforschung. Hamburg, 2002.

Verfolgung, Vertreibung, Vernichtung: Dokumente des faschistischen Antisemitismus 1933–1942. Ed. Kurt Pätzold. Leipzig, 1983.

Vom Generalplan Ost zum Generalsiedlungsplan. Ed. Czesław Madajczyk. Munich et al., 1994.

Wilhelm, Hans-Heinrich. *Rassenpolitik und Kriegführung: Sicherheitspolizei und Wehrmacht in Polen und in der Sowjetunion 1939–1942.* Passau, 1991.

Memoirs

Abramowitch, Maja. *To Forgive ... but not Forget: Maja's Story.* London and Portland, OR, 2002.

Bogdanow, A. A., et al. *Duell mit der Abweh: Dokumentarische Skizzen über die Tschekisten der Leningrader Front, 1941 bis 1945.* Berlin (East), 1971.

Bräutigam, Otto. *So hat es sich zugetragen: Ein Leben als Soldat und Diplomat.* Würzburg, 1968.

Faitelson, Alex. *Im jüdischen Widerstan: Mit Gedichten von Sima Faitelson Hürlimann.* Ed. Charlotte Nager. Baden-Baden, Zürich, 1998.

Gottschalk, Gerda. *Der letzte Weg.* Konstanz, 1991.

Gurewitsch, Arkadij. *Singende Pferde: Eine Jugend im Konzentrationslager.* Hamburg, 1997.

Gurwitz, Percy. *Zähl nicht nur, was bitter war: Eine baltische Chronik von Juden und Deutschen.* Berlin, 1991.

Hörmann, Gustav. "Arbeitseinsatzleiter im Ghetto Kaunas." In *Judenmord in Litauen: Studien und Dokumente.* Ed. Wolfgang Benz and Marion Neiss. Berlin, 1999, pp. 117–132.

Iwens, Sidney. *How Dark the Heavens: 1400 Days in the Grip of Nazi Terror.* New York, 1990.

Kaplan, Israel. "Weapons in the Riga Ghetto." In *Muted Voices: Jewish Survivors of Latvia Remember.* Ed. Gertrude Schneider. New York, 1987, pp. 25–40.

Katz, Josef. *Erinnerungen eines Überlebenden.* Kiel, 1988.

Kaufmann, Max. *Churbn Lettland: Die Vernichtung der Juden Lettlands.* Ed. Erhard Roy Wiehn. (Unverändertes Reprint des Privatdrucks Munich 1947) Konstanz, 1999.

Kits, Abrams. "Zwangsarbeit in Riga, Stutthof, Gotendorf." *Dachauer Hefte* 16 (2000): 18–35.

Kleist, Peter. *Zwischen Hitler und Stalin 1939–1945.* Bonn, 1950.

Kusnezow, N. G. *Am Vorabend.* Berlin (East), 1973.

Lasch, Otto. *So fiel Königsberg: Kampf und Untergang von Ostpreußens Hauptstadt.* Munich, 1959.

Levenstein, Meir. *"Du sollst sterben und nicht leben": Ein Bericht über die Vernichtung der Juden Lettlands.* Münster, Hamburg, 1994.
Lippert, Jules R. "The Return to Riga." In *Muted Voices: Jewish Survivors of Latvia Remember.* Ed. Gertrude Schneider. New York, 1987, pp. 254–267.
Maurina, Zenta. *Die eisernen Riegel zerbrechen: Geschichte eines Lebens.* Memmingen, 1957.
Michelson, Frida. *I Survived Rumbuli.* Washington, D.C., 1999.
Michelson, Max. *City of Life, City of Death: Memories of Riga.* Boulder, CO, 2001.
Muted Voices: Jewish Survivors of Latvia Remember. Ed. Gertrude Schneider. New York, 1987.
Paasikivi, Juho Kusti. *Meine Moskauer Mission 1939–41.* Ed. Gösta von Uexküll. Hamburg, 1966.
Rabinovici, Schoschana. *Dank meiner Mutter.* Frankfurt am Main, 1994.
Ratz, Jack. *Endless Miracles.* New York, 1998.
Rolnikaite, Mascha. *Ich muß erzählen: Mein Tagebuch 1941–1945.* Berlin, 2002.
Salzmann, Jewgenij. "Dieses bittere Glück. Ein lettischer Jude im Ghetto und GULAG." *Dachauer Hefte* 14 (1998): 175–217.
Schellenberg, Walter. *Aufzeichnungen: Die Memoiren des letzten Geheimdienstchefs unter Hitler.* Ed. Gita Petersen. Wiesbaden and Munich, 1979.
Schneider, Gertrude. "Von Riga nach Stutthof." In *Stutthof: Ein Konzentrationslager vor den Toren Danzigs.* Ed. Hermann Kuhn. Bremen, 1995.
Schneider, Karl. "Religiöses Leben der Kölner Juden im Ghetto von Riga nach den Erinnerungen von Karl Schneider." Ed. Hans-Dieter Arntz. *Jahrbuch des Kölner Geschichtsvereins* 53 (1982): 127–152.
Schur, Grigorij, *Die Juden von Wilna: die Aufzeichnungen des Grigorij Schur 1941–1944.* Munich 1999.
Das Schwarzbuch: Der Genozid an den sowjetischen Juden. Ed. Wassili Grossmann and Ilja Ehrenburg. Reinbek bei Hamburg, 1994.
Semenoff, Sasha. "After the Liberation." In *Muted Voices: Jewish Survivors of Latvia Remember.* Ed. Gertrude Schneider. New York, 1987, pp. 231–237.
Sherman-Zander, Hilde. *Zwischen Tag und Dunkel: Mädchenjahre im Ghetto.* Frankfurt am Main and Berlin, 1989.
Silberman, David. "Jan Lipke: An Unusual Man." In *Muted Voices: Jewish Survivors of Latvia Remember.* Ed. Gertrude Schneider. New York, 1987, pp. 87–111.
Sudoplatow, Pawel Anatoljewitsch, and Anatolij Sudoplatow. *Der Handlanger der Macht: Enthüllungen eines KGB-Generals.* Düsseldorf et al., 1996.
The Unfinished Road: Jewish Survivors of Latvia Look Back. Ed. Gertrude Schneider. New York, Westport, CT, and London, 1991.
Warlimont, Walter. *Im Hauptquartier der deutschen Wehrmacht 1939–1945: Grundlagen, Formen, Gestalten.* Frankfurt am Main, 1962.
Winter, Alfred. *The Ghetto of Riga and Continuance: A Survivor's Memoir.* Monroe, CT?, 1998.
Wittrock, Hugo. *Kommissarischer Oberbürgermeister von Riga 1941–1944: Erinnerungen.* Ed. Wilhelm Lenzsen and Wilhelm Lenz jun. Lüneburg, 1979.
Wolff, Jeanette. *Sadismus oder Wahnsinn: Erlebnisse in den deutschenKonzentrationslagern im Osten.* Greiz, 1947.
Yashek, Richard. "'Ich habe immer noch vor Augen, wie der Schnee sich rot färbte': Kindheitserinnerungen an Bad Schwartau, Lübeck und Riga." In *Menora und Hakenkreuz: Zur Geschichte der Juden in und aus Schleswig-Holstein, Lübeck und Altona (1918–1998).* Ed. Gerhard Paul and Miriam Gillis-Carlebach. Neumünster, 1998, pp. 521–529.

Zin, Basja. *Wie ein grauenhafter Traum: Vier Jahre zwischen Leben und Tod. Jüdische Schicksale aus Lettland 1941–1945*. Ed. Erhard Roy Wiehn. Konstanz, 1998.

Memorial Books

Buch der Erinnerung: Die ins Baltikum deportierten deutschen, österreichischen und tschechoslowakischen Juden. Ed. Volksbund Deutsche Kriegsgräberfürsorge, Wolfgang Scheffler, and Diana Schulle. Munich, 2003.
The Holocaust in Lithuania 1941–1945: A Book of Remembrance. Ed. Rose Cohen and Saul Issroff. 4 vols. Jerusalem, New York, 2002.
Jews in Liepaja, Latvia, 1941–1945: A Memorial Book. Ed. Edward Anders and Juris Dubrovskis. Burlingame, CA, 2001.
Pinkas Hakehillot. Encyclopedia of Jewish Communities in Latvia and Estonia. Ed. Dov Levin. Jerusalem, 1988 (Hebrew).

Secondary Literature

Adler, H.-G. *Theresienstadt 1941–1944: Das Antlitz einer Zwangsgemeinschaft.* Tübingen, 1960.
———. *"Der verwaltete Mensch": Studien zur Deportation der Juden aus Deutschland.* Tübingen, 1974.
Aly, Götz. *"Endlösung": Völkerverschiebung und der Mord an den europäischen Juden.* Frankfurt am Main, 1995.
Anatomie des SS-Staates. Ed. Martin Broszat. Munich, 1984.
Angrick, Andrej. "Die Einsatzgruppe D." In *Die Einsatzgruppen in der besetzten Sowjetunion 1941/42.* Ed. Peter Klein. Berlin, 1997, pp. 88–110.
Angrick, Andrej, and Peter Klein. "Riga 1941–1944." In *Orte des Grauens: Verbrechen im Zweiten Weltkrieg.* Ed. Gerd R. Ueberschär. Darmstadt, 2003, pp. 195–206.
Angrick, Andrej, Martina Voigt, Silke Ammerschubert, and Peter Klein. "'Da hätte man schon ein Tagebuch führen müssen': Das Polizeibataillon 322 und die Judenmorde im Bereich der Heeresgruppe Mitte während des Sommers und Herbstes 1941." In *Die Normalität des Verbrechens: Bilanz und Perspektiven der Forschung zu den nationalsozialistischen Gewaltverbrechen. Festschrift für Wolfgang Scheffler zum 65. Geburtstag.* Ed. Helge Grabitz, Klaus Bästlein, and Johannes Tuchel. Berlin, 1994, pp. 325–385.
Antonow-Owsejensko, Anton. *Der Weg nach oben: Skizzen zu einem Berija-Porträt.* In *Berija: Henker in Stalins Diensten. Ende einer Karriere.* Ed. Vladimir F. Nekrassow. Augsburg, 1997, pp. 11–172.
Arad, Yitzhak. *Ghetto in Flames: The Struggle and Destruction of the Jews in Vilna in the Holocaust.* New York, 1982.
———. "Plunder of Jewish Property in the Nazi-Occupied Areas of the Soviet Union." *Yad Vashem Studies* 29 (2001): 109–148.
Arnold, Klaus Jochen. *Die Wehrmacht und die Besatzungspolitik in den besetzten Gebieten der Sowjetunion: Kriegführung und Radikalisierung im Unternehmen Barbarossa.* Berlin, 2005.
Artzt, Heinz. *Mörder in Uniform.* Munich, 1979.
Barkai, Avraham. "German-Speaking Jews in Eastern European Ghettos." *Leo Baeck Institute Yearbook* (1989): 247–266.
Bästlein, Klaus. "'Völkermord und koloniale Träumerei': Das Reichskommissariat Ostland unter schleswig-holsteinischer Verwaltung." In *NS-Gewaltherrschaft: Beiträge zur*

historischen Forschung und juristischen Aufarbeitung. Ed. Alfred Gottwaldt, Norbert Kampe, and Peter Klein. Berlin, 2005, pp. 217–246.

Besymenski, Lew. *Sonderakte "Barbarossa": Dokumentarbericht zur Vorgeschichte des deutschen Überfalls auf die Sowjetunion aus sowjetischer Sicht.* Reinbek bei Hamburg, 1973.

———. *Stalin und Hitler: Das Pokerspiel der Diktatoren.* Berlin, 2002.

Beth, Menahem. "Men and Deeds." In *The Jews in Latvia.* Ed. Association of Latvian and Estonian Jews in Israel. Tel Aviv, 1971, pp. 285–335.

Birn, Ruth Bettina. *Die Höheren SS- und Polizeiführer: Himmlers Vertreter im Reich und in den besetzten Gebieten.* Düsseldorf, 1986.

———. "'Zaunkönig' an 'Uhrmacher': Große Partisanenaktionen 1942/43 am Beispiel des 'Unternehmens Winterzauber.'" *Militärgeschichtliche Zeitschrift* 60 (2001): 99–118.

———. "Heinrich Bergmann – eine deutsche Kriminalistenkarriere." In *Karrieren der Gewalt: Nationalsozialistische Täterbiographien.* Ed. Klaus-Michael Mallmann and Gerhard Paul. Darmstadt, 2004, pp. 47–55.

Blank, Margot. *Nationalsozialistische Hochschulpolitik in Riga (1941 bis 1944): Konzeption und Realität eines Bereiches deutscher Besatzungspolitik.* Lüneburg, 1991.

Blasius, Dirk. "Bürgerlicher Tod: Der NS-Unrechtsstaat und die deutschen Juden." *Geschichte in Wissenschaft und Unterricht* 41 (1990), 3: 129–144.

Bobe, Mendel. "Riga." In *The Jews in Latvia.* Ed. Association of Latvian and Estonian Jews in Israel. Tel Aviv, 1971, pp. 243–261.

Bräutigam, Otto. *Überblick über die besetzten Ostgebiete während des 2. Weltkrieges.* Tübingen, 1954.

Breitman, Richard. *Der Architekt der "Endlösung": Himmler und die Vernichtung der europäischen Juden.* Paderborn et al., 1996.

———. *Staatsgeheimnisse: Die Verbrechen der Nazis – von den Alliierten toleriert.* Munich, 1999.

———. "Friedrich Jeckeln: Spezialist für die 'Endlösung' im Osten." In *Die SS: Elite unterm Totenkopf.* Ed. Ronald Smelser and Enrico Syring. Paderborn, 2000, pp. 267–275.

Broszat, Martin. *Nationalsozialistische Polenpolitik 1939–1945.* Stuttgart, 1961.

———. "Die nationale Widerstandsbewegung in Litauen im Zweiten Weltkrieg (1941 bis 1944)." In *Gutachten des Instituts für Zeitgeschichte,* Bd. 2. Stuttgart, 1966, pp. 311–328.

Browning, Christopher. *Die Entfesselung der "Endlösung": Nationalsozialistische Judenpolitik 1939–1942.* With a contribution by Jürgen Matthäus. Munich, 2003.

Büchler, Yehoshua. "Kommandostab Reichsführer SS. Himmler's Personal Murder Brigades in 1941." *Holocaust and Genocide Studies* 1 (1986): 11–25.

———. "A Preparatory Document for the Wannsee-Conference." *Holocaust and Genocide Studies* 9 (1995): 121–129.

Bullock, Alan. *Hitler und Stalin: Parallele Leben.* Gütersloh et al., 1991.

Chlewnjuk, Oleg W. *Das Politbüro: Mechanismen der politischen Macht in der Sowjetunion der dreißiger Jahre.* Hamburg, 1998.

Cüppers, Martin. *Wegbereiter der Shoah: Die Waffen-SS, der Kommandostab Reichsführer-SS und die Judenvernichtung 1939–1945.* Darmstadt, 2005.

Curilla, Wolfgang. "Schutzpolizei und Judenmord: Die Dienststelle des Kommandeurs der Schutzpolizei in Riga." In *NS-Gewaltherrschaft: Beiträge zur historischen Forschung und juristischen Aufarbeitung.* Ed. Alfred Gottwaldt, Norbert Kampe, and Peter Klein. Berlin, 2005, pp. 247–264.

Dallin, Alexander. *Deutsche Herrschaft in Rußland 1941–1945: Eine Studie über Besatzungspolitik.* Düsseldorf, 1958.

Danker, Uwe. "Der gescheiterte Versuch, die Legende von der sauberen Zivilverwaltung zu entzaubern: Staatsanwaltschaftliche Komplexermittlungen zum Holocaust im "Reichskommissariat Ostland" bis 1971." In *Die deutsche Herrschaft in den "germanischen" Ländern 1940–1945*. Ed. Robert Bohn. Stuttgart, 1997, pp. 159–186.

Daugavas Vanagi. *Who Are They?* Ed. E. Avotins, J. Dzirkalis, and V. Petersons. Riga, 1963.

Dean, Martin. "Seizure, Registration, Rental and Sale: The Strange Case of the German Administration of Jewish Moveable Property in Latvia (1941–1944)." In *Latvia in World War II: Materials of an International Conference 14–15 June 1999 in Riga*. Riga, 2000 (= Latvijas Vesturnieku komisijas raksti, 1. sejums), pp. 372–381.

———. "Die Enteignung 'jüdischen Eigentums' im Reichskommissariat Ostland 1941–1944." In *"Arisierung" im Nationalsozialismus: Volksgemeinschaft, Raub und Gedächtnis*. Ed. Fritz-Bauer-Institut. Frankfurt am Main, 2000, pp. 201–218.

de Jong, Louis. *Het Kroninkrijk der Nederlanden in de TweedeWereldoorlog, Bd. 5/2, Mart 1941–Juli 1942*. Rijksinstitut voor Oorlogsdokumentatie. Amsterdam, 1974.

Die Deportation der Hamburger Juden 1941–1945. Ed. Forschungsstelle für Zeitgeschichte in Hamburg and Institut für die Geschichte der deutschen Juden. Hamburg, 2002.

Die deutsche Herrschaft in den "germanischen" Ländern 1940–1945. Ed. Robert Bohn. Stuttgart, 1997.

Das Deutsche Reich und der Zweite Weltkrieg. Ed. Militärgeschichtliches Forschungsamt. Stuttgart and Munich, 1979–2001.

Deutscher Osten 1939–1945: Der Weltanschauungskrieg in Photos und Texten. Ed. Klaus-Michael Mallmann, Volker Rieß, and Wolfram Pyta. Darmstadt, 2003.

Dieckmann, Christoph. "Das Ghetto und das Konzentrationslager in Kaunas 1941–1944." In *Die nationalsozialistischen Konzentrationslager: Entwicklung und Struktur*, Bd. 1. Ed. Ulrich Herbert, Karin Orth, and Christoph Dieckmann. Göttingen, 1998, pp. 439–471.

Dirks, Carl und Karl-Heinz Janßen. *Der Krieg der Generäle: Hitler als Werkzeug der Wehrmacht*. Berlin, 1999.

Döscher, Hans-Jürgen. *SS und Auswärtiges Amt im Dritten Reich: Diplomatie im Schatten der Endlösung*. Frankfurt am Main und Berlin, 1991.

Evarts, Edvins. "Deutsche Historiker über die nationalsozialistische Okkupationspolitik Deutschlands in Lettland." In *Occupation Regimes in Latvia in 1940–1956: Research of the Commission of the Historians of Latvia in Riga 2001*. Riga, 2002 (= Latvijas Vesturnieku komisijas raksti, 7. sejums), pp. 123–140.

Ezergailis, Andrew. *The Holocaust in Latvia 1941–1944: The Missing Center*. Riga, Washington, D.C., 1996.

Fabry, Philipp W. *Der Hitler-Stalin-Pakt 1939–1941: Ein Beitrag zur Methode sowjetischer Außenpolitik*. Darmstadt, 1992.

Falin, Valentin. *Zweite Front: Die Interessenkonflikte der Anti-Hitler-Koalition*. Munich, 1995.

Fleischhauer, Ingeborg. *Der Pakt: Hitler, Stalin und die Initiative der deutschen Diplomatie 1938–1939*. Berlin and Frankfurt am Main, 1990.

———. "Die sowjetische Außenpolitik und die Genese des Hitler-Stalin-Paktes." In *Zwei Wege nach Moskau: Vom Hitler-Stalin-Pakt bis zum "Unternehmen Barbarossa."* Ed. Bernd Wegner. Munich, 1991, pp. 19–39.

Fleming, Gerald. *Hitler und die Endlösung: "Es ist des Führers Wunsch ..."* Wiesbaden and Munich, 1982.

Förster, Jürgen. "Die Gewinnung von Verbündeten in Südosteuropa." In *Das Deutsche Reich und der Zweite Weltkrieg*, Bd. 4. Ed. Militärgeschichtliches Forschungsamt. Stuttgart, 1983, pp. 327–364.

———. Die Sicherung des "Lebensraumes." In *Das Deutsche Reich und der Zweite Weltkrieg*, Bd. 4. Ed. Militärgeschichtliches Forschungsamt. Stuttgart, 1983, pp. 1030–1078.
Forwick, Helmuth. "Der Rückzug der Heeresgruppe Nord nach Kurland." In *Abwehrkämpfe am Nordflügel der Ostfront 1944–1945*. Ed. Hans Meier-Welcker. Stuttgart, 1963.
Foschepoth, Josef. *Im Schatten der Vergangenheit: Die Anfänge der Gesellschaften für Christlich-Jüdische Zusammenarbeit*. Göttingen, 1993.
Friedlander, Henry. "The Deportation of the German Jews: Post-War German Trials of Nazi Criminals." *Leo Baeck Institute Yearbook* (1984): 201–226.
Friedrich, Jörg. *Das Gesetz des Krieges: Das deutsche Heer in Rußland 1941 bis 1945. Der Prozeß gegen das Oberkommando der Wehrmacht*. Frankfurt am Main, 1984.
Garleff, Michael. "Die kulturelle Selbstverwaltung der nationalen Minderheiten in den baltischen Staaten." In *Die baltischen Nationen*. Ed. Boris Meissner. Cologne, pp. 87–107.
———. "Die Deutschbalten als nationale Minderheit in den unabhängigen Staaten Estland und Lettland." In *Deutsche Geschichte im Osten Europas: Baltische Länder*. Ed. Gert von Pistohlkors. Berlin, 1994, pp. 452–550.
———. *Die Baltischen Länder: Estland, Lettland, Litauen vom Mittelalter bis zur Gegenwart*. Regensburg, 2001.
Genesis des Genozids: Polen 1939–1941. Ed. Klaus-Michael Mallmann and Bogdan Musial. Darmstadt, 2004.
Gerlach, Christian. "Die Einsatzgruppe B 1941/42." In *Die Einsatzgruppen in der besetzten Sowjetunion 1941/42*. Ed. Peter Klein. Berlin, 1997, pp. 52–70.
———. "DieWannsee-Konferenz, das Schicksal der deutschen Juden und Hitlers politische Grundsatzentscheidung, alle Juden Europas zu ermorden." *Werkstatt-Geschichte* 6 (1997): 7–44.
———. "Failure of Plans for an SS Extermination Camp in Mogilev, Belorussia." *Holocaust and Genocide Studies* 11 (1997): 60–78.
———. "DeutscheWirtschaftsinteressen, Besatzungspolitik und der Mord an den Juden in Weißrußland, 1941–1943." In *Nationalsozialistische Vernichtungspolitik*. Ed. Ulrich Herbert. Frankfurt am Main, 1998, pp. 263–291.
———. *Kalkulierte Morde: Die deutsche Wirtschafts- und Vernichtungspolitik in Weißrußland 1941 bis 1944*. Hamburg, 1999.
Gerlach, Christian and Götz Aly. *Das letzte Kapitel: Realpolitik, Ideologie und der Mord an den ungarischen Juden 1944/45*. Stuttgart and Munich, 2002.
Gessner, Klaus. *Geheime Feldpolizei: Zur Funktion und Organisation des geheimpolizeilichen Exekutivorgans der faschistischen Wehrmacht*. Berlin (East), 1986.
Gilbert, Martin. *Auschwitz und die Alliierten*. Frankfurt am Main, 1985.
Gillis-Carlebach, Miriam. "'Licht in der Finsternis' (Fanni): Jüdische Lebensgestaltung im Konzentrationslager Jungfernhof." In *Menora und Hakenkreuz: Zur Geschichte der Juden in und aus Schleswig-Holstein, Lübeck und Altona (1918–1998)*. Ed. Gerhard Paul und Miriam Gillis-Carlebach. Neumünster, 1998, pp. 594–563. (See also Englard, Fanny, "A Light in the Darkness": Jewish Life in Jungfernhof Concentration Camp.")
Gorodetsky, Gabriel. *Die große Täuschung: Hitler, Stalin und das Unternehmen "Barbarossa."* Berlin, 2003.
Grabowska, Janina. "K. L. Stutthof: Ein historischer Abriß." In *Stutthof: Ein Konzentrationslager vor den Toren Danzigs*. Ed. Hermann Kuhn. Bremen, 1995, pp. 8–93.
Greiner, Helmuth. *Die Oberste Wehrmachtführung 1939–1943*.Wiesbaden, 1961.
Gretschko A. A., et al., *Geschichte des Zweiten Weltkrieges 1939–1945*. Ed. for the German edition by H. Hoffmann. Berlin (East), 1978.
Gryglewski, Marcus. "Zur Geschichte der nationalsozialistischen Judenverfolgung in Dresden 1933–1945." In *Die Erinnerung hat ein Gesicht: Fotografien und Dokumente zur*

nationalsozialistischen Judenverfolgung in Dresden 1933–1945. Ed. Norbert Haase, Stefi Jersch-Wenzel, Hermann Simon. Dresden, 1998.

Gutachten des Instituts für Zeitgeschichte. Munich, 1958 and Stuttgart, 1966.

Hachmeister, Lutz. *Der Gegnerforscher: Die Karriere des SS-Führers Franz Alfred Six*. Munich, 1998.

Hartmann, Christian. *Halder, Generalstabschef Hitlers 1938–1942*. Paderborn et al., 1991.

Heer, Hannes. *Tote Zonen: Die deutsche Wehrmacht an der Ostfront*. Hamburg, 1999.

Herbert, Ulrich. "Arbeit und Vernichtung. Ökonomisches Interesse und Primat der 'Weltanschauung' im Nationalsozialismus." In *Ist der Nationalsozialismus Geschichte? Zu Historisierung und Historikerstreit*. Ed. Dan Diner. Frankfurt am Main, 1987, pp. 198–236.

———. "Neue Antworten und Fragen zur Geschichte des Holocaust." In *Nationalsozialistische Vernichtungspolitik: Neue Forschungen und Kontroversen*. Ed. Ulrich Herbert. Frankfurt am Main, 1998, pp. 9–66.

Hesse, Klaus und Philipp Springer. *Vor aller Augen: Fotodokumente des nationalsozialistischen Terrors in der Provinz*. Essen, 2002.

Hiden, John. *The Baltic States and Weimar Ostpolitik*. Cambridge, 2002.

Hildebrand, Klaus. *Das vergangene Reich: Deutsche Außenpolitik von Bismarck bis Hitler 1871–1945*. Stuttgart, 1995.

Hilberg, Raul. *Die Vernichtung der europäischen Juden*. Frankfurt am Main 1990.

Hilger, Andreas, Nikita Petrov und Günther Wagenlehner. "Der 'Ukas 43': Entstehung und Problematik des Dekrets des Präsidiums des Obersten Sowjets vom 19. April 1943." In *Sowjetische Militärtribunale, Bd. 1: Die Verurteilung deutscher Kriegsgefangener 1941–1953*. Ed. Andreas Hilger, Ute Schmidt, and Günther Wagenlehner. Cologne et al., 2001, pp. 177–209.

Hillgruber, Andreas. *Hitler, König Carol und Marschall Antonescu: Die deutsch-rumänischen Beziehungen 1938–1944*.Wiesbaden, 1965.

———. *Hitlers Strategie: Politik und Kriegführung 1940–1941*. Munich, 1982.

Höhne, Heinz. *Der Orden unter dem Totenkopf: Die Geschichte der SS*. Bindlach, 1989.

Holocaust in Litauen: Krieg, Judenmorde und Kollaboration im Jahre 1941. Ed. Vincas Bartusevicius, Joachim Tauber, and Wolfram Wette. Cologne, Weimar, Vienna, 2003.

Hüser, Karl. *Wewelsburg 1933 bis 1945: Kult- und Terrorstätte der SS. Eine Dokumentation*. Paderborn, 1987.

The Issues of the Holocaust Research in Latvia: Reports of an International Conference 16–17 October 2000 in Riga. Riga, 2001 (= Latvijas Vesturnieku komisijas raksti, 2. sejums).

The Issues of the Holocaust Research in Latvia: Reports of an International Seminar November 29th 2001 in Riga and the Holocaust Studies in Latvia in 2001–2002. Riga, 2003 (= Latvijas Vesturnieku komisijas raksti, 8. sejums).

Jäckel, Eberhard. *Frankreich in Hitlers Europa: Die deutsche Frankreichpolitik im Zweiten Weltkrieg*. Stuttgart, 1966.

———. "On the Purpose of the Wannsee-Conference." In *Perspectives on the Holocaust: Essays in Honor of Raul Hilberg*. Ed. James A. Pacy and Alan P. Wertheimer. San Francisco, 1995, pp. 39–50.

Jacobsen, Hans-Adolf. "Kommissarbefehl und Massenexekutionen sowjetischer Kriegsgefangener." In *Anatomie des SS-Staates*, v. 2. Ed. Martin Broszat. Munich, 1984, pp. 135–232.

Jansen, Christian und Arno Weckbecker. *Der "Volksdeutsche Selbstschutz" in Polen 1939/40*. Munich, 1992.

Jansen, Hans. *Der Madagaskar-Plan: Die beabsichtigte Deportation der europäischen Juden nach Madagaskar*. Munich, 1997.

The Jews in Latvia. Ed. Association of Latvian and Esthonian Jews in Israel. Tel Aviv, 1971.
Kaienburg, Hermann. "Jüdische Arbeitslager an der 'Straße der SS.'" 1999. *Zeitschrift für Sozialgeschichte des 20. und 21. Jahrhunderts* 11 (1996): 13–39.
———. *Die Wirtschaft der SS.* Berlin, 2003.
Kaiser, Wolf. "DieWannsee-Konferenz: SS-Führer und Ministerialbeamte im Einvernehmen über die Ermordung der europäischen Juden." In *Täter – Opfer – Folgen.* Ed. Heiner Lichtenstein und Otto R. Romberg. Bonn, 1995, pp. 24–37.
Kalthoff, Jürgen, and Martin Werner. *Die Händler des Zyklon B: Tesch & Stabenow. Eine Firmengeschichte zwischen Hamburg und Auschwitz.* Hamburg, 1998.
Kangeris, Karlis. "Kollaboration vor der Kollaboration? Die baltischen Emigranten und ihre 'Befreiungskomitees' in Deutschland 1940/41." In *Okkupation und Kollaboration (1938–1945).* Ed. Werner Röhr. Berlin and Heidelberg, 1994, pp. 165–190.
Kaufmann, Max. "The War Years in Latvia Revisited." In *The Jews in Latvia.* Ed. der Association of Latvian and Esthonian Jews in Israel. Tel Aviv, 1971, pp. 351–368.
Kingreen, Monica. "Die gewaltsame Verschleppung der Juden aus den Dörfern und Städten des Regierungsbezirks Kassel in den Jahren 1941 und 1942." *Judaica Hassiaca* 3 (2002).
Klarsfeld, Serge. *Vichy – Auschwitz: Die Zusammenarbeit der deutschen und französischen Behörden bei der "Endlösung der Judenfrage" in Frankreich.* Nördlingen, 1989.
Klee, Ernst. *Persilscheine und falsche Pässe: Wie die Kirchen des Nazis halfen.* Frankfurt am Main, 1992.
Klein, Peter. *Die Wannsee-Konferenz: Analyse und Dokumentation.* Berlin, n. d. [1995]
———. "Die Erlaubnis zum grenzenlosen Massenmord – Das Schicksal der Berliner Juden und die Rolle der Einsatzgruppen bei dem Versuch, Juden als Partisanen 'auszurotten'." In *Die Wehrmacht: Mythos und Realität.* Ed. Rolf-Dieter Müller and Hans-Erich Volkmann. Munich, 1999, pp. 923–947.
———. "Strategy or Improvisation? The Ghetto of Riga as the Destination of Deportations from Western Europe." In *The Issues of the Holocaust Research in Latvia: Reports of an International Conference 16–17 October 2000 in Riga.* Riga, 2001 (= Latvijas Vesturnieku komisijas raksti, 2. sejums), pp. 74–82.
———. "Dr. Rudolf Lange als Kommandeur der Sicherheitspolizei und des SD in Lettland: Aspekte seines Dienstalltages." In *Täter im Vernichtungskrieg: Der Überfall auf die Sowjetunion und der Völkermord an den Juden.* Ed. Wolf Kaiser. Berlin and Munich, 2002, pp. 125–136.
———. "Zwischen den Fronten: Die ZivilbevölkerungWeißrusslands und der Krieg der Wehrmacht gegen die Partisanen." In *Wir sind die Herren dieses Landes: Ursachen, Verlauf und Folgen des deutschen Überfalls auf die Sowjetunion.* Ed. Babette Quinkert. Hamburg, 2002, pp. 82–103.
Kley, Stefan. *Hitler, Ribbentrop und die Entfesselung des Zweiten Weltkriegs.* Paderborn, 1996.
Klink, Ernst. "Die militärische Konzeption des Krieges gegen die Sowjetunion." In *Das Deutsche Reich und der Zweite Weltkrieg,* Bd. 4. Ed. Militärgeschichtliches Forschungsamt. Stuttgart, 1983, pp. 190–277.
Krausnick, Helmut. "Hitler und die Morde in Polen." *Vierteljahrshefte für Zeitgeschichte* 11 (1963): 196–209.
———. "Judenverfolgung." In *Anatomie des SS-Staates.* Ed. Martin Broszat. v. 2. Munich, 1984, pp. 233–366.
———. "Kommissarbefehl und 'Gerichtsbarkeitserlaß Barbarossa' in neuer Sicht." *Vierteljahrshefte für Zeitgeschichte* 25 (1977): 682–738.
———. "Hitler und die Befehle an die Einsatzgruppen im Sommer 1941." In *Der Mord an*

den Juden im Zweiten Weltkrieg. Ed. Eberhard Jäckel and Jürgen Rohwer. Frankfurt am Main, 1987, pp. 88–106.

Krausnick, Helmut, and Hans-Heinrich Wilhelm. *Die Truppe des Weltanschauungskrieges: Die Einsatzgruppen der Sicherheitspolizei und des SD 1938–1942.* Stuttgart, 1981.

Der Krieg gegen die Sowjetunion 1941–1945: Eine Dokumentation zum 50. Jahrestag des Überfalls auf die Sowjetunion. Ed. Reinhard Rürup. Berlin, 1991.

Krüger, Gabriele. *Die Brigade Ehrhardt.* Hamburg, 1971.

Kugler, Anita. *Scherwitz: Der jüdische SS-Offizier.* Cologne, 2004.

Künzle, Anton, and Gad Shimron. *Der Tod des Henkers von Riga.* Gerlingen, 1999.

Lager, Zwangsarbeit, Vertreibung und Deportation: Dimensionen der Massenverbrechen in der Sowjetunion und in Deutschland 1933 bis 1945. Ed. Dittmar Dahlmann and Gerhard Hirschfeld. Essen, 1999.

Lammersmann, Birgit, and KarinWißmann. "Nicht nach Riga! Der Überlebenskampf einer Münsterschen Jüdin im Dritten Reich." In *Schon fast vergessen: Alltag in Münster 1933–1945.* Ed. Heinz-Ulrich Eggert. Münster, 1989, pp. 139–183.

Laserson, Max. "The Jews in the Latvian Parliament." In *The Jews in Latvia.* Ed. Association of Latvian and Estonian Jews in Israel. Tel Aviv, 1971, pp. 94–185.

Latvia in World War II: Materials of an International Conference 14–15 June 1999 in Riga. Riga, 2000 (= Latvijas Vesturnieku komisijas raksti, 1. sejums).

Latvijas Okupacijas Muzejs. *Latvia under the Rule of the Soviet Union and National Socialist Germany.* Riga, 2002.

Lenz, Wilhelm. *Die Entwicklung Rigas zur Großstadt.* Kitzingen am Main, 1954.

Lettland unter nationalsozialistischer Herrschaft (1940–1991): Eine Dokumentation des lettischen Okkupationsmuseums. Riga and Cologne, 1998.

Letzte Spuren: Ghetto Warschau - SS-Arbeitslager Trawniki - Aktion Erntefest. Ed. Helge Grabitz and Wolfgang Scheffler. Berlin 1993.

Levits, Egil. "Lettland unter der Sowjetherrschaft und auf demWege zur Unabhängigkeit." In *Die baltischen Nationen.* Ed. Boris Meissner. Cologne, 1991, pp. 139–222.

Longerich, Peter. *Die Wannsee-Konferenz vom 20. Januar 1942: Planung und Beginn des Genozids an den europäischen Juden.* Berlin, 1998.

———. *Politik der Vernichtung: Eine Gesamtdarstellung der nationalsozialistischen Judenverfolgung.* Munich and Zürich, 1998.

———. *Der ungeschriebene Befehl: Hitler und der Weg zur "Endlösung."* Munich, 2001.

Lotfi, Gabriele. *KZ der Gestapo: Arbeitserziehungslager im Dritten Reich.* Stuttgart and Munich, 2000.

———. "Stätten des Terrors: Die Arbeitserziehungslager der Gestapo." In *Die Gestapo im Zweiten Weltkrieg: 'Heimatfront' und besetztes Europa.* Ed. Gerhard Paul and Klaus-Michael Mallmann. Darmstadt, 2000, pp. 255–269.

MacLean, French. *The Camp Men: The SS Officers who ran the Nazi Concentration Camp System.* Atglen, 1999.

———. *The Field Men: The SS Officers who led the Einsatzkommandos – the Nazi Mobile Killing Units.* Atglen, 1999.

Madajczyk, Czesław. *Die Okkupationspolitik Nazideutschlands in Polen 1939–1945.* Berlin (East), 1987.

Mader, Julius. *Hitlers Spionagegenerale sagen aus: Ein Dokumentarbericht über Aufbau, Struktur und Operationen des OKW-Geheimdienstamtes Ausland/Abwehr mit einer Chronologie seiner Einsätze 1933–1944.* Berlin (East), 1970.

Majer, Diemut. "Führerunmittelbare Sondergewalten in den besetzten Ostgebieten," *Verwaltung contra Menschenführung im Staat Hitlers.* Ed. Dieter Rebentisch and Karl Teppe, pp. 374-395.

Maier, Dieter. *Arbeitseinsatz und Deportation*. Berlin, 1994.
Maier, Klaus A., and Bernd Stegemann. "Die Sicherung der europäischen Nordflanke." In *Das Deutsche Reich und der Zweite Weltkrieg*, Bd. 2. Ed. Militärgeschichtliches Forschungsamt. Stuttgart, 1979, pp. 189–231.
Mallmann, Klaus-Michael. "Menschenjagd und Massenmord: Das neue Instrument der Einsatzgruppen und -kommandos 1938–1945." In *Die Gestapo im Zweiten Weltkrieg: "Heimatfront" und besetztes Europa*. Ed. Gerhard Paul and Klaus-Michael Mallmann. Darmstadt, 2000, pp. 291–316.

———. "Die Türöffner der 'Endlösung': Zur Genesis des Genozids." In *Die Gestapo im Zweiten Weltkrieg: "Heimatfront" und besetztes Europa*. Ed. Gerhard Paul and Klaus-Michael Mallmann. Darmstadt, 2000, pp. 437–463.

———. "Der Qualitative Sprung im Vernichtungsprozeß: Das Massaker von Kamenez-Podolsk Ende August 1941." *Jahrbuch für Antisemitismusforschung* 10 (2001): 239–264.
Manvell, Roger. *Die Herrschaft der Gestapo*. Rastatt, 1982.
Matthäus, Jürgen. "Warum wird über das Judentum geschult?" In *Die Gestapo im Zweiten Weltkrieg: "Heimatfront" und besetztes Europa*. Ed. Gerhard Paul and Klaus-Michael Mallmann. Darmstadt, 2000, pp. 100–124.

———. "'Reibungslos und planmäßig': Die zweite Welle der Judenvernichtung im Generalkommissariat Weißruthenien (1942–1944)," *Jahrbuch für Antisemitismusforschung* 4 (1995): 254–274.
Meding, Holger M. *Flucht vor Nürnberg? Deutsche und österreichische Einwanderung in Argentinien 1945–1955*. Cologne et al., 1992.
Menger, Manfred. *Deutschland und Finnland im zweiten Weltkrieg*. Berlin (East), 1988.
Meyer, Winfried. *Unternehmen Sieben: Eine Rettungsaktion für vom Holocaust Bedrohte aus dem Amt Ausland/Abwehr im Oberkommando der Wehrmacht*. Frankfurt am Main, 1993.
Der Mord an den Juden im Zweiten Weltkrieg: Entschlußbildung und Verwirklichung. Ed. Eberhard Jäckel, und Jürgen Rohwer. Frankfurt am Main, 1987.
Müller, Klaus-Jürgen. *Das Heer und Hitler: Armee und nationalsozialistisches Regime 1933–1940*. Stuttgart, 1969.
Müller, Rolf-Dieter. "Von der Wirtschaftallianz zum kolonialen Ausbeutungskrieg." In *Das Deutsche Reich und der Zweite Weltkrieg*, Bd. 4. Ed. Militärgeschichtliches Forschungsamt. Stuttgart, 1983, pp. 98–189.

———. *Hitlers Ostkrieg und die deutsche Siedlungspolitik: Die Zusammenarbeit von Wehrmacht, Wirtschaft und SS*. Frankfurt am Main, 1991.
Musial, Bogdan. *Deutsche Zivilverwaltung und Judenverfolgung im Generalgouvernement: Eine Fallstudie zum Distrikt Lublin 1939–1944*. Wiesbaden, 1999.
Myllyniemi, Seppo. *Die Neuordnung der baltischen Länder 1941–1944: Zum nationalsozialistischen Inhalt der deutschen Besatzungspolitik*. Helsinki, 1973.

———. *Die baltische Krise 1938–1941*. Stuttgart, 1979.

———. "Die Folgen des Hitler-Stalin-Paktes für die Baltischen Republiken und Finnland." In *Zwei Wege nach Moskau: Vom Hitler-Stalin-Pakt bis zum "Unternehmen Barbarossa."* Ed. Bernd Wegner. Munich, 1991, pp. 75–92.
Nationalsozialistische Vernichtungspolitik: Neue Forschungen und Kontroversen. Ed. Ulrich Herbert. Frankfurt am Main, 1998.
Noethen, Stefan. *Alte Kameraden und neue Kollegen: Polizei in Nordrhein-Westfalen 1945–1953*. Essen, 2003.
Nordsiek, Marianne. "Die Deportation Mindener Jüdinnen und Juden 1941 nach Riga." In *Verdrängung und Vernichtung der Juden in Westfalen*. Ed. Arno Herzig. Münster, 1994, pp. 143–155.

NS-Gewaltherrschaft: Beiträge zur historischen Forschung und juristischen Aufarbeitung. Ed. Alfred Gottwaldt, Norbert Kampe, and Peter Klein. Berlin, 2005.

Obenaus, Herbert. "Die Deportation deutscher Juden nach Riga." In *Die vergessenen Juden in den baltischen Staaten: Ein Symposium vom 4. bis zum 7. Juli 1997 in Hannover*. Ed. Ansgar Koscher and Helker Pflug. Cologne, 1998, pp. 85–96.

———. "Vom SA-Mann zum jüdischen Ghettoältesten in Riga: Zur Biographie von Günther Fleischel." *Jahrbuch für Antisemitismusforschung* 8 (1999): 278–299.

Occupation Regimes in Latvia in 1940–1956: Research of the Commission of the Historians of Latvia in Riga 2001. Riga, 2002 (= Latvijas Vesturnieku komisijas raksti, 7. sejums).

Ogorreck, Ralf. *Die Einsatzgruppen und die "Genesis der Endlösung."* Berlin, 1996.

Olshausen, Klaus. *Zwischenspiel auf dem Balkan: Die deutsche Politik gegenüber Jugoslawien und Griechenland von März bis Juli 1941*. Stuttgart, 1973.

Onken, Eva-Clarita. *Revisionismus schon vor der Geschichte? Aktuelle Kontroversen in Lettland um die Judenvernichtung und die lettische Kollaboration während der nationalsozialistischen Besatzung*. Cologne, 1998.

———. *Demokratisierung der Geschichte in Lettland: Staatsbürgerliches Bewusstsein und Geschichtspolitik im ersten Jahrzehnt der Unabhängigkeit*. Hamburg, 2003.

Orski, Marek. "Organisation und Ordnungsprinzipien des Lagers Stutthof." In *Die nationalsozialistischen Konzentrationslager: Entwicklung und Struktur*, Bd. 1. Ed. Ulrich Herbert, Karin Orth, and Christoph Dieckmann. Göttingen, 1998, pp. 283–308.

Orth, Karin. *Das System der nationalsozialistischen Konzentrationslager: Eine politische Organisationsgeschichte*. Hamburg, 1999.

———. *Die Konzentrationslager-SS: Sozialstrukturelle Analysen und biographische Studien*. Göttingen, 2000.

Pajouh, Christine. "Die Ostpolitik Alfred Rosenbergs 1941–1944." In *Deutschbalten, Weimarer Republik und Drittes Reich*. Ed. Michael Garleff. Cologne, Weimar, Vienna, 2001, pp. 167–195.

Pätzold, Kurt, and Erika Schwarz. *Tagesordnung: Judenmord. Die Wannsee-Konferenz am 20. Januar 1942*. Berlin, 1992.

Die Gestapo im Zweiten Weltkrieg: 'Heimatfront' und besetztes Europa. Ed. Gerhard Paul and Klaus-Michael Mallmann. Darmstadt, 2000.

Pick, Hella. *Simon Wiesenthal: Eine Biographie*. Reinbek bei Hamburg, 1997.

Pingel, Falk. *Häftlinge unter SS-Herrschaft: Widerstand, Selbstbehauptung und Vernichtung im Konzentrationslager*. Hamburg, 1978.

Pistohlkors, Gert von. "Die historischen Voraussetzungen für die Entstehung der drei baltischen Staaten." In *Die baltischen Nationen*. Ed. Boris Meissner. Cologne, 1991, pp. 11–49.

Piterskij, N. A. "Die Sowjet-Flotte im Zweiten Weltkrieg." Im *Auftrag des Arbeitskreises für Wehrforschung*. Ed. Jürgen Rohwer. Oldenburg and Hamburg, 1966.

Pohl, Dieter. "Die Einsatzgruppe C 1941/42." In *Die Einsatzgruppen in der besetzten Sowjetunion 1941/42*. Ed. Peter Klein. Berlin, 1997, pp. 71–87.

———. "Schauplatz Ukraine: Der Massenmord an den Juden." In *Ausbeutung, Vernichtung, Öffentlichkeit: Neue Studien zur nationalsozialistischen Lagerpolitik*. Ed. Norbert Frei, Sybille Steinbacher, and Bernd C. Wagner. Munich, 2000, pp. 135–173.

———. "Die Wehrmacht und der Mord an den Juden in den besetzten sowjetischen Gebieten." In *Täter im Vernichtungskrieg: Der Überfall auf die Sowjetunion und der Völkermord an den Juden*. Ed. Wolf Kaiser. Berlin and Munich, 2002. pp. 39–53.

Press, Bernhard. *Judenmord in Lettland 1941–1945*. Berlin, 1992.

Prybil, Lukas. "Die Geschichte des Theresienstädter Transports 'Be' nach Estland." *Theresienstädter Studien und Dokumente* (2001): 148–229.

Raim, Edith. "Die Strafverfahren wegen der Deportation der Juden aus Unter- und Mittelfranken nach 1945." In *Wege in die Vernichtung: Die Deportation der Juden aus Mainfranken 1941–1943*. Ed. Albrecht Liess. Munich, 2003, pp. 178–192.
Rauch, Gregor von. *Geschichte der baltischen Staaten*. Munich, 1990.
Rebentisch, Dieter. *Führerstaat und Verwaltung im Zweiten Weltkrieg: Verfassungsentwicklung und Verwaltungspolitik 1939–1945*. Stuttgart, 1989.
Reichardt, Sven. "Vergemeinschaftung durch Gewalt. Das Beispiel des SA-'Mördersturmes 33' in Berlin-Charlottenburg zwischen 1928 und 1932." In *Entgrenzte Gewalt: Täterinnen und Täter im Nationalsozialismus*. Ed. Herbert Diercks. Bremen, 2003, pp. 20–36.
Reichelt, Katrin. "Profit and Loss: The Economic Dimensions of the Riga Ghetto (1941–1943)." In *The Issues of the Holocaust Research in Latvia: Reports of an International Conference 16–17 October 2000 in Riga*. Riga, 2001 (= Latvijas Vesturnieku komisijas raksti, 2. sejums), pp. 169–184.
———. "Kollaboration und Holocaust in Lettland 1941–1945." In *Täter im Vernichtungskrieg: Der Überfall auf die Sowjetunion und der Völkermord an den Juden*. Ed. Wolf Kaiser. Berlin and Munich, 2002, pp. 110–124.
———. "Der Anteil der Letten an der Enteignung der Juden ihres Landes zwischen 1941 und 1943." In *Kooperation und Verbrechen: Formen der "Kollaboration" im östlichen Europa 1939–1945*. Ed. Christoph Dieckmann (= *Beiträge zur Geschichte des Nationalsozialismus* 19) Göttingen, 2003, pp. 224–242.
———. "Zwei Gesellschaften auf begrenztem Raum – das unfreiwillige Zusammenleben der lettischen und deutschen Juden im Ghetto von Riga zwischen 1942 und 1943." In *NS-Gewaltherrschaft: Beiträge zur historischen Forschung und juristischen Aufarbeitung*. Ed. Alfred Gottwaldt, Norbert Kampe, and Peter Klein. Berlin, 2005, pp. 265–277.
Reitlinger, Gerald. *Ein Haus auf Sand gebaut: Hitlers Gewaltpolitik in Rußland 1941–1944*. Hamburg, 1962.
———. *Die Endlösung: Hitlers Versuch der Ausrottung der Juden Europas 1939–1945*. Berlin, 1979.
Rieß, Volker. *Die Anfänge der Vernichtung "lebensunwerten Lebens" in den Reichsgauen Danzig-Westpreußen und Wartheland 1939/40*. Frankfurt am Main et al., 1995.
Rohde, Horst. "Hitlers erster 'Blitzkrieg' und seine Auswirkung auf Nordosteuropa." In *Das Deutsche Reich und der Zweite Weltkrieg*, Bd. 2. Ed. Militärgeschichtliches Forschungsamt. Stuttgart, 1979, pp. 79–156.
Röhr, Werner. "System oder organisiertes Chaos? Fragen einer Typologie der deutschen Okkupationsregime im Zweiten Weltkrieg." In *Die deutsche Herrschaft in den "germanischen" Ländern*. Ed. Robert Bohn. Stuttgart, 1997, pp. 11–45.
Roseman, Mark. *Die Wannsee-Konferenz: Wie die NS-Bürokratie den Holocaust organisierte*. Munich and Berlin, 2002.
Rückerl, Adalbert. *NS-Verbrechen vor Gericht: Versuch einer Vergangenheitsbewältigung*. Heidelberg, 1984.
Rüter, Christiaan Frederik. "Ost- und westdeutsche Strafverfahren gegen die Verantwortlichen für die Deportation der Juden." In *NS-Unrecht vor Kölner Gerichten nach 1945*. Ed. Anne Klein and Jürgen Wilhelm. Cologne, 2003, pp. 45–56.
Ruth "Sara" Lax, fünf Jahre alt, deportiert nach Riga: Deportation und Vernichtung badischer und württembergischer Juden. Ed. Dorothee Weitbrecht and Volker Rieß. Ludwigsburg, 2002.
Safrian, Hans. *Die Eichmann-Männer*. Vienna and Zürich, 1993.
Sandkühler, Thomas. "Judenpolitik und Judenmord im Distrikt Galizien 1941–1942." In *Nationalsozialistische Vernichtungspolitik*. Ed. Ulrich Herbert. Frankfurt am Main, 1998, pp. 122–147.

Scheffler, Wolfgang. "Zur Rolle der Zivilverwaltung bei der Durchführung der 'Endlösung der Judenfrage' im Reichskommissariat Ostland." In *Täter und Gehilfen des Endlösungswahns: Hamburger Verfahren wegen NS-Gewaltverbrechen 1946–1996.* Ed. Helge Grabitz. Hamburg, 1999, pp. 242–272.

———. "The Fate of the German Jews in the Ghetto of Riga and Surroundings: A Short Survey." In *The Issues of the Holocaust Research in Latvia: Reports of an International Seminar November 29th 2001 in Riga and the Holocaust Studies in Latvia in 2001–2002.* Riga, 2003 (= Latvijas Vesturnieku komisijas raksti, 8. sejums), pp. 39–51.

———. "Das Schicksal der in die baltischen Staaten deportierten deutschen, österreichischen und tschechoslowakischen Juden 1941–1945: Ein historischer Überblick." In *Buch der Erinnerung.* Ed. Volksbund Deutsche Kriegsgräberfürsorge, Wolfgang Scheffler, and Diana Schulle, Bd. 1. Munich, 2003, pp. 1–78.

Scheffler, Wolfgang, and Helge Grabitz. "Die Wannsee-Konferenz. Ihre Bedeutung in der Geschichte des nationalsozialistischen Völkermords." *Studia nad Faszyzmen i Zbrodniami Hitlerowskimi* 18 (1995): 197–219.

Schicksal jüdischer Mitbürger in Nürnberg 1933–1945. Ed. Stadtarchiv Nürnberg. Nürnberg, 1985.

Schlau, Wilfried. "Der Wandel in der sozialen Struktur der baltischen Länder." In *Die baltischen Nationen.* Ed. Boris Meissner. Cologne, 1991, pp. 357–381.

Schmalhausen, Bernd. *Dr. Rolf Bischofswerder: Leben und Sterben eines jüdischen Arztes aus Dortmund.* Bottrop and Essen, 1998.

Schmidt, Hartmut. *Zwischen Riga und Locarno: Bericht über Hilde Schneider, Christin jüdischer Herkunft, Diakonisse, Ghetto- und KZ-Häftling, Gefängnispfarrerin.* Berlin, 2000.

Schmidt, Ute. "Spätheimkehrer oder 'Schwerstkriegsverbrecher'? Die Gruppe der 749 'Nichtamnestierten.'" In *Sowjetische Militärtribunale, Bd. 1: Die Verurteilung deutscher Kriegsgefangener 1941–1953.* Ed. Andreas Hilger, Ute Schmidt, and Günther Wagenlehner. Cologne, 2001, pp. 273–350.

Schneider, Gertrude. *Journey into Terror: Story of the Riga Ghetto.* Westport, CT, 2001.

Schröder, Matthias. *Deutschbaltische SS-Führer und Andrej Vlasov 1942–1945: "Rußland kann nur von Russen besiegt werden". Erhard Kroeger, Friedrich Buchardt und die "Russische Befreiungsarmee."* Paderborn et al., 2001.

Schulte, Jan Erik. *Zwangsarbeit und Vernichtung: Das Wirtschaftsimperium der SS. Oswald Pohl und das SS-Wirtschafts-Verwaltungshauptamt 1933–1945.* Paderborn et al., 2001.

Schulte, Theo. *The German Army and Nazi Policies in Occupied Russia.* Oxford, 1989.

Schwarz, Gudrun. *Die nationalsozialistischen Lager.* Frankfurt am Main, 1996.

Seeger, Andreas. *"Gestapo-Müller": Die Karriere eines Schreibtischtäters.* Berlin, 1996.

Segev, Tom. *Die Soldaten des Bösen: Zur Geschichte der KZ-Kommandanten.* Reinbek bei Hamburg, 1992.

Seidler, Franz W. *Die Kollaboration 1939–1945.* Munich and Berlin, 1995.

Silde, Adolfs. "Die Entwicklung der Republik Lettland." In *Die baltischen Nationen.* Ed. Boris Meissner. Cologne, 1991, pp. 63–74.

Simon, Gerhard. *Nationalismus und Nationalitätenpolitik in der Sowjetunion: Von der totalitären Diktatur zur nachstalinschen Gesellschaft.* Baden-Baden, 1986.

Stopinski, Sigmar. *Das Baltikum im Patt der Mächte: Zur Entstehung Estlands, Lettlands und Litauens im Gefolge des Ersten Weltkriegs.* Berlin, 1997.

Strathmann, Donate. *Auswandern oder hierbleiben? Jüdisches Leben in Düsseldorf und Nordrhein 1945–1960.* Essen, 2003.

Strazas, Aba. "Die Tätigkeit des Dezernats für jüdische Angelegenheiten in der 'Deutschen Militärverwaltung Ober Ost.'" In *Die baltischen Provinzen Rußlands zwischen den*

Revolutionen von 1905 und 1917. Ed. Andrew Ezergailis and Gert von Pistohlkors. Cologne and Vienna, 1982, pp. 315–329.

Streim, Alfred. *Das Sonderkommando 4a der Einsatzgruppe C und die mit diesem Kommando eingesetzten Verbände.* (Unpublished manuscript for the Zentrale Stelle der Landesjustizverwaltungen.)

———. *Die Behandlung sowjetischer Kriegsgefangener im "Fall Barbarossa": Eine Dokumentation. Unter Berücksichtigung der Unterlagen deutscher Strafverfolgungsbehörden und der Materialien der Zentralen Stelle der Landesjustizverwaltungen zur Aufklärung von NS-Verbrechen.* Heidelberg and Karlsruhe, 1981.

———. "Konzentrationslager auf dem Gebiet der Sowjetunion." *Dachauer Hefte* 5 (1989): 174–187.

Streit, Christian. *Keine Kameraden: DieWehrmacht und die sowjetischen Kriegsgefangenen 1941–1945.* Bonn, 1991.

Strods, Heinrihs. "'Salaspils koncentracijas nometne' (1941. gada oktobris–1944. gada septembris)" [with an English summary]. *Latvijas Okupacijas Muzeja Gadagra mata 2000:* 87–156.

Täter und Gehilfen des Endlösungswahns: Hamburger Verfahren wegen NS-Gewaltverbrechen 1946–1996. Ed. Helge Grabitz et al. Hamburg, 1999.

Telpuchowski, Boris Semjonowitsch. *Die sowjetische Geschichte des Großen Vaterländischen Krieges 1941–1945.* Ed. Andreas Hillgruber and Hans-Adolf Jacobsen. Frankfurt am Main, 1961.

Totalitarian Regimes and their Repressions carried out in Latvia in 1940–1956: Research of the Commission of the Historians in Latvia 2000. Riga, 2001 (= Latvijas Vesturnieku komisijas raksti, 3. sejums).

Toury, Jacob. "Die Entstehungsgeschichte des Austreibungsbefehls gegen die Juden der Saarpfalz und Badens (22./23. Oktober 1940 – Camp de Gurs)." *Jahrbuch des Instituts für deutsche Geschichte Tel Aviv* 15 (1986): 431–464.

Tuchel, Johannes, *Die Inspektion der Konzentrationslager 1938–1945: Das System des Terrors* Berlin 1994.

Ueberschär, Gerd R. "Die Einbeziehung Skandinaviens in die Planung 'Barbarossa.'" In *Das Deutsche Reich und der Zweite Weltkrieg,* Bd. 4. Ed. Militärgeschichtliches Forschungsamt. Stuttgart, 1983, pp. 365–412.

———. "Die militärische Planung für den Angriff auf die Sowjetunion." In *Der deutsche Angriff auf die Sowjetunion 1941: Die Kontroverse um die Präventivkriegsthese.* Ed. Gerd R. Ueberschär and Lev Bezymenskij. Darmstadt, 1998, pp. 21–37.

Der deutsche Angriff auf die Sowjetunion 1941: Die Kontroverse um die Präventivkriegsthese. Ed. Gerd R. Ueberschär and Lev A. Bezymenskij, Darmstadt, 1998.

Umbreit, Hans. *Deutsche Militärverwaltungen 1938–39: Die militärische Besetzung der Tschechoslowakei und Polens.* Stuttgart, 1977.

———. "Die deutsche Herrschaft in den besetzten Gebieten 1942–1945." In *Das Deutsche Reich und der ZweiteWeltkrieg,* Bd. 5/2. Ed. Militärgeschichtliches Forschungsamt. Stuttgart, 1999, pp. 3–272.

Die vergessenen Juden in den baltischen Staaten: Ein Symposium vom 4. bis 7. Juli 1997 in Hannover. Ed. Ansgar Koschel and Helker Pflug. Cologne, 1998.

Vestermanis, Margers. "Der lettische Anteil an der 'Endlösung': Versuch einer Antwort." In *Die Schatten der Vergangenheit: Impulse zur Historisierung des Nationalsozialismus.* Ed. Uwe Backes, Eckhard Jesse und Rainer Zitelmann. Frankfurt am Main and Berlin, 1990, pp. 426–449.

———. "Retter im Lande der Handlanger: Zur Geschichte der Hilfe für Juden in Lettland während der 'Endlösung.'" In *Solidarität und Hilfe für Juden während der NS-Zeit,*

Regionalstudien, Bd. 2. Ed. Wolfgang Benz and Juliane Wetzel. Berlin, 1996, pp. 231–272.

———. "Die nationalsozialistischen Haftstätten und Todeslager im okkupierten Lettland 1941–1945." In *Die nationalsozialistischen Konzentrationslager: Entwicklung und Struktur*, Bd. 1. Ed. Ulrich Herbert, Karin Orth, and Christoph Dieckmann. Göttingen, 1998, pp. 472–492.

Vulfsons, Mavriks. "Das lettische Nationalgefühl und die Juden." *Zeitschrift für Geschichtswissenschaft* 43 (1995), 4: 351–357.

Waite, Robert G. "Kollaboration und deutsche Besatzungspolitik in Lettland 1941 bis 1945." In *Okkupation und Kollaboration (1938–1945)*. Ed. Berlin and Heidelberg, 1994, pp. 217–237.

———. "'Reliable Local Residents': Collaboration in Latvia, 1941–1945." In *Latvia in World War II: Materials of an International Conference 14–15 June 1999 in Riga*. Riga, 2000 (= Latvijas Vesturnieku komisijas raksti, 1. sejums), pp. 115–144.

———. "West German Courts and the Holocaust in Latvia." In *The Issues of the Holocaust Research in Latvia: Reports of an International Conference 16–17 October 2000 in Riga*. Riga, 2001 (= Latvijas Vesturnieku komisijas raksti, 2. sejums), pp. 61–73.

Wasser, Bruno. "Die 'Germanisierung' im Distrikt Lublin als Generalprobe und erste Realisierungsphase des 'Generalplans Ost'." In *Der "Generalplan Ost": Hauptlinien der nationalsozialistischen Planungs- und Vernichtungspolitik*. Ed. Mechtild Rössler and Sabine Schleiermacher. Berlin, 1993, pp. 271–293.

Wege in die Vernichtung: Die Deportation der Juden aus Mainfranken 1941–1943. Begleitband zur Ausstellung des Staatsarchivs Würzburg und des Instituts für Zeitgeschichte Munich-Berlin. Munich, 2003.

Die Wehrmacht: Mythos und Realität. Ed. Rolf-Dieter Müller and Hans-Erich Volkmann. Munich, 1999.

Weinberg, Gerhard L. *Eine Welt in Waffen: Die globale Geschichte des Zweiten Weltkriegs*. Stuttgart, 1995.

Weinke, Annette. *Die Verfolgung von NS-Tätern im geteilten Deutschland. Vergangenheitsbewältigungen 1949–1969, oder: Eine deutsch-deutsche Beziehungsgeschichte im Kalten Krieg*. Paderborn et al., 2002.

Wette, Wolfram. "SS-Standartenführer Karl Jäger, Kommandeur der Sicherheitspolizei (KdS) in Kaunas: Eine biographische Skizze." In *Holocaust in Litauen: Krieg, Judenmorde und Kollaboration im Jahre 1941*. Ed. Vincas Bartusevicius, Joachim Tauber, and Wolfram Wette. Cologne, Weimar, Vienna, 2003, pp. 77–90.

Wheatley, Ronald. *Operation Sea Lion: German Plans for the Invasion of England 1939–1942*. Oxford, 1958.

Wildt, Michael. *Generation des Unbedingten: Das Führungskorps des Reichssicherheitshauptamtes*. Hamburg, 2003 (Studienausgabe).

———. "Erich Ehrlinger – ein Vertreter 'kämpfender Verwaltung.'" In *Karrieren der Gewalt: Nationalsozialistische Täterbiographien*. Ed. Klaus-Michael Mallmann and Gerhard Paul. Darmstadt, 2004, pp. 76–85.

Wilhelm, Friedrich. *Die Polizei im NS-Staat: Die Geschichte ihrer Organisation im Überblick*. Paderborn et al., 1997.

Wilhelm, Hans-Heinrich. "Die Verfolgung der sowjetischen Juden." In *Gegen das Vergessen: Der Vernichtungskrieg gegen die Sowjetunion 1941–1945*. Ed. Klaus Meyer and Wolfgang Wippermann. Frankfurt am Main, 1992, pp. 59–74.

———. *Die Einsatzgruppe A der Sicherheitspolizei und des SD 1941/42*. Frankfurt am Main, 1996.

Witte, Peter. "Zwei Entscheidungen in der 'Endlösung der Judenfrage': Deportationen nach Lodz und Vernichtung in Chelmno." In *Theresienstädter Studien und Dokumente* 1995: 38–68.
Wolkogonow, Dimitri. *Stalin: Triumph und Tragödie.* Düsseldorf and Vienna, 1993.
Zamecnik, Stanislav. "Kein Häftling darf lebend in die Hände des Feindes fallen." *Dachauer Hefte* 1 (1993): 219–231.

Films and Television Programs

Die Akte Odessa. Directed by Ronald Neame. Great Britain, Federal Republic of Germany 1975, German version, 120 Minuten.

Die Lüge und der Tod: Die Deportation der Stuttgarter Juden. Directed by Stephan Hermlin. Berlin (East) 1988, 35 Minuten.

Mariannes Heimkehr: Die Jüdin, der Beamte und das Dorf. Directed by Gert Mohnheim and Stefan Röttger. Federal Republic of Germany 2003, 45 Minuten.

Die Präsidenten. Ein Film über Steven Springfield und Alexander Bergmann. Directed by Heike Gläser. Federal Republic of Germany 2001, 89 Minuten.

Verschollen in Riga – Bilder einer Erinnerungsreise. Directed by Jürgen Hobrecht. Federal Republic of Germany 1992, 50 Minuten.

Index of Persons

A
Abel, Xaver, 381
Abetz, Otto, 180, 181, 185, 193, 194
Abkin, Family, 118
Achamer-Pifrader, Humbert, 240
Adler, H.-G., 2, 193, 220, 233, 490
Aismann, Jewish informant, 119, 154, 171
Alletag, Hermann, 451, 464
Alnor, Walter, 270, 284
Altemeyer, Werner, 111, 137, 138, 148, 149, 153, 171, 189, 195, 292, 295, 305, 307, 451
Arajs, Viktor, viii, 8, 33, 66, 67, 68, 69, 70, 72, 73, 74, 75, 76, 81, 86, 88, 89, 90, 108, 116, 117, 118, 129, 137, 154, 155, 156, 157, 160, 166, 169, 170, 172, 197, 220, 221, 222, 331, 332, 334, 336, 341, 453, 454, 455, 456, 457, 464, 465, 467, 475, 484
Arnold, Klaus Jochen, 6, 10, 490
Aron, Kalman, 118, 126, 129
Aufrecht, Hans, 334, 341

B
Babarin, Evgenii, 16
Bachl, Eduard, 108, 126, 473
Bach-Zelewski, Erich von dem, 41, 56
Bag, Yitzchag, 124, 351
Balodis, Jānis, 14, 20
Bamberg, Georg, 271, 282, 283, 320, 360
Bank, Hirsch, 355, 362
Barth, Willi, 76, 90, 384, 387, 392
Bartholomä, Elke, 9
Bartsch, Willi, 342
Batz, Rudolf, 44, 49, 54, 57, 74, 75, 79, 88, 90, 120, 130, 163, 288, 304, 443, 444, 461, 475
Baum, Meta, 318, 334
Baur, Heidrun, 10
Behrmann, Joseph, 105, 120, 124, 349
Behrmann, Sonja, 105, 124
Bender, Horst, 162, 174
Berel, Isidor, 105, 153, 154
Bergmanis, Alexanders, 9
Bermann, Leo, 46
Berner, Charlotte, 46
Berner, Saul Fritz, 46
Berzins, Alfreds, 27, 29
Besekow, Arno, 75, 88, 89, 119, 120, 445, 446, 447, 462, 484
Besen, Wolf, 250, 251, 258
Bilacki, ghetto occupant, 355
Bilder, Sonja, 153, 167, 171
Blankenfeld, Josef, 355
Blaschek, Fritz, 384, 391, 394
Blaumanis, Rudolfs, 69
Blech, Leo (Leib), 115, 128
Blobel, Paul, 405, 406, 427
Bludau, Hans, 314
Blumenau, M., 94, 104, 105, 120, 124
Blumenfeld (Mrs.), 101, 102
Blumenfeld, Dr. Rudolf, 94, 101, 120, 138, 139
Bögner, SS Second Lieutenant, 242, 246
Böhme, Hans-Joachim, 58, 82
Bonin, Eberhard von, 382, 438
Bönner, Egon, 275, 284, 293
Borcke, Hans-Otto von, 275, 284, 373, 378
Borgert, Heinz-Ludger, 9
Borkowski, Bernhard, 76, 89, 90
Bormann, Martin, 180, 193
Botwinik, blacksmith, 352
Brack, Viktor, 187, 188
Bracs, Julius, 71, 87, 88, 117
Braemer, Walter, 138, 166, 190, 268, 271, 304, 369

Index of Persons

Brasch, Friedrich, 139, 166, 291, 292, 293, 294, 305, 306, 307, 323, 452, 464
Brauer, Erich, 412, 427, 428, 430
Bräutigam, Otto, 91, 100, 121, 122, 184, 194, 487, 488, 491
Brodt, Erwin, 360
Bromm, Senior Tax Inspector, 302
Brüner, Hans, 382, 462
Bruhn, Hans, 381, 390
Brüning, Olga, 117, 128
Bruns, Heinrich, 145, 168, 172
Bruns, Hermann, 296, 297, 307, 308, 314, 325
Bruns, Walter, 138, 148, 149, 152, 153, 166, 170, 171
Buchbinder, Salaspils inmate, 415
Bühler, Josef, 191
Bürckel, Josef, 180, 181
Burdach, Brigadier General, 61
Burmeister, Wilhelm, 302, 303, 310, 369, 450

C

Čakste, Janis, 12
Canaris, Wilhelm, 152, 153
Carlebach, Alexander, 212, 436
Carlebach, Dr. Josef, 212
Celmiņš, Gustav, 13, 29, 95, 96
Chemnitz, Arno, 421, 432
Clausen, Theodor, 45, 54, 75, 89
Cromwell, Oliver, 14
Cukurs, Herbert, 67, 116, 137, 153, 155, 157, 160, 453, 454, 455, 456, 457, 464, 465
Cüppers, Martin, 9, 53, 491

D

Dähne, Inspector, 339, 340, 470
Daluege, Kurt, 41, 53, 56
Dankers, Oskars, 27, 33, 96
Dannecker, Theodor, 181, 193
Danskop, Alberts, 114, 137, 160, 166, 306, 307, 361
Dean, Martin, ii, 9, 492
Degenhardt, Herbert, 132, 133, 134, 135, 141, 142, 149, 163, 164, 165, 168, 170, 172, 174, 441, 460, 484
Deglavs, Viktors, 95, 96
Deiftz, Moshe, 90, 103, 126, 307
Deling, German policeman, 396

Denemark, Joseph, 424
Diedrich, Emil, 141, 461
Dierl, Florian, 9
Dietrich, Fritz, 270
Dikmanis, Arveds, 67, 86
Donath, Hans, 237
Donde, 360
Döring, Gustav, 415
Dorr, Max, 79, 90, 95, 107, 109, 110, 237, 238, 244, 266, 267, 268, 269, 271, 272, 274, 275, 281, 282, 284, 285, 325, 339
Draeger, Paul, 441, 442
Dralle, Edgar, 167, 272, 295
Drechsler, Otto-Heinrich, 33, 95, 100, 106, 108, 113, 127, 186, 187, 194, 195, 237, 261, 266, 268, 269, 270, 275, 276, 280, 290, 291, 292, 293, 294, 295, 296, 297, 298, 303, 305, 307, 317, 413, 451, 464, 473, 475
Dreijmanis, Pavils, 97, 103, 110, 291, 306
Dressler, Hans, 66, 84
Dubin, Mordechai, 26, 33, 115
Dubnow, Simon, 139, 167
Dyn, Benjamin, 424

E

Ehle, Paul, 425, 473, 475
Ehrlinger, Erich, 44, 54, 57, 60, 84, 260, 264, 502
Eichelis, Alberts, 28, 34, 457, 465, 484
Eichmann, Adolf, 43, 54, 55, 128, 152, 171, 176, 177, 179, 182, 186, 188, 192, 194, 195, 196, 204, 205, 226, 260, 263, 284, 304, 484, 499
Eicker, Arthur, 285, 307, 341, 348
Einbergs, Bernards, 95, 96
Einstein, camp elder at Salaspils, 250
Ekkelen, see Jeckeln, Friedrich, 439
Eljaschew (Mrs.), 101, 102
Eljaschew, Michail, 93, 94, 119, 120, 137
Eljaschewitsch, Chaim, 355, 362
Elkes, Elchanan, 215
Ellrodt, Friedrich, 79, 90, 272, 284, 450, 463
Esser, Robert, 133, 273
Ezergailis, Andrew, 6, 10, 29, 33, 85, 86, 87, 88, 90, 120, 121, 128, 164, 172, 173, 174, 364, 403, 492, 501

F

Fiedler, SS Staff Sergeant, 407
Finkelstein, O., 101
Finnberg, Emil, 53, 57, 83, 84, 147, 169
Fischel, Lilly, 258, 315
Fischer, Mischka, 353, 356, 362, 363
Fleischel, Günther, 218, 232, 364, 498
Fleming, Gerald, 153, 164, 166, 169, 171, 492
Flick, Carl Gustav, 134, 135, 150
Forsyth, Frederick, 444, 462
Foth, Ewald, 421, 431, 432, 448
Frank, Hans, 179, 181, 183, 184, 191, 367, 369
Frankel, Regina, 114
Frankenberg, Friedrich, 214, 215, 231, 258, 334, 357, 359
Freimanis, Arthurs, 96, 121
Freter, Colonel, 376
Friedrich, Günther, 9
Friess, Käthe, 346, 394
Fründt, Theodor, 121, 151, 280, 292, 293, 294, 304, 306, 323, 450, 451, 463
Furck, Herbert, 128, 167, 168, 169, 170

G

Galanter, Jakob, 389, 394
Gantzkom, Egon, 46
Geese, Karl, 342, 344
Geissler, 62
Genkin, OD member, 358
Gerlach, Christian, 9, 51, 52, 195, 196, 246, 263, 284, 350, 375, 378, 430, 486, 493
Gerrets, Ralf, 342, 344, 345, 349
Gerstein, Solomon, 137, 166, 411, 428, 429
Gewecke, Hans, 282, 289, 304, 305
Gienanth, Carl Ludwig Freiherr von, 368
Gigurtu, Ion, 180, 193
Gimnich, see Gymnich, Max
Ginsburg, Alexander, 115, 166, 364
Gläser, 503
Glaser, Elchonon „Moishe", 399
Glaube, Henri, 424
Glazman, Mordechai, 9, 123
Globocnik, Odilo, 366, 376
Glücks, Richard, 420, 433, 473
Glückson, Moshe, 46
Goebbels, Joseph, 181, 182, 184
Goldberg, Naum, 161
Goldfeld, Otto Isaak, 46
Golender, A., 46
Gonell, Ernst, 439
Göring, Emma, 115
Göring, Hermann, 38, 56, 115, 128, 175, 180, 183, 184, 185, 191, 275, 297
Gottschalk, Gerda, 256, 258, 315, 320, 324, 325, 326, 328, 334, 347, 348, 488
Gottwaldt, Alfred, 9, 491, 498, 499
Grabitz, Helge, 8, 53, 263, 376, 460, 490, 496, 500, 501
Grabowska, Janina, 426, 431, 432, 433, 434, 463, 493
Gräfe, Heinz, 49, 57
Grauel, Erhard, 93, 119, 123, 128
Greiser, Arthur, 177, 181, 184, 185, 194
Groeschel, Max, 387, 388, 389
Grüner, Regina, 9
Grupp, Peter, 9
Gryglewski, Marcus, 233, 493
Gutkin, Samuel, 80, 87, 91, 120, 124, 137, 166, 172, 459
Gutmann, Sara, 157
Gymnich, Max, 330, 358, 363, 364, 441

H

Haar, Rudolf, 215, 231, 334, 357, 359, 364
Haase, member of KdS Riga, 358, 364
Hait, Zelda Riwka, 87, 88, 115, 116, 117, 128
Halder, Franz, 36, 38, 39, 50, 51, 52, 53, 487
Hamann, Joachim, 282, 289, 305
Hamburger, Egon, 415
Hämmerle, Josef, 291, 305
Hampe, Lieutenant Colonel, 360
Hanau, Erich, 250, 445
Hasse, D. I., 101
Haupt, Otto, 423, 431, 432
Heidl, Otto, 419, 420, 421, 423, 432, 448, 449
Heidt, Edgar, possibly Haid, 399
Heise, Karl, 115, 123, 128, 134, 135, 141, 142, 143, 148, 149, 150, 154, 165, 168, 169, 170, 172, 203, 209, 227, 237, 441
Helfsgott, Walter Ernst, 406, 407, 408, 411, 414, 445, 462, 475
Hemicker, Ernst, 133, 134, 145, 164, 165, 441, 442, 460, 461

Index of Persons

Hennewig, Rudolf, 360, 365
Henze, Alfred, 141
Hermann, German administrator, 293, 294, 313
Herzenberg, Erich, 424
Herzfeld, B., 46
Hesfehr, Albert, 106, 141, 142, 154, 168, 171, 272, 306, 312, 313, 323, 330, 442
Heydrich, Reinhard, 19, 40, 41, 42, 43, 45, 46, 47, 48, 49, 52, 53, 55, 56, 58, 66, 68, 72, 98, 122, 140, 147, 148, 152, 169, 170, 175, 176, 177, 178, 179, 180, 181, 182, 183, 184, 185, 186, 187, 190, 191, 192, 193, 194, 196, 200, 260, 261, 262, 264, 269, 281, 284, 305, 333, 366, 368, 375, 437, 438, 439, 473, 476, 486
Heyer, SS First Lieutenant, 302
Heymann, Hermann, 321, 326
Hilberg, Raul, 324, 375, 378, 494
Hildebrandt, Richard, 52, 416
Himmler, Heinrich, 2, 24, 27, 28, 38, 40, 41, 42, 52, 53, 56, 61, 91, 100, 122, 131, 132, 134, 146, 147, 148, 150, 151, 152, 153, 154, 161, 162, 164, 170, 171, 174, 176, 177, 179, 181, 185, 194, 241, 242, 276, 288, 290, 304, 305, 311, 333, 345, 366, 367, 368, 369, 370, 372, 373, 374, 375, 376, 377, 378, 379, 380, 384, 385, 386, 416, 417, 433, 437, 439, 449, 469, 473, 476, 478, 486, 487, 491
Hingst, Hans Christian, 289, 305
Hinrichs, clerk, 421
Hirsch, Karl, 381, 390, 462
Hirschkowitz, Kurt, 250
Hirschland, Herbert, 253, 258, 445
Hitler, Adolf, 2, 4, 14, 15, 16, 18, 19, 20, 21, 24, 26, 28, 29, 30, 31, 32, 35, 36, 37, 38, 39, 41, 42, 47, 50, 51, 53, 55, 56, 83, 84, 91, 95, 96, 113, 120, 131, 148, 152, 153, 164, 166, 169, 171, 176, 179, 180, 181, 182, 183, 184, 185, 192, 193, 194, 226, 263, 290, 302, 305, 306, 325, 368, 377, 378, 408, 430, 437, 439, 440, 476, 486, 487, 488, 489, 491, 492, 493, 494, 495, 496, 497, 499, 500
Hölzl, Martin, 10
Hoppe, Paul-Werner, 418, 419, 420, 424, 425, 430, 431, 432, 433, 448, 449, 463, 473, 476
Höss, Rudolf, 420

Hudal, Alois, 444, 461
Hühnerbein, Willi, 412

I

Iklaws, Peteris, 331, 335
Intelmann, Alfred, 24
Israel, Georg, 424
Israelowitsch, Seika, 358, 360, 365

J

Jäger, Karl, 44, 47, 49, 56, 57, 60, 83, 98, 260, 264, 289, 304, 305, 502
Jäger, Leonhardt, 160
Jagusch, Walter, 245, 302, 303, 369
Jahnke, Friedrich, 106, 114, 125, 128, 129, 154, 163, 164, 165, 167, 168, 169, 170, 171, 172, 173, 441, 442, 460, 461, 484
Jakobson, Alfred, 71
Janowski, Efraim, 69, 87
Javetz, 410, 428
Jeckeln, Friedrich, 41, 48, 52, 56, 130, 131, 132, 133, 134, 135, 136, 138, 140, 141, 144, 145, 146, 147, 148, 149, 150, 151, 152, 153, 154, 155, 156, 158, 159, 160, 161, 162, 163, 164, 165, 166, 167, 168, 169, 170, 171, 174, 196, 240, 258, 261, 262, 270, 292, 293, 304, 350, 361, 370, 371, 395, 397, 398, 405, 427, 438, 439, 441, 451, 459, 473, 477, 482, 484, 491
Jewelson, J., 101
Joffe (Mrs.), 116
Joffe, Michael, 46
Jordan, Fritz, 216
Joseph, Dr., 409
Joseph, S., 123
Joseph, Siegfried, 227, 348
Juchheim, Rainer, 9
Judelis, ghetto inhabitant, 356
Juditzky, Edgar, 291, 306, 307
Jurmann, Esra, 123, 359, 364, 365, 429, 430
Jüttner, Hans, 41, 53

K

Kallmeyer, Helmut, 188
Kaltenbrunner, Ernst, 242, 246, 440, 473
Kamm, Matthias, 9
Kann, Artur, 248, 256

Kaplan, Isidor, 46
Kaplan, Israel, 351, 353, 356, 361, 362, 363, 364, 365, 488
Kaplan, Jacob, 46
Karassek, Alfons, 143
Kassel, Mendel, 161, 338
Katz, Josef, 211, 212, 229, 248, 252, 253, 255, 258, 259, 350, 390, 427, 429, 434, 436, 459, 488
Katz, Leiba, 114
Katzmann, Friedrich, 424
Kaufer, Esra, 94
Kaufmann, Kurt, 214, 218, 230
Kaufmann, Max, 6, 26, 29, 33, 68, 69, 70, 73, 78, 86, 87, 88, 90, 105, 120, 123, 124, 129, 160, 166, 167, 171, 173, 201, 232, 313, 320, 323, 324, 328, 329, 334, 347, 364, 390, 393, 394, 402, 403, 414, 426, 430, 431, 434, 463, 488, 495
Kaufmann, Siegfried, 250, 251, 252, 253, 257, 258, 349, 364, 460
Kaulitz, Sabine, 9
Kauls, Juris, 458, 466, 484
Kehlman, A., 101
Keitel, Wilhelm, 50, 51, 184
Kendziorek, Kurt, 211, 212, 226, 229, 335
Kiesinger, Kurt Georg, 452
Kirchensteins, Augusts, 23
Kirste, Arnold, 45, 49, 55, 57, 79, 87, 120, 125, 167, 263, 264, 323, 444
Kjurbis, Arajs Commando member, 220
Klaus, Edgar, 46
Kleemann, Gustav, 205, 331
Kleemann, Lore, 331
Klein, Peter, ix, x, 9, 52, 53, 56, 83, 86, 169, 170, 193, 246, 263, 282, 284, 335, 349, 486, 490, 491, 493, 495, 498, 499
Klumberg, Wilhelm, 96, 121
Knie, Dimitri, 46
Knobelsdorff, Otto von, 176
Knott, Otto Karl, 421, 423, 431, 432, 433, 448, 449, 463
Kobiella, German policeman, 143, 171
Koch, Erich, 366, 369, 429, 450, 463
Koehler, Paul, 360
Kohl, Rolf, 443
Kohn, Richard, 204, 228, 229
Kopolowitz, Fanny, 416
Koppe, Wilhelm, 185
Kornblum, Aaron, 9

Korotaev, Vladimir, 9
Korsemann, Gerret, 48, 52
Köster, Hermann, 293, 294, 296, 308, 313, 323, 324
Kotze, Hans Ulrich von, 20, 31
Kotzins, Fricis, 22, 32
Kowa, Emilie, 381, 390, 428, 447, 448
Kraujins, Edgars, 116, 128
Kraus, SS Major, 75
Krause, Kurt, 106, 119, 137, 141, 142, 171, 213, 221, 237, 249, 256, 274, 301, 312, 318, 320, 321, 322, 327, 328, 330, 331, 334, 337, 341, 347, 354, 356, 357, 358, 359, 360, 361, 363, 364, 389, 397, 411, 415, 438, 439, 440, 443, 459, 473, 477
Krauss, Hans, 65, 86
Krebsbach, Eduard, 382, 389, 410, 413, 447, 448
Kreišmanis, Ernests, 85, 95, 96
Kremer, Gideon, 114
Kremer, Mark, 114
Kroeger, Erhard, 24, 25, 28, 500
Krüger, Hermann, 156, 164
Kube, Wilhelm, 276, 346, 350, 366, 369, 374, 376, 378
Kuhlmann, Jochen, 8
Kuhn, Gustav, 118, 129
Kuklja, ghetto occupant, 356
Künzle, Anton, 86, 167, 171, 455, 464, 465, 496
Kuppinger, Emmy (Emmy Kowa), 447
Kuzelenkov, Vladimir, 9
Kviesis, Albert, 14

L

Laak, Alexander, 342
Lācis, Villis, 23
Lammers, Hans-Heinrich, 180, 193
Landau, Jakob, 46
Lange, Rudolf, 44, 45, 54, 74, 88, 130, 131, 146, 147, 150, 152, 154, 163, 164, 172, 186, 187, 188, 189, 195, 198, 199, 200, 201, 206, 209, 210, 226, 227, 229, 235, 237, 238, 239, 240, 241, 242, 243, 245, 250, 258, 259, 260, 261, 262, 263, 264, 275, 276, 277, 278, 279, 286, 294, 307, 321, 322, 323, 330, 331, 332, 333, 335, 339, 341, 345, 354, 355, 356, 357, 359, 362, 365, 370, 371, 372, 373, 374, 375, 377, 378, 379, 388, 390, 398, 406,

Index of Persons

407, 411, 414, 431, 432, 439, 440, 443, 445, 460, 473, 477, 495
Lapavok, Olga, 9
Lasch, Otto, 61, 62, 63, 85, 450, 463, 488
Lat, Moisej, 71
Latt, Eliyahu, 352
Lauer, Josef, 424
Leeb, Wilhelm von, 59, 77, 82, 83, 90, 449, 487
Leibbrandt, Georg, 188, 191, 196, 281, 282, 305, 375
Leibowitz, Dora, 46
Leibsohn, 109, 347
Leibsohn, Julia, 46
Leibsoms, Scholom, 46
Leiser, Max, 213, 214, 215, 230, 357, 359, 363, 364
Levi, Lucie, 211, 227, 228, 229, 335
Levie, Erna, 330, 334
Levy, Josef, 208
Lewenstein, Abram, 424
Lewstein, Leo, 46
Lidums, Laimonis, 116, 117, 128
Link, Captain, 354
Lipchin, Abram, 114, 128
Lipke, Janis, 114, 128, 489
Lipowski, Heinz, 223, 233
Lippmann, Günther, 213, 230
Lohse, Hinrich, 95, 97, 98, 100, 112, 121, 122, 131, 136, 148, 166, 187, 188, 189, 190, 191, 196, 235, 238, 258, 265, 266, 269, 270, 271, 276, 280, 282, 287, 288, 289, 290, 292, 293, 296, 297, 302, 304, 305, 306, 310, 317, 346, 369, 374, 375, 377, 378, 413, 429, 450, 463, 469, 473, 478
Lolling, Enno, 420
Lorenz, German policeman, 56, 396
Lorenzen, Johann, 450
Luczak, Boleslav (Dr. Bolek), 410
Lüders, Else, 228, 229, 336, 337, 346, 394, 428
Lünenschloss, Kurt, 109, 126
Lüschen, Johannes, 156, 164, 174
Luther, Martin, 52, 182, 193
Lutrinsch, Matis, 69, 88, 156, 157, 160, 172, 174

M

Maczijewski, ghetto occupant, 355
Mäe, Hjalmar, 61
Maikovskis, Boleslavs, 457, 465
Maisel, Noah, 26
Mallmann, Klaus-Michael, 10, 30, 53, 54, 55, 163, 264, 350, 491, 492, 493, 496, 497, 498, 502
Marx, Frieda, 357, 363, 364, 365
Marzinski, ghetto occupant, 355
Massakas, Alexander, 61
Matthäus, Jürgen, 9, 55, 92, 375, 486, 491, 497
Matthiessen, Martin, 284, 374, 450
Maunz, Gerhard, 452
Mausner, Vera, 220, 233
Maxim, Lev, 139
Maywald, Gerhard Kurt, 88, 89, 109, 126, 200, 201, 206, 222, 224, 226, 229, 248, 250, 255, 256, 259, 274, 321, 329, 331, 334, 347, 445, 446, 462, 470, 478
Medalje, Ella, 68, 86, 87, 157, 160, 171, 172, 173, 174
Meier, Theodor, 419, 420, 421, 427, 432, 493
Meisel, SS First Sergeant, 412
Meixner, Hans, 438, 459
Mendel, Andreas, 251, 252, 259
Mengele, Josef, 444
Metzger, Ernst, 321, 322, 327
Meyer, Alfred, 191, 305, 374
Meyer, Erwin, 28
Meyer, Ernst, 218, 232
Meyer, Theodor, 448
Michalsen, Georg, 170
Migge, Kurt, 211, 213, 226, 228, 229, 230, 302, 330, 358, 359, 364, 365, 373, 378, 440
Milch, Erhard, 147
Minisch, Vera, 313
Minsker, Grisha, 83
Mintz, Jr., M., 94
Mintz, Paul, 26, 33, 73, 123
Model, Walter, 406
Monmillers, Arturs, 114
Moser, Hans Kurz, 440, 460
Möser, Lutz, 9
Moskowsky, Nachmann, 46
Muentz, Paul, 46
Müller, Heinrich, 28, 34, 122, 176, 188, 192, 241, 245, 284, 304, 335, 349, 444, 500

Müller, Lia, 360
Müller, Reinhard, 9
Müller-Oelrichs, Gaby, 9
Munters, Vilhelms, 15, 20, 21
Mussolini, Benito, 14, 180

N

Nakaten, Franz, 69, 87, 109
Namsler, Marion, 9
Nathan, Anatoly, 161, 351, 358
Netler, Werner Georg, 344, 349, 459
Neuendorff, Dr. Willy, 151, 292, 302, 306, 309, 310, 372, 377, 387, 393, 394, 464
Neumann, Erich, 306
Neumann, Max, 143, 155, 168, 312, 318, 363, 441, 442
Neurath, Heinrich, 133, 135, 174, 272, 273
Nickel, Richard, 81, 250, 251, 257, 321, 330, 399, 400, 440, 460, 473
Nieburg, Jacob, 155, 172
Nisse, Agnes, 46
Noim, Herman, 70, 71, 72, 87, 88
Notzke, Carina, 9
Noviks, J., 46
Nurock, Modechai, 26
Nussbaum, Benno, 218, 232

O

Oberwinder, Heinrich, 125, 126, 128, 129, 164, 165, 166, 167, 168, 169, 170, 171, 172, 173, 441, 442, 460, 461, 484
Okun, Ovsei, 352, 360
Oppenheimer, Erika, 325, 410, 411
Oppenheimer, Leo, 9
Oppenheimer, Lore, ix, 9
Orth, Karin, 201, 417, 429, 431, 433, 463, 492, 498, 502
Osis, Roberts, 134, 137, 142, 165, 166, 172
Ostry, 410
Ozols, Edgars, 114

P

Packin, David, 87, 90, 92, 117, 127, 129
Paik, OD member, 353
Panzinger, Friedrich, 375, 378, 405, 427
Päts, Konstantin, 25
Pauli, Max, 416
Perl, Herbert, 359

Pick, Regina, 223, 233
Plensners, Aleksandrs, 95, 96
Pohl, Dieter, 10, 52, 163, 486, 498
Pohl, Oswald, 242, 246, 375, 376, 473, 500
Polis, Alma, 115
Press, Bernhard, 6, 29, 33, 68, 70, 86, 87, 88, 94, 101, 120, 123, 124, 127, 129, 138, 166, 168, 174, 361, 362, 363, 364, 426, 428, 434, 498
Press, Oskar, 101
Primanis, Martin, 28
Pröhl, Günther, 304, 369
Prützmann, Hans-Adolf, 40, 48, 49, 52, 56, 98, 100, 108, 115, 126, 130, 131, 132, 151, 164, 166, 198, 199, 287, 290, 366, 437, 478
Psawka, Jewish prisoner, 399

Q

Querner, Rudolf, 190

R

Rach, Hans, 431, 432, 448
Rachner, 275, 284
Rademacher, Franz, 179, 193
Rage, Moisej, 71, 87
Ramsfelder, Siegfried, 204, 225
Rappoport, David, 46
Rauca, Helmut, 216
Rauter, Hanns Albin, 56, 183
Ravdin, Judiv, 77, 90
Reemtsma, Alwin, 108, 126, 199
Reemtsma, Jan Philipp, ix
Reese, Rudolf, 165, 341, 348, 349, 392, 440, 441
Rehberg, Richard, 135, 150, 154, 155, 156, 165, 171, 172, 173, 461
Reichelt, Katrin, 9, 88, 90, 464, 499
Reznik, Nadia, 410, 428, 429, 431
Ribbentrop, Joachim von, 17, 18, 19, 23, 24, 30, 43, 52, 180, 184, 185, 194, 495
Richter, Gustav, 174, 183
Rintelen, Emil Otto von, 184
Roens, Annemarie, 28
Roens, Karl, 28
Rone, Elvira, 114
Rönne, Latvian intelligence officer, 46
Roppelt, Johann, 416, 430, 432
Roques, Franz von, 37, 77, 96, 120, 280, 449, 463, 478, 482

Roques, Karl von, 37
Roschmann, Eduard, 330, 371, 389, 399, 400, 406, 411, 444, 445, 454, 462, 473, 479
Roseboom, Ruth und Louis, 257, 410, 428
Rosemeyer, Reinhold, 381
Rosenberg, Alfred, 38, 50, 57, 95, 100, 120, 122, 125, 128, 131, 183, 185, 266, 270, 276, 288, 290, 305, 341, 369, 376, 449, 473, 479, 487
Rosenow, Arthur, 75, 89
Rosenstein, Latvian espionage officer, 46, 55
Rosenthal, Heinz, 394, 428
Rosenthal, Michael, 105
Rosin, Rauchmann Ber, 46
Rosowski, lawyer, 46
Rossino, Alexander, 9
Rübsteck, Kurt, 257, 357, 364
Rudow, Boris, 396, 397, 402
Russ, 352, 353, 354, 356, 362
Rybak, ghetto occupant, 355

S
Salitter, Paul, 202, 203, 225
Salnajs, commander of Latvian political police, 46
Salomon, work detail leader, 137, 166, 341
Samunow, H., 46
Sandberger, Martin, 44, 47, 54, 55, 57, 240, 245
Sandel, work detail leader, 353, 354, 355, 362, 363
Sanders, Wiswald, 121
Sauckel, Fritz, 275, 374, 379
Sauer, Albert, 246, 311, 377, 382, 390, 400, 408, 438, 440, 473, 479
Sauer, Werner, 365, 396, 397, 403
Scheffler, Wolfgang, 500
Schellenberg, Walter, 52, 193, 489
Schenker, Harry, 399
Scherwitz, Eleke, 365, 400, 403, 404
Scherwitz, Fritz, 358, 365, 395, 396, 397, 398, 399, 401, 402, 403, 404, 470, 496
Scheucher-Scott, Agnes, 234
Schiebel, Richard, 206, 226
Schiff, Berthold, 259, 322
Schindowski, Hans, 49, 57
Schirach, Baldur von, 181, 184
Schitli, Wilhelm, 385, 392

Schlitter, Austrian refugee, 94
Schlüter, Willy, 381
Schmidt, Hermann, 109, 126, 320
Schmitt, Walter, 194, 460
Schmuljan, Aron, 69, 87
Schmutow, Arkadii, 411
Schmutzler, Administrative Counselor, 237, 246, 272, 285, 286, 337, 339, 341, 348, 371, 372, 373, 374, 377
Schneider, Administrative Assistant, 302, 303
Schneider, Gertrude, 6, 128, 218, 220, 229, 232, 233, 234, 251, 254, 258, 320, 323, 324, 326, 329, 334, 352, 361, 365, 390, 391, 429, 433, 440, 459, 460, 462, 488, 489, 500
Schneider, Hilde, 258, 500
Schnurre, Julius, 16, 17, 30
Schorschik, 355
Schröder, Walther, 131, 162, 163, 464
Schu, Major von, 391
Schulenburg, Friedrich Werner Graf von der, 17, 18
Schultz, Gerhard, 291, 293, 306
Schultz, Herbert, 215, 219, 231, 319, 341, 342
Schulz-Du Bois, Otto, 148, 149, 171
Schwart, Jonas, 424
Schwellenbach, Franz, 389, 390
Seck, Rudolf Joachim, 206, 208, 209, 210, 211, 212, 226, 227, 228, 229, 251, 252, 320, 330, 331, 335, 336, 337, 346, 349, 361, 389, 440, 460, 470, 473, 480, 484
Seeliger, Paul, 371, 373, 378, 384, 452
Sekules, Else, 223, 233
Sekules, Ervin, 394, 446
Seligsohn, OD member, 358
Senulis, Lithuanian captain, 289
Sergius, Metropolitan of Vilnius (Wilna, Wilno), 439
Sherman, Hilde, 203, 225, 324, 325, 326, 328, 334, 364, 365, 409, 410, 428, 429, 434, 489
Shub, Raphael, 72, 88, 129
Sidoroff, Platon, 297, 308
Siegert, Rudolf, 198, 201, 239, 244
Sietina, Jeva, 116
Sigailis, Arturs, 27
Sik, Jindrich, 410, 428
Simons, Sally, 248, 256

Singel, lawyer, 69
Sirewitz, Elias (Eleken), see Scherwitz, Fritz
Škirpa, Kazys, 59, 83
Sollinger, Selma, 320
Soloweitschik, Elisabeth, 46
Sorge, Gustav, 381, 387, 388, 390, 409
Stahlecker, Walther, 42, 43, 44, 45, 49, 53, 54, 58, 60, 63, 64, 66, 67, 75, 76, 83, 84, 86, 88, 98, 100, 113, 121, 122, 127, 130, 131, 134, 135, 140, 169, 170, 186, 190, 198, 199, 200, 201, 239, 260, 261, 264, 268, 333, 437, 438, 459, 473, 480
Stalin, Josef, 4, 16, 17, 18, 19, 20, 21, 24, 26, 28, 30, 31, 32, 35, 91, 120, 487, 488, 491, 492, 493, 497, 503
Standtke, Wartime Administration Counselor, 139, 232, 237, 238, 272, 273, 274, 323
Steckel, Alfred, 69, 87
Štiglics, Roberts, 27, 61, 63, 67, 140, 146
Stradniek, Ernst, 313
Strauch, Eduard, 130, 131, 376
Streckenbach, Bruno, 42, 53, 54, 55, 182, 193, 484
Streim, Alfred, 56, 57, 89, 412, 429, 501
Stüber, Josef, 240, 258
Stuckart, Wilhelm, 180
Subak, Robert, 249, 256
Swikeris, Charij, 221
Szilliensiet, Latvian SS man, 396

T
Taubin, engineer, 46
Teckemeier, Otto, 250, 252, 257, 389, 440, 470
Teidmanis, Herberts, 28, 34
Thaumann, Reinhold, 168, 169, 170, 218, 231, 232, 283
Tollkühn, Karl, 358, 363, 364, 365, 484
Tönnies, Franz-Josef, 9
Trampedach, Friedrich, 104, 124, 189, 195, 304, 375, 376, 451
Trühe, Heinz, 44, 54, 89, 147, 164, 167, 169, 170, 240, 256, 445, 446, 447, 462, 484
Tschierschky, Karl, 44, 54, 76, 88, 89, 98, 99, 121, 130, 164, 445, 446, 447, 462
Tuchel, Otto, 106, 117, 118, 119, 129, 142, 143, 153, 154, 155, 160, 168, 171, 306, 307, 312, 313, 318, 323, 376, 389, 441, 442, 443
Tyas, Stephen, 9, 10, 365, 464

U
Ullmann, Ilse, 410
Ulmanis, Guntis, 458
Ulmanis, Kārlis, 12, 14, 15, 16, 20, 21, 22, 23, 25, 26, 29, 55, 66, 87, 96, 120, 458
Umans, Zanis, 456
Upmalis, Arnis Janowitsch, 220, 222, 223, 224, 233, 234

V
Vabulis, Janis Aleksanders, 87, 116, 117, 128
Valdmanis, Alfrēds, 27, 96, 121
Veiss, Voldemārs, 65, 67, 85, 92, 96
Vester, Lieutenant Colonel, 413
Vestermanis, Margers, 7, 9, 90, 92, 128, 245, 362, 427, 428, 429, 430, 501
Vialon, Karl Friedrich, 297, 298, 299, 301, 302, 303, 308, 309, 452
Vinnik, Yerahmiel, 26
Vogler, Wilhelm, 382, 448, 459, 462
Voigt, Martina, 10, 52, 53, 486, 490
Voldemaras, Augustinas, 25

W
Wachtel, Max, 105, 124, 126, 129, 161, 171, 173, 174, 351, 361
Wagner, Eduard, 41
Waibel, Helga, 9
Waite, Robert, 9, 464, 502
Wand, Max, 351, 359, 364
Wanschaff, Kurt, 360
Wassermann, Rita, 410, 428, 429, 433
Web, Marek, 9
Wedekind, Willi, 156, 164
Weinreich, physician, 410, 428
Weinstein, barber, 410
Welles, Elliot, 349, 446, 457
Wetzel, Erhard, 187, 188, 195
Wichmann, Heinz, 170
Widusch, Albert, 411
Wiesenthal, Simon, 444, 462, 498
Wildt, Michael, 10, 30, 52, 192, 193, 263, 264, 486, 502

Wilhelm, Hans-Heinrich, 10, 31, 33, 52, 54, 55, 56, 57, 83, 90, 121, 125, 127, 166, 174, 201, 427, 461, 463, 488, 496, 502
Willems, Susanne, 9
Willich, German policeman, 142, 143
Wilner, Ruth, 218
Windgassen, Hans, 151, 272, 292, 293, 306, 307, 325
Winter, Alfred, 10, 92, 234, 257, 258, 390, 427, 428, 429, 489
Winter, Franta, 224, 234
Winter, Julius, 315
Winter, Kurt, 203
Wisner, Heinz Günter, 382, 390, 410, 411, 413, 427, 428, 429, 448, 462, 484
Witte, Peter, 52, 194, 333, 335, 486, 503
Wittenberg, Simeon, 102
Wittrock, Hugo, 91, 95, 120, 121, 151, 227, 237, 244, 246, 283, 285, 289, 291, 292, 294, 295, 303, 305, 306, 307, 310, 370, 373, 429, 451, 464, 473, 480, 489

Wolff, Jeanette, 6, 10, 329, 330, 333, 334, 390, 428, 489
Wolff, Karl, 41, 56
Wurz, Hermann, 381
Wysocki, Lucian, 289

Z

Zack, Mendel, 101, 137
Zander, Hilde, 203, 225, 324, 325, 326, 334, 409, 410, 428, 429, 434, 489
Zaneriba, Ira, 9
Zeibots, Viktor, 454, 456, 465
Zeitschel, Carltheo, 185
Zentgraf, Hans, 162
Ziering, Herman, ix, 9
Ziering, Lee, 9
Zik, Max, 410
Zimmermann, Daniel, 10
Zingler, Johannes, 132, 135, 156, 162, 164, 165, 167, 172, 173, 174, 441
Ziwian, Gabriel, 361, 365
Zwidenek, General Eugen, 184

Index of Places

A
Aachen, 115, 361
Abrene (Abrehne), 1, 354, 355
Ahlem, 214
Amsterdam, 182, 183, 424
Angerburg, 1, 149, 153, 228
Argentina, 444, 445
Augšpils (today Vyshgarodok), 354, 355
Auschwitz, 1, 193, 194, 196, 365, 387, 388, 393, 400, 409, 420, 444, 469, 493, 495

B
Babīte (Babbit), 105
Bad Schmiedeberg, 42, 49
Baku, 36
Baldone (Baldohn), 414, 475
Bamberg, 205
Berlin, 1, 4, 7, 9, 14, 15, 16, 19, 20, 22, 24, 42, 43, 44, 47, 49, 54, 55, 56, 57, 58, 60, 64, 67, 73, 76, 83, 96, 98, 99, 115, 123, 128, 137, 146, 147, 148, 150, 152, 161, 162, 163, 167, 169, 170, 174, 179, 180, 182, 185, 187, 189, 191, 198, 200, 201, 204, 208, 215, 216, 219, 223, 224, 225, 226, 228, 231, 234, 239, 241, 250, 257, 261, 262, 264, 273, 293, 297, 320, 329, 333, 342, 344, 345, 350, 374, 375, 394, 395, 396, 398, 400, 401, 404, 437, 439, 440, 446, 457, 460
Bialystok, 1
Bielefeld, 214, 219, 256, 258, 322, 394, 443, 450
Bobruisk, 1, 189, 190, 195, 462, 484
Bochum, 449
Bordeaux, 361
Borisov, 1, 189, 190, 195
Braunschweig, 132, 156, 164, 441, 453
Brazil, 454, 455
Breslau (Wrocław), 83, 84, 177, 461
Brno (Brünn), 1, 43, 215, 216, 220, 225, 250, 257, 261
Brodnica (Strasburg), 425
Bromberg (Bydgoszcz), 426, 431
Brusy (Bruss), 1, 426
Buchenwald, 220, 357, 419
Budapest, 424
Bulduri (Bilderlingshof), 338
Burggraben (today Kokoszki), 424

C
Canada, 457, 458
Chinow (today Chynowie), 426, 433, 434
Cologne, 212, 213, 214, 218, 219, 229, 230, 232, 252, 256, 257, 294, 322, 361, 363, 364, 392, 393, 424, 448, 456, 462, 465
Cracow, 1, 366, 424, 443, 461, 475
Częstochowa, 367

D
Dachau, 400, 419
Danzig (today Gdańsk), 1, 5, 17, 30 , 52, 124, 177, 192, 283, 413, 414, 415, 416, 417, 422, 424, 433, 475, 477, 481, 499
Darmstadt, 10
Daugavpils (Dünaburg), 1, 29, 59, 105, 127, 133, 134, 136, 143, 144, 146, 149, 154, 155, 157, 189, 200, 216, 217, 246, 262, 268, 300, 341, 348, 354, 369, 376, 384, 392, 394
Delmenhorst, 454
Dortmund, 168, 215, 219, 231, 236, 257, 263, 232, 328, 334, 335, 348, 412, 444, 457, 459, 466
Dresden, 223, 233
Düben, 42
Duisburg, 321
Dünamünde (Daugavgrīva), 328, 330, 331, 334, 446

Dundaga (Dondangen), 1, 385, 387, 388, 389, 393, 394, 408, 409, 412, 428
Düsseldorf, 202, 203, 214, 219, 321, 322, 326, 357, 436, 448
Dzintari, 338

E

Eleja-Meitene (Elley-Meitan), 1, 408
Emersacker, 400
Erfurt, 44
Eydtkau (today Chernyshevskoe), 1, 58

F

Fallingbostel, 448, 453, 477
Flensburg, 426
Frankenthal, 440
Frankfurt am Main, 344, 345, 349, 440
Freiburg, 9
Fürth, 205, 225, 226, 482

G

Gargždai (Garsden), 59
Geneva, 361
German Democratic Republic (East Germany), 55, 427, 452
Germany, Federal Republic of (West Germany), 8, 223, 299, 414, 415, 436, 437, 442, 452, 455, 456, 457, 458
Görlitz (East Prussia), 106, 125
Groden (today Grodno), 425
Gutowo (Guttau), 1, 426
Gwiździny (Quesendorf), 426

H

Hamburg, 8, 10, 46, 70, 86, 88, 126, 148, 164, 167, 184, 188, 190, 191, 195, 196, 208, 210, 211, 212, 220, 225, 226, 228, 236, 248, 250, 255, 335, 394, 414, 415, 423, 430, 432, 434, 436, 439, 440, 441, 442, 443, 444, 445, 446, 447, 450, 451, 452, 454, 456, 459, 461, 462, 464, 465
Hanover, 130, 214, 215, 218, 219, 250, 254, 256, 257, 258, 348, 436, 459, 461
Hasenpoth (Aizpute), 270
Heiligenbeil (today Mamonovo), 1, 425
Hendaye, 361

I

Israel, 436, 455, 456

J

Jägala, 342, 344, 345
Jaunjelgava (Friedrichstadt), 344
Jelgava (Mitau), 1, 59, 62, 63, 66, 85, 91, 97, 108, 125, 141, 186, 199, 268, 275, 283, 325, 340, 341, 344, 345, 348, 369, 384, 392, 408, 413, 414
Jessau (today Yuzhnyi), 425
Jugla, 197, 384, 408, 428
Jugla (Strasdenhof), 197, 384
Jurbarkas (Georgenburg), 1, 59
Jūrmala (Riga-Strand), 338, 339, 470

K

Kalevi Liiva, 342, 349
Kassel, 44, 214, 215, 219, 230, 250, 253, 325, 338, 347, 349, 436, 460
Katowice (Kattowitz), 1, 176, 177
Kaunas (Kauen, Kovno), 1, 58, 59, 60, 72, 77, 83, 84, 97, 98, 106, 121, 189, 191, 195, 199, 201, 215, 216, 231, 260, 264, 265, 270, 274, 277, 282, 284, 287, 288, 289, 298, 300, 306, 345, 378, 384, 392, 406, 427, 488, 492, 502
Kiel, 255, 434, 438, 450, 451
Kielce, 177
Kiev, 36, 126, 134, 151, 163, 260, 407, 427
Kirchholm, 279
Kiviöli, 1, 386
Kletsk, 1, 300
Klintholm, 426
Koblenz, 9, 451
Königsberg (today Kaliningrad), 1, 49, 82, 85, 177, 228, 337, 361, 450, 463, 480, 488
Konitz (today Chojnice), 202
Konstantinów Łódzki (Tuchingen), 242
Krasnogvardeisk, 1, 89, 260, 447
Kretinga (Krottingen), 1, 59, 412
Kronstadt, 58
Krzemieniewo (Krumau), 1, 426
Kuldīga (Goldingen), 1, 457
Kurben (Kurbe), 412

L

Landsberg am Lech, 447
Lauenburg (today Lębork), 1, 424, 433
Leipzig, 42, 215, 219, 223, 231, 361
Leningrad (today St. Petersburg), 1, 58, 98, 261, 406

Liepaja (Libau), 1, 13, 19, 59, 62, 97, 122, 123, 127, 164, 174, 262, 268, 270, 300, 340, 341, 348, 376, 377, 384, 385, 392, 412, 415, 417, 424, 430, 438, 459, 490
Łódź (Litzmannstadt), 1, 28, 113, 167, 188, 200, 204, 217, 229, 242, 291, 333, 395, 400, 469, 483
London, 22, 454, 458
Lötzen (today Giżycko), 1, 152
Lübeck, 95, 211, 426, 436
Lublin, 1, 30, 57, 175, 177, 179, 180, 239, 366, 368, 377, 469, 487, 497, 502
Luga, 406
L'viv (Lemberg), 406

M

Madagascar, 175, 179, 181, 193
Majdanek, 1, 239, 242
Majorenhof (Majori), 338, 348
Malmö, 426
Maly Trostenez, 1, 334, 345, 346, 350
Mauthausen, 382, 419
Mazirbe (Klein-Irbon), 385
Melluži, 69
Minsk, ix, 1, 91, 125, 130, 131, 186, 187, 188, 189, 190, 191, 195, 196, 200, 201, 204, 260, 283, 284, 298, 300, 306, 308, 309, 310, 334, 345, 350, 378, 397, 403, 428, 483
Mogilev, 190, 196, 493
Mönchengladbach, 203, 456
Moscow, 9, 11, 16, 17, 18, 19, 21, 22, 23, 24, 25, 29, 35, 36, 189, 195, 352, 416, 453, 463
Mühlenbarbek, 450, 478
Mühlgraben (Milgrāvis), 342, 353, 388, 389, 394, 409, 412, 413, 428
Munich, 83, 399, 401, 458, 459
Münster, 214, 256, 457, 457, 458

N

Nagold, 43, 480
Naguszewo (Nagelstal), 1, 426
Narva, 406
Neustadt, 426
New York, 3, 6, 7, 55, 87, 436, 457
Nisko, 43, 177, 178
Novgorod, 243
Novosel'e, 99

Nuremberg, 9, 121, 166, 170, 171, 204, 205, 206, 211, 225, 226, 227, 235, 257, 280, 436, 439, 449

O

Olaine (Olai), 1, 371, 440
Osnabrück, 214
Ostrava (Mährisch-Ostrau), 1, 176, 177

P

Palanga (Polangen), 1, 59
Palmnicken (today Yantaryi), 1, 425
Paraguay, 445
Paris, 180, 181, 182, 185, 193, 361, 398, 403, 424
Pillau (today Baltiisk), 1, 425
Pölitz (Police), 1, 426
Popervale (Poperwahlen), 1, 412
Poznań (Posen), 1, 28, 177, 439, 440, 460
Prague, 1, 43, 44, 148, 176, 183, 186, 191, 194, 196, 200, 215, 216, 220, 225, 233, 251, 257, 261, 324, 325, 438
Pretzsch, 42, 44, 45, 49, 55, 57
Priedaine, 340
Pskov (Pleskau), 1, 61

R

Raasiku, 1, 342, 344, 345, 349
Radom, 1, 177, 366
Rēzekne (Rositten), 1, 29, 246, 457
Rio de Janeiro, 454, 455, 464
Rogavka, 243, 246
Rome, 64
Römershof, 209

S

Sachsenhausen, 380, 381, 390, 419, 447
Salaspils, 5, 9, 131, 133, 187, 189, 190, 200, 206, 209, 211, 212, 214, 215, 219, 220, 225, 229, 231, 233, 235, 236, 237, 238, 239, 240, 241, 242, 243, 244, 245, 246, 248, 249, 250, 251, 252, 253, 254, 255, 256, 257, 258, 259, 261, 262, 274, 275, 276, 279, 301, 320, 329, 335, 336, 337, 340, 341, 347, 348, 349, 362, 373, 379, 380, 406, 407, 408, 411, 412, 415, 438, 440, 445, 446, 460, 470, 473, 477, 478, 501
Saniki, 335, 437
Sao Paulo, 455

Sauriesi, 211
Schneidemühl (today Piła), 1
Seerappen (today Liublino), 1, 425
Šiauliai (Schaulen), 1, 59, 90, 282, 285, 289, 300, 378, 401, 413
Škirotava, 143, 146, 205, 206, 208, 209, 210, 211, 212, 213, 219, 220, 221, 222, 223, 226, 228, 231, 233, 235, 249, 250, 262, 319, 326, 344, 387, 446
Slamste, 279
Sloka (Schlock), 1, 62, 124, 340, 440
Slutsk, 1, 300
Sophienwalde, 426
Spilve, 277, 285, 345, 373, 383, 387, 389, 391, 408, 412, 414, 428, 430
Starnberg, 451
Stettin (today Szczecin), 1, 33, 179, 192, 365, 483
Strasdenhof (Jugla, Strazdumuiža), 384, 387, 389, 391, 392, 393, 408, 412, 415, 428
Stuttgart, 10, 43, 44, 208, 226, 227, 228, 235, 250, 258, 335, 346, 348, 407, 445, 456
Stutthof (today Sztutowo), 1, 5, 220, 242, 347, 382, 400, 413, 416, 417, 418, 419, 420, 421, 422, 423, 424, 425, 426, 431, 432, 433, 434, 448, 449, 462, 463, 473, 475, 477, 482, 484, 488, 489, 493, 498
Suzi (Suschenhof), 385

T
Tallinn (Reval), 1, 15, 20, 27, 33, 61, 86, 91, 106, 306, 342, 349, 350, 395, 479, 483
Tartu (Dorpat), 1, 54, 117, 174, 325
Taurage (Tauroggen), 1, 59
Tczew (Dirschau), 1, 426
Theresienstadt, 186, 191, 215, 219, 220, 222, 225, 231, 233, 257, 324, 333, 342, 345, 349

Tilsit (today Sovetsk), 1, 49, 56, 58, 201
Tirele, 105
Toruń (Thorn), 2, 228, 406, 412, 425, 426
Trawniki, 379
Treblinka, 1, 367, 444, 469
Tübingen, 42, 43, 431
Tukums (Tuckum), 1, 160, 186, 199, 201, 413

U
United States, 3, 9, 11, 35, 128, 403, 436, 437, 439, 457, 458, 459, 463
Uruguay, 455

V
Valmieri (Wolmar), 1
Ventspils (Windau), 1, 13, 19, 59, 126, 349, 385
Vienna, 1, 41, 43, 44, 83, 176, 177, 181, 182, 183, 185, 193, 195, 208, 215, 219, 220, 222, 223, 224, 225, 231, 233, 236, 246, 249, 257, 263, 328, 334, 345, 348, 349, 415, 436, 446
Vilnius (Wilna, Wilno), 1, 91, 164, 270, 277, 282, 289, 298, 300, 378, 384, 386, 394, 401, 410, 439

W
Warsaw, 1, 44, 102, 167, 245, 257, 259, 285, 326, 366, 367, 368, 369, 370, 372, 375, 379, 395, 450, 469, 483, 487
Washington, 9
Watenstedt, 198
Weimar, 44, 419
Weisswasser, 44, 477
Wesseling, 452
Witten, 448
Würzburg, 204, 205, 207, 226, 256, 337

Z
Zoppot (today Sopot), 24

www.ingramcontent.com/pod-product-compliance
Lightning Source LLC
Chambersburg PA
CBHW071951290426
44109CB00018B/1987